Days of Reckoning

Players Punching Their Ticket Out of Pittsburgh During the Barney Dreyfuss Era

Ronald T. Waldo

Mechanicsburg, PA USA

Published by Sunbury Press, Inc.
Mechanicsburg, PA USA

www.sunburypress.com

Copyright © 2023 Ronald T. Waldo.
Cover Copyright © 2023 by Sunbury Press, Inc.

Sunbury Press supports copyright. Copyright fuels creativity, encourages diverse voices, promotes free speech, and creates a vibrant culture. Thank you for buying an authorized edition of this book and for complying with copyright laws. Except for the quotation of short passages for the purpose of criticism and review, no part of this publication may be reproduced, scanned, or distributed in any form without permission. You are supporting writers and allowing Sunbury Press to continue to publish books for every reader. For information contact Sunbury Press, Inc., Subsidiary Rights Dept., PO Box 548, Boiling Springs, PA 17007 USA or legal@sunburypress.com.

For information about special discounts for bulk purchases, please contact Sunbury Press Orders Dept. at (855) 338-8359 or orders@sunburypress.com.

To request one of our authors for speaking engagements or book signings, please contact Sunbury Press Publicity Dept. at publicity@sunburypress.com.

FIRST SUNBURY PRESS EDITION: September 2023

Set in Adobe Garamond Pro | Interior design by Crystal Devine | Cover by Lawrence Knorr | Edited by Sarah Peachey.

Publisher's Cataloging-in-Publication Data
Names: Waldo, Ronald T., author.
Title: Days of reckoning : players punching their ticket out of Pittsburgh during the Barney Dreyfuss era / Ronald T. Waldo.
Description: First trade paperback edition. | Mechanicsburg, PA : Sunbury Press, 2023.
Summary: Many star diamond performers punched their ticket out of Pittsburgh because of disagreements with management when Barney Dreyfuss owned the team from 1900 through 1932. From Rube Waddell to Dick Bartell, *Days of Reckoning* chronicles why many of the greatest players in Pirates history were traded or released during Dreyfuss's tenure owning the team.
Identifiers: ISBN : 979-8-88819-103-3 (paperback) | ISBN : 979-8-88819-104-0 (ePub).
Subjects: SPORTS & RECREATION / Baseball / General | SPORTS & RECREATION / Baseball / Essays & Writings | SPORTS & RECREATION / Baseball / History.

Product of the United States of America
0 1 1 2 3 5 8 13 21 34 55

For the Love of Books!

Contents

Acknowledgments	*v*
Preface	*vii*
Introduction	*1*

Chapters

1	The Colonel Becomes a Pirate	5
2	The Wayward Pitcher and a Disloyal Veteran	25
3	Et Tu, Brute? Traitors in the Ranks	45
4	Breaking Up the Old Gang, with Help from Gamblers	68
5	A Player to Be Named later and the First Base Jinx	90
6	The Player Pipeline between Pittsburgh and St. Louis	111
7	The Millionaire Kid from Dormont	134
8	Temperamental Players and Malcontents Infest the Pirates' Craft	157
9	Shipping Out the Troublemakers and the Boozers	180
10	A Big Deal Ushers in Harmony and Pennant Glory	204
11	The One Time A-B-C Spelled Mutiny	225
12	The "Inside Story" and a Hero's Fall from Grace	248
13	Disheartening Final Discipline, Broad Fan Support, and Liberation	271
14	Spreading the Buckshot througout the National League	296
15	Bitter Holdouts and Tragedy in the Baseball Family	320

Notes	*343*
Bibliography	*388*
Index	*397*
About the Author	*412*

Acknowledgments

Regarding assistance along the way with some questions that needed answered in this book, I wish to thank a few individuals who supplied invaluable help. First, I wanted to thank Bill Lamb, author of the marvelous biography through the SABR Baseball Biography Project about Pittsburgh Pirates pitcher Albert Leon "Al" Mamaux. Bill graciously answered some questions I posed to him about the Mamaux family history, particularly Al's grandfather Albert Leon Mamaux Sr. I'm also deeply grateful to him for sharing some of the research he used when writing that SABR biography through a document titled, "The Lineage of the Magnificent Nine." Mr. Lamb's information helped clarify a few things related to my section of the book on pitcher Al Mamaux.

Two people deserve heartfelt thanks when it comes to the chapters of this book covering maligned Pittsburgh Pirates outfielder Hazen "Kiki" Cuyler. I want to sincerely thank Michelle Marcouiller, the special collections assistant at the Harrisville branch of the Alcona County Public Library in Michigan. Michelle sent me an article that appeared in the *Alcona County Review* on October 6, 1927, as the Pittsburgh Pirates and New York Yankees battled in the World Series, titled: "Home People Protest Persecution of Cuyler: Dreyfuss Denies Intention to Do Star Player Any Injustice." This article proved invaluable for my research by corroborating that some citizens of Harrisville, Michigan, did send a telegram asking Pirates management to allow Cuyler to appear in at least one game of the 1927 World Series.

I also wanted to extend extreme thanks to KiAnn Kruttlin, Kiki Cuyler's granddaughter, for offering insight regarding her grandfather receiving an oversized baseball glove from the J. A. Dubow Manufacturing Company. Cuyler happened to be one of the major league players who endorsed J. A. Dubow's products. The company gave this glove to Kiki, which was fourteen times larger than a standard mitt, before the 1927 season started.

Finally, thank you to all those people on Facebook who faithfully read the weekly historical baseball perspectives I post on my page. While the names are too numerous to mention, I truly appreciate all the kind support these individuals offer regarding my craft within that realm and the books I've written.

Preface

Much like in everyday life, baseball players who engaged in dubious deeds throughout the game's history usually had to face the consequences of their actions. In many instances, punished individuals felt a harsh penalty didn't prove just for their actions or behavior, which management had deemed unacceptable. Throughout the Deadball Era and the 1920s, well before free agency, club ownership usually held the upper hand in such matters due to their immense power regarding salaries and contracts. Diamond performers exhibiting poor temperament or failing to keep in top condition through chasing the nightlife caused clashes between the two parties. Outside forces sometimes played a critical role as well. Such circumstances led to players riding the pine, receiving fines or suspensions, and eventually, punching their ticket out of town to another organization.

In this book, I chronicle the stories surrounding numerous Pittsburgh Pirates team members who fell out of favor with the organization when Barney Dreyfuss owned the franchise. Dreyfuss controlled Pittsburgh's baseball destiny from the time he joined the ownership group in December 1899 until his death on February 5, 1932. For over three decades, Dreyfuss developed the Pirates into one of the National League's most successful franchises, resulting in six pennants, two World Series titles, and immense financial prosperity. For one reason or another, many players easily classified as the game's stars found new baseball homes throughout Barney's tenure as owner. I share the stories about these events and players who, as a group, could've formed a formidable all-star team.

Articles from many publications, including *Sporting Life* and *The Sporting News*, supplied the material that enabled me to write this story. Books covering that period or players chronicled in my work offered additional information and helped point me in the right direction during the research process. Because of the wealth of data unearthed while researching, each chapter contains substantial footnoting. Audio interviews of Pirates players Glenn Wright and Clyde Barnhart, conducted by Dr. Eugene Converse Murdock, an eminent baseball historian, enhance the book's later chapters.

I've covered a few of the topics in this book in some of my other works. To keep things from being repetitious, I've introduced new information and story angles to differentiate between the current book and my past writings on these subjects. Regarding the topics of players jumping the 1902 Pirates for the American League, the 1926 ABC Affair involving Babe Adams, Carson Bigbee, and Max Carey, as well as the feud between outfielder Hazen "Kiki" Cuyler and manager Donie Bush in 1927, I feel the fresh material and added perspective fully enhances these important stories.

In mentioning Glenn Wright, he has a connection to my family history. As a youngster rooting for the Pittsburgh Pirates in the early 1970s, someone told me a story about my grandfather on my father's side of the family. My grandfather William "Billy" Waldo was a relatively good second baseman who played semi-professional baseball in Pittsburgh in the 1920s. According to the story, while my grandfather worked out at Forbes Field, Wright playfully picked on him, a much shorter person, by pushing my grandfather to the ground. Interestingly, on my mother's side of the family, Glenn was her favorite Pittsburgh Pirates player when it came to grandmother Leona Wallace.

I've always regretted not asking my grandfather more questions about the older baseball eras before he passed away in 1974. Although my father, Arnold Waldo, couldn't remember the particulars surrounding this tale when I recently asked him, he supplied some information about my grandfather playing baseball. According to my dad, Billy Waldo and his younger brother, Charlie, were semi-professional sandlot league ballplayers on the South Side Black Sheep team. My father stated that Charlie received the nickname "Moxie" due to exuding a confident swagger on the diamond. My grandfather played for three different leagues, including the Northside Twilight League. In 1923, the *Pittsburgh Press*, which sponsored that association and many other area sandlot leagues at the time, referred to the Northside Twilight League as Greater Pittsburgh's premier sandlot organization.

Some top Pittsburgh and Western Pennsylvania athletes performed in the league during the 1920s, including future Pittsburgh Steelers coach and owner Arthur "Art" Rooney Sr., who starred in that sandlot organization. In 1922, three Swetonic brothers played for the Northside Twilight League's Bellevue club. Stephen "Steve" Swetonic, who pitched for Allegheny High School and the University of Pittsburgh, performed as a member of the Pirates' staff from 1929 through 1933. My father told me that my grandfather and Mr. Rooney, who happened to be acquaintances, often discussed horserace handicapping.

When I heard the tale regarding Glenn Wright about fifty years ago, my grandfather or another family member told me that he stopped rooting for the Pittsburgh Pirates at some point. From what I remember, the reason given was their sweep at the hands of the New York Yankees in the 1927 World Series. Eventually, Billy Waldo became a St. Louis Cardinals fan because of Stanley "Stan" Musial. As the decades have passed and my interest in baseball history intensified, I've wondered if a reason below the surface could've influenced my grandfather's decision to switch his allegiance. Was it possible that he became disgusted with the mass exodus of phenomenal players out of Pittsburgh to other ball clubs due to disputes with management and ownership?

Wright became one of those players who moved on in a trade to the Brooklyn Robins following the 1928 campaign. After a promising career started blossoming in Glenn's rookie season of 1924, injuries and other issues interrupted his ascension as a great shortstop in Pittsburgh. Like many before him during the Barney Dreyfuss era, Wright found that objectionable behavior usually resulted in punching that ticket out of the Smoky City.

Introduction

From Rube Waddell in 1901 to Dick Bartell in 1930, many players wore out their welcome wearing a Pittsburgh Pirates uniform during the Barney Dreyfuss ownership era. Players sometimes clashed with the manager, whether Fred Clarke during the first decade of the twentieth century or Donie Bush in 1927. On other occasions, team members incurred Dreyfuss's wrath for assorted reasons. One thing usually results when such problems develop. Those individuals at odds with club management and ownership make the journey to a new baseball environment, whether at the major or minor league level. Characters can never compromise team unity and diamond success by exhibiting poor behavior or not conforming to those wielding supreme power.

Regarding confrontational situations, men receive the monikers of antagonists and villains. In some cases, such a description appears justified as a specific player's actions prove detrimental to a baseball team's efficiency and harmony. This attitude was the case for different individuals who played for Pittsburgh when Barney Dreyfuss owned the club. On the other hand, management didn't always appear pious and righteous when dealing with sticky situations. In some instances, when ownership handed Pirates players their walking papers, both sides exhibited terrible judgment and didn't seem to possess any desire to resolve their differences. Ultimately, this tract produced angst and disgust for Pittsburgh's baseball fans who adored the favored diamond performers they believed management tarnished.

Many reasons existed for the numerous clashes that rose to the surface between players and management throughout the thirty-two seasons Dreyfuss owned the club. One was the standard issue at the time, where a player failed to remain in condition, a polite way of explaining that an individual had been boozing, acting as the impetus in some cases. Heated salary disputes between the Pirates' magnate and some hirelings helped to sour and strain relationships. Shortly after taking total control of the club, the upstart American League and their raids on National League teams forced Barney to make tough decisions in 1902 regarding players threatening to jump to the new organization. The events of that summer involving contract jumpers from Pittsburgh's squad read like a detective novel. Although Dreyfuss had been quite generous to his men in terms of salaries and perks, he heartily released stars from his team to maintain the organization's integrity while also striving to uphold baseball values he believed to be profoundly important.

Differences of opinion, substandard performances, and temperamental attitudes supplied other motives for club management jettisoning players from the squad during Barney Dreyfuss's ownership tenure. Sadly, the psyches of a few individuals could only be salvaged through trades to other teams due to the actions of a select group of fans that inhabited Exposition Park and, later, Forbes Field. Throughout most of the period that Dreyfuss owned Pittsburgh, an obnoxious gambling syndicate operated with impunity in these two ballparks. At that time, no other major league city approached the sheer multitude of gamblers present at each game, dedicated to making life miserable for home team members. Some players, targeted by these men through jeering and catcalls, wilted under such abuse. As a result, ownership had to move them to different squads because such treatment compromised their usefulness.

The men who traveled to other baseball lands when Fred Clarke successfully managed the Pittsburgh Pirates included Jack Chesbro, Jesse Tannehill, Kitty Bransfield, Claude Ritchey, Bill Abstein, and Vic Willis. After Clarke retired from baseball following the 1915 campaign, rich-kid star pitcher Al Mamaux, a local product from the Pittsburgh suburb of Dormont, quickly burned his bridges with two Pirates pilots and owner Dreyfuss. Roster purging and transactions necessitated by terrible judgment on the part of some players moved at lightning speed once the 1920s arrived, and dysfunction sometimes acted as an added theme.

A club could've formed an all-star aggregation with the players Barney Dreyfuss and his lieutenants shipped out of Pittsburgh over that decade. Stellar performers such as Rabbit Maranville, Babe Adams, Carson Bigbee, Max Carey, Kiki Cuyler, and Glenn Wright ran afoul with a management hierarchy member who summarily disposed of them. In the cases of Adams and Bigbee, the organization's power brokers deemed the moves insignificant to the club's chances in 1926 because their better days had long passed. When it came to Cuyler's situation in 1927 surrounding his feud with Donie Bush and Barney Dreyfuss, the outpouring of patron support rose to a level never seen when it came to a Pirates baseball player.

Throughout the first decade of the twentieth century, Barney Dreyfuss and Fred Clarke worked beautifully together, bringing tremendous success to a Pirates organization that hadn't seen such a stretch of winning seasons in its entire history as a National League team. The two men had the same mindset regarding personnel moves that best helped keep the Pittsburgh baseball machine humming. This magic touch became elusive after the Pirates defeated the Detroit Tigers in the 1909 World Series. The team floundered and eventually occupied an unaccustomed position in the league's second division in 1914. For the organization, returning to the top of the mountain after Clarke's retirement proved to be a slow process, as the Pirates didn't win another National League pennant until 1925.

It became apparent throughout the 1920s that the organization's power dynamic also included Barney's son, Sam Dreyfuss. Sam's role within the club increased and gained importance as the decade progressed. Someone connected to the Dreyfuss family sanctioned and approved all decisions related to Pittsburgh's baseball team, although most times, making the claim they didn't interfere with how a manager ran the club. By the 1920s, Pirates fans appeared more vocal and louder in expressing their opinion when perceiving ownership had mistreated a beloved player. Pittsburgh area newspapers also presented their stance on specific disputes between players and team management, usually siding with one of the two parties. Depending on the circumstances, the press sometimes supported the organization while they staunchly stood beside the player in other instances. Since Pittsburgh's baseball public constantly craved any tidbit of information about their beloved team, the local newspapers were always more than willing to oblige.

From Rube Waddell to Dick Bartell, many members of the Pittsburgh Pirates punched their tickets out of town during Barney Dreyfuss's time owning the club. The events, stories, and attitudes surrounding these players shaped the organization's destiny throughout that era and influenced how the franchise grew and prospered.

1

The Colonel Becomes a Pirate

Regarding putting together competitive baseball teams that performed capably on the diamond, second-division finishes acted as the standard for the Pittsburgh Pirates' franchise throughout the 1890s. Subsequently, a revolving door of players and managers existed in the quest to find a winning combination. The names may have changed, but the diamond outcome regrettably remained etched in stone. Playing as the National League's Alleghenys in 1890, Pittsburgh firmly entrenched itself in the basement with a horrible 23–113 record. The same result occurred one year later, despite some improvement in the win column.

Following the elimination of the American Association after the 1891 campaign, the Pirates' organization showed some promise, finishing sixth and fourth in a split-season format in 1892 in the new twelve-team National League. Pittsburgh came close to claiming the flag one year later, going 81–48 in 1893, and placing second, five games behind the pennant-winning Boston Beaneaters. This season ended up being the team's high point for the decade, as mediocrity became a common baseball theme in the Smoky City. Following their solid campaign in 1893, Pittsburgh finished sixth once (1896), seventh three times (1894, 1895, and 1899), and eighth twice (1897 and 1898).

A baseball season, decade, and century reached its conclusion for the Pittsburgh organization on the home grounds of Exposition Park on October 14, 1899. Team president and owner William Kerr had taken a calculated risk, deciding a week earlier, while talking to manager Patrick "Patsy" Donovan, to have the Louisville Colonels come into town to play off previously postponed games. When management decided, Pittsburgh had experienced crisp weather, while reports from the West indicated heavy rain appeared likely when playing this slate of games. Despite the poor weather outlook, Kerr maintained the mantra, "Nothing ventured, nothing won," when he decided on this course of action. In the end, Pittsburgh's owner exhibited great instincts, as pleasant weather prevailed for contests on Friday and Saturday.

Over 3,500 fans attended the final game against Louisville on October 14. Colonels hurler George Edward "Rube" Waddell, a local product from Butler County, was the season finale's big attraction. Rube's father, John, who worked as an oil well gauger, mother, Mary, sisters, and relatives from Prospect, Pennsylvania, proudly attended to watch the giant southpaw pitcher take the mound against the Pirates.[1] A steady flow of Butler County inhabitants arrived in Pittsburgh on Friday night and continued coming into the city until game time on Saturday afternoon. Rube held court for two hours at Louisville's Monongahela House lodging before leaving for the ballpark, standing in the corridor shaking hands with friends. William Kerr invited the Waddell family to sit in his private box in the grandstand. While the ladies in the party accepted Kerr's gracious invitation, Rube's father declined since he already had a perfect grandstand seat on a line with the pitcher's rubber and home plate.

The crowd afforded Rube a grand reception when he stepped onto the field for the first time. Butler friends and diehard Pirates fans heartily cheered for him throughout the contest.[2] Waddell's performance was exceptional in all facets of the game. After allowing Pittsburgh to score one run in the first inning, Rube stifled the Pirates' offense for the remainder of the afternoon. Only one Pittsburgh runner reached second base in the final eight innings, as Louisville secured a 4–1 victory. Waddell tossed a complete game, allowed six hits, fanned three batters, walked one, went 2-for-4 at the plate, and stroked a double.[3]

Pittsburgh finished the 1899 season in seventh place, with a 76–73 record. Louisville placed two spots below that, going 75–77. The Pirates played better baseball after ownership named outfielder Patsy Donovan as manager on May 16, succeeding William "Watty" Watkins, who'd resigned. Under Donovan's guidance, Pittsburgh went 69–58. After his team played the final game, Patsy offered a brief assessment of the concluded season, with well-wishes pouring in from local friends.

"Well, I am sure of one thing," said Donovan, with a smile on his face. "We played good ball for the past three months. I remember the time when the club was 13 games behind the .500 mark [their actual low point of 11 games under .500 occurred on May 25]. Now it is three games over it. I guess that indicates that the boys were idling."[4]

It certainly didn't appear to be a sure bet that Donovan would be back managing Pittsburgh in 1900. Team president William Kerr hadn't announced Patsy's retention within that capacity. Donovan had been a Pirates member since 1892. He also piloted the team for the final five games of the 1896 baseball campaign and the entire 1897 season. Patsy's most significant fault while running the squad in 1899 seemed to be allowing players to take advantage of him and playing favorites with select press members while deceiving or betraying other scribes.[5] Days after the season ended, Kerr announced the club's profits for 1899 didn't amount to $15,000, adding that he believed upon perusing all the figures, they wouldn't show a positive balance on the ledger.[6]

William Kerr and partner Philip Auten, a close business associate from Chicago, Illinois, had purchased a stake in the Pirates after the American Association ceased operations following the 1891 season.[7] The two men gained a controlling interest in the franchise on January 20, 1893, when they, along with manager Albert "Al" Buckenberger, bought over four hundred shares owned by William C. Temple, who'd held more than half of the total stock options.[8] A Pittsburgh native, Kerr had received his start within the business world for the Standard Oil Company in Philadelphia, Pennsylvania, before joining Arbuckle's & Company, a local concern dealing primarily in coffee and groceries. William and Philip had also been stockholders in Pittsburgh's Players' League entry in 1890.[9] Friends described Auten as one of the coldest people in business they'd ever known. He'd amassed a great fortune, with the Ford River Lumber Company being one of his most successful ventures.[10]

On October 20, former Pittsburgh manager William Watkins arrived in town and held a brief conference with William Kerr. Watkins asserted his visit had nothing to do with baseball and that he probably would be in town through Sunday to attend to some business matters.[11] That Friday night, Watty took up residence in the familiar room 514 of the Seventh Avenue Hotel, where he'd stayed while managing the Pirates. On Saturday, a rumor made the rounds, claiming that Watkins had arrived in town to inquire about purchasing Pittsburgh's baseball franchise since team vice-president Philip Auten also traveled to the Smoky City. Kerr enjoyed a hearty chuckle when someone mentioned this gossip in his presence.[12] That day, Watkins, Kerr, and Auten did indeed confer behind closed doors for hours. None of the parties involved exhibited a willingness to offer any information about the meeting when pressed by newspaper journalists.[13]

One possible reason put forward by the press for Watty's presence in Pittsburgh was his close relationship with Cincinnati Reds owner John T. Brush.

Writers speculated that Watkins acted as an agent on Brush's behalf to acquire Pirates hurler Samuel "Sam" Leever in exchange for Reds pitcher Emerson Pink Hawley, who'd previously played for Pittsburgh. On October 23, William Kerr gave credence to the gossip surrounding a possible sale of the team, stating that he was amenable to disposing of his interests in the club. Kerr also admitted to receiving an offer to sell those interests but discounted the sincere nature of this proffer due to it being too low. Chicago's *Daily Inter Ocean* reported that Philip Auten planned to transfer the block of stock he and other associates owned to Kerr. According to this newspaper article, Auten wanted to divest from his holdings in the Pirates' organization to join forces with Adrian "Cap" Anson to financially back a Chicago entry in the new American League.[14]

On the evening of October 25, the *Pittsburgh Press* reported that William Watkins was in town for the sole purpose of purchasing the Pittsburgh Pirates. Although Watkins's option to negotiate a deal had expired that day, Kerr agreed to extend it at William's request to allow the former manager's backers to come to Pittsburgh.[15] If the two parties consummated this deal, local patrons would likely condemn it since the possibility existed that John T. Brush happened to be one of Watty's backers. Brush already had connections to more than one National League team, and contaminated syndicate baseball was something Pittsburgh's fans wouldn't be willing to swallow.[16] Syndicate baseball had proved disastrous for the Cleveland Spiders in 1899. As a feeder team for the St. Louis Perfectos, Cleveland resided in the basement with a 20–134 record. Brothers Frank and Stanley Robison owned both teams.

William Watkins's latest foray into Pittsburgh was his third trip to the city in the past month to six weeks.[17] In the end, due diligence attempting to purchase the Pirates from William Kerr and Philip Auten ended up going for naught. Watkins expressed shock and dismay upon being informed on October 26 that no deal would be happening between the two parties. The former Pittsburgh manager exhibited a foul mood when he left for the West that night.[18] During a conference right before noon that morning, the Pirates' magnates had told Watty they would render a final decision later that day once the sellers met with a particular individual. Shortly after 2 P.M., a newspaper journalist informed Watkins that the deal was off. When finding out the news, Watty sat in the Seventh Avenue Hotel lobby, sullen and disappointed.[19]

Upon arriving in Detroit, Michigan, on Friday morning, October 27, before returning to his Wadhams home in that state, Watkins offered a statement about this deal to purchase the Pittsburgh Pirates baseball club, which didn't come to fruition.

"I secured an option which expired at noon yesterday and have been there three weeks getting ready to buy them out," said Watkins. "I had the money with me—that is, $5,000 in cash as a forfeit that the securities would be converted into cash in two days. There were some details which had to be talked over yesterday morning, and when we got through with them it was after 12 o'clock and Mr. Kerr said that the option had expired. I don't believe that Mr. Kerr ever had any serious intention of selling to me in the first place, although he quoted me figures. They were steep, but I met them and the owners did not want to give up.

"I regard Pittsburgh as a splendid franchise, else I would not have tried to buy it, and if I had succeeded I would have done well there. The club played good ball the last half of the year and I have no apprehensions as to next season."[20]

Watkins paused before concluding his statement for the press.

"How much did I offer?" continued Watkins. "Well, the Pittsburgh papers guessed all the way from $50,000 to $90,000. Who was behind me? Well, you can guess again."[21]

Those who had seen Watkins leave the Thursday morning meeting debunked his claim that Kerr acted hastily. Watty appeared agitated and flushed, ignoring a group of acquaintances as he hurried past them without acknowledgment. This reaction indicated that Kerr had already concluded a prudent, thoughtful verdict. Such a decision certainly wouldn't be favorable in the end for Watkins. Throughout this process, newspaper scribes had become annoyed over Watty not being forthcoming or truthful when asked why he was in Pittsburgh.[22] *Cincinnati Enquirer* sports editor Harry Weldon expressed happiness over Watkins failing at his mission. Not enamored with syndicate baseball, Weldon preferred the Smoky City team to continue being owned by upstanding and influential local citizens rather than selling it to a syndicate of outside capitalists.[23] Watty eventually revealed that he wasn't acting on behalf of Cincinnati Reds owner John T. Brush but rather at the behest of the famous Dickson and Talbott theatrical firm, which operated a chain of playhouses in Indianapolis, Indiana.[24]

Kerr and Watkins refused to divulge the critical third party connected to the conference on October 26. They stated it wasn't Louisville Colonels team president Barney Dreyfuss, although the two gentlemen admitted to seeing him in the morning. Knowing that Dreyfuss planned on making the trip to Pittsburgh, Watty met him at the train station and later went to his hotel room. Some theorized that Barney traveled to Pittsburgh so he could sign Colonels players John "Honus" Wagner and Patrick "Patsy" Flaherty, who hailed from the nearby municipality of Carnegie, to contracts for the 1900 season.[25]

Bernhard "Barney" Dreyfuss had risen as a powerful fixture in Louisville after immigrating by boat to the United States from what later became Germany as a seventeen-year-old lad. Born in Freiburg, Baden, on February 23, 1865, Dreyfuss decided to leave his native country due to an aversion to compulsory military training.[26] Barney's father, Samuel Dreyfuss, had lived in America for several years before returning to his home country. Educated in his native land, the younger Dreyfuss worked in a bank in Karlsruhe before making the journey to chase new opportunities in a different country.[27] Upon landing at Castle Garden of New York's Battery, Barney set out for his destination of Paducah, Kentucky, following a side trip to Niagara Falls.[28]

Shortly after reaching Paducah, Barney Dreyfuss briefly worked as a clerk on a steamboat that transported merchandise along the Tennessee River. Dreyfuss secured a job with the Bernheim Brothers distillery through relatives in the Kentucky city.[29] After starting at the bottom of the company ladder cleaning whiskey barrels, Bernheim promoted Barney to an office position. He eventually became the company's head bookkeeper.[30] For his strong expertise with figures, the distillery later elevated him to the chief accountant.[31] A diligent worker, Dreyfuss toiled nine hours a day and stayed up until midnight taking English courses so he became more accomplished in this language.

Barney's health suffered as a result of burning the midnight oil. His Paducah doctor advised outdoor relaxation time, recommending baseball as the perfect activity. Dreyfuss quickly fell in love with the game as a player before becoming intrigued by the front office machinations.[32] Barney joined a semi-professional team in Paducah, learned to play second base, and quickly became the squad's manager.[33] Dreyfuss controlled this baseball club for four years.[34]

When the Bernheim Brothers distillery moved its interests to Louisville in 1888, Barney, a credit man for the company, relocated to that city. Having saved money from his earnings, Dreyfuss purchased a small stock block in the American Association's Colonels baseball team shortly after he arrived in Louisville. In 1890, the Colonels named Barney team treasurer. Four years after Louisville became a member of the twelve-team National League, the organization elected Harry Pulliam as team president in 1896. Dreyfuss served under him as secretary-treasurer. In 1899, after Barney gained a controlling interest in the franchise, the two men switched positions within the organizational hierarchy.[35] Dreyfuss reportedly shelled out $50,000 to purchase the holdings of various partners connected to the baseball franchise.[36] Barney was also a full-fledged Kentucky Colonel.[37]

Speculation abounded that another meeting between William Kerr and Barney Dreyfuss related to player procurement occurred on Saturday, October

28. Kerr expressed an interest in outfielders Honus Wagner and Fred "Cap" Clarke, pitcher Rube Waddell, second baseman Claude Ritchey, and infielder Thomas "Tommy" Leach. He seemed willing to pay top dollar to secure these Louisville players.[38] A Pittsburgh resident claimed the meeting didn't transpire since he'd been with Dreyfuss, and Kerr wasn't in his office when they called on the Pirates' owner. The two men then went to lunch, attended a football game, and ate dinner together.[39] Concerning the alleged summit, this was only part of the story. On October 31, a newspaper report claimed that Dreyfuss now held an option on purchasing the Pirates and had until November 4 to raise the necessary funds to buy the club.[40]

Upon returning to Louisville after his trip to Pittsburgh, Dreyfuss admitted that negotiations were pending between him and Kerr. Because the Louisville franchise expired in two years when the Nationals League's ten-year agreement agreed upon in 1892 lapsed, Barney wanted to dispose of the Colonels since there might not be anything worth selling down the road.[41] Reports stated that Barney controlled a $70,000 option to purchase the Pirates' franchise. A Louisville friend said it wouldn't be a problem for Dreyfuss to raise this money.

"I have known Barney to write out a check for $25,000," stated Dreyfuss's friend, "and reliable information rates his firm as being worth from $500,000 to $1,000,000; so it is not unreasonable to suppose that he can raise $70,000."[42]

Beyond the implications of a leadership change in Pittsburgh, the reduction of the National League circuit from twelve to eight teams hinged on this transaction. According to the *Cincinnati Times-Star*, owners of the Louisville, Washington, Cleveland, and Baltimore squads would be willing to surrender their franchises in exchange for monetary compensation.[43] On Friday, November 3, Barney Dreyfuss returned to Pittsburgh with lawyer D. I. Heyman, intending to hand over the payment to finalize this deal.[44] In the end, Dreyfuss ended up following the same path to ruin and failure previously traveled by William Watkins.

On Saturday morning, November 4, Dreyfuss and William Kerr met in conference. The meeting between the two men continued past noon.[45] When it concluded, Kerr announced the deal was off due to Barney wanting to include a last-minute caveat in the final agreement. Dreyfuss asked Kerr to sign a document in which he assumed responsibility for any liabilities or debts currently connected to the Pirates' franchise.[46] Upon release of this news, many individuals felt that asking for such a commitment was a reasonable request. Kerr stated that he declined to sign this guarantee because of any liability possibly arising if the National League contracted from twelve to eight teams.

Dreyfuss expressed deep disappointment over a deal not being hammered out between the two parties.

"I am sorry that I cannot leave the sum of money I have with me in Pittsburgh," said Dreyfuss. "But Mr. Kerr does not want it, and I guess I'll take it home. I brought it on to pay off the balance on the purchase of the club. Mr. Kerr, however, would not give me a guarantee that there was more than 850 shares of club stock issued [the deal called for Dreyfuss to purchase 825 shares of stock], or that the club debts exceeded $586. He admitted that if he were the buyer in such a deal he would want such a guarantee. He said my agreement as drawn was all right, but still he wouldn't sign anything. So the deal is off. If you ever catch me coming to Pittsburgh again on such an errand please let me know."[47]

Shortly before Barney Dreyfuss left for New York that night, he elaborated on the financial burden inflicted by these deliberations due to his funds not being liquid.

"We had a verbal agreement covering the points raised today," claimed Dreyfuss. "I wanted to put it in writing on October 28, the day it was made, but this was not done. I am sorry the deal fell through. The negotiations cost me a considerable sum, as I do not carry $70,000 in my bank, and in converting securities into cash so quickly I suffered some loss. I will not make another offer for the Pittsburgh team. Had the deal been consummated I am sure this city would have had one of the best clubs in the league."[48]

Love for baseball also played a part in Kerr's calculus behind making this decision. The Pirates' president expressed gladness over not selling, stating he enjoyed the game too much to walk away. Kerr also declared that the main sticking point in Dreyfuss's debt guarantee was a pending lawsuit by former St. Louis Browns owner Chris Von der Ahe against the National League.[49] The *Pittsburgh Press* reported on November 10 that Pittsburgh's owner offered an alternative solution if Barney truly wanted to become part of the Pirates' organization.

"I will gladly give Dreyfuss an interest in the Pittsburgh club for the pick of his players," declared Kerr, "but not the controlling interest. I will give the Louisville president a block of stock, and will also make him president of the Pittsburgh club, if he in return will give the local club the pick of the Louisville players. But the controlling interest will remain where it is at present."[50]

Dreyfuss's right-hand man, Louisville Colonels team secretary Harry Pulliam, had been running point for the magnate regarding a Pittsburgh deal since the baseball season ended. Pulliam also proved instrumental, securing the critical option on the club before Kerr quashed this deal.⁵¹ When Harry spent some time at French Lick Springs, Indiana, before negotiations started, Cincinnati owner John T. Brush also happened to be a guest at the prestigious health resort. At the time, Brush asked Pulliam why Barney Dreyfuss didn't consider purchasing an interest in the Pirates. The Reds' owner explained that William Watkins had struck a deal with William Kerr to sell the club to Fred C. Dickson and Henry Talbott, but the option ran out. Harry immediately made a long-distance telephone call to Dreyfuss and told him about this golden opportunity.⁵²

Following his rejection by Kerr, Dreyfuss traveled to New York to court Giants owner Andrew Freedman, hoping to purchase a stock block in that baseball organization.⁵³ C. L. Moore, who covered Louisville baseball for *The Sporting News*, preferred a deal with New York since it could be more advantageous financially over a merger with Pittsburgh.⁵⁴ When approached at the end of November on the subject of striking an agreement to sell Colonels players to the Chicago Orphans' organization, Barney quickly rejected that notion, saying he'd received plenty of offers, before adding there was nothing new to report surrounding a potential deal.⁵⁵

Shortly after the deal between the Louisville and Pittsburgh owners fell through, the Pirates' magnates offered newspaper journalist and Inter-State League president Charles B. Power that same position within the organization. Power initially accepted and was expected to be elected at the annual organizational meeting on December 12. Charles had a change of heart, informing William Kerr on November 22 of his intention to withdraw his name since it was impossible to accept the position because of some issues rising to the surface.⁵⁶

Charles Power confided to friends that he changed his mind because the position looked too precarious to accept since evidence existed that negotiations had reopened to sell the Pittsburgh Pirates.⁵⁷ Besides assuming the title of team president, there were strong indications that Power would've also received an offer to manage the Pirates in 1900 if he hadn't bowed out.⁵⁸ Such reasoning appeared valid since all the rumors surrounding a Louisville consolidation with New York or Chicago were pure posturing on Barney Dreyfuss's part. This masquerade was a ruse since he never wavered from keeping his eyes on the big prize. When the dust settled, Kerr's suggestion of a stock purchase finally brought an agreement across the finish line.

A deal to purchase the Pittsburgh Pirates seemed to be on once again. From the *Washington Post*, Joe Campbell surmised that renewed talks to buy the Pirates would likely occur at the National League meetings in New York, scheduled to start on December 12, 1899.[59] The *Cincinnati Times-Star* corroborated this premise.[60] Rumors out of New York pointed to various members of the Colonels wearing Giants uniforms in 1900.[61] After returning from a trip to West Virginia on December 6, William Kerr clarified where things stood regarding selling the Pittsburgh Pirates.

"It is up to Barney," said Kerr. "I have received no definite word from him for weeks. When the hitch occurred and he gave up his option the matter of merging the Pittsburgh and Louisville teams was dropped for a while. Later I made Mr. Dreyfuss a proposition and as I do not know positively that he has accepted it I am not in position to talk."[62]

Cloak and dagger mastery dominated as the nineteenth century ended. Weeks earlier, Barney Dreyfuss had resigned as Louisville's team president, with other owners elevating Harry Pulliam to succeed him. Dreyfuss did this so that no conflict of interest existed in conducting negotiations to purchase the Pirates. If doing so as president, he might've forfeited some rights under the National Agreement governing the National League. Telegrams received in Louisville on December 5 from Pittsburgh indicated Barney had purchased that club. This correspondence also declared that the deal called for the pick of players from both teams to combine into a powerhouse unit representing the Smoky City.[63]

On December 8, 1899, representatives from the two organizations finalized a deal at William Kerr's downtown office in the Arbuckle Building, described as one of the biggest in the history of the National Game.[64] Besides Kerr, Philip Auten, Barney Dreyfuss, Harry Pulliam, and Fred Clarke attended the two-hour conference.[65] Following the conclusion of this blockbuster arrangement, Pulliam announced the transaction's particulars. The prize players transferred from Louisville's roster to Pittsburgh included pitchers Rube Waddell, Charles "Deacon" Phillippe, Patsy Flaherty, Walter "Walt" Woods, and Ellsworth "Bert" Cunningham; catchers Charles "Chief" Zimmer and Clifford "Tacks" Latimer; first baseman Michael "Mike" Kelley; second baseman Claude Ritchey; infielder Tommy Leach; outfielder Honus Wagner; and Clarke. The Colonels received $25,000, pitcher John "Jack" Chesbro, catcher George Fox, second baseman John O'Brien, and infielder Arthur "Art" Madison.[66]

The task of molding this star-studded array of baseball talent and gifted Pirates holdovers such as hurlers Jesse Tannehill and Sam Leever, along with outfielder Clarence "Ginger" Beaumont, into a pennant contending team, fell to Fred Clarke, named as Pittsburgh's new manager by ownership. Before leaving for the league meetings in New York, Dreyfuss happily stated that he would immediately be moving his family to Pittsburgh. Barney had always liked the city and expressed delight at becoming a permanent resident. Clarke was also ecstatic that he would be spending the next chapter of his playing career with the Pirates.

"I am more than pleased with the deal," said Clarke, "for I have long desired to play in Pittsburgh. Other members of the Louisville team who are included in this deal will, I know, be delighted with the announcement that they are to become Pirates."[67]

Fred Clarke had debuted with the Louisville Colonels on June 30, 1894, and cracked out five hits in his first major league game.[68] On June 16, 1897, the twenty-four-year-old Clarke succeeded James "Jim" Rogers as the Colonels' manager. Upon being replaced as skipper, stripped of his captaincy, and demoted to a utility role after being the starting second baseman, Rogers asked for and received his release.[69] Fred was lethal at the plate in 1897, batting .390 for Louisville. Clarke's accomplishments as a player were the byproduct of intervention from Barney Dreyfuss. Fred later claimed fate contributed to his great success as a player. As a rookie, Clarke had fallen into the trap of being sidetracked by the external trappings connected to performing as a major league baseball player. In a 1911 interview with a sportswriter, Fred explained how his life had changed through wise advice.

> It all happened in one day. When I first joined the Louisville club I felt very chesty to be among the big leaguers. That was 18 years ago. I was what one might call a fresh cub. There were a lot of men on the team who had reputations as gay fellows and good ballplayers. Their records dazzled me. Their dashing manners fascinated me. Naturally I set out to imitate them.
>
> First I made friends with them. I spent my money freely to have a good time, and I stayed out at night, drinking and chasing around. I was a sincere devil and was living with all the fervor of the temperamental artist. These men were good players, good fellows and rare companions. Why should I not try to emulate them?
>
> Then, one day, after I had been out all night with a merry party, my playing showed the effects of the good time. I could not see the curves break in time and my legs felt as if they were loaded with lead. That was the first time. It happened again and again. I was so foolish that I did not see that it was my life that was pulling me down, slowing me up, tearing my physique apart.

After this had been going on for a time Barney Dreyfuss sent for me one day and I expected to get the call which I so sincerely deserved. I went into the office of the owner of the club with the feelings that I am sure a dog must have when there is a tin can tied to his tail. But I was surprised, relieved, when Mr. Dreyfuss talked only on the most commonplace subjects. After we had chatted for a time he said to me suddenly:

"Clarke, what are you in baseball for?"

I stood first on one foot and then on the other. I was uncomfortable. I hesitated. Then I blurted out: I really have never thought about the matter, Mr. Dreyfuss.

"Have you ever thought of baseball as a mere business proposition?" he asked.

No [Clarke answered].

"Baseball," said Mr. Dreyfuss, "to me is a business, pure and simple. Of course there is a lot of glamour and glory attached to it, but the haloes would soon slip away from the players and the receipts from the box office if the men did not put up their best game. Now, of course, on account of the life you are leading you are not playing fair with me. But put that all aside. Leave me out of it. Are you fair with yourself?

"You can be a top notcher or you can remain what you are—a very ordinary player. You will live in the major league a few years only if you continue to dim your batting eye and weaken your physical self by carousing around. Then you will go back to the minors and be swallowed up, and you never will have been anyone. It's up to you. Think it over."

Clarke proclaimed to the writer that after talking with Barney Dreyfuss, he returned to his hotel room, sat with head in hands, and did hours of soul searching. Fred finally realized that he was wrong and Dreyfuss was right. Although the glare and glitter of the nightlife looked captivating, it ultimately was a dead end. Clarke decided the straight and narrow path was the only logical choice. Fred's ideas about life and baseball changed positively that day, as he slowly stopped associating with companions that would lead him to ruin and forever gave up partying. Clarke owed his success to Louisville's owner.[70] The strong bond, relationship, and friendship between Fred and Barney during their time together in Louisville hopefully would pay dividends for the Pittsburgh Pirates and its fans.

Barney Dreyfuss had astutely navigated the rocky terrain, protecting his financial interests and remaining in the National League as he desired, becoming a partner and stockholder in the Pirates' organization.[71] After consummating the deal, Barney explained he'd made a trip to Pittsburgh two weeks earlier to finalize an agreement with Kerr. He also claimed utmost secrecy had been critical since tipping off the press could've proven to be a fatal blow to these plans.[72] Dreyfuss had informed Louisville sportswriter John J. Saunders about a potential deal. Saunders offered assurances that he wouldn't print anything due to the confidential nature of this information.[73] During the annual meeting of the Pittsburgh Baseball Club in Jersey City, New Jersey, on December 10, the board of directors elected Dreyfuss president, Auten vice president, Kerr treasurer, and Pulliam team secretary (although technically still Louisville's team president).[74]

St. Louis Perfectos owner and team president Frank Robison wasn't happy with this merger. Robison felt Dreyfuss had deceived him when the Louisville man courted Frank about making a potential deal. At the December league meetings in New York, the Perfectos' owner used colorful language during a verbal exchange with Barney. He denounced Dreyfuss's practices of playing different teams against one another and acting in bad faith for the sole purpose of brokering the best possible deal for himself. Robison claimed he'd even talked to Fred Clarke, found him eager to play in St. Louis, and agreed to salary terms in a proposed contract.[75] Regarding league business, the owners established a circuit committee to examine eliminating four clubs from the National League.[76] Technically, the twelve-team organization still had two more years of existence, according to the ten-year agreement signed in 1892.[77]

While visiting relatives in New York, former Pirates manager Patsy Donovan declared that Pittsburgh couldn't sell him without his consent unless he arranged terms with a potential suitor. Barney Dreyfuss responded by saying that he couldn't grant such a request.[78] When Dreyfuss started settling into his new Pittsburgh home, Donovan's friends searched out the team president and vigorously touted Patsy's ability as a player. Although Barney agreed that Donovan was a good man, he declared that Fred Clarke would decide all roster issues.[79] When Clarke arrived from Chicago on January 21, he stated that while he hadn't yet finalized the club roster at this time, the disposal of Patsy and veteran pitcher Bert Cunningham would proceed through sales to the highest bidder.[80] In respect to Donovan, Fred never considered retaining him, feeling it wasn't prudent to employ a man who once had managed the club.[81]

The Chicago Orphans ended up purchasing Cunningham. The bitterness that developed over his treatment led to some adverse and biased decisions against the Pirates when Bert umpired in the National League for two months in 1901.[82] On March 9, 1900, St. Louis acquired Donovan during a league meeting in New York. Team president Frank Robison sang Patsy's praises upon concluding the transaction and immediately inked his signature to a contract.[83] According to a story out of New York, Pittsburgh secured $2,000 from the Donovan sale, debunking an initial report of the Pirates peddling him for $1,000. A Baltimore correspondent claimed St. Louis's cost to acquire Patsy to be $3,000.[84]

Donovan's purchase was a minor footnote to this league meeting. After a three-hour session, following a meeting by National League magnates on the afternoon of March 8, it was decided at midnight, on the recommendation of the circuit committee, that the organization eliminate Louisville, Baltimore, Cleveland, and Washington. Eleven owners signed the agreement on March 9, with New York's Andrew Freedman, who wasn't in attendance but declared in a message that it was an eight-club league or nothing, pledging to do so. Regarding compensation, Louisville received $10,000, Cleveland $15,000, Baltimore $30,000 and the right to sell their players, and Washington $39,000 (a deduction of $7,500 from their original demand of $46,500 for receiving that amount of money peddling three players to the Boston Beaneaters). The settlement also required Washington's remaining players to go into a league pool for disposal.[85]

On March 9, the four individuals sent to Louisville as part of the original transaction "officially" were returned to the Pittsburgh Pirates. This end of the deal had been a phantom inclusion from the start, never intending to be a legitimate part of the big proposal but only temporarily adding names to a pseudo-Colonels roster. At the end of February, Barney Dreyfuss had already disposed of infielder Art Madison. Dreyfuss sold him to the American League's Indianapolis Hoosiers, who William Watkins managed in 1900.[86] When Fred Clarke announced at the beginning of March the twenty-four players who were heading to Thomasville, Georgia, for spring training, that list included pitcher Jack Chesbro.[87] The Pirates released the final two men shipped initially to Louisville, George Fox and John O'Brien.

When the consolidation negotiations had initially concluded on December 8, Carnegie natives Honus Wagner and Patsy Flaherty came to town to sign contracts with their new team for the upcoming season.[88] Upon receiving news about the deal, the two men hustled to downtown Pittsburgh by trolley. Wagner wasted no time posing a critical question to Dreyfuss in conjunction with him playing baseball in his backyard.

"Say, Barney, durst a fellow take a beer now and then next year?" naively asked Honus.

"Course, so long as you do not take too much," responded Dreyfuss.[89]

Performing in his hometown indeed agreed with Wagner. The versatile player, who mainly played the outfield for manager Fred Clarke in 1900, won the first of his eight National League batting titles, leading the league by hitting .381 while also pacing the circuit with 45 doubles and 22 triples. Concerning the Pirates' entire squad, following a sluggish start, which saw them in third place with a 29–28 record at the end of June, Clarke's team caught fire throughout the remainder of the campaign. In the end, Pittsburgh experienced a gratifying season. The year also proved a grand financial success under Barney Dreyfuss's and Harry Pulliam's hands-on stewardship, as the organization turned a profit of at least $40,000 in 1900.

Although Dreyfuss was the largest individual stockholder in the Pittsburgh Pirates, William Kerr and Philip Auten combined controlled 501 out of the 1,000 shares of capital stock related to the organization.[90] Despite immense success on the baseball diamond and in the pocketbook, tension developed between various members within the ownership's hierarchy. Emerging differences of opinion among the three gentlemen started to intensify just as the squad hit their summer stride on the field in 1900. Pittsburgh baseball writer Alfred R. "A. R." Cratty wrote in January 1901 that a Louisville citizen had informed Kerr and Auten of two critical points after consummating the deal on December 8, 1899. He declared that Dreyfuss was a hard-working hustler who disliked playing nice if others didn't recognize him as the undisputed boss.[91]

The flames of discontent became stoked to supernova proportions throughout the off-season, creating so much smoke that Barney Dreyfuss orchestrated shrewd and calculating maneuvers under this thick blanket of uncertainty. In December, Kerr wrote to Cincinnati owner John T. Brush, inquiring about any interest in shipping Pirates hurler Jesse Tannehill to the Reds for one of that team's pitchers. Although Dreyfuss and Fred Clarke likely would be happy to part with the star southpaw pitcher, it seemed interesting that Kerr appeared to be stepping outside his purview as team treasurer, becoming involved in player procurement.[92]

One year earlier, after Dreyfuss and Clarke joined the organization, they considered trading Tannehill, the National League's boss southpaw hurler. These two men were only willing to move the volatile pitcher if they could secure another talented player in the deal. During the National League meetings in New York, Chicago proposed a trade where the Orphans hoped to exchange hurler Clark Griffith for Jesse. Clarke balked, feeling things would go from bad to worse, and Griffith might prove just as challenging to handle as Tannehill.

Chicago's persistence almost won over Pittsburgh's new manager to the degree that he carefully considered the proposition for some time.

Clarke finally decided to go straight to Griffith and directly ask the pitcher if he would genuinely behave himself, given the opportunity to join Pittsburgh's squad. Although anxious to join the Pirates, Fred's accusatory inquiry shocked Clark.

"I cannot see how I deserve these charges," said Griffith. "I have been accused of causing trouble in Chicago, but I think the charges are unjust. I don't believe you will ever have occasion to regret it if you take a chance with me."

Fred looked over Griffith skeptically when Chicago's player offered his assurances. After debating the proposal in his mind one final time, Clarke decided to allow the Orphans to keep Griffith.[93] Any decision to move Jesse Tannehill one year later after the 1900 campaign ended should've been one that rested with Pittsburgh's team president or manager and not the treasurer.

Months of disagreement between partners finally resulted in someone taking decisive action to change the organizational atmosphere. William Kerr and Philip Auten struck a severe blow, ignoring the previous season's positive results, when they decided to remove Harry Pulliam from his post as team secretary.[94] Upon returning to Pittsburgh after being informed the Pirates no longer required his services, Harry stated that although he was sorry that some bosses didn't appreciate his efforts to improve the organization, it seemed best for all parties involved if he moved on. During an interview, Harry intimated on more than one occasion that Auten was the main objector to his further employment, and Kerr only went along with his partner's decision. Newspapers speculated that Frank Balliet, Auten's nephew and the team secretary before Pulliam's election to that post, would hold down the position again.[95]

On December 14, Pulliam requested the Pirates' organization elect a new team secretary, so he didn't remain in limbo and could negotiate with other teams, such as New York or Chicago, to find a new job.[96] When Harry was unsatisfied with this endeavor, he tendered his resignation, which Kerr and Auten accepted on December 21. That same day, a rumor claimed that Fred Clarke and Barney Dreyfuss would likely be the following two people shown the door. A story from Brooklyn claimed that Dreyfuss's two partners expressed interest in securing Superbas first baseman Hugh "Hughie" Jennings to manage the Pirates. Supposedly, Kerr and Auten had regretted not buying Jennings's release two years earlier.[97] This piece of gossip seemed to be a bit disingenuous since Clarke had already signed a contract to play for and manage Pittsburgh in 1901.[98]

The situation regarding Dreyfuss proved a different matter. When Kerr and Auten decided to fire Pulliam, Barney didn't hesitate to express his true feelings about the unjust treatment of his good friend. During a session before the December league meetings officially commenced in New York, while he'd been cordial to his partners surrounding the dismissal, an angry Dreyfuss offered a blistering rebuke of Kerr and Auten to others in the hotel corridors. This tirade included indiscreet comments and a threat to call a meeting of the organization's directors. When asked later whether he'd made such humiliating, disparaging remarks, Barney issued a strong denial. Supposedly, during another fuming moment, he claimed his fellow Pirates magnates belonged to the class of men called "knockers." The original retraction didn't pass muster in the eyes of Dreyfuss's offended partners. They decided the proper course of action was to strip Barney of the presidency at a board of directors meeting on January 12, 1901.[99]

Baseball writers and others connected to the game theorized that Barney Dreyfuss might retain his shares of stock since it most likely would be difficult to find an individual or consortium willing to purchase minority holdings. Having any say in day-to-day management looked unnegotiable, as Kerr and Auten felt Barney had been out of line on different occasions.[100] Despite a gloomy outlook, Dreyfuss was a resourceful individual. When the organizational meeting occurred on January 12 in the Jersey City office of Pirates team counsel Norman L. Rowe, Barney, who presided over the proceedings, used a crafty ploy to stave off being removed as president. Key people attending the meeting were Dreyfuss, Auten, Kerr, Pulliam, Balliet, and Louisville lawyer D. I. Heyman.

Heyman, who possessed ten shares of stock, protested against the meeting's validity. He asserted that according to the charters and by-laws per the incorporation of the Pirates' organization, and the laws of New Jersey, this meeting was illegal. The basis for Heyman's claim centered on the requirement that notices be sent out twenty days in advance of the date of the summit. Heyman further stated that individuals hadn't adequately drawn up the documents. Therefore they weren't binding to any business dealt with at the meeting. Dreyfuss ruled the point well taken and ordered an immediate adjournment. He then rejected Rowe's protest, as the desire to elect a new team president, presumably Philip Auten, was scuttled for the time being. This course of action only emboldened Barney's detractors to remove the Louisville man from his position. A new press report stated that Auten and Dreyfuss had almost engaged in a physical confrontation throwing punches at the December league meeting in New York.[101]

Barney Dreyfuss had called for this particular conference on January 12 and took the appropriate action, knowing he needed to buy some time to set things into motion. At William Kerr's urging, Norman Rowe planned on undertaking court proceedings in opposition to Dreyfuss's decision to adjourn this meeting.[102] Truthfully, Kerr and Auten had committed a significant blunder back in December, when the election of club officers initially was to take place. Barney called for a vote in the regular order established through the by-laws, but his partners acted timidly and refused to do so. Their tentativeness resulted from the National League technically still being in session regarding the yearly meetings in New York while also fearing such action might cause negative repercussions from fans back in Pittsburgh.

This hesitancy proved problematic for Kerr and Auten if a legal proceeding ever reached the New Jersey Supreme Court. Time also appeared to be an issue since the Court didn't meet until February, and Dreyfuss couldn't file an answer until June. The case, at the earliest, most likely wouldn't be settled until the fall.[103] Rowe, a former judge, attempted to expedite matters by asking for a hearing from just one Court member, Justice Gilbert Collins, who lived in Jersey City.[104] Attorney William D. Edwards, who'd offered a brilliant legal perspective at the recent board of directors meeting, represented Barney at this hearing on January 18.[105] Justice Collins, not wanting to decide the matter on his own, told Rowe to apply for relief to the full bench in February. While talking to the press, the Pirates' attorney vowed that Barney had to go, blamed him for Pittsburgh losing the pennant in 1900, and alleged that both players and stockholders disliked Dreyfuss.[106] In discussing what they believed to be a coup by Kerr and Auten, the *Cleveland Plain Dealer* offered a different opinion.

"Dreyfuss is one of the most popular baseball magnates in the country," wrote this newspaper, "both with the players and with the patrons of the game. He is a true sportsman and gave up a business in Louisville which netted him several times as much as would the most prosperous team in the National League."[107]

Such a prolonged time was unfeasible, primarily when irreconcilable differences existed. Regarding utilizing time, Barney Dreyfuss only needed a little breathing room to gain financial backing before making his next move. Dreyfuss issued an ultimatum to William Kerr and Philip Auten, declaring that he would either sell his team stock or purchase their shares since working under the current arrangement proved untenable. In early February, Barney received an option to buy the controlling stock. All the planning and strategizing by Dreyfuss finally resulted in a positive outcome. On February 18, 1901, the two parties consummated a deal where Barney paid $66,150 for the stock options owned by Kerr and Auten. Partnering with Dreyfuss in this colossal deal were businessmen Oliver Hershman, owner of the *Pittsburgh Press* newspaper, and William Kesley Schoepf, manager of the Consolidated Traction Company.

In Trenton, New Jersey, court proceedings immediately ceased due to Dreyfuss buying out Kerr and Auten. At an election of new officers within the Pittsburgh Pirates' organization, Dreyfuss was named president, Schoepf vice president, and Harry Pulliam secretary and treasurer. Besides the $66,150 related to the current deal, Dreyfuss had also put up $47,000 in cash and the cream of the crop when it came to Louisville's players in December 1899.[108]

After almost two years of wheeling and dealing, Pittsburgh's baseball team solely belonged to Barney Dreyfuss, who could now run the show without objection or interference. Although glory and success became the organization's mission statement, individuals were readily present, bucking Pittsburgh's owner throughout this magnificent baseball journey.

On May 16, 1899, Pittsburgh Pirates ownership named outfielder Patrick "Patsy" Donovan to replace William "Watty" Watkins, who had resigned, as manager of the club. Donovan guided the Pirates to a seventh-place finish in the National League standings. Following the huge consolidation of players between Pittsburgh and Louisville on December 8, former Colonels skipper Fred Clarke became the Pirates' manager. Not desirous of having someone on the roster who used to oversee the team, Clarke sold Patsy to the St. Louis Cardinals on March 9, 1900. (Courtesy of the Library of Congress).

2

The Wayward Pitcher and a Disloyal Veteran

As the Pittsburgh Pirates embarked on a new baseball chapter at the beginning of the twentieth century, obstacles cropped up, guaranteeing that a smooth transition wouldn't take place following the addition of Louisville's best players. Cliques developing when attempting to meld two groups together placed team harmony at risk. Those from the old Pirates guard, possibly loyal to former manager Patsy Donovan or ex-president William Kerr, might not be receptive to any changes in methodology instituted by the new people captaining the ship. Any widening divides within the two camps wrecked diamond cohesion and hindered the goal of contending for a National League pennant.

Southpaw hurler George Edward Waddell couldn't be bothered with belonging to one clique or another. Known as "Eddie" and "Rube," Waddell always preferred to march to the beat of his drum in individualistic bliss. When dealing with Rube, each member of Pittsburgh's baseball hierarchy recently transferred from Louisville had an assignment. Manager Fred Clarke played the taskmaster role, while team president Barney Dreyfuss acted within a neutral capacity. Concerning keeping Rube happy, Pirates team secretary Harry Pulliam had the most important job as his friend and boon companion.

From the very moment Waddell joined the Louisville Colonels in 1897, he took a fancy to the genial Pulliam. As a result, where others failed to deal with the eccentric pitcher, Harry was one person who could handle Rube. When Pulliam told Waddell to do something, he usually willingly obliged. Each day during the baseball season, Harry gave Rube twenty-five cents to buy candy, peanuts, and cigarettes. Every morning, Waddell walked into Pulliam's office and received five nickels. Years later, an anonymous baseball player explained how such a strong friendship proved beneficial, especially regarding incidents like one that occurred at Pittsburgh's home grounds of Exposition Park in 1900.

> I remember one day I was in Pittsburgh some six years ago and a crowd of toughs at the Pittsburgh ball grounds were worrying Mr. Pulliam. While bothering with this obstreperous gang, Waddell happened to draw near and spoke to Mr. Pulliam, and as he did so, he noticed the look of worry on Pulliam's face, and he blurted out: "What's eating you, Harry? What are you worried about, and if I can help you, just sing out, and you know me." And Pulliam answered: "Two or three hoodlums are raising Cain outside the office and I would like to have them fired out of the grounds." [Waddell replied,] "Watch me, Harry, and see how quick I'll punch that gang and make them scatter."
>
> The Rube was as good as his word. Jerking off his coat he rushed out of the office, shot out his fists and used his feet to such an advantage that he had them begging for mercy. In five minutes he had the toughs on the other side of the fence, and I never saw such an exhibition of strength from that day to this. When a man will fight for you he loves you, and this is what Waddell will do any day for Harry C. Pulliam.

On one occasion, Pulliam paid Waddell his two-week salary in one-dollar bills as a joke. Rube took this matter very seriously, as he liked walking around with a bankroll in his pocket the size of a baby elephant's trunk. As a result, Waddell insisted in all future contracts that a club paid him this way when the front office doled out semi-monthly compensation. This method kept Harry busy for several days before payday, gathering one-dollar bills. The currency also had to be worn and soiled since Waddell loathed receiving crisp new bills because he believed they looked fresh from a counterfeiter's hands.[1]

In 1900, when the Pirates traveled to a different city during a road trip, the train stopped at a way station at 2:30 A.M. Rube left his berth and searched out Pulliam, and Waddell finally found Harry asleep in his berth. Rube shook the Pirates' team secretary and asked if he could borrow a dollar.

"What for?" queried Pulliam.

"The train's stopped and I want to get some sandwiches," replied Rube.[2]

Whereas Rube Waddell and Harry Pulliam possessed a strong bond, the hurler and manager Fred Clarke had a strained relationship. Shortly after Waddell arrived in Louisville in 1897, Clarke lost patience with his new pitcher and farmed him out to the minor leagues. Upon arriving back with the Colonels in September 1899, Rube went 7–2, supported by a 3.08 ERA. Waddell pitched brilliantly in his first start for the Pirates in 1900 against the Cincinnati Reds at League Park on April 23. Rube tossed a shutout, scattered three hits, and fanned six as Pittsburgh defeated Cincinnati, 6–0. Waddell never lost focus throughout the contest. His teammates constantly encouraged him while forcing the hurler to attend to business and concentrate strictly on the game.[3]

On April 26, the Pirates almost rallied from a 12–4 deficit in the ninth inning, coming up a run short as the Reds claimed victory at Exposition Park. Rube wasn't around at the end, being relieved by Jack Chesbro in the sixth after Fred Clarke gave him the starting assignment.[4] Waddell chalked up two more losses in his next two starts, although five errors by Pirates teammates aided the St. Louis Cardinals' cause in defeating Pittsburgh, 9–2, at home on May 3. A Pittsburgh newspaper called out Pirates catcher Tacks Latimer for his shoddy work, committing one error and two passed balls.[5] Following the Chicago Orphans' triumph over Rube and the Pirates, 7–6, on May 6, the eccentric southpaw didn't receive another start for over two weeks. Amidst this break, Barney Dreyfuss offered a potential plan for Waddell going forward in 1900.

"Fred Clarke has decided not to use Rube Waddell at home at all any more this season," a Cincinnati newspaper quoted Dreyfuss as saying, "but when we get on our long trips Rube will do his fair share of the pitching, and, if necessary, more, too."[6]

When Pittsburgh played on the road, Waddell roomed with Tacks Latimer before the club shipped out the catcher to the Eastern League's Syracuse Stars. Since Tacks's eccentricity sometimes rivaled Rube's, Fred Clarke figured he would spare other players any possible annoyance by having the two men be roommates. Clarke also assumed that either Waddell or Latimer would kill the other by pulling some stupid prank, thus reducing his stress and worry by fifty percent. Early one morning at the team hotel, Fred heard shrieks from their room while passing down the hall. When Clarke smashed the door open, he found Waddell taking careful aim at Latimer with a big rifle.

"He's going to kill me," howled Latimer.

"Yes sir, that's right, Freddie," agreed Waddell, still sighting the gun. "That's just about what I'm going to do unless you make him quit what he does to me."

After much back and forth between the two players of "no, I don't" and "yes, you do," Clarke finally deciphered what problem existed between Waddell and Latimer. Rube alleged that Tacks threatened to cut his throat with a razor each morning. It seemed that Latimer aspired to catch every game that Rube pitched. Knowing this, Waddell sometimes toyed with Latimer by threatening not to permit Tacks to be behind the dish when he appeared on the bump. Whenever Rube wanted some kind of favor from Latimer, he promised Tacks that he could catch the hurler in his next game.

Days before this rifle incident occurred, the two players engaged in a heated debate. As punishment for Tacks not agreeing with him, Waddell reprimanded the catcher, telling Latimer he wouldn't allow him to be his battery mate in any more games. Sullen and glum over Rube's edict, Tacks decided to take action. For three straight mornings, while shaving, Latimer jumped into bed with the razor in hand, awoke Waddell, and threatened to cut his teammate's throat unless he promised to permit him to catch. Clarke found out that over fear of that razor, Rube sent to his home in Butler County, Pennsylvania, for the gun. Upon delivery of the rifle, Waddell loaded it, awakened Latimer, and pointed it at him right before Fred arrived on the scene.[7]

Strange how half of Fred Clarke's worry didn't disappear after he farmed Tacks Latimer out to the minors. Rube Waddell's performance against the Chicago Orphans on June 19 at West Side Grounds sent mixed signals to Clarke. Although Rube exhibited wildness at various points of the game, walking eight batters, he battled throughout the afternoon in a classic pitcher's duel against Clark Griffith. Waddell also struck out a dozen Orphans as neither team pushed home a run through thirteen innings.[8] Rube worked out of many jams by utilizing a dazzling array of speed pitches and weird curveballs.

While Pittsburgh didn't mount any serious threat through the final five innings, Chicago always seemed to be on the brink of claiming victory. The Orphans finally secured the win in the fourteenth frame. After retiring the first two batters and firing two strikes past William "Billy" Clingman, Rube became too deliberate and issued a walk. Griffith stepped up to the plate and slapped a soft fly ball to left. Three Pirates players desperately chased the baseball, but it fell out of their reach and rolled into foul territory. Clingman quickly made it around the bases to score the game's only run.[9] The baseball correspondent for *Sporting Life*, who went by the nom de plume of Circle, wrote that Waddell performed as Pittsburgh's hero that day. He also stated a deserved victory likely would've swelled Rube's head but that it was okay to swell lads of this kind.[10]

The fall from grace for heroes can sometimes be relatively swift. Waddell lost his next start against the Philadelphia Phillies on June 29 at Exposition Park, 4–2. At home versus the New York Giants on July 5, Rube suffered a 7–3 defeat. Although Waddell only lasted four innings, second baseman Claude Ritchey experienced a more arduous day, committing three errors. Clarke didn't fault Ritchey, saying he shouldn't have even played in the game. Pittsburgh's manager noted that Claude, nearly prostrated from the heat, had stretched out on the sod until fifteen minutes before the contest started.[11]

On July 7, Pittsburgh newspapers announced that manager Fred Clarke had suspended Rube Waddell indefinitely without pay. The *Pittsburgh Post* reported that Waddell insisted on doing all sorts of things and staying out at all hours, greatly affecting his pitching. A lecture by Clarke didn't bring about the desired result.[12] Fred missed dinner that afternoon to make the trek from the ballpark across the Allegheny River to downtown team headquarters to inform Barney Dreyfuss of this decision. Clarke explained he'd taken the action of suspending Waddell and then left without offering a reason. Dreyfuss and Harry Pulliam, who called on the telephone to ask his boss to confirm the suspension rumor, were both in the dark, not knowing the details behind Waddell's situation.[13]

One reason immediately put forward regarding the suspension was that Clarke had tired of hearing stories about Rube's drinking escapades one day earlier on Friday night while entertaining different people.[14] This facet possibly fit into "the last straw" category as a newspaper report on July 8 offered further evidence supporting Fred's decision. People close to Clarke asserted the manager became perturbed over Waddell's claim that he suddenly suffered from rheumatism. Fred later heard that his pitcher had habitually been playing baseball games on back lots against scrub teams. During one of those games, Rube badly stove his finger while performing as a catcher.

Clarke sent for Waddell on the morning of July 7 and demanded an explanation for his behavior. According to the *St. Louis Republic*, Rube flew into a rage, alleging that other Pittsburgh players were attempting to drive him out of the baseball business. Waddell claimed his teammates didn't offer proper support behind him when he pitched, forcing him to do all the work. Rube then provided that he'd struck out 82 opposing batters in 12 games to prove his point. This allegation led to the player and his manager exchanging harsh and angry words.[15]

Rube's suspension was good news for Meyran Avenue inhabitants in the Oakland section of Pittsburgh. Each evening on a back lot in this neighborhood, Waddell engaged in friendly scrub games following his regular duties at Exposition Park. Since the club returned home after a four-game series in Chicago ended on June 20, Rube had missed supper every night, opting to play pick-up baseball until dark. Waddell, who performed the hero role on many occasions, loved playing every position on the field, especially catcher. One night as he worked behind the bat, Rube injured his pitching hand from a foul tip while catching a newsboy hurler.[16] Besides playing with young lads,

Waddell also engaged in games against upstanding local business people on this lot in front of his Oakland boardinghouse. Rube denied injuring his hand while engaging in this activity.[17] During the heated meeting between Fred Clarke and Waddell, the Pirates' manager told his pitcher that the Pittsburgh club would pay him salary no longer to afford amusement to businessmen and small boys in Oakland.[18]

Before Clarke issued this proclamation, he'd repeatedly warned Rube that the Pirates paid him to pitch, and the southpaw twirler should take no unnecessary risks which could result in injury. At the time of his suspension, Waddell had posted a 4–8 record while also fanning 81 opposing batters in 12 games.[19] Since he no longer drew a salary from the Pirates, Rube looked toward alternative means to earn money. On July 9, Waddell secured $25 while pitching for a team from the nearby borough of Millvale in a shutout victory over the Punxsutawney, Pennsylvania, squad.[20] On July 10, Rube played center field and hit a home run that accounted for Millvale's only tally against Punxsutawney. One day later, Pittsburgh newspapers announced that Waddell had signed a contract to play for Punxsutawney throughout the remainder of the season. As Rube traversed around Western Pennsylvania playing baseball, he seemed to have forgotten about his new bride, Florence Dunning Waddell. *Pittsburgh Chronicle Telegraph* editor Alfred R. Cratty notified the public about Mrs. Waddell's current dilemma.

"They say that Rube left his wife without a word as to her future home," said Cratty. "Forgetting that he has a better half has been the big fellow's trick lately. Whenever Mrs. Waddell came along, Rube overlooked that he had a boardinghouse on Meyran Avenue, and hung his hat up somewhere in Allegheny [the municipality where Exposition Park was located that is now the North Side (Northside) section of Pittsburgh]. The club will pay no attention to the big fellow."[21]

Mrs. Waddell hoped to return to her parents' home on Michigan Avenue in Columbus, Ohio.[22] Before the Pirates left for an eastern swing that started in Philadelphia on July 19, Rube's wife reported her unfortunate situation to secretary Harry Pulliam. She requested money for train fare to Columbus. Understanding that the prodigal pitcher might continue throwing his tantrum for some time, Pulliam graciously gave Mrs. Waddell the money for her trip. When baseball writer Circle reported this news in his *Sporting Life* article, he commented about one critic in town claiming the Pittsburgh club helped enable Rube. The writer then said that the policy of some people had been to play Waddell for a freak, and such an approach gave opposing players and managers ammunition for throwing Rube off his game. Brooklyn Superbas skipper Edward "Ned" Hanlon offered a simple explanation when asked why his team diligently harassed Rube and sent him up into the air when playing against Pittsburgh.

"Well," responded Hanlon, "you have been playing him for a fool, and therefore we have the right to go after him on that lay."[23]

Rube Waddell certainly played the fool pitching for Punxsutawney on July 12. While kicking against the umpire over a decision, hoping to get the grandstand crowd on the home grounds revved up, Rube's heel slipped on home plate, and he fell heavily, seriously twisting his neck. As Waddell suffered yet another silly injury, manager Connie Mack of the American League's Milwaukee Brewers was in Pittsburgh dickering for the pitcher's services.[24] Barney Dreyfuss consented to Mack taking Rube for his team and trying to do something with him.[25] A bulletin from Milwaukee on July 21 stated that Waddell indeed would be joining the Brewers and that Mack had practically purchased his release.[26] Pirates team treasurer William Kerr appeared pleased over Rube joining Milwaukee.

"I have an idea that Connie Mack will take good care of the man," said Kerr. "He will use some of his salve on the big fellow. I think that there is a way to handle Rube."

Manager Fred Clarke certainly was happy he no longer needed to deal with Waddell's antics. Fred wouldn't be required to search for Rube when a game started, and the southpaw hurler was off tending bar in some saloon. One time, Waddell had been running around an Indian show just outside Exposition Park's grounds, forgetting his manager selected him to pitch that afternoon. The writer known as Circle alleged that the only solution to Rube's constant unserious behavior was to treat him like a freak. On one occasion when he'd made a trip to Pittsburgh, Rube's father, John Waddell, admitted that his son sometimes acted a trifle light-headed. Years earlier, when hurler Pink Hawley played for the Pirates, he met John Waddell at a tavern and bought him a beer. Hawley seemed a bit perplexed over John's comment offering sincere gratitude.

"My, if my boy only had a head like yours," said John Waddell.[27]

Rube Waddell did dazzling work on the mound for Connie Mack and Milwaukee, winning ten out of thirteen decisions.[28] Unfortunately, for Mack and Brewers fans, Rube's one afternoon of brilliance attracted attention through sports page headlines across America. On August 19, Waddell established a record by pitching twenty-two consecutive innings and securing victories for the Brewers in both games of a doubleheader against the Chicago White Stockings.[29]

The first contest lasted seventeen innings, as Rube claimed a 3–2 decision over Chicago. Before the second game started, both teams agreed to limit the proceedings to five innings. Mack walked up to Waddell with a proposition. Connie told Rube he could skip Milwaukee's next trip to Kansas City, Missouri, and instead go fishing at Pewaukee Lake in Wisconsin if he pitched the second game. Waddell heartily concurred and defeated the White Stockings once again.[30]

Barney Dreyfuss read the story about Rube's outstanding performance in the newspaper.[31] Following Milwaukee's first game in Kansas City, Mack found a telegram at the hotel from Dreyfuss, officially recalling Waddell to Pittsburgh. The Pirates were involved in a hot pennant race in the National League, and Barney believed Rube's pitching could help the team.[32] Manager Fred Clarke, apprehensive about the upcoming eastern trip and desiring to strengthen his pitching staff, agreed with his boss regarding Waddell's return to Pittsburgh.[33] Mack immediately telegraphed Rube at his fishing camp, telling his pitcher that Dreyfuss had recalled him. Rube balked at the order, declaring he would quit baseball before pitching for the Pirates. Rube told Connie he would join Milwaukee when they moved to Indianapolis after playing in Kansas City.

Mack wrote back to Dreyfuss explaining where matters stood. He suggested that Pittsburgh's owner send somebody to Indianapolis to take care of things personally since Waddell could never be bothered with letters or telegrams.[34] Clarke selected catcher Chief Zimmer to handle this delicate task since he experienced good rapport with Rube.[35] Zimmer recently had been lying flat on his back earlier in the month with a kidney problem. The *Pittsburgh Press* joked that Chief suffered more from this illness than when Rube usually crossed him up an average of six times a game when the two worked together as batterymates.[36]

Zimmer arrived in Indianapolis on August 31.[37] Waddell wouldn't listen to reason. He refused to accompany the Pirates' catcher so both men could join the team in Boston. Concerned his trip would be a failure, Chief asked Mack for help convincing Rube to leave. Explaining that he'd taken the wrong approach, Connie offered a few suggestions to Zimmer, including buying Waddell a fancy new wardrobe. The following morning, Chief was waiting for Rube when he came downstairs to the hotel dining room for breakfast. Zimmer immediately whisked Waddell away for a shopping spree where he bought the hurler a new suit of clothes, shoes, shirts, collars, and ties.[38] Chief finished things off with the cherry on top by purchasing a new leather traveling bag for Rube.[39]

Decked out in his new duds, Rube Waddell returned to the hotel. All earlier objections vanished as he eagerly accompanied Zimmer to the train station and left for Boston that night.⁴⁰ The two players rejoined their teammates in Ashtabula, Ohio, as they traveled from Pittsburgh to Boston.⁴¹ Waddell pitched the second game of a Labor Day doubleheader against Boston on September 3 at South End Grounds, breezing past the Beaneaters, 14–1. Although Rube lacked speed, he constantly fooled the Beaneaters' batters with his wicked curveball.⁴² Waddell tossed a complete game, allowing four hits, walking one, and striking out four.⁴³

Pittsburgh experienced a highly successful eastern swing, going 13–3 on the road trip. Upon returning home on September 20, the Pirates stood in second place with a 70–51 record, leaving them four games behind Brooklyn. When they arrived at Union Station that morning, the conquering heroes received a rousing reception from about 20,000 people. The crowd constantly increased in size from 7 A.M. until the train arrived about two hours later. Many of these joyous fans wore badges labeled "Royal Rooters." The Duquesne Greys Band led a parade throughout the city once Pittsburgh's players exited the train. Fans were most keen on searching out and cheering local favorites Honus Wagner and Rube Waddell. The wagon leading this procession contained clever signs such as, "What club is this? Ask Hanlon!" and "Wagner of old was the greatest in music; Wagner of today is the greatest willow musician." A celebratory banquet at Newell's Hotel on Fifth Avenue concluded the festivities.⁴⁴

Six thousand three hundred fans were at Exposition Park that afternoon as Pittsburgh defeated the St. Louis Cardinals in seven innings, 10–4. When the Pirates batted in the first frame, the umpire stopped play so rooters from the Bloomfield section of the city could present Fred Clarke with a floral horseshoe. Waddell appeared taken aback when he also received a gift from fans.⁴⁵ Two small boys handed Rube a big box and ran away. Waddell opened it and then pulled away with a loud howl, kicking over the hat box as it fell to the ground. A dozen crabs ventured out of the box and started moving around. Rube called for help and corralled the crustaceans, returning them to the container.⁴⁶

Waddell turned the tables as the season's end neared. He'd been quite the road warrior in 1900 but found little success pitching at home. On October 11, Rube performed masterfully against Chicago at Exposition Park. He secured a 2–1 victory and fanned twelve Orphans batters. Waddell started the contest by striking out three out of the first four opposing hitters. Rube also struck out the side in the eighth inning. This sublime performance was the first time in the ballpark's history that any hurler had singlehandedly fanned that many batters.⁴⁷ Waddell's father, John, watched his son's excellent pitching achievement from the grandstand.⁴⁸

Pittsburgh finished the 1900 campaign in second place with a 79–60 record, 4½ games behind pennant-winning Brooklyn. These two teams squared off in a postseason series played at Exposition Park and sanctioned by the *Pittsburgh Chronicle Telegraph*. The newspaper donated a $500 solid silver trophy cup to be presented to the series winner.[49] Fred Clarke gave Rube the starting assignment in Game One on October 15. The Superbas prevailed over the Pirates, 5–2. In the eighth inning, with Joseph "Joe" McGinnity at third base and Fielder Jones on first, Brooklyn's William "Willie" Keeler tapped the ball to Waddell. McGinnity broke for the plate before realizing that Rube was running like a holy terror and would beat him to that destination. Joe retraced his steps as Waddell chased him at full speed.

Conditions proved unconducive for nimble maneuvers. McGinnity slipped in the mud, dropping hard to the ground. As Brooklyn's pitcher fell, his head struck the oncoming Rube's knee. Although unconscious for a few minutes, the groggy star Superbas player eventually stood up and finished the game.[50] Brooklyn claimed this series, three games to one, by defeating Pittsburgh, 6–1, on October 18. Waddell came on in relief for starter Sam Leever in the fifth inning and allowed two runs and two hits. Following the game, during a meeting at the Superbas' Monongahela House lodging, at the suggestion of outfielder and team captain Joseph "Joe" Kelley, a unanimous team vote awarded the silver bowl to McGinnity for his gilt-edged work in this series. Pittsburgh Mayor William Diehl presented the trophy to Kelley that evening in between the first and second acts of a play at the Alvin Theater.[51]

Although Rube went 8–13 in 1900, with a league-leading 2.37 ERA, Pittsburgh management immediately started working on trading him to another team after the season ended. When this news reached Waddell, he became indignant, stating he would accept a smaller salary and pitch for the local Homestead team rather than leave Pittsburgh.[52] On March 29, 1901, the *Boston Daily Globe* reported that the National League's Beaneaters had purchased Waddell's release from Pittsburgh at the suggestion of new catcher Malachi Kittridge, who previously played with Rube in Louisville.[53] Boston officials vehemently denied signing Waddell, although interest seemed genuine, and the Pirates appeared intent on selling him to the Beaneaters.[54]

A recent agreement between National League owners and Protective Association of Professional Baseball Players members, of which Chief Zimmer acted as the president, thwarted efforts to sell Waddell. One concession the players achieved from the magnates was that an individual couldn't be suspended or fired from a team for refusing transfer to another organization.[55]

Newspapers reported on March 30, 1901, that Rube had refused a trade to the Boston Beaneaters. Although he wasn't a card-carrying member of the Protective Association, Waddell still received shelter under this new bargaining standard.[56] Barney Dreyfuss found it interesting that Rube unabashedly said, "I don't want to go to Boston," despite them offering to pay him $2,500 a year while he earned $1,500 in salary playing for Pittsburgh.[57]

Rube Waddell remained a member of the Pittsburgh Pirates when the 1901 baseball campaign opened. His first start came against St. Louis at League Park on April 23. The Cardinals hammered Rube and defeated Pittsburgh, 10–4. Surprisingly, Fred Clarke didn't blame Waddell for his poor performance and breaking down against St. Louis.

"Eddie has been up against the same brand of weather that has made us all stiff and slow, and it is not surprising that he failed to make good," declared the manager. "The time for criticism has not arrived. The players cannot be expected to reach a high standard until the weather improves."[58]

The time for criticism eventually arrived quickly. Rube didn't see action again until the Pirates played a practice game against Pittsburgh College (now Duquesne University) on the campus bluff on April 26. Pittsburgh secured an easy 17–3 victory over the Collegians.[59] Waddell left the team before the season's home slate was about to begin, matriculating to his stomping grounds in Prospect, Pennsylvania, with numerous stops to quench his thirst during the journey. John Waddell brought his son back to Pittsburgh on May 1. Clarke decided to start Rube in the game that afternoon against Chicago.[60] Waddell's erratic outing proved a joke, as nine batters faced him in the first inning before Pittsburgh's manager replaced him with Jack Chesbro. Four Orphans reached base on walks, three recorded hits, and four tallies crossed the plate before Fred pulled him with the bases loaded.[61] Chicago won the game, 8–3.

Fred Clarke's patience had reached its limit. Hours after the game on May 2, Clarke stormed into Barney Dreyfuss's office. The irate Pirates manager demanded Pittsburgh's owner sell Waddell, release the hurler, or drop him off the Monongahela Bridge, so long as Dreyfuss got Rube the hell off his team.[62] Barney acquiesced to Clarke's wishes, arranging to move the pitcher to Chicago. Dreyfuss finalized the deal with skipper Thomas "Tom" Loftus, who'd previously managed Rube in the minor leagues. About thirty minutes after the two parties completed this deal, Fred walked into Barney's office a second time and heartily laughed at Loftus.

"Well, I bet a cigar that I get work out him," retorted Tom as he smiled back at Clarke.

Loftus arranged to have a meeting with Waddell at his boardinghouse. When Chicago's manager and Dreyfuss arrived after walking through a rainstorm, they found only his wife, although Rube was supposed to be at his residence. Barney remained outside in the rain as Mrs. Waddell told Loftus that her husband had gone downtown to take care of some outstanding matters. Tom encountered Waddell the following day, signed him to a contract, and shipped the hurler to Chicago on an early train. Much like prophets in the Bible being unwelcome in their hometown, Rube also became resigned to this fact when it came to Pittsburgh. He certainly would miss his old friend Harry Pulliam.[63]

Barney Dreyfuss kept the deal with Chicago a secret until Friday evening after Rube left. An earlier announcement might've made things more difficult due to potential blowback from the pitcher's supporters. Pittsburgh's players were happier now that Waddell had gone since his unpredictability proved a constant nuisance. Catcher John "Jack" O'Connor refused to work behind the plate when Rube pitched.[64] Before leaving Pittsburgh, Waddell had come to Dreyfuss's office and demanded that he receive half of the purchase price paid by the Orphans. Years later, Barney explained how he honored this request.

"I just reached over to my desk and picked up the stogie that had been given to me by the Chicago manager and said: 'You can have it all, Rube,' and gave him the cigar," stated Dreyfuss.[65]

Ironically, one year earlier, a Pittsburgh cigar dealer had marketed the Rube Waddell cigar, placing a picture of the southpaw hurler on every box.[66] Peace of mind didn't last long for Fred Clarke following Waddell's sale to Chicago. Another matter quickly rose to the forefront, forcing the purge of a second player from Pittsburgh's roster. One day after Rube's debacle on the mound against the Orphans, youngster Charles "Truck" Eagan started at shortstop on May 2, in place of veteran William Frederick Ely. The thirty-seven-year-old Ely, known as "Fred," "Bones," and "Father Time," hadn't been in shape because of illness or injury since being sidelined during spring training at Hot Springs, Arkansas. Days earlier, in a game against St. Louis at Exposition Park, Bones played horribly, committing two throwing errors and not turning around to make a play at the plate after receiving a toss from the outfield.[67]

Fred Ely had joined the Pirates when Connie Mack, who managed the club at the time, acquired him from the St. Louis Browns in January 1896. Although revered by local fans for his staunch fielding, Fred gained a place in Pittsburgh baseball folklore because of something he did as a batter. In a game against the Boston Beaneaters on June 27, 1899, Bones stepped up to the plate in the ninth inning with two outs and the Pirates trailing 3–2. Ely connected against a pitch and drove the ball to Exposition Park's left-center field fence. Despite suffering from a charley horse, Bones motored around the bases with reckless abandon. Upon reaching third base, Ely decided to gamble and chugged for home. He beat the relay throw with time to spare. Pittsburgh won the game with a run in the tenth inning. After the contest, fans talked effusively about their new hero.[68] A Pittsburgh newspaper adorned Bones with more glory by authoring a poem titled "Ely's Great Home Run."[69]

In 1901, Ely continued to be hampered by illness and injury. On June 29, outfielder Fred Clarke shifted to shortstop in a game against the Philadelphia Phillies at National League Park and committed three errors. Bones once again covered that position in the next game two days later. On June 28, Clarke had received word that both Ely and third baseman Tommy Leach were disabled and likely couldn't play for one week. To offset these injuries, Barney Dreyfuss purchased Lewis "Lew" Carr from the New York State League's Troy Washerwomen/Trojans.[70] Carr received praise for his solid work after joining the team and being placed at shortstop.[71] Lew remained in the lineup until a fastball from William "Bill" Dinneen drilled him in the arm when Pittsburgh played Boston on July 10 at Exposition Park. Bones received hearty cheers from the crowd upon replacing Carr. Ely immediately electrified the patrons, gobbling up grounders and making sparkling throws to first base. Some supporters reasoned Carr's injury might be a blessing in disguise if Bones maintained this level of play.[72]

Clarke mystified those in the pro-Ely camp when he installed Tommy Leach to play shortstop against the Cincinnati Reds on July 23. Lineup changes became necessary due to the emergence of outfielder Alfonzo "Lefty" Davis, who'd performed brilliantly since becoming the starting right fielder at the end of June, shortly after signing with the club following his release from Brooklyn. The new retooled infield of William "Kitty" Bransfield playing first and Claude Ritchey manning second, with Honus Wagner and Leach handling the left side, appeared to be a formidable unit.[73] Fred initially intended to play Wagner at short, but Honus's reluctance resulted in him remaining at third base.[74]

On July 25, Fred Clarke boarded the train, taking his team to St. Louis. Before leaving that evening, he announced two roster moves to the press. First, the Pirates' skipper revealed that management had given veteran shortstop Fred Ely his unconditional release. Clarke then stated that to bump the Pirates back up to the 16-player limit permitted by the National League, the team signed free agent hurler Edward "Ed" Doheny, who'd been cut loose by the New York Giants ten days earlier.[75] Ely's release certainly surprised many Pittsburgh rooters. Pirates management offered no reason for the dismissal, simply stating the club no longer required his services. Pittsburgh waived their claim to the shortstop for ten days and paid him in full as per his contract. Ely planned on remaining in Pittsburgh for a few days before returning to his Ohio home.[76]

By July 26, Bones had received telegrams from various clubs in both the American and National leagues, asking him to consider signing with their team. Ely also fired back against the Pirates, claiming personal reasons were the impetus behind his release from the squad.

"I'm going up to Girard [in Erie County, Pennsylvania] and lay in Lake Erie for a week," said Ely. "After that I'll accept one of the offers I received today. Dreyfuss is determined to get rid of the Kerr men on the team. Tannehill will be the next to go, and after him will be several others. It was purely spite work on Dreyfuss's part. When Carr joined the team in Philadelphia Dreyfuss gave Manager Clarke orders to play him even if he was only half as good as I. Dreyfuss came to the park yesterday and handed my release to Clarke, with instructions to deliver it to me. Fred refused to take it, and Barney handed it to me myself. My game was as good as any shortstop in the league."[77]

Dreyfuss's initial comment regarding the release offered a contrasting point of view. Barney stated that the organization made this move because he figured his club was more likely to win the National League pennant with Leach at shortstop and Wagner playing third base.[78] Fred Clarke wasted no time refuting Ely's claims, writing out a detailed statement for the press on July 27, explaining his decision.

> I am, and have always been the manager of the Pittsburgh Club. In fact, as well as in name, and every member of the team is on the team on my judgment. I am striving always for the best interest of the team and the city of Pittsburgh in a baseball sense, and am willing to be judged by the results accomplished. Ely's release was with my approval and consent. I consider Tommy Leach a better man for the team.
>
> Ely's statement that I refused to tender him his notice is absolutely not true. His statement that he or any other member of the team was released or is to be released on account of the so-called Kerr clique is untrue.
>
> In making up the team I know no man's influence or objection, be it Captain Kerr or any other man. I am looking for the best results and every man is tried only by his own merits.
>
> His statement that I am to release Tannehill is untrue. In conclusion I wish to state that while some may criticize my action I, by my constant work

with the team, am in a better position to judge a player's ability and work and decide on the advisability of his presence on or off the team.

I am willing to let my judgment stand the test of final results, which, after all, in baseball, like in other vocations, speak louder than words.

The alleged interview with me in today's *St. Louis Star* was a fake pure and simple. I never saw a reporter on this newspaper.

—Fred C. Clarke, Manager Pittsburgh Ball Club.[79]

Regarding being in the best position to judge a player's ability and work, Clarke's desire to move Honus Wagner to shortstop became a reality in the game against St. Louis on July 27. Regarding Bones Ely, Pittsburgh's players weren't very pleased over him grumbling about his release. Pirates members firmly declared they had no input into the decision regarding the veteran shortstop's discharge from Pittsburgh and didn't deserve the criticism he hurled their way.[80] Ely seemed to be singling out Claude Ritchey, making disparaging remarks about the Pirates' little second baseman.[81] One team member, who asked to remain anonymous, admonished Bones for his childish behavior in a Pittsburgh newspaper article.

"Ely knows why he was released," said the anonymous player. "He also knows that he is not in Hans Wagner's class in fielding, batting, or base running. I don't blame him for being sorry that he was let out, for this is a good team to play with. After he was released why didn't he take his medicine like a man and not go around telling tales out of school and trying to hurt the men who played beside him. If we wanted to talk we might make Mr. Ely crawl into his hole. A ballplayer who carries a hammer is making a mistake."[82]

After mulling over his offers, Fred Ely signed with Connie Mack's Philadelphia Athletics and played his first game in the rival American League against the Boston Americans at Columbia Park on August 3.[83] Hashing out the reason why Ely indeed drew his release mirrored Rube Waddell's situation one year earlier when he received a suspension, as a myriad of incidents explained the shortstop's dismissal. One theory behind the release surrounded a clubhouse confrontation between Fred Clarke and Bones following a game against the Brooklyn Superbas at Exposition Park on July 19.[84] That contest, which Pittsburgh lost, 5–4, ended when umpire Robert "Bob" Emslie called Clarke out at second base on a stolen base attempt.

Clarke immediately jumped to his feet, seething with rage.[85] "What, calling me out?" shouted Fred. "Why I was on the bag before he got the ball near me." Fred then tore off his cap, threw it on the ground, spiked it, and lurched toward Emslie.[86] Several hundred bleacher fans rushed onto the field and surrounded the two men.[87] Clarke shook his fist under the umpire's nose. He then pushed and jostled Emslie, yelling, "You know it was not out." Brooklyn team members rushed to assist the arbiter. They escorted him to the dressing room, with the mob following close behind. One of these angry fans stole Emslie's mask that lay on the diamond.[88] In the clubhouse after the game, the two Freds had an altercation over the conduct of Pittsburgh's manager toward the umpire. Although an original rumor about a physical fight proved unfounded, they did indeed have a fiery argument. The two men didn't exchange words after this, leading to speculation that a rift had developed between Ely and Clarke.[89]

Another plausible reason for Bones's release proved a bit more nefarious. During the previous off-season, Barney Dreyfuss and Clarke had attempted to trade Ely to different teams. St. Louis spurned an offer of Bones and another good player for Cardinals shortstop Roderick "Bobby" Wallace. New Cincinnati Reds skipper John "Bid" McPhee turned down a deal of Ely and a star Pirates pitcher for hurler Frank "Noodles" Hahn and shortstop Thomas "Tommy" Corcoran. Boston manager Frank Selee laughed at Clarke when he suggested a straight-up transaction of Bones for shortstop Herman Long. Fred concluded that every other National League manager considered their shortstop superior to Ely.

A .208 batting average during his time with the Pirates in 1901 corroborated these baseball leaders' assessments. Although diminishing skills were unavoidable for a veteran player, disloyalty by a disgruntled employee was never acceptable under any circumstances. Following his release from the Pirates, Ely's good friend in the newspaper business unleashed a bombshell, alleging that the organization jettisoned the shortstop from the roster for conspiring with the enemy as an American League agent. This individual felt compelled to step forward with the truth because Bones didn't accept his dismissal gracefully, instead opting to squeal and complain. This associate offered stark commentary about Ely's insubordinate activities over the past few weeks.

"Probably the principal cause for the release of Ely was the connection of his name with an American League team in this city next year," said the former shortstop's friend. "If the National and the American leagues do not amalgamate or come to an amicable understanding at the close of this season it is certain that Pittsburgh will be represented in the opposition league next year and Ely is slated for manager. Local capitalists with plenty of money are ready to buy an American League franchise and put the strongest team in Pittsburgh that money can obtain. It is said that grounds have been located within five minutes ride from the downtown section and if the American League does not consolidate with the National, there will be two big league clubs in Pittsburgh next season."

Another friend of Ely's claimed that an American League agent had approached Bones two weeks earlier, asking him to sign a contract to play in their organization. Ely stated that he couldn't discuss such business until his current contract expired in October. Abiding by these words was the honorable action, rather than possibly helping secure grounds for an American League team or convincing a few players to jump the Pirates. This tract indicated that some quid pro quo most likely existed as payment for services rendered.[90] Front office people also traced Bones's movements one stormy night to the residence of former Pittsburgh owner William Kerr. Kerr and onetime partner Philip Auten might be eager to become owners again, believing the Smoky City's baseball pie was big enough to divide between two teams.[91]

Bones Ely's treachery certainly affected the Pirates' play on the field. When Pittsburgh returned home for a game against Cincinnati on August 3, newspapers in the city friendly to Kerr pumped out the propaganda, roasting the organization for releasing Fred. This unfair criticism made some Exposition Park fans hostile toward the home team.[92] A third potential reason behind Ely's summary dismissal became known four years after he played his final game in a Pittsburgh uniform. In 1905, Fred Clarke offered insight surrounding what had motivated him to dump Bones from the team.

"We once had a great shortstop—Fred Ely," said Fred Clarke in August 1905. "He had a sore finger one day and said he couldn't play. I told him I had no one to put in his stead. I teased him, but it was of no avail. The upshot was that I went in and played the position, but you may depend on it that Ely was released. He showed that he did not have his heart in his work—a trait indispensable in a winning ballplayer. Pluck is absolutely indispensable in practically every sport, but particularly in the game of baseball, where you must display sand and grit to accomplish anything worthwhile. The man who has those qualities and can play will invariably win out."[93]

Clarke elaborated on this account in 1911 when discussing the spirited attitude of his second baseman that year, John "Jack" Miller, who refused to leave the lineup although he'd injured his finger. In telling this story about Bones Ely, Fred confused the years, mistakenly claiming it occurred during the pennant drive of 1900 when it happened in the summer of 1901. According to Clarke, while the team was on their eastern swing in late June, Bones injured the finger on his throwing hand. In Fred's opinion, such an injury would only present a minor inconvenience for an ordinary baseball player. Clarke expressed shock when Ely told his manager he couldn't play against Philadelphia on June 29, 1901, leading Fred to refuse to permit him to miss the game. Bones then whined that his finger hurt too much to play that afternoon.

The Pirates' skipper attempted to coax him to take the field, but after this didn't work, he simply said, "Well, if you don't play today you'll never play for the Pittsburgh club again." A stubborn Ely didn't participate in pre-game practice, and once the contest started, he remained in uniform on the bench. Clarke received harsh criticism from the press for his action, although Ely did return to the starting lineup on different occasions throughout July. While relating this story, Clarke alleged that Barney Dreyfuss and Harry Pulliam initially appeared stunned when the manager arrived at his decision to release Bones. Clarke described what happened concerning the Ely affair during a meeting of the three men at the Pirates' club offices.

"I want you to write out Ely's release he cannot play for me again," Clarke began when talking about the incident that happened a decade earlier.

> Then there was trouble. President Barney grew pale at the very thought of canning his great shortstop. Pulliam gaped in astonishment, knocked his tie away and forgot to straighten it out again.
>
> "You're crazy!" he yelled at me; "you're batty even to dream of such a thing! Why, the public would boycott us."
>
> Mr. Dreyfuss at first refused to listen to me. Finally he attempted to expostulate; he tried to get me to change my mind. But I was determined and when, after a little confab, Ely's release was denied me, I walked over to a desk, sat down, and commenced to write.
>
> "What are you writing?" inquired the president after a few minutes had elapsed.
>
> "I am writing my resignation as manager of the Pittsburgh Baseball Club," I replied.
>
> This brought them to time. When I left I had Ely's release in my pocket.

On the subject of Honus Wagner, Fred Clarke claimed he was scared to death to make a move to shortstop, fearing the home fans would roast him unmercifully for replacing a beloved player like Bones Ely. Clarke finally issued an ultimatum before the game against St. Louis on July 27 that Honus either play shortstop that afternoon or not at all. Pittsburgh's manager exhibited shrewdness by making this change when the Pirates played on the road for a few days.

While the squad lined up at Exposition Park before the first home game since Ely's release against Cincinnati on August 3, the crowd heckled and booed both Clarke and Wagner. This attitude was short-lived, as Honus's brilliance at that position changed those jeers to cheers, with Pittsburgh's fans yelling louder for Wagner than they ever had for Bones.[94]

One man not directly close to the situation offered his opinion on what most likely greatly impacted Fred Ely's release. After spending Thanksgiving in Cincinnati, eating dinner with his father and mother on November 28, 1901, American League president Byron Bancroft "Ban" Johnson hustled back to Chicago. While offering an organizational status update before the upcoming league meeting at the Auditorium Hotel on December 2, Johnson also weighed in on Ely's actions the previous summer.

"Barney Dreyfuss was frightened by the visit of Frank Hough [a sportswriter and American League agent], who wanted to land a couple of his men for Connie Mack," said President Ban. "At that I think that Hans Wagner is the only Pirate who was ever approached. Colonel [William] Kerr sent for Hough. The Colonel is ambitious to get back into the game, but I never figured Pittsburgh as a good place for two clubs. Both of them nearly starved to death in '90 [Pittsburgh had teams in both the National League and Players' League in 1890]. Still Barney was scared, and Fred Ely lost his head, doubtless because he was too good a friend of Colonel Kerr."[95]

According to Ban Johnson, overzealousness and excessive hubris led to the discovery of Bones Ely's motives related to him sneakily colluding with the American League. On efforts such as those perpetrated by Ely and Frank Hough attempting to steal Pirates players, Johnson planned on being front and center, causing more problems for Barney Dreyfuss and Fred Clarke in 1902.

Although Pirates fans revered him for his staunch fielding, shortstop Bones Ely achieved folklore status in Pittsburgh for hitting a clutch inside-the-park home run at Exposition Park on June 27, 1899. A little over two years later, on July 25, 1901, the Pirates handed Ely his unconditional release. One reason for this move centered on Bones acting as an agent for the rival American League, working against the organization that paid his salary. A second explanation for the release, courtesy of manager Fred Clarke, resulted from Ely refusing to play in a game because of a sore finger. In this photo of the 1896 Pittsburgh Pirates, Bones is standing on the far right, in the top row. (Photo in the Public Domain).

3

Et Tu, Brute? Traitors in the Ranks

Every successful baseball team possesses an individual who toils anonymously, delivering the goods each day and leading his squad to victory while not necessarily garnering attention in the press or receiving plaudits from the fans. Although sometimes inconspicuous to the outside world, these men who act as a squad's unsung heroes certainly are appreciated by the baseball brothers who perform beside them on the diamond. When it came to the fortunes of the 1901 Pittsburgh Pirates and the literal survival of that entity as a viable contending franchise, a name unknown to Fred Clarke and his players acted as that team's true unsung hero. G. L. Richards of Galesburg, Illinois, rightfully earned that title in the eyes of Pirates owner Barney Dreyfuss.

Richards, a former Pittsburgh resident, was instrumental in helping Dreyfuss thwart an effort by Ban Johnson and the American League to curry favor with members of the Pirates, hoping to entice them to jump to that organization. Up to this point, Pittsburgh remained practically unscathed when it came to players switching to Johnson's association which functioned as a major league in 1901 after holding down minor league status in 1900. In the spring of 1901, the Baltimore Orioles' John McGraw swooped in and grabbed Pirates third baseman James "Jimmy" Williams, who'd arrived early at Hot Springs, Arkansas, to work out before the team's training session started. During an interview with Albert "Al" Abrams of the *Pittsburgh Post-Gazette* decades later in 1931, Dreyfuss recalled Richards's critical assistance toward revealing that traitors had become embedded among the Pittsburgh Pirates.

> While the other clubs were being riddled right and left in 1901 by raids from the American League, Ban Johnson gave out the impression that the

Pittsburgh team would not be tampered with. We didn't allow this to fool us and kept a watchful wake at every turn.

Although I knew that efforts were being made to get in touch with my players, the first real intimation that I received came through a letter to me from former Pittsburgher, G. L. Richards of Galesburg, Ill., in 1901. While I didn't know him, Mr. Richards wrote me that he had information that was of great importance to me.

He stated, that while staying in the Walton Hotel [Hotel Walton] in Philadelphia on a recent trip, his room happened to be above one, from which he could hear voices very plainly. He said that the radiator pipes were unscrewed, and that he heard everything that was said in the room below. The names of [Honus] Wagner, [Claude] Ritchey, [Jesse]Tannehill, and [Jack] Chesbro came up in the conversation, and this was enough to tell Richards that a raid was being planned on the Pittsburgh club. The name of Jack O'Connor was prominently mentioned and it was revealed that he was doing the undercover work for the American League while receiving his pay as a catcher on our club.

After "listening in" on the full conversation, Richards heard the men preparing to leave their room, and immediately stepped out himself, getting on the same elevator with them. He described one as "small and dark complected," another "heavy set and blustering in his actions and talk," and another "tall and very thin."

I concluded from this that they were Tom Shibe [son of Philadelphia Athletics owner Benjamin "Ben" Shibe], Ban Johnson and Connie Mack. There was another, whom I later found out to be Jim McAleer, then manager of the St. Louis Browns and later pilot of the Cleveland Indians [McAleer managed the Cleveland Lake Shores in 1900, the Cleveland Blues in 1901, and then the Browns from 1902 through 1909].

Armed with this critical information, Barney Dreyfuss acted swiftly. He ushered Bones Ely into his office and called him out for working as an American League agent against the Pirates, which played a partial role in his release from the team. Dreyfuss also cleverly rented out three different pieces of property that might be attractive as potential ballpark sites to Ban Johnson if he placed an American League team in Pittsburgh. Barney procured old Recreation Park, which local National League and American Association teams had used from 1884 through 1890, vacant ground on Craft Avenue in the city's Oakland section, and a big empty lot on Liberty Avenue in the Lawrenceville district.¹ Dreyfuss's most cunning move involved signing his players for the 1902 season.

While talking with Cincinnati sportswriter Charles "Charlie" Zuber, pitcher Jesse Tannehill revealed that Dreyfuss had approached the players at the end of July and informed them of his willingness to sign every person at their salary terms for the upcoming campaign. Each player, other than Tannehill, wrote down their figures, and Barney signed them for 1902. Speculation pointed toward these being personal contracts rather than baseball documents. Jesse declared he didn't want to sign, believing he could be traded during the off-season. An American League agent seemed surprised when newspapers reported this story.² Tannehill finally came into line on August 6.³ The astute Dreyfuss had re-signed every Pittsburgh team member, irrespective of the high price, to keep his stellar baseball squad intact.⁴

The generosity of Pittsburgh's owner, coupled with brilliant foresight when circumventing American League overtures toward his players, paved the way for harmony and success. Months after being sold by Pittsburgh to the Chicago Orphans, former hurler Rube Waddell offered his impressions on where the Pirates stood as pennant contenders. Although Rube claimed he wasn't a knocker, the eccentric pitcher predicted Pittsburgh would never win the pennant because the men didn't play well together and did too much wrangling to execute consistent, winning baseball.⁵ Waddell ended up being incorrect, as the Pirates secured their first National League pennant in franchise history. The 1901 squad posted a 90–49 record, placing them 7½ games in front of the second-place Philadelphia Phillies.

Receiving extremely credible intelligence from G. L. Richards and rooting out a traitorous despot such as Bones Ely were vital factors in Pittsburgh's achievement. While Ely had packed his bags and moved on, another man frequently mentioned during that meeting at the Hotel Walton remained on the Pirates' payroll. Regarding catcher Jack "Peach Pie" O'Connor, Dreyfuss possibly clung to the old axiom of "keep your friends close and your enemies closer." A fifteen-year veteran who'd received his start in 1887 with the American Association's Cincinnati Reds, the Pirates purchased O'Connor from the St. Louis Cardinals for $2,000 on May 22, 1900. In his first entire season with the team in 1901, Jack batted .193.

O'Connor was a throwback from the rough-and-tumble days of nineteenth-century baseball. As a member of the American Association's Columbus Solons in 1891, the team suspended Jack indefinitely without pay on July 1 for conduct unbecoming a gentleman and a baseball player. His assaults and vindictive actions against opposing players on the home grounds caused a steep drop in attendance. O'Connor had also been drinking to the point that it affected his diamond performance.[6] The root cause behind Columbus's recent poor play seemed to be Jack's behavior, leading the front office to issue a resolution calling for manager Gustavus "Gus" Schmelz to suspend the catcher. O'Connor, whose foul language on the field had become unbearable, played the part of a scapegoat since an investigation showed other players had also engaged in behavior that destroyed their usefulness to the organization.[7]

Jack never gave any quarter, even against former teammates. In the first game Pittsburgh played, after Bones Ely's release, against St. Louis on July 26 at League Park, O'Connor was involved in a confrontation against his prior club. Jack became upset when Cardinals players interfered with his effort to grab the baseball, which had rolled under the St. Louis bench following a poor throw from Pirates first baseman Kitty Bransfield. O'Connor finally secured the ball, rushed toward home plate, and joined his teammates in an argument with umpire Henry "Hank" O'Day. As some Cardinals players participated in the exchange, Jack started swinging his fists at manager and outfielder Patsy Donovan. St. Louis pitcher Edward "Ed" Murphy surprised O'Connor and landed a vicious knockout punch to the catcher's chin that left him motionless, lying on the ground. When Jack regained consciousness, he jumped to his feet and attempted to reach Murphy, but members of both teams thwarted that effort.[8]

Jack O'Connor experienced one of his best seasons at the plate in 1902, batting .294. Being able to remain intact proved beneficial for Barney Dreyfuss and his team as the Pirates steamrolled over all National League opposition in 1902. After Pittsburgh swept the St. Louis Cardinals in three straight games at League Park to open the season, the *St. Louis Star* contemplated whether the Pirates could win all 140 games on their schedule.[9] Although Pittsburgh didn't achieve an undefeated record as this newspaper suggested, they performed brilliantly in 1902, posting a 103–36 mark. The Brooklyn Superbas finished in second place, 27½ games behind the Pirates.

Under cover of victories and diamond success, O'Connor deftly attempted to execute his disruptive plan, working the levers of power like a politician. Such a delicate task required help, and southpaw Pirates hurler Jesse "Tanny" Tannehill proved more than happy to supply support when the time came as his able lieutenant. Tannehill, who first joined Pittsburgh in 1897, was considered one of the top left-handed twirlers in baseball. Jesse had reached the twenty-victory plateau for three consecutive seasons from 1898 through 1900. While Tannehill only went 18–10 in 1901, his 2.18 ERA led the National League.

Jesse lowered that to a 1.95 ERA in 1902, as he posted a 20–6 record. Nobody ever questioned that Tannehill possessed immense talent and ability. On the other hand, it seemed fair to scrutinize his attitude and personality.

In 1899, then Pirates manager Patsy Donovan experienced a problem with Jesse. For two weeks in September, Tannehill didn't appear in a game for Pittsburgh. Jesse had informed Donovan that he wasn't in shape to take his regular turn on the mound. Patsy acquiesced to his hurler's wishes, believing it better to save a piece of valuable baseball property rather than lose it. Some people thought Tannehill was faking his injury and didn't want to work. This situation represented the most significant transgression committed that year by players taking advantage of Donovan due to his benevolent nature. Patsy's passive approach to handling Jesse's case caused a divide to develop between him and owners William Kerr and Philip Auten.[10]

A new management team of Barney Dreyfuss and Fred Clarke being in place for 1900 didn't change Tannehill's mindset. As the season progressed, Jesse claimed he couldn't work for one reason or another when, in reality, the southpaw hurler became unenthused when reaching the point in the campaign where he felt he'd toiled enough to earn his salary.[11] Regarding the postseason Cup Series against the Brooklyn Superbas, Jesse claimed Clarke hadn't asked him to participate in any of the games. At the same time, the Pirates' manager alleged the southpaw refused to pitch.[12] Earlier that year, a verbal confrontation occurred between Tannehill and Pittsburgh's manager during a game.

"Barney understands that you are lazy," said Clarke. "Get a hustle on you."

"That's all right," retorted Tanny. "You go and play left field and I'll pitch the game."

Fred Clarke and Jesse Tannehill had also become involved in a fight on one occasion while the Pirates held spring training in Hot Springs, Arkansas.[13] After Bones Ely's release on July 25, 1901, *The Sporting News* correspondent, who went by the penname Duquesne, offered information about one of the veteran shortstop's chums on the Pirates. Duquesne stated that a pitcher, friendly to Ely, was supposedly sick in one instance that season and too ill to report for a critical practice session called for by Clarke. This hurler suddenly became well enough to attend an all-day picnic and stand on his feet for two hours umpiring a baseball game.[14] It wasn't a leap for Pirates fans to deduce that the pitcher in question was likely Tannehill because of his strong friendship with Bones.

Jesse's obstinate and abrasive temperament made him a prime candidate to stir up trouble whenever the mood suited him. Near the end of his career, Tannehill offered insight into what may have molded him into the type of player some categorized as a disruptive force against team harmony. Jesse seemed to be a jaded individual due to the treatment he'd received after breaking in with the Cincinnati Reds in 1894 as a nineteen-year-old and pitching a beautiful game in his second start with the team.

> After I had pitched that game for them, and went to the Cincinnati park the next morning, I thought I had made a mistake and got on the wrong grounds. Why, for a time I thought the players on the team had forgotten me. At first not a member of the team spoke to me. They passed me by without so much as a nod of the head. Those who did look at me did so with a stare as much as to say, "What are you doing here, anyhow?" I was only a green kid and this kind of treatment nearly broke my heart. I felt that I couldn't do anything on that team. Indeed, it looked as though the old-timers hoped I wouldn't succeed. I believe this is the way most youngsters are treated.
>
> I know I would have been in for the same dose at Pittsburgh if I had stood for it. When I went to that team the old-timers started to give me the same treatment I had been accorded at Cincinnati, but I returned as good as they sent. I answered stare with stare. I was as cold as they were and I didn't try to warm up a bit. I said to myself, "I have come to paddle my own canoe; I shall do my part and that is all anyone can ask of me." In short time I was on par with the best of them. A youngster who expects to have easy sailing when he comes into the big league is going to be fooled. When he takes his place it means that someone has got to go. There is no telling who will succeed. Self-preservation is the first law of nature and a ballplayer is not going to dig his own grave. The first two or three months in a big league are the hardest in a player's experience. If he wins—oh, well, everybody knows the answer.[15]

In response to his shabby treatment at the hands of veteran players in Cincinnati and Pittsburgh, Jesse Tannehill thought it best to be one of the individuals who broke youngsters' hearts. When Ginger Beaumont debuted with Pittsburgh in 1899, Tannehill was part of the clique, including Bones Ely and outfielder Thomas "Tom" McCreery, who constantly poked fun at him. They believed Beaumont to be the funniest thing they'd ever witnessed. The treatment and hazing Jesse administered toward Ginger were particularly severe and harsh. This type of behavior certainly didn't elevate his popularity among some team members.[16]

One Pittsburgh baseball writer observed that when Tannehill first arrived in the Smoky City, he was an ambitious young man with a cheerful disposition. Noting a change as time passed, with Jesse becoming prone to sneer at reporters, this scribe cited the pitcher's comment about those in his writing profession during a discussion in the sleeper car of a train, saying, "They are like umpires—all bad." Another remark that Tannehill made to a young Pirates member revealed the true motives surrounding his priorities.

"You will come near making a record," exclaimed the youngster admiringly.

"Record be blamed," retorted Jesse. "It's the money I'm after. I am too old to be looking for the records."[17]

Ban Johnson and the American League acted as the beautiful road paved in gold for those who fantasized about grabbing unimaginable riches. The first visible sign of problems in the Pirates' camp regarding treacherous intentions emerged while the team played in Brooklyn. On the evening of June 11, 1902, sportswriter Harold Lanigan's dispatch from a St. Louis newspaper claimed that catcher Jack O'Connor and shortstop Honus Wagner had signed to play for the American League's Browns team from that city. For the remainder of the evening, phones at Pittsburgh newspaper offices rang as reporters attempted to verify the integrity behind this claim. By 8 P.M., ridiculous rumors abounded that every Pirates player had jumped to the American League other than O'Connor, Wagner, and manager Fred Clarke. Jack vehemently denied that he planned on heading to the American League, while Honus calmly stated that Barney Dreyfuss could answer for him.[18]

Despite his denials, those residing in O'Connor's hometown of St. Louis understood for some time that Jack was dissatisfied with his berth in Pittsburgh. The *St. Louis Republic* later reported that the premature publication of this story was the only thing that prevented Pirates players from joining the St. Louis Browns.[19] Dreyfuss started an investigation regarding the O'Connor allegation and found that the newspaper report was accurate. The colossal error this inquiry unearthed was that Wagner acted as Jack's partner in crime. Initially, American League sympathizers offered Honus twice as much as O'Connor regarding salary before telling him he could name any amount he wanted regarding money and contract length. Wagner remained loyal to the man many considered to be the most generous employer in baseball.[20] After the team completed a series in Chicago on June 26 and prepared to leave for Cincinnati, Pittsburgh outfielder Lefty Davis revealed that individuals had contacted him about jumping leagues.

"Just before we left Chicago for Cincinnati on Thursday I was approached by a representative of the Chicago American League Club and asked to make my price for playing under [Charles] Comiskey next season," said Davis. "I had no figure to give them, for I am well satisfied with Pittsburgh and know that President Dreyfuss will pay me all that I am worth."[21]

Barney Dreyfuss immediately utilized detectives to track Jack O'Connor's movements.[22] While recuperating from an injury for nearly two weeks at his St. Louis home, Jack conducted conferences with American League officials on more than one occasion.[23] After the Pirates concluded a long road trip on August 14 that started in Chicago and eventually shifted through the league's eastern cities, Fred Clarke announced that American League agents had approached every team member during their time away from Pittsburgh. Clarke also stated that through this exhausting endeavor, each player received a promise of a higher salary than they earned playing for the Pirates.[24] One rumor alleged that Pittsburgh's manager had been guaranteed $20,000 over three years for switching leagues.[25]

As that road trip wound down in Boston, Honus Wagner came to Barney Dreyfuss's hotel room one night at 1 A.M. According to Dreyfuss, decades later, Wagner earned $10,000 a year in salary, a fact unknown to the general public or bad actors. Honus requested a contract from Barney that night. Pittsburgh's shortstop had grown tired of the constant hounding by agents about jumping leagues. Since Wagner always responded that he'd already signed a Pittsburgh contract (the personal contracts from 1901 were two-year deals), Honus wanted to make it official. Having no contracts in his possession, Dreyfuss placed a blank piece of paper before him, which Wagner signed without knowing how much salary he would earn.[26] Honus became one of the first players to fall in line, committing to the Pirates for 1903 and 1904.[27]

The time had arrived for the American League to make their bold and daring move. Pirates magnate Barney Dreyfuss exhibited supreme preparedness thanks to a multi-layered intelligence apparatus that included a network of loyal operatives. In his 1931 interview with Al Abrams, Dreyfuss explained how the wheels of deceit started moving into motion.

> O'Connor came to me one day while in Boston and asked for leave of absence to go to Brooklyn to see his sick wife. I consented, and still can recall that day. I was sitting on the sidewalk in front of the hotel when O'Connor came rushing out in a hurry to catch his train. His pockets were bulging with baseballs and two of them fell out as he dashed past me. I picked them up, but by that time he had crossed the street. I called to him, that he had dropped something, but not wanting to miss his train and somewhat

abashed for taking the balls he asked me to throw them to him, after I had suggested that he return and get them handed to him.

I forgot to mention that I was in charge of the club on that eastern trip, as Fred Clarke, the manager, was badly spiked and was forced to stay home [Clarke actually did accompany the squad on the road trip and suffered an injury in the final game on August 14], and Harry Pulliam, then our secretary, was spending a well-earned vacation at Saratoga Springs.[28]

Being in the right place at the right time proved beneficial, helping Dreyfuss receive direct evidence of the American League's plans from an unexpected source. On August 15, Pittsburgh finished its long journey across the country by relaxing at the shore and playing an exhibition game in Atlantic City, New Jersey. The Pirates crushed a local team, 18–1.[29] Jesse Tannehill collected five hits in the game while playing right field for Pittsburgh. The *Pittsburgh Press* reported that Jesse injured his right arm after the game. Tannehill swung his limb awkwardly while exiting an omnibus at the team hotel and threw it out of joint. The newspaper reported that Pittsburgh's owner accompanied his pitcher to a local hospital, where a doctor restored Jesse's arm to its proper condition.[30]

It turned out that the explanation given out explaining Tannehill's injury was a deliberate fabrication. A newspaper exposed the actual story in print after the season ended, when National League owners held a meeting in Chicago about brokering peace with the American League. Jesse had injured his shoulder after locking arms with teammate James "Jimmy" Burke in a wrestling tussle. Burke balked at witnessing the surgical procedure required to fix the athlete's painful injury. As a result, Barney Dreyfuss solely accompanied Jesse to the hospital. After medicos administered ether to Tannehill before the operation, Dreyfuss became shocked and astounded when his player started mumbling about a raid against the Pirates. Jesse revealed just enough details of the plot to confirm that many suspicions Barney held happened to be accurate and galvanized him into action.[31]

Jack O'Connor wasn't with the team in Atlantic City since he supposedly had traveled to Brooklyn to be with his sick wife. Continuing his 1931 conversation with Al Abrams after discussing O'Connor's leave of absence, Dreyfuss related how all the pieces fell into place in his efforts to outmaneuver disloyal members of the Pirates and American League representatives.

> We were playing an exhibition game in Atlantic City the next day with
> a picked team of collegians. After the game Jess Tannehill and Jimmy

Burke got into a fight. I can't recall if it was friendly or not. Burke pinned Tannehill's arms behind his back, knocking the left arm, the one he twirled with, out of its socket.

I took Tannehill to the Atlantic City hospital, where three men were forced to keep him down before an anesthetic could be applied and his arm put back in place. While under the ether Tannehill spilled the whole story in the presence of myself and the doctor, as to the planned raid of the American Leaguers; of his talk with Ban Johnson, and named the different players that were to be approached.

When we were leaving Philadelphia later that night I was met at the station by Tim Hurst, the umpire, and he informed me that he had seen O'Connor at the Gilsey House [a hotel in New York City] in conference with Ban Johnson and other American Leaguers.

I ran across O'Connor a few minutes later, but after trying to dodge me I caught up with him and asked him to see me the next morning in my office at 10 o'clock. He didn't show up, however, and while I was leaving the building after waiting for some time I was called by a telegraph operator in an office on the main floor and informed that O'Connor had been there and sent out a wire, which I later found out was sent to Ban Johnson and reads as follows: "The jig's up. Come here at once."

In the afternoon of the same day, an answer came to this telegram, but was delivered to the press box in the ballpark. Operator friends of mine intercepted the wire and informed me of its contents which read: "Will be on Cleveland flyer tomorrow." Signed by Ban.[32]

Setting up the timetable of events, upon returning home from the East, Pittsburgh swept a doubleheader against the Philadelphia Phillies at Exposition Park on August 16. The team then made a Sunday trip to Cincinnati for a single game on August 17, losing to the Reds, 2–1. Pittsburgh returned to Exposition Park, defeated Philadelphia, 7–4, on August 18, and beat the New York Giants on August 19, 5–4. Jack O'Connor performed the hero role against Philadelphia, smacking an eighth-inning shot into right field that bounded to the scoreboard for an inside-the-park home run with two teammates on base.[33] Two days later, Jack played the villain as American League president Ban Johnson, along with vice president and Cleveland Broncos owner Charles Somers, arrived in Pittsburgh to execute their plan.

Although rain caused a postponement of the game between Pittsburgh and New York on August 20, baseball-related activity remained prevalent throughout the city.[34] The unsung hero for Pittsburgh in 1902 happened to be a young man named Walter Smith, who worked for Barney Dreyfuss in the Pirates' team offices. On the evening of August 19, Smith, entrusted with this critical sleuthing assignment, followed Jack O'Connor to the Pennsylvania Station (Union Station) and witnessed him meeting both Johnson and Somers. While walking behind the group, the Pirates' employee couldn't hear their conversation but picked up the words "Lincoln Hotel," offering insight into their destination.[35]

This reconnaissance mission verified pieces of information that came to the attention of team secretary Harry Pulliam. Harry had received a tip about this trip from a Cleveland man who always appeared well versed on such matters. Pulliam also felt the two men would lodge at the Lincoln Hotel (Hotel Lincoln) since the manager of that establishment, Frank Probst, formerly ran the Hollenden Hotel in Cleveland and was friends with Somers and many ballplayers. Before traveling to Pittsburgh, the American League's vice president had shaved off his little mustache to hide his identity.[36] Armed with this credible information, Pulliam and Barney Dreyfuss started their stakeout at the Lincoln Hotel on August 20, while manager Fred Clarke assumed responsibility for keeping watch in Allegheny, where Jesse Tannehill resided.

On August 21, Dreyfuss announced that O'Connor had drawn his release from the Pirates for being a traitor.[37] This swift action by Pittsburgh's owner came after he suspended Jack for violating Section 5 of his contract.[38] In a statement to newspapers, Barney offered an account of the previous day's activities surrounding this evil mission to disrupt his baseball team.

> The causes leading up to this summary action on my part have been brewing for some time, but the crisis was reached yesterday, when I was compelled to take this step in order that I might meet the issue in the attempt that is being made to wreck the Pittsburgh Club.
>
> Tuesday night Charles W. Somers, who is the vice president of the American League, came to Pittsburgh on a gumshoe mission. Accompanying him was one Ban B. Johnson, the president of that league, who came to aid his partner in his dirty work. O'Connor, I know, visited the Union Depot at the time of the arrival of the Cleveland train, from which place this worthy pair came, which in itself was significant to what followed.
>
> Somers and Johnson, evidently ashamed of their mission, made their way carefully to the Lincoln Hotel. Johnson waited behind a lamppost while Somers went in, and after seeing, as he thought, that his tracks were covered, registered as J. A. Benham, Saginaw, Mich. He did not register Johnson at

all, such were his dark-lantern methods. Yesterday morning the plot began to unfold when O'Connor appeared on the scene with one of our unsigned players. After a protracted conference both players departed, and O'Connor returned a short time afterward with another of our players, whom he conducted to the hiding place of this precious pair. The scene was then transferred to a room in Allegheny, where another meeting was held with two more of our players, with O'Connor again present.

Upon his return from Allegheny Mr. Somers, alias Benham, arranged to leave on the 6 o'clock train for Cleveland. By this time, however, he became aware that his presence in Pittsburgh was known to the officials of the Pittsburgh Baseball Club, and he tried all he could to save his co-conspirator; Johnson, from public view. He first ordered a closed carriage for himself and Johnson to make the trip to the depot, but changed his mind at the last moment and drove away, leaving Johnson still undercover.

As both had to make the same train, Johnson, to cover his retreat, had the porters bring him down by the freight elevator hidden among a lot of garbage cans. He then sneaked out by the back alley and trudged his way on foot to the Ft. Wayne Depot in Allegheny, where he waited undercover until the train came along which Somers, alias Benham, had boarded at the Union Station. I mention these details to show the dark-lantern and sneak thief methods employed by this worthy pair.

I don't believe they signed any of our players, and I hope the net results of their efforts will be shown in the future to be nothing. I have treated our men well and am willing to pay them as much as anybody can honestly promise to pay.

If, notwithstanding, any of our players at the expiration of their contracts choose to leave the Pittsburgh Club, well and good. But I will not stand for any treachery or disloyalty from anybody while in my employ. No player can be a stool pigeon for the American League and draw salary from the Pittsburgh Club at the same time.

I don't object to legitimate competition for the services of ballplayers, and had Johnson and Somers come here and acted in an honorable manner I would have been perfectly willing to have had them meet our unsigned players to talk business. But I do object to such people coming in between two days in disguise and using one of our players to accomplish their ends.[39]

The *Pittsburgh Press* reported that a third unidentified individual traveled with Ban Johnson and Charles Somers. This newspaper also stated that Somers wore a disguise to conceal his identity while finding humor in a large man like Johnson attempting to hide behind a lamppost.[40] Dreyfuss explained in 1931 that he and Harry Pulliam had secured rooms on either side of Somers and his boss at the Lincoln Hotel. These two men had been placed in adjoining rooms after Somers registered under the alias of Benham. Diligent surveillance eventually paid off for Pittsburgh's owner.

"At that time there was some sort of ventilator contraption in the doors," explained Dreyfuss, "that if pushed aside, one could hear what is being said in the next room, although unable to see what is going on. We kept a close vigil at our doors for a while and hearing no one come in, went outside and waited near the elevator doors, hiding behind newspapers while watching everyone that came in and went out. It wasn't very long afterwards that O'Connor came up and along with him [Jesse] Tannehill, [Tommy] Leach, [Jack] Chesbro, [Harry] Smith, [Lefty] Davis and [William "Wid"] Conroy. They went straight to Johnson's room and we took up our watch at our god-send ventilation device and listening post."

The American League emissaries offered each player $1,000 upfront if they agreed to jump to their organization in 1903 and play for a team in New York.[41] Johnson and Somers hustled over to Jesse Tannehill's apartment in Allegheny when they realized Pirates officials were monitoring their activities. Once there, Jack O'Connor started ushering in Pirates players to that dwelling. Fred Clarke had already positioned himself when the second wave of this gambit got underway. After some players arrived, Clarke walked up to the door, gave the correct signal when knocking, and received permission to enter the room. The plotters were surprised to see their manager enter the premises.[42]

According to Barney Dreyfuss, in 1931, Clarke walked into Tannehill's room at the Library Apartments and found a group of his players conferring. After concluding negotiations with these men, Johnson hid in the lavatory when Fred entered the room. Dreyfuss marveled over the fact that Clarke made himself feel right at home for five hours, circumventing these players' intentions while also forcing Ban to remain cowering in the bathroom, afraid to show his face.[43] When Fred arrived, his players changed the subject and discussed anything other than their purpose for gathering in Jesse's apartment. Some men left before Clarke, while others exited the apartment with their manager. Tannehill appeared to be alone when Fred extended him a fond farewell, but the Pirates' pilot knew this wasn't the case, although Jesse believed he'd fooled him.[44]

One week after the top members of the American League's hierarchy trekked to Pittsburgh, Chicago White Sox pitcher and manager Clark Griffith arrived in the Smoky City to talk with numerous Pirates players. Detroit Tigers catcher James "Deacon" McGuire, who'd jumped his contract with the Brooklyn Superbas to join the American League in 1902, assisted Griffith.

Newspaper reports stated that Griffith traveled to Pittsburgh to talk with two pitchers, two infielders, and one catcher from the Pirates.[45] Griffith spent six hours in conference with individuals at the residence of a disgruntled southpaw hurler at Library Place.[46] When Al Abrams interviewed Barney Dreyfuss in 1931, the Pirates' owner revealed that an American League agent also came to Pittsburgh at around the same time to deliver on the promise of a $1,000 incentive for each player agreeing to jump their contract.

"A week after the six players had signed with Johnson, an American League agent came here to pay the $1,000 guaranteed to each man," said Dreyfuss in 1931. "His every move was shadowed and his style was hampered like the others. He was originally supposed to meet the men at the Boyer Hotel [Hotel Boyer], but seeing too many of us around, held an impromptu session with the group under the Sixth Street Bridge, behind one of the many shacks that used to stand up there—but all this was under our observance."

Barney also claimed that some players, except for Jesse Tannehill and Jack Chesbro, eventually handed their checks over to him.[47] This strike against his franchise came on the heels of various people from the American League attempting to convince Dreyfuss to transfer the Pirates to that organization. Weeks earlier, an American League magnate visited Barney while he vacationed in Bedford Springs, Pennsylvania, discussing his plan for Pittsburgh to switch leagues. Dreyfuss heard this man out and then politely refused.[48] Individuals had also followed the little magnate all over Western Pennsylvania, trying to convince him to embrace the American League while also denouncing the National League. Barney declined to discuss the proposition and thanked them for the invitation. Vows of friendship and an agreement to respect each entity's rights left Dreyfuss with the false impression that he happened to be dealing with honorable men possessing integrity.[49]

Ban Johnson rapidly reacted to Barney Dreyfuss's accusation that he and Charles Somers performed a gumshoe mission on August 20. During an interview in Cleveland, Johnson said that the Pirates' owner certainly shouldn't have expected a brass band announcing their arrival in Pittsburgh.[50] Besides releasing Jack O'Connor, Dreyfuss left instructions with the gatekeepers at Exposition Park for not permitting the former catcher to enter the baseball grounds under any circumstances.[51] This edict stood even if Jack happened to possess a purchased ticket. One day after acting as the conduit between some of his teammates and Ban Johnson, O'Connor remained sequestered in his hotel room.[52] When Jack did venture out, he avoided the city's main streets, fearing possible encounters with angry baseball fans.[53] Although unwilling to face the music regarding hostile patrons, this didn't prevent O'Connor from attempting to absolve himself from blame.

"Dreyfuss was wrong in his action," said O'Connor, "and he will find it out. It looks now as if I was entirely to blame in this matter, but you will hear a different story in a few months from now. I met Johnson and Somers while they were in Pittsburgh, but there was no sneaking on my part to get to them. Neither did I take any of the other players on the team to the American League officials. I told him some time ago I would sign where I could get the most money. He goes on what Clarke and Pulliam tell him, and the manager and secretary have had little use for me for some time."[54]

Contrary to O'Connor's statement, people across the country commended Barney Dreyfuss for his actions while condemning the ungrateful and traitorous catcher for his behavior.[55] New York baseball writer John B. Foster admonished Jack and praised Barney for his courage. Foster stated that Dreyfuss paid his players liberal salaries, allowed them to receive half of the profits from the gate realized in exhibition games, and always set them up in the best hotel accommodations when the team traveled around the country.[56] Rather than becoming involved in a war of words with his former catcher, Pittsburgh's owner simply said that the O'Connor incident was closed as far as he was concerned. Fellow backstop Chief Zimmer didn't react so kindly. Zimmer, who'd also been O'Connor's teammate for seven years on the Cleveland Spiders, cried upon hearing the news and wrote Jack a letter severing their friendship.

"I have cut O'Connor's acquaintance for good," said the old player on the evening of August 21. "He had a good thing in Pittsburgh and why Jack should have become so foolish I cannot say. He and I are through."[57]

Once Jack O'Connor brought the large hammer down upon himself, the other dominoes started falling over time. Due to injuries and uncertainty, former Boston Beaneaters outfielder Frederick "Fred" Crolius was abducted from his desk in downtown Pittsburgh on August 22, signed, and played the doubleheader that afternoon against Brooklyn at Exposition Park.[58] On August 26, Dreyfuss purchased catcher Edward "Ed" Phelps from the Eastern League's Rochester Bronchos for $1,500 to replace O'Connor.[59] Pittsburgh's owner announced days later that any player who hadn't agreed to play for Pittsburgh in 1903 by September 3 was considered a former team member, with a new individual acting as a replacement. Dreyfuss also claimed that he'd undergone a change of heart surrounding a possible postseason series proposed by him between the Pittsburgh Pirates and any potential American League pennant winner, citing Ban Johnson's and Charles Somers's actions in Pittsburgh as his reason.[60]

Dreyfuss believed that every contract signed by his players in 1901, which happened to be two-year mutual agreements, would stand up in any court.[61] Concerning bringing individuals into line for 1903, team members wanting to remain in Pittsburgh agreed to abide by these original documents.[62] Upon deciding to stay with the club, the Pirates' magnate required that each player sign an affidavit saying he'd read the contract, understood the same, accepted the terms, and swore to carry out its provisions.[63] Barney's early September deadline allowed for some flexibility as management pondered decisions regarding which diamond performers stayed in Pittsburgh and who would be cut loose. Subtractions eventually rose to the forefront as Dreyfuss handed some individuals connected to the American League plot one-way tickets out of town.

Outfielder Lefty Davis was the second player, unfaithful in his obligation to the Pittsburgh baseball club, shown the door. Of all those who listened to promises of rich contracts from Ban Johnson, Davis might've sealed his fate before that memorable day on August 20. Lefty hadn't played since breaking his ankle while stealing second base in a game against the New York Giants at Exposition Park on July 11.[64] Before suffering this injury, Fred Clarke briefly benched Davis in June because of indifferent work.[65] Lefty made some bad choices after blazing a trail of consistency for Pittsburgh in 1901 by batting .313 in 87 games.

Davis decided to room with Jesse Tannehill in Allegheny in 1902. Besides being a troublemaker, Jesse was known for keeping convivial nighttime habits. On the American League raid evening, Dreyfuss and Harry Pulliam took a late-night stroll through the city. While turning down a side street, they came upon Davis, hanging out with a group of revelers engaging in activities detrimental to a baseball player remaining in condition. Pirates management became so unhappy with Lefty that he needed to request practice balls at club offices three times on one occasion.[66] In another instance, Davis hobbled into team headquarters when Barney Dreyfuss was present. He immediately acted like a victim, criticizing the local newspapers' coverage of the American League raid in Pittsburgh.

"Some of these newspaper men are going to have a lot to answer for," said Davis. "Their pipe dreams are ever that a lot of players are going to jump. I'll swan if I have ever heard of a single man who is going to leave."

"Well, if you haven't I have," snapped Dreyfuss.

Sensing an irritated tone in the owner's voice, Lefty picked up his cane and left. After condemning the press, Davis whined to a Chicago reporter that the Pirates didn't allow him to sign for 1903 after he'd rejected American League overtures earlier in the year in the Windy City.[67] Of course, Lefty recently sounded out Ban Johnson about playing for an American League team in New York. Dreyfuss hadn't approached Davis about signing because Pittsburgh didn't want him. This point became quite apparent when the Pirates' owner called Lefty into conference on September 2. Once again, Davis had decided to utilize the press and, in the process, roasted his boss. One hour after the broadsheet hit the streets, Barney requested a meeting with Lefty in his office and then showed him the paper.

"Did you say this?" Dreyfuss asked.

"Yes, sir," responded Davis.

"Well that will be about all for you with Pittsburgh," replied Dreyfuss. "Get another position and quickly. I don't want you on the Pittsburgh team, but because of your injury you may remain on the payroll until the end of the season if you cannot locate."

After leaving the office, Davis complained about this treatment being unjust because he'd spurned a previous offer from an American League agent in Chicago.[68] Following his decision relative to the Davis situation, Barney Dreyfuss issued a brief statement for the press.

"If Davis stays for the rest of the season," said Dreyfuss, "we will pay his salary, because he was hurt in our service, but if he can land a position at once I will not interfere. Davis was let go for managerial reasons. He roomed with one of the twirler's who is going to the American League, and certain rules of training were not observed."[69]

When an individual in Pittsburgh took up Lefty Davis's cause, Dreyfuss quickly extinguished the figurative fire this person attempted to create. Barney said Davis had nobody but himself to blame for his situation. Pittsburgh's owner declared that Lefty had been warned over his reckless behavior earlier in the year but didn't listen to the advice. This conduct resulted in punishment, which didn't have the desired effect since Davis returned to his old tricks. Dreyfuss said, "Mr. Davis was paid for playing ball and not for having a good time."[70] Before leaving for a meeting of the baseball owners in New York on the evening of September 23, Barney announced that since Lefty's ankle had healed, the club gave the outfielder his ten days' notice of release.

Dreyfuss also stated that another player might be eliminated from the roster before the week ended. Newspapers speculated that Jesse Tannehill was that other individual.⁷¹ Management also told Davis to remove his clothing from Exposition Park's locker room. Rumors had pointed to Tannehill receiving his notice before Barney traveled east, but this didn't happen for some reason.⁷² Jesse's attitude had certainly been insufferable after he performed his duties as Jack O'Connor's able assistant. Upon returning to action against Brooklyn on August 25, following his unfortunate injury in Atlantic City, Tannehill refused to pitch versus the Chicago Cubs on August 30. Clarke ordered the southpaw to throw under threat of suspension.

"Better warm up another one," said Tannehill as he started, "I won't last very long."

"You'll last the full game and win it, too," said Clarke. "If you don't I'll know why."⁷³

Jesse pitched all twelve innings of this contest at Exposition Park, defeating Chicago, 3–2. Newspapers reported that Clarke was pushing Tannehill to the limit as punishment for getting in bed with the American League.⁷⁴ Management also planned on playing Jesse in the outfield when he didn't pitch to get as much work as possible out of him.⁷⁵ Such an approach wasn't to Tanny's liking since the southpaw twirler certainly didn't want to risk being damaged goods when the time came to collect a big payday. When Cincinnati's batters hit Jesse harder than usual in a game the Reds won, 6–4, on September 13 at Exposition Park, he received a vicious roasting from the crowd.⁷⁶ Tannehill's conduct had been bad enough before the Pirates started east on September 1, but it worsened as the season's final weeks progressed. Some wondered why Barney Dreyfuss tolerated the behavior of such an ingrate.

When Pittsburgh stopped over in New York for a series, rain caused the postponement of their game against the Giants on September 9.⁷⁷ Revealing that deadlines could be somewhat flexible, Barney Dreyfuss decided to hold a meeting with hurlers Jesse Tannehill and Jack Chesbro at the team hotel, regarding what it would take to sign them for the 1903 season.⁷⁸

"I want a two years contract calling for $17,000," said Chesbro.

"I will sign for the same amount," said Tannehill.

These contract demands staggered Dreyfuss. He'd foreseen a huge salary ultimatum by these two pitchers, but even this amount far surpassed the owner's comprehension. "I will see you again in an hour," Dreyfuss responded after gathering his composure. When the group came together again an hour later, the Pirates' magnate handed each player a contract paying them $11,000 over two years.

"This is as far as I will go," said Dreyfuss. "You can take it or leave it. This is a big increase on your present salaries. If you think you can do better in the American League, go ahead."

Tannehill and Chesbro walked away with the contracts in their pockets. The two pitchers later returned to tell Dreyfuss they'd decided not to accept his offer. The pair also readily admitted that these salary terms were $1,000 more than Ban Johnson's organization had offered them. When asked about the attitude of his two players following this generous proposition, he refused to discuss personalities and stuck to the facts.

"I have made them their final offer," stated Dreyfuss. "That is all I will say, but Pittsburgh, with or without them, will have a team next season that will be fighting for the pennant from flag-fall to finish."[79]

Giants manager John McGraw also made news when he claimed that Jack O'Connor had acted as his liaison when snatching Jimmy Williams from Pittsburgh for the Baltimore Orioles in 1901. Dreyfuss immediately declared that he didn't believe McGraw's charge.[80] Regarding those final contract offers to Tannehill and Chesbro, one correspondent felt that players were perfectly within their right, "making hay while the sun shines."[81] Pirates management took a different approach to these individuals, given one final chance after being disloyal to the people who'd treated them splendidly. Club management ordered Jesse to remain in Pittsburgh while the rest of his teammates participated in a series of exhibition games in late September against Eastern League teams. The significance of this punishment was that Tannehill would lose his share of the receipts from these contests.

Management also required Jesse to report to team headquarters each day, although it was an unnecessary exercise. Barney Dreyfuss planned on requiring Tannehill to follow this directive until his contract expired on October 15. This decision prevented Jesse from participating in barnstorming trips such as the All-Nationals jaunt organized by Joseph "Joe" Cantillon. The *St. Louis Republic* felt Pirates management did this to drive Tannehill to insubordination through jumping the club. Such action would then eliminate the team's salary obligation.[82] A baseball writer from Kansas City felt Dreyfuss acted petty and vindictive toward Tannehill. This scribe believed Barney's behavior shattered the sportsmanlike persona he usually exhibited.[83] A month earlier, when various Pirates players had entertained offers from the American League, the *Cincinnati Enquirer* wrote that the National Game needed more men like Barney Dreyfuss.[84]

Lefty Davis, Jesse Tannehill, and brother Lee Tannehill remained at the Library Apartments residence while Pittsburgh's players conducted their exhibition excursion.[85] Dreyfuss didn't leave Jesse dangling in limbo until his contract expired. On October 4, Barney handed Tannehill his unconditional release and paid him in full for the remainder of the season. Like Davis, the organization ordered Jesse to immediately remove his baggage from Exposition Park. Since Tannehill had severed all ties with the Pirates, he wasn't permitted to participate in the field day benefit event at the ballpark on October 6. The boss hurler also wouldn't be on the roster for an upcoming series against an all-star aggregation of American League players.[86] Pittsburgh's owner revealed that Jesse's discharge would've coincided with Jack O'Connor's if the team hadn't needed him due to numerous injuries.[87] Dreyfuss made a brief statement when he announced Jesse's release that evening.

"Tannehill has my best wishes," said President Dreyfuss. "He is a good pitcher, but we are well supplied in that department."[88]

Following his release, Tannehill confided to a friend that he'd acted as the real American League agent and Jack O'Connor only helped him with the task of disrupting Pittsburgh's team.[89] Jesse also stated weeks later that he and Dreyfuss never did get along.[90] Tannehill believed he'd greatly assisted with the biggest coup of the American League affair due to the strong influence he possessed over fellow hurler Jack Chesbro, who in 1902 went 28–6, supported by a 2.17 ERA. Although dubbed with the "Happy Jack" nickname throughout most of his baseball life, Chesbro received the monikers of "Algernon" and "Algy" in Pittsburgh. Jesse's sway with Jack aside, Chesbro exhibited intense indecisiveness about the direction he wanted to go, much like the title of the popular 1980s song by The Clash. After Jack and Tannehill had requested two-year contracts worth $17,000 from owner Barney Dreyfuss, the *Boston Post* reported Chesbro had considered asking for $20,000.[91]

Although Dreyfuss rejected his salary request, Chesbro didn't give up on attempts to remain in Pittsburgh. At one point, Jack's wife, Mabel Shuttleworth Chesbro, brought her husband to team offices to see the Pirates' owner about re-signing him, but Barney refused.[92] Chesbro and Dreyfuss also had an impromptu conference at Tim Hurst's Irish Fair in Pittsburgh on the evening of August 29. The discussion became contentious based on both men's body language.[93]

Player and owner held a combative meeting at Pirates headquarters on October 7.[94] When Chesbro again suggested being paid the $7,500 per year Johnson had offered; Barney laughed at him in the crowded office in the Smith

Building. Jack took this chortling on Dreyfuss's part to mean the owner didn't believe him to be telling the truth. As the discussion became very heated and contentious, others beckoned Harry Pulliam to come in and restore peace. Harry and Algy expressed friendliness toward each other when they left the office. However, the meeting's outcome seemed to indicate the end of this relationship, as Barney had wished Chesbro "good luck" and "goodbye."[95]

Pittsburgh Dispatch baseball writer Frank B. McQuiston surmised that Jack Chesbro might hesitate about jumping to the American League because he realized much of his success as a pitcher resulted from the solid team playing behind him. Uncertainty regarding New York's American League squad possibly justified his wanting to remain in Pittsburgh.[96] Besides other Pirates members, players left over from the Baltimore Orioles would join the New York Americans. Unfortunately, not much remained regarding quality players after the Orioles' carcass had been picked clean by National League owners John T. Brush and Andrew Freedman, along with Giants manager John McGraw. Over time, Barney Dreyfuss tired of Algy's wishy-washy posture. During the Pirates' September trip to New York, Chesbro had asked Dreyfuss to grant him a three-day vacation. Barney offered a brief response to his out-of-favor pitcher.

"I don't care if you never come back," Dreyfuss seriously replied.[97]

Dreyfuss's sentiment finally became a reality, courtesy of every team member who played for the Pittsburgh Pirates. On October 8, Pittsburgh's players decided to ask Jack Chesbro to pitch in that afternoon's game of the postseason series against the American League team of All-Americans. Jack initially promised to do so but then reneged on that pledge.[98] Chesbro's teammates believed he was afraid to pitch in the game. Jack offered a lame excuse about being sick, although he looked like a healthy and husky youth before and after the game.[99] Fearless hurler Deacon Phillippe pitched magnificently in the contest for the Pirates, holding the All-Americans to no runs and three hits.[100] Algy refused to play in this game under American League rules and vowed he would work when the series switched to Cleveland under National League rules. When informed by teammates that he would take the mound in Pittsburgh or they would cut him out of the monetary proceeds realized for this series, Chesbro laughed.

After the game on October 8, the players held a meeting and branded Jack a deserter who didn't deserve to reap any monetary benefit from this series. They also ordained Chesbro as a quitter and told him he no longer was a team member regarding these games against the All-Americans.[101] Before the series started, Barney Dreyfuss had allowed his players to take complete charge of the entire event and dictate how they divided up the gate receipts.[102] Jack appealed his case to Dreyfuss, who told the hurler there was nothing he could do and he supported the stance taken by the other players. Chesbro responded by serving notice about severing ties with the Pirates' baseball organization. He left Pittsburgh on the evening of October 10 for Chicago to join the barnstorming All-Nationals squad bound for the West Coast. Dreyfuss certainly didn't convey sadness upon finding out that his misguided pitcher had quit the team.

"Chesbro is gone," said Dreyfuss, "and I am glad of it. He showed himself a quitter when he had a chance to help the boys out. He refused to go in under American League rules. I wish the American all kinds of luck with him, but no more of him in Pittsburgh."[103]

Barney Dreyfuss also vowed that Jack Chesbro would never again play on any team he controlled.[104] The fourth and final domino had finally fallen. In August, when Dreyfuss bounced Jack O'Connor from the squad and Pittsburgh sportswriter A. R. Cratty guessed that former catcher Tacks Latimer might return to fill the void, manager Fred Clarke exhibited astonishment over such a suggestion. He then offered a tongue-in-cheek response.

"At that," said Clarke, "if I had Rube back I would grab Tacks."[105]

Moving forward proved a preferable baseball option rather than looking back and going in reverse.

Following their sneaky trip to Pittsburgh on August 20, 1902, hoping to secure players for the American League, the organization's president, Ban Johnson, and vice president, Charles Somers, convinced a group of team members to jump the Pirates and play for a club in New York in 1903. One of the players captured by Johnson and Somers, star hurler Jack Chesbro, posted a 28-6 record in 1902, supported by a 2.17 ERA. In this photo of the 1900 Pittsburgh Pirates, Chesbro is standing second from the right in the top row, next to manager Fred Clarke, who is dressed in a suit and derby hat. Fellow jumper and stellar hurler Jesse Tannehill is second from the left sitting in the front row. (Photo in the Public Domain).

4
Breaking Up the Old Gang, with Help from Gamblers

Having despicable defectors afoot didn't detract from the many erstwhile Pittsburgh Pirates players who pledged their loyalty to the organization. Not all appeared lost when it came to the raid perpetrated by Ban Johnson and Charles Somers on August 20, 1902. Three players, who sounded out these individuals and Clark Griffith a week later, had a change of heart and decided to remain in Pittsburgh rather than cast their lot with the American League. Third baseman Tommy Leach, catcher Harry Smith, and infielder William "Wid" Conroy regretted their decision to accept $1,000 from the American League. These three players, believing the syndicate agents had deceived them, returned the drafts to Somers. While the Pirates played games in Cleveland against the American League All-Star aggregation, Pittsburgh owner Barney Dreyfuss again condemned Charles for unsuccessfully tampering with Leach and Smith a second time.[1] Team secretary Harry Pulliam unequivocally vowed that these three players would wear Pirates uniforms in 1903.

"You can bet all you're worth that Leach, Conroy, and Smith will play with Pittsburgh next season in spite of the fact that the American League has them on their list," said Pulliam. "Should they play with the American League next season, which is out of the question, then they would be contract jumpers. All the Pittsburgh players in 1901 signed two-year contracts, straight contracts which will hold good in any court of law."[2]

After eliminating troublemakers from the equation, the Pittsburgh Pirates' organization decided to make its stand regarding these three baseball players. American League representatives countered by declaring that special ironclad contracts bound Tommy Leach, Harry Smith, and Wid Conroy to play for that organization's New York team in 1903. Given the choice of compliance or shirking their responsibility, Cleveland Broncos team president John Kilfoyle stated that these three individuals would be playing baseball in the American League or not at all.[3]

In an attempt to curry favor for his organization's stance, Ban Johnson alleged, after the season concluded, that Leach had acted as the liaison between him and Pittsburgh's players. Barney Dreyfuss, who offered guidance to all three repentant Pirates members on this matter, fired back. He stated that Johnson, Somers, Jack O'Connor, Jesse Tannehill, Lefty Davis, and others had browbeaten and intimidated Tommy until he signed an American League contract.[4] Dreyfuss made sure he refreshed everybody's memory regarding the actual conspirators behind committing this dastardly deed against his baseball team.

> I have known for weeks, in fact, ever since Leach decided that he would not jump his contract, that the American League was going to try to make him unpopular with the Pittsburgh rooters, simply for revenge. He was the man that the trust wanted and now that it knows that he can't be bribed, it is trying to make trouble for him.
>
> Tannehill first circulated the story that Leach was the syndicate's agent. Leach came at the time of the charge and asked me to investigate it thoroughly, because it was not true. I knew every move that had been made and that Leach was not guilty, so I sent him away happy by assuring him that an investigation was not necessary.

Dreyfuss then reminded baseball fans about the facts related to this case. He again affirmed that Jack O'Connor had met Johnson and Somers at the train station, not Tommy Leach. Paid for his deceitful work, O'Connor escorted the two American League executives to the Hotel Lincoln. Jack then traveled to Allegheny, picked up Leach, and guided him to that hotel. According to Barney, it was also O'Connor who took Johnson in a cab over to Jesse Tannehill's apartment in Allegheny after the group realized Pittsburgh's owner and Harry Pulliam had discovered their activities. Jack, not Leach, then escorted various Pirates players to Tannehill's room. American League propaganda wilted under the intense scrutiny of truth.

"We know other details about the conspiracy that convince us that we did not make any mistake in blaming O'Connor and Tannehill," concluded Dreyfuss, "but I have mentioned enough to prove that Ban Johnson has trumped up the latest charge against Leach to punish Tommy for being too honest to jump his Pittsburgh contract."[5]

In mid-November, Jack O'Connor explained in an interview that the American League had never employed him to act as an agent for their interests. O'Connor claimed that former Cleveland Spiders teammate James "Jimmy" McAleer, who currently managed the St. Louis Browns, had talked with the catcher about playing for his team in 1903. Jack promised McAleer he could eventually bid for his services. They also discussed the positive and negative points related to Pittsburgh's players. O'Connor stated the two did this in passing rather than him offering an opinion on who would be suitable for the American League. Jack also alleged that every Pirates member had been mulling over the financial question after operatives approached them throughout 1902 about switching leagues. O'Connor had even asked Honus Wagner if any agent courted him about moving to the opposition organization.

"Nothing doing yet," Wagner had replied, "but I want you to help me get the money."

"That's easy for a player of your reputation," O'Connor had remarked. "You ought to be getting the top-notch figures. I don't see how I can help you, but all you have to do is name your salary, and if these people don't take you up, get in line with those who think you are worth more to them than Barney does."

O'Connor continued, saying he stopped offering such advice after two or three more Pirates members requested his input since he believed these men were reporting back to team management. Jack condemned the tactic of Barney Dreyfuss commissioning spies to follow him, feeling it would've been more honorable if he and Pittsburgh's owner had talked directly about stories circulating in the press. O'Connor concluded by claiming he went about his business, meddling with nobody and always looking out for himself.[6] Two players who weren't part of the group that O'Connor and Tannehill brought to Ban Johnson remained loyal to Dreyfuss through different circumstances.

Second baseman Claude "Little All Right" Ritchey had joined the Pirates along with other members of the Louisville Colonels following the consolidation on December 8, 1899. Considered one of the top fielders at his position in the National League and Pittsburgh's best clutch hitter, Ritchey had performed brilliantly in 1901, batting .296 while driving home a career-high 74 runs. Although Claude proved faithful to the Corsairs' cause, this didn't mean despicable individuals hadn't made overtures to corrupt his mind. O'Connor constantly attempted to persuade Ritchey to consider a more significant payday playing for the American League. During his 1931 interview with Al Abrams,

Dreyfuss remembered with pride how Claude handled such badgering on the night in 1902 that Honus Wagner had begged to sign a contract for 1903.

> That same night in Boston, my room happened to be next to that of Ritchey's and O'Connor's who were rooming together. The transom being open, I overheard their conversation, in which O'Connor was trying to work on the faithful Ritchey in an effort to get him to quit the team for a more lucrative salary with an American League team. I can still remember hearing Ritchey's Pennsylvania Dutch voice raised in a high pitch [Ritchey hailed from Emlenton, Pennsylvania], saying to O'Connor, "You've been in baseball something like 18 years, and you don't have a cent to show for it, as you admit. I've been in the game about ten years, and I've got about $25,000 put away. Now, you're trying to tell me what to do."
>
> That was a complete squelcher for Mr. O'Connor and offered me plenty of satisfaction to hear Ritchey talk in that manner.[7]

The other player who rejected the temptation to leave Pittsburgh and remained firm in his convictions was first baseman Kitty Bransfield. Purchased from the Eastern League's Worcester Farmers, Bransfield sizzled in his 1901 rookie campaign, batting .295 and knocking in 91 runs. That year, while Philadelphia played a July series in Pittsburgh, star Phillies outfielder Edward "Ed" Delahanty arranged a meeting between him and Kitty at his hotel. Delahanty then escorted Bransfield for a rendezvous with *Philadelphia Inquirer* sportswriter Frank Hough to discuss the topic of Kitty joining the Philadelphia Athletics. Bransfield requested time to mull over the offer but re-signed with Pittsburgh.[8] In the fall of 1901, Ed, Hough, and a Pittsburgh reporter bounded about the city, attempting to grab players for the American League.[9]

On that fateful August day in 1902, Kitty wasn't in Pittsburgh when Ban Johnson and Charles Somers made their pitch. Bransfield relaxed at home in Worcester, Massachusetts, recuperating from a knee injury he'd suffered in the first game of a doubleheader against the Boston Beaneaters at South End Grounds on August 13, which occurred while tripping over the bag running to first base.[10] This temporary inconvenience didn't deter Johnson from doing due diligence, as the American League president made a journey to Bransfield's home on August 30.[11]

During his 1931 interview with Abrams, Barney Dreyfuss explained that he'd received a reliable tip regarding Johnson's intentions. Harry Pulliam immediately boarded a train in Pittsburgh destined for Worcester. Pulliam and

Ban ended up on the same train in a quirk of fate, although the Pirates' team secretary wasn't aware of this fact until the locomotive stopped in Ashtabula, Ohio. Harry deviously devised a plan to circumvent Johnson's motives. Pulliam somehow gained possession of Ban's shoes, which he hid from him that night. When the train reached Worcester, a dumbfounded Johnson experienced a delay leaving since he couldn't find his shoes. Harry hustled to Kitty's residence, signed him to a Pittsburgh contract, and started for home before Ban arrived at Bransfield's domicile.[12]

Over time, loyalty only carried a player so far, as was the case for Claude Ritchey and Kitty Bransfield. These two players eventually saw their careers end in Pittsburgh for different reasons, although one common thread existed. When it came to the young man who replaced Lefty Davis as Pittsburgh's right fielder, a challenge against the highest-ranking member of the Pirates' organization resulted in predictable consequences for such misguided action. In 1903, concerns over players switching leagues after being promised high salaries abruptly became ancient history. Realizing that following the current path was unsustainable for both parties, leaders from the American and National leagues met to hammer out a deal that could garner mutual consent.

On January 10, 1903, in Cincinnati, the two associations brokered a peace agreement that allowed both leagues to operate as co-equal organizations. Before the two sides reached a consensus, one of the discussion points centered on the division of sixteen disputed baseball players claimed by both leagues. The parties hammered out a satisfactory resolution where the Pittsburgh Pirates retained their rights to Tommy Leach and Harry Smith while awarding Wid Conroy to the New York Highlanders.[13] On January 22, at 2 A.M., the eight National League owners ratified the peace agreement. However, New York Giants magnate John T. Brush initially dissented by presenting a minority report on the deal.[14]

Pittsburgh continued its National League dominance in 1903, winning a third consecutive pennant. Things were slightly tighter than the previous year, as the Pirates finished at 91–49 and outpaced second-place New York by 6½ games. In the first modern World Series arranged by Barney Dreyfuss and owner Henry Killilea of the Boston American League champion team, the Americans prevailed over the Pirates, five games to three. Hurler Deacon Phillippe did exceptional work on the mound for Pittsburgh, tossing five complete games and going 3–2. Fred Clarke only had one viable option in Phillippe since an arm injury hampered fellow twenty-five-game winner Sam Leever. At the same time, southpaw hurler Ed Doheny was unavailable and at home in Massachusetts due to suffering a mental breakdown.

A host of pitchers received opportunities to ease the burden of losing Jack Chesbro and Jesse Tannehill and their forty-eight combined wins in 1902. Most of the ten men other than the big three of Phillippe, Leever, and Doheny failed in this quest, accounting for twenty-five total victories in 1903. Proving that some selfish people never changed their ways, Highlanders manager Clark Griffith suspended catcher Jack O'Connor for the remainder of the season on August 21, 1903.[15] Concerns over team dissension intensified through the belief that Chesbro and Tannehill had sided with their former Pirates teammate. Griffith exhibited unflappable deportment when explaining why such discipline occurred when New York played in Jack's hometown.

"O'Connor deserved all he got," said Griffith. "I am manager of the club and will maintain discipline among the players so long as I hold the position.

"O'Connor did not keep in condition, and at St. Louis reported on the field in citizen's clothes late for a game in which he was scheduled to catch. Any baseball man knows that that sort of thing cannot be tolerated."[16]

After the season ended, the Highlanders shipped Jack O'Connor to the St. Louis Browns on October 6. Pitcher Jesse Tannehill, who supplied a mediocre 15–15 record with a 3.27 ERA for New York, found a new home in Boston, being traded on December 20, 1903, to the Americans for fellow hurler Thomas "Tom" Hughes. The 1904 baseball campaign was a lost year for Pittsburgh, as injuries and discord ended their three-year reign atop the National League. The Pirates came home in fourth place with an 87–66 record, putting them 19 games behind the pennant-winning New York Giants. Continuity and leadership were issues as stellar field general Fred Clarke remained on the sidelines for most of the season.

Clarke suffered an injury in game two of a Fourth of July doubleheader against the Chicago Cubs at Exposition Park. Fred collided at first base with Cubs pitcher Herbert "Buttons" Briggs. Clarke sustained an injury when the spike from Briggs's shoe tore into the flesh and ligaments of his left leg, thus exposing bare the bone. After the game, Pittsburgh's manager bound the long gash in his leg and then paid little attention to it, not comprehending the severe nature of this mishap. In a home series against Philadelphia that began on July 13, Clarke complained of severe pains in his leg. In the contest against the Phillies on July 15, he made a spectacular somersault catch, sliding headfirst across the ground. When Fred came to the bench after the inning concluded, he realized the gash in his leg had reopened.

Pirates trainer Edward "Ed" LaForce dressed the wound before Clarke left the ballpark to return home. That night, Fred became seriously ill, and a doctor arrived by request at the residence on Saturday morning, July 16. The physician ordered Pittsburgh's manager to remain in bed after an examination. That afternoon, Clarke's condition became quite alarming, leading to this doctor returning to his domicile. When the medico entered, Fred exhibited symptoms of delirium, with a 105-degree temperature. At the behest of Barney Dreyfuss, two physicians arrived on Sunday and attended to Clarke for many hours. By that evening of July 17, the administered opiates had taken effect, and Fred finally rested comfortably. The prognosis called for Clarke to remain confined to his bed for an extended period. Besides suffering from blood poisoning and a slight attack of typhoid fever, Clarke had also experienced a rupture that left his body badly swollen, and he temporarily couldn't use his lower limbs.[17]

Fred remained in bed, lying on his back for four weeks. When Clarke ventured to Exposition Park for the first time after being able to get around again, sportswriter A. R. Cratty expressed shock over the great player's anguished appearance. Over thirty pounds were missing from Fred's athletic frame, and his eyes possessed the stare of a fever patient. Clarke hobbled about on crutches with his left leg bandaged and never touching the ground, even when walking. Fred had been through a dreadful ordeal that required continued recuperation. According to well-wishing friends, further participation in the season seemed very unlikely.[18] This ended up being the case, as Clarke didn't appear in another game except for two late-season appearances as a pinch hitter.

Fred covered his left field position in a postseason series against the Cleveland Naps, who finished fourth in the American League race in 1904. Clarke recorded two hits in the five-game series. Fred couldn't showcase his standard skillset, seemed tentative in the series' early games, and never was able to get up to speed at this supreme level of competition.[19] Cleveland claimed the series, winning two games, while Pittsburgh achieved a single victory, and the other contests ended tied.[20] Shortly after Clarke had suffered his injury, Barney Dreyfuss changed the leadership hierarchy. On July 19, Dreyfuss discussed with Tommy Leach the prospect of replacing Honus Wagner as the squad's assistant manager. Honus, who'd held this position for four years, became unhappy handling these duties, and the team wasn't pleased with his work while running things. Leach accepted the berth to oversee the Pirates in Fred's absence.[21]

Each of these individuals who worked in positions of power impacted critical events related to Pittsburgh's disappointing 1904 season. Internal problems immediately rose to the surface when the campaign began. While traveling by train for their season opener against the St. Louis Cardinals on April 15, pitcher Frederick "Bucky" Veil became ill with fever and chills after playing an exhibition game in Des Moines, Iowa. Catching a cold in Des Moines, Veil's condition deteriorated on the train as he started hallucinating from his feverish condition. Bucky recovered sufficiently to accompany the team on their bus to the Southern Hotel, but he experienced a relapse after being assigned a room.[22] A doctor examined Veil and concluded that he suffered from a bad case of the flu.[23]

Before the Pirates played the final game of their series against St. Louis on April 17, Bucky ventured to the hotel lobby, where some of his teammates had assembled. Harry Smith asked Veil how he felt before Ginger Beaumont inquired if the pitcher might be ready to resume playing baseball. Bucky said the prospect seemed unlikely, although his health was improving. Veil then offered that he might attempt to eat a meal. Sitting in the lobby reading a newspaper, Tommy Leach sarcastically encouraged him to do just that. A perturbed Bucky responded by asking his teammate if he happened to have a problem with that decision. Tommy replied that he didn't have a problem before snidely telling Veil to enjoy a nice lunch at owner Barney Dreyfuss's expense while the rest of the team went to the ballpark and earned their salaries. Leach then suggested Bucky was a slacker before posing that question in a biting tone to his teammate.

Being branded a slacker didn't sit well with Veil, who sprang into action.[24] A vicious fistfight between the two ensued that left Leach badly beaten.[25] Fred Clarke talked to both men about the incident. Clarke discussed team unity with Bucky and received assurances from his pitcher that such behavior wouldn't occur again.[26] After going 5–3 with a 3.82 ERA in 1903, Veil only appeared in one game in 1904. On April 25, Clarke handed Bucky his notice of release. The Pirates' organization hoped rest would help Veil regain his health since sickness had handicapped him since joining Pittsburgh.[27] This sporadic illness stunted Bucky's ambition, and his teammates were constantly worried over the hurler's physical appearance. It came as quite a surprise when, rather than engage in a recovery period, Veil signed to play for the baseball team in his hometown of Altoona, Pennsylvania.[28]

Although the Pirates cast Bucky adrift, the repercussions of his fight with Leach still lingered. Following the incident, players took up sides as to who they supported. The strongest in the Veil camp was Pirates outfielder James "Jimmy" Sebring, the pitcher's best friend on the team. Sebring defended Bucky at all times. Following his friend's release, Jimmy declared there were worse players on the squad who also happened to be in high favor with team management. Sebring suggested that Veil still would be a Pirates member if Tommy had whipped his buddy in the fight. Such open defiance wasn't a smart career move, especially when Barney Dreyfuss became aware of his outfielder's grievances.[29]

Sebring, a native of Williamsport, Pennsylvania, had joined the Pirates in September 1902 to replace right fielder Lefty Davis. Jimmy appeared in 19 games and batted .325. Sebring swung the willow in his 1903 rookie campaign at a .277 clip. The speedy outfielder became the fans' darling during a contest against St. Louis at Exposition Park on April 23, 1903. In the second and fifth innings, the youngster, also known as "Jeems," raced around the bases for inside-the-park home runs as Pittsburgh defeated the Cardinals, 8–4.[30] Sebring etched his name in the annals of baseball history on October 1, 1903, when he became the first player to smack a home run in a World Series game. Jimmy connected off Boston hurler Denton "Cy" Young in the seventh inning at Huntington Avenue Baseball Grounds, blasting a drive to deep center field and racing around the bases for an inside-the-park four bagger.[31]

Despite some pitfalls, Jimmy Sebring and Barney Dreyfuss engaged in a kind and friendly relationship.[32] Pittsburgh's owner also attempted to look after his young outfielder in financial affairs. Shortly after marrying Elizabeth Milnor in the summer of 1903, Sebring started freely spending money on his new wife, leaving him broke. When Dreyfuss handed out the checks for each player's share of the postseason World Series money amounting to over $1,300, he made Jimmy's out to Mrs. Elizabeth Sebring. This decision supposedly angered Pittsburgh's player.[33] A rational approach by Dreyfuss proved prudent. When the Pirates held spring training at Hot Springs, Arkansas, in 1904, Sebring touched up his boss, borrowing $50. An hour later, Jimmy returned with enough souvenirs to start a museum. These mementos included ornaments, crystals from Hot Springs caves, and carved wooden Indians. By that night, Sebring had spent all the money he borrowed from Pittsburgh's owner.

After much urging and pleading by Dreyfuss, Jimmy allowed his boss to accumulate $400 in salary in a savings account for his new daughter, Mary. She was born at the beginning of the 1904 season. Following numerous persistent requests by Sebring, Barney eventually permitted the player to draw money from that account.[34] The caring relationship between the owner and his young player started disintegrating when Jimmy became involved in confrontations with the player elevated above all others regarding diamond ability and importance to the team. On June 29, 1904, Honus Wagner had charge of the squad when they played an exhibition game in Youngstown, Ohio, against a local semi-professional team called Ohio Works. The angry crowd relentlessly hurled insults toward Wagner and jeered him as the uninspired Pirates suffered a crushing 9–1 defeat.[35] At one point in the game, Honus criticized Sebring for his lazy approach when an opposing batter smacked a ball to his position in right field.[36]

The following day, when the Pirates defeated a team from the Pittsburgh municipality of Homestead, Wagner rode his players extremely hard after the previous afternoon's humiliating outcome. Honus once again confronted Jimmy over his lackluster and disinterested performance.[37] A Pittsburgh sportswriter later reported that Wagner and Sebring patched their differences following these two incidents.[38] Directly challenging this reconciliation, problems arose again during a game against the St. Louis Cardinals at Exposition Park on July 26. The two players engaged in fiery exchanges early in the contest as each individual muffed plays.[39] Jimmy was peeved over one particular game situation, where he made a bad throw from right field, and Honus, stationed at second base, just stood there with outstretched hands as the baseball sailed about forty feet wide past him.

A heated quarrel commenced when the Pirates reached their dugout once the inning ended. Sebring alleged that Wagner had purposely tried to show him up regarding the play. Jimmy then attempted to assault Honus, but their teammates stopped him. Sebring spewed vicious, bitter words as he vowed to get the big fellow when an opportunity presented itself. Wagner responded that any time was okay with him.[40] Engaging in an all-out war with the squad's best player certainly wasn't a wise career decision. On the morning of July 27, Barney Dreyfuss summoned Sebring into his office for a meeting.[41] Jimmy remained sequestered in that room for almost an hour. A Pirates official offered an engaging narrative when asked about this little session in Barney's inner sanctum.

"Oh, Barney handles Sebring's finances for him and is fixing up a deal to make him some money," stated the club official.[42]

This narrative, of course, wasn't the case. Dreyfuss scolded and lectured Jimmy Sebring for his conduct. Barney told Sebring that he must be on his best behavior and wouldn't tolerate friction between players on the Pirates under any circumstances.

"We never have permitted factions in our club," Dreyfuss told him, "and I do not propose to have men on the team who cannot work in perfect harmony at all times."[43]

Jimmy seemed to be a conflicted soul in 1904, having stated earlier in the season that he wasn't in love with baseball life and would venture into another business as soon as he could secure adequate capital to achieve this purpose.[44] Everything related to this tumultuous year reached a tipping point for Jimmy a few days after his altercation with Honus Wagner. While running to first base in the first inning of the game against the Cincinnati Reds at the Palace of the Fans on July 31, Sebring sprained his ankle.[45] Barney Dreyfuss sat in the private box of Reds owner August "Garry" Herrmann, along with Dr. E. W. Walker, a well-known Cincinnati practitioner and surgeon. Dr. Walker agreed to accompany Barney to Pittsburgh's clubhouse to look at Jimmy's injury. The physician offered his prognosis and treatment recommendation following an examination.

"Merely a turned ankle," said Dr. Walker. "Just bathe it in cold water and at night pack ice around it."

Sebring rejected this doctor's opinion in Dreyfuss's presence.

"Oh no, it hurts," wailed Sebring. "I want to go home. I am going home."

"Home? Where, Pittsburgh?" queried Dreyfuss.

"No, Williamsport," retorted Jimmy.

"You go with us," shot back Barney.

Following the game, before leaving to return to Pittsburgh, Dreyfuss arranged to have the railroad company place cracked ice in the team's car on the train. That night, Sebring ignored Dr. Walker's treatment recommendations and played cards with some teammates. The following morning Jimmy disobeyed orders to meet with the Pirates' team physician, Dr. Gustav Berg. That afternoon at Exposition Park, as Pittsburgh prepared to play the Chicago Cubs before embarking on a trip through the East, sportswriter A. R. Cratty came upon player and owner discussing Sebring's injury when he entered the grandstand. Jimmy walked with a cane and limped. Barney turned to Cratty and offered up the result of their conversation.

"I know where he wants to go," said Dreyfuss. "He wants to go home."[46]

During this chat, Sebring had requested to remain behind since the injury caused him great pain. Jimmy also reasoned that riding on trains and sitting around hotels would only magnify his suffering. Sebring felt the best remedy was recuperating in Williamsport with his wife and child. Dreyfuss rejected Jimmy's request.[47] Sebring arrived at Union Station that Monday evening of August 1 with his grip packed, where Pittsburgh would leave by train and travel to New York for a series against the Brooklyn Superbas.[48] Still reluctant to make the trip, Jimmy suddenly decided he wanted to remain in Pittsburgh. Handing the valise carrying his uniform to teammate Harry Smith, Sebring remarked that he guessed he would return to his home in Allegheny.[49]

Jimmy again engaged Barney Dreyfuss, who handed him his ticket for an upper berth in the sleeper car. Sebring reiterated that he wanted to travel to Williamsport and recuperate at home for about ten days. Jimmy felt it useless to go to New York since he couldn't play. This insistence on not traveling with the team brought about harsh words between both men and a definitive resolution.[50]

"Well, I want you to go, and you'll go," said Dreyfuss angrily.[51]

These two gentlemen exchanged more dialogue before Sebring emphatically told Mr. Dreyfuss that he wasn't going on the team's road trip. Days following the incident, Jimmy shared what happened after he issued this proclamation to Pittsburgh's owner.

"He instantly told me that I could quit," said Sebring, "and I replied that was all right. When the train pulled out I started for my boardinghouse. I deny that I have jumped the team. Mr. Dreyfuss while angry told me to quit the club, and I, while in a similar frame of mind, took him at his word. Our relations have always been pleasant and this thing is not to my liking."[52]

Jimmy parsed his words when alleging that Dreyfuss told him to quit since many newspapers used terms such as desertion and suspension to describe the situation.[53] Sebring set out for his Williamsport home. In an interview at his hotel room in Altoona on the evening of August 2, Jimmy declared he was through with the Pittsburgh baseball team due to the unjust treatment he'd received. Sebring stated the Pirates could come begging if they wanted him to return to the squad.[54] Jimmy also visited his good friend Bucky Veil while in Altoona. Upon arriving home in Williamsport on Wednesday afternoon, Sebring issued a denial when a reporter asked him if he'd jumped his contract. Sebring also explained that Dr. Berg wanted to put his leg in a cast two days earlier but told the physician that wasn't possible since Pittsburgh's owner had required him to join the team on their road trip. Lastly, Jimmy refuted his statement from the Altoona interview about being through with the Pirates.[55]

Newspapers sent mixed messaging in articles about Sebring's relationship with acting manager Tommy Leach. In one piece, Sebring asserted that since he supported his friend Bucky Veil after the fight with Leach, the jealous veteran Pittsburgh player never neglected taking an opportunity to knock him.[56] As newspapers printed stories about that earlier confrontation, Sebring classified Leach as one of his best friends on the Pirates' squad. On August 4, Jimmy also pronounced he planned on rejoining Pittsburgh when they reached Philadelphia on August 6.[57] At this point, Sebring's declaration about preparing to rejoin the team seemed of little consequence to Barney Dreyfuss, as team officials ignored his correspondence.[58]

On the evening of August 7, a three-team transaction was finalized that involved the Pittsburgh Pirates. After Cincinnati Reds owner Garry Herrmann shipped outfielder Michael "Mike" Donlin to New York for Harry McCormick, a second deal followed. In that transaction, the Reds traded outfielder McCormick to the Pirates for Jimmy Sebring.[59] Upon hearing that Pittsburgh had dealt him, Sebring said he knew nothing about the deal and that Pirates officials would be required to consult him before finalization. A relative of Jimmy's claimed the player would probably refuse a move to Cincinnati since he didn't like the city.[60] An announcement soon followed that Sebring had signed a contract to play for the Tri-State League's Williamsport Millionaires, although his good friends cautioned against such a rash move.[61] Jimmy eventually came to his senses and reported to the Reds. On August 18, Sebring also exhibited maturity by calling Dreyfuss on the telephone and apologizing for his behavior.[62]

While Barney Dreyfuss handled the Sebring situation, manager Fred Clarke still performed on the diamond when problems arose for first baseman Kitty Bransfield. In 1904, Bransfield appeared to be a former shell of himself thanks to the disgusting efforts of a small but boisterous group of gamblers who made life miserable for him at Exposition Park. One day, Kitty made a play that offended these bettors, and from that time forward, they didn't give him a moment's peace.[63] Dreyfuss had attempted to devise numerous plans to circumvent their activities, but none seemed to work. At one point, Barney refused to sell tickets to such individuals, but they still found a way to gain entrance into the ballpark. These gamblers often bet on the Pirates. When the home squad failed to win, or a particular player committed an error, severe verbal abuse cascaded down upon that individual. These disloyal, selfish, corrupt tin-horn gamblers repulsed devoted baseball patrons.

No player, not even the great Honus Wagner, was exempt from their abuse. At the beginning of the 1904 season, in Pittsburgh's second series against Cincinnati on the road, Wagner became ill with tonsillitis. A physician conducted an examination and recommended Honus remain in his hotel room. Finding this course of action unacceptable, Wagner reported for duty the following day. Although the illness eventually settled in Honus's back, making it necessary to apply plasters that limited his mobility, Pittsburgh's star shortstop remained in the lineup. Wagner continued playing when the Pirates returned home. Honus committed two errors in the game against the Reds on April 23 at Exposition Park but still helped Pittsburgh secure an extra-inning victory with his bat. True baseball fans were stunned and angry as the malicious gamblers constantly hissed at Wagner over his two miscues on the field.[64]

Kitty Bransfield chafed under the constant abuse he received. His batting average for the season reached its high point on opening day in St. Louis on

April 15, when he went 1-for-4 at the plate. For many of the season's early months, Bransfield's average swung like a pendulum on either side of the .200 mark. After hitting .305 (1902) and .265 (1903) the previous two seasons, Kitty could only muster a .223 mark in 1904. Bransfield also wasn't playing up to his usual standards in the field and lacked focus on many occasions. Against Cincinnati on May 27 at Exposition Park, Fred Clarke temporarily sent Kitty to the bench and installed catcher Frederick "Fred" Carisch at first base. Clarke, who praised Carisch for his work as Pittsburgh defeated the Reds, 2–0, explained his decision behind the lineup change.

"Bransfield has not been playing his game either at the bat or on first, and we decided to give him a chance to get at himself," said Clarke. "I don't know how long he will be off. Carisch played good ball today. I will lay any man on the team off who is not playing his game—that is, if I have a man who can take his place. Baseball, not sentiment, will rule here."[65]

Although Barney Dreyfuss preferred that Clarke keep Bransfield out of the lineup for a more extended period, his skipper reinstalled him at first base after only a few games. Pittsburgh's manager reasoned that such punishment proved counterproductive since it caused Kitty to brood even more than usual. Bransfield's biggest problem was that he sulked and moped when mired in a slump, which only caused him to become more anxious. While Kitty seemed to lack nerve and couldn't quickly recover from a batting slump, no player on the team ever worked harder than the big first baseman.[66] One Pittsburgh baseball writer, who'd always given Bransfield praise for his excellent work but felt compelled to issue some criticism as the player experienced his current problems, conveyed amazement when Kitty stopped talking to him over this latest evaluation.[67]

Reinstatement into the lineup didn't mean Fred Clarke wouldn't lose his patience over boneheaded plays. In the second inning of the game against Brooklyn at Washington Park on June 4, Kitty reached first base on an error. When Jimmy Sebring followed by ripping a single, Bransfield only advanced to second for some unexplainable reason. While working the coaching line, Clarke berated Kitty, using pretty strong language that caused a chorus of boos from the crowd over his response.[68] In the game against St. Louis on June 23 at Exposition Park, Clarke lifted Bransfield after he made a dumb play and replaced him for the second time with Fred Carisch. The stupid maneuver occurred in the fourth frame, with Fred and Honus Wagner on base and two outs. Kitty swung at the first pitch, a high, wide offering, and fouled out.[69]

At the beginning of June, a newspaper story claimed that Clarke took great joy in criticizing and panning Bransfield whenever he committed a boneheaded play. This article also stated that one evening from his residence at the Monongahela House, Kitty acknowledged he'd grown tired of his manager disparaging him and would welcome a move to another team.[70] Pittsburgh sportswriter Ralph S. Davis stated that no such problem existed between Clarke and Bransfield, who were close friends.[71] In respect to Carisch replacing Kitty in the game on June 23, Barney Dreyfuss declared the reason to be that the first baseman suffered from a sore hand, which the owner became aware of after the contest ended. To back this claim, Dreyfuss stated he saw Bransfield show Clarke his hand before making the change at first base.[72]

Whether friction existed between Fred Clarke and Kitty Bransfield, Pittsburgh's first baseman possessed a gloomy disposition as he attempted to battle through adversity.[73] The gamblers in Exposition Park's right-field grandstand added to Kitty's angst through their constant, vicious criticism. These fellows, who wagered a dollar or two on a game, and a dime or a nickel on a particular play, had found fault with Bransfield when making an error on one occasion and launched a campaign to belittle him at every turn with rude epithets. According to an article in the *Pittsburgh Dispatch*, Clarke had attempted to ease Kitty's burden by proposing a trade with the Boston Beaneaters for first baseman Frederick "Fred" Tenney. Pittsburgh's manager discussed the proposition with Bransfield, who welcomed the opportunity to play near his home. When the deal ended up not reaching fruition, Kitty vowed to jump in and give his best efforts for the Pirates.[74]

Bransfield's star-crossed season received another jolt on August 8 while the team played in Philadelphia. As thirteen members of the Pirates departed the Aldine Hotel in a horse-drawn bus headed for National League Park, the rear wheel of the coach broke free, causing it to wobble and throw players from the carriage. Pitcher Roscoe Miller received severe contusions to his right arm. Horrible bruises about his body resulting from this accident prevented Kitty from playing in the game against the Phillies that afternoon. One Pirates player jokingly claimed the accident occurred due to local baseball loyalist sabotage.[75] A man named Hayes, who acted as the proprietor of this service, had been taking players in many leagues to Philadelphia ballparks for nearly twenty years. In the past, Hayes had relished giving Pittsburgh's players a scare through close calls regarding a collision.[76]

The gamblers at Exposition Park, who lost a few pennies on the outcome of their bets from blunders by Bransfield, roasted the first baseman and called him vile names throughout the 1904 season. According to the *St. Louis Republic*, eliminating this band of miscreants from the stands would go a long way toward

Kitty returning to form. At the same time, the club shouldn't make a sudden change unless they could secure a better first baseman.[77] A trade seemed likely if the story about Bransfield and Honus Wagner engaging in a fight on the final eastern trip of the season were true.[78] Ralph S. Davis declared this rumor false since, on the evening in question regarding a confrontation, he witnessed Wagner and Kitty being on friendly terms while playing cards in the same room. Bransfield bid his teammate a fond "goodnight" when the game ended.[79]

For two months after the season concluded, Fred Clarke pondered what future direction he wanted to take the Pirates. Barney Dreyfuss had tasked Clarke with remolding the squad.[80] Before leaving for the December league meetings in New York, Pittsburgh's manager officially announced that Kitty Bransfield wouldn't be playing for the Pittsburgh Pirates in 1905. Clarke admitted to having a few trades in mind but didn't divulge players of interest before explaining the decision related to Bransfield.

"I consider Bransfield one of the very best first basemen in the business," said Clarke. "He can play first-class ball, but at times he did not do it last year. He was not playing his game, and the action of some patrons of the park who seemed to take delight in going after him, seemed to effect him. Kitty always had his ear open for criticism. He would complain to me, and I advised him to pick out the offenders and I would have them excluded from the park."[81]

Clarke orchestrated his first deal in New York on December 14, trading twenty-five-year-old catcher Ed Phelps to Cincinnati for thirty-four-year-old backstop Henry "Heinie" Peitz.[82] Ed, very popular with Pittsburgh's fans, readily admitted he'd experienced a tough year in 1904.[83] In a game against Boston at Exposition Park on July 11, Beaneaters hurler Charles "Togie" Pittinger had drilled Phelps in the head with a pitch in the third inning that struck him in the temple above the left eye.[84] Ed fell to the ground eliciting an agonizing scream. Dr. Gustav Berg jumped out of the grandstand and attended to the player. Phelps was taken unconscious to the dressing room, where Dr. Berg applied ice to his head. Ed's wife, Mary Bills Phelps, and son, Eddie Jr., left their grandstand seats and stood by his side in the dressing room. A requested carriage reached Exposition Park to take Phelps to his home, where prescribed quiet and rest returned him to good health.[85] While discussing this trade, Clarke said that he acquired a player nearly nine years older than Phelps out of necessity.

"I'll tell you why I traded Phelps," said Fred Clarke after the deal had been closed. "We have a bunch of quiet fellows on our team. I am the only man who can say anything on the lines and we need a coacher. Heinie fills that bill all right. He is also a good—level-headed catcher and while he is not fast I think he will prove all right for us."[86]

The inevitable finally happened when Fred swung his second deal that same day. He shipped Kitty Bransfield, Harry McCormick, and utility player Arthur "Otto" Krueger to Philadelphia for outfield prospect George "Del" Howard, whom the Phillies had drafted from the Western League's Omaha Rangers, and a player to be named later.[87] Although Howard still hadn't played in a major league game, Pirates fans appeared satisfied with the acquisition.[88] Clarke immediately refuted reports regarding the fallacy that he moved Kitty because of an alleged quarrel with Wagner.[89] Owner Barney Dreyfuss backed both deals, trusting his manager's judgment and baseball knowledge. Dreyfuss claimed changes were necessary since the Pirates' expenses, including payroll, were higher in 1904 than any team in either the National or American leagues.[90]

Pittsburgh bounced back nicely in 1905, going 96–57. The Pirates placed second, nine games behind New York. With transition becoming evident, the gamblers occupying Exposition Park's right-field grandstand altered how they went about their business. Since Kitty Bransfield no longer played on the club, different players needed to be the object of their fury. Pirates officials had made headway by preventing wagers from being made in the ballpark. Unfortunately, these club representatives and Allegheny police couldn't thwart gamblers from betting outside the grounds and entering to watch games. These seedy individuals had also shifted gears and now usually bet against the Pirates. One grandstand spectator, who'd placed a wager of $200 for the Phillies to win on June 17 and was quite open about it, started having conniptions when Pittsburgh rallied late in the game. This gambler began pulling his hair when the Pirates tied the contest in the ninth frame and fainted after Tommy Leach scored the winning run an inning later.[91]

Although his production at the plate declined, faithful servant Claude Ritchey continued plugging along at second base for Pittsburgh. After batting .287 in 1903, Claude saw those numbers drop to .263 (1904) and .255 (1905). Rumors abounded about Ritchey's status after the 1905 campaign ended. One story claimed Claude would be sent to the bench and supplanted by David "Dave" Brain, whom the team had acquired from St. Louis over the summer. Barney Dreyfuss dismissed such silliness, citing Ritchey's solid work the previous season. Barney also stated that Claude had served him well within the baseball realm.[92] The ludicrous nature of this suggestion was hammered home when Fred Clarke included Brain as part of the package of players shipped to Boston for pitcher Victor "Vic" Willis on December 15. The concept of

"Claude Ritchey for sale or trade" remained strong throughout the off-season. Dreyfuss responded to a rumor that the Cardinals wanted to acquire Ritchey.

"So, St. Louis wants Ritchey," laughingly repeated Barney Dreyfuss. "Yes, they seem to think that all they have to do is to offer a man for him and it will be accepted, but if I was betting it would be that the tobacco squirter stays here."

In his December article for *Sporting Life* quoting Dreyfuss, A. R. Cratty also wrote about Ritchey: "At times the little fellow from up river may do things which are not the best for himself, but he does not seem to suffer to an extent that the habit forces any deterioration in his work."[93] That habit, of course, surrounded partaking in alcohol. Although Ritchey didn't say much, his teammates often quoted the squad's resident humorist, who possessed a dry wit when making one of his classic comments.[94]

Claude played second base for third-place Pittsburgh in 1906 and batted .269. The National League campaign that year consisted of seven teams choking on Chicago's dust. The Cubs cruised to the pennant with a 116–36 record before losing to the crosstown Chicago White Sox in the World Series, four games to two. As this season wound down, Ritchey refuted a claim regarding unhappiness over his current berth and planning on retiring in the fall to devote his attention toward business interests in Emlenton that included very successful oil wells.

> That story about my being dissatisfied with the players on the Pittsburgh team is a pipedream. I never said any such thing, either, but you can't speak these days without being quoted as wanting to retire. I'm good for a few more campaigns yet, I guess, and I'm not anxious to admit that I am a "hasbeen," even if some of my dear, kind friends do think that of me.
>
> I've been in Pittsburgh a good while now, and I haven't had any employer but Barney Dreyfuss for so long that I don't think I could get along with any other. I've never had any trouble with Barney. I always try to do my work for him, and he has never told me he didn't like what I did. I told Barney just a few weeks ago I was going to play for him till he kicked me off the team, and I meant what I said.[95]

There must've been something in the Allegheny River water near Exposition Park, as retirement rumors abounded as the season closed. This possibility surrounding Clarence "Ginger" Beaumont didn't surprise Pirates management, who felt the outfielder might walk away from baseball. Barney Dreyfuss offered fascinating insight when commenting on this prospect.

"Well, Clarence may be going to quit but I don't notice him doing it just now," said Dreyfuss. "Seems to me he is reporting for his checks all right. Of course, I cannot stop any man who wants to try another occupation and I don't mind saying that some would not cause me any regret by retiring."[96]

Dreyfuss's final comment seemed quite telling since manager and outfielder Fred Clarke had been the only other person considering retirement until he signed a new contract when the league meetings commenced on December 11 in New York.[97] Clarke's three-year, $22,500 deal had expired when the 1906 season ended. Through discussions with Fred's close friends, baseball writers ascertained that Pittsburgh's manager thought he deserved $10,000 a year.[98] Although the Pirates' owner didn't release a salary figure, many sources believed the deal satisfied Clarke and made him the highest-paid diamond leader for 1907.[99] Two days after inking his signature to the document, Fred announced the contract called for him to manage Pittsburgh next year exclusively. He promised to play in case of accident or injury to any starting player, but the agreement didn't require him to appear in games unless he desired to take the field.[100] On opening day in 1907, Clarke took his position as Pittsburgh's starting left fielder.

The Pirates also had a new second baseman when the 1907 baseball season commenced. Shortly after Fred Clarke and Barney Dreyfuss agreed on contract terms, Pittsburgh's manager held a conference with Boston skipper Fred Tenney. An announcement surrounding the results of that meeting came later on December 11, as the Pirates shipped Claude Ritchey, pitcher Patsy Flaherty, and a player to be named later to the Beaneaters for infielder and Latrobe, Pennsylvania, native Edward "Ed" Abbaticchio.[101] A shortstop by trade in Boston, Abbaticchio, who hadn't played in 1906, would be expected to replace Ritchey at second. "Abby," as he sometimes was called, had retired from baseball to run a lucrative hotel in Latrobe. This establishment proved to be a moneymaker since Ed had obtained a coveted liquor license for his hostelry. Gaining this document was a considerable coup since Pennsylvania liquor license laws were very stringent.

Pittsburgh had attempted to secure Abby the previous year. Both parties had agreed to a plan where Abbaticchio would at least play home games if Judge Lucien Doty, Westmoreland County licensing officer, granted permission to allow a capable manager to be in charge of the hotel. A vital individual from Charleroi, Pennsylvania, made a special request to Judge Doty on Abbaticchio's behalf, leading to him receiving approval for a leave of absence during the baseball season. Ed declined to consider the proposition, stating his parents wanted him to leave baseball forever. Things changed in 1906 after George Dovey purchased the Beaneaters. Dovey traveled to Latrobe on many occasions to visit his elderly mother. He often met with Abby and finally convinced the player to come out of retirement and help the Boston organization through a trade with the Pirates.[102]

Following the deal, *Pittsburgh Dispatch* sports editor Charles B. Power praised Claude Ritchey for his brilliant work at second base for seven years with Pittsburgh. Power claimed fans watching games from the grandstand heartily cheered when Claude made dazzling plays around the keystone sack. He also declared that Boston, requiring the services of a first-class second baseman, received a just reward in this transaction.[103] As 1906 concluded, a New York newspaper loyal to Highlanders baseball owner Frank Farrell's racetrack interests, commenting on Claude Ritchey's willingness to go to Boston, said, "Who wouldn't be glad to get away from Pittsburgh?"[104]

Dedicated fans occupying Exposition Park's grandstand had applauded Ritchey's every move around second base. The rude and crude bettors at the ballpark jeered Claude in many instances rather than cheer for him. Before the 1907 season started, while the Beaneaters held spring training in Thomasville, Georgia, Ritchey stated that he'd told Barney Dreyfuss in 1906 that he wanted to be transferred to Boston if George Dovey purchased the team. Claude also declared he wouldn't have played under any conditions that season in Pittsburgh.[105] Ritchey enraged Pittsburgh's baseball patrons after categorizing the local fans as unfair and rabid. One fan, who'd attended most of the games at Exposition Park over the past five years, called the *Pittsburgh Press* offices and stated that he couldn't remember when Ritchey didn't receive applause after making an exceptional play.[106]

When Boston and Pittsburgh made the deal, A.R. Cratty claimed in his *Sporting Life* article that Claude never thrived under criticism and couldn't understand the purpose behind cheers one time and boos in another instance. Ritchey was a quiet, reserved man, whether attempting not to appear in a 1901 parade when Pittsburgh won their first National League flag or being reluctant to doff his cap after receiving plaudits for an exceptional play. The little second baseman once threatened to "lick" a reporter in a fight who'd referred to him as "Dope."

Cratty also said that Claude refused to extend his hand to the writer at the beginning of spring training in 1906. Ritchey's reason appeared to be his exaggerated perception that the writer had intimated in winter articles that he was always loaded. Cratty later wrote that Claude was among a group of players reportedly drinking more than the rules allowed at the end of the 1906 campaign. According to the writer, such an allegation came as no surprise. Rumors had pointed to Ritchey enjoying his beverage of choice daily after a game for many years. Cratty pointed out that such indulgence never affected his performance on the field.[107]

After insulting every fan who attended games at Exposition Park, Claude finally blamed the true culprits behind the strong desire to shake Pittsburgh's dust from his shoes. With the 1907 season being almost two months old, the *Philadelphia Telegram* quoted Ritchey as saying that gamblers had been responsible for driving him out of Pittsburgh.[108] This declaration by Claude certainly didn't come as a surprise, as Barney Dreyfuss had echoed that sentiment in April.

"All the knocking against the Pittsburgh players that is heard at Exposition Park is done by these cheap gamblers," said Dreyfuss. "They bet a few nickels on the game and then proceed to hammer the home team, the result being that the visitors are given the impression that all Pittsburgh fans are disloyal. These knockers made life miserable for Claude Ritchey, than whom no more faithful player ever lived, keeping after him until he was driven to desperation and welcomed a chance to go to another club."[109]

The activities of knocking gamblers had ruined the thriving careers of two Pittsburgh players, driven to desperation by their gross behavior. Following Claude Ritchey's trade to Boston, only six men, Fred Clarke, Honus Wagner, Tommy Leach, Ginger Beaumont, Deacon Phillippe, and Sam Leever, remained from the first pennant-winning team of 1901. In short order, that number swiftly would be reduced to five.

In a game against the Cincinnati Reds on April 23, 1904, gamblers occupying Exposition Park ruthlessly heckled Honus Wagner, who played despite feeling the effects of tonsilitis, for making two errors. Wagner also had a rough time while managing the Pittsburgh Pirates in exhibition contests throughout the season. On July 19, teammate Tommy Leach replaced Honus as the club's assistant manager, a position he'd held for four years. Wagner appeared unhappy doing this job while the organization hadn't been pleased recently with his work. Honus also experienced problems with Pirates outfielder Jimmy Sebring, who threatened to fight the star shortstop on one occasion. (Photo in the Public Domain).

5

A Player to Be Named Later and the First Base Jinx

A manager or owner utilizing the concept of "a player to be named later" to keep a potential trade alive was a critical mechanism for agreement on such proposals during the Deadball Era. This little caveat proved very helpful for breaking the logjam when negotiations stalled between representatives from two baseball teams, or when a potential transaction seemed to be falling apart. While throwing in money also offered a viable alternative to sweeten the pot, having the option to add a player to be named later helped bring many trade propositions across the finish line to the satisfaction of all parties involved in these discussions.

When Pittsburgh proposed shipping Claude Ritchey to the Boston Beaneaters, a minor sticking point developed regarding potential players the two clubs wanted to exchange. Upon hearing rumors that the Pirates might trade him, outfielder Otis Clymer met with manager Fred Clarke to receive assurances that he wouldn't be dealt or sold. Otis missed most of the 1906 campaign after suffering a broken ankle against the St. Louis Cardinals on April 27 at Exposition Park.[1] Clymer, who'd been the player to be named later involved in the Kitty Bransfield deal with the Philadelphia Phillies in December 1904, had a solid rookie season for Pittsburgh in 1905, batting .296. Otis didn't appear to be particularly enamored with making a move to Boston.

"I'm going to have a little to say about where I go if the Pittsburghs decide to dispose of me," said Otis Clymer. "I heard there was talk of trading me, so I just came over from Lebanon, [Pennsylvania,] to look into the matter. If any deals are made for me and I don't like them, I will notify the intending purchaser that he'd better not carry it out, as I won't go along. There was talk of me going to Boston, but I would rather play outlaw ball than play there. Neither would I play in Brooklyn or St. Louis. I have no objections to any of the management or players, but just don't like the town. I have no trouble with my injured leg and feel as good as I ever did. If Dreyfuss thinks I can't do good work the coming season I will fool him badly."[2]

Because of this stance, Clymer wasn't a viable candidate to be included in the Ritchey trade. Upon closing the deal, a rumor surfaced that outfielder Robert "Bob" Ganley would likely be included in the transaction as the player to be named later.[3] This possibility became moot when the Pirates sold Ganley to the Washington Senators on December 31, 1906. Months after the completion of the deal between Boston and Pittsburgh, the final piece of the puzzle shifted between these two teams. On February 28, 1907, Barney Dreyfuss released longtime Pittsburgh outfielder Ginger Beaumont so he could move on to the Doves, as the team was now called, as the third and final Pirates player involved in this transaction.

When Fred Clarke had announced days earlier that Beaumont might be released, Dreyfuss opened communications with Boston owner George Dovey about the outfielder being that player to be named later. Dovey accepted the offer after his manager, Fred Tenney, agreed to assign Ginger an outfield berth. Beaumont consented to join the Doves and play his best for that organization. Dreyfuss thanked Ginger for the interest he'd always exhibited in the team's success as a Pirates member and wished him well in all future ventures. Beaumont had played eight seasons in Pittsburgh. Debuting in 1899, Ginger batted .352 during his rookie campaign. He recorded a 6-for-6 day at the plate and scored six runs in a game against Philadelphia at Exposition Park on July 22. A few weeks later, on August 9 versus these same Phillies at National League Park, Beaumont smacked a single, a double, and three triples.[4] In 1902, Ginger earned the crown as the National League's batting champion when he hit .357.

In recent years, injuries had taken their toll on Beaumont. Rheumatism in the legs had become a general concern before Ginger suffered a debilitating injury in 1905.[5] Beaumont only saw sporadic action in the campaign's final two months due to a puzzling situation. He could walk on his heel without any problem, but when running, Ginger lost all power in his leg. On December 10, Beaumont arrived in Pittsburgh from his home of Honey Creek, Wisconsin, and traveled east with Barney Dreyfuss and Fred Clarke to see a specialist about his leg. No mystery existed over how the Pittsburgh outfielder's injury had occurred months earlier while the Pirates made an eastern swing in July.

"I hurt my heel in the East last season and I can recall the time and place well," said Beaumont while discussing his trouble. "Sam Leever and I were at a roof garden show, and after it was over we were coming down a flight of steps when I missed my footing and slipped four steps before I caught myself. I did not pay any attention to the accident at the time, and it was not for some time afterward that I noticed the effect of the injury. I had trouble with my right knee for two or three seasons, but that injury finally gave way to treatment and didn't bother me."[6]

University of Pennsylvania athletic trainer Michael "Mike" Murphy identified Ginger Beaumont's ankles as the problem and prescribed a work regimen instead of rest.[7] Christmas Clune, a professional athletic trainer from Canada who Pittsburgh's International Hockey League team recently hired to condition its players, said such treatment would prove futile.

"All the specialists in the world cannot cure Beaumont," emphatically declared the Canadian. "The only thing that will do Beaumont any good is this."

Christmas Clune mimicked the movements of a masseur's hands for effect. "I'll wager that I can put the big ballplayer in first-class trim by manipulation of the affected part," he continued, "and I don't think a specialist can do that much."[8]

Beaumont's issue persisted into the 1906 baseball campaign. The outfielder only appeared in one game as a pinch hitter against the Cincinnati Reds on April 19 at Exposition Park before he sought another opinion regarding the injury. Dr. Harley Parker, a former major league pitcher and current team physician for the Chicago Cubs, who also coached Northwestern's college baseball squad, saved the day for Ginger. Dr. Parker discovered the area of concern and started treating Beaumont for a spine ailment. On May 24, the physician declared that Ginger would rejoin his team on June 3 in Chicago, take his place in center field once again, and ably assist the Pirates in their fight to claim a pennant.[9] As promised, Beaumont returned to the starting lineup against Boston on June 5. For the first time since 1900, Ginger failed to top the .300 mark at the plate, batting .265 in his final season with the Pirates.

Like former teammates Kitty Bransfield and Claude Ritchey, grandstand plungers who worked crooked numbers of their own during baseball games at Exposition Park had also subjected Beaumont to catcalls.[10] With Ginger and Bob Ganley's removal from the picture, Otis Clymer certainly should've gotten an opportunity to fool Barney Dreyfuss badly if Pittsburgh's owner didn't think he could give the Pirates quality work in 1907. Unfortunately, Otis's ankle wasn't as strong as he'd hoped at the beginning of the season. Disheartened and discouraged, Clymer informed Fred Clarke that he'd firmly considered quitting baseball. His ankle didn't play a role regarding limited diamond action for Otis. The outfielder suffered a charley horse injury during spring training, and, later, stomach problems prevented Clymer from playing and practicing.[11]

Otis's perceived illness helped usher his exit from Pittsburgh. Clymer enraged Clarke by declining to follow his manager's orders in a game when Fred asked Otis to pinch hit for the pitcher. The Pirates' skipper became shocked and amazed when Clymer refused to follow his directive because he had a stomach ache. Incensed over Otis's attitude, an outraged Clarke offered a stern warning to owner Barney Dreyfuss.

"You might as well ask for waivers on that man," said Clarke. "I won't put him in another game as long as I have anything to do with the Pittsburgh team."[12]

Otis Clymer wasn't familiar with the legend of Bones Ely and his sore finger. Ten minutes after Clarke issued this demand, Dreyfuss requested waivers on Clymer over the wire. Seven clubs immediately responded, inquiring about his services. Barney ended up selling Clymer to the Washington Senators on a thirty-day trial basis for $2,000, with one-half of that amount paid shortly after consummating the deal.[13] On the evening of June 20, Dreyfuss sent a wire to Senators manager Joe Cantillon, asking him to call up long distance on the telephone at 10 A.M. the following day. Early in their conversation, Dreyfuss broached the subject of Otis.

"By the way," said Dreyfuss, "would you like to have Clymer?"

"What's the matter?" replied Cantillon. "Has he broken his leg or his neck that you want to let him go. He is a grand ballplayer and I certainly would like to have him."

"No, he is all right," replied Dreyfuss, "but he and Fred Clarke got into a row at the clubhouse yesterday and Fred sprained a couple of fingers. He is mad all the way through and says he won't have him around the park."

"But can you get waivers on him?" asked Cantillon.

Barney Dreyfuss assured his counterpart that although three clubs had refused to waive Clymer, he'd gotten everybody in line. Joe expressed a desire to want Otis and inquired about the cost. Dreyfuss claimed he needed to check with Fred Clarke first to see if he was still mad, and if so, Pittsburgh's owner would place a second phone call about the price. At 2 P.M. on June 21, Cantillon received a telegram explaining the details, and he immediately wired back his acceptance. The telegram also stated that Clymer would report to Joe in Philadelphia on June 24. When concluding his earlier telephone conversation,

Barney told Washington's manager that Otis might be another gem for them, like Bob Ganley. Dreyfuss added that while neither individual played their best in Pittsburgh, Cantillon seemed capable of getting everybody to do their best.[14] Dreyfuss struck a more subdued tone when talking to Pittsburgh's press corps members about the deal.

"I wish Clymer luck," commented Dreyfuss. "We could not use him, Washington can. That's all."[15]

Otis Clymer didn't join Washington until the morning of June 27, and he played that afternoon against the New York Highlanders at Hilltop Park. Clymer offered his explanation for why things didn't work out in Pittsburgh.

"I was glad to get away from Pittsburgh," said Clymer. "Things were not congenial there, and I could not give the club my best efforts. I believe that I am just as capable now as I ever was to hold my own in the big league, and I will prove that in a very short time."[16]

Concern arose for the Pirates shortly after Otis joined the Senators. Although Clymer got off to a blistering start at the plate for Washington, he experienced a disagreement with manager Joe Cantillon during a game against the Chicago White Sox at South Side Park on July 11. Otis, who furiously bristled over criticism from any manager, ended up riding the pine for two weeks. When informed of the Chicago report, Barney Dreyfuss replied, "I hope they don't send him back to me."[17] Dreyfuss's mind rested at ease when the Senators didn't renege on the deal and kept Clymer on their team.

Amidst roster upheaval, Pittsburgh came home second in the 1907 National League race with a 91–63 record, placing them 17 games behind the Chicago Cubs. For the past three years since Philadelphia acquired Kitty Bransfield, the station at first base proved a work in progress for the Pirates. After management found William "Bill" Clancy severely lacking at the major-league level in 1905, Del Howard moved from the outfield to first base that summer. Howard's elimination from the equation came that off-season when manager Fred Clarke traded him on December 15, 1905, with infielder Dave Brain and pitcher Vivan "Vive" Lindaman to Boston for veteran twirler Vic Willis. Weeks before making this deal, Fred believed he'd solved his first base problem.

On the evening of November 13, 1905, a long-awaited letter from California detailing the signing of first baseman James Joseph "Joe" Nealon arrived in Pittsburgh. Clarke had composed this correspondence on the train ride back to his farm in Winfield, Kansas, since he'd been too busy pursuing Nealon in San Francisco to write. Joe was a hot piece of baseball property that had also drawn interest from the Cincinnati Reds, Boston Americans, and

New York Highlanders. James Sr., a wealthy San Francisco businessman and Nealon's father, helped handle negotiations between his son and potential suitors. Anybody hoping to sign Joe also needed James Nealon's consent. Although other teams bid higher to purchase the big first baseman, Pittsburgh secured the youngster. James Nealon had hoped to make the best business arrangement for his son while also being keen on Joe going to a good baseball organization with the proper companions. Clarke's responses regarding these points swayed Mr. Nealon. Joe also told his father that he preferred signing with the Pirates.[18]

Joe Nealon received a hefty salary for a rookie in 1906, getting $6,000 a year to play for the Pittsburgh Pirates.[19] A late-season batting slump didn't diminish Joe's contribution to the Pirates' cause that year. Nealon batted .255 in 1906 and tied for the National League lead with Chicago's Harry Steinfeldt, by knocking in 83 runs. Joe also did splendid work around the first base sack, pacing the circuit in putouts and double plays. Sadly, everything came crashing down one year later for many reasons, some of which were unavoidable and others categorized as self-inflicted. Over the winter, Nealon suffered a fractured hand at his San Francisco home. When Joe arrived in Hot Springs for spring training, his hand remained stiff from the injury.[20] Nealon had also tipped the scales at 216 pounds when the squad held preliminary training in West Baden Springs, Indiana, prompting him to hike five miles once or twice each day when rain and flooding interfered with other workout activities.[21]

Joe averted a severe injury once the regular season began. Nealon twisted his ankle, sliding into second base in the game against Chicago at Exposition Park on April 18. Patrons initially feared that Joe had fractured his ankle, but he eventually rose to his feet and hobbled off the field.[22] Five years earlier, Pirates outfielder Lefty Davis had broken his leg doing the same maneuver at that vexed diamond spot. Nealon supplied a horrendous performance for Pittsburgh at the plate in 1907 before pushing his average up to .257 with an August batting surge. Disciplinary issues, placing Joe at odds with management, also rose to the surface.

The big first baseman consistently indulged himself in alcohol throughout the 1907 campaign. Near the conclusion of Pittsburgh's final trip through the East in August, Nealon and pitcher Albert "Lefty" Leifield were sent home to Pittsburgh early for engaging in activities that didn't take the team's best interests to heart. Leifield was one of the few Pirates who'd received a salary increase in 1907, based on going 18–13 with a 1.87 ERA one year earlier. Lefty's decline on the bump, which had started a few weeks earlier, could be attributed to his more carefree nighttime lifestyle. Shortly after the two men left the team and returned to Pittsburgh, an anonymous Pirates player came to Joe's defense. This individual stated that the gambling element's rank behavior throughout sections of Exposition Park supplied enough anxiety to drive any ballplayer to sullenness and depression. He reasoned that no young player would ever be developed in Pittsburgh until management silenced such bettors.[23]

These problems regarding Joe Nealon and Lefty Leifield first appeared when Pittsburgh played at home. Bored with the mundane existence of living in Allegheny, the two roommates decided to move to a hotel in the city. Both men immediately became caught up in the fast life at their new residence, causing them to lose focus on essential matters such as winning baseball games. Owner Barney Dreyfuss viewed their conduct with dismay and consternation. Dreyfuss demanded that both players leave the hotel at once and move to a quiet boardinghouse.[24] After starting at first base for the Pirates against the Cubs at Exposition Park on September 6, Nealon only made one more appearance in 1907 as a pinch hitter.

Joe appeared to be the picture of despair throughout the season's final weeks, sitting daily in the hotel annex lobby, yearning to return home. Several false reports claimed that an illness had sidelined Nealon, although the only ailment he seemed to be experiencing was homesickness. Joe, who preferred the cooler California climate, resembled a beaten-down individual during games played in summer's heat. When the sun's rays ruthlessly tormented Nealon while performing on the diamond, he lacked ambition and practically dragged himself up to home plate to bat. Dreyfuss offered a short remark about Joe's future with the Pirates.

"I haven't had a talk with Fred Clarke as to his disposition," replied Dreyfuss.[25]

On February 1, 1908, Pittsburgh's owner received a letter from Joe confirming a report that he wouldn't play baseball the upcoming year. Nealon planned on devoting his time to helping his father erect a large public building in California after James Nealon had received a contract from the state for this construction project. Joe also requested that Pittsburgh place his name on the club's reserve list and wished his teammates the best of luck in 1908.[26] People believed Nealon likely would've been released or sold because of his poor habits and rule-breaking in 1907 if he hadn't retired.[27]

Upon signing Joe in 1905, Fred Clarke had promised James Nealon that he would look after his son and attempt to steer him away from the bad vices that sometimes resulted from fame and fortune. In 1907, Joe, who'd never previously shouldered the burden of heavy responsibilities due to his social standing, took a strong liking to the wild and glittering nightlife. Clarke soon found it to be an impossible task to keep tabs on the youngster. Before the campaign reached halfway, stories related to Nealon's activities abounded throughout Pittsburgh. Besides being charged with failing to remain in top condition, Joe was also guilty of leading at least two other Pirates players astray, including roommate Lefty Leifield.[28]

As was the case for Joe Nealon, conditions for creating a broken spirit remained ripe in Exposition Park's stands. In July 1908, Fred Clarke and Pirates ownership threw down the gauntlet, condemning those fans who always found fault with Pittsburgh's players. This attempt at a policy change wasn't directed toward truly devoted patrons but rather at the despicable clique of cheap gamblers who made life unbearable for Pirates team members. Individuals of this ilk had also become bolder, denigrating opposing players when an adverse outcome ruined their wager. The organization issued a cease and desist mandate with backing and assistance from local law enforcement.

These objectionable bettors had become more contentious because Pirates management prevented them from making wagers inside Exposition Park. They still placed bets outside the ballpark before a game since police and team officials couldn't possibly circumvent such activity away from Exposition Park. Thanks to the vigilance of Pittsburgh Police Superintendent Thomas McQuaide and his officers, these individuals could place no wagers inside the facility. The Pirates' organization needed to employ more rigorous measures regarding the disgraceful knocking and roasting during a game. Clarke appealed to Barney Dreyfuss that his players receive critical protection from such abuse.

> My men are fast going up in the air because of the unreasonable fault-finding by a few who attend the games at Exposition Park. We must have protection for them, or I will not stand responsible for the consequences. The players on the Pittsburgh team are not hoodlums—they are all upright, self-respecting citizens, but I have had my hands full at times restraining some of them from jumping into the stands and personally avenging the insults which have been heaped upon them.
>
> The jeering that has followed the making of a single error has been in more than one instance responsible for two or three misplays that have followed. "Rooting" may do a team some good, but it is certain that "knocking" does incalculable harm. If the fans cannot applaud our good plays without roasting us for our mistakes, then I would prefer to play all the games

without a single word of encouragement. We are doing our best, and we cannot stand for the insults and abuse that have been hurled at some of us.

Interestingly, Fred Clarke didn't single out gamblers as the culprits who used abusive and foul language toward his players. Dreyfuss immediately consulted Superintendent McQuaide after speaking with the Pirates' manager. Arrangements were made to place plainclothes officers in the stands for the game against the New York Giants on July 11.[29] The first base jinx also thrived in 1908, as Clarke used Warren Gill, James "Jim" Kane, Alan Storke, and Harry Swacina at that position. None of the four men staked a claim to that spot, as their numbers were unimpressive. Despite questionable fan support and holes in the lineup, Pittsburgh remained in the National League pennant hunt until the final day of their season. The Chicago Cubs ruined the team's hopes of raising the fourth flag in the decade when they defeated the Pirates, 5–2, on October 4 at West Side Grounds. Pittsburgh posted a 98–56 record in 1908, leaving them tied for second place with New York, one game behind Chicago.

The Pirates again made an effort in 1909 to subvert the first base jinx. The organization chose rookie William "Bill" Abstein as the latest person to hopefully man the initial sack in a manner not seen in Pittsburgh since Kitty Bransfield's departure. Barney Dreyfuss had discovered Abstein, a native of St. Louis, Missouri, while playing for the Southern Association's Shreveport Pirates in 1906. Nicknamed "Big Bill," William received a trial with Pittsburgh late that season, appearing in eight games as an outfielder and second baseman. Abstein spent the 1907 and 1908 campaigns playing first base for the Eastern League's Providence Grays.

Fred Clarke was so happy with Bill's progression in 1907 that he almost invited the youngster to spring training one year later at Hot Springs but had a change of heart and allowed him to remain at Providence for more seasoning. When the Pirates had an idle Sunday in 1908 while playing in the East, Clarke spent two nights on a train's sleeper car to travel and watch Bill play for the Grays. Dreyfuss became pleased with Abstein's attitude upon reading a letter that arrived at team offices on January 23, 1909, with the player's signed contract.

"Fred Clarke will not have to worry about a first baseman after he sees this big German hustling around that bag," claimed William Abstein in his letter to Barney Dreyfuss.[30]

Although a positive attitude by a rookie baseball player should've always been something to welcome and admire, nagging injuries acted as a counterbalance to even the most upbeat outlook. When spring training commenced at

Hot Springs, Abstein introduced soccer as part of the morning practice session, which acted as a lovely diversion for Pittsburgh's players.[31] As the regular season approached, the Pirates' manager shifted Bill from playing first base for the Regulars in practice games to manning left field for the Yanigans due to a sore throwing arm.[32] Concern existed that Abstein wouldn't be able to play in the opener against the Cincinnati Reds on April 14 at Palace of the Fans.[33] Bill did suit up on opening day, going 2-for-4 at the plate and driving home one run as Pittsburgh prevailed over Cincinnati, 3–0.

While Abstein's teammates traveled by train on May 10 to Philadelphia to begin a series the following afternoon against the Phillies, he remained behind, suffering from tonsillitis. Team physician, Dr. Gustav Berg, advised Bill to go to the hospital where he could receive proper treatment to eliminate the affliction. Abstein started complaining about his throat as the team prepared to return home from Cincinnati on the evening of May 9.[34] Rain had led to the postponement of Sunday afternoon's game between Pittsburgh and the Reds.[35] In June, Bill informed his manager that the pain in his throwing arm, which he believed to be rheumatism, had worsened after hoping it would subside by continuing to play. Clarke examined Abstein's arm, found the problem to be a displaced ligament, and ordered him to go see the exceptional Youngstown, Ohio, muscle specialist and doctor, John "Bonesetter" Reese.[36]

From July 6 through July 18, Bill only made two pinch-hitting appearances during that time due to suffering from a split finger on his hand.[37] Shortly after Abstein returned to the lineup, staff ace Samuel Howard "Howie" Camnitz, who went 25–6 in 1909, supported by a 1.62 ERA, suffered ptomaine poisoning while the Pirates played in Boston.[38] Setbacks didn't deter the Pirates in their quest to experience a remarkable season in 1909. The summer proved bittersweet for owner Barney Dreyfuss. On June 30, Pittsburgh hosted its first game at its brand-new baseball palace, Forbes Field, located in the Oakland section of town. In this festive inaugural event, Chicago defeated Vic Willis and the Pirates, 3–2.

Sadly, Dreyfuss lost a dear friend weeks after exposing the baseball world to the beautiful crowning jewel of his tenure owning the Pittsburgh Pirates. On the night of July 28, Harry Pulliam, who'd been National League president since 1902, shot himself in the head at his apartment in the New York Athletic Club in New York City. Pulliam passed away the following morning.[39] Pirates star shortstop Honus Wagner was disconsolate and wept when doctors informed him that he couldn't make the trip by train to attend Harry's funeral in Louisville on August 2. Concerns over any jostling to his injured side being problematic for Wagner's heart or permanently sidelining him from the game predicated no traveling by train.[40]

Dedication and perseverance paved the way for a glorious baseball season in Pittsburgh. After losing three out of four contests at Forbes Field in a crucial series against Chicago that started on Labor Day, the Pirates reeled off a sixteen-game winning streak. The game of that series, which the Pirates won over the Cubs, 6–2, on September 7, saw numerous Chicago players banished from the grounds by umpire William "Bill" Klem, including manager Frank Chance for arguing that Bill Abstein's blast in front of the left-field bleachers wasn't a home run. The following day, new National League president John Heydler informed Chance and Cubs shortstop Joseph "Joe" Tinker that he'd fined each player $50. Heydler also ordered third baseman Harry Steinfeldt to fork over $25.[41] When Klem banished Frank from the ballpark the previous afternoon, thousands of Forbes Field fans stood and cheered the umpire. Chance swallowed his tongue until reaching the stands behind first base, where individuals hurled the most ignorant, vindictive remarks.

"Crap shooters!" yelled Chance.[42]

Given Forbes Field's expansive size, Pirates officials initially were gleefully optimistic that the days of being enslaved to the gang of harsh gamblers should be over. They believed the acoustics wouldn't be conducive since these new baseball quarters weren't as tight-knit as at Exposition Park. Unfortunately, such changes didn't deter the gambling element assembled in one section of the new ballpark from making their voices heard. In the closing game of a series against the Brooklyn Superbas on August 6, these despicable individuals hurled ugly words toward Pirates players from one of Forbes Field's concourses. Team members kept a brave front, although shaken by the mean-spirited epithets. One day earlier, fans had vociferously roasted John Owen "Chief" Wilson when he stood and took a called third strike from Superbas hurler George Bell, with the bases loaded, that ended the game. Patrons also jeered pinch hitter extraordinaire Robert Hamilton "Ham" Hyatt when he fanned in the contest versus Brooklyn on August 4.[43]

As the 1909 season concluded, this group of miscreants focused their venom on William Abstein. The husky first baseman attempted to remain strong. In the fourth inning of the second game of a doubleheader against New York at the new Oakland baseball temple on September 27, Giants third baseman Arthur "Art" Devlin tried to give Bill the shoulder as he rounded third base on a single by teammate George Gibson. Abstein, a former football player, placed one arm around Devlin's neck and sent him sprawling to the ground as he continued toward home plate.[44]

Pittsburgh prevailed in the National League race, going 110–42 and finishing 6½ games ahead of second-place Chicago. The Pirates locked horns against the Detroit Tigers in an intense seven-game World Series that included many spikings and collisions on the base paths. The Pirates prevailed in the series because of the heroic performance of rookie pitcher Charles "Babe" Adams, who led Pittsburgh to victory in Games One, Five, and Seven. Twirler Nicholas "Nick" Maddox claimed Game Three as the trio of Vic Willis, Howie Camnitz, and Lefty Leifield, who had combined to win sixty-six contests during the regular season, pitched horribly against Detroit. On the opposite end of the spectrum to Adams's monumental effort was Bill Abstein's performance, as Pittsburgh's first baseman ended up being the series' undisputed goat. Abstein batted .231 in the World Series, struck out nine times, committed five errors in the field, and made numerous base-running blunders.

Bill's most egregious mistake occurred in Game Six at Bennett Park on October 14. Trailing 5–3 heading into the ninth inning, Pittsburgh mounted a furious rally to take the lead and possibly clinch the championship. The frame started splendidly for the Pirates as rookie second baseman Jack Miller and Bill Abstein struck back-to-back singles. Chief Wilson laid down a bunt and then collided viciously with Tigers first baseman Thomas "Tom" Jones while running to the initial sack, knocking him out cold. Miller, also called "Dots," raced home from second base. For some reason, Abstein stopped at third and gazed over at Jones lying on the ground rather than continuing to the plate and scoring the tying run effortlessly. Abstein then committed his second boneheaded play moments later when George Gibson smacked a groundball to Detroit's new first baseman, Samuel "Sam" Crawford. Bill hesitated briefly before bolting for home plate. Crawford threw him out by four feet.[45]

Compounding matters for Bill regarding this poor decision was the fact that Fred Clarke, while working the third base coaching line, ordered his player not to make a break for home on any batted ball that didn't leave the infield.[46] For the first time in modern World Series history, the championship battle went the distance. On October 13, the Pirates had secured Game Five over Detroit at Forbes Field, 8–4. That same day, major league baseball officials conducted a coin toss to decide who hosted a potential seventh game in this World Series. According to newspaper reports, John Heydler of the National League called "heads," but the coin came up "tails," thus awarding the Tigers a seventh game at home, to be played on October 16 after Barney Dreyfuss recommended a Friday off day between Games Six and Seven.⁴⁷

Over four decades later, in an interview with Joe King of the *New York World-Telegram and Sun* for a three-part article in *The Sporting News*, Clarke claimed Pittsburgh had won the coin toss but elected to play the game away from Forbes Field. Fred had reasoned that everybody at home would pull for the Pirates while the fans would ride his players in Detroit, and Clarke believed that particular team played their best when incensed and provoked.⁴⁸ Did the possibility exist that ruthless gamblers occupying Forbes Field may have also played a role in the decision? It's hard to say since many of the individuals from this seedy group of cheap sports had traveled to attend the games at Bennett Park.

Bettors openly wagered thousands of dollars on the 1909 World Series in Pittsburgh and Detroit. The depth of this activity reached proportions many times greater than had ever been witnessed before in the Fall Classic. Authorities made practically no effort to curb gambling. Encouraged by the police's failure to pretend they wanted to crush such betting, gamblers opened handbooks in the lobbies of numerous Detroit hotels.⁴⁹ Around 3,000 rooters had made the trip from Pittsburgh to Detroit by train to watch Games Three and Four at Bennett Park.⁵⁰ Pittsburgh police detective Ted Dillon happened to be one of those individuals. Detective Dillon traveled to the Michigan city to offer assistance to law enforcement there in identifying known criminals connected to gambling from his hometown.⁵¹

One man, considered the best-known sporting authority on betting in the Pittsburgh area, claimed that rumors about manipulation of this World Series from a box-office standpoint, rather than the concept of the best team gaining victory, possessed validity. This individual anonymously offered his impressions for Western Pennsylvania newspapers following the Tigers' Game Four victory on October 12.

> I am absolutely satisfied that the Pittsburgh-Detroit games are being played for the box office instead of trying to honestly have determined which is the best club. Until last Saturday [when the two squads played Game Two of the World Series at Forbes Field on October 9], I always discredited rumors of crookedness in connection with the National League. However, I have not met anyone who can explain why Camnitz was sent to the slab.
>
> That Camnitz was not physically fit for duty no one understood better than the officials of the Pittsburgh club. He had recently undergone an

operation that resulted in greatly reducing his weight and vitality. Not only was he permitted to enter the box but he was kept there after his work disclosed the fact that he could not make good. This piece of 'generalship' gave each club a victory.

Pittsburgh won Monday, so Leifield was put in today. He has been out of condition for weeks and could be depended upon to maintain the box-office equity. He did, though the game [Detroit hurler George] Mullin pitched would probably have won anyway. But with Leifield in the box for Pittsburgh nothing was left to chance.

It now looks as though the next two games would break even, which will insure the playing off of the tie, and conclude the entire series of seven games scheduled.[52]

At the beginning of the World Series, the betting line favored Pittsburgh, 2 to 1. By the final contest on October 16, speculation had swung in Detroit's direction at 10 to 8 odds. This change didn't occur due to an overwhelming feeling that the Tigers were the better team but rather so gamblers could hedge their action.[53] This Pittsburgh gambling expert proved correct about Howie Camnitz, who'd suffered from a slight case of quinsy at season's end, which required a doctor's treatment.[54] Fred Clarke, who believed such talk about a box-office first policy to be nonsense, offered an opinion asserting proof after his team and Detroit's players battled gallantly in Game Six at Bennett Park on October 14.

"The game was really one of the most desperate I ever saw," said Clarke, "and I only wish that some of these malcontents who have claimed the result of this series was pre-arranged could have seen it. I know that the silly idea doesn't exist here. Had it gained a foothold, today would surely have dispelled it. These two teams are so evenly matched that it's like tossing a coin to guess the winners when they meet."[55]

Some of these gambling malcontents had started making life unbearable for Bill Abstein during the campaign's closing weeks, causing the young man to lose his nerve when performing on the diamond.[56] For some unfathomable reason, one Exposition Park rooter loathed Abstein at the season's start and immediately made the rookie first baseman his object of scorn with taunts. Friends of this rowdy spectator quickly joined in the knocking chorus.[57] Gamblers soon found fault with the youngster, calling him "bonehead" as the season progressed. When these bettors wagered against Pittsburgh, they bullied the first baseman. If their money was on the Pirates, they roasted the initial sack's guardian again. Even the strongest-willed individual would likely succumb to this pressure after receiving such abuse daily. Detroit manager Hughie Jennings quickly realized that Bill was Pittsburgh's weak link.[58]

Members of the Pirates' organization readily admitted that Abstein had played a significant role in helping secure the National League pennant. When Bill started performing poorly in the World Series, teammates quietly took up a cry against him to deflect attention from their mistakes. As the series progressed, many Pirates players shunned Abstein.[59] In the presence of newspaper journalists and a group of friends, Barney Dreyfuss severely chided Bill over his performance, although he never approached the lad to discuss the situation. Fellow St. Louis citizen and friend Robert "Bobby" Byrne, who Pittsburgh had acquired from the Cardinals on August 19, acted as the only person attempting to boost Abstein's confidence by constantly cheering for him.

One day after the Tigers tied the World Series, a Detroit afternoon newspaper reported that during a special Friday team meeting at noon on October 15, Bill stood up and affirmatively announced that he was through with his teammates for good after the last man was retired in Saturday's game. Fred Clarke swiftly reacted by claiming this story to be false.

"We had a meeting at noon," said Clarke, "but Abstein did not even attend. So far as I know, not a member of the team has said anything to him about the mistakes he has made in the series. We all may have thought a lot, but I have heard no one give him a 'call.' Bill has been overanxious and has not played his game. But he was a great help to us in winning the National League pennant and was especially strong against the Chicago club."[60]

A Pittsburgh newspaper corroborated Fred Clarke's claim that Bill Abstein hadn't been present when holding this summit but waited for other team members in the hotel lobby.[61] A baseball discussion wasn't even the reason a meeting occurred. Pirates players, headed by Fred, visited Detroit Mayor Philip Breitmeyer after he'd requested meeting the squad.[62] Abstein also happened to be a marked man from the perspective of Detroit's players because he'd spiked Tigers catcher Charles "Boss" Schmidt on his fateful ninth-inning dash to the plate one day earlier.[63]

Clarke invited the entire team to his hotel room the night before Game Seven to ease the tension. In his sitting room was a table full of sandwiches with tubs of beer and soda pop around it. The Pirates' team engaged in eating, drinking, telling stories, and starting an entertaining barbershop quartet. Pittsburgh's manager also invited Barney Dreyfuss to the festivities to partake in a beer. At 10 P.M., Fred sent his players to bed, telling them to get a good night's sleep while also declaring that no matter what happened, if they won or lost, to hell with it.⁶⁴ During practice before Game Seven started on the afternoon of October 16, substitute Ham Hyatt appeared on first base for Pittsburgh.⁶⁵ That morning, sportswriter Ralph S. Davis, in his dispatch to the *Pittsburgh Press*, stated that Hyatt would play first base as a replacement for Bill Abstein.

Readers accused Davis of making a false claim when Abstein took his position at the initial sack in the bottom of the first inning. This lineup change occurred due to Bobby Byrne getting hurt in the top of the frame and being unable to continue after Detroit's George Moriarty spiked Pittsburgh's player when he slid into third base. Clarke initially planned on placing Ed Abbaticchio at first base after shifting Tommy Leach to third and Hyatt to center field. Fred then changed his mind again, deciding to substitute Bill at first.⁶⁶ Clarke performed some lineup gymnastics by placing Ham in Byrne's leadoff spot, although he was already in the lineup, and putting Abstein in his usual sixth position since that slot hadn't yet come up in the batting order.

Pittsburgh's players took care of business in a big way, defeating Detroit in Game Seven, 8–0. Babe Adams continued his mastery over the Tigers, giving up six hits, striking out one, and allowing one walk. Bill Abstein drew a walk in the second inning and then doubled in the third. After Fred Clarke closed his glove on Tom Jones's fly ball to left field to end the game, joyous Pittsburgh fans in attendance rushed onto the field. The exuberant crowd tossed Tommy Leach into the air like a cork. When part of the frenzied mob attempted to accost Honus Wagner, he pointed to a slim, young Adams trying to escape the field through a gate under the grandstand.

"There's the fellow, get him," said Wagner. "He did it."

Pittsburgh's rooters madly dashed toward the young hero, shouting, "Babe, Babe," as they ran. These devoted patrons reached Adams before he could flee and dragged him back onto the field to join in the celebration.⁶⁷ Bill Abstein's friends who watched the contest were ecstatic that the first baseman gave an outstanding performance in the final World Series game. The big fellow's all-around work proved magnificent, and Bill was robbed of a second hit in the contest when David "Davy" Jones speared his blistering line drive to left field in the eighth inning.⁶⁸

On the evening of October 18, the city of Pittsburgh and the surrounding area held a grand celebration that ended at Forbes Field to honor baseball's new champions.⁶⁹ Pennsylvania Congressman James Francis Burke called each team member to the front of the staging platform. Pittsburgh Mayor William Magee introduced them to the crowd before handing over a check for their share of the World Series money.⁷⁰ When Abstein's turn came, he received a rousing reception from the people, requiring him to rise numerous times and bow to the crowd before these proceedings continued.[71]

Once the celebrations ceased, information about Bill's shortcomings in 1909 came forward. Abstein's most apparent deficiency seemed to be his habit of making incorrect decisions during critical moments.[72] While conceding that Bill was a fair mechanical player, he didn't appear mentally sharp when reacting to game situations. Pittsburgh sportswriter Ralph S. Davis declared that on at least five occasions during the 1909 campaign, Abstein cost Pittsburgh victories in baseball games when he cut off throws from right fielder Chief Wilson, headed toward home plate. Although Wilson possessed an accurate cannon arm and usually pegged laser-like darts to Pirates catchers, Bill couldn't resist the temptation of intercepting his teammate's throws.[73]

Abstein possessed another harmful habit that grated on Fred Clarke's nerves. When the opposing team had a runner on first base with less than two outs, Bill, without fail, stepped on the initial sack after a batter smacked a sharp groundball to him. Although Fred schooled Abstein numerous times about throwing to second and forcing the runner before covering the bag to receive a return toss, hoping to turn a double play, Bill failed to understand or follow his manager's instructions.[74] Abstein also didn't appear very stable on baseballs thrown to his left while manning the first base bag as a runner bore down upon him. Bill had also made a glaring boneheaded mental mistake during the inaugural game at Forbes Field on June 30 that aided Chicago in claiming victory. Barney Dreyfuss readily admitted that Abstein had done a fine job as a batter in 1909, although he tended to make wild and crazy decisions on plays in front of him that tempered the owner's belief that Bill could be a first-class first baseman. Clarke also gave his stark opinion of the situation in early June.

"Get rid of him," proclaimed Clarke to Pittsburgh's owner.[75]

News that the Pirates planned on releasing Bill Abstein gained traction shortly after the World Series ended. The inevitable occurred near the end of the year when Pittsburgh asked for waivers on Abstein. On Christmas, Bill received the discouraging news that every National and American league team had expressed no interest in obtaining him. On the other hand, ten minor league clubs put in a claim for Abstein's services.[76] Surprisingly, things took a positive turn for Bill. On January 7, owner Robert L. Hedges and manager Jack O'Connor of the St. Louis Browns announced they'd purchased and signed Abstein to play first base for the team in 1910. Both men engaged Barney Dreyfuss during a league function in Cincinnati and acquired Pittsburgh's first baseman. Hedges didn't release the price paid to secure Bill.[77]

O'Connor and Hedges believed Abstein to be an accomplished hitter. The Browns' owner had also asked Cincinnati manager Clark Griffith's opinion about Bill and received a positive endorsement of the player's ability. Discussing his previous season's work with the Pirates, Abstein said he considered it satisfactory and of such quality that he remained with a pennant-winning team like Pittsburgh the entire year. When it came to the World Series, Bill concurred that he'd performed abysmally. Abstein then offered insight into some of the problems he experienced while playing for the Pirates.

According to Bill, trouble arose between him and longtime team trainer Ed LaForce. Abstein claimed that Tommy Leach and Fred Clarke sided with LaForce regarding this disagreement. From that point forward, Bill experienced misery and gloom while playing baseball.[78] Personal issues with Leach and two other teammates festered as the season progressed. Tommy constantly berated Abstein from the third base coaching box when the giant guardian of the initial sack ran the bases. As the campaign advanced, Bill became so timid and terrified of making a mistake while playing the field that he started receiving throws from Pirates infielders at first base on his knees over fear that the baseball might elude him. If Abstein's lifelong friend, Bobby Byrne, hadn't joined Pittsburgh, Bill possibly wouldn't have lasted the entire season. Byrne's friendship acted as a counterbalance against Abstein's detractors, giving him the courage to persevere.

Barney Dreyfuss stated that Pittsburgh released Abstein for mixing up the team's plays.[79] In the early stages of the 1909 campaign, Bill had played great baseball, solidified the infield defense, and was heralded as the year's find. This brand of baseball ended when the gamblers started torturing him every day.[80] Clarke had an explanation regarding Abstein's demise that sounded eerily similar to comments he made back in 1904 when Pittsburgh's manager had announced that Kitty Bransfield's days with the Pirates were over. Fred offered his impressions shortly after the 1910 season started, blaming fans who'd attended games at Exposition Park and Forbes Field.

> Abstein is a grand fellow and a good ballplayer. He always gave the best he had throughout the season of National League playing and was a mighty good man on the initial corner. Not until the big series with Detroit did "Bill" fall down in his work. Abstein made quite a few bobbles. The "fans," as everyone knows, were out in force to witness the playing of these battles. When "Bill" made his breaks the crowd got after him. Unlike most ballplayers, "Bill" could not stand for the severe call-downs handed out by the

"fans." His one weakness was brought out in decided fashion and Abstein played his poorest ball of the entire 1909 season.

I was willing that Abstein should come back. But, remembering that if Bill made a few bobbles or a bad play of any sort, it would prove worse than ever, I decided, rather than take any chances with the fans or on the ability of Abstein to play tip-top ball, to let him go. Yes, I might say it was sentiment entirely that caused Abstein to lose his job in Pittsburgh.

Clarke also stated that Pittsburgh had experienced problems finding a solid first baseman in recent years but expressed confidence that John Flynn and Bayard "Bud" Sharpe would do fine work at that position in 1910. Fred also believed his team had a good chance of repeating as National League pennant winners.[81] Things didn't turn out much better for Bill Abstein with the St. Louis Browns. The *Pittsburgh Press* reported on May 15 that the Browns would likely release Bill. Manager Jack O'Connor had asked American Association minor league clubs to bid on him but found no interested parties. This scenario left selling him to a Class B or Class C organization as the likely option.

Scribes covering the Browns during their spring training session in Houston, Texas, readily noticed Abstein's deficiencies but ignored them, hoping he'd improve once the season started. Such hope was misguided as Bill's performance deteriorated. Finally, team members held a conference and decided they wouldn't permit Abstein to handle any ball that one of the other Browns players could reach in the future. This strategic decision meant that Jack O'Connor only inserted him into the lineup for his bat, which didn't make sense since Bill hit .149 in 25 games that year. In an article, writer Ralph S. Davis took a brutal stance toward Abstein, suggesting an alternative occupation.

"It is too bad, but Abstein has simply missed his calling," wrote Davis. "He never was a ballplayer, and never will be a successful one. He might flourish in some bush organization, but he would probably make more of a success as a clerk in the corner grocery, if he could concentrate his mind on the business sufficiently not to hand a customer a pound of coffee when she asked for a quart of milk."[82]

Bill Abstein made his final appearance in a game for St. Louis on June 2 before moving on to play for the Eastern League's Jersey City Skeeters. It's possible to glean three points from Abstein's tragic tale. The first is that Bill's 1909 season exhibited the first base jinx still strongly prevailed in Pittsburgh. The second feature is that Fred Clarke wasn't being straightforward as to sentiment acting as the reason for Bill's liberation from the mean and nasty gamblers through his sale to the Browns. A story about another Pittsburgh Pirates player's demise in 1909 proved this point. Lastly, the Abstein sale, this other individual's downfall, and future events indicated that a strong relationship was developing regarding deals involving the Pirates and major league teams from St. Louis.

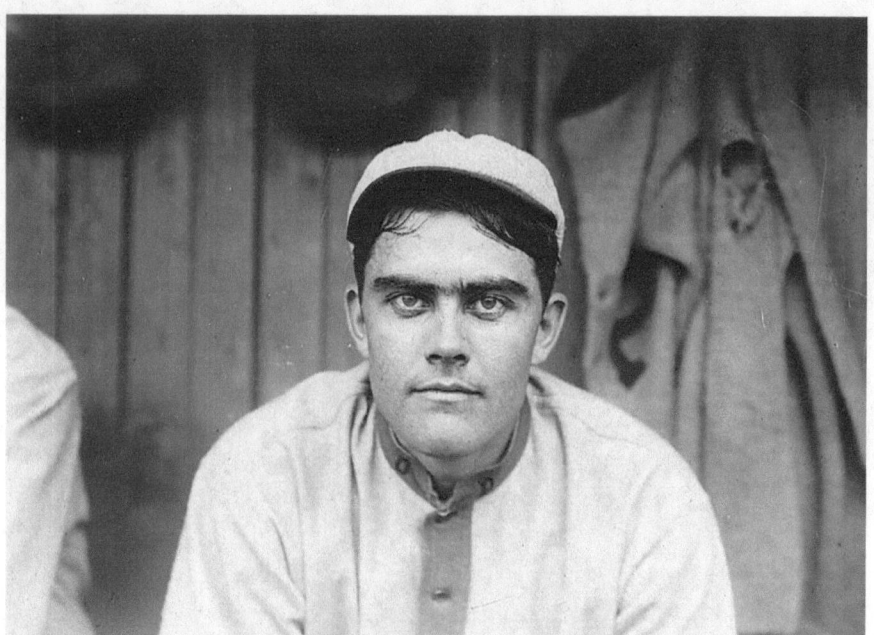

Pittsburgh Pirates hurler Babe Adams gave a heroic performance on the bump against the Detroit Tigers in the 1909 World Series. Babe posted a 3-0 record, defeating Detroit in Games One, Five, and Seven. Pittsburgh claimed the title by beating the Tigers, 8-0, on October 16, at Bennett Park. After the contest ended, Adams failed in his attempt to hurriedly exit the field before joyous Pirates fans caught up to him. While Babe acted as Pittsburgh's hero, first baseman Bill Abstein performed the goat role, batting .231, striking out nine times, committing five errors in the field, and making numerous base-running blunders. (Courtesy of the Library of Congress).

6

The Player Pipeline between Pittsburgh and St. Louis

More changes loomed in Pittsburgh following the sale of first baseman Bill Abstein to the St. Louis Browns. As the second decade of the twentieth century progressed, Smoky City citizens could make a strong case for christening the Pirates' organization with a theme song for moving players to other organizations. The 1904 hit song "Meet Me in St. Louis, Louis" seemed appropriate.[1] In quick fashion, a star performer on Pittsburgh's squad followed Abstein out the door, going to that city's National League entry. Longer term, the most significant trade ever orchestrated with Barney Dreyfuss and Fred Clarke at the helm involving the St. Louis Cardinals brought about a new low period for Pirates baseball in the twentieth century.

Since his acquisition from the Boston Beaneaters on December 15, 1905, pitcher Vic Willis had successfully fulfilled the role as Pittsburgh's staff ace. Willis performed brilliantly on the bump, topping the twenty-victory plateau in 1906 (23–13, 1.73 ERA), 1907 (21–11, 2.34 ERA), and 1908 (23–11, 2.07 ERA). Before spring training commenced at Hot Springs, Arkansas, in 1909, Vic sent a surprising letter from his home in Newark, Delaware, to a Pittsburgh friend. In this correspondence, Willis intimated he was tired of the game and planned on quitting baseball.

"I am doing very well here," wrote Willis, "and can make more money in my present venture than I can playing baseball. I do not intend to leave Newark again, for I can make more here summer and winter than I get in Pittsburgh in the summer."

This friend, shocked that Vic seemed to be considering retirement, wrote back asking for specific information about this life-changing decision. When a baseball writer approached Dreyfuss about this matter on the evening of January 23, 1909, the Pirates' owner appeared surprised upon hearing the news.

"I know absolutely nothing about it," replied the Pittsburgh magnate. "Willis has never written anything about retiring to me, but I can't prevent him, or any other player, from retiring if he wants to. We club-owners all have to stand for plays like this from the men in the wintertime."

When the writer asked Barney if he felt Vic seemed sincere about retiring, the Pirates' owner replied that he didn't know. Dreyfuss cautioned this scribe that Willis had also talked about quitting in the fall of 1907.[2] The story regarding Vic ending his major league baseball career amused some Newark inhabitants. With a smile, one of the hurler's friends asked, "What would Vic do here to make even the amount that Dreyfuss has offered him this year, let alone the $4,000 proposition?" Many baseball fans and writers believed Willis wanted to receive at least $4,000 a year to pitch for Pittsburgh in 1909. The organization had paid him a salary of $3,500 in 1908, along with a $400 bonus given by Pittsburgh's owner for outstanding work that season. Manager Fred Clarke sent Vic a letter stating that he expected the veteran twirler to be in attendance when preliminary training started in West Baden Springs, Indiana.

Back home in Newark, Willis pitched outside when nice weather prevailed and worked out in a Delaware college gymnasium on cold days.[3] Barney Dreyfuss's statement about standing for such plays during winter seemed prophetic. Vic's retirement talk acted as a negotiation ploy since he hoped to earn $5,000 in 1909, while Dreyfuss had offered a contract for $4,000. Willis wished to work out an agreement in the middle for $4,500. A story claimed that the notion of purchasing a Newark hotel and affording that establishment his full attention as an alternative to baseball was a pure bluff.[4] As the holdout dragged on, Barney constantly reiterated that he'd paid Vic all the pitcher was worth in 1908.[5] On the morning of April 9, Dreyfuss and Willis held another conference and finally hammered out a deal. While both sides appeared pleased, the terms of the agreement weren't made public.[6]

Before signing his contract, Willis exhibited unhappiness over how his holdout had progressed. While on his way to join the Pirates' entourage in Memphis, Tennessee, Vic met up with members of the New York Giants during a stopover in Louisville, Kentucky. According to New York sportswriter Samuel "Sam" Crane, being desirous of severing his relationship with the Pirates and Barney Dreyfuss, Willis asked how Giants manager John McGraw was lined up for pitching when it came to the upcoming season. Vic expressed disappointment when some of New York's players informed him the squad looked strong in that area. Willis then asked where he might find McGraw since he was anxious to be traded and wanted to join the Giants. New York's manager denied discussing a deal involving the Pirates with Vic.[7]

Vic Willis went 22–11 for Pittsburgh in 1909, supported by a 2.24 ERA. Although Howie Camnitz supplanted Vic as the staff ace, fans expected big things from him in the World Series against the Detroit Tigers. After Camnitz faltered in his Game Two start at Forbes Field on October 9, Fred Clarke summoned Willis to the mound to relieve in the third inning. Detroit held a 4–2 lead, with Tyrus "Ty" Cobb occupying third base and James "Jim" Delahanty perched on second. Cobb immediately started toying with Vic as he faced George Moriarty. As he usually did when contemplating a theft of home, Ty slowly moved up the line at third before running halfway to home in an attempt to distract the pitcher. After a slight hesitation, Cobb bolted for home as Willis methodically followed through with his delivery. The low toss to Pirates catcher George Gibson appeared to beat Ty to the plate. Umpire William "Billy" Evans originally called Cobb out before reversing his decision after realizing that Gibson had failed to tag the runner.[8]

This victory buoyed the confidence of Detroit's players since none of Howie Camnitz's offerings puzzled them in Game Two, and they wouldn't be fearful of Vic Willis regarding future encounters.[9] Fred Clarke handed Willis the ball in Game Six, hoping to secure the championship. Vic's work proved substandard, as he allowed four earned runs in five innings before being pulled in favor of Camnitz. The Tigers saddled Willis with the loss, claiming a 5–4 victory. After Babe Adams had won Game One over Detroit, Vic boasted to his teammates that the Tigers looked like easy money, and if he didn't beat them when given an opportunity, he would "eat his uniform." When Willis failed in Game Six, many teammates reminded the hurler of his dare and suggested engaging in the gastronomic feat he'd promised to undertake.[10] Adams's dominance over Detroit in Game Seven eased the sting of Vic's poor performance.

A new city would be where Willis made any future glib assertions about eating uniforms if he didn't conquer a perceived inferior opponent. Pirates management placed Vic on the open market during the off-season. The Cincinnati Reds expressed interest in the tall hurler, but the player offered didn't suit manager Fred Clarke, who preferred receiving money for Willis.[11] On February 15, 1910, Pittsburgh sent Vic to the St. Louis Cardinals in a straight cash sale, with the purchase price remaining a secret. Those within the Pirates' camp had understood for some time that Clarke deemed Willis's convivial nighttime habits detrimental to team discipline.[12] This lifestyle had hampered Vic, who wasn't in proper condition to pitch at any point during the World Series.[13] Barney Dreyfuss offered a straightforward reason for selling Willis to the Cardinals.

"Fred Clarke decided in December to use his younger pitchers and was willing to allow Willis to go to any second division team," said Dreyfuss. "He considered Willis too strong to be sent to a first division club. We have no fault to find with Willis. The records show that he did excellent work for us."[14]

Barney also told writer A. R. Cratty that although the money received for Vic happened to be below market value, he accepted it to help out the old pitcher.[15] This deal also contained a fascinating proviso. Neither Cardinals owner Stanley Robison, nor manager Roger Bresnahan, could ever transfer Willis to the New York Giants or Chicago Cubs, Pittsburgh's main rivals.[16] In respect to Dreyfuss saying he and Clarke found no fault with Vic, this wasn't totally accurate. It was no secret that while Barney appreciated Willis's talent and work as a pitcher, he disliked the tall twirler.[17]

Clarke had two reasons for eliminating Vic from the team. The first regarded his policy of punishing those individuals who didn't follow the rules and tenets of discipline throughout the baseball season. Reports claimed that Willis's behavior during part of the summer and October resulted in harsh condemnation from his manager. Rather than appreciating his responsibilities as a veteran hurler of a pitching staff that included many youngsters, boozing was a distinct failure that management couldn't tolerate.[18] Fred's second reason contradicted two statements he'd made about the situation regarding Bill Abstein during the 1909 World Series.

Following Pittsburgh's loss in Game Six of the World Series to Detroit, an incident occurred between Bill and Vic at the team hotel. As Abstein entered the hotel lobby following that critical contest, Willis bitterly criticized him over his boneheaded blunders throughout the Fall Classic. Bill's anger reached a boiling point, and the two men fought violently. The situation incensed Fred Clarke, who couldn't afford to lose any players because of a petty clash with a crucial seventh game pending. Clarke vowed to get rid of both players once the postseason ended.[19] When Vic joined the National League team in Abstein's hometown, the first baseman praised his former teammate, stating he still was a great pitcher in the prime of his career. Bill also claimed that Willis had exhibited a strong desire to leave the Pirates the previous year.

"He wasn't at all pleased with his berth in Pittsburgh," said Bill Abstein. "He wasn't exactly dissatisfied, and he pitched his best possible, and a 22–11 record isn't bad for any twirler. But Vic would have preferred to play in some other town. He made this known, and that's the only reason he was let go."[20]

Barney Dreyfuss, Fred Clarke, and Bill Abstein offered their reasons for Vic Willis's sale to St. Louis. An individual close to the situation tamped down the assertion that Willis enjoyed a too vigorous nightlife, claiming that unfounded rumors blew these stories out of proportion. While this observer readily admitted that Vic consumed alcoholic beverages on occasion while in the company of another veteran pitcher and an infielder, he never indulged to the point that it interfered with his performance on the mound.[21] Before the 1910 season started, Cubs manager Frank Chance predicted his team would claim the National League pennant by a wider margin than Pittsburgh had done in 1909. Chance also alleged that Clarke made a severe mistake selling Willis to St. Louis. Frank believed the Pirates would miss Vic's veteran presence when the tough pennant race started heating up.[22]

Chance proved correct on all counts as Chicago claimed the pennant, and Pittsburgh mounted no serious challenge, finishing a disappointing third with an 86–67 record. As the campaign progressed, some pundits felt the Pirates wouldn't have been so far down in the standings if Willis had remained on the team. One writer stated that Barney Dreyfuss and Fred Clarke, whom he referred to as an unforgiving stern taskmaster, weren't happy with Vic's constant rule-breaking and decided to cast their lot with a group of young pitchers.[23] As the 1910 season moved into September, a Pittsburgh newspaper started trumpeting the perception that management didn't welcome having careless men on the Pirates' roster. Removing Willis and his negative influence from the equation didn't make a difference, as hurlers Howie Camnitz, Lefty Leifield, and Nick Maddox performed poorly on the mound.[24]

Near the season's conclusion, Dreyfuss refused to pay Camnitz a $1,200 bonus, aside from his $3,000 salary, for failing to abstain from drinking intoxicating liquors for one year. Howie deserted the club and returned to his Kentucky home. Camnitz also claimed Pittsburgh's owner had reneged on a promise to several Pirates about receiving $500 bonuses for securing the 1909 National League pennant.[25] After winning 25 games in 1909, Howie went 12–13 one year later, supported by a 3.22 ERA. Although Cubs owner Charles Murphy expressed interest in acquiring Camnitz during the off-season, the hurler remained in Pittsburgh.[26] Howie bounced back for the Pirates in 1911, posting a 20–15 record along with a 3.13 ERA.

Pitchers weren't the only team members called out during the 1910 season. In his rookie campaign one year earlier, second baseman Dots Miller flashed brilliantly on the baseball scene, batting .279 and driving home 87 runs. Miller performed miserably in 1910, as his batting average plummeted to .227. When the season concluded, Barney Dreyfuss summoned Jack into his office and told Miller that he'd supplied insufficient and unsatisfactory work that year. Dreyfuss explained to Dots that he needed to take better care of himself and deliver the goods consistently to remain employed by the Pirates. Manager Fred Clarke, who undertook an intervention of his own, attempted to trade Miller over the winter but couldn't work out an acceptable deal. When Clarke handled contract negotiations with Dots, the two men clearly understood what the pilot expected from Pittsburgh's second baseman.[27]

No player was exempted from feeling management's wrath after the disappointing 1910 season, not even star shortstop Honus Wagner. Much like Miller's situation, Dreyfuss and Clarke displayed intense unhappiness over the behavior of that youngster's best buddy. In the fall of 1910, Pittsburgh's manager had talked to Wagner and didn't mince words when he offered the National League's premier batsman an ultimatum: "No booze or no baseball." Honus promised at the time to reform his ways, and the 1911 campaign offered proof that the man from Carnegie, Pennsylvania, had returned to prime condition once again.[28] That season, Wagner won the eighth and final batting title of his illustrious career by pacing the league with a .334 average.

In 1911 and 1912, New York claimed the National League pennant before falling to the Philadelphia Athletics and Boston Red Sox in each World Series. Pittsburgh finished third in 1911 and came home second one year later. On June 30, 1912, the Pirates shipped veteran Tommy Leach and hurler Lefty Leifield to Chicago for pitcher Leonard "King" Cole and outfielder Arthur "Solly" Hofman. As the Giants claimed their third consecutive pennant in 1913, Pittsburgh regressed, falling to fourth place with a 78–71 record. Fans expected the purge, which started that summer, to escalate in the off-season. Two more important members of the 1909 championship team moved to a new club on August 23, when previous talks between Fred Clarke and Philadelphia Phillies manager Charles "Red" Dooin finally brought a definitive resolution.

After the Pirates played a doubleheader that day in Philadelphia, Clarke traded third baseman Bobby Byrne and pitcher Howie Camnitz to the Phillies for third baseman Albert "Cozy" Dolan and cash. Dolan expressed delight over the deal and looked forward to being a member of a potential pennant contender. On the other hand, Byrne and Camnitz were both disheartened that their careers in Pittsburgh had ended. Teammates also appeared upset over two popular Pirates players in the locker room leaving the squad. Camnitz, who received a tip earlier that day about the transaction, didn't attend the twin bill at National League Park and instead boarded a train for Pittsburgh. Before leaving that night for the Smoky City to pack his belongings for transport to Philadelphia, Byrne bid team members a fond farewell.

"Believe me, I do hate to leave this club," said Byrne. "You all seem like brothers to me and Pittsburgh seems like my home, but baseball is baseball and all I can do is go to Philadelphia and give them the best that's in me. That's exactly what I've tried to do at Pittsburgh."

Although neither side divulged the amount of money given along with Cozy Dolan, scribes understood on good authority that Pittsburgh received $4,500 in the deal.[29] This proved false, as Dooin weeks later placed the amount at $1,500, which Barney Dreyfuss corroborated.[30] Cozy soon found that replacing a fan-favorite such as Bobby Byrne was a challenging situation. In his first game at Forbes Field against Chicago on August 29, Dolan appeared nervous while working at the hot corner and had trouble handling several balls teammates threw to him. This problem resulted from Cozy losing a nail on one of his fingers while fielding a batted baseball in practice that took a bad hop. Although not serious, the injury caused much pain. Clarke wanted to keep Dolan on the bench, but the new player insisted on being in the lineup.[31]

Such dedication meant little to Forbes Field's patrons, who were angry over Pittsburgh trading two well-liked players to another team. Throughout the remainder of the campaign, many regular fans, rather than the gambling element, shamefully criticized Cozy, using vile language deemed unacceptable on the street. Pittsburgh baseball writer Ralph S. Davis believed Dolan could never prosper in Pittsburgh under the circumstances, and the club should consider moving him to another organization over the winter. Davis also felt it unfair to Cozy that he replaced Byrne, as fans should place the blame at Fred Clarke's feet.[32]

An angry rooting populace, disgusted with poor results, usually galvanized baseball organizations to make off-season changes. It seemed that the adage of "nobody is sure of his job" applied to almost every member of the Pirates heading into the 1914 season. Outfielder Chief Wilson was at the top of the list regarding players who might be changing addresses shortly. In 1912, Wilson established a major league record that still exists today by smacking 36 triples. One year later, Chief consistently failed when he stepped up to the plate by striking out with runners on base.[33] After hitting .300 in 1911 and 1912, Wilson's average dropped to .266 in 1913.[34] Chief also exhibited a polite demeanor and didn't possess a rough edge on the diamond. This personality trait had prompted Chicago's Frank Chance to explain why he didn't like Wilson years earlier. One time, during a game between the Pirates and the Cubs, Frank sat down and took off his shoe after being spiked.

"I hope you're not hurt," remarked Wilson as he passed Frank.

"I don't like that kind of a chap," said Chance. "He ought to have said, 'I hope you lose your leg next time.'"[35]

In December, Fred Clarke and Barney Dreyfuss went to the league meetings in New York, intending to reshape the Pittsburgh Pirates' roster. Shortly after arriving, Clarke received an offer from Red Dooin, where he would trade Bobby Byrne and Howie Camnitz back to the Pirates for Cozy Dolan. Fred immediately refused, declaring he always took his medicine when getting the worst of the bargain in a player transaction. Fred then told Pittsburgh scribe Ed F. Balinger that he intended to keep Dolan for 1914. Clarke sympathized with Cozy's plight, as the Pirates' third baseman played great baseball on the road in 1913, even if his performance suffered at Forbes Field due to fan abuse. Fred had offered Dolan his staunch support when the home crowd started jeering Cozy during preliminary practice before a game.

> I told him to go out there and play—that I was manager and had every confidence in him. I told him to let them yell all they pleased and try not to mind it. He still played badly, but this was only to be expected, for he wasn't getting a word of encouragement from the fans. With all due regard for the public—and they must be given their share of consideration—I have a right to my opinion as they have a right to theirs. I cannot always side in with the fans. They may be right and I may be wrong in many things, for we all make mistakes, but in this case I realize just how hard a matter it was for Dolan to try to fill Byrne's place before the people at Forbes Field and I certainly admire his gameness.
>
> The people of Pittsburgh have one of the greatest players in baseball and right there is where they too often forget themselves in sizing up a new player. They measure every man on the ball field by comparing him with Wagner. If a player is not up to the Wagner standard then they pronounce him poor. This is very unjust. Wagner is as nearly perfect as a player perhaps as any person living. Others have this fault or that fault. It remains to be seen whether or not Dolan's speed will counterbalance a pair of poor hands. As long as I cannot see a good chance to strengthen the team by letting Dolan go in a deal, I expect to keep him.[36]

On December 9, Jack Miller made the trip from his home in Kearny, New Jersey, to New York. Dots promised to take Clarke on a spin in his automobile the next day around his hometown. Fred joked that Miller needed to guarantee he would follow the speed limit after police pulled him over for driving too fast. Since 1912, Dots had done an admirable job after transitioning from second base to the initial sack. When a reporter at the league meetings suggested that Clarke might try Miller at third base in 1914, Jack offered the type of response expected from a player who placed the team above himself.

"I will play where Clarke puts me," Miller said. "I never played first base before until he put me there. I will do the best I can wherever they put me."

If a position change looked to be in the offing for Jack Miller, it would happen with a different organization. On the evening of December 9, when pressed by newspapermen about a potential deal between New York and St. Louis for first baseman Edward "Ed" Konetchy, Cardinals manager Miller Huggins stated that the Giants had made no offer. He added that Konetchy, also known as "Koney," could be traded to Pittsburgh for Miller, an outfielder, and a pitcher. When approached about Huggins's statement, Clarke countered that St. Louis's pilot hadn't yet consulted him about any such transaction.[37]

On December 12, St. Louis's and Pittsburgh's managers engaged in close discussions the entire afternoon at the Waldorf Astoria Hotel until 4:30 P.M. about brokering a deal. Initially, the two sides agreed on Miller and Chief Wilson going to St. Louis for Konetchy before adding other players to the mix as talks progressed. With the parameters of the deal in place, Clarke left at 5 P.M. to return to his winter home in Winfield, Kansas. The only thing required to close the transaction was approval from Cardinals ownership. This hurdle was cleared shortly after 8 P.M. when someone summoned Barney Dreyfuss to the phone booth. St. Louis team president Schuyler P. Britton, the husband of owner Helene Hathaway Robison Britton, informed him by a long-distance call that he'd consented to the deal.

In this blockbuster trade, Pittsburgh shipped first baseman Jack Miller, outfielder Chief Wilson, infielders Arthur "Art" Butler and Cozy Dolan, and hurler John Henry "Hank" Robinson to St. Louis for first baseman Ed Konetchy, third baseman Harry Harlan "Mike" Mowrey, and pitcher Robert "Bob" Harmon. Dreyfuss beamed excitedly after talking on the telephone with Britton and remarked, "Well, the deal has gone through."[38] Pirates fans most likely wouldn't be concerned over Wilson's departure since some individuals from this group had urged Clarke to get rid of him. Patrons never accepted Dolan into the fold, and Butler was also unpopular with spectators at Forbes Field. These rooters had been clamoring for many years to find a way to secure Koney's stellar services for Pittsburgh's baseball team.[39]

Following the Bill Abstein fiasco in 1909, rumors had cropped up shortly after the World Series ended that Ed Konetchy would wear a Pirates uniform in 1910. Barney Dreyfuss tamped down such nonsense at the time by stating that no chance existed of reaching any such agreement.

"The owners of the Cardinals think so highly of Konetchy," said Dreyfuss with a smile in 1909, "that they would not swap him for any man in the business—unless it should be Wagner."[40]

Although the St. Louis Cardinals' organization thought highly of Konetchy in 1909, this didn't mean that Fred Clarke and Barney Dreyfuss couldn't continue coveting the star first baseman from afar. Clarke had attempted to secure Koney after the 1912 campaign ended, but Miller Huggins rebuffed him.[41] When Pittsburgh's manager and Dreyfuss discussed brokering a potential deal in 1913, the Pirates' owner said that he'd only excluded Honus Wagner's inclusion from the current roster in any trade.[42] From the Cardinals' perspective, Dots Miller acted as the centerpiece of this transaction, based on his play in a June series at Robison Field months earlier. Miller did excellent work chasing long foul balls from his position at first base. In one game, Dots made six sensational catches. This marvelous performance caught the attention of St. Louis ownership, who agreed with Huggins following the final contest between the two teams that Miller looked mighty sweet.[43] After making the trade with Pittsburgh, St. Louis's manager offered his rationale for moving Konetchy in a letter to baseball writers.

"Konetchy is a star," wrote Huggins, "but he hasn't been doing good work in St. Louis. His heart hasn't been in the game, and when such is the case a man is of no value to a team, no matter how brilliant a natural player he might be."[44]

One key question stood out in the minds of Pittsburgh's baseball fans. Would Ed Konetchy's heart be in the game as a Pirates member? A potential problem involving one of the other players secured from St. Louis in this deal rose to the surface. Within the realm of history repeating itself, a new organization known as the Federal League planned on staking its claim to relevance within professional baseball. On Saturday, January 10, 1914, Barney Dreyfuss opened a letter from Mike Mowrey claiming he'd received a lucrative offer to play for the Federal League. That same evening, Mowrey sent a wire to Pittsburgh's owner asking that the two meet in Harrisburg, Pennsylvania, the following day. Barney didn't respond to the message, but the two men conversed by telephone on Sunday. Mike admitted to possibly considering a Federal League offer to play in Baltimore, the original home of his wife, Nannie K. Hammel Mowrey, who wanted to live there.

When interacting with the press about this development, Dreyfuss said he couldn't prevent Mowrey from jumping. He then likened the situation to Jimmy Williams abandoning the Pirates for the American League's Baltimore Orioles in 1901.[45] On January 17, Barney, Mike, his wife, and the National League president, Pennsylvania Governor John Tener, held a conference in Harrisburg early that afternoon. After talking for less than an hour, Mowrey signed a contract with a hefty salary increase above what St. Louis paid him in 1913.[46] Upon Tener's general recommendation for contracts where certain conditions warranted, Mike signed a three-year deal.[47] Days earlier, on January 14, Ed Konetchy admitted he'd also signed a 1914 contract while in Cincinnati. Konetchy's meeting with Dreyfuss only lasted a few minutes, as Ed balked at the Pittsburgh owner's first offer before making a counterproposal that Dreyfuss happily accepted.

Koney promised to give Fred Clarke and the Pirates his best in 1914. Ed readily admitted to experiencing a bad year at the plate for the last-place Cardinals in 1913, hitting .276. He'd experienced worrisome moments over this hitting slump. Konetchy also declared he didn't attempt to steal the managerial job from Miller Huggins as some suggested and never usurped his authority.[48] The additions of both Koney and Mike Mowrey helped offset two defections to the Federal League. On January 27, Barney Dreyfuss announced that pitcher Claude Hendrix and catcher Michael "Mike" Simon had joined the Federal League's ranks. The situation surrounding these two individuals looked uncannily similar to the war years of 1901 and 1902. Dreyfuss stated that each man had signed Pirates contracts in 1913 containing options that carried over to the next season.

Simon's case baffled Barney since he eventually met the catcher's demand to be paid $3,000 to play for Pittsburgh in 1914. When he called Mike's home in North Vernon, Indiana, on January 26, his wife, Jessie Belle Swarthout Simon, answered the telephone. She informed the owner that her husband had signed a three-year deal to play for a Pittsburgh team in the Federal League (he joined the St. Louis Terriers). Simon also performed the coward's role, as his wife notified Dreyfuss her husband didn't want to talk to him.[49] Regarding Hendrix, he experienced a considerable decline in production the previous season after going 24–9 in 1912, supported by a 2.59 ERA. Claude had exasperated Fred Clarke when the Pirates' manager traveled to Kansas City, Missouri, to sign his pitcher, causing him to announce that he was through with Hendrix.[50] In respect to Claude jumping to the Federal League, Barney issued a statement reminiscent of his feelings over a decade ago about Jesse Tannehill's services no longer being required back in 1902.

"If it is true that Claude Hendrix has jumped to the Federal, all that I can say is—let him go," said Dreyfuss. "My best wishes go with him. I'm not worrying about his actions."[51]

When the Pirates held spring training in Hot Springs, baseball writer Hugh Fullerton sat down with Fred Clarke to talk about the big trade he'd orchestrated the previous December. Clarke said a baseball player who didn't fit into the team wasn't any good. He deemed such individuals, even if they happened to be quite accomplished at hitting, running, and throwing, as not belonging. Fred also classified them as losing baseball players. Fred qualified this opinion, declaring that not all the fellows he traded to St. Louis were misfits, just some of them. Clarke claimed the deal helped both teams before discussing two of the players Pittsburgh acquired from St. Louis.

> It was this way. I have thought for years that Konetchy is one of the greatest ballplayers in the world—only out of place—I knew that if I could get him away from St. Louis he would fit into the Pittsburgh team perfectly and give us his best. I knew Mowrey would.
>
> I felt certain Koney, who is a clean, decent fellow, was disgusted with the way things went at St. Louis; that if his ambition was aroused he would be a leader and a great help. A man who works to win, who is wild to win, loses a lot when he is surrounded by careless, slip-shod players and who sees the bad habits of some hurting the team's chances. Put that same man on a fighting, hustling team, with everyone behaving and working hard, and he will break a leg to help the team win. I figured it that way with both Konetchy and Mowrey—and they'll make good for me.[52]

Once the 1914 baseball campaign started, Clarke stated that while he wasn't guaranteeing any National League pennant, Pittsburgh's manager believed he'd never commanded a better bunch of fighters and hard workers than the current squad. Fred added that every player earnestly went about their work, and the team possessed great ability.[53] These words initially didn't ring hollow, as the Pirates blazed a glorious path of success in the early going, posting a 15–2 record by May 7. Sadly, Pittsburgh couldn't keep up this torrid pace. When talking with Hugh Fullerton, Clarke offered a standard baseball premise put forward throughout the game's history that the trade he orchestrated with the Cardinals helped both teams. Unfortunately, this wasn't one of those times.

The conduct of some former Pirates players indicated that St. Louis may have gotten the worst of this deal. Shenanigans involving various team members included individuals who once called the Smoky City home. On June 24, 1914, the Cardinals started a four-game series against Pittsburgh at Forbes Field. That Wednesday morning, before the game, Jack Miller, Cozy Dolan, Art Butler, and outfielder Leo "Lee" Magee decided to relax by playing a round of golf at Schenley Park's beautiful course. Around the same time these four baseball players started their match, a gentleman named Kelly arrived at the links with a party of three women.

Everything appeared to be moving along quite nicely until the fourth hole. One of the shots from a member of these two parties stopped a few feet from another golf ball. Mr. Kelly's caddy picked up one of the balls, although a member of the ballplayers' group claimed it to be his. The young caddy alleged he'd picked up the correct golf ball and refused to hand it over. At this point, one of the players used physical force to retrieve the ball. The boy broke free from his grasp, still holding the golf ball in one hand and covering up a black eye with the other. Other caddies at the Schenley Park course, who tended to be territorial and defended each other's rights, came to the aid of their friend. A melee ensued as the three women in the Kelly foursome quickly headed to the clubhouse with fingers in their ears so they didn't hear the rank language hurled by the combatants.[54]

This incident only provided the opening act for one or two members of the Cardinals, as a much different confrontation occurred that night after St. Louis beat Pittsburgh in the afternoon, 3–0. The following day, the *Pittsburgh Press* reported the activities of a well-known baseball player at a house on Lawn Street in the Oakland section of Pittsburgh. A man burst into the Forbes Street (Avenue) police station that night, claiming his wife and other women were entertaining major league baseball players at that residence. Offering proof of his suspicions, the man had brought a pair of trousers with him that belonged to one of the ballplayers as evidence. This individual suspected things weren't right at that house as he watched the place that night and observed these players enter the dwelling.

This gentleman quickly entered the premises and found the bedroom door locked. A male had tossed his outer apparel on a chair in an adjoining room. At this point, the husband grabbed a pair of trousers and rushed to the police station to sound the alarm. Sensing trouble, the baseball players decided to vacate the building hurriedly. Unable to find his pants, one ballplayer borrowed a pair of pajamas belonging to the husband, then donned his coat, vest, and hat before hastily departing. Those procured trousers contained that person's most recent paycheck, bearing a name and revealing his identity. Initial newspaper stories reported that police had arrested one of the individuals at the house.[55]

Manager Miller Huggins offered a stern warning and severe reprimand the following morning regarding how team members were supposed to behave.[56] This wasn't the first time Cardinals players in Pittsburgh had exhibited a free-for-all mentality. Three weeks earlier, some St. Louis team members, during a stopover in the Smoky City as the squad traveled east, carried private refrigerators onto the train with them before departure. One player attempted to bring a case of lager onboard, while another carried bottles of beer in each hand as he entered the train.[57] Baseball writer Ralph S. Davis referred to Jack Miller as "Gay Lothario" while describing a triple he blasted in the series' final contest on June 27, which helped substantiate the suspicion that Dots happened to be one of the people present at the Lawn Street home nights earlier.[58]

Speculation became fact when William D. Casper of 310 Federal Street, the husband who'd held a stakeout of the Lawn Street residence, filed a suit for divorce from his wife, Mrs. Clara Casper, on July 8. The husband also named Cardinals first baseman Jack Miller in the lawsuit. Mr. Casper alleged that his wife was guilty of infidelity with Miller on June 24 and had similarly conducted herself with different men on other occasions. The couple, married on February 21, 1906, hadn't lived together since April 21, 1912. The account contained within this court filing slightly differed from the earlier newspaper story.

Mr. Casper had gone to his wife's apartments at 362 Lawn Street around midnight on June 24. The *Pittsburgh Press* had correctly described everything about the scene inside the building. Facts about this incident's final actions proved quite different. Neighbors heard a great commotion near the back of the dwelling when two men, mostly undressed, threw the husband into the backyard. Officer Tibbit, a nearby resident and a member of the mounted police force, rushed to the scene and raided the dwelling as a disorderly house. The police officer took Mr. Casper and two women into custody while the other scantily attired men escaped through the front door. The arrested individuals were subsequently released from the Oakland police station. The filing also asserted that Mrs. Casper had arrived at the Lawn Street apartments at 10 P.M. in the company of two men before meeting another woman on the porch.[59]

Some newspaper accounts covering this unseemly scene claimed that Jack Miller and Mrs. Casper had been friendly when Dots played for the Pittsburgh

Pirates.⁶⁰ In response to her husband's claim, Mrs. Casper stated in a petition to the Common Pleas Court on July 31 that she had never been unfaithful in her marriage vows. Clara, who now listed her residence as 3352 Fifth Avenue in Oakland, planned on contesting the divorce proceedings. Mrs. Casper denied being intimate with Miller on June 24 or any other date while stating this to be the case regarding other people. Clara claimed that her husband, William, manager of a Federal Street café, had broken up their home on April 21, 1912. Since then, she'd boarded at various residences. Mrs. Casper also alleged that the couple had discussed reconciliation from time to time, but she now believed her husband had no intention of following through with this plan. Mrs. Casper declared that this trumped-up charge surrounding June 24 acted as a mechanism for her spouse to avoid his responsibility for paying alimony.⁶¹

Miller was easily identifiable at the scene due to the famous trousers containing a paycheck bearing his name, while he left behind an inscribed watch at Mrs. Casper's apartment.⁶² When the Cardinals returned to Pittsburgh for a brief September series, Jack and Cozy Dolan exited the city early to avoid subpoenas issued against them so the two players wouldn't miss any games during the hot pennant race.⁶³ The court handed down these subpoenas to both men on assault charges concerning William Casper's divorce case. Dolan became incensed over being included in connection with the case, claiming to be asleep in bed on the night in question. Initially, Cozy thought the court proceedings had something to do with the Schenley Park golf course incident since the young caddy had threatened to have Dolan charged with assault because the ballplayer slapped his face.⁶⁴

When the Cardinals arrived back in Pittsburgh at month's end, Miller and Dolan appeared before Alderman J. J. Kirby on September 30. Kirby decreed that the charge of aggravated assault and battery filed against the two players by William Casper would go to a grand jury. Casper also made an affidavit exonerating Cozy from any involvement in the incident.⁶⁵ On October 13, 1914, this Pittsburgh grand jury ignored the assault charges against Miller and Dolan. The action in Jack's case surprised many people, while the prosecutor had made that earlier agreement to ask the grand jury to disregard the bill against Cozy.⁶⁶ Judge Ambrose B. Reid then freed Jack from the indictment in criminal court on January 12, 1915, based on Miller and Casper reaching an agreement where the ballplayer paid for the cost of prosecution and any damages the plaintiff had suffered.⁶⁷ Months later, Judge Thomas D. Carnahan removed William Casper's divorce case from the trial docket, at the request of Clara Casper's attorneys, due to a filing error by her husband.⁶⁸

After the judge voided the indictment against Miller, some of Jack's friends stated that he didn't know Mrs. Casper was a married woman when visiting her home.[69] Surprisingly, when examining this lousy behavior by former members of the Pirates, passionate and knowledgeable Pittsburgh baseball fans still couldn't honestly assert that the St. Louis Cardinals got the short end of the stick in the trade on December 12, 1913. For the Pirates, the deal ended up being transformative in a very negative way. Pitcher Bob Harmon gave consummate effort for his new team in 1914, going 13–17 with a 2.53 ERA. Pittsburgh's great start at the beginning of the campaign proved a mirage. The team played poorly and descended into uncharted waters never before seen during the Fred Clarke and Barney Dreyfuss era by falling into the National League's second division. The Pirates finished in seventh place with a 69–85 record as Mike Mowrey and Ed Konetchy significantly contributed to this rapid decline.

In Mowrey's case, a newspaper article from 1913 should've tipped off Clarke to the type of player coming into the fold. In this interview with Mike, the writer explained that his St. Louis Cardinals teammates referred to him as "Iron" Mowrey since the third baseman never experienced nervousness during a game. Mike discussed his major league debut with Cincinnati on September 24, 1905, at Palace of the Fans, to hammer home this point about not being anxious, regardless of the game's magnitude. The Reds played the Brooklyn Superbas that day in a Sunday afternoon doubleheader on the home grounds.

> Well, that day I made five errors, but it never bothered me a bit. All I would do was to laugh. And the funny part of it all was that not a fan hooted me.
>
> After making a few bobbles I had almost every one of the fans with me. And that's just the way I would act in a World's Series game. I don't consider them a bit harder than a regular contest in the National League.
>
> To make up for my errors I banged out five safeties [Mike actually only recorded two hits in game two of the twin bill after taking a collar in the first contest], so it was even up—five errors and five base hits the day I made my debut in the National League.

Mowrey did say that although he laughed while bobbling and kicking baseballs around the diamond during those two games, he was the sorest person on earth that night and never wanted to see a baseball park again.[70] A fine line prevailed between possessing nerves of steel and appearing to be a baseball player who loafed and didn't care. Forbes Field's fans certainly wouldn't refrain from hooting and hollering when it came to the latter. Adding injuries to the mix didn't aid Mike in his plight. In the sixth inning of a game against Chicago at Forbes Field on May 7, which Pittsburgh won 7–1, Mowrey felt a sharp pain in his left leg while running to first and beating out a groundball he hit to Cubs third baseman Henry "Heinie" Zimmerman. Mike remained in the game and painfully reached second on Honus Wagner's single. Mowrey couldn't continue further as Fred Clarke lifted him for Joseph "Joe" Leonard.

Mike left for Youngstown, Ohio, shortly after the game so Bonesetter Reese could offer his diagnosis and treatment regarding the injury. Mowrey believed it to be nothing more than a charley horse, while some feared a torn ligament in his leg.[71] Mike played in great agony after visiting Reese before the ailment finally forced him from the lineup. After examining the player on May 21, a Pittsburgh physician placed his injured left leg in a plaster cast. Mowrey's injury was worse than first suspected as this doctor found that two tendons in his leg had been torn loose at the hip. Damage also occurred to the hip joint. Stabilization of the limb with the cast occurred by bending Mike's knee almost back to the hip to assist with realigning the muscles in their proper position.[72]

Mowrey returned to the lineup on June 5. When the injury sidelined him, Mike's batting average stood at .286. Over the next two months, his hitting mark slowly sank to .253. Injury aside, Mowrey tended to loaf on too many occasions to suit patrons and Pirates management. In a 21-inning game against New York on July 17 at Forbes Field, Mike failed to hustle to first base on a groundball to third baseman Milton "Milt" Stock, with teammate Max Carey occupying third. Loafing aside in this instance, Mowrey put on a sensational fielding display at the hot corner the entire afternoon.[73] Amazingly, both pitcher Babe Adams and New York hurler Richard "Rube" Marquard went the distance as the Giants prevailed, 3–1.

Throughout the 1914 campaign, fans at Forbes Field became disgusted as Mowrey deliberately walked away from batted balls he easily could have reached and failed to run out hits that would've placed games in the win column for the Pirates. Mike appeared unconcerned about whether Pittsburgh won or lost. Fred Clarke often called him out for this intentional laziness, and Honus Wagner reprimanded his teammate for a lapse when the squad played in Philadelphia.[74] Mowrey believed he was in a no-lose situation with the Pirates. After getting a huge salary boost from Barney Dreyfuss, Mike acted like nothing mattered in Pittsburgh and that he could give no diamond effort. He was confident that the Federal League always provided a viable option if things didn't work out.

Mike Mowrey's indifference at times stunned management and fans. One illustration of his boneheaded capabilities occurred during a five-game series against the Brooklyn Robins at Ebbets Field that started on July 30 and ended on August 3. In the series' final contest, Brooklyn's Zachariah "Zack" Wheat batted with two outs and the bases loaded. Robins pitcher Don Carlos Patrick "Pat" Ragan was the runner on third. Zack smacked a ball down to Mowrey at the hot corner. All Mike needed to do was move about five feet toward third base and step on the bag to record the inning's final out. Mowrey became confused when Ragan stood still rather than heading for home plate. Mike instead threw wildly to first base, hoping to retire the speedy Wheat. Ed Konetchy made a great play to grab the errant toss and fired home to force Ragan. After the game, when approached by a sportswriter, Mowrey laughed and claimed that when Wheat hit the baseball, he didn't know how many men were on base or the count regarding outs.

Manager Fred Clarke considered this incident the final straw.[75] On August 15, the Pittsburgh Pirates tendered Harry Harlan "Mike" Mowrey his unconditional release, with every major league club waiving on the third baseman.[76] Clarke also failed to sell Mike to a minor league organization.[77] An individual who talked with Mowrey in early October 1914 offered some insight into things that occurred behind the scenes regarding the third baseman.

> Mowrey is the maddest gent in seventeen states. Before signing with the Pittsburgh Nationals he turned down a three-year contract with the Baltimore Feds calling for $4,000 per annum. The Feds were suspicious of Mowrey's bad leg and had an x-ray photograph taken of it. The examination cost the Baltimore Feds $200, but they figured it money well spent until Mowrey backpedaled on them and signed with Pittsburgh.
>
> Mowrey's relatives made him sign with the Pirates. They convinced Mike that Pittsburgh had a cinch on the National League pennant and that Mowrey would be foolish to overlook a chance to share in the World's Series money. Mike took the bait, hook-line and sinker, and signed a Pittsburgh contract with the ten-day rule in it bigger than life. Dreyfuss served Mowrey with a ten-day notice when the club slumped and the management decided to cut down expenses. Dreyfuss said he had no objection to paying big salaries to first-division ballplayers, but he couldn't see himself handing over fancy money to tailenders. Mowrey lost his job when the economical spirit hit the club.[78]

Although finances might've been a consideration, Dreyfuss released Mike Mowrey for giving a lackluster and uncaring effort on the diamond.

Unfortunately, the centerpiece of the trade with St. Louis happened to be from the same mold, as first baseman Ed Konetchy's performance in 1914 proved an abject disappointment. Expected to be a run producer, Koney, also called the "Big Train," only drove home 51 teammates, which wouldn't have been bad if he'd mustered something better than a .249 average. In fairness to Konetchy, other players also performed well below expectations. From a strategical standpoint, Fred Clarke instituted a flawed batting system for the Pirates, as his men constantly took too many good strikes. Opposing pitchers knew in advance what Pittsburgh's players would do when a situation arose. This defect was illustrated in a game against Chicago on June 3 at Forbes Field, when Cubs second baseman William "Bill" Sweeney shouted instructions to hurler Albert "Bert" Humphries while Koney batted with a count of two balls and one strike.

"Lay it right in there now," yelled Sweeney, "he'll let this one pass."

Koney did just that and took the pitch for strike two.[79] While some classified such a system as archaic and unoriginal, Konetchy proved predictably inadequate when stepping up to the plate with men on base and consistently failing in the pinches.[80] Another foreseeable outcome in correlation to Ed being such a blatant underachiever surrounded him receiving abuse from the knockers stationed near first base at Forbes Field. This tradition had started a decade earlier with Kitty Bransfield at Exposition Park.[81] The inept play of his team, and Konetchy specifically, even caused Barney Dreyfuss to voice his opinion strongly on one occasion. Beaten down by the constant losing, Dreyfuss made his way to Forbes Field's clubhouse, pushed open the door, popped his head in, and hollered, "K-witters! And for you, Konetchy, it goes double."[82]

The relentless Forbes Field knockers felt Ed played careless ball in 1914 because of his unhappiness over the unfriendly treatment he received from the people of Pittsburgh. They also maintained that Koney's huge downfall occurred when Federal League emissaries made him an appealing offer to join their organization, based on the conditions that they still existed on Memorial Day and Independence Day. Fans contended that following a bright start, Konetchy slumped after Decoration Day. *Pittsburgh Post* baseball writer Ed F. Balinger challenged this assertion, pointing out that Ed consistently supplied mediocrity the entire season. Balinger, while conceding that Koney had a lousy year, disagreed with some patrons' perception that the first baseman quit on the team.[83] Barney Dreyfuss probably didn't subscribe to this writer's assessment.

Pirates baseball fans correctly opined about Konetchy's attitude toward those who lived in Pittsburgh. Neither Ed nor his wife, Aubrey Seawel Konetchy, particularly enjoyed Pittsburgh. They didn't dislike the steel metropolis but rather their social environment after moving to the Smoky City. While playing for St. Louis, Ed and his wife had been treated like royalty and pampered by an adoring populace. Individuals constantly shepherded them to restaurants, paid for their meals, picked up drink tabs, and took the couple on automobile drives. None of this happened in Pittsburgh, and Konetchy constantly complained to Barney Dreyfuss about such a slight. The resulting monotony following Ed being lionized, entertained, and taken for automobile spins throughout the countryside as a member of the Cardinals contributed to his uninspiring diamond effort. In one instance, Dreyfuss attempted to offer a positive spin on Konetchy not being spoiled and coddled by Pittsburgh's baseball patrons.

"You had to reciprocate occasionally, didn't you?" innocently commented his employer.

"Sure thing," said Koney just like that.

"Well, it cost you money, didn't it?" asked Dreyfuss.

"Sure thing," Koney once again responded.

"You'll have money in the bank when you're through here," was his boss's parting shot.

When it came to money, Ed Konetchy also expressed unhappiness over the fact that Barney Dreyfuss had only signed him to a one-year contract rather than a three-year deal. Back in January, when reaching an agreement, Dreyfuss told Konetchy to deliver the goods in 1914, and a financial reward would follow next year.[84] Ed's 1914 salary called for him to make $6,300 with a $300 option clause to remain property of the Pittsburgh Pirates for the following season. Shortly after the 1914 campaign started, Fred Clarke lamented having made the trade with St. Louis. During a doubleheader against Cincinnati at Redland Field on May 31, the squad couldn't pull out a victory in either contest as the Pirates were in the midst of a losing streak that reached ten games. Pittsburgh lost the first game, 2–1, and didn't muster anything better than a 5–5 tie in the nightcap when they held a four-run lead at one point.

That night Clarke wrote to Dreyfuss, conveying dissatisfaction with his squad and urging the owner to bring in new players. Fred also admitted that the deal he'd made with the Cardinals in December was a complete disaster.

"We have received in our deal with St. Louis," wrote Pittsburgh's manager, "some of the worst boneheads it has ever been my misfortune to run up against. No wonder St. Louis usually finished near the bottom; I wouldn't be surprised if Pittsburgh finished seventh or eighth with the material we have to work with."

The Pirates asked for waivers on Ed Konetchy in June. Somehow, Koney found out he was on the market, which galvanized him to start hustling, but to no avail. Following Mike Mowrey's release, individuals overheard Ed remarking that he "guessed he would be the next to be canned." A few days later, Dreyfuss was in a small room of Forbes Field's clubhouse adjacent to the players' dressing quarters. While there, Barney overheard Konetchy attempting to persuade pitcher Arley Wilbur Cooper, second baseman James "Jim" Viox, and other players to jump to the Federal League. Koney had already agreed to desert the Pirates and join the new organization. When it came to Konetchy's desire to bolt from Pittsburgh, Dreyfuss firmly declared that the contract his first baseman had signed included a $300 option for his services in 1915.[85] That document also contained no ten-day clause.

A potential reason for Koney's peevish behavior and his thinking behind jumping to the Federal League came to light after the season ended. Konetchy claimed he primarily jumped the Pirates to join Pittsburgh's entry in the new league because Dreyfuss had declined to sell his release for $15,000 to John McGraw's New York Giants that summer.[86] Rumors indicated that the Giants demonstrated a willingness to pay $18,000 for Ed and pitcher Martin "Marty" O'Toole or send outfielders John "Red" Murray and Frederick "Fred" Snodgrass, first baseman Carl Frederick "Fred" Merkle, and $10,000 to Pittsburgh for Koney. Concerned that people might believe he could be helping New York win another pennant, Barney turned down the propositions.[87] In November, Dreyfuss offered cover to his manager for acquiring someone who ended up acting as a Federal League spy.

"There are defects in some players which it is impossible to detect until the men are working for you," said the Pirates' owner. "When Koney appeared here as a Cardinal, he looked like a fine ballplayer, but it didn't take us long, once we had him on our roster, to discover that he had weaknesses which were fatal to a great performer."[88]

Although Ed Konetchy agreed to join the Federal League, he hadn't officially notified Fred Clarke or Dreyfuss.[89] Clarke visited Konetchy in St. Louis in December and offered him a first-class contract. Koney refused to discuss the matter, telling Pittsburgh's manager he'd cast his lot with the Federal League.[90] Ed had inked his signature to a three-year deal for $21,000, while wife Aubrey received $1,000 for influencing him about making a change. Fred threatened Konetchy with a court injunction prohibiting him from playing Organized Baseball in 1915 if he didn't renounce the Federal League deal.[91] Dreyfuss wasn't concerned that Ed flew the coop, declaring he possessed a much more intelligent player named Honus Wagner ready to play first base. Barney then belittled Koney's behavior for effect while concluding an interview with a reporter.

"I wish other affairs worried me as little as this Konetchy business," concluded the Pirates' magnate. "The Feds are welcome to him."[92]

For the record, St. Louis experienced their best finish in the National League race since 1901, placing third with a mark of 81–72 in 1914. Jack Miller batted .290 for the Cardinals and knocked in 88 runs. Shortly after being traded by the Pirates to St. Louis in 1913, Miller had said he was just another victim of the first base jinx but held the position longer than anyone since Kitty Bransfield.[93] The Pirates' first base jinx thrived in 1914, thanks to Ed Konetchy. Connections to the days of triumph and success sadly faded, although a young local prodigy arrived on the scene that flamed out just as quickly as he blazed a path of glory.

Previously hoping to acquire Ed Konetchy on numerous occasions, the Pittsburgh Pirates finally secured the St. Louis Cardinals' first baseman on December 12, 1913. Pittsburgh traded Chief Wilson, Dots Miller, and three other players to the Cardinals for Konetchy, third baseman Mike Mowrey, and hurler Bob Harmon. Following this deal, the Pirates reached a new low for diamond ineptitude in 1914, finishing in seventh place with a 69-85 record. Ed proved a big disappointment, batting .249 that season. Although the club held an option for his services in 1915, Konetchy signed a three-year deal for $21,000 with Pittsburgh's Federal League team. (Courtesy of the Library of Congress).

7

The Millionaire Kid from Dormont

Becoming stuck in an unaccustomed position after years of success could fracture the psyche of even the most devoted diamond warrior. After flourishing in the National League's first division for fourteen straight seasons upon arriving in Pittsburgh in 1900 to manage and play for the Pirates, even Fred Clarke's resolve dissipated throughout the hugely disappointing 1914 baseball campaign. Many who covered that industry for newspapers across the country considered Clarke a taskmaster and stern disciplinarian regarding players who weren't in sync with the organization's goals and objectives. Things changed in 1914 as Fred became more lenient while adjusting to his new station in life. In the summer of 1914, an anonymous Pirates member claimed to St. Louis sportswriter W. J. O'Connor that Clarke took it too easy when dealing with his players.

"Fred is a prince," said this player, "but I believe he's too nice for his own good. I've had him tell me when I started for the plate in a pinch: 'Just go up and have a swing, if you miss it, alright.' That's pretty soft for the player, don't you think?"[1]

When faced with flawed players like Mike Mowrey and Ed Konetchy, apathy was bound to set in. Although poor play slowly shattered Fred Clarke's resolve throughout the 1914 season, Pirates owner Barney Dreyfuss appeared as feisty as ever, harkening back to the war days between the National and American leagues. During December league meetings in New York, Dreyfuss exhibited no inhibition, offering his opinion about Konetchy making the Federal League jump. During a discussion with Chicago Cubs vice president and Pittsburgh native Harry Ackerland, Barney passionately expressed his feelings on this critical matter that affected the entire National League in fighting for their rights.

No contract jumper can ever play baseball for me. I have always taken this stand, and I shall never recede from it. In the American League war I released several players outright when I heard they were dickering with the other side. I have always believed that a player who would jump once would jump again, and I want nothing to do with such a man.

So far as Ed Konetchy is concerned, he has been guilty of an unlawful, a crooked act, and he knows it. If ever any man was bound under a contract, he was bound to me. Yet he accepted $5,000 advance money from the Feds before our season closed.

I knew what he was doing, and I would have released him long ago but for the fact that I knew it would result in a lot of adverse criticism because of the way my team was going at the time.

Ackerland then raised a hypothetical question, asking Dreyfuss what he would do if the Pirates' organization sued Konetchy in court and won the case, meaning that such a judgment awarded the player to Pittsburgh.

"I would release him outright," was Barney's spirited rejoinder. "Having proved his perfidy, I would turn him loose. Let him see, then, whether he could gouge the Feds for a three-year contract at $7,500 a year!"

Mr. Ackerland commended Barney Dreyfuss for taking such a noble stand. Dreyfuss also stated that he agreed with Eastern League president Edward "Ed" Barrow, who believed a ballplayer that jumped a contract would also throw a baseball game.[2] In another interview, Barney professed that the bad fellows in baseball received all the money while the good guys suffered harm and injury. He reiterated not wanting contract jumpers on the Pirates while adding that he and the general public weren't interested in individuals who sold their souls and jeopardized their honesty.[3] Pirates manager Fred Clarke, regretting the foolishness of baseball players that jumped to the Federal League, stated these unfortunate men only injured themselves. Clarke also condemned the tempters who made generous offers to ballplayers. Fred believed these crafty individuals, who'd scarred lives and damaged the game, should be the ones to suffer.[4]

Barney Dreyfuss's threat of fighting in court to retain Ed Konetchy loomed large as 1914 wound down.[5] Before the 1915 season started, Federal League officials still feared that action might be taken against them by Organized Baseball, related to three players slated to debut in their circuit within a week. Uncertainty perplexed the Feds since they didn't know what Organized Baseball intended to do. One prominent individual connected to Organized Baseball admitted he wasn't sure of Dreyfuss's plans regarding Konetchy. Pittsburgh's owner, who staunchly refused to discuss the matter, wanted to employ the tactic of unpredictability and force the other side to sweat things out until the very end.

"Let the other side do the worrying," said Dreyfuss when asked to supply a statement. "I do not intend to say that I will prosecute Konetchy, or that I will not do so."[6]

Posturing and bluffing withered away once the baseball season started. Ed Kontetchy suited up for the Federal League's second and final campaign in 1915 without any legal pushback from his previous employer. Former Pittsburgh Pirates and St. Louis Cardinals teammate Mike Mowrey also joined Ed on the Pittsburgh Rebels. Offering evidence that breaking old, bad habits proved tricky for players, the *Pittsburgh Leader* criticized Mowrey shortly after the season commenced. While intimating that Mike didn't like to work extra hard, the newspaper criticized the third baseman for missing some smashes in the field that might've been gobbled up by showing any effort. The *Pittsburgh Leader* also condemned Mowrey for loafing in the home opener against the Kansas City Packers on April 17, 1915, at Exposition Park, while running out a groundball to first that would've been an infield hit had he hustled.[7]

Amidst all the turmoil one year earlier, in 1914, a youngster born on May 30, 1894, in Dormont, a borough adjacent to Pittsburgh, played his first entire major league baseball season. Albert Leon Mamaux saw action in 13 games for the Pirates during his rookie campaign. Mamaux had debuted with Pittsburgh on September 23, 1913, when he pitched three innings of relief against the Brooklyn Superbas at Forbes Field. As he'd previously done on many occasions with young pitchers, manager Fred Clarke used Al sparingly throughout his inaugural campaign. Such a strategy proved wise, given Pittsburgh's poor showing in 1914. Clarke exhibited more confidence in the youngster as the season progressed, giving Mamaux four starts during its latter stages. Al finished with a 5–2 record, supported by a 1.71 ERA.

Besides being a gifted athlete, Al enjoyed the good fortune of having been afforded many opportunities in life due to his last name. His father, John Mamaux, was a prosperous businessman and well-known tent and awning manufacturer in Pittsburgh. In his younger days, John had starred as a semiprofessional hurler in the area but now preferred total involvement in the family business rather than pursuing a big-league career.[8] Albert Leon Mamaux Sr., Al's grandfather, had started the company, later known as A. Mamaux & Son, with his father, Eugene, in Pittsburgh after the Civil War. The elder Albert had served as chief gunner's mate on the USS *Lehigh* during the war.[9] When young Al became old enough to grip a baseball, his father took him out into the yard and started showing him how to pitch. By age sixteen, Al performed against teams of grown men. Father and son attended Pirates games so the youngster could study hurlers and batters.[10]

Known as "Abbie" to his friends, Mamaux later acquired the nickname "Smokes" because of his speed on the mound. Al played for area teams in the Crafton church league, Brookline, West Liberty, and other top-notch amateur squads. When pitching for a team managed by former Pirates player Tom McCreery, Mamaux defeated Vandergrift in a titanic battle. While hurling for Brookline, Smokes only allowed four hits against Beltzhoover in a nineteen-inning game.[11] As a student, Al attended city public schools, moved on to East Liberty Academy, and finished his studies at Duquesne University.[12] Mamaux pitched magnificently for Duquesne and also played football for the college.[13]

Potential aside, Al experienced trouble sticking with the teams he played for around Dormont at the early stages of his development. Although some felt his son was an ordinary pitcher, John Mamaux sincerely believed the lad possessed extraordinary talent, which he anxiously desired to develop appropriately. After managers fired Al from numerous squads, John purchased a franchise in an amateur league, secured a piece of property, laid a field, built a grandstand, organized a team, and bought the players glistening new uniforms. John seemed confident this course of action guaranteed that nobody would boot his son from the squad. Unfortunately, the awning business prevented John from devoting as much time as he wished to this venture, so he hired a manager to take charge of the baseball team. One of the first things this new skipper did was bounce Al from the club.[14]

In 1912, at eighteen, Al Mamaux signed a contract to pitch for the Wilkinsburg club of the Allegheny County League, an organization composed of semi-professional players with moderate ability. While there, Al became known as Smokes because of his bewildering speed.[15] As a member of Wilkinsburg's team, Mamaux averaged 10 to 12 strikeouts per game and tossed a no-hitter in a contest that didn't last the full nine innings.[16] Al's family offered crucial assistance in helping the young lad receive an opportunity to reach the next level. One day, Barney Dreyfuss walked into his office and started opening a stack of mail. A letter in a pile was from a Pittsburgh native who admired Fred Clarke and the Pirates. Albert Mamaux Sr. had written this correspondence, talking about his grandson's exemplary record as a sandlot pitcher while urging the Pirates to give the youngster a tryout.[17]

John Mamaux also applied pressure by bringing his son to Pirates headquarters and asking Dreyfuss to give his kid an audition.[18] Fred Clarke invited the young Mamaux to don a Buccaneers uniform and practice with the team. Al worked out for several weeks, participating in pregame drills. Mamaux's curveball so impressed Clarke that Pittsburgh's manager offered the hurler a contract and added him to the Hot Springs spring training list for 1913.[19] After Barney had forked over $22,500 in 1911 to purchase disappointing hurler Marty O'Toole, homegrown Al Mamaux cost Pittsburgh's owner nothing. Unless he sent the lad's grandfather a small stipend for recommending the young pitcher.[20]

Following spring training in 1913, Pittsburgh initially farmed out Al to the Central League's Fort Wayne Champs. Former Pirates player Jimmy Burke, who managed the team, wasn't impressed with Mamaux and returned him to Pittsburgh. The Pirates then shipped Al, dubbed the "Millionaire Kid" due to his family's wealth, off to the Ohio State League's Huntington Blue Sox, where he started realizing his potential before being recalled when the minor league campaign ended.[21] Brimming with endless possibilities as a major league player, after doing good work on the bump in 1914 in a limited capacity, the first round of drama surrounding Mamaux burst onto the scene shortly after the baseball season ended.

On October 15, 1914, Al's mother, Julia Wiseman Mamaux, became involved in a physical confrontation with her husband, John, in New York. Julia attacked John Mamaux with an umbrella Thursday night at the Hotel McAlpin. The force of the blows knocked her husband down to the ground as a crowd gathered to view the scene. The reason for the assault revolved around Mrs. Mamaux's accusation that John had registered at the hotel with another woman. Julia felt justified in taking such action and immersed her son Al into the whole sordid situation while being interviewed by the *Pittsburgh Press* two days after the incident occurred.

"I have borne his attitude toward me and my three children too long," said the still-angry wife. "For the last two years he has inflicted a constant succession of various indignities on me, through his actions. During the year he has been away from me he has insulted the name of 'husband' innumerable times. I have been too quiet. I am glad that I had the courage to attack him as I did. And I am glad also that my oldest boy was not with me, or I think my husband would have received the thrashing of his life."

According to his wife, John Mamaux habitually engaged in the company of other women. The couple, married for twenty-two years, had been separated for about twelve months before Julia Mamaux finally took action.[22] The woman accompanying John to New York, in this instance, happened to be Helen Wilson, also known as Mrs. M. E. Sherman, from Detroit, Michigan. In August, Mrs. Mamaux confronted her husband and Wilson at a cottage on Cass Lake in Michigan. Julia had sworn a warrant against John with local authorities, but the sheriff moved too slowly, serving it after the two individuals left the area. On May 29, detectives hired by Mrs. Mamaux had traced John making a trip by train from Pittsburgh to Cleveland. Once there, he met Helen Wilson at the station, and the two then traveled together over the Lake Shore Railroad to Chicago. They registered as "John J. Mamaux and wife" at the LaSalle Hotel, which gave them room 1002. They remained there through the Memorial Day holiday before going to Detroit on June 1.

Julia Mamaux told the newspaper that she attacked her husband at the Hotel McAlpin in New York out of desperation. While on her way to the hotel lobby's elevator to visit John's room, she encountered him when the doors opened, and he exited. Mrs. Mamaux immediately struck him with her umbrella and knocked him to the ground. She smacked John about twenty times and then shouted that she was Mrs. John J. Mamaux of Pittsburgh, and the man she was accosting happened to be her husband, who'd registered at the hotel with another woman as his spouse. Julia offered some final particulars for the *Pittsburgh Press* newspaper article.

> The hotel manager asked my husband if I was his wife and he acknowledged I was and the manager ordered him to leave the hotel immediately. My husband was attending the annual convention of the Awning and Tentmakers' Association of the United States in New York this week, and when I learned that he had another woman with him I became angry and went to New York to thrash him, which I did.
>
> My husband is supporting me and the children, but he is not giving us enough money, when one considers his means and the amount of money he spends on himself. I already have entered legal proceedings to compel him to pay me more. I have had private detectives watching him for months and their evidence is entertaining, indeed. The world would be surprised to know the inside history of John Mamaux. I lose patience when I see the "front" he puts on in Pittsburgh and the big show he makes. Well, perhaps he will not be so much in evidence after this. For decent men and women will have little to do with him. And that is only just to me and my children.

Mrs. Mamaux stated her husband, who gave $200 a month in support, wanted a divorce. She didn't intend to allow John to follow through with this action.²³ In September 1892, Julia Wiseman and John Mamaux had eloped to Cumberland, Maryland, to get married. Although they'd dated for some time, neither group of parents approved of the couple's plans for matrimony, favoring them to delay the nuptials. Julia required the consent of her father and mother because she wasn't of legal age in Pennsylvania. John's parents had been visiting his father's original hometown of Philadelphia for the past two weeks. Once in Cumberland, the potential bride and groom experienced no problem obtaining a marriage license. A Catholic priest initially hindered their plan when he refused to perform the ceremony after intensely questioning Julia. Undaunted, the two found a Protestant minister who officiated the ceremony. This decision angered both sets of parents, strict Catholics who understood their son and daughter would need to engage in a public penance, so the church didn't consider them excommunicated.²⁴

While vitriol and animosity remained at a premium in the Mamaux household, things took an even uglier turn on November 17, 1914. Police arrested Pirates pitcher Al Mamaux in his mother's Dormont home at 2946 Belrose Avenue. Al's father charged that his son had threatened his life two days earlier and feared that the lad might do such harm in the future.²⁵ Constable Murray Edlis arrested Mamaux on a warrant charging surety of the peace as sworn out by his father. Al's grandfather, Albert Mamaux Sr., posted the $300 bail for his grandson's release from jail.²⁶ Julia Mamaux, who had no reservations over discussing private family matters, supplied the course of events for a Western Pennsylvania newspaper.

"My husband has caused the electric lights to be taken out of our house and has attempted to have the gas shut off in this freezing weather," said Mrs. Mamaux from the home she occupied with her three sons.

"This petty move angered my son Albert and he went to his father's store, 644 Penn Avenue, to make protest. My husband says that Albert 'shook him up and down in his chair,' but that I can hardly believe, although perhaps the provocation was great."

This scenario became more interesting because Albert Mamaux Sr. sided with the daughter-in-law against his son, leaving John Mamaux ostracized by the entire family.²⁷ Besides living at the Belrose Avenue residence in Dormont, Julia Mamaux had sometimes resided with Al in his room in the Hotel Anderson and his West View apartment.²⁸ On November 18, Al Mamaux appeared before Alderman J. J. Kirby for a hearing.²⁹ Kirby freed the young pitcher and ordered him to pay court costs, which his grandfather handled after the lad promised the alderman he wouldn't commit any illegal act against his father.³⁰

John Mamaux filed a bill of particulars in his divorce suit against Julia Mamaux in February 1915. In that document, Mamaux alleged that his sons Albert and John Jr. had assaulted him at his place of business on Penn Avenue on November 15, 1914, after being prompted into doing so by his wife. Regarding attempts by Julia to do bodily harm to him on occasions other than the Hotel McAlpin incident, Mr. Mamaux asserted that she'd struck him in the face at their Dormont home on March 16, 1913. On June 14 of that same year, at his place of business, Julia hit him on the face, breast, neck, and back while tossing an ink well and umbrella at him. John Mamaux's filing further proclaimed his wife threatened his life on June 18, 1914, at their home, and she assaulted him again at the office one day later.[31]

In the libel of divorce proceeding, John charged his wife with "cruel and barbarous treatment." Julia refused to apply for divorce for religious reasons and other factors.[32] In December 1915, a master agreed with the wife, declining to grant John J. Mamaux a divorce from Julia V. Mamaux based on that legal arbitrator's recommendation.[33] John eventually received justice in July 1916 when the Pennsylvania Superior Court in Philadelphia reversed the original ruling in the Mamaux case from Allegheny County and granted the divorce.[34] Oddly, while Al's father and mother's domestic spat raged, his grandfather, Albert Leon Mamaux Sr., was also involved in a contentious divorce case. In the spring of 1913, Albert Sr. had filed a suit of libel against his second wife, Nora H. Mamaux (his first wife, Catherine, had passed away on March 13, 1907), charging her with subjecting him to indignities to his person and cruel treatment.[35]

Nora Mamaux offered an answer on May 10, 1913, to this divorce suit on the grounds of cruel and barbarous treatment.[36] In her response filed with the court, Nora requested alimony and counsel fees while accusing her husband of neglecting to provide financial support. Nora claimed Albert Sr.'s worth to be between $75,000 and $100,000, while he earned an annual income of $12,000. The awning manufacturer denied this in a response filed on May 17. Albert Sr. alleged his worth to be about $25,000 while netting slightly less than $5,000 a year. The Mamaux patriarch also declared that shortly after the two married, his new bride spurned living at his Hamilton Avenue residence. He then secured a home on Wightman Street with a $13,000 mortgage. Albert Sr. stated that Nora still lived there and had refused to vacate the premises.[37]

Albert Mamaux Sr. and Nora married on October 6, 1909, and then traveled to California for a honeymoon.[38] Nora vehemently denied all the charges against her, claiming she had never threatened to shoot her husband as alleged if he refused to make a large property settlement for her. The wife also contended that Albert Sr. had deserted her. She disavowed ever treating her husband disrespectfully and took extreme exception to the charge of not fulfilling her marital vows. Nora also lobbed heavy salvos in son John Mamaux's direction. After vacationing in the Pocono Mountains in Pennsylvania, at her husband's urging, Nora returned to find Albert Sr. stricken with pneumonia. Upon arriving home, two doctors, a male nurse, John, and an aunt, Mrs. Susan Moore, were in attendance.[39]

Throughout her husband's illness, Nora visited his bedside daily while cooking meals for the nurse and John. Nora criticized her stepson for being controlling, rude, and ignorant throughout the ordeal. She charged that John Mamaux attempted to turn Albert Sr. against her. She even ordered John to leave the house once, allowing him to return the following day.[40] Regarding divorce proceedings, Albert Mamaux Sr. objected to a jury of his peers hearing the case because of concern over a public court spectacle tarnishing his community standing. His pretty young wife requested that a judge grant a jury trial. The husband filed a petition in Common Pleas Court on May 17, 1913, to have a master decide the case.[41]

After being granted his wish, the case's outcome ended up disappointing Albert Sr. On December 16, 1914, attorney David L. McCann, appointed the master to decide the divorce case, declared that he couldn't find any evidence, facts, or testimony to substantiate the charges brought forth by the husband. McCann filed his report, dismissing the case and denying Mamaux a divorce from his wife, Nora. When the master handed down his decision, Albert Sr., who now lived at 4742 Maripoe Avenue (Street) in Bloomfield, was sixty-six years old, while his wife was about half that age.[42] Following an appeal, Common Pleas Court Judge John C. Haymaker, on March 13, 1915, upheld McCann's previous decision after hearing the evidence.[43] Sadly, the man who'd built the A. Mamaux & Son dynasty passed away almost two months later, on May 9, 1915.[44]

Before leaving for spring training at Dawson Springs, Kentucky, young Al Mamaux visited the kids recuperating in the children's ward of West Penn Hospital. Al regularly frequented this institution, and the youngsters always gave him a warm reception. Mamaux distributed gumballs to all the children, while one lucky group received an authentic major league baseball. Al also captivated the kids for hours with diamond tales about Honus Wagner, Fred Clarke, and George Gibson, as they exhibited gaping mouths the entire time. These happy children, ecstatic over Mamaux taking the time to spread a little joy, referred to him as the "baseball doctor." [45]

Although this visit offered a therapeutic moment, Pirates pitcher Al Mamaux had experienced a tumultuous off-season. Things didn't start so beautifully for him once the 1915 baseball campaign commenced. Al felt slighted when Pittsburgh opened the season on April 14 against the Cincinnati Reds at Redland Field. There weren't enough road jerseys for all team members, so one or two players had to wear tattered garments from the previous year. Mamaux happened to be one of those players. He felt gravely disrespected by such treatment and couldn't be bothered with the thrilling opening day atmosphere. He saw recruits, who eventually would be discarded, wearing sparkling new jerseys while he modeled a uniform held together by safety pins. Al sulked on the bench, brokenhearted.

"I ought to have had one of those uniforms," he muttered.

Mamaux sat there, his head down, watching the neatly clad rookies cavorting about the diamond. Suddenly, Al decided to stop feeling sorry for himself, jumped to his feet, and ripped off his sweater coat.

"Doggone them, I'll show 'em who has the best right to a new uniform," exclaimed Mamaux.

Al then proceeded to join his Pirates teammates wearing the patched-up garb. Mamaux pitched to batters in practice, fielded bunts, and did everything possible to make himself useful. Al gained the support and admiration of the Cincinnati crowd through exhibiting such pep and ginger during the pregame practice session.[46] Whether strong determination, borne out of anger from being snubbed, or talent blossoming forth, Mamaux experienced a monumental season in 1915. Al went 21–8 on a Pittsburgh team that finished fifth in the National League standings with a 73–81 record. Mamaux also placed third in the circuit with a 2.04 ERA. Following this grand campaign, baseball experts rated Al in the same class as stalwart hurlers Walter Johnson and Grover Cleveland Alexander.[47] Manager Fred Clarke's prediction from the previous year when a baseball writer asked about the youngster's ability rang true in 1915.

"He's going to be one of the best pitchers in the country," said Clarke.

"What's he got?" further queried the writer.

"Brains," responded Pittsburgh's manager.[48]

Al Mamuax's performance in 1915 certainly caught the Federal League's attention. Sensing an opportunity to exploit his nephew's rise to fame, Al's uncle, Dick Wiseman, proclaimed that he acted as the pitcher's agent. Uncle Dick approached both Federal and National League team officials, alleging he was authorized to negotiate contract terms for his nephew as if Mamaux were a free agent. When Wiseman met with Barney Dreyfuss at Pirates team headquarters, the owner politely but firmly showed him the door. Pittsburgh's owner had received word that Uncle Dick worked all angles for his nephew.[49] According to Dreyfuss, Federal League representatives also hounded Mamaux in Pittsburgh for some time before the Pirates embarked on an eastern trip that started in Philadelphia on August 18.[50]

When the Pirates reached New York, representatives from the Brooklyn Tip-Tops futilely pestered Al about signing with their team for next season. Manager Fred Clarke conferred with his pitcher on this matter of being pursued by the renegade league.[51] Barney Dreyfuss traveled east to handle some league business in Boston, while Clarke had kept his boss abreast of the situation concerning Federal League overtures toward Mamaux. On August 26, Fred took Al to Dreyfuss's New York hotel room. After a fifteen-minute conference, Mamaux readily agreed to sign a contract that allowed the hurler to remain with the Pirates.

When Dreyfuss announced striking a deal, he stated Al had asked for a contract at the meeting. Pittsburgh's owner explained to the pitcher what the team would pay, and Mamaux found these terms satisfactory. Barney claimed Al told him he wanted to take care of this matter so the annoyance of being constantly badgered wouldn't be repeated when the team returned to Pittsburgh. Although Dreyfuss didn't reveal the salary figure, he admitted it to be less than those numbers thrown about by the Federal League.[52] The document signed by Mamaux bound him to Pittsburgh for 1916, 1917, and 1918.[53]

Upon learning that Al Mamaux had signed a contract to remain with the Pirates, Ennis Telfair "Rebel" Oakes, manager and outfielder of the Federal League's Pittsburgh Rebels, stated that the hurler had initiated contact with him. According to Oakes, he didn't want to interfere with Al getting as much money as possible for his services, so he kept the outcome of a private meeting between the two a secret. Now that Mamaux had cast his lot with the Pirates for three more seasons, Rebel saw no harm in breaking his silence.

> In the first place, neither I nor anyone else connected with the club hunted him up and lured him away. Mamaux approached me, instead, and wanted to know what I had to offer.
> Mamaux declared to me that he was not getting enough for a pitcher that was leading the league with a club that could hardly keep at .500, and wanted to know what we had to offer. He declared that he was being paid $250 a month [$1,500 a year] by the Pirates, with the promise of a bonus

if he made good. He said that he had just come from Mr. Dreyfuss's office, where he had asked for his bonus.

Mamaux said Mr. Dreyfuss told him he would have to wait until the end of the season.

"How much will I get at the end of the season?" asked Mamaux.

"I'm going to give you $300," is what Mamaux said Dreyfuss replied.

"How about next year's contract?" asked Mamaux.

"You'll get $2,700," so Mr. Drefyuss said, according to Mamaux. Albert says he started for the door, but was called back and offered $3,000. Then he hunted me up.

Rebel Oakes then told Al Mamaux what his organization would be willing to pay as long as the pitcher could join the team free from legal entanglements related to prior contractual obligations. Mamaux promised to think it over before the two men parted company. Oakes stated he hadn't heard back from Al since that conversation.[54] An obstacle appeared, circumventing Al's quest to collect that $300 bonus at the season's end. On September 18, reports out of Pittsburgh indicated that Mamaux would miss the remainder of the campaign due to appendicitis.[55] Al ignored the doctors' advice by refusing to go to the hospital and vowing to finish the season. He planned on receiving the operation a few weeks after the campaign ended. Mamaux pitched with great difficulty as the season wound down, stunting the youngster's efficiency before suffering the attack.[56] When Al eventually entered West Penn Hospital, he became particularly fond of an attractive nurse who cared for him. The following season, she occupied a Forbes Field box each afternoon Mamaux pitched.[57]

Ten days before Al had been told to remain on the sidelines, Pirates pilot Fred Clarke made a significant pronouncement. On September 8, 1915, Clarke announced that effective at the season's end, he planned on retiring from baseball as team manager. Fred had acted primarily as a bench manager for the Pirates since 1912. Clarke claimed that no friction existed between him and owner Barney Dreyfuss.[58] Following the glorious 1909 World Series victory, Fred had wanted to retire then, but Dreyfuss refused to let him go.[59] When Clarke purchased a sizeable flouring mill a few years ago, he realized that making this business venture a success would require him to leave baseball eventually. After weeks of contemplation over a proper course of action, Barney induced Fred a second time to remain with the organization.[60] Clarke also offered insight into his decision while offering a fond farewell to faithful Pirates fans.

My mind was made up to quit baseball long before the Pirates were out of the running, but even if they had won the pennant, I would have retired at the end of this season. One year ago, it was my intention of stepping out, but Barney Dreyfuss would not listen to such a thing. After thinking it over for a long time, I decided that I owed it to Mr. Dreyfuss, as well as the fans of Pittsburgh, to make one last effort to give the city a winning ball team.

In this attempt I failed and now I'm going to step down and I sincerely hope my successor will give the public what it wants and what it deserves—a winning club. I never was cut out to be a bench manager. When I was in there playing, it was different, but the strain of sitting inactive and directing the battle from the bench proved too much for my nature.

Some time ago I consulted physicians, who informed me that unless I gave up the sport soon, my health would be endangered. I am sorry the Pirates did not make a better showing during my last year.

It is hard to leave Pittsburgh, where I have had so many happy associations, and, furthermore, I regret having to part from President Dreyfuss, whom I consider one of the fairest and best employers it has ever been my good fortune to meet. However, there will always be a warm place in my heart for Colonel Barney, Forbes Field and the Pittsburgh fans.[61]

Although Fred Clarke regretted that the Pirates didn't perform better in his final season, he'd claimed four National League pennants as leader of the squad and one World Series title. Clarke also posted a lifetime managerial record of 1,602–1,181 from when he took control of the Louisville Colonels in 1897 until overseeing his final game for Pittsburgh on October 3, 1915. On December 16, Barney Dreyfuss announced that he'd hired a former pitcher from the Chicago clubs in both major leagues and onetime White Sox skipper James "Jimmy" Callahan to run the Pirates. Callahan, also called "Nixey" and "Cal," had recently accepted a position to manage the Pacific Coast League's Los Angeles Angels. John "Johnny" Powers, an owner of that ball club, released Cal from the obligation since Callahan's in-laws weren't happy with the West Coast move. Powers, a life-long friend of Jimmy's wife, Josephine Hardin Callahan, didn't want to cause family discourse. Following a discussion between Cal and Johnny, Powers called off the proposition, freeing Callahan to join Pittsburgh.[62]

As the Pirates' organization prepared to launch a new season without Fred Clarke at the helm for the first time in seventeen years, Al Mamaux experienced an off-season filled with positive and adverse events. Mamaux started at fullback for the Dormont football team on Thanksgiving Day. Upon hearing that his star pitcher had participated in a gridiron contest, Barney Dreyfuss instructed Al to cease playing for the Dormont squad immediately. Dreyfuss cited that Mamaux's recently signed contract prevented him from participating in winter sports where he might suffer an injury that could wreck his baseball career.[63] Sorrowfully, on December 17, 1915, Al's maternal grandmother, Catherine L. Wiseman, died.[64]

In February 1916, Mamaux started utilizing talents unrelated to his baseball skills. Al happened to be an accomplished violinist and a grand singer. Initially pushing back against suggestions that he consider performing on the stage, Mamaux cited that the "big time" might be a bit overwhelming. He finally agreed to appear onstage for the fun of it with new manager Jimmy Callahan in a one-week engagement. Al proved a smashing success, prompting manager Harry Davis of the Davis Theatre in Pittsburgh to sign him up for a seven-day vaudeville show featuring the hurler at his establishment. Mamaux declared he could sing any melody recommended when inundated with song suggestions. Al opened up his engagement at the Davis Theatre on February 17, 1916, performing each day in shows in the afternoon and evening. Mamaux had done private singing stints before in Pittsburgh and made appearances in other National League cities.[65]

Any possible rapport between player and manager onstage didn't possess longevity as the baseball campaign progressed. Al picked up where he left off the previous year on the mound by pitching sensational ball for the Pittsburgh Pirates. When Mamaux defeated the Chicago Cubs, 1–0, in the second game of a Fourth of July doubleheader at Forbes Field, he pushed his record to 13–3, supported by a 1.61 ERA. Everything then came tumbling down due to self-inflicted circumstances. Later that month, Jimmy Callahan called out his men for partying too much at night; when the Pirates played at home. The press rationalized that since amusement parks closed at 10:30 P.M. and theaters weren't open later than 11 P.M., no reason existed for his players to wander home several hours after midnight. Cal threatened a heavy fine and suspension for any individual willing to challenge him on this point.[66]

On August 17, Al pitched horribly against the Brooklyn Robins in the contest at Forbes Field, allowing four earned runs before Callahan pulled him after four innings of work. The 5–1 loss against the Robins dropped Mamaux's record to 17–9. In between games of a Saturday twin bill on the home grounds with Brooklyn on August 19, a local sports scribe rushed to the Pirates' dugout after receiving some juicy information from an out-of-town colleague.

"What's this about Mamaux being suspended?" queried the scribe.

"Nothing that I know," parried Cal.

"You must know something of it," replied the writer.

"Where did you hear of it?" asked Callahan.

"Mamaux told the Brooklyn players and newspaper boys, and it doesn't look exactly square to us to keep us in the dark," responded the scribe.

"Good night!" exclaimed Callahan, throwing his hands up in the air. "Well, I guess we've got to go through with it."

Pittsburgh Post baseball writer Florent Gibson said that Thomas "Tom" Rice of the *Brooklyn Daily Eagle* informed him and his colleagues that Al Mamaux had appeared at the Schenley Hotel the previous evening. The young man told Brooklyn's players and scribes that he drew a ten-day suspension for violating club rules. According to Mamaux, the team alleged that they took this action since he stayed out all Wednesday night before pitching in Thursday's game. During the doubleheader's second game, angry writers in Forbes Field's press box besieged team business manager Peter Kelly. Unfortunately, Kelly knew nothing about the suspension. Following Barney Dreyfuss's and Callahan's early silence, Peter announced on September 20 that Pirates management stood firmly in suspending Al for ten days and that the punishment had started on August 18. If not for being caught hiding information that Al leaked, it's possible the sentence initially acted only as a bluff by Pirates management, aimed at coercing the young hurler into changing his ways.[67]

Al Mamaux bitterly denounced his suspension and railed against what he viewed as unwarranted punishment.[68] Mamaux also wouldn't be paid throughout the ten-day suspension. While not denying the charges against him, Al indignantly threatened that he could possibly quit the team.[69] On the heels of this potential refusal to rejoin Pittsburgh once club officials lifted his suspension, a rumor surfaced, claiming Mamaux seemed eager to join the New York Giants or some other eastern club. Months earlier, Giants manager John McGraw had bestowed lavish praise upon the Pirates' pitcher.[70] This action was no surprise to Smoky City patrons who knew Al wasn't taking care of himself for some time.[71] When finally pressed for the reason behind Mamaux's suspension, Jimmy Callahan simply replied, "For an infraction of club rules." Although Cal offered no further details, he stated Al's reprimand wasn't related to drinking alcohol.

A member of Pittsburgh's gambling fraternity offered some insight into the rule-breaking that Mamaux had committed. As he traveled by streetcar to view the game Al pitched on August 17, this individual told companions that he planned to bet on Brooklyn that afternoon. When pressed for a reason, this gambler declared he possessed knowledge that Mamaux had engaged in the pleasurable but frivolous activity of "tossing the ivories" the previous night. The gentleman sharing this inside information claimed Al didn't retire to bed until the morning, or not at all. This gambler deduced that Mamaux would be in no condition to pitch against the Robins. Other sources corroborated these details surrounding Al's late night, where the young pitcher actively participated in a game of dice shooting and had lost large chunks of his semi-monthly paycheck.

Mamaux denied his night of revelry, maintaining he'd remained home sick on Wednesday night. This accusation also caused him to make the impulsive statement to friends that he was through forever with the Pittsburgh club.[72] Regarding his denial, Al added that he wasn't out late that night but had become ill around 3 A.M. and then taken a walk for about an hour before returning to bed. *Pittsburgh Press* sportswriter Ralph S. Davis mocked such a preposterous claim, wondering if the alleged leisurely walk had led him to the vicinity of Fifth Avenue and Fernando Street, where he met a man named Klein, who happened to be running a dice game.[73]

Davis classified Mamaux's assertion of innocence as laughable and an attempt to garner sympathy. The writer also believed that not having sustainable available income would curtail this activity Al had been engaging in for many weeks. Davis reasoned that if Mamaux had returned home on the morning in question by 5 A.M., the youngster could justify in his mind that he wasn't out all night, although thirteen minutes acted as the margin for supporting its legitimacy. The young hurler also vowed to pitch for two years without receiving any salary if management proved their charge against him. Davis held the opinion that Pirates management should've suspended Mamaux sooner.[74]

Pirates owner Barney Dreyfuss expressed his feelings when reached by telephone at the Westmoreland Country Club on the evening of August 19. Dreyfuss asserted that the organization reacted slowly in announcing the suspension to the press because they wanted to protect their player, if possible. However, this became a moot point when Al sought sympathy from Brooklyn's team members.

> Mamaux has made the crack that he will never pitch another ball for my club. I agree with him—unless he comes back to us at the end of his period of suspension in good physical condition, and ready to give us something for the money we pay him.
>
> We have the goods on him, and we don't propose to bother anymore with him unless he sees a light, and does his duty. He thought he could fool us, but he was caught at his tricks, and he had to be punished. There is no

use trying to deal leniently with a man of Mamaux's makeup—and we do not propose to shield him any longer.

He will live up to the rules made for the government of players on the Pittsburgh club, or he will not play any more baseball. That is final. His suspension is for ten days, but if he does not toe the scratch at once, cut out his bad habits and do as he knows he should, he will be suspended again when the present penalty expires.[75]

A rumor that Al and outfielder Daniel "Dan" Costello, his good friend and frequent nighttime companion on the Pirates, planned on traveling to Atlantic City was unfounded. Jimmy Callahan also denied that Costello, nicknamed "Dashing Dan," had been fined and suspended for speaking out against management regarding the Mamaux situation.[76] On August 26, Pittsburgh released Dan to the International League's Toronto Maple Leafs for showing a poor attitude toward club officials and their policies.[77] Costello refused to report and declared his intention to retire from playing baseball.[78] Callahan initially suspended Dan but then had a change of heart and wired him on September 4 to report back to the Pirates the following day.[79] Costello didn't rejoin Pittsburgh, opting instead to retire and enter Harvard University to study law.[80]

Before experiencing an epiphany about his conduct, Al Mamaux claimed someone had impersonated him and also done so on other occasions.[81] When Philadelphia rolled into town for a series at Forbes Field after Pittsburgh played Brooklyn, Al asked Phillies manager Patrick "Pat" Moran for fatherly advice. Moran told Mamaux that there was only one thing to do; get back into a Pittsburgh uniform. Jimmy Callahan also stated that he wouldn't hold a conference with a committee of fans sympathetic to the hurler's plight who wanted to discuss his suspension.[82]

Al initially had been quite vicious, commenting on Callahan and his managerial ability.[83] Mamaux finally repented, understanding the gravity of his offense and promising to behave in the future. He admitted to being terribly at fault and acknowledged his punishment was justified. On August 24, the Pirates' manager dispelled rumors of Al's early reinstatement, although he admitted the hurler now worked out with the team. In conclusion, Jimmy reiterated his comment from days earlier about the Mamaux incident being closed in his mind.[84] Al fulfilled his entire ten-day sentence and returned to the mound in the first contest of a doubleheader at Forbes Field on August 28, tossing a complete game and defeating the Boston Braves, 5–1. After losing his final five decisions, Mamaux finished the 1916 campaign with a 21–15 record and a 2.53

ERA. Despite tough sledding at season's end, Al now appeared to be in good standing with team management.[85]

Once the campaign concluded, the stench of hypocrisy tainted Pittsburgh's air. When Mamaux served his ten-day suspension, Philadelphia's *Evening Ledger* newspaper reported that people close to Barney Dreyfuss felt that Jimmy Callahan was about to be fired. Although Dreyfuss remained confident that Cal would make good running the club if given time, Pittsburgh's players and fans demanded a change. These patrons, who weren't attending games at Forbes Field, believed the team should've been performing better in the National League race.[86] Outfielder Max "Scoops" Carey, one of the players at odds with Pittsburgh's manager, didn't get along with him. At one point in the season, relations became so strained that various team members didn't speak to each other for two weeks. When baseball writer A. R. Cratty told Barney Dreyfuss at the end of the campaign that a specific individual was verbally trashing the organization, the owner declared he could name the player with one guess. After incorrectly deducing it to be a particular young prodigal pitcher, Dreyfuss didn't miss on his second attempt.

"Carey could be the only other man," shouted the magnate.[87]

Stories surrounding a falling out between Barney Dreyfuss and Jimmy Callahan resurfaced at the end of October. According to sportswriter H. C. Hamilton, the two had almost reached a parting of ways the previous summer due to an incident involving Pittsburgh's manager.[88] Pundits didn't realize that Dreyfuss knew of Jimmy's indiscretion because Callahan had informed him about everything related to deserting the club for a week.[89] Months after issuing his July threat to suspend and fine any player caught partying through all hours of the night, Callahan was guilty of breaking that very rule.

Frustrated over his team's ineptitude, Cal had met up with some friends in Philadelphia and then deserted the Pirates as they prepared to open a six-game series against New York at the Polo Grounds on September 16. Honus Wagner managed the team during Jimmy's absence of several days. Team secretary Peter Kelly and newspaper journalists worked to suppress information regarding Callahan's disappearance. Kelly stated that Barney would have to hear the news from someone other than him. Dreyfuss did find out, and he fired Kelly for being more loyal to Cal rather than the man who paid his salary.[90]

In February 1917, the Pirates' owner initially named former Pirates scout William "Billy" Murray to succeed Peter.[91] One month later, newspaper reports stated that Murray was coming back within a scouting capacity.[92] When the season started, Barney announced that current scout William "Cap" Neal would take on the added responsibilities of the organization's temporary business manager. Dreyfuss cited not burdening himself with extra expenses as the reason for naming no permanent successor, given baseball's uncertain status following the United States's entry into the Great War.[93] With talk swirling about a potential baseball strike by major league players that never unfolded, Al Mamaux said in January that he felt no worry or concern over other players discussing a possible work stoppage.

"This strike business isn't bothering me in the least," said Mamaux. "I am signed for next season. And when the time comes for reporting, you can bet I'll be on the job. Moreover, I am going to work harder than ever before. Mr. Dreyfuss and I had a few differences last season, but I realize now that I was in the wrong. I was not as earnest about my work as I might have been. But this is all past. I am going to give the club my best efforts this coming summer, and I think I'll be able to win a lot of games."[94]

This kind of talk was cheap when actions didn't match those words. Al did take a positive step toward a more grounded future. On March 8, 1917, the *Brooklyn Daily Times* announced his engagement to a fashion model from that area. Mamaux was to wed Miss Alice Johnson of 946 St. Marks Avenue in Brooklyn. Miss Johnson announced these nuptials the previous Wednesday evening after Al had proposed Tuesday night. Alice also gained fame in the fall by winning first prize at the Winter Garden Fashion Show.

The two had been introduced the previous summer at Ebbets Field by Marie "Dearie" McKeever, daughter of Stephen McKeever, part-owner of the Brooklyn Robins. The McKeevers were friends with Alice's parents. Mamaux, who'd visited his fiancée numerous times since the season ended, left directly for spring training at Columbus, Georgia, after she accepted his marriage proposal, ending this one-week stay at the Johnson home. While talking to a Brooklyn newspaperman about this good news, he recoiled when the writer mentioned his "Millionaire Kid" nickname.

"I have no fortune but my arm," said Al. "My father is well-to-do. He is in the tent and awning business in Pittsburgh. The story started when I first went South with the Pirates. My father gave me a generous allowance, as I was only 19 [18], and a Pittsburgh sporting writer played the fact that I was comparatively rolling in money for a good yarn. It spread like wildfire."[95]

When a reporter called the Mamaux Dormont home on the telephone in Pittsburgh, John Jr., who went by "Jack," said his brother wasn't there. Jack also stated he'd heard nothing about his sibling's engagement and that it would be best if this individual spoke to Al directly to receive answers to any questions.[96] Mamaux's decision to marry his sweetheart turned out to be the highlight of what became a very turbulent year. In June, newspapers reported that Al was being sued for $12,000 in damages in a Pittsburgh court for running over a small boy with his auto. The accident had occurred in May 1915, and the lad's parents filed suit since they alleged their son had never recovered from his injuries.[97]

Sportswriter Paul Purman also wrote an article asking, "Will Al Mamaux eat himself out of baseball?" Purman started his story by stating that Mamaux had failed to show any ability reminiscent of his stellar mound effectiveness from the past two years. According to the writer, although Al didn't drink alcohol, he dissipated in another manner by possessing an insatiable appetite for food. Purman claimed Mamaux was prone to eating anything at any given time. The mishmashes were quite weird, as Al sometimes combined lobster and ice cream at night while consuming too much candy and rich foods, jeopardizing his digestive system's health. Paul compared Mamaux to former outfielder Elmer Flick, who used to eat a heavy meal before participating in a baseball game. At the same time, other ballplayers usually consumed a light repast of a bit of soup or a bowl of milk. Purman also wrote that Al had lost his first five decisions that year.[98]

The 1917 season proved horrendous for the Pirates' team, as they finished in the basement with a 51–103 record. With the club listlessly floundering at the season's early stages, Barney Dreyfuss handed manager Jimmy Callahan his walking papers at noon on June 30. Barney made this move despite Callahan containing a non-release clause in his contract that lasted through October 10. Pittsburgh's owner named Honus Wagner as the club's interim manager.[99] Wagner only ran the team for five games until Hugo Bezdek, who'd gained fame as a football player and coach, supplanted him. Before being appointed Pittsburgh's manager, Hugo worked as a coach and scout for the organization.[100] Dreyfuss had first met Bezdek during Pittsburgh's spring training trip to Hot Springs in 1908 when he coached the University of Arkansas football team. Since that time, Hugo had recommended baseball talent to the Pirates.[101]

Pittsburgh's baseball fans immediately condemned Barney Dreyfuss for hiring an inexperienced man like Bezdek to manage the Pirates. Although these rooters had lobbied for Jimmy Callahan's dismissal, they felt a pragmatic candidate steeped in baseball knowledge should succeed Jimmy.[102] On July 10, Callahan met with Dreyfuss to discuss a satisfactory settlement related to what the organization owed the former manager on his contract.[103] Upon reaching an agreement with Pittsburgh's owner, Jimmy declared that when he took the job of leading the Pirates, certain conditions beyond his control had already existed, which he couldn't rectify.[104] Although Cal wouldn't say following this conference what severance amount the two sides agreed on, Callahan admitted to compromising on the matter so he wouldn't be required to report to team headquarters each day to fulfill the contract's obligation to be paid. As Jimmy boarded a train bound for his Chicago home, he took a parting shot at Dreyfuss.

"If the general public knew all the insides of the running of the Pirate team they would say I did as well as any living man could do," declared Callahan. "Why, the Pope, the Kaiser, nor Providence could do any better under the ownership of Barney Dreyfuss. The greatest punishment we can mete out to the Hohenzollern monarch after the war is over is to sentence him to manage the Pirates."[105]

Fans criticizing Jimmy Callahan's brief time as Pittsburgh's manager alleged he made a mistake trading third baseman Howard Douglas "Doug" Baird shortly before his dismissal and had blundered disciplining Al Mamaux in 1916.[106] These detractors also severely chastised Jimmy for having the audacity to suspend the star hurler. Callahan received vindication when it came to that criticism.[107] On July 22, while the Pirates were in New York playing the Giants, Hugo Bezdek suspended Mamaux indefinitely for violating club discipline. Al had been ordered to travel to Pittsburgh immediately but didn't leave until one day later. On Saturday night, July 21, Mamaux failed to return to the Ansonia Hotel, where the team lodged. This rank insubordination and other delinquencies forced Hugo to render his punishment. Some of Al's buddies claimed the pitcher had been that night's guest of friends in Brooklyn. However, Mamaux hadn't requested management's permission to leave the hotel.

Barney Dreyfuss hadn't been particularly pleased over Al's cheery and content demeanor whether he won or lost baseball games.[108] Mamaux certainly didn't achieve much of the former, as he went 2–11 with a 5.25 ERA in 1917. Dreyfuss had held a conference with Bezdek in New York on Saturday to discuss Mamaux's case. Hugo had a hunch that his pitcher was breaking the rules and planned on taking swift, drastic action when he caught Al in the act. Barney replied that the Pirates' manager shouldn't have trouble finding out before offering a brief comment.[109]

"If you catch him in the act, do as you see fit," suggested Dreyfuss.[110]

Hugo Bezdek stated that it grieved him to take such action against any player on his squad. As of 10 P.M. on the day the Pirates' organization issued the suspension, Al Mamaux still hadn't returned to the Ansonia Hotel.[111] An angle to this situation put forward by one newspaper story claimed that Mamaux deliberately violated team rules to force a trade to a different team. Supposedly, when the Giants last played in Pittsburgh five weeks earlier, Al had approached New York manager John McGraw and asked him to buy his release since the hurler had grown tired of playing in Pittsburgh.[112] When Bezdek handed down his penalty, the Pirates' manager told Mamaux that the punishment's length depended entirely on the pitcher's behavior. Al's reaction to the reprimand perplexed Hugo, as the youngster refused to don a uniform for several days, although asked to do so, and instead devoted his time to playing cards in the clubhouse.[113]

On August 3, a dispatch from Chester, Pennsylvania, stated that Mamaux had signed a contract to pitch for the Delaware County League's Upland team. After local newspapers picked up this story around 10 P.M., Barney Dreyfuss and Hugo Bezdek stated they didn't know Al had signed with an independent outlaw league. When called on the telephone, Mrs. Julia Mamaux said this was news to her, adding that her son wasn't home and she didn't know where to reach him. Shortly after 3 P.M., some people had seen Al leaving the Western Union Station on Fifth Avenue, below Wood Street, in downtown Pittsburgh. At 6 P.M., dining patrons witnessed Mamaux eating dinner in a downtown restaurant. When asked to comment on this report, Bezdek said that he felt sorry for Al if the youngster had taken this step since it meant that Organized Baseball would blacklist him.[114]

The report from Delaware County League headquarters also claimed that Upland planned on paying Mamaux the $5,000 per year salary he received with the Pirates. On August 4, Al quashed this story as being untrue and without foundation while adding he planned on making the best of his opportunities in the future.[115] Mamaux cleared the hurdle bringing about expulsion weeks later. On August 20, the National League automatically blacklisted Al under Organized Baseball's rules. If a player under contract performed for an outfit beyond that institution's purview, the individual received an automatic suspension. Mamaux fell under that criterion after he pitched for Al Grayber's semi-professional squad at Esplen in the West End section of Pittsburgh one day earlier. Barney Dreyfuss refused to address the matter and declined to talk to his misguided player. This ban could only be lifted through a player petitioning the National Commission for reinstatement.[116] When Grayber had contacted Dreyfuss to receive permission to use Mamaux, Pittsburgh's owner offered a definitive response.

"I don't care what Mamaux does," said Dreyfuss. "We're through with him."

In true Al Mamaux style, manager Al Cerceo of the Bradley Eagles' semi-pro baseball team claimed he had talked to a person on the telephone about playing for his squad, who he believed to be the pitcher, but possibly could've been an imposter.[117] The combination of temperamental behavior, poor performance, and banishment indicated Al's major league career's possible end of the line. Nonetheless, Mamaux didn't plan on going quietly into the night.

In 1915, a product from the Pittsburgh suburb of Dormont, who also played for Duquesne University, achieved the status as one of the National League's top pitchers. Hurler Al Mamaux posted a 21-8 record for the Pittsburgh Pirates that year, along with a 2.04 ERA. Although Al went 21-15 in 1916, Pirates manager Jimmy Callahan suspended the young pitcher on August 18 for breaking club rules. Mamaux was guilty of pulling an all-nighter participating in a game of dice shooting in one of Pittsburgh's neighborhoods. In 1917, new skipper Hugo Bezdek also suspended Al while the Pirates played a series in New York, for failing to return to the club's Ansonia Hotel lodging on the night of July 21. (Photo in the Public Domain).

8

Temperamental Players and Malcontents Infest the Pirates' Craft

Hurler Albert Leon Mamaux never hesitated to speak his mind when he perceived that an entity such as the Pittsburgh Pirates' organization attempted to harm him somehow. When it came to Al's early days as a youngster, when he couldn't stick with local baseball squads, had the possibility existed that his attitude was the problem rather than lack of talent? Weeks after Hugo Bezdek suspended Mamaux, *Pittsburgh Post* sportswriter Harry Keck interviewed him on the evening of August 20, 1917. Al told Keck that he objected to being branded something he wasn't and that the Pirates' management hierarchy had labeled him with many unpleasant things. Mamaux's primary goal in granting an interview was to be vindicated by the fans over his alleged responsibilities for the problems he experienced that season.

> The club announced that I was suspended for "breach of the rules of discipline and training." It has not gone into detail to tell the nature of the infraction or infractions. It has left it up to the public to judge for itself, and anyone knows what the public thinks when an athlete is suspended for breach of training rules.
>
> Everywhere I go, I see people go off in pairs and whisper about the "high life" I am living. They avoid me on the streets, looking to the side as they pass me or going to the other side of the street if necessary to keep from meeting me. I might think I had done something criminal if I wasn't sure that I hadn't.

One of my friends, a lawyer, has written me from San Francisco advising me to "lay off the booze." Other people are throwing similar hints at me. And yet, I defy Barney Dreyfuss, Manager Bezdek, Jim Callahan or anybody else to prove that I have been indulging in drink or in any other way living a wild life. I defy them to prove that I have not tried to work for the club's interests.

I have been made to appear in a bad light as a result of my suspension. Nobody has ever stopped to consider my side of the case. The club's word is taken for everything and the public is led to believe that I am a good-for-nothing bum and loafer; and, as a result, I am being treated that way.

I am through with the Pirates for good. I would not work for the club for a million times the salary I was getting. Barney Dreyfuss told me his club had gotten along without Al Mamaux before and would get along without him now. Very well, Al Mamaux got along without the Pirate club before also, and will get along without it now.

Al Mamaux told Harry Keck he'd been considering becoming a salesman for a local clothing company. Al also mentioned the possibility of pitching independent baseball on the weekends, which he'd already done the day before this newspaper interview. Mamaux didn't care whether he ever pitched another game in Organized Baseball. Al declared to be an obedient employee who didn't fuss when Hugo Bezdek issued the suspension, claiming to have worked out with the team for ten days while not on the payroll. At that time, feeling he'd exhibited repentant conduct, Mamaux went to Barney Dreyfuss and asked to be reinstated to the squad. Al alleged that Dreyfuss replied to his request, saying, "Talk is cheap." Given his circumstances, Mamaux reasoned no chance existed that the organization would ever lift his suspension. He wondered why the club hadn't utilized a fine of something like $500 instead if Pittsburgh's owner truly believed the pitcher so horribly sinned. Al finished the interview by offering some final parting shots at the organization.

The only reason I can see for my getting in bad with the club is that I was costing it too much money. I had a contract calling for $5,000, and, because I couldn't get going in my best form, I guess they figured I wasn't earning that pay. There are quite a few other pitchers on the team who have records of three or four games won and 13 or 15 lost, but nothing is said about them.

Barney Dreyfuss wanted to "get" me and he did. I know for a fact that he told Manager Bezdek to get me the first time he got the goods on me, whatever he meant by the "goods." Of all the members of the club, I was singled out to be watched day and night in all my actions. The manager and others had orders to "get" me.

I have read that I was given warning that I was violating the rules. I don't know when I was ever warned this season that I was doing anything wrong until the suspension came.

This spring I was "ridden" almost to death. Callahan called me into the office every day and warned me that Dreyfuss might take drastic action in my case because I was not going well. It got to be a joke with the players.

Just make it strong that the Pirates are no more through with me than I am with them. All I care for is a vindication from the people and the way to get that vindication is for Dreyfuss to take away his blanket charge of breaking the club rules and state specifically what I have done that I should merit my very severe punishment.[1]

Al's primary issue with what he believed to be an excessive penalty centered around being ostracized in the town where he grew up and the false perception that the young hurler acted like a boozer. Mamaux proved entirely accurate about one thing. The Pittsburgh Pirates were through with him. While exhibiting temperamental behavior and acting selfish and privileged at times, he didn't endear himself to those who controlled his destiny as a major league player. On January 9, 1918, Barney Dreyfuss shipped Mamaux, fellow hurler Burleigh Grimes, and infielder Charles "Chuck" Ward to the Brooklyn Robins for second baseman George Cutshaw and outfielder Charles Dillon "Casey" Stengel.

Upon announcement of the deal, stories surfaced surrounding Al Mamaux's unwillingness to pitch his best for the Pirates in 1917 in hopes of forcing a trade to another team. The New York Giants had made several efforts to purchase Al the previous summer, but Dreyfuss rebuked them each time. Barney supposedly had turned down a $20,000 offer from John McGraw to bring the young hurler into the Giants' fold. When rejecting these overtures, Dreyfuss repeatedly declared that Mamaux was grievously mistaken if the pitcher thought he would be rewarded for his shoddy work on the mound by being traded to a championship club.[2] Upon learning about the move to Brooklyn, Al appeared thrilled over leaving Pittsburgh.

"Am I glad to get away from the Pirates?" shouted Al, repeating the query that had been put to him. "Well, you can bet your Liberty Bonds I am glad. Why shouldn't I rejoice to break away from a lot of unpleasantness.

"I was willing to take my share of the blame for any rules I may have broken, but, personally, I think I was mistreated. And some of my own teammates seemed to be in league with the management."

Mamaux also declared he would experience great pleasure over beating the Pirates when he pitched against them in 1918. Al promised to deliver his best efforts for Brooklyn while stating he liked manager Wilbert Robinson and felt his new boss would give him a square deal.[3] Mamaux also guaranteed his pitching arm sound, contradicting self-proclamations as the previous year progressed; his limb was weak, and he couldn't throw a curveball. This declaration created the impression that Al had lied about his salary wing being lame to expedite a trade to another team.[4]

Brooklyn owner Charles Ebbets and manager Wilbert Robinson quickly witnessed Mamaux's temperamental behavior. The Robins offered to pay Al a $3,200 salary in 1918. He reportedly had received $3,400 from Pittsburgh in 1917 after Barney Dreyfuss savagely slashed $2,600 off the pitcher's $6,000 salary earned in 1916. Mamaux decided to hold out for the $200 difference between what he would have netted with the Pirates in 1917 if no suspension had occurred and Ebbets's proffer. The Robins' owner only placed this figure in a contract after Al didn't respond to the magnate's letter. In this correspondence, Charles asked Mamaux how he was doing and invited him to submit fair terms for playing in 1918.[5]

The unique aspect of Al's previous contract with Pittsburgh compounded matters for all involved parties. Stating that he wanted to help Mamaux if the lad truly was dedicated to working hard and behaving, Dreyfuss sent for the hurler and his mother in the spring of 1917 and made an intriguing offer. Pittsburgh's owner proposed that Al receive $200 per month in salary over the next two years. Rather than be paid for only six months under a standard policy, Mamaux would receive his installments over twelve months. Dreyfuss suggested the remainder of any salary Al was entitled to be invested by the Pirates' owner at his discretion. According to Barney, if Mamaux fulfilled the two-year contract to his satisfaction, he would turn over that money to Pittsburgh's pitcher in a lump sum. Failure to live up to team rules resulted in forfeiture of everything other than the $200 a month Al had received.

At the time, Mamaux had been short on cash and financially in such dire straits that he found any proposition appealing. Al accepted these terms without a word of dissent and signed the agreement, which received approval from the National Commission.[6] In the end, when it came to the stalemate between Mamaux and Ebbets, Dreyfuss rode in on his white horse and saved the day. Brooklyn management immediately refuted Al's claim that he was a free agent. The Pirates' owner stepped into the breach, holding a conference in New York with Mamaux and his Pittsburgh lawyer, Thomas L. Kane, and making concessions regarding back pay from his suspension in 1917. As a result, people believed that Ebbets agreed to pay Al a $1,400 signing bonus, the total amount Pittsburgh's baseball organization owed him. Many people surmised that Dreyfuss slipped the cash amount to Brooklyn's magnate to preserve some dignity in the affair.

This ordeal for both organizations reached its conclusion when Al Mamaux heartily signed the contract. He seemed tickled to death to join forces with Robinson and felt the excellent baseball mind would improve his pitching ability. Al also expressed happiness for his mother, who would be pleased to hear that her son would again be back playing baseball. Most importantly, Mamaux's new opportunity in life made him ecstatic. Al beamed with joy when interviewed at New York's Waldorf Astoria Hotel, looking as happy as any person possibly could while celebrating by drinking buttermilk due to being a temperance lad.

"This is the happiest day of my life, and so forth," said Mamaux.[7]

On March 16, 1918, the National Commission reinstated Al Mamaux to active status after the player applied for readmittance in good standing. The commission assessed no fine, feeling the player's long layoff had been a teachable lesson.[8] Mamaux only appeared in two games for Brooklyn in 1918. On May 2, Al didn't report to Ebbets Field for an afternoon contest against the Boston Braves. That evening, Mamaux boarded a train for Boston.[9] Once arriving there, Al hoped to assist with the war effort and obtain a job at the Fore River Plant of the Bethlehem Shipbuilding Company in nearby Quincy.[10] Mamaux defended his decision, declaring he needed to support a younger brother and his mother since sibling Jack had already entered military service.[11] Sadly, that brother, William, passed away on June 7, 1919, at age thirteen.[12]

"I am not trying to avoid the draft," Mamaux said. "I am looking out for my future. I feel that I no longer am the pitcher I used to be and that I would not be of much use to Brooklyn. It is up to me to look ahead as I have a mother and a small brother to take care of. I think I can do that and at the same time do something to help win the war by working at shipbuilding. If the country wants me to fight I'll enlist in the Navy rather than be drafted. I prefer the Navy to the Army, and if I enlist I shall ask to be sent overseas at once, where I can get action. I have no desire for a soft job when there's a chance for real work."

On the morning that Mamaux abandoned his team, Danny Comerford, charged with overseeing Ebbets Field's clubhouse, told Wilbert Robinson that Al had removed his belongings from his locker after Wednesday's game. Early that same afternoon, Charles Ebbets received word from the National Commission, through Cincinnati Reds owner Garry Herrmann, that Mamaux owed St. Louis Cardinals third baseman Doug Baird $290. The hurler incurred this debt when the two played for Pittsburgh, and Herrmann wanted that amount of money taken out of Al's paycheck. When Ebbets told Robinson that he wished to speak to Mamaux, Charles's anger reached a boiling point upon being informed that the pitcher had abandoned the team.

Ebbets found Al receiving his semi-monthly paycheck before leaving for Boston to be particularly irritating.[13] He also publicly warned Mamaux that military authorities had sternly decided such employment in munitions plants wouldn't qualify as an excuse for baseball players hoping to escape the draft. The local draft board in Pittsburgh had given Al a Class 1A designation but hadn't yet called him for service to participate in the Great War in Europe.[14] Although Mr. Mamaux was now Ebbets's headache, Barney Dreyfuss needed to confront some of the issues surrounding one of the players he acquired in the trade with Brooklyn.

After the Pirates and Robins finalized their deal, the *Brooklyn Daily Eagle* reported that Casey Stengel had sent word from his home in Kansas City, Missouri, that he might balk at the transfer and was pondering the possibility of enlisting in the Army.[15] In another dispatch he sent to the newspaper, Casey expressed joy regarding the move. Stengel conveyed disappointment over leaving Brooklyn's fans before stating he was delighted to be getting away from Charles Ebbets, whom the player had previously criticized. Ebbets responded to this comment, declaring that when Casey came to Brooklyn one month earlier to discuss his contract, the player had threatened to join the Navy if he didn't receive a raise from his 1917 salary of $4,000. When Charles told the player that he wouldn't prevent any member of the Robins from enlisting and didn't plan on adding a nickel in potential salary to any individual's contract possibly contemplating fighting for their country, Stengel changed his tactics.

Rebuffed in his effort to garner more money by using the patriotic ploy, Stengel then demanded that Ebbets trade him to either the New York Giants or Chicago Cubs. Brooklyn's owner told Casey that transferring the outfielder would be a move to the organization that offered the best players in return while also striking down the possibility of any cash sale.[16] Stengel joined the Pirates for the 1918 campaign and appeared in 39 games. When Pittsburgh completed a June series against the Robins, Stengel remained behind as the team traveled to Boston. Casey decided to enter the Navy. Stengel expected to be drafted and had easily passed his physical tests administered by the Army.

"The doc took a look at me and pronounced me a perfect man," said Stengel when it came to the Army physical.[17]

After the Great War ended on November 11, 1918, Barney Dreyfuss soon realized what Charles Ebbets had to deal with regarding Casey negotiating a contract. Stengel claimed he didn't want to play in Pittsburgh and requested a trade. To grant Casey's wish, the Pirates' owner couldn't make an acceptable deal that improved his ball club. Barney then tendered Stengel a contract in the mail, but the outfielder ignored it. Dreyfuss communicated with Casey once before deciding to give him the silent treatment so the player could contemplate his action. Although Stengel remained a holdout and didn't join his teammates in Birmingham, Alabama, for spring training, club officials weren't concerned since they knew Casey worked out daily with the American Association's Kansas City Blues.

The silent treatment had the desired effect. Dreyfuss received a telegram from Stengel on the morning of April 10, telling his boss he'd accepted the original terms offered him while also asking where he should report to join the team.[18] This didn't prevent Casey from griping over his salary situation as the season progressed. Barney had tired of dealing with men who constantly bickered and haggled over the money situation. A considerable part of the breach between Dreyfuss and former hurler Al Mamaux came about because of the Dormont lad's insistence on constantly asking for more money. According to Barney, Mamaux believed he should receive a salary boost for each victory he achieved on the mound. When such raises weren't forthcoming, a temperamental Al displayed indifference in his deportment. Such behavior greatly annoyed Dreyfuss.

Pittsburgh's owner approved offering salary increases to players earning the hike on merit. Over time, he'd become disgusted with the ballplayers who incessantly complained since these individuals usually didn't deserve salary increases as frequently as they asked.[19] In Dreyfuss's eyes, Al Mamaux and Casey Stengel were cut from the same cloth. Just as he'd done with Mamaux, Barney disposed of his latest problem. On the night of August 9, 1919, the Pirates' club announced they'd shipped Casey to the Philadelphia Phillies for the multipurpose George "Possum" Whitted, who played the outfield, first base, and second base.

Throughout the 1919 season, Stengel's dissatisfaction became evident and affected his play. Occasional loafing by Casey even turned the right-field bleacher fans against him, who had been supportive when others at Forbes Field harshly roasted the outfielder. During Stengel's spring holdout, Dreyfuss had informed the outfielder he was at liberty to make any deal for himself, provided the team, in return, received equal value. Casey couldn't pull anything together besides a cash bid from New York, which Barney rejected. This stance further peeved Stengel, who never seemed happy playing in Pittsburgh.[20] Pirates fans generally expressed little regret over Casey's transfer to the Phillies.[21] These same patrons probably weren't surprised when Stengel initially refused to report to Philadelphia.[22]

Subsequently, Pittsburgh wasn't getting a truly model citizen in return, as George Whitted, too, had been a disgruntled employee. Before the 1919 season started, Whitted had vehemently declared to Phillies owner William Baker that he no longer wished to play in Philadelphia. To appease George, Baker stripped popular, diligent first baseman Frederick "Fred" Luderus of the captaincy and elevated Whitted to that position. George performed admirably for manager Clifford "Gavvy" Cravath after he took control of the reins from John "Jack" Coombs on July 9. Since Cravath didn't want any unhappy players on his squad, he jumped at the opportunity to trade Whitted to the Pirates.[23] Sportswriter James "Jimmie" Isaminger of the *Philadelphia North American*, a harsh critic of the Phillies' owner, panned the pretext behind shipping George to Pittsburgh.

"Whitted incurred Baker's displeasure and has been a marked man for several weeks," commented Isaminger. "He has been accused of being a disorganizer, when, as a matter of fact, he is one of the best-liked players in the profession. Whitted has ever been an inspiration to his pals. Bubbling over with good humor at all times, he was always a pleasing personality in the clubhouse and on the road. Players of the Whitted type help a team, but of course, once Baker conceived a dislike for him, he had to go."[24]

George Whitted helped the Pirates immensely in 1919, appearing in 35 games and batting .389. Dan Daniel, a sportswriter for New York's *The Sun*, felt this trade might be a precursor for a managerial change in Pittsburgh. He reasoned that the Pirates had acquired Whitted as a candidate to replace Hugo Bezdek as the squad's field leader. Daniel held that while Hugo recently took a two-week leave of absence for his health, outfielder Max Carey, with second baseman George Cutshaw's assistance, hadn't displayed overwhelming leadership or experienced stellar success overseeing the squad.[25]

On July 22, while the Pirates completed an eastern swing in Philadelphia, Bezdek left the team and returned to his Pittsburgh home. His wife, Victoria Benson Bezdek, had implored her husband, who suffered from a nervous attack, to come home to recuperate.[26] Hugo consulted a specialist who recommended he take a long rest or suffer a physical breakdown.[27] Although newspapers reported the true nature of Bezdek's sickness, Barney Dreyfuss alleged that he'd never received any explanation from the manager regarding his situation. Carey took control of the club after not playing for weeks due to an abscess on his arm. Once Hugo rejoined the Pirates, rumors abounded that he planned on resigning as manager and that Max likely would be named as his successor.[28]

Although under contract through the 1920 season, Bezdek seemed committed to quitting baseball and entirely focusing on collegiate athletics. Hugo also remained contracted as the head of athletics at Penn State University until the fall of 1920. Some believed he might return to Oregon University under the same title, where Bezdek experienced previous success as coach of that program's football team. Hugo had done exemplary work for the Pirates, despite having no prior experience managing a professional baseball team. He'd taken control of a disorganized, rag-tag lot of players and nurtured a semblance of order from the chaos.[29] Pittsburgh proved a solid basement dweller in that first year of 1917 when Bezdek received his managerial appointment in July. During the war-shortened 1918 season, Hugo brought the Pirates home fourth with a 65–60 record. Pittsburgh maintained that spot in the standings in 1919, going 71–68.

Hugo Bezdek seemed more determined than ever to walk away from baseball because he'd become quite a favorite of both fans and administrators at Penn State.[30] Throughout his more than two years managing the Pirates, Bezdek experienced a few confrontations with Barney Dreyfuss over the team since Pittsburgh's owner wasn't always the most pleasant boss to work beside. One scribe suggested that Fred Clarke had gotten along with Barney because he shouted louder than the diminutive Pirates magnate.[31] Barney accepted Hugo's resignation after the campaign ended. Bezdek, who'd suffered a nervous breakdown the previous summer, decided this to be a sensible move from a health standpoint. Hugo also wanted to devote energy to drilling Penn State's football team throughout the year.[32]

Newspapers mentioned former Cubs second baseman John "Johnny" Evers as a possible successor, along with current Pirates player George Cutshaw.[33] New York sportswriter Joseph "Joe" Vila wrote that Dreyfuss shouldn't overlook brilliant Giants infielder Lawrence "Larry" Doyle when considering candidates.[34] While in Cincinnati attending World Series games between the Reds and the Chicago White Sox, Barney held conferences with Evers on several occasions. Pittsburgh's owner denied these discussions had anything to do with

Johnny coming aboard as his manager. Evers still seemed to be the odds-on choice to be offered the job.[35] In the end, it wasn't Johnny or either of the two Georges named Cutshaw and Whitted who took control of the team. A different George with a previous connection to the organization ended up being Dreyfuss's choice to manage the Pirates in 1920.

On the afternoon of December 8, 1919, team secretary Leslie Constans announced that former catcher George Gibson had agreed to pilot Pittsburgh. "Gibby," as referred to during his playing days, had carefully mulled Barney Dreyfuss's offer before accepting the position. This announcement didn't come as a surprise since Pirates fans knew negotiations were ongoing between the two parties. George had also resigned as manager of the International League's Toronto Maple Leafs, a team he brought home second in 1919. A simple, concise telegram, sent by Gibson from his Mount Brydges, Ontario, home to Dreyfuss, sealed the deal.

"Your terms accepted," wrote Gibson. "More than pleased to be with the Pirates again. Will meet you in New York Wednesday."[36]

The *Pittsburgh Post* reported that official efforts to bring Gibby aboard only occurred after Hugo Bezdek had rejected Barney Dreyfuss's ultimatum. Pittsburgh's owner had told Bezdek that if he wanted to continue as Pirates manager, Hugo would be required to sever all ties with Penn State.[37] Gibson planned to meet Dreyfuss in New York so the two men could discuss important matters regarding the team and spring training. George had been a consistent performer for Pittsburgh as a player from 1905 through 1916.[38] On August 15, 1916, Gibson had drawn his release to the New York Giants. Gibby initially refused to report since he felt the organization should've afforded him the courtesy of receiving his unconditional release as a player with ten years of major league service. He finally joined the Giants in 1917 after agreeing to terms with John McGraw. Gibson's job description included coaching pitchers as the New York manager's lieutenant.[39]

In 1916, George had acted as Al Mamaux's personal catcher since the two experienced great rapport and proved a successful combination. Manager Jimmy Callahan surprised Pirates fans when he split up that winning ticket in a game against New York on August 2 at the Polo Grounds. Walter Schmidt worked behind the plate as the Giants routed Mamaux and defeated Pittsburgh, 6–2.[40] Gibson's time in a Pirates uniform ended weeks later when the team asked for waivers on him, and New York placed a bid for his services. Since Barney Dreyfuss had promised to release Gibby unconditionally when that time in his career came, the veteran catcher felt he should receive the waiver price as a bonus for joining the Giants. George temporarily retired when Pittsburgh's owner refused to consent to this wish. Dreyfuss claimed he never intended to sell or trade Gibson when making the waiver request but only followed league regulations before liberating the catcher.[41]

In his first season at the helm in 1920, George Gibson guided the Pirates to a fourth-place finish with a 79–75 record. Sensing that Pittsburgh possessed a weakness at the shortstop position, which various individuals had covered since Honus Wagner retired in 1917, Gibson focused his energy on eliminating that massive hole in the lineup during the off-season. Gibby finally acquired the player that had been on his radar for months. On January 23, 1921, the Pirates traded outfielders William "Billy" Southworth and Fred Nicholson, along with infielder Walter Barbare, to the Boston Braves for spunky shortstop Walter "Rabbit" Maranville. Owner Barney Dreyfuss also included a check for a generous amount that he didn't make public to close the deal (later reported to be $15,000). When asked to divulge how much cash he'd given Boston, Barney only smiled and said it was enough to make that organization very happy.

Negotiations regarding this transaction had been ongoing for months.[42] Shortly after consummating the deal, a Cincinnati newspaper claimed that a "hypnotized" Dreyfuss had planned to hand over 77 percent of Pittsburgh's playing strength to Braves owner George Grant before Gibson intervened, nixing this alleged deal. Such an absurd suggestion caused Gibson to smile since Pittsburgh's owner never participated in the Maranville negotiations. When George started talks during a baseball meeting in Kansas City, Missouri, Dreyfuss assured the manager that he backed his instincts regarding the matter. Discussions commenced at the December league meetings in New York before Gibby made his final offer while the National and American organizations held joint sessions in Chicago. Dreyfuss only rendered final approval when Grant accepted Gibson's terms.[43]

Those who believed that Max Carey or George Whitted might be involved in a transaction for Rabbit Maranville throughout this ongoing process ended up guessing incorrectly.[44] Maranville had debuted with Boston in 1912 and played an integral role in the Braves' 1914 pennant-winning season and subsequent victory over the Philadelphia Athletics in the World Series. Although Rabbit acted as a sparkplug on the field, he tended to be a livewire away from the diamond. When informed by telephone at his home in Springfield, Massachusetts, about the trade, Maranville didn't seem overly thrilled about joining the Pirates.

"I want to play baseball in Boston more than I want to play it in any other city," stated Maranville. "I want to know all about this trade before I do a thing. But I do not want to leave Boston and I do not want to go to Pittsburgh, and I don't think I'll go. You bet they will have to talk to me about this trade business."[45]

Pirates management appeased Maranville by talking to him about the contract business. On January 30, Barney Dreyfuss and George Gibson quietly left Pittsburgh for New York. Before making this excursion, the two Pirates representatives contacted Rabbit and asked him to meet them there on January 31. When Maranville arrived at the hotel where Gibson and Dreyfuss lodged, Pittsburgh's owner handed the pint-sized shortstop a document already filled out with specific numbers. Rabbit briefly perused the contract, found it satisfactory, smiled as he declared approval over the terms, picked up a pen, and signed his name in the proper spot. That night, Pirates team treasurer Samuel "Sam" Dreyfuss, Barney's son, announced this colossal news about Maranville signing a one-year deal to the press.[46]

The younger Dreyfuss's involvement in the operational side of the club started after he graduated from Princeton University in 1919 and quickly became team treasurer in 1921. Born on November 9, 1896, in Louisville, Kentucky, while his father was part-owner of that city's Colonels franchise, Sam received his early education at the Liberty School after the family moved to Pittsburgh. He then attended Shady Side Academy and graduated in 1915.[47] Since his younger days attending grade school, Sam spent a good deal of time around the Pirates.[48] Upon returning home from Princeton for Thanksgiving in 1917, Samuel informed Barney of his intention to enlist in the United States Army Aviation Corps after showing an interest in airplanes and flying at college. Pondering his son's decision, Pittsburgh's owner concluded that Sam could now think for himself since he'd passed out of boyhood. Barney consented, expressing great pride in the spirit of patriotism his son demonstrated.[49]

Although expectations ran high for 1921 and a possible pennant seemed within grasp, in the end, problems plagued the Pirates' organization as fans turned on the players as they had in the past. Of course, these rooters weren't without justification for engaging in jeering and razzing. With the potential for success came a renewed desire by gamblers to make their voices heard at Forbes Field. Difficulty in extricating these pests from the ballpark became rampant for many reasons. Before the home opener on April 21 against Cincinnati, Pittsburgh Public Safety Director Robert J. Alderdice and Police Commissioner John C. Calhoun of the Oakland district decreed that all gambling at Forbes Field must desist. To enforce this directive, these officials planned on working hand-in-hand with the team to root out such evil.

Both parties agreed upon one hundred uniformed officers and twenty plainclothes policemen stationing themselves at various parts of the ballpark for the home opener. These law enforcement officials acquainted themselves with known convicted gamblers and then expelled these individuals from the grounds if they succeeded in gaining entrance past the gatekeepers. Officers then furnished ticket-takers with the names and descriptions of those arrested so guilty parties could be refused admission in the future. This anti-gambling crusade by Pittsburgh police aligned with the policies of authorities and political leaders from other major league cities.[50] Barney Dreyfuss once said to Al Mamaux that talk is cheap. This dynamic was apparent when it came to cleaning up corruption related to betting on baseball in Pittsburgh.

After receiving little or no assistance from local police officials, Dreyfuss, on June 9, declared war against all known gamblers who frequented Forbes Field, vowing they wouldn't gain admittance to the baseball facility.[51] Barney contended that despite twenty policemen being assigned as a detail to assist Pirates officials, gamblers still carried out their activities in various ballpark sections. Dreyfuss levied further charges that most likely aroused the attention of Allegheny County District Attorney Harry Rowand and Thomas Carroll, the new Pittsburgh superintendent of police.

> Gamblers, mostly of the gutter-snipe class, although there are others, gamble openly in the ballpark. They even make bets outside the door of my own office, as well as the streets surrounding the park.
>
> I have repeatedly appealed to the police, but get no satisfaction.
>
> There seems to be some unseen power at work, protecting gamblers here. I have found gambling conditions in no city as they exist in Pittsburgh. They seem to act with impunity; plain evidence to me that protection money is being paid to someone "higher up."[52]

The recently elected baseball commissioner, Judge Kenesaw Mountain Landis, promised his assistance after Dreyfuss alerted him that police magistrates quickly discharged Forbes Field's gamblers following their arrest. Committed to eradicating all types of gambling from baseball on the heels of the 1919 World Series scandal involving the Chicago White Sox, Landis made a trip to Pittsburgh on June 20 and met with Pittsburgh's owner at the Schenley Hotel.[53] As always, the commissioner struck a straightforward tone upon telling reporters he intended to handle this problem. Judge Landis exhibited the scrappy demeanor of a boxer when offering his opinion regarding magistrates discharging gamblers on orders from their political bosses.

> Mr. Dreyfuss has explained the whole situation to me. The Pittsburgh club has the ground thoroughly covered by police officers who it pays $5 a day. Crooks caught violating the anti-gambling law have been taken to the police station, a block from the park, and there discharged by whoever is authorized by Pennsylvania law or city ordinances to turn criminals loose.
>
> Mr. Dreyfuss will have all the support I can give him. I have a suspicion that, politics or no politics, we'll put a stop to this gambling.
>
> I haven't decided whether I shall call upon Mayor Babcock myself, but baseball can get rid of undesirable elements in its ranks or around its baseball parks whether the police aid or not.[54]

Pittsburgh Mayor Edward V. Babcock, who didn't kindly receive Judge Landis's harsh accusation, angrily replied, "It was your city, Chicago, not Pittsburgh, that produced the national gambling scandal." Babcock railed against Landis for not arranging any meeting with him before levying such charges.[55] In a statement to the press, Pittsburgh's mayor alleged that the commissioner's comments were both unfair and based on false information. Babcock invited Landis to visit him before the latter returned to Chicago.[56] Councilman W. Y. English also expressed his displeasure over these allegations, saying that if wagering indeed existed at Forbes Field, it should be closed down just like the activities in any gambling house.[57]

As was the case when perceived corruption existed, evil perpetrators sometimes utilized deflection as a critical tool. Commissioner John C. Calhoun stated that all his officers reported under the command of Milton Bailey, a former Pittsburgh inspector of police employed by Barney Dreyfuss. Calhoun also said his men conveyed that no evidence of gambling existed in the ballpark.[58] Strained relations between the Pirates' organization and local police reached a breaking point in July. Barney Dreyfuss discontinued friendly outreach with Pittsburgh's police department over Public Safety Director Robert J. Alderdice's refusal to allow his officers to arrest grandstand patrons who persisted in keeping foul balls hit into that section. On July 30, team secretary Samuel "Sam" Watters explained the organization's new policy regarding plainclothes officers, city detectives, and policemen gaining permission and access to enter the ballpark through the pass-gate.

"Plainclothesmen and city detectives come here in droves and are admitted on their badges," said Watters, "with the idea that they would break up the gambling evil alleged to exist at Forbes Field, but they have never done a thing to stop it. They don't even locate themselves in the territory where the bettors are, but find themselves in nice boxes on the roof of the stand and enjoy the game. Hereafter they will have to pay their way in."[59]

The gravy train reached its end for Pittsburgh public servants taking advantage of Barney Dreyfuss. Prime seats were essential to paying customers since the Pirates looked to be a strong contender to win the National League pennant. On the night Watters issued this statement about the organization's new policy, Pittsburgh and New York stood atop the standings, tied with 60–35 records. A solid August run allowed the Pirates to break free and pad a decent lead over their longtime rival. When Pittsburgh started a five-game series against the Giants at the Polo Grounds on August 24, their margin in front of New York stood at 7½ games. The Giants eradicated months of hard work and sweat in just four days as they swept the series. In the process of suffering such a devastating setback, a disappointing precipitous fall of their doing started, which Buccaneers team members quickly found couldn't be reversed.

Before the game against New York on August 25, the team met in manager George Gibson's hotel room. The group discussed club matters where they explored errors of omission and commission in an unforgiving fashion related to the performance in a doubleheader one day earlier when the Giants outscored them 17–2 in the two games.[60] The eastern trip initially appeared to be salvaged when Pittsburgh secured victories in two out of three contests against Brooklyn.

Throughout the 1921 campaign, four Pirates players entertained Forbes Field's fans with musical interludes before games. This frolicsome harmonious quartet consisted of Possum Whitted, Rabbit Maranville, second baseman James "Cotton" Tierney, and first baseman Charles "Charlie" Grimm.[61] Harnessing that vaudevillian spirit, Gibson changed things up for pregame practice before the series finale against the Robins on August 30 by abandoning standard protocol.[62]

Pittsburgh's manager had the infielders pitch to hitters in batting practice to relieve the tension and pressure while permitting every pitcher to take their cuts at the plate. Tierney, Grimm, third baseman Clyde "Pooch" Barnhart, and others tossed pitches as the hurlers slammed baseballs all over Ebbets Field. When Rabbit's turn came on the bump, he donned catcher Walter Schmidt's mask. Pitchers Lyle Bigbee and Charles "Whitey" Glazner cracked a few balls over the fence while Gibson slammed some of Barnhart's offerings for clean hits. This unique diamond burlesque show pleased the spectators and worked wonders for the Pirates' confidence as they battered the Robins, 8–2.[63] A merry atmosphere prevailed when the team boarded the train to return home to Pittsburgh, as various players tuned up guitars, mandolins, banjos, and ukuleles in celebration of the victory. Pittsburgh's manager sanctioned such behavior as a fantastic, stress-relieving outlet.

"That's just what I want you to do," remarked Gibby, "try to divert your thoughts momentarily from the game, for worrying has made you overanxious."

Encouraged by Gibson, the musicians cut loose, and when a cornet entered the ensemble, the loud jazz music quickly drowned out any noise made by the locomotive.[64] Upon returning home, poor diamond performance quickly extinguished that loose atmosphere when Pittsburgh played a doubleheader against the St. Louis Cardinals at Forbes Field on September 1. After the Cardinals scored three runs in game one's first inning, a razzing chorus started cascading from the stands. One fan shouted, "Take Maranville out and drown him," while the angry patrons subjected other players to similar vicious taunts.[65] The bulk of the abuse in the first contest came from gamblers stationed in the ballpark's grandstand. By the time the second game concluded, as the Pirates succumbed to St. Louis by scores of 10–4 and 8–0, regular male rooters became so disgusted with the display that they started heckling the squad. A person attending from outside the city might've believed that Pittsburgh took up residence in the cellar rather than being pacesetters.

Leading the league, albeit by only one game over New York, appeared to be of little consequence to these angry fans, who'd become aware of stories about wild nighttime parties and broken training rules that resulted in substandard diamond execution. Rumors frequently mentioned Rabbit Maranville as one of these offenders.[66] As was the case with all major league squads, injuries and illness presented a problem as some individuals dealt with various issues. Tonsillitis briefly sidelined stalwart catcher Walter Schmidt. Following a Labor Day doubleheader split with Cincinnati at Forbes Field on September 5, the Pirates had three days off from major league games (they participated in two exhibition contests) to recharge the batteries before resuming their schedule against Chicago.[67]

Many of the players relaxed on September 6 by playing golf. Barney Dreyfuss invited some of his men to the Westmoreland Country Club while others enjoyed a round at different courses. Possum Whitted, Cotton Tierney, and former Pirates player Hoke "Hooks" Warner played thirty-six holes at the

Schenley Park golf course. Pitcher Moses "Chief" Yellow Horse followed the others around the links before finally trying the game for the first time on several tees.[68] The rest didn't help much, as Pittsburgh lost to Chicago, 8–5, when the squad resumed playing on September 9.

According to William A. White of the *Pittsburgh Post*, some people in town believed the Pirates shouldn't be criticized or knocked. While these individuals stated patrons had razzed Pittsburgh's players on various occasions, White contended that paying rooters had likewise been subjected to such treatment by watching an inferior diamond product. The writer then compared baseball to a store. William asserted that when a customer walked into an establishment and shelled out good money to purchase a high-end product, the person expected that the item worked and functioned as advertised. When a product didn't meet that standard, White felt an individual had the right to object or complain. He then asked why the same rule didn't apply to baseball. If the fans were willing to pay high prices to watch these gifted athletes, the expectation existed that players should perform up to their capabilities.

White further concurred that when a baseball owner paid generous salaries to these men, that magnate expected maximum performance for their money. Players who failed to keep in condition through dissipation cheated their employer and the fans. William concluded that various Pirates team members better wake up to the fact that the public had caught on to their shenanigans. The time had come for these individuals to go to bed at a reasonable hour and abandon the lifestyle of partying at night, visiting roadhouses, and other unsavory places. Such behavior proved detrimental for any athlete, let alone a pennant contending baseball team player. White understood that it was unreasonable to expect baseball players not to slip up occasionally during a long season. He believed such an approach to be counterproductive when it started becoming habitual.[69]

Some of the reasons behind William White's comments in his article came to light in the *Pittsburgh Press* as the Pirates prepared to open a critical series against New York at Forbes Field on September 16. In a letter to sports editor Ralph S. Davis which appeared in that newspaper, a North Side resident named Mr. McCullough wrote that Pittsburgh had no chance of winning the National League pennant unless they secured two victories over the Giants. McCullough then referenced the two previous occasions in 1921 when New York visited Forbes Field and captured three out of four games each time. He claimed that a person connected to the Giants' organization in both instances had taken several Pirates team members out for nighttime jaunts where the liquor flowed freely. These boozers had to be put to bed each time, and Pittsburgh proved no match for the Giants. Although Mr. McCullough stated that he supported the Pirates and always rooted for them to win, the players couldn't expect everybody to remain by their side after pulling such stunts.[70]

A fellow local baseball fan who read Mr. McCullough's letter penned his correspondence that appeared in Davis's column on September 19. While talking with a friend on the day Pittsburgh opened their series against New York, his buddy told the letter writer that on the night of September 15, some of Pittsburgh's players visited a club in his neighborhood where they heavily consumed alcohol. This person's friend concluded the Pirates wouldn't defeat the Giants due to such behavior.

The letter writer opined that if such stories happened to be accurate, why hadn't the offenders been suspended for breaking training rules? This devoted patron concluded by stating that the club should clear their names if these players were innocent. If guilty, they hurt baseball as much as the Black Sox did in the 1919 World Series and should receive punishment.[71] The *Pittsburgh Press* didn't want to be the judge or jury regarding boozers. McCullough had supplied the names of Pittsburgh's players and New York's nocturnal entertainment agent in his letter, but the newspaper refused to print them, although many Western Pennsylvania citizens knew their identities.[72]

Upon arriving in Pittsburgh, the Giants issued an interesting request regarding the drinking water at Forbes Field. The home club usually was responsible for providing drinking water for visiting players, but manager John McGraw wasn't happy with this arrangement.[73] McGraw called up a local company that supplied bottled water and ordered them to send a large quantity to Forbes Field for the series. One of the conditions insisted upon by the Giants' organization was that they wouldn't pay for the water unless each bottle remained sealed and the stamp hadn't experienced any tampering when they received the shipment.[74]

New York's manager also mandated that none of his men associate or commiserate with Pittsburgh's players or fans throughout the series' duration. The Giants remained sequestered in their hotel the entire time, other than when appearing at Forbes Field. They endured isolation from outside forces in the morning and evening.[75] John tasked coaches Jesse Burkett, Hughie Jennings, John "Hans" Lobert, and Cozy Dolan with enforcement of this directive. McGraw exhibited paranoia when possessing provenance over drinking water, fearing poison or knockout drops could end up in the aqua pura by following standard procedure.[76] This concern resulted from possible retaliation by Pirates team members or fans because of Giants agents' underhanded tactics of luring some players to roadhouses on previous trips to Pittsburgh.[77] George Gibson's troops expressed stunned disbelief and resented the implication that they might resort to deceitful measures to beat their adversary.[78]

Anger over such a charge didn't translate into fire and brimstone on the diamond as New York secured two out of the three contests. The Giants now led the race by 3½ games. Their record stood at 90–55, while the Pirates were in second with a mark of 85–57. As the Corsairs floundered down the home stretch, many questioned how things had reached this point. On September 18, *Pittsburgh Post* sportswriter Regis M. Welsh wondered how a team that had been in the lead by 7½ games less than a month ago found themselves 4½ behind New York. He pondered that even when taking excessive drinking into account, such a collapse seemed incomprehensible. Besides blaming the players for their horrible performance over the past two weeks, the writer also found much fault with coach William "Bill" Hinchman and manager George Gibson.

Welsh claimed that Hinchman worked the coaching lines at third base horrendously, costing the club runs throughout the 1921 campaign. Bill either sent runners to their demise at the plate when caution appeared to be the correct strategy or exhibited too much prudence holding up players at third when chances to secure a tally proved better than 50 percent. Welsh mentioned that third base at Forbes Field had been appropriately named "Suicide Corner." Regis then criticized Gibson over pitching decisions and a reluctance to play small ball by bunting to gain early momentum in games by pushing a run across home plate. Welsh cited the use of rookie William "Bill" Hughes in relief against Boston at Forbes Field on September 15 (Hughes's only major league appearance) to back the claim that Gibby mishandled his pitchers. Regis also detailed the crushed spirit of Pittsburgh's players when they took the field in the seventh inning of that contest. With heads down, dawdling to their positions on the diamond, they looked like someone had forced them from the bench with a whip.[79]

George Gibson addressed questions over his team's collapse, rumors about players drinking excessively, and criticism regarding his managerial decisions. Gibson spoke to local press members on the evening of September 19, after Pittsburgh gained their single positive result of the New York series, beating the Giants that afternoon, 2–1.

> The Pirates have not quit. We are not out of the pennant race by any means and do not intend giving up until the last game is played.

There is one thing that happens to every ball team and that is what is known as the slump. Seldom ever in a season does any club escape it. The Pirates were no exception this year, but unfortunately our slump came at a period in the race when it hurt the most.

As for these stories which are being circulated about the players, people are liable to say anything when a ball team is losing. The ballplayer, in the heat of a close game, often gets worked up to such a high tension that he makes remarks on the spur of the moment, that he would not think of making under ordinary circumstances. The fan may say things just the same as do the players, for all have their heart in the game and hate to see matters going bad. But such remarks do not hurt the fans as badly as they hurt us.

I also will state that I am not opposed to hearing that one of my players has taken a glass of beer, but it is a positive fact that not one of the Pirates this entire year has appeared on the ball field when he was not in condition to give his best efforts to the team. While I do not lay claim to having a Sunday school team, I know that these Pirates take better care of themselves than 90 percent of all the ball clubs in the business. But it is what the men do upon the field, that concerns me.[80]

Pittsburgh's fans might contend that the Pirates were no longer contenders in the race. Patrons and sportswriters attempted to answer one probing question as pennant hopes flickered. Why didn't Pittsburgh win? One answer, accepted by many as quite logical, contended that the feisty Pirates played well above their heads throughout most of the season and simply folded when the truly threatening squads confronted them. The second plausible response to this query was team members performing like a group of cowardly quitters. A third and most likely option surrounded the contention that numerous players happened to be despicable ingrates who threw away pennant glory in the pursuit of alcohol and nights of pleasure.[81] In the wake of the Chicago White Sox scandal, many followers believed false tales about the players purposely selling out and possessing crooked intent. Sportswriter Ralph Davis received many letters from patrons who felt the team didn't try to win the pennant.[82]

In their final 12 games, following the victory over New York on September 19, the Pirates' record was 5–6, with umpires stopping another game after nine innings with the score tied, 4–4. Before St. Louis smacked down Pittsburgh, 12–4, at Sportsman's Park on September 30, Cardinals star second baseman Rogers Hornsby received an odd telegram from an alleged Pirates baseball fan. The telegram read, "Everyone in Pittsburgh is pulling for you to beat out those spineless pie-rats."[83] As the Pirates' players trudged through the mud to the clubhouse after defeating St. Louis, 4–3, in the season finale on October 2, they shouted in unison, "It's over." The juxtaposition seemed eerie when compared to a month ago. At the beginning of September, all the glitz and grand trappings of a possible World Series appearance danced in their heads, while a cold, driving rain greeted them, in the end, during this meaningless contest.[84]

Pittsburgh finished with a 90–63 record in 1921, good for second place, four games behind pennant-winning New York. As the campaign mercifully concluded, many rooters probably echoed *Pittsburgh Post* sportswriter Regis M. Welsh's sentiment that he hoped the Pirates' musical quartet had sung their last refrain.[85] Ralph S. Davis of the *Pittsburgh Press* took this idea further. Davis felt Barney Dreyfuss should include an anti-singing clause in all 1922 player contracts. He contended that the "Singing Quartet" became very unpopular as the season progressed.

Some fans interpreted this desire to constantly sing as meaning these diamond performers lacked interest in doing the job Barney Dreyfuss paid them to undertake. Davis alleged that the clown antics and monkeyshines appeared novel for about one day. These shenanigans originally supplied laughs for a few patrons, but the ordeal became monotonous over time. The writer decreed that if baseball lovers wanted to see vaudeville, they could go to variety houses and didn't need exposure to it at the ballpark. Davis concluded by writing that Dreyfuss paid his men to play baseball, not to make fools of themselves on the sidelines or the diamond.[86]

After the Pirates played their final game, Ralph S. Davis reported that another key reason behind the team's demise was the existence of too many cliques on the squad since the season opened. Certain players were inseparable, exclusively eating and socializing with each other. This particular faction resented any attempt by other teammates to wedge their way into the exclusive group. This group snubbed both regulars and substitutes. Some second-stringers didn't appreciate being shunned and not permitted to gain entry on the inside and resented such treatment. Early in the season, a fistfight involving three or four players had broken out in the clubhouse following a game. This disharmony continued to fester throughout the campaign, as management didn't intervene and allowed members of the Buccaneers more freedom than any other major leaguers received.[87]

Another story surfaced about Pittsburgh's players' excessive drinking in the Prohibition Era. The report claimed that when New York made their final trip to the city, three Pirates team members and three or four Giants players became entangled in a raid on a notorious inn in the city's heart. According to some accounts, John McGraw drank at the establishment but escaped arrest, while Giants players Casey Stengel and Arthur "Art" Nehf received severe beatings amidst the chaos. Police escorted Pittsburgh's involved players to the police station before releasing them on forfeit. Police remained silent about the incident, and the press could glean no accurate version of the events. One plausible account was that some local independent baseball players had been captured and then gave out the names of Pirates and Giants players to hide their identities.[88] So much for McGraw's men remaining sequestered throughout that final series if this theory about independent baseball players didn't pass muster.

In anticipation of a potential World Series at Forbes Field, Barney Dreyfuss had architects draw up designs to expand the ballpark's seating capacity by building stands in left and center fields. The Pittsburgh baseball organization expected these improvements to increase the capacity by 10,000 fans beyond the 30,000 that currently existed. At the end of August, Dreyfuss had gone to New York to discuss these plans with league president John Heydler.[89] This precise planning went for naught. As the season concluded, several Pirates players declared they'd been invited to participate in an off-season barnstorming trip to Cuba. Others stated they planned on playing in California over the winter to earn some extra money.[90] Barney scuttled all these intentions, announcing that none of his players would be permitted to play winter league ball or participate in barnstorming trips.[91]

Barney Dreyfuss paid his players quite handsomely in 1921. On good authority, scribes and fans believed Pittsburgh's salary list was one of the largest in major league baseball. Furthermore, its team payroll was the highest in the organization's history. This fact didn't seem to satisfy many of the Pirates' players. As Ralph Davis wrote in his column on October 3, "Perhaps they think they did too much for the club this year. Instead of losing the pennant in September, perhaps they figure they should have lost it in May."[92] With disappointment, turmoil, and mayhem pervasive and counterproductive, changes to the squad became inevitable. Fallout over the team's failure in 1921 went far and wide. Regrettably, it took years to sift through the rubble and move all the perpetrators out of Pittsburgh.

On December 8, 1919, Pittsburgh Pirates team secretary Leslie Constans announced the hiring of George Gibson to replace Hugo Bezdek as the club's manager. Gibson, a former catcher, played for Pittsburgh from 1905 through 1916. In 1921, the Pirates appeared poised to win the National League pennant until the New York Giants swept them in a late August, five-game series at the Polo Grounds. Pittsburgh stumbled throughout September and finished in second place. Critics blamed George for the late-season collapse, stating he mishandled his pitchers and didn't crack down on rule breakers who engaged in drinking alcohol. During a press interview, Gibson stuck up for his players and declared that every baseball team slumped at some point during the season. (Courtesy of the Library of Congress).

9

Shipping Out the Troublemakers and the Boozers

Many devoted followers of the Pittsburgh Pirates felt devastated when the squad faltered and failed to win the 1921 National League pennant. One of the area's most ardent fans was Charles "Chilly" Doyle, a Pittsburgh *Gazette Times* sportswriter. For years after this disappointing course of diamond events, Doyle refused to forecast the Pirates' chances of copping the flag. When it came to the Singing Quartet's musical interludes in 1921, courtesy of Charlie Grimm, Cotton Tierney, Rabbit Maranville, and Possum Whitted, Chilly, years later, offered a straightforward reason for the team's failure in that fateful August series against the New York Giants.

"We came in to New York singing and went out dying," recalled Doyle.[1]

Fans and sportswriters had offered many reasons for Pittsburgh's inability to stave off the ferocious attack mounted by the Giants. For those of a superstitious nature, in a sport where the performers usually didn't want to tempt the gods of fate, another explanation related to that late-season collapse seemed plausible to this group of people. Twelve years earlier, when the Pirates secured their last National League pennant in 1909, *Pittsburgh Press* sportswriter Ralph S. Davis had made a special request to manager Fred Clarke before his squad clinched the title. Davis asked if a photographer from his newspaper could snap a group picture of the eventual league champions. Clarke looked back at the sportswriter as if he'd lost his mind.

"Say, a lot of my fellows would jump in the river rather than pose for a picture like that at this time," said Clarke. "Don't you know that the average ballplayer considers it a hoodoo to have a group picture made during the season? Come around the day we cinch the pennant and I'll let you snap 'em a dozen times."

The same thing happened in 1921 when Pittsburgh prepared to play New York in a doubleheader on August 24 at the Polo Grounds. Several photographers pestered Pirates manager George Gibson to allow his players to pose for a group photo, and he reluctantly consented to their wishes.[2] Weeks later, before the contest between these two squads on September 19 at Forbes Field, a cameraman requested the Giants' players assemble for a team picture. Understanding the jinx component behind such an action, the team members threw up their hands in horror and refused to accommodate this photographer. The cameraman then appealed to Giants skipper John McGraw, who responded that he wouldn't dream of ordering his men to do something against their will. A New York inhabitant attending the game offered insight into each team's response when confronted with the same circumstances.

> I guess you remember what happened when the Pirates appeared at the Polo Grounds last month. A squad of 15 or 20 newspaper photographers and movie men followed Gibson and his fellows and snapped them in every conceivable position. Many of them objected to having their pictures taken—especially before the game.
>
> Gibson pleaded for them not to take any snaps, explaining that the pennant was yet a long way from being clinched, but the snap shooters were persistent, and with reluctance, the players finally marched out and posed in a group. The Pirates lost five straight, and they have dropped 16 of the 25 games they have played since that New York incident.
>
> Can you blame the Giants for dodging the cameramen? They feel sure that if they were to pose now it might bring them the same luck.[3]

Years ago, when acting as National League president, former Pirates front office official Harry Pulliam had a little placard hanging over his desk that read, "Take nothing for granted in baseball."[4] Taking nothing for granted in baseball had different applications related to the Pirates. It most certainly signified a stern, cautionary message for players to keep delivering supreme effort each day from the season's start to finish, without allowing hijinks or a zest to enjoy the nightlife to offer interference. Pulliam's message also pertained to players not assuming they had a guaranteed roster spot, especially after ceding a pennant to a despised rival such as the Giants. While problems seemed plentiful, the organization needed pragmatic solutions that acted in its best interests. Striking a balance between a complete overhaul and tweaking critical areas offered the best remedy for keeping Pittsburgh competitive. This approach led to removing harmful elements from the team being a slower process for ownership than in the past.

The rumor mill started churning out its off-season butter related to Pirates players who possibly could move on to new baseball pastures. This group included outfielders Max Carey and George Whitted; pitchers Moses Yellow Horse, Earl Hamilton, and Harold "Hal" Carlson; staff ace Wilbur Cooper; veteran second baseman George Cutshaw; and infielder Cotton Tierney. Although Rabbit Maranville had been a hero to Pittsburgh's baseball fans early in the season, they wanted his hide by the campaign's end. Local rooters floated a possible trade, including him and third baseman Clyde Barnhart to Cincinnati for hot corner guardian Henry "Heinie" Groh. A deal involving catcher Walter Schmidt, for either cash or another player, appeared likely.[5]

Fans' disgust over Wilbur Cooper seemed interesting since he went 22–14 with a 3.25 ERA in 1921 after doing stellar work one year earlier, posting a mark of 24–15, supported by a 2.39 ERA. Although considered one of the National League's top southpaw hurlers, fans didn't appreciate Cooper because of his temperament and penchant for sulking and brooding. Wilbur's 1921 contract stipulated that he receive a bonus for winning 25 games. Once Cooper realized the opportunity to earn this extra money was slipping away, he became miserable and angry. Pittsburgh's baseball fans rightfully chafed over this attitude.[6] Many of the hurler's character traits didn't endear him to the paying public. Constantly acting like Barney Dreyfuss underpaid him, although the Pirates' owner had treated Wilbur fairly when it came to salary, added another demerit in the rooters' eyes.[7]

Sportswriter Regis M. Welsh of the *Pittsburgh Post* understood from a credible rumor that one of the Singing Quartet's members likely would be discarded from the roster for the serious charge of insubordination.[8] Speculation also abounded as to whether George Gibson would run the team in 1922. Fans found fault with Gibson's handling of pitchers on the diamond and his hesitance to crack the whip when it came to some players' activities away from the ballpark. George possessed a cheery disposition and always preferred to look at the positive side of any issue. Gibson certainly wasn't a taskmaster, as he preferred encouraging his troops rather than scolding or threatening them.[9] When whittling down the accurate list of likely players to be traded or released, it included Schmidt, Tierney, Whitted, Barnhart, Cutshaw, and pitcher James "Jimmy" Zinn.[10]

George Gibson failed to pull off a deal while he and Barney Dreyfuss attended the National Association meeting in Buffalo, New York. To acquire third baseman Milt Stock from St. Louis, Gibson became flabbergasted when Cardinals manager Wesley Branch Rickey countered with the players he wanted from Pittsburgh to seal an agreement. Rickey requested Walter Schmidt, Wilbur Cooper, outfielders Max Carey and Carson Bigbee, and one or two Pirates players in exchange for Stock. This demand abruptly ended negotiations between the two men as Gibson offered a parting comment.

"Why not ask Barney to throw in Forbes Field?" responded Gibson before he walked away.[11]

Pittsburgh's manager then became a little overzealous at the winter league meetings. When talking with Brooklyn Robins skipper Wilbert Robinson, Gibson asked for outfielders Zack Wheat and Henry "Hi" Myers in exchange for Schmidt. Robinson didn't appear receptive to moving two of his star outfielders for the catcher. When Gibby tossed George Whitted into the mix to break this logjam, Wilbert instead asked for an infielder, which the Pirates' skipper rejected.[12] When it came to potential holdouts by National League players, Barney Dreyfuss expected to suffer his share of difficulty signing up some of his men for the upcoming season. Dreyfuss likely would harbor bad memories of the late-season collapse when he mailed out contracts for the 1922 campaign.

As per new provisions in all major league contracts instituted the prior year, players who failed to report for spring training properly would receive fines. Unsigned players also weren't permitted to report for spring training workouts. Commissioner Kenesaw Mountain Landis was the final arbiter in any player and team management dispute.[13] Disgruntled and dissatisfied, Walter Schmidt was a likely candidate for the holdout camp. The issue seemed deeper than money, based on his tone in letters he mailed to Pittsburgh friends throughout the winter. In some of these writings, Walter declared he couldn't get along with manager George Gibson and disagreed with his methods. A letter penned to a friend from the city's East End section contained one or two tidbits about things that happened in 1921, with Schmidt adding, "No wonder we didn't win the pennant."

Barney Dreyfuss expressed no optimism over having Walter in the fold for 1922. Pittsburgh's owner figured it better not to have Schmidt on the Pirates rather than allow an agitator to disrupt team harmony. Dreyfuss and Gibson agreed that youngster John "Johnny" Gooch would work out fine as Pittsburgh's first-string catcher.[14] *Pittsburgh Press* sportswriter Ralph S. Davis believed Walter was in a unique position since he didn't need to worry about playing baseball to earn money. Schmidt owned various properties in Modesto, California, while connected to lucrative business ventures. He'd just sold two of his farms, one of them a 40-acre piece of land that garnered him $24,000 in cash. Another individual purchased the second place, a 24-acre plot of fruit and grapes, for $10,000. When it came to letters harshly criticizing the Pittsburgh Pirates' organization, one that Walter wrote to sportswriter Chilly Doyle in January exposed the catcher's deeply-rooted animosity.

> After what I have been reading in the papers, it looks to me like Gibson has been discussing the team. If Gibby starts to fight his players it will be a bad condition, and I will bet you a $75 suit of clothes we don't finish one, two, three under such a handicap. Remember just what I write in this letter, next fall, and see.
>
> The boys all played their heads off last season, and a fifth place club finished second just because they hustled. But, mind you, I am telling you that the players will not stand being belittled. I like Gibby and held up for him all year. The players are sore because we did not get the pennant, with the extra money, and absolutely can't see why certain players should be blamed for it. Baseball players of this day will not stand for the bunco stuff. Now the moguls are starting to howl about tough times ahead. That is to cover up the fans, and make them forget the good seasons' baseball has had in the past two years.
>
> I notice they have me traded to several clubs, along with Carey and Cotton Tierney. Nothing would suit me better than to be traded, as our club won't have much chance, under present methods. If they sent me to any club outside of the Phillies, I would have a chance to be put in the race. The Pittsburgh club made a lot of money last year. I have been in the game quite a while, and I'm not fooled in these matters. They are all jumping McGraw because he advertises and buys players. He goes out and gets all the grapes, and the others sit back and howl.[15]

Walter Schmidt certainly didn't hold back, offering his critique of manager George Gibson's work in 1921. It wasn't a secret that Schmidt disagreed with his manager regarding team policy and had been open about these feelings in the past.[16] News on March 7 that Walter turned down the latest contract offer from Barney Dreyfuss didn't surprise local fans. Schmidt stipulated that he wouldn't sign for less than $10,000 a season, requiring the contract's term to run for at least three years.[17] Gibson exhibited no concern over Walter's holdout, believing the Pirates' catching corps to be in capable hands.

"By the Fourth of July Walter Schmidt will be forgotten," said Gibson when discussing Schmidt's holdout one day after he rejected the organization's latest contract offer. "I have one of the classiest catching staffs ever rounded up, and should Schmidt fail to appear, he will not be missed by midseason."

George also considered Schmidt's decision to hold out a foolish choice.

"He has not more than two or three years at a high salary ahead of him," continued the manager. "If he is now earning enough money in the winter to meet his expenses, his baseball salary would be 'velvet' for three years. He could lay away his annual wages, and he would be on Easy Avenue when his major league career is over."[18]

After the Chicago White Sox defeated Pittsburgh, 11–5, in a spring exhibition game on March 19, Barney Dreyfuss declared that he didn't plan on making any further proposals to sign Schmidt. He also stated that if Walter accepted management's terms, the club would suspend the catcher at the appropriate time for failing to report on the designated date for the training session. Dreyfuss claimed he'd grown tired of Schmidt's holdout tactics and couldn't go any higher in the salary matter for his catcher.[19] As it turned out, the situation surrounding a piqued Walter Schmidt ended up being the undercard compared to punishing one of the singing Pirates accused of insubordination.

On March 14, the Pirates' organization announced they'd sold outfielder and Durham, North Carolina, native George "Possum" Whitted to the Brooklyn Robins for the $2,500 waiver price.[20] Some in the press thought it odd that such an accomplished player couldn't bring back more than the waiver price in a transaction. Like teammate Walter Schmidt, Whitted had been a stubborn holdout for many weeks. *New York Tribune* sportswriter W. J. McBeth felt the monetary return for George didn't make much sense unless Barney Dreyfuss took this action to discipline and humiliate this particular player. McBeth also mentioned that Pittsburgh could've recalled the waivers when Brooklyn placed their claim for him. Citing Dreyfuss's thoughtful and wise manner in handling his baseball empire, the writer stated that Pittsburgh's owner didn't usually hand out gold passes to regular customers.

McBeth alleged that individuals close to the situation insisted Whitted had been a thorn in Barney's side this past year. George had been a member of the clique of players who seemed unconcerned when the Pirates experienced their late-season flop in 1921. The writer also commended Brooklyn manager Wilbert Robinson for securing a star player who offered versatility. When reporting this deal, the *Pittsburgh Chronicle Telegraph* praised Whitted's work from the previous year, pointing out that he'd hugely factored in the team's success.[21]

Others felt this transaction signaled that rumors about George's dissatisfaction over playing for Pittsburgh were true. Some hinted that Whitted and Dreyfuss had been at odds since the Pirates' owner never allowed George to manage the team. Supposedly, numerous National League squads had attempted to deal for Whitted the previous summer, but Barney and George Gibson rebuffed them each time while also denying the player was unhappy. Possum appeared to be the scapegoat for all that had ailed Pittsburgh's baseball team in 1921.[22]

As expected, George Whitted didn't appreciate being a fall guy. Whitted issued an explosive response shortly after the 1922 season opened. George talked to *Philadelphia North American* sports editor James Isaminger while the Robins played in town in a series against the Phillies. Although rain postponed the contest between these two clubs at the Baker Bowl on April 19, Whitted issued a fiery comeback to insinuations and charges that he'd been the complicit goat regarding Pittsburgh's problems one year earlier. In naming the true culprit, he lobbed a volley of fireworks that landed squarely in team management's tent.

> We were accused of committing every crime on the calendar, but I never saw a better-behaved team. There were no hooch parties, as charged. Do you think we players would be foolish enough to kick away several thousand dollars that were in our grasp?
>
> We lost that pennant because of the Pittsburgh high command and nothing else. You can draw your construction from those words and I won't go into any details, but it is the truth.
>
> Barney Dreyfuss sent for me last fall and bawled me out. We had a big fuss and I demanded that he trade me. To belittle me he sent me to Brooklyn and announced I went for the waiver price.[23]

Robins manager Wilbert Robinson wasn't happy over Whitted, giving the impression in this interview that readers might perceive a move to Brooklyn as a demotion. The two men held a conference where George apologized, saying he hadn't meant to insult the Robins' organization but was motivated by wanting to criticize Barney Dreyfuss. Whitted then talked to *Brooklyn Daily Eagle* writer Thomas Rice, telling the scribe he was glad to be with Brooklyn, desperately wanted to leave Pittsburgh, and always wished to play under Robinson. A furious Dreyfuss wasted no time responding to these comments from his disgruntled former employee. Barney claimed he treated George fairly while with the Pirates and released him for valid reasons.

> We had some trouble on our team at a certain stage of the 1921 season, because all of our rules were not lived up to. I have never discussed that matter very fully, because I did not care to show up any of the men who failed to do right.
>
> However, Whitted was the ringleader of that gang. One notable incident occurred while we were playing in New York. Whitted took several other members of the team with him on a gay expedition. That settled him with me. We were in the thick of the pennant fight at the time, and I was naturally angered when I heard the details.
>
> I made up my mind then that Whitted was through as a Pirate, and I got rid of him at the first opportunity. I do not want to go into details, for there are certain men still on our roster who were mixed up in that defiance of the rules.
>
> They will remain with us as long as they do what is right, but the moment there is a break on their part, they will be dealt with as they deserve.[24]

Although most people knew that George Whitted and George Gibson had numerous significant disagreements in 1921, newspaper stories had never previously mentioned Possum as a player who didn't abide by the club's rules of conduct.[25] Dreyfuss added more context regarding the Whitted situation one day after making his initial statement when responding to the Pirates' former player.

> I only "bawled out" Whitted, as he terms it, on one occasion, and that was in New York, when he led some of the other players on a gay excursion, which extended far into the night, and I caught them coming home at 2:30 in the morning. "I'm not under contract, and I'm not a boozer, so it doesn't matter why I was up at that hour." It did matter about the ballplayers, and I let Whitted know what I thought about it.
>
> He got $6,000 here last season, and wanted $9,000. He didn't play $1,500 ball. That is why he was waived off the Pirate roster.[26]

Griping during this encounter about not yet having a contract for 1922, George Whitted lost credibility since he still received paychecks for playing in 1921. Whitted didn't last long in Brooklyn. The Robins placed him on waivers in May, and no major league team put in a claim for his services. This destined George to continue his baseball career in the minors, although he contemplated retiring to oversee business interests in the South.[27] Whitted played for the American Association's Toledo Mud Hens in 1922. With one discontented player now removed from Pittsburgh's roster, the situation regarding Walter Schmidt remained in limbo. There appeared to be some hope on the horizon for a resolution between the two parties. According to news leaked from Pirates offices on April 21, the attitudes of both Schmidt and his boss seemed to change abruptly, thanks to Dreyfuss's letter from the catcher.

Walter's correspondence responded to a letter the club mailed him, informing the catcher that an automatic suspension from Organized Baseball would take effect on April 22 if he didn't sign a contract by that date. From that point forward, Judge Kenesaw Mountain Landis would need to rectify the situation. Schmidt's letter appeared more conciliatory than ones in the past, which possessed a bitter tone. Walter had held out in the spring of 1921 but reached terms before the season opener. Pittsburgh's owner and George Gibson decided to freeze out Schmidt with the silent treatment in 1922 to avoid controversy. Dreyfuss seemed delighted over Walter's latest correspondence, although nobody knew whether he would respond.[28]

Such gossip supplied false hope for those who anticipated that Walter Schmidt would again don a Pirates uniform in 1922. On April 22, the National League officially placed Schmidt on Organized Baseball's suspended list, meaning he wouldn't be permitted to play until Judge Landis reinstated him. Although many felt the suspension started that afternoon, Dreyfuss believed it kicked in at midnight on April 21 since it happened ten days after the season opened. The Pirates' owner admitted that extreme bitterness existed between him and the catcher before reiterating that the organization didn't want Walter.

> We planned long ago to get along without him. That is why I bought three new catchers. I didn't want to invest so heavily in backstops, but I was determined to be prepared for every emergency. I intended to call Schmidt's bluff. He has written me several insulting letters, in which he said that he hated me. Under the circumstances there is small chance of any change in his status.
>
> Gooch will in no time be a better catcher than Schmidt. He is not so brittle. Walter was continually getting hurt, especially just when we needed him most. With every year he will become more easily injured, and it will take him longer to recover.
>
> A number of weeks ago, he told me in a letter that several clubs were willing to pay him what he asked. I told him to name the clubs, and I would try to trade him, but he didn't do so.

Then I asked for waivers on him, and two clubs put in claims, but neither of them was willing to pay a cent above the waiver price. One of them was a club which I have suspected several times of trying to make him dissatisfied, the same club, by the way, which I think meddled with another player, who we have since let out.[29]

The player alluded to by Barney Dreyfuss was outfielder Davis "Dave" Robertson, whom the Pirates had acquired from the Chicago Cubs on July 1, 1921, for hurler Charles Elmer Ponder. Robertson, a holdout, drew his unconditional release at the beginning of the 1922 campaign. He immediately signed with the New York Giants, an action that Dreyfuss felt might lead to a tampering inquiry. Davy ended up being persona non grata regarding the Pirates because of several stories connected to him and insubordination in 1921.[30] Despite dumping two problem players from the squad and having another malcontent relaxing in California, the general malaise that gripped the Pirates near the end of 1921 lingered into the 1922 season.

Pittsburgh rolled out the gate with a 7–8 April record, leaving them in fifth place. The club rebounded nicely by going 17–8 in May but fell on tough times throughout June. Following their sixth loss in a row on June 17, a 2–1 ten-inning defeat at the hands of New York at the Polo Grounds, the third-place Pirates possessed a 27–25 record, leaving them eight games behind the league-leading Giants. One rumor claimed the reason behind this sudden skid revolved around an exhibition game against the Eastern Canada League's Montreal Royals on Sunday, June 11. The teams couldn't play the contest because of rain. Pittsburgh had defeated Boston the previous afternoon, 9–1, at Braves Field. Assertions from the Hub alleged Pittsburgh's players didn't want to make the trip to Montreal and weren't thrilled over spending two nights in train sleeper cars. George Gibson denied the tale and wrote Barney Dreyfuss that none of his players had offered any complaints.[31]

Poor performance wasn't the only problem confronting Gibson. Many of those unnamed individuals Dreyfuss had mentioned when talking about George Whitted being the carousing ringleader still played for the team. Although Barney didn't reveal these players' identities, Pittsburgh and Western Pennsylvania inhabitants were aware of who happened to be the rule breakers. Moses "Chief" Yellow Horse and Rabbit Maranville took their place front and center. Yellow Horse, a member of the Pawnee tribe from the reservation in Pawnee, Oklahoma, debuted for the Pirates in 1921. Moses exhibited a pleasant personality and always made others laugh. After appearing in ten games for the

Pirates in 1921, Yellow Horse primarily performed as a reliever the following year while taking the bump twenty-eight times in 1922. On one occasion, first baseman Charlie Grimm decided to have some fun at his teammate's expense.

"How's the old bullpen going, Yellow Horse?" asked Grimm.

Moses turned toward Grimm and waved at him to be silent.

"One more week of that stuff," the pitcher said, "and I'm going to change my name to Chief Sitting Bullpen."[32]

Things weren't rosy for Yellow Horse, as he sometimes became subjected to prejudice due to his heritage. Rumors also abounded that a fistfight had occurred between him and fellow hurler Wilbur Cooper in 1921.[33] Like many of his teammates, Moses enjoyed drinking alcohol at times.[34] One time, this desire to quench his thirst happened during a game. According to Grimm, when he later related this tale to Chicago sportswriter Warren Brown, drinking water didn't suffice for Yellow Horse during a contest on a sweltering summer afternoon. As the game progressed, Moses took the mound to begin a later frame and refused to pitch as Pittsburgh's catcher flashed various signals. Becoming angry, George Gibson yelled to Charlie, who happened to be the player closest to him.

"Go over and see what in hell's wrong," Gibson ordered.

Grimm strolled over to the bump to ask Moses about his issue, causing him to delay the game.

"I'll not throw another ball until I get a shot of liquor," said the pitcher.

Charlie stood there perplexed since he didn't have a solution to this problem. Pittsburgh's catcher, and fellow infielders Cotton Tierney and Rabbit Maranville, quickly joined the conclave. Maranville inquired about the holdup, and Grimm responded that Yellow Horse wouldn't continue until he received a shot of alcohol. Rabbit thought the idea a marvelous one and asked if any of his teammates were carrying a flask with them. Somebody did have a decanter of liquor tucked away in their uniform. Everybody huddled around Moses as he satisfied his thirst, while Grimm claimed another player possibly took a shot since the opportunity presented itself. The meeting finally broke up, and play continued. When the inning concluded, Gibson waited at the dugout entrance to talk to Charlie, the first player walking toward him.

"What was the matter out there?" Gibson wanted to know.

Before Grimm could utter a word, Maranville, strolling in one step behind the first baseman, answered in his unique, eloquent way.

"The guy's supporter was binding him," Rabbit said, "and he didn't know what to do about it out there in front of all those people."[35]

One night during the 1921 baseball campaign, Yellow Horse caused a disturbance in the Oakland section of Pittsburgh. After partaking in a few beers, Moses took some swigs of hard liquor from a container passed around among his group of partiers. The introduction of this liquid into his system changed Yellow Horse's disposition. Unable to find a bottle opener, Moses bit off the top of a beer bottle, causing his lip to bleed. The boisterous pitcher became involved in a fight with a baseball fan on the street corner. A witness reported that Yellow Horse pulled out a knife during the scrap. The pitcher denied this, claiming he didn't need or use knives because of being very capable with his fists. A teammate whisked Moses away from the scene and made sure he went to bed.[36]

That fellow Pirates player was most likely pitcher Drew Rader, Moses Yellow Horse's roommate. Years later, in discussing his best friend on the team, Rader commented on Moses being a fine fellow when appropriately treated. He then remarked about witnessing one fight involving Yellow Horse where the other combatant acted extremely mean and ignorant. Moses told the man to stop being abusive and then only dropped the harasser with one punch after he persisted.[37] The morning following his involvement in this brawl, Yellow Horse went to Barney Dreyfuss's office and informed him of the incident. Moses figured Pittsburgh's owner would find out the details from someone, so he felt it sensible to explain the situation and apologize for acting in that manner. Impressed by the hurler's candor, Dreyfuss only provided a brief lecture and didn't fine Yellow Horse.[38]

Since Drew Rader didn't play for the team in 1922, Rabbit Maranville became Moses's new bosom buddy. The duo's exploits started a chain reaction of events that reshaped the Pirates' organization. When Pittsburgh made a late-June trip to Chicago, Barney accompanied the team. Although the Pirates claimed three out of the four games, Dreyfuss was displeased when he witnessed one of his players in an intoxicated condition while there. Barney shared this with George Gibson, who calmly responded everything was all right.[39] Things grew tenser when the team traveled home by train after the final game at Cubs Park on June 28.

Before the train departed, Rabbit Maranville and Moses Yellow Horse had enough time to duck into an illegal establishment near the station and guzzle a few beers. The alcohol on empty stomachs gave both players a nice buzz. Once on the train, they spied Dreyfuss at the far end of the dining car and decided to have some fun. Much to the shock of everyone seated in the diner, Yellow Horse stood up and introduced Maranville as the great Pittsburgh Pirates shortstop. Chief added that his teammate was a sweet fellow who minded his business and never got into any jams. Rabbit then arose and reciprocated, presenting Moses to the crowd and exclaiming that he was a fine pitcher and the best scrapper in Pittsburgh. Dreyfuss, unamused over this poor attempt at vaudeville comedy at his expense, told George Gibson his players had gotten beyond his control and that he better do something to rectify the situation.[40]

Following an 8–5 defeat at the hands of the St. Louis Cardinals at Forbes Field on June 29, Barney and his manager engaged in a contentious verbal confrontation where each individual exchanged words that weren't pleasing to the other. Dreyfuss later denied that any such incident occurred.[41] Fans at Forbes Field had exhibited surprising patience throughout the 1922 campaign, displaying devout loyalty even in the face of substandard diamond performance. This restraint ended during the game against the Cardinals on June 30, when Pittsburgh lost 6–0. The razzing and heckling reached proportions that Forbes Field's spectators and players hadn't witnessed in many years.[42] After the contest concluded, Gibson entered the clubhouse with a deliberate expression rather than the usual smile. Gibby aborted the Pittsburgh players' standard trek to the showers.

"Wait a minute, fellows!" he sang out. "Before you go in there to the showers I want to say something to you!"

None of the players had the slightest idea what their manager intended to discuss. Some expected a lecture, while others wondered if they were about to be released from the team. Gibson shocked and stunned the players when he informed them that he planned on handing in his resignation.[43] George stated that he believed the Pirates could possibly do better work with a different manager at the helm. Gibson told his players that no blame existed with them for this action. He wished the men good luck and hoped they would move up in the standings under new leadership. Gibby walked out of the clubhouse and went to Barney Dreyfuss's office to tender his resignation. The fact that Dreyfuss accepted it without offering any rebuttal indicated that ownership most likely desired a change.[44]

George had been disgusted with the squad's performance for some time. All the pilot's experiments to shake the Pirates out of their funk failed, and the recent slump led to his team sliding out of the first division.[45] When talking to his squad before resigning, Gibson thanked the entire group for all they'd done. An anonymous player seemed remorseful while discussing Gibby's sudden departure with a reporter.

> Not one of us had the slightest inkling that Gibby was going to resign. We were knocked so completely off our feet by what he said, that nobody could

say a word. Since I've been thinking it over, I regret that I did not go to him and express my regret, but as a matter of fact I was rendered absolutely speechless and that appears to be exactly the same way all the rest of the players felt. We all like Gibby. He has been with us so long and has always been on the level. He played no favorites but treated us all just the same as if we were his brothers. When we made mistakes, he never hesitated to shoulder the responsibility. We never can find a better friend in the whole wide world.

One of the stunned people sitting in that clubhouse was Wilkinsburg, Pennsylvania, native William "Bill" McKechnie, who'd played for the Pirates in 1907, 1910 through 1912, and again in 1918 and 1920. Following a season with the American Association's Minneapolis Millers in 1921, McKechnie rejoined the Pirates to coach the infielders during spring training at Hot Springs. Bill stuck with the team as an assistant to George Gibson once the season started. Following Gibson's resignation, Barney Dreyfuss appointed McKechnie as Pittsburgh's new manager. When pressed to release a statement later that day, Bill asked reporters to excuse him from conducting interviews due to still being extremely shocked over recent developments.[46]

Not wishing to air dirty laundry, George slipped quietly out of town without talking to reporters. Sportswriter Ralph S. Davis didn't mince words when he stated that Gibby proved too easygoing and never ruled with an iron fist when players constantly defied club rules. Gibson allowed the situation to grow so bad that when he attempted to clamp down on some players moderately, such efforts ended up being impossible. Factions still existed in the club, although alleged ringleaders no longer played for the team.[47] Weeks after the managerial change, baseball writer Thomas Rice of the *Brooklyn Daily Eagle* ventured into the territory where George had been hesitant to travel as he shook Pittsburgh's dust from his feet.

Rice started his article by writing that Barney Dreyfuss had been unjustly condemned and slandered by some individuals because the team failed in 1921. The writer targeted George Whitted and Walter Schmidt as the guilty parties. According to Rice, Whitted had intimated in his earlier interview with James Isaminger that Dreyfuss didn't want to win the pennant in 1921. The former outfielder and Schmidt had insinuated that Gibson purposely mismanaged his pitching staff and other players. These two felt George enacted this course of action upon secret orders from the Pirates' owner. Whitted and Walter based this premise on the misguided notion that Dreyfuss believed winning the National

League flag would be bad for business. They reasoned Barney acted under the impression that fan reaction in ensuing years, when this pennant-winning team experienced an inevitable decline, likely would cost him more at the gate than could be gained by playing in the World Series.

As someone who'd known Dreyfuss for many years, Rice declared such an accusation ludicrous. Brooklyn's writer vowed that Barney was a dedicated fighter who always wanted to win the pennant. Upon encountering Dreyfuss early in the 1921 campaign, when the Pirates overachieved, Rice said that the longtime owner acted as proud as a new papa. As the two men crossed paths later in the season, the writer thought Barney looked like a nervous wreck. A newspaper colleague, usually unfriendly to Dreyfuss, who'd seen him at the World Series in New York, feared the magnate might end up in the hospital. The Brooklyn writer also shared the inside story surrounding former second baseman George Cutshaw. Rice claimed that Gibson didn't want Cutshaw on the team any longer, and Dreyfuss heeded the manager's wishes.

Barney, who always admired Cutshaw, lent him the necessary money in 1921 for a California real estate deal. Dreyfuss spoke with pride that Pittsburgh's second baseman expeditiously paid back every cent. When Gibby decided on Cutshaw, Barney attempted to find a managerial position for him in the Pacific Coast League, but no vacancies existed. After the 1921 season, Detroit Tigers manager Ty Cobb met Cutshaw while playing in the Pacific Coast Winter League. Cobb informed Dreyfuss that he would love to secure the brainy veteran. Barney consented to the idea and approved a deal after Ty agreed to pick up George's Pittsburgh contract. Dreyfuss refused to accept the $2,500 waiver price from Detroit for Cutshaw. It seemed likely instead that the Tigers gave the money to George as a bonus for signing with them.

Discussion about Walter Schmidt's attitude proved critical since the first decision made by Bill McKechnie as Pirates manager was to enter into negotiations with the holdout catcher. Throughout the 1922 campaign, veteran Pittsburgh hurlers lamented the absence of Schmidt's steadying influence. Thomas Rice reported that Barney Dreyfuss wanted Walter on the team in 1922, but George Gibson adamantly refused. Against his friends' advice and better judgment, Dreyfuss allowed Gibson to keep Schmidt off the squad. Rice also claimed that Gibby didn't notify Pittsburgh's owner face-to-face about his decision to leave the organization but rather through writing a brief note.[48]

Pittsburgh's baseball fans expressed delight when Schmidt agreed to contract terms and became a member of the Pirates again. These patrons realized one of the reasons for the club slumping resulted from inadequate contributions by the catchers. Many believed Dreyfuss had met Walter's terms from last spring for $10,000 a year and felt the backstop might receive back pay from his time on the sidelines.[49] Bill McKechnie handled the negotiations, which moved at breakneck speed. Schmidt immediately gave resounding approval and said he would join the club once Judge Kenesaw Mountain Landis reinstated him. In his column, sportswriter Ray Coll Jr. asserted that Walter's holdout had been done to camouflage the fact that he wouldn't join the club as long as Gibson served as manager.

Ray Coll Jr. stated the two men suffered a strained relationship. George, a former catcher, had specific ideas which he passed on to Walter. Schmidt resented these suggestions, feeling he knew more about playing that position than his manager. As a result, the two constantly remained at odds. Walter didn't like how his skipper handled Pittsburgh's twirlers, while George wasn't pleased with how the veteran catcher coached the hurlers on pitching to certain opposing batters. Many heated, quarrelsome arguments occurred after games between Schmidt and Gibson. Following one of these disputes during the 1921 season, Coll claimed Walter confided in him that he would never return to the Pirates while Gibson managed the team.

The writer also offered some information surrounding the previous year's problems between Gibby and George Whitted. As a veteran player, Whitted thought he should be permitted to use his judgment on some issues and disagreed at times with Gibson's philosophies. However, the player's main beef with his manager centered on Gibby's edict prohibiting Pirates team members from playing golf during the baseball season. George had implemented this new rule following a spring exhibition game against the Western League's Oklahoma City Indians. The morning before the contest, Whitted, an avid golfer, Coll, and another writer played a round at a local course.

Possum placed premium mental and physical effort upon the morning golf game, resulting in the veteran player having little energy left for that afternoon's diamond clash. This sluggishness was apparent in Whitted's performance. Gibson called him out for such a horrible display, and the two exchanged heated words, prompting Pittsburgh's manager to institute his new rule forbidding golf. Things blew over briefly until Possum violated the order numerous times later in the 1921 season. As punishment, Gibby benched Whitted for a few games of the critical August series against New York at the Polo Grounds.[50] When Pittsburgh had their three-day break from the National League schedule that year after Labor Day, it seemed most of the team had broken this no-golf rule, including Barney Dreyfuss's guests at the Westmoreland Country Club.

Although Walter Schmidt had rejoined the fold to offer some stability and guidance to a vital facet of the Pirates' team, new manager Bill McKechnie still had to contend with that dynamic duo of Rabbit Maranville and Moses Yellow Horse. Before the squad embarked on an eastern swing in late July, Dreyfuss summoned McKechnie into his office and asked how the manager planned on dealing with these two rascals on this long road trip. Bill expressed utmost confidence to his boss by declaring everything would be fine since the skipper planned on rooming with the two naughty players. When Pittsburgh arrived in New York for the first phase of this trip against Brooklyn, McKechnie held a team meeting where he prohibited bootleg liquor and established a midnight curfew. Bill then said that although he didn't plan on ruling with an iron fist, he intended to be firm in his discipline and expected reciprocation regarding his respect for his players.

Maranville and Yellow Horse behaved at the start of this trip, never challenging the curfew time. Things continued to work smoothly when the squad lodged at New York's Ansonia Hotel during a series against the Giants.[51] Following one of the games against New York, McKechnie ate dinner, saw a movie, and returned to the hotel at 10 P.M. When Bill entered his hotel room, Rabbit and Moses were in bed, sound asleep.

"Aha," McKechnie thought. "It works."

Bill then walked over to the closet to change into his nightclothes. When he opened the closet door, a flock of pigeons flew out and navigated past him into the room. The loud commotion stirred Maranville from his slumber while Yellow Horse, oblivious to the noise, continued sleeping.

"Don't open the other closet, Bill," Maranville said. "The Chief's got his pigeons in there and, boy, he'd really be mad if you let 'em out."[52]

While Bill had enjoyed dinner and a movie, the two players implemented their prank. Maranville and Yellow Horse somehow got the hotel to send a few beers to their room. After polishing off the alcohol, the two went over to a window, and while holding Rabbit by the ankles, Moses lowered him down to where pigeons roosted on the coaming several feet below. Fifteen stories above the street, Maranville navigated several sorties, holding a pigeon in both hands each time as Yellow Horse pulled him back up and through the window. McKechnie had threatened to slap a $250 fine on the two men if they weren't in bed by 11 P.M.[53] Technically, the pair did obey their manager's orders.

Bill McKechnie did an excellent job after being handed the keys to the Pirates' car. Under Bill's tutelage, Pittsburgh went 53–36. In August, a wild story with origins in New York claimed the Giants planned on purposely losing the National League pennant. This crazy rumor intimated New York decided to lay down so Pittsburgh could claim the bunting as repayment for the Buccaneers tanking the 1921 campaign. Believers of this tale cited gambling money shifting from the Giants and St. Louis Cardinals to Pittsburgh as proof that a fix existed. Individuals connected to Organized Baseball said, "It's an infernal, malicious fabrication." The predictable comeback from those skeptical people who thought such a scenario creditable responded, "Remember the Black Sox."[54] Diamond events ended up disproving this theory. New York claimed their second straight National League flag, as the Pirates placed third with an 85–69 record, eight games behind the league pacesetter.

On September 26, Barney Dreyfuss publicized that McKechnie had signed to be Pittsburgh's manager in 1923. While not divulging Bill's salary, Dreyfuss stated he expedited an announcement on this appointment to spike rumors that catcher Walter Schmidt might be named to oversee the Pirates.[55] According to this gossip, Schmidt had written a letter telling friends in Modesto that he would be the Pirates' new pilot, with Bill receiving a promotion to the business manager position. Walter indicated in this prose that he would earn around $25,000 in salary for his new job, a massive increase above the $8,000 a season the catcher supposedly received in a three-year deal when signing months earlier.[56]

Before announcing McKechnie's retention as Pittsburgh's manager, Barney declared on September 25 that Schmidt hadn't been a contender for that job.[57] Dreyfuss became enraged when receiving news of Walter's possible letter, calling the notion a fabrication and a pipe dream.[58] Bill and the catcher were very close friends, and many understood that McKechnie would task Schmidt with handling Pittsburgh's pitchers once again in 1923.[59] Walter unequivocally denied ever writing such a message to any friend and feared somebody concocted the story as a joke. The Associated Press, who first broke the story, vouched for its authenticity, stating they corroborated the information before sending it over the wire. Schmidt countered this narrative by declaring he wouldn't consider usurping McKechnie's authority.

"I have never given any thought to managing a club," said Schmidt when interviewed in Pittsburgh. "I am loyal to Bill McKechnie, and have no desire whatsoever to take his job. He is a fine fellow, we get along together well, and I am extremely sorry that this tale came out, for it puts me in a bad light with the manager."[60]

When Bill McKechnie took control of the club, he constantly pressed upon his players that he wouldn't tolerate upheaval and discord while in charge. He followed the mantra, "You are either for me, or you will go elsewhere." During his few months at the helm, Bill had proven he knew how to handle men and was a gifted diplomat.[61] On October 11, Barney Dreyfuss intimated to press members that Walter Schmidt possibly wouldn't be with the Pirates in 1923.

"No contract has been offered Schmidt," said Dreyfuss. "When I said goodbye to him nothing was mentioned about terms for next year."[62]

One player who definitely wouldn't be on Pittsburgh's roster in 1923 was pitcher Moses Yellow Horse. In the middle of December, the Pirates packaged Moses in a deal along with fellow hurler Bill Hughes, infielder Claude Rowher, outfielder Harry Brown, and $7,500 cash to the Pacific Coast League's Sacramento Senators for pitcher Earl Kunz. The transaction was provisional, depending on how Kunz performed in spring training (George remained with the Pirates in 1923). When Yellow Horse first joined Pittsburgh, he quickly became a fan favorite. Over time, that staunch support waned. Originally, shouts of "Put Yellow Horse in" were genuine as patrons clamored to see their latest darling enter a game. By the end of his second campaign with the Pirates, fans hollering that same request did so out of mockery.[63]

When Barney Dreyfuss mailed out contracts to his players in January 1923, many Pittsburgh rooters expected perennial holdout Walter Schmidt to be among the dissenters.[64] Schmidt worked behind the plate when the Pirates opened the season on April 17 with a 3–2 victory over Chicago at Cubs Park. Pittsburgh offered up a mediocre brand of baseball throughout the season's early stages, hovering around the .500 mark. When the Pirates arrived in Philadelphia to start a series with the Phillies on May 21, rumors swirled about a potential trade between the two teams since Dreyfuss traveled with the club. Stories regarding Phillies hurler Henry Lee Meadows possibly joining Pittsburgh seemed unlikely since the New York Giants had been courting Philadelphia management about swinging a deal for the pitcher.[65]

Following the game between the Pirates and Philadelphia on May 23, the two teams pulled off their big swap. Pittsburgh acquired Lee Meadows, also called "Specs" because he wore glasses, and second baseman John "Johnny" Rawlings. The Pirates shipped out hurler Whitey Glazner and another member of the Singing Quartet, second baseman Cotton Tierney.[66] Rawlings had refused to report to the Phillies when they claimed him off waivers from New York on May 11.[67] After doing great work for Pittsburgh in 1921, going 14–5 with a 2.77 ERA, Glazner regressed in 1922, doing no better than 11–12, supported by a 4.38 ERA. Tierney had developed into a very accomplished hitter, batting .345 in 1922, with 7 home runs and 86 RBIs. Bill McKechnie looked slightly emotional when he told newspaper journalists that the club had completed the transaction.

"This is the only real tough part of baseball," said Bill freely. "You work up a friendship for fine boys like Cotton and Whitey and then these things come along."

Tierney accepted the switch philosophically, while Glazner appeared visibly upset over the move. Team treasurer Sam Dreyfuss exclaimed it to be a mighty good trade that he was pleased the club put through.[68] Pittsburgh's baseball rooters were also delighted about this deal. Although the Pirates had moved a great hitter in Tierney, Rawlings's addition strengthened the infield defense. Many figured Rabbit Maranville's performance at shortstop should also immensely improve with Johnny playing second base. As Tierney's close friend, Rabbit attempted to cover up his buddy's defensive shortcomings, which affected Maranville's performance, and his play suffered.[69] When it came to his work at the plate, the raw numbers showed that Rabbit did a commendable job, batting .294 in 1921 and .295 in 1922. A closer look concerning 1921 revealed that his execution as a batter precipitously declined after July 2, when his average stood at .362.

Constant indiscretions circumvented a positive stance over those numbers. On May 18, 1923, while the Pirates played a series in Boston against the Braves, Maranville ran afoul with police in the suburb of Brookline. An officer arrested the player between 8 and 9 A.M. as he returned to the team's lodging at the Brunswick Hotel. Rabbit was the passenger in the back seat of an automobile driven by a friend who'd been drinking. To help his friend at the time of this traffic stop, Maranville claimed he'd been driving the car and revealed his identity, feeling this might influence the arresting officer into letting both men off. It didn't work.

Bill McKechnie received news about the arrest a little after 9 A.M. and rushed to the police station. McKechnie became surprised and worried upon arriving and being informed that they'd already released Rabbit. His concern resulted from an earlier report that Maranville had been detained at the police station for nine hours under the influence of liquor and might require hospitalization. Upon returning to the hotel, Bill, amazed over finding Rabbit there, confronted his shortstop. After Maranville admitted to drinking beer the previous night, McKechnie fined him. Intending to play Jewel Ens at shortstop that afternoon, Bill changed his mind following a sincere apology by Rabbit.[70] Because of being charged with driving an automobile while intoxicated, the court required Maranville to make an appearance for a hearing the next time Pittsburgh made a trip to Boston.[71]

Maranville had his day in multiple courts on July 19. He appeared before a magistrate in the Boston suburb of Brookline, who fined him $100 for operating an automobile while under the influence of alcohol.[72] The arrest report alleged that Rabbit had also been speeding through this area inhabited by millionaires. A lawyer representing Maranville at the proceeding asked for mercy, claiming the Pirates' organization had adequately punished the ballplayer by imposing a fine on Rabbit over his behavior. Maranville's counsel also attempted to use his standing in major league baseball as leverage against punishment, declaring Rabbit to be a great ballplayer.[73]

The lawyer then cited Maranville's performance in Pittsburgh's game against Boston on May 18 as proof that his client had been sober when arrested. His attorney argued that Rabbit handled nine chances in the field flawlessly, and his only error that day was detention in police custody. Counsel, possibly laying it on too thick about Maranville's innocence, finished by confirming that he'd delivered the winning hit in the ninth inning, which secured Pittsburgh's 4–3 victory. The judge, possibly a Braves fan, immediately rendered a guilty verdict and instructed him to pay the fine.[74] After Maranville handed over $100 in Brookline, another hearing awaited him at a court in nearby Newton. That town had charged Rabbit with refusing to stop his automobile on May 18 when ordered to do so by a traffic officer. Newton police had filed a second speeding charge, and another judge ordered him to pay a $25 penalty.[75]

Due to these two arrests and convictions, the State Registrar of Motor Vehicles in Massachusetts revoked Maranville's license, forbidding him from driving in that state for one year.[76] Although Rabbit still had friends back in Pittsburgh who supported him, many rooters considered the player a detriment rather than an asset.[77] Amidst a team slump, Forbes Field's fans finally voiced their frustration. During game one of a doubleheader against Brooklyn on August 8, with Maranville's legal issues burned in their minds, patrons viciously heckled the shortstop over his general lethargy and lack of hustle on the field.

Manager Bill McKechnie also levied some sharp criticism, telling Rabbit in between games of the twin bill that he expected more from him while demanding immediate improvement in his play and effort.[78] Barney Dreyfuss certainly hadn't been pleased with Maranville and happily would ship him to another team if it didn't weaken the Pirates.[79] Dreyfuss and McKechnie focused on breaking in a new shortstop in 1924. Pittsburgh's scouts had already found three potential candidates.

Rabbit Maranville wasn't the only offender in excessively drinking alcohol. In 1923, hurler John "Johnny" Morrison rose to the Pirates' best pitcher status, going 25–13 with a 3.49 ERA. On the evening of July 28, before a series started against New York at Forbes Field two days later, an intoxicated Morrison, after consuming copious amounts of liquor at a Pittsburgh saloon, boasted that when given the opportunity, he would easily handle the Giants. He offered to wager money to back up his bragging. When given a chance in game two of a doubleheader on July 30, Johnny didn't make it out of the third inning as the Giants slaughtered the Pirates, 17–2.[80]

Pittsburgh came home third in the National League race in 1923. The Pirates posted an 87–67 record, leaving them 8½ games behind pennant-winning New York. Disgusted with the performance of some high-salaried players, Barney Dreyfuss dedicated himself to making changes to his squad for 1924. In the owner's crosshairs was Maranville, leader of a club faction that had constantly disrupted team spirit and performance.[81] When discussing qualities a new shortstop should possess, Barney mentioned one key attribute.

"I'd like to get a shortstop with a voice like a rusty brake," said Dreyfuss. "Music has cost me too much in the last couple of years."[82]

In January 1924, the Boston Braves inquired about reacquiring Maranville. Although eager to rid himself of a problem, Barney suspected Boston's intentions. Dreyfuss, skeptical over the Braves needing Rabbit because recently secured David "Dave" Bancroft from New York was slated to hold down the shortstop position, felt the Boston organization had an ulterior motive. He believed Maranville's time in the Hub to be fleeting, with a second trade to the Giants a likely outcome. Since Dreyfuss never wished to strengthen his biggest rival, he rejected this proposition.[83] Things started positively for Pittsburgh in 1924 as Walter Schmidt joined the team in Paso Robles, California, for spring training.[84]

The Pirates battled gallantly to claim the pennant in 1924. An influx of talented rookies, such as pitchers Remy "Ray" Kremer and Emil Yde, outfielder Hazen "Kiki" Cuyler, infielder Graham Edward "Eddie" Moore, and shortstop Forest Glenn Wright, joined Pittsburgh. These five performers, veterans, and young third baseman Harold "Pie" Traynor, who became a starter in 1922, helped the Pirates remain in the hunt for most of the season. Rabbit Maranville shifted to second base and performed marvelously for the Pirates. He also behaved compared to past years. Maranville's career experienced a rebirth after Bill McKechnie moved him to second. The switch also allowed the highly touted Wright to take over at short, as his hitting, fielding and throwing proved to be as advertised from his time playing with the American Association's Kansas City Blues.[85]

This change also made sense to McKechnie since Rabbit had slowed a bit at shortstop. Bill never wavered, even when Wright struggled at the beginning of his rookie campaign.[86] Offering veteran insight by helping the youngster, Rabbit graciously tutored his replacement on the nuances of playing shortstop in the major leagues.[87] Sadly, absolute harmony didn't exist in 1924, as old problems resurfaced. The Pirates made it a trifecta of third-place finishes, going 90–63 and finishing three games behind pacesetting New York. When the season ended, the *Pittsburgh Press* reported tales of players boozing at establishments in the Western Pennsylvania boroughs of Bellevue, Braddock, and Etna. A breach of team rules also occurred when Pittsburgh played an August exhibition game in Warren, Ohio.[88] On August 17, the Pirates defeated the Warren Moose semi-pro team, 14–3.[89]

Pittsburgh's baseball fans resoundingly held Bill McKechnie responsible for the Pirates' faltering in capturing the 1924 National League pennant. However, Barney Dreyfuss exhibited total satisfaction with how McKechnie operated and brought him back to direct the club in 1925.[90] Amid harsh criticism from devoted Pirates fans, Bill executed a preemptive strike, purging the final remnants of those connected to Pittsburgh's disappointing 1921.

Following the Pittsburgh Pirates' late-season collapse in 1921, manager George Gibson and many players received harsh criticism for the squad's downfall, as the rival New York Giants claimed the National League pennant. Gibson shocked his players when he gathered them in Forbes Field's clubhouse after a loss to the St. Louis Cardinals on June 30, 1922, and announced his intention to resign as Pittsburgh's manager. Following this decision, some in the press blasted George for not cracking down on players who enjoyed carousing at night drinking alcohol. One person singled out for leading this type of lifestyle was shortstop Rabbit Maranville. In this photo, George Gibson is in the foreground engaging a fan, with Rabbit Maranville standing behind him. (Courtesy of the Library of Congress).

10

A Big Deal Ushers in Harmony and Pennant Glory

Sometimes, to buck the status quo, bold measures became necessary for changing a baseball team's chemistry and their potential diamond proficiency. For an overabundance of young talent to thrive and take that next step toward baseball stardom, the proper balance of roster additions and subtractions helped achieve the ultimate goal of winning a pennant. For Pittsburgh Pirates fans, coming close each year wasn't good enough, especially since the rival New York Giants had claimed four consecutive National League flags. These devoted patrons expected better results, particularly since youngsters such as Pie Traynor, Glenn Wright, Eddie Moore, and Kiki Cuyler had started developing into legitimate star performers. Sensing the essential nature of a change to Pittsburgh's composition toward achieving this objective, manager Bill McKechnie pulled off a blockbuster deal with that goal in mind shortly after the 1924 season ended.

On October 27, 1924, the Pirates traded second baseman Rabbit Maranville, first baseman Charlie Grimm, and pitcher Wilbur Cooper to the Chicago Cubs for second baseman George "Boots" Grantham, pitcher Victor "Vic" Aldridge, and first baseman Albert "Al" Niehaus. Upon learning of the deal, Pittsburgh's fans seemed divided over its merits. They agreed that this transaction looked no worse than an even swap, exchanging pitchers and second basemen. The sticking point hinged on trading away one of the league's best fielding first basemen in Grimm for an unknown quantity, such as Niehaus, who hadn't yet played a major league game. To rooters, this part of the deal appeared to be risky.

Whether he played the infield or outfield, the heavy-hitting Grantham seemed like a better baseball asset than Maranville at this stage of his young career. Although Rabbit performed exceptionally for the Pirates in 1924, most fans didn't regret his departure due to off-field conduct detrimental to team morale. Rooters also felt that Aldridge could capably fill Cooper's shoes. As had been the case with other hurlers, patrons appeared turned off by Wilbur's passive approach on the mound at times, despite always giving Pittsburgh his best efforts. On the other hand, Charlie Grimm happened to be a fan favorite whose work around the initial sack was a thing of beauty to behold. Grimm experienced terrible luck as a hitter, swinging a robust bat but seeing his drives gobbled up by opposing players.[1]

The day after consummation of this deal, around half of Pittsburgh's population felt the Cubs had fleeced the Pirates. Over the next week, that stance softened a bit. In Chicago, baseball followers hailed team president William "Bill" Veeck and manager William "Bill" Killefer as astute traders who pulled off a transaction that propelled the Cubs into pennant contenders for 1925. Barney Dreyfuss exclaimed that he felt great satisfaction over the trade and would make it again if the opportunity presented itself. Time would tell who gained the upper hand in this transaction and whether the faction of approving or disapproving Pirates fans received validation for being correct in the end.

Pittsburgh sportswriter Ralph S. Davis declared that Maranville's fate had been sealed years earlier because of his many off-field indiscretions. Davis also cited a contentious argument between McKechnie and Grimm the previous summer, following Charlie's effort to be paid a higher salary in the spring, as a possible reason for the first baseman's inclusion in this transaction. Concerning Cooper, the scribe conceded Wilbur to be one of the best southpaw pitchers in baseball. According to Davis, despite this phenomenal natural ability, Cooper never achieved great popularity among Pittsburgh's fans due to his moodiness and the bad habit of exhibiting open dissatisfaction when things went terribly in a game. Wilbur's friends in the city alleged patrons misunderstood him, claiming this personality trait resulted from his strong passion for winning.[2]

The shipping of Charlie Grimm and Rabbit Maranville removed the final two members of the Singing Quartet, who once had regaled the masses with their perceived musical ability before games. After completing this trade, Bill McKechnie stated that Eddie Moore, who batted .359 in a limited role the previous year, would be penciled in to replace Maranville at second base. Bill also said that George Grantham wouldn't be used as an infielder but would receive a chance to crack Pittsburgh's starting outfield.[3] Ten days before Christmas, McKechnie offered insight behind his reasoning for pulling the trigger on this colossal deal.

When I sent Maranville, Cooper and Grimm to Chicago, I broke up a good combination, but I did so in the hope that in another year or so I will have a better one. We have come close to winning the pennant three times since I have had charge of the club, but I realized we never would win it unless I make a shakeup. Frankly, I didn't want to part with Grimm, but I had to include him in the deal or see it fall through.

Of Maranville and Cooper I have only this to say. Both are fine ballplayers, but they didn't fit in the plans I have mapped out for the Pirates. Maranville, shifting over to second base last season, did remarkably well, and I believe he has more than one or two good seasons left. I expect him to play a fine game for the Cubs and I told Bill Killefer so when we made the deal. Cooper is far from through, and the change of scenery undoubtedly will help him, as it helps many a veteran. Good ballplayers, both of them—but not for me.

As I see it we got the best of the deal. If I hadn't thought so all along I wouldn't have made it.[4]

When Maranville returned from a hunting trip, he engaged the press about the deal. Rabbit planned to give the Cubs his best services, just as he'd done while playing for the Pirates. Maranville declared his intention to make Pittsburgh his permanent home since his daughter, Betty, attended school there, and he had made many friends in the city. He planned to remain in Chicago during the baseball campaign and live in the Smoky City during the off-season.[5] Rabbit currently worked a winter job for a Pittsburgh newspaper's circulation department.[6] Because of the desire to remain in Pittsburgh, Maranville became involved in one final incident because of that decision.

On the night of November 19, the car which Rabbit was driving struck five-year-old Frank Smayda (Smozda), of 75 Bates Street, in the Oakland section of Pittsburgh. An ambulance took the young boy to Mercy Hospital in serious condition with a fractured skull. The accident occurred on Bates Street near Wilmot Street.[7] Maranville surrendered himself at the local police station, where authorities charged him with reckless driving. Police released Rabbit on $1,000 bail pending the outcome of the boy's injuries. Maranville explained to the officers that a group of boys had been playing on the sidewalk when someone pushed Smayda into his automobile's path.[8] Witnesses corroborated Rabbit's account, attesting that the accident was unavoidable.[9]

In January 1925, the insurance company through which Maranville held a policy paid out a $700 cash settlement to the boy's parents. Young Frank, hit in front of his Bates Street home by Rabbit, had been confined to Mercy

Hospital for one month with a fractured skull. A hearing in Oakland police court still loomed for Maranville.[10] Rabbit only remained with Chicago for one season before being waived after the 1925 campaign ended and claimed by the Brooklyn Robins. Maranville signed with the St. Louis Cardinals on December 23, 1926, months following his release from Brooklyn. Rabbit played for the Cardinals' minor league affiliate Rochester Tribe of the International League for most of the 1927 season before a September call-up to the big club.

Maranville experienced an epiphany while playing for Rochester. One morning that spring, Rabbit awoke with a brutal hangover. When Maranville approached the mirror in his hotel room, the victim of too much partying didn't like seeing what stared back at him. Rabbit observed heavily lined, bloodshot eyes and a puffy face. Maranville realized that drinking alcohol had him down for the count like a boxer. At that moment, he vowed never to consume another drop of alcohol again.[11] Back with the Boston Braves in 1929, Rabbit expanded on this lifestyle change during an interview with a reporter. Maranville admitted that his career could be longer if he'd never fallen victim to alcohol's allure. It took him years to learn that lesson, but the truth of the situation finally brought about enduring change.

> I never cared about the taste of liquor. I only cared about the feeling it gave me after I drank it. One drink didn't give me any feeling. I took five or six, and then I'd take more.
>
> I finally got to the stage where I realized that I couldn't stay out all night drinking, and hope to compete with the fellow who was sober, who got the required amount of rest, and whose brain was clear and legs steady the next afternoon.
>
> So I got to saying "No." It wasn't so easy at first, but I got used to it, and I never touch drink anymore.

Maranville then discussed his past drinking code, which dispelled allegations that he acted as the boozing ringleader during his Pittsburgh Pirates days.

> I never took a ballplayer out of an evening and got him drunk. I've been accused of it, though. Why, when I was at Pittsburgh, I was accused of keeping the whole team drunk.
>
> If one of the boys came into the hotel lobby to the accompaniment of the rattle of milk cans, the manager would spot him, and say: "Aha, out with the Rabbit again, eh?"

But I never did that. I did my own drinking, and let the other fellow do his. Perhaps, I did too much of it. In fact, I know I did. I am still playing ball, but I know I would be better today if I had never taken liquor.[12]

In the wake of the big deal put forward by Pittsburgh and Chicago, the Pirates jettisoned another problem player from their roster. On December 16, the Pirates unconditionally released catcher Walter Schmidt. Although many who followed Pittsburgh's baseball fortunes had expected this news for several months, they appeared surprised by how the organization terminated Schmidt. Pirates fans assumed the club might transfer him to another major league squad. Attempts to find a potential trade partner at the league meetings in New York had failed. The Buccaneers requested waivers on the player, with all fifteen major league teams passing on Schmidt. The purchase of fellow backstop Earl "Oil" Smith from the Boston Braves on July 14, 1924, made Walter expendable. Barney Dreyfuss afforded the catcher a nice gesture, despite Schmidt not being a ten-year man in terms of major league service. In appreciation for Walter's years of playing for the Buccaneers, Dreyfuss allowed his catcher to broker a deal as a free agent instead of assigning him to the minors.[13]

Rather than shift Schmidt to a minor league team, as was their right, Pittsburgh handed the catcher his unconditional release. It appeared that Barney didn't consult Bill McKechnie about the move since Pittsburgh's skipper had included Walter in a discussion at the league meetings about the Pirates' future. During this interaction, McKechnie claimed Schmidt would get the bulk of the work behind home plate in 1925.[14] Walter had undoubtedly lasted much longer with the club than many troublemakers preceding him. Despite writing letters to Dreyfuss expressing hatred for Pittsburgh's owner, Schmidt remained with the squad three more seasons since blaming George Gibson and team ownership for the Pirates' failure in 1921. *Pittsburgh Post* sportswriter William "Bill" Peet offered proof that Barney's disdain over Walter constantly holding out for big money proved a critical factor behind this decision.

> When McKechnie telegraphed Schmidt in July 1922, asking him to come east, Walter's characteristic reply was. "Yes, but the old boy will have to come across with the salary I want."
>
> Barney Dreyfuss gave Schmidt what he wanted, made him satisfied with the financial arrangements and Schmidt has been with the club ever since at a salary said to be $12,000 a year.

The Pirate management gave Schmidt his unconditional release after every club in both leagues had waived claims.

Schmidt is a good catcher, one of the best in the league, and I for one am sorry he is not with the Buccos for the 1925 campaign, but the tip-off is obvious. Schmidt is too expensive a proposition. He places a valuation upon his services that does not appeal to the club owner. He is now a free agent, and if he comes back to the big show it will have to be at a reduction in pay.

Walter Schmidt always preached the gospel of "Get all you can out of the club owner, while the getting is good."

He was paid the limit right here in Pittsburgh. I do not know of a catcher in either league today who draws $12,000 a year.[15]

Walter Schmidt signed on with the St. Louis Cardinals for 1925 in what ended up being his final season as a major leaguer. In Pittsburgh, it became a work in progress, meshing the new players in with youngsters and a dash of veterans sprinkled in on the squad's roster. After experiencing a bumpy April where the Pirates went 5–8, the team played much better in May, going 16–9 that month. Regarding the big deal with Chicago, one of the acquired players' time as a team member proved brief. On May 30, Pittsburgh shipped first baseman Al Niehaus, who only hit .219 in 17 games, to the Cincinnati Reds for veteran hurler Thomas "Tom" Sheehan. Although he'd never played the position, George Grantham manned the initial sack when the National League raised the curtain on the 1925 baseball campaign.

Grantham gave a solid effort in his first season with the Pirates, playing 114 games and batting .326. For Bill McKechnie having a platoon option at first to give George, a left-handed batter, a day off, he and Barney Dreyfuss signed veteran right-handed swinging first baseman John "Stuffy" McInnis. While appearing in 59 games for Pittsburgh, McInnis hit a blistering .368. Vic Aldridge, the third player secured in the Cubs' deal, complemented holdover pitchers Lee Meadows, Johnny Morrison, Ray Kremer, and Emil Yde beautifully, going 15–7, supported by a 3.63 ERA. Of the eight starters in the lineup, on days when Earl Smith handled catching duties, second baseman Eddie Moore was the only player who didn't top the .300 mark. As Pittsburgh's leadoff hitter, Moore batted .298 and knocked in 77 runs.

Outfielder Kiki Cuyler continued his ascension to stardom for Pittsburgh, batting .357, smacking 18 home runs, and recording 102 RBIs. Cuyler also led the National League in runs scored (144), triples (26), hit-by-pitch (13), and tied four other players in games played (153). Veteran center fielder Max Carey experienced his best year at the plate, batting .343 while leading the circuit with 46 stolen bases. Shortstop Glenn Wright tied Kiki in the home-run department, batted .308, and drove in 121 runs. Third baseman Pie Traynor also wielded a deadly stick, hitting .320 and knocking in 106 runners, while outfielder Clyde Barnhart experienced a career year, batting .325 and bringing 114 teammates across the plate. Barnhart had shifted from third base to the outfield when Traynor placed a permanent stranglehold on that position in 1922.

One of the early season highlights for the Pirates occurred on May 7 in a game against St. Louis at Forbes Field. Vic Aldridge walked both James "Jimmy" Cooney and Rogers Hornsby to start the frame in the top of the ninth inning. Cardinals first baseman James "Jim" Bottomley stepped up to the plate and smacked a blistering line drive toward second base after receiving the hit-and-run sign. Both Cardinals runners were in motion when Pittsburgh shortstop Glenn Wright snagged the line drive in his glove as it appeared to be heading into center field. Wright's momentum guided him toward second, where he stepped on the keystone sack to retire Cooney. Glenn then tagged out Hornsby, who approached him at the bag, before St. Louis's star player could reverse course and attempt to return to first. Although the Pirates lost the game, 10–9, Wright had pulled off the thrilling maneuver of executing an unassisted triple play.[16]

Fans at Forbes Field also experienced the treat of another exhilarating moment a month after witnessing this rare unassisted triple play. On June 6, as part of the National League's Golden Jubilee Celebration, current Pirates team members played a short contest against former players from the 1901 aggregation before Pittsburgh's scheduled clash against the Philadelphia Phillies. In the three-inning game, the 1925 Pirates defeated the old guard from 1901, 5–3. Thousands of devoted Pittsburgh baseball fans received the grand opportunity to witness Honus Wagner, Tommy Leach, Claude Ritchey, and Kitty Bransfield cavorting on a baseball diamond. Fred Clarke managed and played left field for the 1901 squad. Proving that time indeed healed all wounds, even players such as Jack Chesbro and Jesse Tannehill, who'd fallen out of grace with Pirates management over two decades ago, were invited to participate in this festive occasion and attended.[17]

This celebration also helped set the wheels in motion for one of the most significant figures who ever donned a Pittsburgh uniform to return to the organization. On June 12, Barney Dreyfuss announced Clarke's hiring to rejoin the Pirates as an assistant to him, the team president, and manager Bill McKechnie. Under Fred's title of vice president, his responsibilities also included overseeing the club's scouting department. Conferences between the two men had been ongoing for the past few weeks. Serious negotiations started when Clarke came to Pittsburgh for the Golden Jubilee Celebration, and the two sides hammered out minor details before the announcement. Fred, who'd wanted to own a major league franchise, also purchased a block of team stock.

Pirates fans exuded an ecstatic outlook over the fiery Clarke rejoining the organization. These devoted patrons always expressed fondness for the man who'd previously guided the team to four National League pennants. His experience and insight should greatly assist McKechnie, while Fred's diplomatic nature hopefully could help nurture Pittsburgh's players into achieving great things.[18] In the past, Clarke had offered assistance when the Pirates held spring training in Hot Springs, helping George Gibson in 1922 and then Bill in 1923.[19] This would be the first time Fred's input directly impacted the team's fortunes since he retired from baseball following the 1915 season.[20] While pronouncing Clarke's coming aboard Pittsburgh's baseball ship once again, Dreyfuss stated that running a club was becoming too much of a strain for an individual his age. He wanted to shift some of that responsibility to a trusted person.[21]

Although some critics of Pittsburgh's team equated the club's summer surge with Clarke's arrival, Bill McKechnie's troops had started trending upward back in May. It didn't seem fair to blame McKechnie when the Pirates had been mired in the second division in April and then single out Fred's influence once things started jelling. "Wilkinsburg Bill" had been the man who assembled what appeared to be one of the greatest clubs in recent baseball history. The inspiration of Clarke's personality behind the Pirates' manager was the final ingredient in this winning recipe.[22] Pittsburgh pulled away from rival New York in the race by setting a scorching August pace, posting a 21–10 record that month. This stellar performance allowed the Pirates to increase their narrow one-game lead at the end of July to 7½ games when August ended.

Veteran infielder Johnny Rawlings received much credit for Pittsburgh's success that month.[23] McKechnie yanked second baseman Eddie Moore from the starting lineup for the contest against the Brooklyn Robins at Ebbets Field on August 18. The excuse put forward by Pittsburgh's manager as the determining factor alleged that Eddie suffered from a lame leg. This explanation appeared inadequate once Bill declared that Moore would play the outfield when the Pirates faced a southpaw pitcher. McKechnie benched Eddie, who didn't always approach his work seriously, for mental lapses and poor defensive work at second base.[24] After playing right field two days before his benching because Max Carey suffered an injury, Moore eventually returned within that capacity, briefly rejoining the reconfigured outfield.[25]

Sadly, an injury snuffed Rawlings's steadying influence during a game against St Louis at Forbes Field on September 5. In the sixth inning of that contest, while running from first base to second on Kiki Cuyler's groundball to the Cardinals' Jim Bottomley at the initial sack, Johnny's left foot twisted underneath him while sliding into the bag. Pittsburgh's players quickly rushed toward their teammate, indicating the injury's severity. Team physician, Dr. Gustav Berg, conducted a quick initial examination before left-handed twirler Emil Yde carried Rawlings off the field on his shoulder. A thorough medical analysis in the clubhouse by Dr. Berg and another physician revealed that Johnny had broken the fibula bone on the outer left ankle. The two medicos consulted advocated a six-week recovery period, effectively ending Johnny's season. Doctors placed a plaster cast on the leg before Rawlings went to St. John's Hospital on the North Side for X-rays.[26]

Despite Johnny Rawlings's unfortunate injury, Pittsburgh claimed the National League pennant, finishing with a 95–58 record, 8½ games ahead of second-place New York. The Pirates opposed the defending champion Washington Senators in the World Series. When it came to enormous worries for Bill McKechnie and Fred Clarke on the eve of the Fall Classic, Rawlings's absence topped the list. Following Johnny's injury, Eddie Moore returned to second base, while youngster Lafayette Fresco Thompson also saw time in that position. Many people believed that, if healthy, Rawlings likely would've been Bill's selection as the starter at the keystone sack due to the "good luck charm" factor and his ability to shine when the stakes proved their highest. If Johnny hadn't broken his ankle, he would've been an excellent insurance policy in the event the managerial tandem of McKechnie and Clarke had played Moore at second.[27]

In the big scheme of things, everyone connected to Pittsburgh's baseball organization should've been most concerned with Washington star hurler Walter Johnson. In Game One of the 1925 World Series at Forbes Field on October 7, Johnson throttled the Buccaneers, going the route and striking out ten batters as the Senators claimed a 4–1 victory. With the score tied 1–1 in Game Two the next afternoon, a hero emerged for the Pirates in the bottom of the eighth inning.

Leading off the frame against Washington starter Stanley "Stan" Coveleski, Eddie Moore reached first base on an error by shortstop Roger Peckinpaugh. Max Carey stepped to the plate for Pittsburgh and failed to push Eddie to second on two successive sacrifice bunt attempts. In the end, Carey did his job, as Moore moved up a station when Max grounded out to Senators second baseman Stanley "Bucky" Harris on a hit-and-run play.

Kiki Cuyler strolled into the box to face Coveleski. Stan worked carefully against the deadly Cuyler, who also exhibited supreme patience at the plate. Kiki refused to bite at Coveleski's first two pitches on the inside part of the plate that umpire Clarence "Brick" Owens called balls. Sensing he would see a sweet offering with a 2–0 count, Cuyler attacked the next offering and blasted a ferocious drive between Washington's Joseph "Joe" Harris and Edgar "Sam" Rice into right-center field. Much closer to Harris, the shot flew by him quickly, bounced near the stands, and skimmed the railing before landing among the temporary right-field seats' fans for a home run, as per rules from that period.[28] Pirates starter Vic Aldridge finished his masterful mound performance after loading the bases to start the ninth inning, preserving a 3–2 Pirates victory.

The importance of Cuyler's clutch home run and a victory in Game Two couldn't be understated since Washington claimed the first two contests on their home turf at Griffith Stadium. Johnson muzzled Pittsburgh's attack for the second time in Game Four on October 11, beating the Pirates 4–0. Before Game Five on October 12, McKechnie made a lineup change, benching George Grantham and replacing him with Stuffy McInnis. The veteran first baseman's steadying influence quickly became apparent as Aldridge won his second contest of the World Series, defeating the Senators, 6–3, and sending the teams back to Pittsburgh.

Before Game Six started at Forbes Field on October 13, Pirates second baseman Eddie Moore injured his hand during batting practice. After this occurred, former diamond icon Honus Wagner, who wrote a syndicated column throughout the World Series, came upon Moore underneath the grandstand. Eddie stood there crying while holding his badly bruised hand.

"Does it hurt so much?" Wagner asked him.

"I'm not crying because of any pain," Moore replied, "but I'm afraid I won't be able to bat at my best, and I want to help the boys win today."

Wagner offered the young player words of encouragement. As the game progressed, Moore most likely forgot about his sore hand, with feelings of joy replacing tears of regret.[29] Moore came up to lead off the bottom of the fifth inning, with the game tied, 2–2. Washington pitcher James Alexander "Alex" Ferguson began working on Eddie by throwing a low pitch that the batter let pass for ball one. Ferguson tossed a shoulder-high inside curveball that Moore took a mighty cut at with his bat. Eddie's bat connected against the pitch and sent the baseball screaming to deep left field.[30] Moore's drive soared over the temporary bleachers' new left-field screen for a homerun.[31] The crowd roared as Eddie's blast that gave Pittsburgh a 3–2 lead disappeared into the mass of humanity. As Moore crossed home plate, his teammates grabbed the second baseman, shook his hand, and patted him on the back.[32]

This score stood as Pirates hurler Ray Kremer's efficiency on the bump kept Washington's offense in check. The 1925 World Series now stood tied at three games apiece and headed for a decisive seventh contest. One day after Pittsburgh claimed Game Six, local newspapers reported about the organization securing two Pacific Coast League phenoms in a high-priced deal. Although Barney Dreyfuss and Bill McKechnie wouldn't confirm completing such a transaction, an authoritative source stated the Pirates acquired infielder Harold "Hal" Rhyne and outfielder Paul Waner from the San Francisco Seals for $100,000. Within the reported parameters of this deal, Pittsburgh expected to hand over $85,000 in cash and three players to be named later in exchange for Rhyne and Waner.[33]

Commissioner Kenesaw Mountain Landis ended up postponing Game Seven on October 14 at 2:30 P.M., after it had rained for one hour with no indication that the weather would improve.[34] Although a steady rain fell in Pittsburgh the following day, Landis checked out Forbes Field's conditions at 10 A.M. and decreed them to be satisfactory enough in his mind for playing Game Seven unless the poor weather continued.[35] The judge, anxious to complete the World Series after two previous postponements, disregarded his initial premise, allowing the contest to start and play out to its conclusion. However, a cold drizzle greeted players from both teams for the first pitch. A steady downpour replaced these light rain showers as the game progressed.[36]

The wet, sloppy, muddy conditions made life difficult for starting pitchers Vic Aldridge and Walter Johnson. Aldridge didn't make it out of the first inning as Washington pushed four runs across the plate. Johnny Morrison and Ray Kremer entered the fray and did fine work as the Pirates battled back throughout the contest. Down 6–4 heading into the bottom of the seventh inning, Pittsburgh plated two tallies to tie the score. Shortstop Roger Peckinpaugh restored the Senators' lead when he smacked a solo home run in the top of the eighth. As the rain intensified, things looked bleak for the Pirates when Johnson retired Glenn Wright and Stuffy McInnis to start the home half of the eighth.

Catcher Earl Smith gave Pittsburgh's fans something to cheer about when he stroked a double to right field. Hurler Emil Yde replaced Smith as a pinch runner at second base. Carson Bigbee, announced as the pinch hitter for Kremer, promptly blasted a two-bagger to the left-field screen that scored Yde and tied the game. Walter Johnson, exhibiting fatigue, walked Eddie Moore. Max Carey, who'd already played a critical role in the Pirates' comeback with a single and three doubles, entered the batter's box. Carey hit a ground ball toward Peckinpaugh at short. With the speedy Moore hustling to second base, Roger rushed his throw. Because of that haste and the slippery ball, Peckinpaugh's off-the-mark toss caused Senators second baseman Bucky Harris to leap in the air to catch the sphere. As Harris came down on the bag, he felt Eddie's foot underneath his. All runners ended up safe because Roger committed his eighth World Series error.

"King Ki-Ki," as sportswriter Ralph S. Davis referred to Kiki Cuyler in his column the day following Game Seven's completion, stepped up to the plate. Johnson had fooled Cuyler in the first inning, striking him out, while Pittsburgh's outfielder smashed a run-scoring double in the fifth.[37] A titanic battle ensued between these two players. The count reached two balls and two strikes, with Kiki pushing the drama to heightened proportions by fouling off many pitches. Cuyler then watched a close fastball go by that home plate umpire William Joseph "Barry" McCormick called ball three. The umpire's decision perturbed Walter and battery mate Herold "Muddy" Ruel. Johnson's next offering was too "fat" for a lethal hitter like Kiki, who took a mighty cut and clobbered the baseball.[38]

Cuyler's drive rocketed down the right-field line into restricted territory. The speedy Kiki darted around the bases, past first, second, third, and then home as he crossed the plate behind his three Pirates teammates. The umpires conferred, ruling the hit a double and sending Carey back to third base and Cuyler to second.[39] Arbiters based their decision on Forbes Field's ground rules since the baseball had become trapped underneath the tarp in foul territory when Washington's right fielder, Joe Harris, attempted to retrieve the sphere.[40] After Johnson retired Clyde Barnhart, the eighth inning ended with Pittsburgh in front, 9–7.

Bill McKechnie summoned southpaw hurler John "Red" Oldham to finish the game. Oldham had joined the Pirates in August after pitching for the Western League's Des Moines Demons. Red started the ninth inning by fanning the Senators' Sam Rice. Bucky Harris then lined to second baseman Eddie Moore for the second out. Leon "Goose" Goslin entered the batter's box. Goslin quickly got behind in the count as he took one of Oldham's tormenting crossfire pitches for strike one. Goose swung mightily at the second offering and came up empty. Red wound up one final time and fired the baseball. Goslin couldn't pull the trigger as umpire Barry McCormick signaled strike three. The Pittsburgh Pirates wore the crown as baseball champions for the first time since 1909.[41]

The list of Pirates heroes in the 1925 World Series proved a long one, as Vic Aldridge, Ray Kremer, Eddie Moore, Pie Traynor, Max Carey, and Kiki Cuyler positively impacted the proceedings. Carey received accolades as the top star, leading both teams at the plate with a .458 batting average. Max gave a remarkable performance since, unbeknownst to Pirates fans, he played the final two games in extreme agony.[42] Carey suffered a debilitating injury in Game Five when he collided with Bucky Harris while running from first base to second. The force of the impact rendered Max unconscious. Upon regaining his faculties, Carey continued in the contest. Bill McKechnie declared that had Game Seven not been pushed back one day because of inclement weather, Max probably would've remained on the bench.[43]

Carey endured and performed at an elite level despite excruciating pain and being wrapped in heavy bandages. Max's ribs troubled him throughout Game Seven, but he still frolicked about Forbes Field as if everything was fine. Following the World Series, Carey's ribs continued bothering him, and lumbago also confined him to his home briefly.[44] Max ended up being admitted to Mercy Hospital. Physicians stated they would restrict Carey's activities for an undetermined period until he recovered from pleurisy and the effects of damaged ribs. One doctor cautioned that because of the bad condition of his ribs, the Pirates' player needed to take every necessary precaution to avoid complications.[45] Max certainly didn't suffer from loneliness, as many visitors called on him at the hospital on October 27, including former mayor and current Allegheny County commissioner, Edward V. Babcock, who was also convalescing at the facility. Carey commented that day on his greatest joy since entering Mercy Hospital.

"The best thrill I have felt since I came here was experienced today," said Carey. "I was the recipient of a bouquet of beautiful roses. The flowers were pretty, but I got more of a kick when I looked at the donor's card. On it was the name of the Pirate batboy—Joe Snyder, an Oakland kid."[46]

In early November, speculation suggested that second baseman Eddie Moore might be waived out of the major leagues, going to San Francisco as partial payment in the deal to bring Hal Rhyne and Paul Waner to Pittsburgh. Such a rumor seemed preposterous since waiving Moore through the National League without either Chicago or Brooklyn putting in a claim appeared highly unlikely, even if the Pirates held a genuine interest in getting rid of him. Although Waner possibly could win a starting berth in Pittsburgh's stocked outfield, Rhyne definitely wouldn't supplant Glenn Wright at shortstop. Uncertainty existed over Hal, proving to be an upgrade over Eddie. It seemed likely that Rhyne would decorate the bench in a utility role.[47]

Deliberations over finding a place for a hot prospect such as Hal Rhyne aside, his purchase from San Francisco negatively impacted Pittsburgh's 1926 baseball season. Most importantly, sublime harmony existed within the Pirates' family in 1925. The earliest clue alluding to this not continuing one year later happened once the team gathered for spring training in Paso Robles, California. Moore arrived in camp with a bad cold, and Stuffy McInnis suffered from slight stomach trouble. George Grantham showed up a day late after stopping in Los Angeles, California, to visit a doctor about an old shoulder injury he'd suffered while playing for Chicago. Max Carey didn't even make it to Paso Robles. Stricken with a severe cold on the train ride, he exited the locomotive during a stopover in St. Louis, Missouri, and gained admission to the Deaconess Hospital.

A fear of pneumonia possibly occurring because of a previous illness related to suffering cracked ribs in the World Series precipitated such action. Luckily, this much direr diagnosis didn't happen, and Max hoped to join his teammates in a few days.[48] Carey did spend time on the sidelines as Pittsburgh prepared for the upcoming campaign by playing exhibition games. Eddie Moore also couldn't break into the lineup due to a bad ankle. This injury proved problematic for the Pirates' second baseman since rookie Hal Rhyne provided solid execution at the keystone sack in his place. *Pittsburgh Gazette Times* sportswriter Chilly Doyle declared the peppery Rhyne's performance at second to be a pretty sight, while his overall team play looked smoother than Moore's. In comparing the two men, Doyle also claimed Hal smacked the ball in a hard and timely manner, supplying an added point in his favor. Chilly surmised that Rhyne had won a job by making such a good impression on manager Bill McKechnie.[49]

Eddie started at second base for the Pirates on opening day, as St. Louis defeated Pittsburgh, 7–6, at Sportsman's Park on April 13. Moore experienced a wretched April, batting only .179 for the month. McKechnie replaced Eddie in the starting lineup with Hal on April 27 as the Pirates opposed Chicago at Cubs Park. Following sparse action in May as a pinch hitter and a pinch runner, Moore emerged as a regular again in early June but couldn't bump his batting average above .237. Eddie didn't act as the sole transgressor in this department. Max Carey floundered around the .200 mark, and fellow outer gardener Clyde Barnhart struggled while reaching an average of .165.

The pattern played out similarly for the 1926 Pirates compared to the previous season. The team had a rough time in April, posting a 7–10 record for the month before rebounding in May and going 16–8. Things regressed in June as Pittsburgh accrued an 11–12 mark that month, while the club soared throughout July, setting a blistering 21–10 pace. On June 10, the Pirates found themselves slightly in first place with a 27–19 record, putting them a minuscule seven percentage points ahead of the Cincinnati Reds. That day, Barney Dreyfuss began an exciting vacation adventure, something out of character for him since taking over ownership of Pittsburgh's baseball team. That Thursday, Dreyfuss, and his wife, Florence, embarked on the SS *Christopher Columbus* steamer in New York for Europe.

Barney planned to visit his childhood home in Germany during this long overdue vacation. Exhibiting their affection for Pittsburgh's magnate, the Pirates' players got together and crafted a farewell message to their boss.[50] The telegram, handed to Dreyfuss as he boarded the steamship on the night of June 9, exhibited a true sentimental spirit that exuded among the men at that time. Most players signed the bon voyage message using their first names or nicknames rather than surnames, adding a beautiful personal touch.

"Every good wish for a refreshing and comfortable voyage and a safe return to find us leading the league by a pennant-winning margin," read the message. "Appreciating the confidence you repose in us during your absence, we, by our personal signatures to this message, mutually pledge to each other and to you the very best that is in us to bring another pennant and world championship to Pittsburgh. We can win and we will."[51]

This group of players, highly confident in their abilities, truly believed they would win another National League pennant and World Series in this expression to Barney.[52] When it came to appreciating the confidence one reposed in a group during that leader's absence, actions indeed supplanted hollow words. In early July, rumors about poor behavior and disharmony found their way into print. One baseless tale claimed pitcher Vic Aldridge and shortstop Glenn Wright engaged in a fistfight. The outcome of this encounter supposedly explained the reason behind Wright's brief absence from the lineup. Tales of other clubhouse brawls sustained the gossip machine. Due to the wide circulation of such stories, gullible fans didn't question unsubstantiated fabrications.

The usual stories involving all-night parties and carousing accompanied such tales of internal dissent. While most of these accusations proved false, two team members engaged in occasional drinking excursions and never attempted to hide that fact. Team management didn't forbid the consumption of an occasional glass of beer, but these two players crossed that line by drinking hard liquor. They didn't even try keeping their behavior a secret, being quite open and proud about it, leading to further rumors of more expansive partying.[53] Things reached a problematic juncture for Pittsburgh when issues festering for some time interfered with playing the game between the lines on a baseball diamond.

On July 14, the New York Giants swept a doubleheader from the Pirates at Forbes Field by scores of 12–8 and 5–2. Following the double loss, manager Bill McKechnie fined second baseman Eddie Moore and pitcher Emil Yde.[54] McKechnie doled out a stiff $100 penalty to Moore, while Yde's fine amounted to $50. This punishment arose from the manager charging the two players with indifferent play. He'd repeatedly warned both individuals that a lack of conscientious diamond effort would bring severe consequences. This lackluster attitude had pushed Bill's patience beyond the breaking point. Rabbit Maranville was the last team member fined for indifferent play or egregious conduct off the field. Maranville had received his penalty for breaking training rules.[55]

Sportswriter Ralph S. Davis believed McKechnie had ulterior motives for doling out these two harsh penalties. Davis felt this was a warning shot to others who'd exhibited indifference and weren't always giving their best effort.[56] Regarding Moore's situation, the writer alleged he'd displayed indifferent play well before receiving a reprimand. In one instance during the series' first game against New York on July 12, Eddie made a listless attempt when an opposing player smacked a groundball in his direction. Although fans had been cheering all season for Moore each time he batted, and some even encouraged him in this lazy moment, keen observers realized the second baseman appeared to be developing into a slacker who didn't offer supreme effort.[57]

McKechnie had also placed too much faith in Hal Rhyne since his spring brilliance proved a mirage. When Bill decided to bench Hal, the sulking Moore received his opportunity. Rhyne returned to the lineup at shortstop when injuries sidelined Glenn Wright, forcing Johnny Rawlings to replace Eddie after Pittsburgh's manager punished him. Moore threatened to quit the club, incensed over being docked $100 in pay. Eddie's bad attitude had started early in the season. Moore believed that since he'd performed as the 1925 championship team's starting second baseman, management should've afforded him more respect while also perceiving they'd ignored him and bestowed too much attention on Rhyne. *Brooklyn Daily Eagle* sportswriter James J. Murphy pondered whether McKechnie possibly erred in selling second baseman Fresco Thompson to the International League's Buffalo Bisons before the 1926 campaign began.[58] Thompson ended up hitting .330 for Buffalo that year.

Moore had also incurred Barney Dreyfuss's wrath through an incident the previous year, either during the World Series or shortly after it concluded. It wasn't a secret that Dreyfuss turned on individuals who either didn't follow the straight and narrow path or committed some unacceptable offense. In more than one instance this past off-season, the team had asked for waivers on Eddie.[59] In response to the recent incident, rather than hold onto Moore until the campaign ended and attempt to make a trade, the management trio of Bill McKechnie, Fred Clarke, and Sam Dreyfuss, tasked with running things in the owner's absence, placed the player on waivers shortly after being fined. More than a half dozen clubs from both major leagues submitted a claim for Eddie's services.[60]

Due to being the National League's resident cellar dweller, Boston secured Moore's services on July 20 for the $4,000 waiver price. Eddie immediately joined the Braves, who'd just finished up their series against Pittsburgh at Forbes Field, and traveled with his new team to Cincinnati. One area newspaper described the move as coming to fruition because Moore had criticized McKechnie's strategy system. Although deeming Eddie undesirable, *Pittsburgh Press* sportswriter Lou Wollen believed management had allowed feelings and emotions to cloud sound judgment. Wollen reasoned that holding onto an asset and involving that player in a transaction to address an area of need after the season concluded seemed more logical.[61]

During his brief time with the Pirates, Eddie Moore gained a reputation for being high-strung and irritable. This personality trait most likely resulted from nervousness and his self-conscious temperament while manning the keystone sack for Pittsburgh. Sportswriter Norman E. Brown argued that Moore experienced a daunting task due to his fellow infielders. Immediately after arriving on the scene with Eddie in 1924, shortstop Glenn Wright absorbed a substantial portion of the spotlight. Many classified third baseman Pie Traynor as an indisputable star performer. A nervous Moore realized he needed to keep pace with these teammates or suffer in the many newspapers' daily reviews. Brown also felt that because of Traynor's value at the hot corner, Bill McKechnie avoided validating a suspicion that Eddie might be better suited to play third base rather than second.[62]

In 1978, when interviewed by Dr. Eugene Converse Murdock, chairman of Marietta College's history department at the Ohio educational institution, Wright graded Moore as the best second baseman he'd ever played alongside. Glenn also told Dr. Murdock that Eddie acted hot-tempered and had a fuse that burned quickly.[63]

If Bill McKechnie levied fines against Eddie Moore and Emil Yde as a wake-up call to other team members who weren't toeing the line, it didn't work. Pitchers Vic Aldridge and Johnny Morrison both fell victim to justified organizational jurisprudence for breaching club rules.[64] On July 22, team treasurer

Sam Dreyfuss announced that the club fined Aldridge $50 for violating the Pittsburgh organization's rule requiring pitchers to immediately report to the clubhouse after being removed from a contest.[65] In game two of a doubleheader against Brooklyn at Forbes Field on July 21, the Robins knocked Vic and his ailing arm out of the box in the first inning after pitching to just three batters, leading Bill McKechnie to replace him with Leslie Ambrose "Bullet Joe" Bush. Aldridge walked to the clubhouse, changed out of his uniform into street clothes, and left the ballpark. The rule Vic broke also mandated that each player appear in the locker room before every contest.

Pirates management fined Aldridge for being absent without leave when the doubleheader concluded and thus breaking a team rule. Vic evidently was disgusted with his performance, went to the clubhouse, changed out of his uniform, and stormed away without asking if he could leave. McKechnie found this excuse to be insufficient and, to maintain strict discipline, plastered the fine. The organization slapped a suspension on Morrison for assuming he possessed carte blanche to do as he pleased.

Johnny recently had a procedure to remove his tonsils. Upon leaving the hospital, he went home and convalesced at his apartment. On July 22, Pittsburgh baseball officials found that Morrison had returned to his off-season dwelling in Owensboro, Kentucky. He disobeyed club regulations by not seeking permission to leave the city. Sam Dreyfuss wired Johnny that the club would fine him unless he returned by train at a designated time. Morrison's slow recovery from the effects of his operation exacerbated the situation.[66]

Problems existed within the Pirates' ranks. When Pittsburgh started an eastern road swing against Brooklyn on July 25, the team held a five-percentage-point advantage over the Cincinnati Reds, with six games in hand. St. Louis stood third, 3½ games behind the leaders. The long road trip, which ended and started with a series versus the Robins, proved inconsistent for the defending world champions. They split two games with Brooklyn, swept both contests against New York, and claimed two out of four affairs versus Philadelphia.

Following a 14–0 shellacking at the hands of lowly Boston in the first game of a doubleheader on August 4, Pittsburgh secured the nightcap, 5–2. Things seemed to stabilize when the Pirates won two successive close games, defeating the Braves 4–3 on August 5 and 5–4 on August 6. The bottom fell out on August 7, as Pittsburgh failed to score a single run in either game of a doubleheader against seventh-place Boston. The Braves shocked the Pirates, claiming both contests by 2–0 scores, as umpires ended the second battle after eight innings because of rain.[67]

Pittsburgh rebounded nicely at the plate as their long journey wound down in another series against Brooklyn. The Pirates secured the first two games, scoring a combined 19 runs. Although Bill McKechnie's squad had only posted a 10–6 record thus far on this trip, their lead over the second-place team jumped to three games, where the cushion had only been five percentage points when Pittsburgh ventured east.[68] St. Louis, the new second-place team instead of Cincinnati, did gain ½ game in the standings over that time. In the Pirates' 10–2 victory over the Robins on August 10, outfielder Kiki Cuyler ended a 0-for-15 slump with an infield single in the ninth inning.[69] On August 11, Brooklyn defeated Pittsburgh, 4–2, to finish the team's road trip.

Before returning to Pittsburgh, McKechnie divided the squad into two groups. The first party, consisting mainly of battery men, boarded a train for the Smoky City. At the same time, other team members, under the supervision of coaches Jewel Ens and John "Jack" Onslow, remained in New York before traveling to New Haven, Connecticut, for an exhibition game on August 12.[70] The contest on August 13 at Forbes Field between Chicago and the Pirates ended up being postponed, despite the team chartering a special train so the remaining group of players could return home.[71] The Cubs' entourage couldn't arrive in time for the game since conditions stranded them in New York. Heavy rain in the Big Apple the previous night and that morning caused flooding in the city. The barnstorming group of Pirates had returned from their exhibition game against New Haven. At the same time, poor weather led to the postponement of Chicago's final contest versus New York at the Polo Grounds. The Buccaneers' train finally pulled out of New York at 7:07 A.M. on August 13, one hour after the Cubs had departed.[72]

As these players traveled by train back to the Smoky City, the *Pittsburgh Press* broke a sensational and astounding story about dissension spreading like cancer throughout the team, courtesy of several veteran team members. The newspaper reported that once this entourage reached the city, a meeting involving all the players, Bill McKechnie, Fred Clarke, and Sam Dreyfuss would be held that evening at Forbes Field. McKechnie, Clarke, and Dreyfuss had conferred at Pirates offices in the morning and concurred such a summit to be essential for dealing with a critical problem, which, if permitted to magnify, could ruin Pittsburgh's pennant aspirations. At the root of this trouble was whether Fred should be permitted to remain sitting on the dugout bench.

Clarke demanded that the alleged ringleaders of this revolt, veterans Babe Adams, Carson Bigbee, and team captain Max Carey, be punished for their role. Sam Dreyfuss initially preached caution in the matter, as the owner's son indicated he most likely would seek league president John Heydler's counsel before making a rash decision. Supposedly, six men voted in favor of Fred losing the right to remain in the dugout as manager Bill McKechnie's assistant. *Pittsburgh Press* sportswriter Ralph S. Davis phoned Carey at his home that morning to get his side of the story.[73] Max, as well as Pittsburgh's manager and vice president, wasn't part of the entourage that made the trip to New Haven.[74]

> I feel that a statement is due myself and the other veteran members of the team, who only have its best interests at heart.
>
> Anything that we did was done because we wanted to see the club win. After we lost that doubleheader in Boston, McKechnie suggested that a meeting be held to discuss the welfare of the club. A time was set for the session, but about a half hour before it was to be held, McKechnie called it off.
>
> Later Clarke came to the clubhouse, and said he would not appear again on the bench if he was not wanted. The next day a vote was taken by the players as to whether he should be asked to retire. That is all there is to it.
>
> But I feel that Manager McKechnie should make a statement, setting forth my part and that of other players in the matter. We simply wanted to get results.
>
> No team can thrive under two managers. That is not said with any special reference to Fred Clarke, for he and I are good friends, but it is a general baseball proposition that holds true on any club. There were conditions existing on our club which were losing games for us, and it was primarily with a view of getting better results that we jumped at McKechnie's suggestion to hold a meeting and try to iron out our difficulties, regardless of what they might be.

Fred Clarke did leave the bench for the August Brooklyn series after finding out about a potential uprising orchestrated by those working against him.[75] Acting within his capacity as team captain, Max Carey believed these actions to be honorable and done for no other reason than the team's best interests and success. Max had been with the Pirates since 1910. He certainly should've known that this issue wasn't dead despite his comment about taking a vote, and that was all there was to it. A baseball icon's bruised ego, an individual's effort at saving his job, and a young man attempting to exhibit courage when dealing with a crisis for the first time dictated that wouldn't be the case. This action resulted in the administration of swift and decisive action, leading to the downfall of the National League's best team.

Pittsburgh Pirates second baseman Eddie Moore played the hero in Game Six of the 1925 World Series against the Washington Senators on October 13 at Forbes Field. With the game tied 2-2 in the bottom of the fifth inning, Moore connected against a pitch from Washington hurler Alex Ferguson and blasted a home run that ended up being the contest's deciding marker. Following a solid season in 1925, Eddie fell out of favor with Pirates management one year later. Due to exhibiting a lackluster attitude in the first game of a doubleheader against the New York Giants at Forbes Field on July 14, 1926, manager Bill McKechnie fined Moore $100 for indifferent play. The Boston Braves claimed Eddie after Pittsburgh placed him on waivers. (Courtesy of the Library of Congress).

11

The One Time A-B-C Spelled Mutiny

Just as baseball had evolved on the diamond since the Deadball Era, athletes performing at the major league level differed from their predecessors. In these changing times, baseball players felt more independent and freer to speak their minds on essential topics related to the sport. This newfound determination allowed for seamless deployment in matters that affected the organization's well-being that paid their salary. Deadball Era performers had also made their voices heard, but the dynamic for handling and dealing with a major league player changed as the game evolved into the lively-ball era of the 1920s. Fred Clarke last directed a squad a decade earlier before rejoining the Pittsburgh Pirates' organization as vice president and assistant manager in 1925. Clarke's methods, which garnered him much past success, especially throughout the twentieth century's first decade, were not necessarily prudent or always likely to be accepted by players in the current baseball environment.

Discord had taken root in the Pirates' backyard due to a conflict between some players and part of Pittsburgh's management hierarchy. This discontent threatened to derail the club's aspirations to repeat as National League pennant winners in 1926. Fred's presence in the dugout as an advisor to manager Bill McKechnie didn't enthrall some team members. Pirates captain Max Carey believed that two managers on any baseball team were one too many. As a result, the players voted regarding whether Fred should be permitted to remain on the bench. On the morning of August 13, Clarke, McKechnie, and treasurer Sam Dreyfuss conducted a conference at the team's Forbes Field office to address this situation.

Those press members outside the room's doors heard a loud discussion throughout the meeting. Reporters standing nearby in the corridor struggled to ascertain who said what, except when Clarke's raised voice repeatedly exclaimed, "I want." Writers couldn't understand what Fred exactly wanted, although he likely insisted on enforcing some kind of disciplinary measures on the guilty parties. At one point, Clarke refused to leave the room when asked to do so. Upon exiting the club office, McKechnie told reporters that no statement would be forthcoming on his part until after the Pirates' players arrived back in Pittsburgh around 5 P.M.

"As soon as the players get in," said the manager, "there will be a meeting, and following that session I will probably have a statement to make. Until that time I have nothing to say."

Although he didn't delve into the particulars surrounding resolved team policy in this case, Bill had offered some general comments when pressed that morning.

"I don't know what I will do yet," said Bill. "I want to protect the best interests of the club alone. I am interested in winning another pennant for Pittsburgh, and I am going to be governed accordingly. Whatever I may have to say will be said after full consideration has been given to every point."

A reporter followed up by asking McKechnie about the extent of Fred Clarke's power relative to the organization.

"He is supreme," Bill replied. "He is the president of the club right now. Mr. Dreyfuss gave him full authority when he left for Europe."

"Does his authority extend over you?" a scribe asked.

"I would say that it does," answered the manager. "But I want to make it strong that Fred has never exercised it, as far as I am concerned. He has been fine with me, and we are the closest and best of friends. We have never had a word of difference. He has never tried to dictate to me. I have managed the club according to my own ideas, though, of course, Fred and I have conferred daily."[1]

Once the players arrived at Forbes Field's clubhouse, they engaged in a ten-minute session with organizational figureheads that brought about a stunning and shocking resolution. When the dust settled, three longtime team members walked the plank for leading a purported mutiny against the baseball team's best interests.[2] Before the conclave started, Sam Dreyfuss stated he would do the talking on behalf of team management.[3] This decision made sense since he represented the Dreyfuss name synonymous with Pittsburgh Pirates baseball since 1900. Once all the players gathered, Sam read a statement announcing the remedy for such blatant action by the group of mutineers, mutually agreed upon by him, Fred Clarke, and Bill McKechnie.

I have been chosen to talk to you about a most serious matter and I assure you all that I am not at all tickled over the task which is certainly a tough one and naturally I do not like to be the one to have to tell it to you. Bill McKechnie and myself both felt that the attack made upon Fred Clarke was totally unnecessary and unwarranted, and a step which could only lead to trouble. It is entirely beyond me how a group of men could, after giving any thought to a matter of that kind, go through with the proposition. Surely they must have foreseen the trouble it was bound to cause the rest of the team and the management, as well as the rest of the public.

It is something that we think must be stopped at the source and stopped quickly. We have engaged or hired our players to play ball as well as to give their very best services both on and off the field. Clarke, McKechnie and myself are paid to run the ball club, each having his respective duties to perform, whatever they might happen to cover.

We considered the matter of what should be done in this particular instance, with extreme care, and reached the firm and unalterable conclusion that for those spokesmen or ringleaders of the insurrection, Adams is unconditionally released, effective at once, and Bigbee also is unconditionally released, to take effect immediately.

Carey is suspended without pay pending waivers which were asked on him today. His services will go to the claimant whose club is the lowest in the standing of the teams, or otherwise he will be sold at the waiver price.

It was a particularly hard thing to do to these men who were the oldest players on the team in point of service, but we considered the situation most carefully and this step was considered for the best interests of the baseball public, the players and the club owners.

Manager McKechnie and myself both firmly believe that if those players who have been loyal to their fellow players and employers will continue to bear down every day, the club will finish on top, where it belongs.

Sam Dreyfuss concluded his speech by saying the matter was closed and no appeal of this decision would be forthcoming. Dreyfuss then handed Adams and Bigbee their unconditional releases and notified Carey of his suspension.[4] Barney Dreyfuss's son also named third baseman Pie Traynor to replace Carey as the Pirates' team captain.[5] Pittsburgh's players resembled a sad, dejected group as they filed out of the room after the conference ended, looking as if they'd just attended the funeral of a dear friend. As sportswriter Ralph S. Davis described it, they knew this action resulted from Fred Clarke's "mailed fist" approach bringing about such a harsh penalty. These men also realized Fred's word to be law and that Bill McKechnie performed a role subservient to Pittsburgh's vice president. After the meeting, McKechnie looked downtrodden and brokenhearted despite agreeing with the punishment.[6]

Reaction within baseball circles came swiftly. Former Pirates greats Honus Wagner and Deacon Phillippe expressed extreme confidence in Clarke and McKechnie, declaring a pennant-winning baseball squad must preserve a sound system and harmony.[7] Pittsburgh's baseball fans seemed divided over the action taken by team officials in casting three players aside who'd given the organization a combined forty-six years of loyal service. Many on one side believed the organization treated Babe Adams, Carson Bigbee, and Max Carey like scapegoats. In expressing their concerns to Pittsburgh's manager regarding their teammates' feelings about Fred, they did so under the impression that it was a majority consensus from the squad. Other patrons felt management had followed the proper course maintaining discipline on a team battling for the pennant by releasing these insurgents.[8]

Fans interviewed by the *Pittsburgh Press* one day after the three veterans' dismissal offered contrasting views on this roster purge. Almost everyone expressed positive insights about Fred Clarke and the trio of players as individuals and good baseball men. Burke F. Reed stated, "Fred Clarke forgot more baseball than those three men will ever know." J. A. McKee of Canonsburg, Pennsylvania, took issue with Clarke's statement about desiring to bring the pennant to Pittsburgh. If so, McKee wanted to know why hurler Alvin "General" Crowder wasn't sporting a Pirates uniform but instead wearing the Washington Senators' spangles.[9]

Crowder had exhibited promise during spring training after Pittsburgh purchased him on an option from the Southern Association's Birmingham Barons. This option included a second payment if he remained on Pittsburgh's roster after May 1, 1926. Barney Dreyfuss called their bluff when Birmingham tried to increase the price of that final sum, believing Alvin likely would stay with the Pirates. The Pirates' owner sent Crowder back to the Barons without any stipulations or strings attached.[10] Besides lamenting Alvin slipping away, this Canonsburg native also wanted to know that if Dreyfuss truly placed Clarke in charge while vacationing in Europe, why did Fred insist on scheduling so many exhibition games? McKee reasoned that such meaningless contests played during the sweltering summer weather in 1926 negatively affected the players' conditioning.

Another Pirates fan classified Adams's, Bigbee's, and Carey's discharges as "One of the most cold blooded and ridiculous performances of which he has ever heard." One disgusted patron, who didn't offer his name, submitted the most scathing indictment of Fred Clarke from those interviewed by the *Pittsburgh Press*.

> Why Fred Clarke should have dictatorial powers over the Pittsburgh club is beyond me. There is no question that he was a great baseball player. As a manager, however, I fail to see that he ever was a wonder. Nearly a quarter of a century ago the Pittsburgh club won three pennants, with Clarke as manager. The club of that day was formed by a consolidation of the Pittsburgh and Louisville clubs, bringing together such a galaxy of stars that their failure to win pennants would have been one of the wonders of baseball.
>
> As soon as the combination of that day began to break up pennants went elsewhere and it was not until 1909 that another pennant came to Pittsburgh. I know it is the opinion of many fans that the Pittsburgh club of that year was not in the same class with the present club or the clubs that won pennants for Pittsburgh some years earlier.
>
> After 1909 Pittsburgh waited until 1925 for another pennant, Clarke being the manager for many of the seasons during that period. Clarke could win pennants when a ready-made team was handed to him. I could never see him as a developer of young players or as a handler of a team to be mentioned in the same breath with numerous other managers.[11]

Sportswriters from Pittsburgh's newspapers also weighed in on the controversy. Havey J. Boyle of the *Pittsburgh Chronicle Telegraph* surmised that if, when acting as a team spokesman, had Max Carey believed he was leading a rebellion, the veteran outfielder never would've gone through with his plan to oust Clarke. Max trusted that most of his teammates agreed they would perform better with just Bill McKechnie on the bench while also feeling his manager shared this sentiment. Boyle reasoned that since players favored Clarke in their vote, Max, Adams, and Bigbee were wrong in their actions. Chilly Doyle of the *Pittsburgh Gazette Times*, gauging the fans' reaction, felt most of these patrons expressed deep sympathy for the three players' plights. Doyle also stated a sad note in management's decision persisted and that many people perceived Carey to be a victim rather than an instigator.

James J. Long of the *Pittsburgh Sun* deeply regretted that such a situation ever arose in Pittsburgh baseball. Long backed those patrons who believed removing these three players was the only logical solution. From a baseball standpoint, the writer also thought it a warranted course of action to sacrifice playing strength for team harmony. Sports editor Ralph S. Davis of the *Pittsburgh Press* advocated for the three players, offering a scathing opinion regarding the hypocrisy surrounding Max Carey's banishment.

"The Pittsburgh club officials' action in asking for waivers on Max Carey," wrote Davis, "in punishing him for any part he may have had in the rumpus over the presence of Fred Clarke on the bench was not without a tinge of commercialism. No attention was paid to the fact that Carey for years has given his best. But the club isn't going to be entirely rid of him. It will get at least the waiver price of $4,000. Had Carey been unconditionally released as were Adams and Bigbee, he could have dickered with other clubs for his services—but the club wanted that $4,000, and Max will probably land with the tailenders."[12]

Davis further stuck to his convictions, guaranteeing he most likely wouldn't be invited to any Pittsburgh Pirates organization Christmas party. The writer categorized this dismissal of three loyal players, who'd always aligned themselves with the organization's best interests, as too severe a penalty. He found it inconceivable to the average fan that Babe Adams, Carson Bigbee, and Max Carey, paradigms of virtue and integrity, would ever resort to being troublemakers disrupting team harmony. Davis also understood that a valuable asset such as Carey could've brought a fortune to the Pirates on the open market.[13] He felt Fred Clarke had overreacted in demanding such a severe punishment, believing a fine and standard suspension the proper reprimand for this type of offense. Such a course would've vindicated management's power while also serving as a lesson to Carey, so the veteran outfielder wouldn't offer further opinions or act on them. In this case, Max believed he did it with the team's best interests in mind.

Davis conceded that Adams's and Bigbee's releases didn't come as a great surprise since such a fate probably awaited them due to having outlived their usefulness with Pittsburgh. Although Pirates management vehemently considered this a concluded case, the writer pondered this claim's validity regarding the other three undisclosed players who voted for Fred's removal from the bench. He reasoned that nothing could prevent Clarke, a true fighter throughout his baseball career who bristled over anyone usurping his authority, from attempting to discover their identities. Davis wondered if the club's vice president might dole out further punishment by once again using a "mailed fist" policy through an action such as making life difficult for these individuals come contract time over the winter. The *Pittsburgh Press* sports editor also claimed that many Forbes Field patrons believed the crisis likely would've been averted if Barney Dreyfuss wasn't vacationing in Europe.[14] For Fred's part, he thought it best for everybody involved to move on from this closed incident.

"The only thing for us all to do," said Clarke, "is forget it."[15]

In the eyes of devoted Pirates fans and the three fired players, such finalization wasn't feasible. One day after Sam Dreyfuss issued the organization's edict, New York Giants manager John McGraw indicated he might claim Max Carey at the waiver price.[16] McGraw asserted that he held no interest in picking up Babe Adams or Carson Bigbee. That same afternoon, Cincinnati Reds skipper John "Jack" Hendricks stated his team wouldn't bid for the services of any of the three deposed players.[17] Upon receiving the news shortly after Max had been placed on waivers the previous night, St. Louis Cardinals manager Rogers Hornsby declared he wanted to acquire the outfielder for his team. Hornsby planned on putting in a waiver claim, although it seemed highly unlikely St. Louis possessed any chance of bringing Carey into the fold since the Cardinals currently occupied second place in the National League.[18]

Pirates fans were disappointed, hoping for clarity from manager Bill McKechnie on what had led to this drastic action. His only statement following the decision was, "We all had better try to forget things."[19] Many rooters believed McKechnie made a grave mistake by not handling the matter differently, pointing out that Pittsburgh's skipper should've immediately thwarted the movement to criticize Clarke. A majority of these fans, gravitating toward the players' side, felt the club belittled Max by requesting waivers on him and thus banishing him to the league's lowest club willing to pay $4,000.[20] One day after their removal from Pittsburgh's roster, Carey, Bigbee, and Adams remained in seclusion that Saturday, preparing a formal statement offering their side of the sordid affair. Following this confab, the trio decided to hold off making comments since the timing didn't seem right, determining that a statement wouldn't be forthcoming any earlier than Monday.[21]

On the morning of August 14, Max Carey left his home at Louisa Street and McKee Place in the Oakland section of Pittsburgh shortly after breakfast. He drove to Babe Adams's Morrowfield Apartments residence in that same neighborhood. The hurler and Carson Bigbee awaited Max when he arrived. The three men conferred for many hours before appearing in the Morrowfield dining room at noon to eat lunch. Before sitting down to dine, Carey stopped for a moment and offered a brief statement to newspaper journalists.

"Our consciences are clear," declared the deposed Pirates captain. "We all had a good night's rest. We couldn't ask for more. We were working for the success of the team and if we are killed for that it is something we could not avoid."

Amid constant discussion about the incident in newspapers and throughout Pittsburgh, Fred Clarke reiterated that the affair was a closed book.

"The incident is closed as far as I am concerned," Clarke averred. "The guilty players have been punished and I believe that the club will win the pennant for the second consecutive year. I will be on the bench henceforth."

Fate certainly could be fickle at times, as team management hoped to turn the corner and bring diamond action back into the consciousness of local baseball fans. Over 20,000 patrons attended Forbes Field on August 14, desirous of watching the Pirates play a doubleheader against Cincinnati. Intermittent showers and a final steady downpour crushed those hopes as club officials announced a postponement at 4 P.M. Max declared they planned on awaiting further developments before issuing any public statement regarding the trio of alleged malcontents.[22] In the end, Adams, Bigbee, and Carey didn't reveal this "inside story" until the Pirates' season concluded.[23]

Regarding Fred Clarke's return to the bench, he'd demanded that all offenders who clashed with his wishes in this respect receive heavy penalties before rejoining the Pirates' team in the dugout. Clarke claimed to be surprised and saddened to learn such a movement against him had existed.[24] Supposedly, the request by these three individuals, related to Fred's interference, stunned Bill McKechnie when they approached him about the problem. Bill immediately engaged Fred in a conference. When Clarke asked what he should do, McKechnie feebly offered no immediate solution, replying that he needed to thoroughly think over things in his mind before responding.

Pittsburgh's vice president met with Adams, Bigbee, and Carey in his hotel room on August 12. Clarke told them why he'd occupied the bench and that it wasn't to criticize or interfere with the manager but only to assist in helping the team win. Fred then asked the trio to honestly and openly articulate their grievances, and their response remained a secret.[25] This conference certainly didn't assuage Clarke's bruised ego, as the organization implemented his vindictive request for a punitive admonishment. Although Carey, the spokesman for the three jettisoned players, didn't initially release a statement about the "inside story," he decided to appeal his case to a higher power to clear both his name and those of his two teammates when it came to instigating a rebellion. New York sportswriter John B. Foster reported that Max planned on traveling to that city on August 16 to see Judge Kenesaw Mountain Landis and plead his case before the commissioner. Landis had stated he would meet with Carey if the ostracized player called on him.

Foster also revealed the crucial incident, which galvanized Pirates team members to take action against Fred Clarke. The pivotal event occurred when Boston swept a doubleheader from Pittsburgh at Braves Field on August 7, holding the Pirates scoreless throughout that afternoon. Clarke occupied his place on the bench during the first contest. Fred prearranged leaving before the second game started to catch the boat train to New York. As Clarke rose from the bench to depart, he turned toward Bill McKechnie and offered a suggestion regarding the nightcap contest and a slumping Max Carey.

"Better get someone out there to play center field," said Clarke. "Max is having a hard time of it."

"I haven't got anybody," McKechnie replied.

"Put somebody out there, even if it is a pitcher," suggested Clarke.[26]

The Pirates' manager heeded his boss's advice, shifting Kiki Cuyler to center field and playing Carson Bigbee in left in that second game. A later report alleged that Clarke had responded to McKechnie by saying, "Put the batboy or anybody else in instead of Carey. The batboy could do more hitting than he can."[27] In respect to the first version, maybe Fred was reflecting on those early golden days of baseball as Pirates player and manager, thinking the squad possessed someone like southpaw hurler Jesse Tannehill, who'd been at his disposal to play in the outfield. In either case, some players on the bench heard the disrespectful comment and related the story to Max. The squad's three elder statesmen then determined to conduct a meeting to address the advisability of Clarke remaining on the bench. These veterans prevailed upon all other Pirates players to attend the conference, who then selected Adams, Bigbee, and Carey as the group's spokesmen tasked with bringing this to Bill McKechnie's attention.[28]

According to Max, McKechnie called for a meeting after their three-person committee advised him several times that they thought something was holding back the club. After agreeing to conduct this conference, Bill eventually called off the session.[29] McKechnie didn't permit this meeting, scheduled to be held in Kingston, New York, as the team traveled to New York City to start a series against Brooklyn, to move forward. At this point, Carey believed the issue to be dead until Pittsburgh's manager resurrected it again in New York City.[30] Max asserted that McKechnie later advised the players that a meeting would occur. Clarke, present at this gathering, insisted the players take a vote on the matter of him remaining on the bench. Management cautioned each player not to discuss the issue verbally but rather to offer a verdict secretly by writing their selection on a piece of paper.[31]

Fred also told the committee spokesmen, the remaining players, and others connected to the club that he expressed no desire to continue sitting on the bench if they didn't want him there. Clarke stated he only occupied a place in the dugout because he thought his presence helped the team. Of course, Fred's attendance at this conference came about because McKechnie had alerted him to the danger brewing, linked to possible dissension. Bill's determination to pass this information on to a superior officially placed the matter at ownership's feet since Clarke operated as the highest-ranking representative in Barney Dreyfuss's absence.[32] Fred expressed his thoughts on why he participated in daily game-related activities for the Pirates.

"Bill McKechnie requested me to sit on the bench when I became associated with the club in an official capacity last year," said Clarke. "I would not have embarrassed Bill by taking a seat without an invitation. As far as the management of the club goes, the players know that I do not attempt to hamper McKechnie. On one or two occasions I have spoken advice to a player about something, but these matters had nothing to do with Bill's policy of running the club."[33]

Astute Pittsburgh baseball fans supportive of Babe Adams, Carson Bigbee, and Max Carey pulled out the rulebook to justify the action taken by these three men. They asserted that rather than engaging in a despicable coup, this trio only upheld Rule 21 of the National League, governing which individuals possessed permission to sit on a dugout bench. The rule stated: "Under no circumstances shall the umpire permit any person except the players and substitutes in uniform, coaches in uniform, and the manager of the team entitled to its exclusive use, to be seated on a bench." The *Pittsburgh Press* questioned whether Fred Clarke had ever signed a coach's contract allowing him to sit on the bench. Even Barney Dreyfuss wasn't permitted to do so under this tenet. Although Clarke wore a uniform in the dugout, this didn't necessarily entitle him to be there. Such an individual would only be obligated to vacate the premises if the umpire enforced that rule.[34]

On August 16, in his "Down the Line" column, *New York Herald Tribune* sportswriter W. O. McGeehan penned an article addressing the Pirates' situation titled "The Soviet in Baseball." McGeehan wrote that Pittsburgh's baseball team seemed interested in experimenting by applying the Soviet system to the National Pastime. He opined that the Pirates acted as members of a debating society, passing resolutions during baseball games, with few of them carrying forward. As a result, three players had been cut loose from the squad, and one of baseball's finest clubs seemed in disarray. McGeehan stated that the Pirates operated on a dual managerial system, a gambit made more difficult by the players giving themselves the powers of initiative, referendum, and recall.

The *New York Herald Tribune* sportswriter declared that such a thing always happened to an army composed entirely of generals. Each individual carrying that high rank thought everybody was out of step but him. *New York*

Times sportswriter James R. Harrison felt something more to this story was lurking beneath the surface. The scribe surmised that Barney Dreyfuss likely would investigate the affair after returning from his European vacation.[35] In Pittsburgh, this incident became known as the "ABC Affair" (Adams-Bigbee-Carey) because of the three individuals who organized a movement to preserve the squad's harmony and effectiveness on the diamond.[36]

Lou Wollen of the *Pittsburgh Press* imagined that things might've been different if individuals such as Pie Traynor, Glenn Wright, and Kiki Cuyler had been guilty of participating in what Pirates officials classified as a mutiny. Although according to Wollen, they had no involvement, the writer wondered if management would've unceremoniously dumped these three young stars with such little regard as had been the case with Babe Adams, Carson Bigbee, and Max Carey.[37] Sportswriter Gene Kessler of the *Washington Daily News* echoed that sentiment, claiming management kicked the three older players to the curb because better days had now passed in the twilight of their careers.[38]

Treasurer Sam Dreyfuss had stated the organization took no action against the other three individuals that voted for Fred Clarke's removal from the bench since they happened to be younger players who didn't fully comprehend the dire consequences of a so-called rebellious venture. Lou Wollen felt that long and faithful service counted for nothing. Wollen also believed that management's failure to search out and punish the other three individuals indicated that only those men who didn't hurt the organization's bottom line deserved condemnation. When it came to Traynor, Wright, and Cuyler, Lou believed it a good bet that their involvement in the matter would've resulted in either minor discipline or no punishment.[39] Including one of these players in the writer's prose became interesting when future events started unfolding. The younger Dreyfuss also seemed to be exerting more influence in his father's absence, as he supposedly had sanctioned the earlier fines against Eddie Moore and Emil Yde rather than Bill McKechnie.[40]

Max Carey left late Sunday night for New York to meet with Judge Kenesaw Mountain Landis on August 16. Babe Adams and Carson Bigbee decided against joining him, allowing Carey to present their side of the case. Max made the trip after the trio received a response to a telegram written by one of them, asking Landis to travel to Pittsburgh and conduct a hearing since they didn't receive due process in the case.[41] Baseball's commissioner explained why he requested Max talk with him in New York.

"My telegram to Carey was in response to a wire sent to Chicago and phoned to me here, asking me to come to Pittsburgh to give the players a hearing, as they had been punished without being given a chance to state their side of the matter," Commissioner Landis said. "It was impossible for me to go to Pittsburgh because of business that will keep me in the East for four or five days."[42]

Besides wanting vindication for him, Adams, and Bigbee after Pittsburgh management labeled the three as agitators and mutineers, Carey also had a personal motive for taking his case to baseball's highest power. The question had been broached, asking if Max could go to court if every National League team waived on him. Concerns over being blackballed indeed posed a legitimate problem for Carey. Reds manager Jack Hendricks had expressed no interest in claiming Max. Early in the evening of August 13, after Sam Dreyfuss announced his intentions regarding Carey, skipper Dave Bancroft of lowly Boston immediately waived on claiming the player. Philadelphia Phillies manager Arthur "Art" Fletcher stated he would pass on Max. Upon making his decision, Dreyfuss had asked National League president John Heydler to set aside the standard five-day waiver rule so he could directly dispose of Carey. Heydler denied his request.[43]

When Max Carey held a conference with Judge Landis in New York, baseball's commissioner told him he wouldn't take any action on the case until Heydler had conducted a hearing. Carey then conferred with the National League president, presenting his side of the story that resulted in the Pirates' organization disciplining him, Babe, and Carson, because of their efforts to remove assistant manager Fred Clarke from the bench. John concurred with Landis's decision, claiming the affair to be a league matter under his purview. He also believed in quickly handling the issue, scheduling the hearing for 11:30 A.M. on August 17 at the William Penn Hotel in downtown Pittsburgh. Heydler decided to conduct the inquiry in Pittsburgh for the convenience of all involved parties.

When asked by a reporter on the night of August 16 to offer his opinion on this hearing, treasurer Sam Dreyfuss calmly stated there would be no change in the club's attitude toward these men. Fred Clarke also confirmed that he, Dreyfuss, Bill McKechnie, and team secretary Sam Watters would represent the Pittsburgh Pirates' organization at this meeting.[44] When it came to putting good old-fashioned newspaper sleuthing into practice, an erstwhile *Pittsburgh Gazette Times* reporter pulled off a significant coup by interviewing McKechnie that evening. This individual engaged Bill while he sat puffing a cigar on the porch of his beautiful brand-new home on the William Penn Highway, about a mile from Wilkinsburg. The reporter wasted no time digging for a story, asking McKechnie if he would ever consider resigning his post as Pirates pilot.

"If I ever leave the Pirates, I'll have to be fired," said McKechnie. "I have too good a job to think of resigning. I have only one business, and that is baseball."

"What power has Heydler to intervene in this matter?" McKechnie was asked. "Isn't it strictly a club affair?"

"I don't know what Heydler can do," replied Bill. "It is the first time such a situation has arisen, so far as I know."

The newspaperman then talked of a rumor percolating in the city that Bill planned on refusing to attend John Heydler's hearing the following day. McKechnie declared he didn't believe this gossip.

"It isn't necessary that you should," responded the writer. "Are you going to be there?"

"I certainly am, but what concern is it of yours?" responded Bill with a belligerent look. "Who sent you out here?"

"My paper," replied the reporter. "Don't you think the public, which pays the freight, is entitled to know what is back of all this?"

"I have nothing to say to the public at this time," said McKechnie. "I have not talked to any newspaper for publication. Whatever I have to say will be said to President Heydler. He may issue a statement then. I will not issue a statement then or at any other time."

When this *Pittsburgh Gazette Times* writer challenged McKechnie by stating the fans wanted to know all about it, Pittsburgh's manager responded that he didn't plan on telling them, as he glared defiantly at the surrounding landscape. The reporter shifted gears, questioning whether government ownership of baseball or a national subsidy is more effective. He then returned to the matter regarding the patrons' right to know who bore fault in this sordid affair. Bill glared a second time and briefly remained silent before saying tomorrow's hearing would reveal such information.[45] McKechnie became more talkative when the discussion pivoted to the players' vote to oust Fred Clarke from the bench.

"Do you know what three players, besides Carey, Adams and Bigbee voted against Fred Clarke's presence on the bench?" asked the reporter.

"I do not know sir," replied McKechnie.

"But there were six votes in favor of Clarke's remaining away from the bench, were there not?" pressed the journalist.

"Yes," said Bill. "That is correct."

"You called off the players' meeting that was to have been held in Kingston, N. Y.?" asked the writer.

"I did," answered McKechnie. "There was no other meeting called except the one which I called in New York, at which the vote was taken."

"It was a secret ballot?" queried the newspaperman.

"Yes, sir," said Bill. "And six of the 24 players on the team voted against Clarke. I don't know who any of the six were."

Upon the writer again attempting to discover the actual cause behind this rebellion, Bill McKechnie continued deferring to John Heydler's hearing. When asked whether he felt satisfied having Clarke help him on the bench, McKechnie answered affirmatively, stating he invited the team vice president to sit there.

The reporter then asked about Fred's stock ownership in the club and a rumor which alleged he could succeed Barney Dreyfuss, who might retire after returning from Europe due to ill health, as president. Bill didn't know how much interest Clarke owned in the club and hadn't heard any crazy story about Barney's retirement. McKechnie hammered home the point that Fred acted as president pro tem in the owner's absence. When asked if Sam Dreyfuss was a good baseball man, Bill answered, "He is a pretty shrewd baseball man." The *Pittsburgh Gazette Times* reporter then posed a question that likely shocked McKechnie.

"Had you heard the report that Barney Dreyfuss, during a conversation in the Westmoreland Country Club, shortly before he sailed for Europe, blamed you for losing a game by your poor coaching at third base?" asked the newspaperman.

"What was that?" queried McKechnie.

"Barney was asked whether it was the runner's fault he stopped at third when he should have scored," replied the reporter. "His answer is said to have been: 'No, that's another of McKechnie's bonehead blunders.'"

"I was not at the Westmoreland Country Club that night," responded McKechnie.

"Have you had any intimation that Dreyfuss was dissatisfied with your work as manager?" asked the pundit.

"I do not think he is dissatisfied," answered Bill. "If he were, I would not be where I am."

The writer then queried McKechnie about the Pirates' pennant chances. Pittsburgh's manager responded positively, adding that the probability would be greatly enhanced once injured shortstop Glenn Wright returned to the lineup. When the writer posed another question asking for comment on the ABC Affair, Bill bid his interviewer a polite goodbye.[46] Some in Pittsburgh believed McKechnie's time managing the Pirates would likely end once the season concluded. One of the most frequent guesses for a replacement revolved around a veteran player who'd not been with the team long. When approached about this prospect, an individual generally well versed in Pittsburgh baseball affairs offered a negative shake of the head. He also predicted the club could drop another player within a week due to the recent trouble.[47]

In deciding to hold a conference in Pittsburgh, John Heydler cited Max Carey's exemplary and remarkable sixteen-year record in baseball and the fact that this had been the first charge brought against him. Heydler expressed confidence in reaching a resolution that satisfied all concerned parties.[48]

The National League president banned a group of more than a dozen reporters from attending the hearing on the eleventh floor of the William Penn Hotel.[49] At 11:20 A.M., the session formally started with Heydler presiding and secretary Cullen Cain beside him taking notes, although they didn't enter the stenographer report of this meeting into the record. Barred reporters stood near the room's closed door, hoping to glean some snippets of dialogue. At one point, they heard Carey's and his former manager's excited voices while engaging in a heated verbal exchange.

Press members believed Max denied a charge, regarding the meeting related to Fred Clarke's removal from the bench, of going over McKechnie's head in calling for the gathering and subsequent vote, which favored the Pirates' vice president, 18–6.[50] In another instance, they overheard Carey requesting Bill to tell what feeling he had in his heart toward him. Although newspapermen couldn't discern McKechnie's answer, they heard Max's audible voice inquiring, "Didn't I ask you in your room a second time?" A reliable source told journalists that Carey sat directly next to Fred throughout the hearing.[51] When the inquiry ended shortly after 1 P.M., Pittsburgh's club officials emerged from the room together while the three players remained behind for a few minutes. Clarke, Sam Watters, and Sam Dreyfuss appeared in good spirits. On the other hand, the Pirates' manager looked like someone who'd just been through an unpleasant experience. Bill's drawn and pale face showed wrinkles as two tense cheek muscles twitched with apparent agitation.

Upon arriving in Pittsburgh, John Heydler put the Rule 21 scenario to rest, stating that Fred Clarke had signed a coach's contract, entitling him to sit on the bench.[52] Following the hearing, Heydler informed the press he'd issue his formal statement at 7 P.M. John and Cullen Cain appeared a half hour late, handing out the written verdict to reporters. After Cain had typed up the material, Heydler first called in Clarke and Dreyfuss to receive their copies. Heydler appeased both parties' wishes in this case. The conference also revealed that McKechnie didn't only ask Fred to sit on the bench; Barney Dreyfuss had ordered him to do so. The league president believed that this bound Clarke to obey such a directive from a superior officer.[53] Heydler termed the action "mistaken zeal" on the three players' part and offered a statement about the decision. Nothing in this prepared declaration shed light on the contended "inside story" of the case.[54]

"I cannot go back on the right of the officials of a league club to release, suspend, or ask waivers on any of its players," said Heydler, "nor would I wish to do so if I had the right; but it is my opinion after a most complete and thorough hearing of this case that none of the three players—Carey, Bigbee and Adams—has been guilty of insubordination or malicious intent to disrupt or injure his club."

Heydler also adamantly revealed that Max Carey's purpose in requesting this hearing was to clear his name and those of Babe Adams and Carson Bigbee regarding the insubordination charge. The trio accomplished this goal, as the league president stated that all three players could move forward with their good names intact. He claimed that misunderstandings led to dissension following the double defeat against Boston on August 7 and that Adams, Bigbee, and Carey made a mistake in how they attempted to rectify a problem hurting the club. The fact that Heydler didn't interfere pleased Pirates management in upholding their decision to deal with this particular problem.

"The Pittsburgh club feels that Mr. Heydler has conducted this hearing in a fair and impartial manner," stated Sam Dreyfuss. "We accept his findings in good faith and consider the matter a closed incident."[55]

Sam Dreyfuss, the heir apparent to someday taking control of the Pirates' organization, had navigated through his first crisis as part of the management trio running things in his father's absence. Years ago, during Samuel's youth, Barney Dreyfuss used to take great delight in telling reporters a story about his boy. One day, father and son happened to be discussing the young lad's future.

"What do you want to be when you grow up?" Barney asked his young hopeful.

"I want to be a streetcar conductor," promptly replied Sammy.

"Why do you want to be a streetcar conductor?" asked his father.

"Because he gets all the money," was Samuel's reply.

Over the past few days, Sam Dreyfuss probably wished he'd chosen that profession for his life's work. Although Fred Clarke had been left in command during Barney's vacation and dictated the order penalizing the three players, Sam received his fair share of criticism from fans. The young man understood his role in this crisis, supposedly having remarked, "But father's over there, and we're over here, and we have to run things."[56] Management believed the final page of this story to be written upon the resolution of Max Carey's situation. The New York Giants and Brooklyn Robins had filed a waiver claim for Carey.[57] Because of their lower place in the standings, the league accepted Brooklyn's claim on August 18, making Max a member of the Robins.[58]

Following a week of inactivity, the Pirates finally hit the diamond again on August 18, splitting a doubleheader against Boston at Forbes Field. Manager Bill McKechnie received a mixed reaction from fans. Some heckled Bill with raspberries, while others offered up resounding cheers. In the fourth inning of game one, McKechnie foolishly waved home slow pitcher Ray Kremer as he ran from second to third on a single. Fans universally roasted Pittsburgh's skipper when the Braves effortlessly cut down Kremer at the plate.[59] The crowd's most ambitious rooters reveled in hurling sarcastic remarks toward Pittsburgh's bench. Anytime Bill or Fred Clarke appeared on the field, the loud comments from patrons could be heard all over the ballpark. Fans directed mocking quips throughout the afternoon toward McKechnie when he assumed his position on the coaching lines.

"Did Clarke tell you to come out?" yelled a fan in one instance, while another shouted, "Better make sure of your orders, Bill."

Pittsburgh Press sports editor Ralph S. Davis found it interesting that the Pirates had already removed Babe Adams's, Carson Bigbee's, and Max Carey's pictures from scorecards sold at Forbes Field during the doubleheader versus Boston. Davis wrote that on some occasions, the photograph of a released player remained in the program for months after he departed. The scribe reasoned that Pirates officials wanted local fans to quickly forget Adams, Bigbee, and Carey. However, their memories remained fresh in devoted patrons' minds without the benefit of pictures on paper as a reminder.[60] Davis also opined on Barney Dreyfuss most likely thinking four or five times before ever deciding to enjoy another vacation in the future. For the past twenty-seven years, Dreyfuss immersed himself in his life's true pleasure: the Pittsburgh Pirates. Past holidays had been spent with his players, joining them on an eastern tour or the spring training trip. For the first time since becoming the Pirates' owner, Barney didn't accompany his squad for the spring session in 1926.

According to Sam Dreyfuss, his father knew nothing of the recent controversy concerning his beloved franchise. Sam also refused to give reporters his dad's address in Paris, France, since the son didn't want him to be worried or bothered about the matter.[61] Barney knew something about this entanglement, as he finally issued a statement from Paris on Saturday, August 21. Pittsburgh's owner anxiously wanted to be back home to prepare for another World Series in

Pittsburgh. On Monday, he planned on beginning the return trip to the United States aboard the SS *Christopher Columbus* steamer. Barney, more concerned over poor weather in major league cities rather than the release of three veteran Pirates, offered his first opinion on the ABC Affair.

"I am a sentimental fellow," Dreyfuss said, "and therefore I feel deeply the departure of these players, but sentiment has no place in baseball. The fans insist on a winning team and won't tolerate a loser. I thoroughly approve of anything done by McKechnie, and my son, who offered to handle my affairs in order to permit me to have a vacation. They did not consult me. I got only a brief telegram from my son saying the releases were necessary. I saw the details in an American newspaper in Paris."

Barney Dreyfuss alleged that Max Carey's departure at the $4,000 waiver price cost the organization $96,000 since he could've sold the player for $100,000 after the previous World Series. The owner also claimed no signs of any team dissension were present before leaving for Europe in June. When commenting on the long period Adams had been connected to the organization, Barney exclaimed that he'd considered appointing Babe as pitching coach to keep him on the payroll. Dreyfuss also refused to comment on whether he was considering replacing Bill McKechnie as the team's manager to re-establish order and peace among the players.

"I keep my managers on one-year contracts," Dreyfuss said. "That makes them work harder. They have the temptation to sit back when they have a long-term contract in their pocket. I have not yet considered the question of a manager for next year."

Barney also unwaveringly declared the Pirates to be the National League's best team while adding that it certainly wasn't a three-man club, a direct reference to the released veteran players.[62] It was telling that Dreyfuss didn't offer a ringing endorsement for Bill McKechnie's continued employment or even mention Fred Clarke in his initial statement. Throughout the past week, thousands of Pittsburgh baseball fans had expressed their opinion about Clarke's role in the sordid affair. A large majority concluded Fred to be out of place taking any part in managing the club. Ralph S. Davis alleged that everything didn't always run smoothly when Clarke previously piloted the Pirates. He never even allowed Barney to step on his toes and had several bitter quarrels with his boss. While Pittsburgh's squad exhibited harmony in 1925, that wasn't the case a year later, as one Pittsburgh correspondent pointed out: "The club has had more trouble with its players, more fines, suspensions, releases, etc., for indifferent playing, men not being in proper condition, insubordination, etc., whereas heretofore the club was noted for its tranquility, harmony among players with the management, etc."[63]

Upon returning to his Forbes Field office on August 31, Barney Dreyfuss told reporters he didn't plan on reopening the case surrounding Max Carey, Carson Bigbee, and Babe Adams. He declared that what the three individuals left in charge decided during his absence stood.

"I could not do anything even if I wanted to and I do not want to do anything," Dreyfuss told reporters. "I put Clarke, my son and McKechnie in charge when I went away and told them I didn't want to know what was going on while I was away."

Barney explained he didn't know the details regarding the case. He'd spoken to his son on the telephone, who'd traveled with the team to St. Louis. Sam planned on explaining things in person, as his father hoped to join the entourage in three days in Chicago. When asked if he would see Babe Adams and Carson Bigbee if they requested a meeting, Dreyfuss responded that he would welcome anyone that called on him. Barney then expressed puzzlement over Babe's involvement in this affair. Dreyfuss acknowledged that he kept Adams on the roster for two years at a high salary when the hurler did little work for the Pirates and followed this course purely out of sentiment. The owner informed the press he didn't intend to issue any formal statement on the matter. When told that the three departed players expressed kind sentiments toward him, Barney exhibited no surprise over this revelation.

"Why shouldn't they," he replied. "I have always treated them well, and I do not see how they could feel otherwise than kindly toward me."[64]

That same day, Adams, Bigbee, and Carey conferred with Dreyfuss at his office. Nobody from either camp issued an initial statement about the meeting. The following morning, Max confirmed that Pittsburgh's owner received the trio cordially and exhibited friendliness throughout their conversation. Carey planned to return to Brooklyn that night.[65] Max's assessment seemed curious, given Dreyfuss's comments when his interview with writer Francis "Frank" Wallace of the *New York Evening Post* appeared in the *Pittsburgh Press* on September 14. Ralph S. Davis believed Wallace secured this interview because an individual sometimes expressed to an outsider things he wouldn't divulge to the home folks, especially those newspapermen who'd criticized the organization throughout their moment of crisis.[66]

Wallace started by claiming that the general impression around the country regarding Pittsburgh's baseball team seemed to be that the recent mutiny caused the players to fight amongst themselves, thus killing any chances of the club winning the National League pennant. Dreyfuss responded that the affair did the team well, and the trouble regarding its current third-place position stemmed from an injury sidelining Glenn Wright for seven weeks. The New York sportswriter then mentioned various rumors, such as Kiki Cuyler being the only team member to occupy a training table during the spring session months ago. Frank also claimed a split existed among the Pirates' players over religion and that Max Carey had been jealous of Cuyler and wanted to get rid of him for three years.

Regarding the training issue, Barney stated that while in Paso Robles, California, he didn't witness such neglect from the entire team (Dreyfuss hadn't accompanied his team on the spring training trip in 1926). The Pirates' owner adamantly professed he never hired a man for his religion and asserted Max hadn't told him about Kiki.[67] When the conversation shifted to an effort by the three dismissed players to tell Dreyfuss their side of the story regarding the ABC Affair, hoping he exonerated them, the owner contradicted Carey's earlier perception of this meeting. Wallace vowed that Barney related to him that he told the trio, "You will wait until your beards grow long before I exonerate you, or even listen to you." According to the writer, Dreyfuss then expanded on this point.

"They pulled a boner by not waiting until I came back before they did anything," proclaimed Dreyfuss. "They made a mistake, and they know it now. Whatever happened in my absence was handled by the men I left in charge. I never even asked my son Sam about his side of it."

Wallace also alleged that Pittsburgh's owner closed the interview by stating Carey fell down in performance and the player's illness was his fault. Dreyfuss claimed he wired Max to remain in the hospital and recover, but Carey ignored that advice and arrived at spring training prematurely. This final comment, if true, astonished Ralph S. Davis, who reminded his readers that Max's sickness resulted from his valiant effort at the tail end of the 1925 World Series against the Washington Senators, playing despite damaged ribs.[68] When Carey had made his first appearance for Brooklyn against the Pirates in game one of a doubleheader on August 23, Forbes Field's rooters afforded him numerous standing ovations. Max performed grandly in the Robins' 7–3 victory, rapping out a single, drawing two walks, and reaching on a beautiful bunt hit toward first base.[69]

By eliminating Babe Adams, Carson Bigbee, and Max Carey from Pittsburgh's roster, Pirates officials probably thought the moves insignificant because these three men hadn't contributed much to the diamond cause in

1926. Their stance proved risky since relying upon batting averages and mound victories didn't consider cohesion. Team spirit needed consideration, and it became apparent that tearing apart the inner soul of the Pirates contributed to a disappointing finish that year. When Sam Dreyfuss handed the three mutineers their sentence on the evening of August 13, Pittsburgh occupied first place, two games ahead of St. Louis with a 61–45 record. From that point forward in the campaign, the Pirates could do no better than a mark of 23–24. In the end, the Cardinals claimed the National League pennant as the Pirates came home third, 4½ games behind the pacesetters.

Things became so bad that a hurler tossed a no-hitter against the Pirates in an exhibition game at Akron, Ohio, on August 22. Twirler Charles Ketchum of an industrial league team, called Akron General Tire, didn't allow a hit and defeated a Pittsburgh lineup including many regulars, 6–0.[70] Harold Sloop, a high school athlete from that city rehabilitating his shoulder following a football injury, pitched batting practice for this team, also known as the Akron Generals. According to Sloop, Ketchum utilized chewing gum and emery dust in a hole in the middle of his glove to add more break to his pitches. When the umpire alerted Bill McKechnie to Charles's general practice before starting the game and asked if he wanted the hurler called out for it, Pittsburgh's manager replied to let him throw. To preserve the no-hitter, with two outs in the ninth inning, Ketchum intentionally walked the dangerous Paul Waner, who batted .336 for the Pirates in his rookie campaign. This strategy worked beautifully, as shortstop Joseph "Joe" Cronin grounded out to end the game.[71]

Pittsburgh's players endured the insufferable exhibition game blues throughout the tail end of the season. Many of the Pirates expressed a disgruntled attitude over playing an exhibition contest in Bridgeport, Connecticut, on September 26, one day after the club's final games on the National League docket. Other team members offered sarcastic remarks when someone mentioned the extra trip, while a group of men laughed about it. The players expressed unhappiness over performing in front of a bush league crowd after playing their last official league game, preferring to start for their winter homes. Unfortunately, the contracts of Pittsburgh's players required them to be available for exhibition contests until Boston and Philadelphia played the National League slate's final scheduled games in a doubleheader on September 29. Management gave hurler Ray Kremer permission to miss the contest so he could return to the Smoky City and prepare for the long journey to his home in Oakland, California.[72]

After the Pirates finished their league campaign with a twin bill against Boston at Braves Field on September 25, a move alluded to over a month ago finally happened. That evening, Sam Dreyfuss announced the club had given first baseman Stuffy McInnis his unconditional release.[73] Barney Dreyfuss also broadcast this information for newspapers in Pittsburgh, stating that under the release, the club permitted McInnis to leave immediately for his home in Gloucester, Massachusetts.[74] Back in August, when players voted on removing Fred Clarke from the bench, Bill McKechnie threatened to drop anyone from the team who carried news of what happened at that meeting to the press.[75]

Someone attending that conference had leaked the story to the press. Many believed this release pointed toward Stuffy as the culprit behind circulating news about a revolt by Pittsburgh's players.[76] Those accepting this premise felt McInnis revealed the information because of his strong friendship with Clarke. Ill feelings existed between Stuffy and some of his teammates. On the season-ending trip, a day or two before McInnis received his walking papers, the first baseman and some teammates almost became involved in a fistfight. A sensational scene occurred late one night when two Pirates players visited Stuffy's hotel room and a heated argument broke out.[77] Barney Dreyfuss decried that releasing McInnis had no connection to the August uprising.[78]

After Pittsburgh's season ended, sports editor Chester L. Smith of the *Pittsburgh Gazette Times* mused over who the other players might've been that voted for Clarke's removal from the bench. In a column, Smith wrote that many squad members, including Eddie Moore, George Grantham, and Kiki Cuyler, hadn't fancied Clarke's methods or approach.[79] Moore certainly didn't cast a vote since he'd already moved on to Boston. Shortstop Glenn Wright most likely supported Fred. When interviewed by Dr. Eugene Converse Murdock in 1978, Wright told the historian that Fred Clarke was a great second father to him.[80] Supposedly, Grantham approached Carson Bigbee after problems arose from the vote. George said that since he'd taken as much of an active role in the insurrection as the three punished players, he would be willing to tell the world about it. Bigbee recommended George keep quiet because enough damage had already occurred, adding that Grantham was a young man with a prosperous career ahead of him.[81]

Now that the Pirates' campaign had concluded, the banished trio could tell the "inside story" since doing so at this time wouldn't damage the club's pennant chances. More fallout beckoned as two more people connected to the ABC Affair awaited their fate. A fan-favorite also fell out of favor, much to the disillusionment of devoted rooters who offered him the most extraordinary outpouring of support ever witnessed regarding a Pittsburgh athlete.

Upon rejoining the Pittsburgh Pirates' organization as vice president on June 12, 1925, former skipper Fred Clarke received praise for being a key factor behind the club winning the National League pennant and World Series. One year later, Clarke's presence on the bench as an assistant to manager Bill McKechnie caused problems and led to a vote by the players, requiring him to leave the dugout. That vote overwhelmingly favored Fred, 18-6. The fallout from this action occurred on August 13, when Sam Dreyfuss announced the organization had released Babe Adams and Carson Bigbee, while placing Max Carey on waivers. McKechnie received criticism for not properly handling this action put forth by these veteran players. In this photo, left to right, are Bill McKechnie and Fred Clarke (Courtesy of the Library of Congress).

12

The "Inside Story" and a Hero's Fall from Grace

Now that the 1926 Pittsburgh Pirates' season had ended, fans anxiously awaited the revolters' "inside story" promised by Max Carey, Babe Adams, and Carson Bigbee. Exhibiting a steadfast commitment to the squad's pennant fight, although released from the Pirates in August, these three men remained silent until after the campaign closed. Since a statement hadn't been readily available from the trio, other possibilities behind this action taken against them filled the void. Former *Pittsburgh Ledger* and *Pittsburgh Gazette Times* sports editor Richard "Dick" Guy offered up one such unfathomable story after receiving this information from a source near the season's conclusion.[1] Besides his career in the newspaper business, Guy also owned the Pittsburgh Collegians traveling baseball team.[2]

"I was told that the friction between Max Carey and assistant manager Fred Clarke of the Pittsburgh Pirates, was due to religious differences, as unthinkable as that may appear," said Guy.[3]

Before Max Carey became a professional baseball player, he attended Concordia Seminary as a divinity student. This institution acted as a training school for the Missouri Lutheran ministries. Max seemed destined to become a minister, if not for convincing himself that he might be a more accomplished baseball player than a preacher. A true gentleman, Carey never used profane language and made prayer part of his daily regimen. After the Pirates defeated the Washington Senators in the 1925 World Series, Max acted as one of the speakers at a banquet by Wilkinsburg's citizens to honor manager Bill McKechnie. In his speech, Carey credited God for lending a helping hand with the squad's World Series victory.

"You hear a lot about luck in baseball, and I suppose there is a certain amount of it," said Carey while speaking at the banquet. "But what some folks call luck, I call something else. I have a firm belief in divine guidance, and I believe that God Almighty had more than a little to do with our winning from Washington. I know I prayed to him as sincerely over that matter as I ever did over other problems that bothered and worried me."[4]

Fans pushed rumor and conjecture aside as clarity ultimately rose to the surface. Pirates owner Barney Dreyfuss spoke first, finally giving out an interview locally to the *Pittsburgh Gazette Times* on the evening of September 26. Dreyfuss immediately denied that team dissension and internal strife acted as the catalyst for Pittsburgh's failure to repeat as National League pennant winners. Barney attributed the club's fall to third place to Clyde Barnhart's weak hitting (a decline from .325 in 1925 to .192 in 1926), an injury sidelining Glenn Wright near the campaign's close, and hurlers Ray Kremer, Vic Aldridge, and Johnny Morrison missing time due to injury or illness. When asked about the three dismissed players, Dreyfuss declared the revolt issue a settled case.

"The Carey incident is closed forever, and will never be reopened," said the Pirates' president, smiling good-naturedly. "The players who made trouble for themselves are gone and will not come back. That is all there is to it. All the questioning in the world will not get me to reopen that subject."[5]

Dreyfuss also quashed this correspondent's theory about Stuffy McInnis when asked if the first baseman's release happened because he'd snitched to the press about the meeting in New York where the players took a secret vote related to Fred Clarke's status.

"Absolutely not," said Mr. Dreyfuss. "McInnis was given his unconditional release because we had no room for him and could not carry him any longer. Grantham is doing all right at first base, so we did not need McInnis."

Upon being probed about Bill McKechnie continuing as Pittsburgh's manager in 1927, Barney replied he didn't care to comment and that any announcement about this or other team matters would be made public through the newspapers. Dreyfuss also told the writer that he'd appointed Clarke as his representative during his absence in Europe and had informed the manager, team captain, and Pittsburgh's players about this decision.[6] When pressed on the rumored reason for McInnis's release a second time, Barney declared that tracing any alleged leak on the matter to Stuffy to be an impossible exercise. He reiterated that since Grantham did such good work, no place on the Pirates' roster existed for the veteran first baseman. When asked whether he'd heard Clarke's remark to McKechnie in Boston on August 7 about replacing Max

Carey with the batboy, Pittsburgh's owner then queried the correspondent about the incident, laughed, and declared he knew nothing about it.[7]

Two weeks earlier, when Frank Wallace of the *New York Evening Post* interviewed Dreyfuss, the sportswriter had questioned him about a rumor claiming that star outfielder Hazen "Kiki" Cuyler wanted the club to trade him to another team. During that exchange, Barney professed he hadn't heard anything about any such desire on Cuyler's part.[8] The *Pittsburgh Gazette Times* reporter also honed in on this subject while interviewing Dreyfuss.

"Some of Hazen Cuyler's friends are said to have declared he wants to be traded and has said he cannot do his best work as a Pirate, under present conditions," said the newspaperman. "Has he made any such request?"

"He has not made any such request to me," said Mr. Dreyfuss. "Besides, I see he was quoted in an interview in Philadelphia, the other day, as having said he had no intention or desire in the direction of leaving Pittsburgh."

Barney Dreyfuss then denied rumors about the Pirates shipping Cuyler to the New York Giants for second baseman Frank "Frankie" Frisch or moving George Grantham to that same team for first baseman George "High Pockets" Kelly. Dreyfuss also exclaimed "bosh" about a story alleging that young infielder Joe Cronin's pending release would occur due to his bad habit of cutting under the ball as a hitter. Barney also added that Cronin batted as well as any other team member during the campaign's final weeks.[9] This analysis from the Pirates' owner gave passionate, hungry Pittsburgh baseball fans something to digest for a few days. The long-awaited banquet of information about the actual "inside story" regarding the ABC Affair finally became available on September 30, 1926. In a statement released by Babe Adams, Carson Bigbee, and Max Carey, the three players claimed internal dissension started festering during the pennant-winning days of 1925.

These three gentlemen declared that a prevailing negative sentiment existed toward Fred Clarke practically upon his return to the organization. They claimed the first problem arose when the time came after the World Series victory to divvy up the winner's share of money for claiming the championship. According to Adams, Bigbee, and Carey, an initial vote about doling out the spoils granted nothing to Clarke. Carey then prevailed upon his teammates to cut Fred in on sharing the World Series melon, leading to a second close vote that awarded a $1,000 check to Clarke. Supposedly, the team vice president returned the money with a statement that he'd received it with ill feeling before later accepting the check after being encouraged by other Pittsburgh management team members to keep it.

The departed trio alleged this incident brought about a strained relationship between Fred and Bill and friction between Clarke and some players. The temperature increased during the 1926 season when second baseman Eddie Moore demanded one day that Fred "Get off the bench." Before that, when Fred offered batting tips to George Grantham, the player asked Clarke to "Keep off him" because the assistant manager made him nervous. Adams, Bigbee, and Carey insisted that Fred handicapped rookie outfielder Paul Waner for a long time by changing his batting style.[10] On numerous occasions, Kiki Cuyler repeatedly told teammates that he couldn't hit the way Clarke wanted him to. The three castoffs declared that nearly every regular player, including Grantham, Cuyler, Waner, Pie Traynor, Glenn Wright, Hal Rhyne, Johnny Gooch, Johnny Rawlings, Emil Yde, and Lee Meadows, believed that Fred's presence on the bench held back the club through his interference, although perceived as unintentional.[11]

These three individuals said that the manager initially agreed to a meeting within their capacity as committeemen when they approached Bill McKechnie, following consultation with coach Jack Onslow. He later called it off, saying, "Secretary Sam Watters and I have a diplomatic way of eliminating Clarke from the bench." Adams, Bigbee, and Carey alleged that Bill misstated facts to Fred before Pittsburgh's vice president offered a threat during a team meeting ahead of a game against Brooklyn on August 9.

"I may leave the bench, but I am still vice president, and you must see me next winter," asserted Clarke, referring to contract time.[12]

As the three players released their statement, Bill McKechnie happened to be hunting in Elk County and planned on attending a banquet in St. Marys, Pennsylvania, that evening.[13] Barney Dreyfuss refused to talk to newspaper reporters about this proclamation, and his son, Sam Dreyfuss, officially spoke on behalf of the Pirates' organization.

"The Pittsburgh Baseball Club has nothing to say in regard to the statement made public today by Max Carey, Babe Adams and Carson Bigbee, three players who were let out by the club toward the end of the season," said Sam Dreyfuss.

The younger Dreyfuss also emphasized that the organization didn't care what these players had to say. Bucking the organization's official stance, Fred Clarke wasted no time answering these accusations in his defense through an interview with the *Pittsburgh Gazette Times* later that day following the release of the trio's statement. Fred told the reporter he wouldn't sit on the player's bench this upcoming season and could decide to dissolve his current association with the Pirates' organization permanently.[14] While talking with this newspaperman at his Iroquois Apartments residence in the Oakland section of Pittsburgh, Fred stated that although not yet deciding on his responsibilities related to team affairs, he wouldn't again undertake this past season's impossible role. In refuting Adams, Bigbee, and Carey's statement, Clarke affirmed that he never interfered with McKechnie's strategic decisions as alleged when it came to bunting, the hit-and-run, or a general battle plan. He never offered strategy suggestions or told players to ignore the manager's signals from the coaching lines, as had been contended.

Clarke admitted to making recommendations to batters experiencing a slump, telling them what they happened to be doing wrong, just as he and other baseball men had done for years. Fred denied ever taking to task any of these individuals, and he told the writer what had occurred with George Grantham.

"I suggested to Grantham that he hold his bat low when at the plate, as he seemed to hit low balls better when he did so," said Clarke. "I said something of the kind to him one day, and then he went up to the plate and struck out. When he returned to the bench, he said: 'I wish you wouldn't say anything to me.' I replied: 'All right, George, I won't.' And I never mentioned the matter to him again."

Clarke also denied that Eddie Moore had told him to "Get off the bench" and never intimated, as far as Fred knew, that he didn't want him there. Clarke stated he only pried positively, patting Eddie on the back and encouraging him when fans viciously badgered the second baseman. The team vice president claimed to help Vic Aldridge similarly, reassuring the hurler during a rough time. While reading this account offered by the three disgruntled former players, Clarke smiled when he came across the paragraph about holding back Paul Waner because he insisted on changing the outfielder's batting style.

"Too bad about Waner," he remarked. "He just about burned up the league, as it was. I wonder what he would have hit if I hadn't interfered with him."

Clarke also responded to the allegation that trouble started when he returned the $1,000 check for his share of the World Series money. In the initial player's proxy on this matter, Max Carey didn't vote on this ballot since it wouldn't have figured in the outcome. Max then suggested giving Fred something since players had voted the team secretary, the trainer, the clubhouse boy, and the groundskeeper a portion of World Series money. Someone proposed $1,000, which passed in Clarke's favor by a slim one-vote margin. According to Carey, Babe Adams, and Carson Bigbee, when Fred became aware of this, he went to Barney Dreyfuss. Clarke told the owner he didn't think the players wanted him there. Dreyfuss called Bill McKechnie into his office and asked why there seemed to be a problem, wondering if enough honor and glory didn't exist for everyone. McKechnie then spoke to Clarke and offered him some kind, reassuring words.

In their statement, the three players asserted that Fred returned the check to Pittsburgh's owner with an accompanying letter indicating ill feelings on the part of Pittsburgh's team members. Clarke then requested to present the money to Bill with compliments before Dreyfuss convinced Fred to accept the check. Clarke denied that bitter sentiments existed between him and McKechnie at any time. Fred also declared that he'd returned the $1,000 check to Bill because he felt all the active players deserved that money. Clarke believed he didn't warrant a share since he wasn't a player. Clarke stated that nobody possibly could hold a clearer conscience than him surrounding this matter. The team vice president believed events had placed him in an impossible position as an assistant to the manager since a scenario evolved where he didn't receive credit when things went well. Still, criticism followed if a plan or strategy failed. Fred also showed displeasure over coach Jack Onslow's inclusion after the fact, alongside the mutineers for the first time, at National League president John Heydler's hearing.

"That sounded to me like 'sour grapes,'" said Clarke. "They were trying to drag Onslow into the mess. We were not inclined to take the word of three convicted wrongdoers against a man they accused after their own conviction."

Fred Clarke readily admitted to suggesting to Bill McKechnie on August 7 in Boston about removing Max Carey from the lineup. Clarke vowed he did so to help both Carey and the club. Although hitting the ball hard, Max consistently smacked it at enemy competitors, and Fred reasoned slumping players benefitted from such a rest. Clarke also denied ever crossing McKechnie or issuing a harsh word to any Pirates team member. For those who wondered why he didn't leave the bench voluntarily during the first sign of trouble, Fred affirmed he couldn't disobey his boss's orders and also didn't want people accusing him of running away while under fire. Clarke seemed surprised these three men had started the trouble, counting them among his best friends. Fred also adamantly refuted the allegation that he and McKechnie threatened or coerced the players through speeches before that fateful vote regarding the question of him remaining on the bench.

"There was no intimidation about it," said Clarke. "I gave the boys to understand that I expected them to work, because, as Barney's representative and as part owner of the team myself, as well as in justice to the public, it was my business to see that they did work. The players are paid to play ball, not to manage the team. The manager runs the team. That is my idea of it and I plainly told them so, but I made no threats and did not try to intimidate anybody."

Fred and his family planned on leaving for his "Little Pirate Ranch" in Winfield, Kansas, the following morning. Clarke told the correspondent that he shared his statement with much reluctance. Fred had also already officially resigned as assistant manager and attempted to do so on numerous occasions since it proved a disagreeable job but stayed on each time at McKechnie's urging. He still retained his executive position within the organization. Clarke also refuted rumors about becoming Pittsburgh's manager, stating he didn't want to hold down that job again.[15]

On the day the ABC Trio released their statement, Max Carey packed up his belongings and departed the Smoky City with his family in his automobile. They planned to spend the night in Zanesville, Ohio, before visiting Carey's mother in Terre Haute, Indiana. From there, St. Louis would be the final destination, where Max and his father-in-law operated a gasoline filling station business.

Before leaving his Pittsburgh apartment, Carey called upon a neighbor's home to retrieve the family's pet canary, Geraldine. Upon reaching that house, the woman who'd been kind enough to look after the bird informed Max, his wife, Aurelia Behrens Carey, and their two children that Geraldine had died.

"It's been a hard year, Mr. Carey," the neighbor sympathized.

"It has, for a fact," said Carey, "but next year will be another year."[16]

It certainly had been a challenging year for many members of the Pittsburgh Pirates. Things were about to get rougher for a few more people. Neither side was cloaked in glory regarding team dissension and the uprising. In his statement, Fred Clarke talked about being placed in an impossible position, sitting on the bench as an assistant to Bill McKechnie. Weeks after the uprising, St. Louis sports journalist John B. Sheridan declared that owner Barney Dreyfuss had placed McKechnie in an untenable situation when he asked Clarke to join the team in the dugout. Sheridan believed that at the time of this appointment, Bill possessed the capability of winning the 1925 pennant without any assistance from another party since he was an intelligent baseball man. The decision dumbfounded the scribe that such an astute person in business like Dreyfuss could make the colossal mistake of having two managers in the dugout. Sheridan also described Fred's comments about Max Carey in Boston as rough stuff for a sensitive, high-strung individual who'd been sick most of the 1926 season.

John B. Sheridan felt McKechnie should've resigned when Pittsburgh's owner appointed Clarke to assist him on the bench.[17] In the end, Sheridan's suggestion from months ago became a reality through a different avenue. On October 18, 1926, Barney Dreyfuss announced that Bill wouldn't be returning as Pittsburgh's manager in 1927, a kind way of saying he'd fired him. Dreyfuss stated that although breaking the news during a meeting between the two men proved a difficult undertaking, his decision had been a necessary one demanded by Pirates baseball fans.[18]

> It was an unpleasant task. It is always unpleasant to cut a man loose from a job. McKechnie was a hard, conscientious man who did the best he could. It was unfortunate that his best did not prove quite enough. Our session was a friendly one. I have high regard for McKechnie as a man and I still have warm friendship for him.
>
> The public, however, wants a winner, and it is my duty to take whatever steps I can to see that a winner is established here. Judging from the attitude of the fans, they had lost confidence in McKechnie, and there was only one thing to do.

Sportswriters expected a deluge of applicants to inquire about the job after Dreyfuss's announcement. Upon questioning the certainty that Fred Clarke wouldn't receive consideration, Barney replied that the team vice president didn't want the job. When asked if a managerial change affected Clarke's position within the organization, Dreyfuss stated he wasn't aware of Fred's plans for 1927.[19] This quelled a rumor in the *Yonkers Herald* claiming it wouldn't be surprising if Clarke managed the Pirates next year. The newspaper's article on the subject intimated that Fred had fancied himself more as a manager in 1926 rather than a front-office executive. The publication reasoned that the old warhorse, in helping guide the 1925 team to a World Series victory, once again relished the pleasure of sitting on a dugout bench wearing a uniform and spikes, watching the game unfold in front of him.[20] Bill McKechnie uttered no words of dissatisfaction toward Pittsburgh's owner after Barney relieved him of his duties, an action which even he seemed to have anticipated.

"He treated me fine all the time I worked for him and I haven't a word of complaint to utter," said McKechnie. "I realize that many of the fans have turned against me, and that I was being criticized as a result of the dissension which broke out in the club during the past season. My only comment is that I always did my best."[21]

Dreyfuss stated the previous season's trouble didn't influence his decision regarding Bill's discharge.[22] Barney acknowledged that McKechnie hadn't delivered the winner that Pittsburgh's baseball fans expected.[23] The whole ABC Affair had been beyond Bill's scope, as he told friends at the time, "My head was all in a whirl," and, "This thing is too big for me."[24] When reporters asked Dreyfuss if McKechnie might find other employment within the organization, the owner stated that the two men didn't discuss this during their meeting. Barney also affirmed he decided to give Bill plenty of opportunity to attain a job with another team. When broached on a report that Owen Donie Bush, manager of the American Association's Indianapolis Indians, might replace McKechnie, Dreyfuss replied that many rumors probably would come forward before he made a final selection. Barney deemed such guessing fruitless since he hadn't made up his mind on a definitive candidate.[25]

Press members presented many choices when speculating on Pittsburgh's next manager. Reporters believed recently deposed Philadelphia Phillies manager and former Giants shortstop Art Fletcher held the inside track. Onetime major league catcher and Rogers Hornsby's able assistant on the St. Louis Cardinals, Bill Killefer, also received consideration from the press. Former Cincinnati Reds outfielder Alfred Earle "Greasy" Neale made the pundits' list, as did skipper John "Jack" Lelivelt of the American Association's Milwaukee Brewers. Manager Casey Stengel of that league's Toledo Mud Hens seemed to be a longshot choice given his past problems with Pittsburgh's magnate. If Dreyfuss wanted to go with a player/manager, current Boston Braves shortstop and pilot Dave Bancroft might fit the bill.[26] Inhabitants of the Morrowfield Apartments in Oakland also penned a letter to *Pittsburgh Press* sports editor Ralph S. Davis, suggesting former Pirates pitcher and tenant Babe Adams as the Pirates' next manager.[27] Many other baseball patrons in the city supported this idea.[28]

Newspapers also mentioned Donie Bush as a candidate to take control of Pittsburgh's baseball destiny.[29] A former major league shortstop for the Detroit Tigers from 1908 through 1921, Washington claimed him off waivers on August 20 of that year. Bush managed the Senators in 1923 and oversaw Indianapolis for the next three seasons. Those newspapermen feeling Donie looked like a favorite to grab this job certainly had offered the correct prediction. Pittsburgh Pirates scout Bill Hinchman made a trip to Indianapolis, which also happened to be Bush's hometown, to visit with the Indians' manager. Hinchman wasted no time getting to the heart of his reason for calling on Donie.

"How would you like to manage the Pirates?" Hinchman asked.

Bush quickly nodded his head affirmatively. Bill told Donie that Barney Dreyfuss had sent him to Indianapolis, and the two swiftly hammered out a potential deal that made all parties happy.³⁰ On the evening of October 25, 1926, Dreyfuss announced Bush's hiring to manage the Pirates in 1927. Donie signed a one-year contract to come aboard after the two sides finalized negotiations that afternoon. Supposedly, if Bush hadn't reached an agreement with Pittsburgh, Barney would've turned to Greasy Neale as his next choice. Pittsburgh's owner issued a brief statement on this hiring to the press.

"We favored Bush for the management for several reasons," said Dreyfuss. "I have known him since he played against the Pirates in the World's Championship in 1909. Bush is a hustler, he knows baseball, his record at Indianapolis has been very good and he is of excellent habits. It is up to him to succeed or fail in his new appointment. He will be given as much cooperation as we can give him. The new manager will have the authority to pick his own aides, and all that sort of thing. We think we have made a good selection, but, of course, nobody knows this for a certainty."³¹

Three days after this announcement, Barney Dreyfuss declared that he'd given Donie Bush unfettered authority to run Pittsburgh's baseball team. The Pirates' owner confirmed that Bush possessed supreme command without any interference or input from advisors.³² Donie did excellent work with Indianapolis from 1924 through 1926, as the Indians finished second in the American Association each year. Bush's Washington tenure lasted only one season due to differences with owner Clark Griffith. Former Buccaneers skipper George Gibson acted as Donie's coach for part of that season before departing after not meshing with the front office hierarchy.³³ Bush vowed to work hard at his new post.

"The fans of Pittsburgh will never be able to accuse me of not hustling," said Bush. "I will give them my best at all times. If that isn't good enough, then I'll be ready to step out. But as long as I'm in charge, the Pirates will give the fans a run for their money."³⁴

The puzzle's final piece fell into place one day after Barney Dreyfuss hired Donie Bush to manage his club. Since the 1926 season ended, fans had clamored for Fred Clarke's exit from the scene. Bill McKechnie's firing reinforced this sentiment.³⁵ These patrons held Clarke and his meddling responsible for dissension in the ranks breaking out and the team's woes. They believed no manager could motivate his players to succeed when a czar-like advisor constantly offered advice.³⁶ Ownership had booted Max Carey, Babe Adams, Carson Bigbee, Stuffy McInnis, and McKechnie all out the door. As the last direct person remaining connected to the Pirates' family feud this past summer, Fred decided to be proactive rather than reactive.³⁷

On October 26, from his home in Winfield, Kansas, Clarke notified Dreyfuss about severing his connection to the Pirates' organization, resigning as vice president and club director.[38] Pittsburgh's owner received Fred's letter that night. Barney announced other club directors would act upon the resignation during a meeting the following day. If accepted, Clarke would sell his stock in the Pittsburgh Athletic Company. Dreyfuss seemed shocked and surprised over Fred's decision.[39] The following evening, after having this meeting, Barney declared that if the organization needed a vice president, he planned on acting within that capacity. It probably wasn't a coincidence that Dreyfuss stated that he placed the sole power and authority of running the Pirates in Bush's hands after accepting Fred's resignation. Barney asserted his intention to retain scouts Bill Hinchman, Charles "Chick" Fraser, and Joseph "Joe" Devine since their responsibilities didn't fall under the manager's purview.[40]

When Barney Dreyfuss fired Bill McKechnie, he believed normalcy should return after last season's stormy period with a new manager on board.[41] Sadly, harmony remained elusive, as a grudge continued festering, related to one team member on the peripheral when it came to the ABC Affair. Through three full seasons in a Pirates uniform, Hazen Cuyler had developed into one of baseball's top outfielders. Known as "Kiki," "Ki," the "Flint Flash," and the "Michigan Flash," Cuyler seized his opportunity when given a chance to start in 1924, batting .354 in his rookie campaign. Kiki proved even better during the championship season of 1925, hitting .357 and establishing a franchise record for home runs shared with Glenn Wright that year when both players smacked 18 four-baggers.

Pittsburgh's baseball fans elevated Cuyler on a pedestal for his heroics in Games Two and Seven of the 1925 World Series against Washington. Forbes Field's rooters loved Hazen's speed, bold style, and dedication to winning. After setting a blistering pace at the plate in the summer of 1926, Cuyler tailed off amidst the turmoil swirling throughout the squad, hitting .321 and appearing in every game for the second consecutive season. Before that campaign started, Kiki engaged in what some people perceived to be contentious contract negotiations with owner Barney Dreyfuss. When Cuyler visited the team's Forbes Field office shortly after the Christmas holiday as his all-star basketball team from Flint, Michigan, traveled around the area playing games, he failed to sign a contract following a conference with Dreyfuss.[42]

Later in January, newspapers reported that Kiki had also returned unsigned contracts from his off-season home in Flint on two occasions. Although the press designated Cuyler a holdout, Pittsburgh's outfielder denied this to be the case, claiming it was a matter of business and that the two sides hadn't yet reached terms.⁴³ *Pittsburgh Gazette Times* sportswriter Chilly Doyle intimated that Glenn Wright and Vic Aldridge might also be holdouts.⁴⁴ Dreyfuss refuted this claim before leaving for a trip to the East on the night of January 28. Although Pittsburgh's owner didn't reveal whether Aldridge and Wright had signed contracts, he declared the two weren't holdouts and would be in camp once spring training started at Paso Robles, California.

Accompanied by his wife, Florence, and son, Sam, Barney departed for Philadelphia, where he planned on spending two days before traveling to New York. Once there, two members of the Dreyfuss family would be attending a special banquet at the Hotel Astor on February 2, 1926, commemorating the conclusion of the National League's Golden Jubilee Celebration.⁴⁵ The Pirates' entourage included twenty-five people to be honored as world champions at the Tuesday night celebration.⁴⁶ Pittsburgh baseball officials expected Kiki Cuyler to reach New York the night before or the morning of the festivities. Barney Dreyfuss stated on the day of the banquet a willingness to talk terms with Cuyler if he so wished.⁴⁷

"I'll see Cuyler if he desires to see me," said Dreyfuss, "but I didn't know there was any controversy over his contract."⁴⁸

Those espousing this controversy theory most likely would've expressed disappointment if they knew that Kiki and his employer exhibited a friendly relationship throughout these negotiations.⁴⁹ According to reliable reports, Cuyler earned $6,000 while playing for the Pirates in 1925. A group of press members speculated that Kiki hoped to receive a salary bump of at least $10,000 a year, or a maximum of $14,000 per season.⁵⁰ Following a conference between Cuyler and Dreyfuss at the Waldorf Astoria Hotel on the afternoon of February 2, Pittsburgh's star outfielder signed a contract for the 1926 campaign. Both men had cause for jubilation when they attended the Golden Jubilee celebration that night at the Hotel Astor.⁵¹

The two parties withheld figures surrounding this critical agreement. Reporters guessed that Hazen might receive around $12,000 for playing this upcoming season, give or take $1,000, after earning $6,000 in 1925.⁵² Barney Dreyfuss sent a telegram to Pittsburgh declaring that practically all members of his championship team, including Cuyler, had signed contracts for the 1926 campaign.⁵³ One New York writer believed $12,000 to be the accurate figure, while another newspaperman surmised that $10,000 a year seemed more logical based on Kiki's salary the previous year.⁵⁴ Being a star outfielder on a pennant-winning team certainly brought about unlimited press coverage regarding a contract dispute. Such fanfare didn't exist one year later after the Pirates' disappointing 1926 season. Widespread media exposure disappeared, as the announcement on January 11, 1927, that Kiki Cuyler and veteran hurler Bullet Joe Bush had signed contracts to play this upcoming campaign went largely unnoticed.[55]

At the beginning of the 1927 season, J. A. Dubow Manufacturing Company presented Cuyler, who endorsed their baseball gloves, as did some other major league players, with the largest fielder's mitt in the world. This oversized mitt was about fourteen times bigger than a standard glove. Kiki kept that glove with him during the entire campaign while traveling from city to city. A sentimental sort, Cuyler had every player from his club and the other seven National League teams autograph that fielder's mitt.[56] This conscientious endeavor possibly turned out to be the highlight of Hazen's baseball campaign.

When Babe Adams, Carson Bigbee, and Max Carey released their statement about the "inside story" after the 1926 season ended, they mentioned ten other teammates who also believed Fred Clarke's presence on the bench held back the team.[57] When the time came to put things on the record, some of these players must've gotten cold feet since the squad members' vote favored Clarke, 18–6. Cuyler also received a direct connection to this incident through the trio's declaration and in an article written by Chilly Doyle of the *Pittsburgh Gazette Times*.

A contentious relationship immediately developed between Kiki and new Pittsburgh Pirates manager Donie Bush. While traveling by train to Paso Robles for spring training, Cuyler harmlessly stated that Pittsburgh's new skipper happened to be just a "busher," a reference to possessing minor league capabilities in his current vocation. Players who heard the remark passed this information along to Bush.[58] The Pirates' new skipper approached Kiki to discuss this comment, and the two men amicably ironed things out regarding the player's stated opinion.[59] While talking to hometown friends in Flint after the 1927 campaign ended, Cuyler revealed that Bush immediately tinkered with how he approached different game phases once the training session started.

"Bush asked me to change my style of leading off second base while in camp in California," said Cuyler, "and I did as he suggested. He wanted me to face the pitcher instead of having my back toward third base, a position taught me by Max Carey."[60]

Many considered the speedy Hazen to be Carey's successor in leading the National League in stolen bases, which Cuyler did by swiping 35 bags in 1926. Although Kiki accepted altering his method for leading off second base, he balked at other changes that occurred once the season started. Donie Bush shuffled his batting order for the May 3 game against St. Louis at Forbes Field, moving Cuyler from the third slot to the number two spot. Believing he wasn't successful batting in the two-hole on rare occasions in other years, Kiki developed a superstitious aversion to that spot. However, while doing so in 1925, he'd recorded a hit in nine consecutive games. On July 24, in the second tilt of a doubleheader against New York at the Polo Grounds, Cuyler entered the game as a left-field replacement after playing a few games in right. Two days earlier, Paul Waner moved back to right field after primarily seeing action at first base for ten straight contests, as Clyde Barnhart occupied left. Bush kept Lloyd Waner in center, where he'd done marvelous work since May.

During his first season with the Pirates, Lloyd batted .355, while older brother Paul, in his second year, led the National League in hitting with a .380 average. Decades later, during an interview, Donie Bush explained his rationale for these changes regarding Kiki Cuyler and Pittsburgh's baseball team.

> Cuyler had played center field and batted third in 1926. He wanted to do the same thing in 1927. I started the season with him in center and had him hitting third.
>
> Later I decided he should play left field and hit second. He fretted over this all the time. My reason for making the change was that Lloyd Waner had joined the club and I regarded him as a better center fielder than Cuyler.
>
> Lloyd was a good hitter, probably a better one. But the main point was that Lloyd was faster and had a better arm.[61]

After appearing in every game for Pittsburgh the past two seasons, Hazen Cuyler saw that streak end. On May 28, in a contest against the Cardinals at Forbes Field, Cuyler retired after injuring his ankle, sliding into third base in the seventh inning.[62] Initially believed to be a broken leg, a second X-ray allayed those fears. Pirates team physician Dr. Gustav Berg announced on the evening of May 29 that Kiki had severely torn the ligaments in his right foot. Although this dispelled earlier reports of broken bones, Dr. Berg cautioned that the injury's severity could keep Cuyler on the sidelines until mid-June.[63] In Kiki's absence, Bush gave veteran outfielder Clyde Barnhart an opportunity in left field.[64]

Cuyler's injury and Barnhart's inclusion in the starting lineup precipitated Lloyd Waner's move to center field. On the afternoon Kiki suffered his injury, the Pirates won their tenth consecutive game, defeating St. Louis, 6–4. While

Clyde did an excellent job replacing Cuyler until his leg healed, the Pirates posted a 13–9 record while he remained out of the starting lineup. When Kiki made a grand return as an everyday regular on June 22 versus the Cincinnati Reds at Forbes Field, he batted second, played right field, and went 3-for-5 at the plate, hitting two singles and a triple, as the Pirates claimed an 11–9 victory. Bush also eventually shifted Cuyler mainly to the fifth and sixth spots in the batting order for about a month before permanently placing him back in the two-hole at the beginning of August.

Tension continued to build between player and manager as the season progressed. On July 5, Pittsburgh demolished St. Louis at Forbes Field, 14–2, as Kiki went 3-for-4. Despite this positive result for everyone connected to the Pirates' club, Cuyler incurred Donie's wrath on a play in the fourth inning. After drawing a walk, which moved teammate Pie Traynor to second, Kiki started tearing around the bases when Clyde Barnhart cracked a double to left field. Although Bush flashed the halt sign as the hustling Cuyler approached third, he ignored his boss's orders and aggressively headed for home plate. Kiki crossed the dish without regard for his recently mended foot and ankle. For several minutes, Donie stood in the third base coaching box seething, shaking his head and loosening the turf with his spikes over defiance of his instructions.[65]

Everything that had built up finally reached a climax in a game at Forbes Field versus the Giants on August 6. New York efficiently handled the Pirates, 9–2. In the fourth inning, Cuyler drew a one-out walk. He took off for second base when Paul Waner rapped a groundball to Giants first baseman William "Bill" Terry. Kiki's swiftness allowed him to beat Terry's throw to second, hoping to cut down the lead runner. Rather than slide, Cuyler approached the bag standing up. As New York shortstop Travis Jackson dropped Bill's toss, he overran the base. Given a reprieve, Jackson picked up the ball and tagged Kiki out. Pie Traynor followed with a single that might've scored Cuyler if perched at the keystone sack.

In the sixth frame, Kiki's attempt to utilize his speed again resulted in unfortunate consequences. Cuyler tapped a slow roller down the third-base line. Giants catcher Albert "Al" DeVormer grabbed the baseball and heaved it over Terry's head at first base. Kiki blazed around the bases as the ball struck Forbes Field's grandstand. He foolishly attempted to reach third base and was gunned down with yards to spare by outfielder George Harper's accurate throw to Andrew "Andy" Reese. An article in the *Pittsburgh Press* described Cuyler's performance as lurid and woozy baserunning.[66] Pirates manager Donie Bush deemed such a bush-league display unacceptable.

Bush wasted no time punishing Kiki Cuyler, as Pittsburgh newspapers reported two days after the incident that the manager fined him $50 for failure to properly run the bases. Donie contended that Cuyler wouldn't have gone past second base in the fourth inning of the New York game if he'd hooked the bag sliding. Upon announcing this fine, Bush made it clear that such future boneheaded actions by any of Pittsburgh's players might receive a similar evaluation. Donie pronounced there were some things big league ballplayers should know, and they deserved punishment when not performing at their best under this diamond doctrine. This action possessed a dual purpose, penalizing Kiki for his indiscretion and acting as a warning to other players.[67] Owner Barney Dreyfuss fully supported Bush's decision to fine Cuyler.

> Whatever action Manager Bush has seen fit to take is O. K. with me. I hire a man to run my ball club and if he believes a player in his charge needs to be punished, it is his right and duty to penalize him. I never butt into running of the club on the field. I haven't been on the field this year and I don't intend to even intimate to Manager Bush what he shall or shall not do insofar as getting the most out of his players is concerned.
>
> I don't know how Bush decided upon the $50 fine for Cuyler and I don't care to ask him about it. All I know is that Cuyler didn't play as he should—that much was evident to anyone who saw Saturday's game from the grandstand. As far as I am concerned, it is a closed incident. It looks like Manager Bush tried his pat-on-the-back methods and, as has often been the case before, found it didn't work and had decided upon a more drastic way of urging him on.
>
> I might also say that it isn't the player who talks the loudest about himself who is the most indispensable. I think by far the majority of ballplayers who prove of inestimable value to their teams are the ones who do the best they know how on the diamond and after the game, forget all about it.[68]

Dreyfuss also chuckled and scoffed over the opinion of some anonymous Giants players who felt Pittsburgh management had mistreated Kiki Cuyler. These individuals declared Bush made a mistake in doling out such punishment.[69] This group of men who played for John McGraw also stated they'd welcome Cuyler into the fold, although realizing such a scenario wasn't possible until the season ended since the trade deadline had passed.[70] Pittsburgh's owner cited a recent story from several years ago regarding tampering and coercion on the part of a New York official (former coach Cozy Dolan). This representative asked a Pirates player (Pie Traynor) how much salary he received and then said something like, "They don't appreciate you in Pittsburgh, my boy. Why, if you were playing for New York, you'd be getting twice as much money."[71] On this occasion, when it came to stirring the pot in the heat of a tight pennant race, placing a further wedge between Kiki and management seemed more practical than taking a bunch of Pirates players out drinking, as nefarious Giants team members had done in 1921.

Butting in when it came to his managers proved a touchy subject after a St. Louis newspaper brought up the time in 1914 that Barney called his players, especially Ed Konetchy, quitters. Dreyfuss categorized this tale as a lie, stating he hadn't visited the dressing room in ten years.[72] When it came to local newspapers' opinions, sportswriter Regis M. Welsh of the *Pittsburgh Post-Gazette* explained that the parting of ways in the baseball life of one of the Pirates' greatest players had finally arrived after a long delay. Welsh pointed out that besides Donie Bush docking Kiki Cuyler $50 in salary for being the goat in Saturday's game against the Giants, he would also be "riding the wood" when Pittsburgh played New York on August 9. Clyde Barnhart took the Flint Flash's place in left field, with the Waners brothers holding down the other two outfield posts.

This sportswriter also tackled what usually happened to Pirates players fined by management. Welsh stated that only pitchers Vic Aldridge and Emil Yde had been fined in the past and survived that reprimand by remaining on the club.[73] Regis hearkened back to the 1924 season when Kiki received a pay boost of $50 per month from Dreyfuss after almost single-handedly winning a series for Pittsburgh against the Giants. Nobody questioned Cuyler's place in the lineup until later that year when he struck out six times in two games as New York swept three September contests with pennant implications at the Polo Grounds. Murmurings from those close to front office personnel echoed the sentiments of Hazen being "yellow" and "hitting over his head." This opinion existed despite confirmation from a Boston physician that Kiki had seriously injured his shoulder in a collision with second baseman Frankie Frisch in an August game against the Giants.[74] Cuyler couldn't even play this series' middle contest on September 24 because cold weather caused excruciating pain in his shoulder when batting.[75]

Welsh wrote in his 1927 article that Kiki stood up running to second in the game against New York on August 6 to interfere with the completion of a double play, just as the Giants' Royce "Ross" Youngs and other intelligent players had done for years. Cuyler claimed he made the correct decision on that play, although he readily admitted that he used poor judgment trying to reach third base on an overthrow later in the game. Regis reasoned it appeared inconsequential who happened to be right or wrong about this play. According to Welsh, within the bigger picture, this incident afforded Pirates management a ready excuse to get rid of a player they'd been looking to move for three years.[76]

Upon completing their home stand against the Giants on August 10, Pittsburgh traveled to St. Louis to begin a series against the Cardinals one day later. The Pirates currently stood in second place with a 61–43 record, putting them 3½ games behind the Chicago Cubs. When the team arrived in St. Louis, Donie Bush stated that Kiki Cuyler wouldn't play in the series. Pittsburgh's manager refused to comment on rumors of a suspension or possible trade regarding Cuyler. The Pirates' greyhound outfielder claimed the club hadn't suspended him, as far as he knew. Such trade speculation resulted from a *New York Evening Post* story claiming the newspaper possessed credible, authoritative information that Pittsburgh planned on trading Kiki to the Brooklyn Robins for outfielder Max Carey once the 1927 season concluded. This article inferred that Carey would manage the Pirates in 1928.[77]

The newspaper story declared Barney Dreyfuss was interested in bringing Max back to the club. It also professed that although Dreyfuss supported the action against those who instigated a mutiny one year earlier to maintain discipline, he regretted Carey's release to Brooklyn. The *New York Evening Post* revealed their source of information to be close to the Pirates' club while also expressing the belief that such a move resulted from the feud between Cuyler and manager Donie Bush.[78] Team secretary Sam Dreyfuss responded to this report by characterizing it as "Too silly for comment." Noncommittal on whether Kiki would stay or go after the campaign finished, Sam's father denied this particular rumor.

"Mr. Cuyler will not be traded for anybody," emphatically stated Barney Dreyfuss. "If Cuyler doesn't want to play ball for Pittsburgh he can quit. I'm not satisfied with him or his playing and I don't think anybody else is for that matter."[79]

Contrary to Barney Dreyfuss's statement about people exhibiting dissatisfaction over Kiki Cuyler's performance, many fans sided with the player. Legions of admirers throughout Pittsburgh and the surrounding area supported Kiki. They afforded him the kind of adulation commensurate with that received by Honus Wagner when he played for the Pittsburgh Pirates. One such rooter devoted to Cuyler's cause expressed his feelings in a letter to the *Pittsburgh Press*. This individual, reacting to another letter in that newspaper offering advice for committing the sin of "indifferent base running," wrote that Kiki couldn't show improvement in this area while languishing on the bench. He stated Bush's intention for issuing the fine wasn't to benefit Cuyler.

Concerning Kiki's boneheaded play disgusting the other reader, this individual declared there were instances when Pie Traynor, Glenn Wright, George Grantham, Lloyd Waner, and even Paul Waner disgusted him. The letter writer confirmed that to err was human, and nobody doubted that Pittsburgh's players were human. This person then countered against the tired, stale phrase of "indifferent play," used as a broad brush to condemn a baseball player who committed one mistake.

> But did it look as if Cuyler was indifferent to his club's welfare when he made such a wild dash into third base to avert a force out in May that he injured his ankle? Did it look like he was indifferent when he remained in the game for another inning despite the fact that he was in the hospital before the day was over? Did it look like indifference when he pleaded later on to watch the team play, promising to return to the hospital cot afterwards? Did it look like indifference when a few weeks later, Cuyler went in as a pinch hitter several times though he could hardly walk, let alone run?
>
> Did it look like indifference to his team when Cuyler, though injured to the extent that he couldn't play, yet warmed up pitchers, pitched to batters and for hours, had extra batting practice of his own on the sidelines? Did it look like indifference when Cuyler was so anxious to play again that he aggravated his ankle before it was entirely healed? Did it look like much indifference when he made seven hits in the three days previous to his being fined? Last but not least, did it look like indifference when Cuyler, by an exceptionally clean life, strove to keep in top form for everyday play?

The letter's author acknowledged that no conclusive evidence supported Cuyler's indiferrence. This ally said that the majority of fans held the opinion that Donie Bush, desirous of benching Kiki anyway, made him the goat to urge on the other boys.[80]

When Barney Dreyfuss commented on the trade rumor regarding Kiki shifting to Brooklyn for Max Carey, Pittsburgh's owner said that Mr. Cuyler could quit if he didn't want to play ball for Pittsburgh.[81] Usually, the true definition of playing for a team meant that an individual participated on the field. For the next month following the fine, Cuyler only made rare appearances late in games as a pinch hitter, a pinch runner, or a defensive replacement. That briefly changed due to an unfortunate set of circumstances involving a teammate. Before the morning contest of a Labor Day doubleheader at Forbes Field on September 5, Lloyd Waner split the middle finger on his right hand while fielding a groundball during preliminary practice. Pittsburgh's trainer, George Asten, taped up the injured area, and Lloyd played in the contest, which Cincinnati won, 8–6.

Waner's finger became too sore for him to participate in the afternoon tilt versus the Reds.[82] Team officials expected Lloyd to be sidelined a few days from this minor injury—a bruised finger.[83] Donie Bush restructured his lineup for the second game, placing George Grantham in the leadoff spot usually occupied by Waner and rushing Kiki into the side as the center fielder and number two batter.[84] The Reds defeated Pittsburgh in the nightcap, 4–3. When Cuyler batted for Grantham in the first game's eighth inning, he received rousing applause from Forbes Field's patrons before hitting a single to right field.[85] This encouragement by the large afternoon crowd continued throughout the second contest.[86] In four trips to the plate in game two, Kiki legged out one scratch infield hit to Cincinnati shortstop Horace "Hod" Ford.[87]

That night after these two squads opposed each other, the *Pittsburgh Press* gained some information they claimed to be reliable that the Pirates and Reds planned on pulling off a big deal after the season concluded. The article, which appeared in print the following day, stated that Pittsburgh had proposed trading Kiki Cuyler and possibly pitcher Johnny Morrison to Cincinnati for first baseman Walter "Wally" Pipp, catcher Eugene "Bubbles" Hargrave, and hurler Adolfo "Dolf" Luque. Regarding the source of this intelligence, the *Pittsburgh Press* affirmed that it came from a trustworthy and credible informant. Club officials had vigorously discredited previous rumors surrounding trade speculation. One of Pittsburgh's players mentioned in this story told his friends that he was aware of the proposal and seemingly delighted over including his name in this potential deal due to unhappiness over his current surroundings.[88]

Any hope Kiki Cuyler may have harbored over remaining in the Pirates' starting lineup during Lloyd Waner's absence came crashing down quickly. On the morning of September 6, Sam Dreyfuss announced the recall of outfielder Adam Comorosky from the Western League's Wichita Larks to replace the injured Waner in center field.[89] Donie Bush confirmed that he planned on starting Comorosky in that afternoon's contest against the Reds, meaning that Cuyler would be decorating the bench again in favor of a rookie.[90] That day, Barney Dreyfuss also announced he'd retained Bush to manage Pittsburgh in 1928. For the first time, Donie spoke openly about his disagreement with Kiki. Bush alleged Cuyler's performance failed to keep pace with other outfielders on the team, thus necessitating a lineup change. Donie also stated nothing personal existed regarding his attitude toward Kiki. Bush wanted all the other players, as well as Cuyler, to know that he took the correct action against him by levying a $50 fine.

"However," Bush said, "it is a fact that Cuyler has not been playing up to the caliber of Barnhart and the Waner brothers and therefore it has been necessary to keep him out of the game. Anytime I feel he will be of assistance in helping us to win I will immediately rush him back into the lineup."[91]

In discussing Clyde Barnhart's proficiency, Donie Bush seemed to be living in the past. Barnhart certainly experienced a hot streak after Hazen Cuyler suffered his injury, batting .421 in June. Clyde saw a slight drop-off for July when he hit .341. That downward trajectory continued as Barnhart batted .273 in August. Bush's confidence in him and a quick rush to judgment about Cuyler might've left fans perplexed as Clyde couldn't produce anything better than a .209 mark in September. Donie's insight about the Waner brothers proved correct, as they experienced sensational seasons in 1927. According to a close friend of one of Pittsburgh's players, this led to a jealous streak on Kiki's part.

This insider stated on September 9 that Cuyler expressed displeasure over how Paul and Lloyd had thrust themselves into the limelight. Newspapers chronicled their grand success every day, although the two brothers hadn't asked for this type of publicity related to their diamond capabilities. The team member's buddy declared that Kiki didn't like playing second fiddle and having the two Waner boys steal his thunder. This individual contended Cuyler also felt slighted that Donie Bush didn't immediately place him back into the starting lineup after recovering from his leg injury. Doing so would've been difficult for Pittsburgh's manager since it meant removing either Lloyd or Barnhart from the lineup, both of whom had played great baseball at the time. Although the possibility existed that there happened to be no truth to this story emanating from Forbes Field, people nonetheless continued circulating it throughout the city.[92]

Throughout the final month of the 1927 campaign, Pittsburgh battled New York and St. Louis in a spirited pennant race. The victor in this baseball exercise gained the privilege of opposing the mighty New York Yankees, who barreled through the American League like a runaway freight train, posting a 110–44 record. Sportswriter Carl L. Turner commended Pirates manager Donie Bush for keeping his players focused on the prize while dealing with a similar situation that tore the team apart under Bill McKechnie in 1926. Turner believed that when Donie put his fist down in this instance, benching

Kiki Cuyler over the perception that he didn't play to win, a satisfactory outcome resulted for the squad. To show all team members he was the undisputed boss, Bush pulled one of the greatest outfielders in baseball from the starting lineup as if he was a green rookie. For Donie, maintaining discipline proved paramount to diamond success.

"I may not be fortunate enough to develop a winner," Bush said, "but I will have harmony on any club I manage, regardless of who may need disciplining."[93]

Following a 3–1 loss against New York at Forbes Field on September 24, *Pittsburgh Press* sports editor Ralph S. Davis received letters criticizing Bush and Barney Dreyfuss for not using Kiki Cuyler in the series against the Giants. Davis commented that outfield defects proved very noticeable in the crucial four-game engagement where Pittsburgh only pulled out a single victory. In one of the games, Clyde Barnhart played miserably and resembled a bush leaguer. In another, Paul Waner badly misplayed a ball hit to right field. Lastly, brother Lloyd lacked his usual precision in one of the contests. Throughout the four games, a dejected Cuyler resembled a figure from a Greek tragedy, slumped down on the bench looking as if saddened, with a broken heart. After game one of a doubleheader versus the Giants on September 22, which the Pirates won, 5–2, every player briefly trekked to the clubhouse, except Kiki, who remained alone sitting on the bench.[94]

Pittsburgh weathered the challenge put forward by their two worthy foes, claiming the National League pennant by defeating Cincinnati, 9–6, at Redland Field on October 1.[95] The following afternoon, the Pirates lost a meaningless game to the Reds, 1–0. Bush played substitutes at every position but one. Lloyd Waner remained in center field, as every other starter received a day off, and Cuyler occupied his usual spot on the bench. Such a decision regarding Lloyd appeared risky with an upcoming battle against the Yankees looming, given that he missed a few games in early September due to an injured finger. The Pirates finished with a 94–60 record, placing them 1½ games ahead of St. Louis and two games in front of New York.

Disgusted Pittsburgh Pirates fans lamented the treatment afforded favorite son Hazen "Kiki" Cuyler. Many rooters pondered the possibility of another "inside story" related to the "Cuyler case." Upon firing Bill McKechnie, Barney Dreyfuss had declared he answered the demand of Pittsburgh's baseball fans to bring in a new manager.[96] These same patrons planned on making their voices heard even louder this time, as it became painfully evident that action mandated by them only applied when it suited management's goals or purposes.

On September 30, 1926, the three banished players who instigated the ABC Affair, Babe Adams, Carson Bigbee, and Max Carey, released a statement regarding the affair's "inside story." In this statement, the three former Pittsburgh Pirates players claimed problems started with Fred Clarke in 1925 and continued to fester one year later. In 1926, Eddie Moore supposedly demanded to Clarke that he "Get off the bench," while George Grantham and Kiki Cuyler had problems batting the way Fred advised. Carey, shown in this photo, starred in the 1925 World Series and played the final two games against the Washington Senators with severely damaged ribs. Max acted as the spokesperson for the three disciplined players throughout the entire ordeal. (Courtesy of the Library of Congress).

13

Disheartening Final Discipline, Broad Fan Support, and Liberation

Disciplining a player could be tricky, especially if baseball fans strongly disagreed with that course of action. In Donie Bush's case, the decision to fine and bench Kiki Cuyler served a twofold purpose. While Bush had disciplined Cuyler for his insubordination, the Pirates' manager also wanted to communicate to other players that he was the supreme boss and wouldn't tolerate similar behavior. What better way for Donie to hammer home this message than by relegating one of the club's star players to a nonparticipant role in the season's final two months. However, this decision came with consequences, as some team members and most of Pittsburgh's baseball fans opposed such a drastic measure. It also caused a dilemma for the Pirates' pilot, who possibly had reached a point of no return because Donie needed to follow through with this punishment. Reinserting Kiki into the lineup came at a possible cost if the outfielder performed at his past elite level, and such an outcome might feed the angry mob who'd questioned this benching from the outset.

Before Pittsburgh started the World Series against the New York Yankees at Forbes Field, catcher Johnny Gooch, who also happened to be Cuyler's roommate on the road, and other players, prepared a petition asking Bush to use the benched player in the upcoming Fall Classic.[1] A day or two before the World Series began, a group of men from Kiki's hometown of Harrisville, Michigan, sent a telegram to the Pirates' manager, pleading with him to at least play Cuyler in one contest for the sake of his aged parents. Each person also signed the message. Upon delivery of the telegram to the team's Forbes Field headquarters, Barney Dreyfuss intercepted the correspondence and instead answered it rather than turning it over to Bush. Dreyfuss replied that Donie was very busy and thought it best he didn't bother him over this request. Pittsburgh's owner responded that only nine men could play at one time, and Cuyler would receive a chance in a game if a spot presented itself.[2]

The outlook certainly looked gloomy for Kiki Cuyler seeing action in the 1927 World Series. At a luncheon honoring the Pirates, given by Pittsburgh's Chamber of Commerce, one club official referred to Kiki as a "good ballplayer who is having a bad year."[3] A report regarding Cuyler's eight-year-old son, Harold, being seriously ill with bronchitis compounded the outfielder's diamond plight.[4]

When Pittsburgh's players participated in hitting and fielding practice at Forbes Field on October 4, one day before Game One of the World Series, Kiki arrived on the diamond wearing a dazzling green shirt. Cuyler's face was sad as he helped his teammates prepare for the big battle against George Herman "Babe" Ruth, Henry Louis "Lou" Gehrig, and the mighty Yankees. When approached by a sportswriter who asked him about maybe playing in one of the contests, Kiki offered a short response, indicating he'd become resigned to his fate.

"Guess there ain't a chance," Cuyler said with a wry grin, glancing surreptitiously across the diamond to where manager Donie Bush hustled about with unwavering enthusiasm, drilling those players who would play a prominent role in the series.

When the scribe approached Bush and asked about the possibility of him relenting and swallowing his prejudices to allow the dashing Cuyler to get into the World Series and perhaps help Pittsburgh win, the Pirates' skipper confirmed his player's outlook.

"Not a chance," echoed Donie.

Bush, whose word was final on the diamond, also insisted that the Pirates were a better ball club without Cuyler.[5] Although Donie functioned as the ultimate authority related to his managerial duties, thousands of Forbes Field fans believed they acted as the final and most essential judges regarding the local team's baseball fortunes. Passionate patrons offered the greatest demonstration of support ever witnessed for one player when the World Series between Pittsburgh and New York commenced on October 5. Fans carried pennants and homemade banners to support the maligned Kiki Cuyler. Throughout the game, these rooters chanted, "We Want Cuyler," and "Put Cuyler In."[6] They also booed and cursed Bush at every opportunity.[7]

A giant streamer hanging from Forbes Field's concrete bleacher section read, "We Want Cuyler," in flaming bright lettering. The banner disappeared for a brief time before it reemerged once again. When those responsible for voicing their opinion in giant, written form permanently removed the streamer, others in the ballpark didn't know whether they'd done this voluntarily or on orders from Pirates management.[8] While not overly sensitive, Donie Bush certainly felt the brunt of this adverse sentiment on the part of many Pittsburgh baseball fans. American League umpire Billy Evans had always admired Bush when he played shortstop for the Detroit Tigers. Although not working the World Series as an umpire, Evans covered the event for his popular syndicated newspaper column. While Billy chatted with Donie on the Pirates' bench before the opening game started, the grandstand banner supporting Kiki entered the conversation.

"Look out there in left field, Bill, and read that banner," said Bush, pointing in that general direction at the sign which read, "We Want Cuyler."

"I doubt if they get him," continued Bush. "Each club can have only one manager. Just as long as I am working for Mr. Dreyfuss I am going to be the pilot of the Pittsburgh club.

"I am going to make mistakes, but I am willing to ride along with my judgment and accept the verdicts."[9]

Pittsburgh's baseball fans handed down their first verdict against Donie Bush late in Game One of the 1927 World Series. The highly anticipated power display by the Yankees' batters didn't occur in the first fixture, as both teams engaged in a tightly contested battle. The Pirates outhit their opponent, nine to six, as New York claimed a 5–4 victory. Down a run heading into the bottom of the ninth inning, hurler John "Johnny" Miljus led off for Pittsburgh. Throughout the contest, Kiki Cuyler had worn his sweater over the jersey and nervously changed seats in the dugout. When the bottom of the ninth arrived, Kiki stood at the mouth of the dugout, hoping to answer the call that didn't come.[10] Rooters throughout Forbes Field vociferously clamored in deafening fashion for Bush to send Cuyler up to the plate as a pinch hitter.[11] Instead, Donie selected left-handed hitting rookie outfielder George Frederick "Fred" Brickell to bat for Miljus.

Yankees hurler William Wilcy Moore induced Brickell to hit a weak grounder back to the mound, which he quickly tossed to first base for the out.[12] Moore then retired Lloyd Waner and Clyde Barnhart to end the game. An article in the *Pittsburgh Post-Gazette* severely criticized Bush for leaving Kiki languishing on the bench in the ninth inning. The publication reasoned that sentiment swayed many of Forbes Field's fans in demanding Cuyler enter the game. The *Pittsburgh Post-Gazette* alleged that necessity and baseball logic dictated this move at such a critical juncture of the contest. The newspaper also added that most patrons in attendance would've preferred witnessing Kiki strike out rather than watching Fred tap weakly to the pitcher because Cuyler was the better player.[13]

Pittsburgh Press sports editor Ralph S. Davis reasoned in his column that when Fred Brickell batted for Johnny Miljus in the ninth inning of Game One, this signaled Kiki Cuyler wouldn't see action in the Fall Classic under any circumstances. Davis wrote that Kiki resembled a pathetic figure all afternoon. During hitting practice, since he didn't take a turn in the batting cage with the regulars, Cuyler elicited the assistance of Pirates batboys on the side. According to Davis, Kiki perched himself on the rim of the dugout for most of the game, his eyes exhibiting a distant gaze.[14] Following this defeat, the question of why Pittsburgh didn't use Cuyler dominated the conversations of baseball fans.

One rumor regarding this query suggested Sam Dreyfuss and his father Barney had demanded that Cuyler take a seat on the bench. This gossip claimed that differences between player and ownership, rather than a problem with Donie Bush, resulted in the decision to remove Kiki from the lineup. Amidst some criticism on this front, Pittsburgh's team treasurer clarified the situation by giving out a statement to the Associated Press.

> It is solely an issue between Cuyler and Bush. Bush is manager of the club. What he does in handling the team is not dictated by my father or myself. If Bush wants to play Cuyler at any time, he is free to do so. There is absolutely no dark, deep or mysterious reason for keeping Cuyler on the bench.
>
> The club's executives, however, share Bush's conviction that there is no reason for inserting Cuyler in the regular lineup for the simple fact that Barnhart is playing better ball. I think Barnhart proved himself one of the stars of the opening game.
>
> So far as using Brickell as a pinch hitter instead of Cuyler is concerned, I think that also was advisable. Brickell, left-handed batter and fast, was the proper man to send against Moore, a right-handed pitcher. Cuyler is a right-handed batsman.

Bush refused to discuss Cuyler's case other than repeating that he intended to use him when needed.[15] Although Sam Dreyfuss definitively declared that Donie solely acted as Pittsburgh's manager, it was intriguing that he offered alibis behind Bush's Game One decisions.

When it came to the over 41,000 fans who attended that contest at Forbes Field, a man who knew something about leading the Buccaneers into battles on the diamond happened to be among the multitude, fighting through ballpark entrances while clutching his precious tickets. Former skipper and player Fred Clarke made the trip from Winfield, Kansas, along with a friend, onetime Pittsburgh citizen, and Oklahoma oilman Louis "Lew" Wentz, to be honored by the Amen Corner at a dinner in the William Penn Hotel. The man connected to the Pirates' only two diamond championships exhibited a genuine appreciation for his new role as a private citizen.

"You know I got sort of a kick out of it, being pushed around, asked to show my ticket and all the other things a spectator is subject to in a thing of this kind," said Clarke in a *Pittsburgh Post-Gazette* interview. "And then to sit among the fans and hear their chatter, ideas, suggestions, boosts and knocks; well, it makes a fellow feel that baseball is worthwhile after all.

"I don't think I'll ever be a part of baseball again like I once was, but I'll always be at a ball game when the chance offers."[16]

While sitting in Forbes Field's stands, Fred Clarke undoubtedly heard chatter, ideas, and suggestions demanding Kiki Cuyler be permitted to play in the contest. For Game Two at the same venue on October 6, New York Yankees manager Miller Huggins selected George Pipgras to oppose Pittsburgh on the mound. In 1922, Pipgras had been Cuyler's teammate on the South Atlantic League's Charleston Pals. It's worth noting that no newspaper articles chronicling this game mentioned Bush asking Kiki during a skull session or team meeting to offer any information regarding the hurler's strengths or weaknesses. Cuyler certainly would've been able to present intelligence about George that might help his teammates. No reports on this point didn't mean nobody requested such advice, although it seems unlikely since newspapers thoroughly covered every aspect of the 1927 World Series.

After allowing Pittsburgh to tally one run in the first inning, Pipgras performed brilliantly on the mound for the Yankees. Lackluster work at various points of the game proved an obstacle too massive for the Pirates to overcome, as New York secured a 6–2 victory.[17] *Brooklyn Daily Times* sportswriter Thomas W. Meany wrote in his column that a significant demonstration of support existed from Pittsburgh's fans toward Kiki throughout the game at Forbes Field. Meany also recalled that such chants favoring Cuyler had cascaded throughout the ballpark as he decorated the bench during a September series at Forbes Field between the Pirates and Brooklyn Robins.[18]

Fans' yells for Kiki became louder as Pittsburgh's prospects dimmed later in the game. When Earl Smith pinch-hit for hurler Michael "Mike" Cvengros in the eighth inning, the cries for Kiki intensified. These shouts turned to groans after Smith grounded out to New York's first baseman, Lou Gehrig. As Clyde Barnhart stepped up to the plate that same frame, the chorus favoring Cuyler started again. Pooch quieted the crowd by slamming a single to center field that moved Lloyd Waner from first to third.[19] Before not seeing action for the second consecutive afternoon, Kiki utilized his pocket camera, snapping pictures of each Pirates teammate. The *Pittsburgh Press* felt this a pitiful sight, witnessing a once valuable player lining up each team member for a photo. Cuyler's friend explained this behavior, believing that the outfielder wouldn't be permitted to appear in another game for Pittsburgh.

"He wants something to remember them by," said the friend as he watched Ki.[20]

During the Fall Classic, Kiki Cuyler also had each New York Yankees team member sign the oversized mitt given to him by the J. A. Dubow Manufacturing Company.[21] As the World Series shifted to New York, newspaper stories attempted to explain the disagreement between Cuyler and Pirates management. The tale about Kiki's jealousy when it first came to Paul Waner grabbing the spotlight at his expense and then little brother, Lloyd, resurfaced. Reporting introduced a new angle that Cuyler had been one of the charter members of the clique in 1926 who pursued ousting Fred Clarke. When Donie Bush took charge of the club at spring training in 1927, he firmly informed his players that he wouldn't tolerate such cliques.[22] Associated Press sportswriter Brian Bell felt Bush most likely welcomed a change of scenery away from Pittsburgh. Bell reasoned the multitude at Yankee Stadium attending Game Three on October 7 didn't care whether Kiki played or autographed baseballs, his primary occupation recently at Forbes Field.[23]

Thomas Meany offered a different assessment than Brian Bell. After ordaining Pittsburgh's patrons as the most interested fans in the country in following baseball, the writer also declared they happened to be at the top of making life difficult for players and managers. Meany stated that New York's rooters might also show a display expressing support for Cuyler. Thomas alleged these fans, much more sportsmanlike than their Pittsburgh counterparts, likewise felt that the Pirates' manager had treated Kiki shabbily, regardless of being right or wrong in holding this opinion. Since Meany believed New York's baseball patrons to be true sportsmen, he felt this designation demanded such action.[24]

Yankees southpaw hurler Herbert "Herb" Pennock pitched exceptionally against the Pirates in Game Three of the 1927 World Series. Through the first seven innings, Pennock didn't allow one Pittsburgh runner to reach base as New York built up an 8–0 lead. Babe Ruth connected for a home run in the seventh frame when the Yankees put the contest out of reach by placing six runs on the scoreboard. Ruth, who'd smacked 60 round-trippers during the regular season, blasted a three-run bomb off lefty Pirates reliever Mike Cvengros. Pittsburgh finally ended Herb's perfect game in the eighth when Pie Traynor singled to left field and then scored the contest's final run on Clyde Barnhart's double to right.[25]

In the eighth inning, Donie Bush sent up third-string catcher Roy Spencer to bat for Johnny Gooch. Starting the ninth frame, utility infielder Heinie Groh pinch-hit for Cvengros. Heinie had only batted 35 times in 1927 after signing a contract on July 2. Both players failed horribly at their tasks.[26] Sam Dreyfuss didn't release a statement after the game explaining why Bush didn't use the right-handed batting Kiki Cuyler against a southpaw pitcher. While three consecutive losses against New York wrecked the nerves of devoted Pirates fans, a large crowd still jammed their way before the electronic newspaper scoreboards on a Saturday in Pittsburgh to receive updates regarding Game Four on October 8. Although rooting for the Pirates to be victorious, these spectators also hoped Ruth might clout another homer. Strangely enough, Smoky City rooters talked more about Cuyler's benching than previous games' outcomes. At Forbes Field, the crowd had channeled its focus in the second contest toward booing and hissing Pittsburgh's manager.[27]

These rooters back in Pittsburgh received their wish. In front of a crowd of nearly 58,000 spectators, Babe smacked a two-run home run in the fifth inning off Pirates hurler Carmen Hill to give New York the lead, 3–1.[28] Pittsburgh battled back in the seventh inning, scoring two runs off Yankees pitcher Wilcy Moore. Earl Smith started the frame by reaching the initial sack when Moore muffed the throw from first baseman Lou Gehrig after fielding a grounder off the Pirates' catcher's bat.[29] With Hill scheduled to bat for Pittsburgh, Yankee Stadium's fans loudly shouted for Kiki Cuyler to enter the fray. When Donie Bush rebuked this demand from the masses by selecting Fred Brickell to pinch hit and sending Emil Yde in to run for Smith, those cheers turned into a wild chorus of boos.[30]

Brickell reached base on an error by New York second baseman Anthony "Tony" Lazzeri, which moved Emil to second. Lloyd Waner pushed the runners to second and third with a sacrifice bunt. Yde scored on Clyde Barnhart's single to center, and Brickell crossed the plate on Paul Waner's sacrifice fly.[31] Bush's strategy in the eighth inning appeared questionable as he permitted relief pitcher Johnny Miljus to bat with two men on and two out. Moore then fanned him. Many in attendance felt that Cuyler might've been a good option at the plate to give Pittsburgh the lead.[32] Miljus ran into trouble in the bottom of the ninth when he started the inning by walking Earle Combs before Mark Koenig reached first on a bunt single to third. Both runners moved up one bag with Ruth at the plate when Johnny uncorked a wild pitch. Miljus then opted to load the bases by intentionally passing Babe.

Pittsburgh's pitcher rose to the occasion, striking out both Lou Gehrig and Robert "Bob" Meusel in succession. Tony Lazzeri, whom St. Louis Cardinals hurler Grover "Pete" Alexander had fanned in a similar situation with the bases loaded in Game Seven of the 1926 World Series, strode to the plate. As was the case one year earlier, Tony crushed an offering that curved foul into the left-field stands. Home plate umpire Emmet "Red" Ormsby called Johnny's ensuing pitch a ball.[33] Miljus wound up and fired his next offering toward home plate. As the toss came in wide of the dish, Pirates catcher Johnny Gooch lunged at the baseball. The sphere smacked off the tip of his mitt and bounded to the stands behind home plate. Combs chugged across the dish with the run that won Game Four and the World Series.[34] Yankee Stadium's official scorer charged Pittsburgh's hurler with a wild pitch. This decision didn't stop Gooch from taking responsibility for the blunder.

"The ball that Miljus threw to Lazzeri which allowed the winning run to score was a passed ball," said Gooch two days after the deciding game. "Nine times out of ten I would have caught it, but I was squatting and the ball went a little high and wide.

"That ball should have been caught. The official scorer made a mistake. It was no wild pitch. The 'boot' should have been charged against me."[35]

While saddened over the outcome, many Pirates fans viewing the giant electronic scoreboard in downtown Pittsburgh cheered when New York scored the deciding run that crowned them as world champions.[36] After Game Four ended, Pittsburgh's players dejectedly trudged to the clubhouse. As Pirates team members hit the showers, Kiki Cuyler exhibited consummate sportsmanship during this heartbreaking moment. Rather than express his feelings that things might've been different if Donie Bush had permitted him to play in the World Series, Cuyler exhibited a reassuring tone as he approached each teammate and offered consoling words.

"You sure fought 'em today," said Cuyler to each player standing near him. "They had the breaks, that's all."

Whether Kiki's presence in the starting lineup could've helped his team is pure conjecture. The main advantage to having the flamboyant former World Series hero on the field might've been no more than psychological against the tremendous and mighty New York Yankees.[37] Syndicated sports columnist Frank

G. Menke held an interesting opinion about the 1927 World Series, suggesting the Yankees hadn't been so strong in their clash against the Pirates but rather played mediocre baseball while winning in a rout. Menke classified Pittsburgh's performance as terrible and listless, displaying the type of diamond dysfunction that would've disgraced a sandlot league. He also offered a unique take on why the Pirates' players appeared lackluster, especially in Games Two and Three, when they seemed to be doing nothing more than going through the motions.

Frank asked a serious question about the feud between Kiki Cuyler and Donie Bush. Did the failure of Bush to use Cuyler in the first game take the spirit out of the team? Menke wondered if many of the Pirates, who were Cuyler's friends, resented the manager's action of not using this player noted for delivering in the pinches at a critical time in Game One. The writer opined whether Bush's decision in that contest led to Pittsburgh's players not giving their best effort in Games Two and Three, possibly due to the perception on their part that punishing a player trumped winning. Menke deliberated over the possibility that Kiki's teammates played uninspired ball on purpose, hoping to hammer home the point to Donie that the team needed Cuyler's batting expertise when pinch-hitting situations inevitably arose.

According to Frank, the Pirates' players fought gallantly in Game One and then in the final contest with their backs up against the wall. Menke continued that New York didn't seem to have enough power to annihilate Pittsburgh four straight times, without favorable luck on two occasions and inexplicable decisions assisting them two other times.[38] Once the World Series ended, Bush explained his rationale behind never using Kiki against the Yankees.

"The only reason Cuyler was not used was because I didn't figure there was a spot for him," said Bush. "I used in the series the team that had won the National League pennant for me, and I think that that was the logical thing to do. I think those boys were entitled to play. That's the reason I used them and the only reason I didn't play Cuyler."[39]

Devoted Pittsburgh rooters, craving any information about an "inside story" surrounding the "Cuyler case," finally received snippets of details courtesy of the star outfielder. That evening, following the Pirates' defeat in Game Four of the World Series against the Yankees, Kiki offered his version of the case through the Associated Press. A brilliant man, Cuyler astutely articulated the points from his perspective about this unfortunate situation.

> To tell the downright and whole truth, the whole thing is a mystery to me. There are some things to be told, without doubt, but it is not I who can tell

them. In my own heart I have felt some things, and they may or may not be true, but as for what might be called the facts of the case, they will have to come from my employers.

However, I have decided to tell what I know and some of what I feel, and I do it solely because Barney Dreyfuss, the owner of the Pirates; his son, Sam Dreyfuss, and Donie Bush, manager of the team, have each and often told their sides of the case. As long as the Pirates were after the National League pennant and while they were in the World Series, I kept still. I have been reported as saying this and that. I said nothing. Now that is all over. Furthermore, I think I have played for the last time in a Pirate uniform. Not because I don't want to play in that uniform, but because my employers, I have heard, have other plans.

First of all, it should be said that I have no ill feeling for Donie Bush. I am sure that whatever he did, even where he did things that didn't make me feel any too good, he did for the best; did them because he was convinced that he would help the team. For my part, I was as strong for the team as Bush or Dreyfuss, but, perhaps, we did not agree on the best way to help the team.

Kiki then indicated that although the "Cuyler case" generally started when Donie Bush fined him $50 after failing to slide into second base during an August game against the Giants, the seeds of discontent possibly had been sown before that contest at Forbes Field. Cuyler once again defended his decision to run toward second base, standing up to better prevent a potential double play by interfering with the throw to first. Kiki stated that despite overrunning the bag and then being tagged out by shortstop Travis Jackson after he initially dropped the ball, New York indeed failed in executing a double play. Because Pittsburgh's newspapers quickly learned of the fine, Cuyler denied Bush's claim that he'd alerted the press to his situation. Kiki argued to possess no legitimate reason for leaking the story. However, he didn't understand the problem behind such information reaching newspaper reporters since management had informed them when fining players in the past.

Cuyler declared this false assertion led to a misconception that he happened to be balking over his punishment. As time passed, Kiki felt he'd paid for his mistake, whether right or not, and should've gained permission to start over with a clean slate. In the end, things didn't work out that way. Cuyler also touched on his "yen," as he described, for playing left field and batting second in the order. Kiki claimed that playing left field was the worst thing he did on a baseball diamond. Cuyler informed Donie about his trepidation toward those two things. Pittsburgh's manager said he needed him to bat in the second spot. Kiki acquiesced, declaring he tried as hard as ever in his life to succeed while batting second, although the player felt statistics validated his failure to hit in the two-hole. In the end, Cuyler understood that approaching his manager on this topic hadn't been wise.

> I made the mistake, I see now, of speaking about these two things. I should have batted second and played left field without saying anything, but I wanted to help and felt I could be of more help in center and batting in any other position than second.
>
> No doubt I have been guilty of things that might be held against me, but I never loafed and I was always trying to do my best. I still think Bush a great fellow, and there is no extreme bitterness in my heart. I, quite naturally, feel that I should have been permitted to play, but who knows that I would have done as well as the man who played my position? Clyde Barnhart played a good game, and he and I are not enemies in any way.
>
> I have heard that the whole matter will be thrashed out soon, and I will be as happy as anyone to find out what is the real trouble. No one feels the team's defeat any more than I do. No one pulled harder for them to win.

Other Pirates players expressed extreme dissatisfaction over Cuyler's benching since it dampened team harmony. These individuals pointed out Kiki's percentage of runs scored figured against times at bat, which happened to be among the league leaders, his powerful throwing arm, and speed on the bases as other valid reasons to be included in the starting lineup. After Game One, Cuyler's supporters also questioned Sam Dreyfuss's statement that Donie Bush benched him because Clyde Barnhart played better baseball. They cited that Sam didn't explain why Adam Comorosky, a raw recruit, replaced Barnhart on occasion when he couldn't play during the season's final month because of an injury. While allowing the Associated Press to offer his account, Kiki also laughingly related the story about an offer to perform on a vaudeville stage for the next two weeks.

"Accept it," a friend advised.

"What could I do on the stage?" Cuyler asked.

"Well," one of Pittsburgh's players said, "you can just go out there and take that bench with you and sit on it with a gag in your mouth while they play the spotlight on you, just as you did in the World Series."[40]

A New York newspaper writer talked to numerous Pirates players during their stay in the Big Apple. These individuals claimed problems existed between Kiki Cuyler and Barney Dreyfuss before Donie Bush arrived to manage Pittsburgh's baseball team. This reporter alleged they told him that Cuyler immediately asked Bush who ran the squad, him or Dreyfuss. The newspaperman continued that Donie did everything in his power to appease Hazen, who insisted on being petulant, leading the manager to remark, "Well, when you make up your mind what you will do, come around and see me." *Pittsburgh Press* sports editor Ralph S. Davis also asked an anonymous Pirates player a point-blank question.

"Do you think that the Cuyler business hurt your chance in the Yankee series?" Davis asked. "By that I mean, did the players resent his absence and did it affect their morale?"

"I don't think so," replied the Pirates' player. "Cuyler is a fine fellow. I like him and I am sorry he is in trouble. But I don't believe the players have taken sides in the case to any extent, and I don't believe they allowed it to influence them in any way. Clyde Barnhart is one of our most popular players. He is quiet, modest and well-liked by all of us. If Cuyler had been in, Clyde would have been out. We can't resent the moves made by the manager. It's up to him and most of the boys are willing to let him run the club."[41]

A key point made by this anonymous player about most of the boys, and not all, being willing to let Donie Bush run the club revealed that factions or cliques truly existed regarding the "Cuyler case." The assertion by some players that Kiki and Barney Dreyfuss had been at odds before Bush joined the organization received corroboration through an article by sportswriter Edward "Ed" Hughes in the *Brooklyn Daily Eagle*. An unidentified, well-known baseball scout, claiming his knowledge to be accurate, acted as Hughes's informant, explaining to the writer on October 11 that the ABC Affair of 1926 had soured Cuyler's attitude.

> Cuyler and Bush were practically at loggerheads the moment Donie took charge of the team. Kiki immediately faced Bush and demanded to know just how he stood with the new pilot of the Pirates.
>
> "You know where I stood in that Carey-Bigbee-Adams thing," Cuyler told Bush. "I was with those players and against McKechnie. Now, what I want to know is how you feel about that, Bush, and what effect it is going to have on your treatment of me during the season?"
>
> Bush answered that McKechnie's troubles of the past did not belong to him, that he considered them a closed book. Cuyler, according to the

manager, would be given as fair treatment as any member of the team. Bush explained that he had no thought other than of winning ball games and that he would use every method at hand to score victories.

This did not seem to wholly satisfy Cuyler, who demanded further satisfaction. To which Bush declared that he was going to be the sole boss of the team and that he alone would be responsible for every order affecting the welfare of the team. Cuyler rather strongly hinted that Bush would do no such thing and that Barney Dreyfuss would have more than a little to say about such matters. All of which did not set well with Mr. Bush, nor was it of great cheer to Cuyler. Kiki felt that Dreyfuss still regarded him with some rancor on account of his support of Carey, Bigbee and Adams.

The scout alleged that Donie Bush immediately understood that Kiki Cuyler planned on being at odds with his theories and ambitions as a manager. Although Bush believed Cuyler would be a difficult player to handle, this gentleman thought Donie did his best to appease and work with the star outfielder. The conflict between these two reached a tipping point when Kiki failed to slide into second base against the Giants in August. According to the scout, more harsh words followed on Cuyler's part about ill-treatment and who happened to be Pittsburgh's boss. To prove he wielded uncompromising authority, Bush benched Cuyler, although the player still supposed this mandate had come from Barney Dreyfuss's office.[42]

When the downcast Pirates entourage returned from New York on October 9, only a few fans welcomed them at the train station. Manager Donie Bush offered no statement to the press about Pittsburgh's defeat at the Yankees' hands. Owner Barney Dreyfuss likely wouldn't return from New York until the following day. A final team meeting, focusing on divvying up the loser's share of World Series money, was scheduled for October 10 at Forbes Field. Reports indicated that Bush, Cuyler, and Dreyfuss might hold a conference after this gathering to resolve the situation.[43] Donie also held a clubhouse session with the players at 11:00 A.M. Once this meeting concluded, Bush responded to scribes about Kiki's comments to the Associated Press following Game Four of the World Series.

"Cuyler's own statement convicts him," said the Buccaneers' boss. "I would have been foolish to use in the World Series a player who acted the way Cuyler says he acted in his own statement.

"I think the Cuyler statement is its own answer, and requires no comment on my part."

Donie had just finished dealing with a delicate situation at the conference with his players. Bush possessed a letter, which one of his men had written to *Pittsburgh Press* sports editor Ralph S. Davis. The unsigned correspondence severely criticized the conduct of both Donie and owner Barney Dreyfuss. Bush read the following letter, supporting Cuyler, to the entire squad.

> There have been chances to win games thrown away by Bush not using Cuyler, and still Cuyler was silent. In fact, I believe they expected him to pout, and are sorry because he didn't.
>
> They threatened to send him home from St. Louis because several men were riding Bush for the fine, and they blamed Cuyler for telling it when it was common gossip around town before the papers got it, and the only reason Bush and Dreyfuss didn't want it to get out was because they didn't want to be shown up.
>
> In my opinion Dreyfuss was sore at Cuyler for holding out in 1925 [related to his 1926 contract], and also sore because someone found out that he gave him a measly $50 raise for getting a regular job in 1924.
>
> Bush was sore at Cuyler because Cuyler showed him up at a meeting, where he made a wrong play and tried to make Cuyler the goat. But this is what made my blood boil: Cuyler asked if he could be shifted to his regular position out of left, because the sun was hard on his eyes. This was proven by an eye expert in New York, who stated that Cuyler's eyes were strong, but subject to strain when in bright light and suggested Cuyler being away from the sun field as much as possible. Center field didn't get the direct light like left field. This Bush refused, and he made Cuyler play all the sun fields on the eastern trip, or as much as he was in there.
>
> I also know that Barney Dreyfuss refused to let men in on Cuyler's passes, etc., but what did Cuyler do in return? He took Comorosky out in center field, and showed him how to play different batters and said he would do anything he could to help him.

After reading this letter out loud, Donie Bush asked the author to identify himself. Dead silence pervaded the room. Bush then turned to Kiki Cuyler and inquired if he knew who wrote this letter. Cuyler responded that he did but refused to divulge the individual's name.[44] Upon possessing this communication, Donie started a vendetta to discover the author and punish that individual. Kiki expressed happiness and relief that Davis hadn't originally printed this blistering epistle in the *Pittsburgh Press* since revealing the player's identity would've guaranteed his exit from Pittsburgh through a trade.[45] Pirates ownership offered no clarification about this continuing big story in the press. Before leaving New York on the evening of October 9, Barney Dreyfuss refused to comment on Cuyler's status and stated that Bush oversaw the team for him. Secretary Sam Watters offered little response when pressed to give his opinion on Kiki's statement released through the Associated Press.

"I have nothing to say," said Watters, "because there is no club side to the story. There is no 'Cuyler case' except what the newspapers have made of it."[46]

On October 11, Kiki packed up his belongings and started for his home in Flint, Michigan.[47] Before leaving Pittsburgh, Cuyler told the whole story surrounding his predicament while also addressing some rumors in circulation and not yet reported by exclusively writing three articles for Universal Service titled "Why I Was Kept on the Bench." The first installment appeared in select Western Pennsylvania newspapers on October 10. The editor hoped this series might add some clarity regarding the two sides of this story; one that Kiki had engaged in insubordinate actions or his friends' contention that Donie Bush didn't handle the temperamental star correctly. In the first article, explicitly related to his interactions with the Pirates' skipper, Cuyler rehashed some of the ground covered in his statement to the Associated Press after the World Series ended.

Kiki said that although Pittsburgh wasn't his native city, he considered it his native baseball city. Regarding the aversion to batting second in the lineup, Cuyler professed that no cross or ugly word ever passed between him and Donie on that point. Kiki made no demands, only suggesting it might be better for the team if he batted elsewhere in the order. Bush didn't express any anger over this suggestion and said, "I am going to show you you are wrong about the two hole." Cuyler denied ever kicking over playing left field, claiming he only mentioned to his boss on one occasion about it being the worst spot for him to play. Kiki dropped the matter forever when Donie explained that Lloyd Waner was more proficient in center field than left. Cuyler also talked about another incident before Bush fined him $50 in August, which his teammate had addressed in the supportive letter.

> Prior to my being fined there was just one other conflict between Bush and myself. Bush blamed me for getting caught off third in a Giant game at the Polo Grounds. I was doubled on a line hit to [shortstop Travis] Jackson who whipped the ball to [third baseman Frederick "Freddie"] Lindstrom. I was playing off too far but I played off too far because Bush had insisted against my advice that I take a couple of extra steps from the bag in playing off.

When Bush took me to task about being caught off I believed he was wrong in doing it. I don't say it was his fault I got caught off third; maybe it wasn't anybody's fault. But certain I don't believe I should have been "panned" because I had followed instructions.

Kiki also talked about the play at second base that led to Donie fining and benching him. In the clubhouse after that contest against New York on August 6, Cuyler clarified to Bush his reasoning behind the decision to run into second base standing up. Donie responded that he didn't want to hear any alibis. Kiki claimed he then explained to the manager he only wanted to tell him what he thought of the play.

Now was I a loafing, stubborn, insubordinate ballplayer for all this? Well, anyway, there was no one more anxious to play and to help the club win. A few days after the fine I was advised by a friend in St. Louis to act like a good soldier and be a good sport and to go to Bush and to apologize. This I did in St. Louis. "If I've done anything," I said to the Pirate manager, "I want to apologize for it. I'm sorry."

Bush replied, "I have nothing personal against you. You're too good a fellow for me to hold anything personal against."

In the article, Cuyler also mentioned that Clyde Barnhart was an excellent player and a good friend. Kiki's final point in the first installment centered on a false insinuation that he stirred up the fans to get them to support his position in the "Cuyler case." During a game toward the season's end, Cuyler sat in the Pirates' dugout in the open part, not on the bench. Kiki had waved to a friend in the stands who briefly spoke to him. Bush walked up to Cuyler and offered a harsh reprimand.

"Get in out of here," said Bush tersely. "Get on the bench. Your friends all know you are here."

A sensitive Kiki Cuyler, claiming this false accusation hurt him more than past exchanges, obeyed his superior's directive.[48]

Part two of Cuyler's prose focused on his relationship with Pirates owner Barney Dreyfuss. Kiki understood that Dreyfuss never cared very much for him. Although Cuyler refused to critique his playing ability, declaring non-partisan judges should decide that point, he figured that diamond skill or perceived lack thereof caused him to fall into disfavor with his employer. Kiki announced that he'd only spoken to Barney four or five times since joining the Pirates, with one of those moments occurring in New York more than a year ago when the two agreed on contract terms for the 1926 campaign. Cuyler claimed to have heard Dreyfuss beginning to exhibit a wrong impression about his capabilities as a player when he struggled at the plate in a late-season series against the Giants in 1924.

Kiki admitted that he couldn't hit in that critical series. Cuyler also reminded readers that although suffering from a bad shoulder at the time, he played at manager Bill McKechnie's urging since his presence on the field would've made a positive impact with the regular lineup remaining intact. Earlier that summer, when Kiki's performance proved instrumental toward a sweep of New York at Forbes Field, the Pirates' owner sent for him and offered a $50 a month bonus in his paycheck. Cuyler then told some team members who asked him how much of a boost in pay he received. Kiki also later confirmed this to a Pittsburgh reporter. When a story on the subject came out, Cuyler feared Dreyfuss believed he might be complaining about getting such a small stipend, which he stated to be untrue. Kiki reasoned that Barney didn't need to give him anything extra and that he genuinely appreciated the gesture. Following these two incidents, Cuyler heard rumblings that the front office didn't view him favorably.

Kiki rejected rumors about stormy encounters with Dreyfuss, a critical statement on his part given future allegations. Cuyler also disavowed a ridiculous story about demanding a bonus in 1927 since Pittsburgh's owner had given teammates extra money for good work. Kiki stated he certainly wouldn't request a bonus because individuals superior to him on the diamond received them. It was the owner's prerogative of how he spent his money. Cuyler hypothetically asked on what grounds he could've justified requesting a bonus that year. Kiki denied that he'd ever queried Donie Bush about who directed the Pittsburgh Pirates; him or Barney Dreyfuss. Hazen once again reiterated that he never attempted to whip the fans into a frenzy but appreciated the support given by kids in the bleachers and a host of friends in the stands that loyally stood by him.[49]

In his final article, Kiki Cuyler tackled how he got along with his teammates. Kiki quickly answered by declaring that he honestly believed he possessed no enemies among the Pirates' players. Cuyler also refuted the silly suggestion that the Waner boys caused him to turn green with envy. Kiki again dismissed false contentions regarding his anger over teammates receiving bonuses, naming Lloyd Waner and Glenn Wright as those individuals. Regarding jealousy toward Lloyd and brother Paul, Cuyler acknowledged that an appearance on a Pittsburgh broadcasting station at the beginning of the season rebuffed this notion. During that radio talk show, Kiki referred to Paul Waner as an expert batsman, the best he ever saw, and predicted he would lead the National League batters this upcoming season.

Cuyler also declared that besides possessing great diamond ability, the Waner brothers happened to be two of the finest boys that ever walked onto a baseball field. Why should he be jealous of a kid like Lloyd, who did such remarkable work in his rookie season? Kiki also commented that when a return to the starting lineup didn't happen when good friend Pooch Barnhart suffered an injury, he helped youngster Adam Comorosky by teaching him the nuances of playing the outfield against different batters. Because Cuyler considered Adam a talented youngster, the maligned veteran offered assistance since he'd always welcomed advice from his elders to gain experience when breaking in at the major league level. Kiki also referenced in this final article that he'd stopped a potential repeat of the ABC Affair from happening in 1927.

> Friendliness shown toward me came from various players. While I was on the bench one player came to me and said: "I'm going to the front for you and ask Bush to put you in the lineup to help us win."
>
> Later this was repeated by another member of the squad. Still later two other players came to me to say they were going to ask for a meeting at which time Bush would be asked to use me in the interest of the club.
>
> It was when these last two came to me that I sensed the danger of such a proceeding. I was certain it would do no good for a series of events had shown me all too plainly that I was through forever as a Pirate and to these friends said, "Now don't do that. It will bring no good results and it is dangerous to you fellows and to the club in general. It might start a general rumpus which would be a repetition of what happened in 1926 when trouble arose over a meeting and our pennant chances were ruined.
>
> "Whatever you do, no matter how strongly you feel, don't go through with your idea. That would just about ruin the pennant chances for the boys."

In conclusion, when pondering the common suggestion that Cuyler would be glad to escape Pittsburgh, Kiki expressed sorrow over going to another team. Leaving the Pirates meant the loss of many valued friendships and moving to another city where he would be among strangers.[50] Upon reaching Flint, Cuyler told his hometown pals that he never refused to take an order from Donie Bush. Cuyler also stated that his troubles batting in the lineup's two-hole led him to be nicknamed "Double O" after hitting into so many double plays. Some players, and even Bush, laughed over his misfortune.[51] After Kiki's first two articles appeared in print, Donie displayed little concern over any "inside story" presented by the Pirates' star outfielder.

"There is nothing in them so far except what everyone knows," said Bush. "Cuyler is telling the truth as he always has. In fact, I don't think the boy knows how to tell a lie."[52]

Donie's thoughts and opinions on the matter also found their way into print. Through various interviews with the *Pittsburgh Post-Gazette* during the summer, Bush had expressed views on Kiki Cuyler and his ability as a player. By mutual agreement, the publication withheld these conversations from being printed until after the season ended.[53] On one occasion, Donie told the newspaper that he didn't consider Cuyler to be his style of a ballplayer. Bush added that Kiki preferred doing what he wanted rather than what the manager told him to do. Donie also talked about receiving a warning on the spring training trip that "Cuyler was the sort of player who he needed to handle with kid gloves." Bush added that he liked Kiki as a boy without any bad habits, who maintained exemplary conduct, except for flashes of temperament.[54]

Regarding benching Cuyler, Pittsburgh's pilot also declared Lloyd Waner would remain in the lineup even if he only hit .275 due to being such a valuable player. At the same time, Clyde Barnhart's hot batting made it impossible to remove him. After the Pirates had returned from a long trip in the East in late July, Bush told the *Pittsburgh Post-Gazette* writer that Kiki cost the team two games on the recent excursion because he made throws from the outfield to the wrong base. Donie called out Cuyler in front of the entire club, not harshly, but rather to stress that the outfielder needed to start playing smart, heads-up baseball. Bush then explained how Kiki reacted to his criticism.

"Then Cuyler said," Bush told the reporter, "'Well, why don't you get someone in there who can throw.' My infield will tell if you ask them, that they were instructed to yell at him as to the base he was to return the ball."

Pittsburgh's skipper had also offered a comment one day after he fined the sulking outfielder $50 for his performance against the Giants on August 6.

"I fined him right in front of all the club and everyone on the club knew why he was fined," declared Bush. "And the biggest reason was to get him out of the almost melancholy rut he was in."

This article also cited rumors about Kiki smacking one of the club executives in the face over being fined, or that Barney Dreyfuss had issued an ironclad order to Donie not to use Cuyler under any circumstances, as ridiculous.[55] Other comments attributed to Bush found their way into print courtesy of

William "Billy" Smith, a former minor league manager who worked as a scout for the Washington Senators' organization. According to Smith, Kiki Cuyler remained on the bench of his own volition.[56] Billy had been present when Donie talked to *Washington Daily News* sportswriter Gene Kessler in New York during the World Series. Smith related this insight for the benefit of a curious public.

> Cuyler was mumbling to himself and acting dissatisfied early in the season. I never could understand his action, and apparently he didn't care to understand mine. Then came that incident when he failed to slide into second base and I fined him $50. Naturally I benched him at the time.
>
> Later I went to Kiki and told him the incident was closed and that he could return to the game and forget about the past. I told him I wanted him to play left field and bat in second place. He said he couldn't do either, as the positions weren't natural to him.
>
> I told him he'd have to do as I said. I explained to him that Lloyd Waner was too good to be removed from center field and that Paul Waner was hitting so well in third place I couldn't change him.
>
> "If that's the way you feel about it I'd just as soon not play at all," Cuyler replied very sharply. So I told him I'd keep him on the bench until I was ready to put him in the lineup.
>
> "Remember this," I said to Cuyler. "I'm boss of this team. My job means as much to me as yours to you, and I'm not going to let you run me out of it by dictating the way this team should be run."

According to Billy Smith, Donie Bush told Gene Kessler the case ended there.[57] Decades later, during another interview with Nashville sportswriter Fred Russell, Bush claimed that the actual reason behind benching Kiki Cuyler revolved around the outfielder's habit of overthrowing the cutoff man. One afternoon during a game, after Kiki's throw to home plate allowed a runner to reach second base, who eventually scored on a single, Donie asked Cuyler when he came to the bench, "Won't you ever learn to throw the ball low?" Cuyler responded to Bush about getting somebody else if the skipper didn't like the way he played. While talking to Russell, Donie alleged this remark to be the valid reason for banishing Kiki to the bench. Bush also spoke of having the utmost respect for Cuyler as a player, his great natural ability, and a strong desire to always be in top physical shape. Donie then cited temperament and bullheadedness as the player's two main flaws.

Bush asserted that if Kiki had apologized to him, he would've put the outfielder back in the lineup.[58] When it came to apologies, Donie possibly suffered a memory lapse since Cuyler claimed in 1927 that he expressed regret on the advice of a St. Louis friend.[59] After newspapers printed Kiki's articles, Bush said that Cuyler always told the truth and didn't know how to lie.[60] When covering opinions and sentiments over time, decades after retiring, third baseman Pie Traynor stated that Kiki and Donie acted like little children in 1927. Pie added that the silly quarrel between these two made things unhealthy for the entire team.[61] When Dr. Eugene Converse Murdock interviewed Glenn Wright in 1978 and asked him about the "Cuyler case," the former Pirates' shortstop claimed to have heard at the time that Kiki went to a newspaper reporter in defiance of Bush. Wright also commented that Cuyler was a great hitter and fielder, had a great arm, and was a beautiful runner.[62] While talking to Clyde Barnhart in 1979, Murdock received little information about the dispute from the man who'd replaced Kiki in the lineup.

"I don't know what it was," Barnhart told Murdock. "They didn't get along too good together."[63]

A sliver of hope existed for friends and fans of the speedy outfielder, who wished Hazen somehow could remain in a Pittsburgh Pirates uniform. On October 11, a newspaper report alleged that Oklahoma oil promoter Lew Wentz planned on buying the Pirates from Barney Dreyfuss for $3 million. If true, and Wentz made the trip to Pittsburgh to close a deal, Fred Clarke would likely accompany him. Dreyfuss and team secretary Sam Watters issued a joint statement affirming nobody had offered to purchase the team, and none was forthcoming.[64] According to sports columnist Frank Getty, under a partnership between the Oklahoma oilman and Clarke, the former player and manager most likely would direct the squad's diamond destiny. Before leaving for Pittsburgh, both men detailed plans under their stewardship, including Kiki playing center field for the Buccaneers.

Although the pair admitted Lloyd Waner was an excellent ballplayer, Clarke and Wentz felt left field suited him best, with Cuyler moving back to center and Paul Waner a fixture in right. Fred, certainly planning on keeping Cuyler in the fold, objected to any trade while he and Lew negotiated a potential deal.[65] Sadly for the Flint Flash's devoted fans, this annual report about an impending Pirates sale proved false. On the night of October 11, Lew Wentz issued a statement from Pittsburgh denying this rumor. Wentz and Clarke, traveling from New York, where this story originated, stopped in the Smoky City before continuing to their homes in the West. Lew confirmed he'd asked Barney Dreyfuss some time ago about selling Pittsburgh's baseball franchise, but the magnate refused to name a price or show interest in such a transaction.

"I regret the report of my purchase of the Pirates," Wentz said in his statement.[66]

A consistent outfield of Kiki Cuyler, Lloyd Waner, and Paul Waner possibly could've been the best in baseball since Tristram "Tris" Speaker, Harry Hooper, and George "Duffy" Lewis patrolled the outer garden for the Boston Red Sox. Since no change in the Pirates' ownership exhausted any hope of Kiki remaining with Pittsburgh, trade rumors littered newspaper columns throughout the country. One such story claimed Cincinnati would be willing to part with second baseman Hugh "Hughie" Critz and first baseman Wally Pipp for Cuyler.[67] Another report declared Reds manager Jack Hendricks might bring Kiki aboard for infielder George Kelly and pitcher Dolf Luque. Some gossip pointed toward a move with the Philadelphia Phillies, where the Pirates acquired pitcher Frank "Dutch" Ulrich and catcher James "Jimmie" Wilson. Brooklyn could possibly enter this high-stakes poker game for Cuyler's services by dangling southpaw hurler Jesse Lee "Jess" Petty.[68]

Of course, eliminating some National League clubs from the list of potential suitors made sense based on those managers who supported Donie Bush's action of not playing Kiki Cuyler in the World Series. Giants skipper John McGraw declared that ownership paid players to bat where a manager desired, and play the position he deemed necessary. Hendricks of Cincinnati asserted, "Any big league manager who doesn't run the ball club to suit himself will shortly be looking for a new job."[69] A possible deal also hung in limbo since Barney Dreyfuss spent a week in Memphis, Tennessee, at the end of October, to attend the wedding of his son, Samuel, to Miss Carolyn Wolf of Arkansas.[70]

With still no movement on the trade front through most of November, sportswriter Thomas Holmes of the *Brooklyn Daily Eagle* cited a revelation from colleague Lou Wollen of the *Pittsburgh Press* in his column. According to Holmes, Wollen surprisingly admitted that Dreyfuss hadn't received a single offer for Cuyler's services from a rival club owner since the season closed. Pirates ownership seemed worried that other astute baseball men didn't rank Kiki as highly as the general public. Holmes wrote that the National League wouldn't allow Cuyler to slip away into oblivion even if he'd insulted both Barney and his son, thus forcing Pittsburgh to send him to the bush leagues.[71]

James "Jimmie" Isaminger, the *Philadelphia Inquirer* sports editor, had made a similar statement in his column shortly after the World Series ended, lambasting Donie Bush for so harshly punishing Kiki. In that article, Isaminger related the unconfirmed story that Cuyler had been abusive during a conference with Dreyfuss shortly after being docked $50 in the pocketbook, and Pittsburgh's owner ordered Bush to bench the outfielder permanently.[72] In November, New York's *The Sun* sportswriter Joe Vila reported that Kiki had abhorrently insulted both Barney and his son, Sam, at Pirates headquarters. Vila claimed the two men planned on further punishing Cuyler by requesting permission from Judge Kenesaw Mountain Landis to place the player on the suspended list for 1928. Kiki supposedly responded that he would counter such action by appealing through the courts.[73]

One newspaper account alleged that Kiki commented on Dreyfuss's Jewish heritage during a heated confrontation, infuriating Pittsburgh's owner.[74] Cuyler had already disputed such a claim in the second article he penned a month ago, stating that he respected Barney as a good baseball man. At the same time, he alleged the two never exchanged cross words or engaged in any heated arguments.[75] Throughout this agonizing ordeal, Kiki admitted to being in the dark and mystified over the whole situation.

"I don't know what it's all about," Cuyler said. "I'm like the guy without a country—as far as baseball is concerned."[76]

Kiki Cuyler finally found a baseball nation to call his own once again. On the night of November 28, 1927, owner Barney Dreyfuss announced Cuyler's trade to the Chicago Cubs for second baseman Earl "Sparky" Adams and outfielder Floyd "Pete" Scott. That day, Cubs president William L. Veeck and manager Joseph "Joe" McCarthy quietly arrived in town to hold a conference with Dreyfuss. The group held their meeting away from Forbes Field's headquarters to preserve secrecy in these discussions. Donie Bush, who'd already participated in preliminary negotiations with Chicago's management hierarchy, remained at his Indianapolis home. After finalizing the transaction, Veeck and McCarthy boarded a train and returned to Chicago. Both parties appeared satisfied and felt they benefited from the deal. Adams's acquisition addressed a deep concern for the Pirates at second base.[77]

Kiki's many friends and admirers certainly regretted not seeing the outfielder's constantly smiling face in a Pittsburgh uniform ever again.[78] A reporter from the *Pittsburgh Post-Gazette* communicated with Cuyler by telephone at his home at 1313 Avenue B in Flint to chronicle the player's reaction shortly after Dreyfuss released his statement about the deal. Although expected, Kiki claimed the news still came as a shock.

Gee, whiz, I haven't had time to give it much thought. Only tonight at dinner Mrs. [Bertha Kelly] Cuyler and I were talking about winter plans and we agreed that nothing much could be done until I had some definite idea of my future.

There is only one thing you can say for me right now, and that is that no matter where I go or where I play I will do just as I did in Pittsburgh—give my best at all times. You ask me if I like the idea of leaving Pittsburgh. Well, to that I can only say yes—and no. During my stay in Pittsburgh I made a lot of friends, real friends, who stood by me from the first game I played until the last. Naturally, I hate to leave them.

But, baseball calls for some queer twists in a fellow's life. I guess this is mine. The only break that I got was to know long enough in advance what was going to happen, even though I didn't know what it would be. In that way I sort of steeled myself for this shock. But, nevertheless, I am sort of befuddled right now, when I realize that the moment I have been looking forward to has actually arrived.

Kiki Cuyler said he planned on giving the Chicago Cubs his best as a player. He also revealed that his son, Harold, and wife, Bertha, had recovered from their recent illnesses.[79] The Cuyler saga in Pittsburgh, which possessed so many angles that it possibly caused even architects to experience dizziness, had finally ended. When it came to Pirates rooters feeling disappointment and pain, this move acted as just the beginning, as Donie Bush dismantled a championship team, and another star player took up residence in management's doghouse.

Pittsburgh Pirates outfielder Kiki Cuyler and manager Donie Bush started feuding from the outset once the former Detroit Tigers shortstop took control of the club in 1927. After Bush fined Cuyler $50 for poor base running in the game on August 6 against the New York Giants at Forbes Field, the stellar outfielder found a place on the bench. Although Kiki had been a 1925 World Series hero, he never stepped on the field in the 1927 Fall Classic as the New York Yankees swept the Pirates. Throughout games at Forbes Field as the season progressed and during the World Series, fans showered Cuyler with the greatest expression of support ever given for a Pittsburgh athlete. In this photo from 1925, standing left to right, are New York Giants manager John McGraw and Kiki Cuyler. (Courtesy of the Library of Congress.)

14

Spreading the Buckshot throughout the National League

Opinions and insights quickly poured in after the Pittsburgh Pirates traded Hazen "Kiki" Cuyler to the Chicago Cubs. The consensus of many individuals connected to baseball from New York and other areas of the country pointed toward the Pirates outsmarting Cubs manager Joe McCarthy in acquiring Sparky Adams and Pete Scott for Cuyler. New York Yankees general manager Ed Barrow believed Pittsburgh received a high return for practically nothing while fortifying an area of need at second base, where a glaring weakness had progressed during the previous World Series. Ed also reasoned that Pittsburgh lost no strength to their club since management didn't plan on using Kiki. New York Giants manager John McGraw also felt the Pirates emerged as winners in this transaction.

"I think the Pirates got all the better of the deal," said John McGraw. "Adams is a dangerous ball player, always getting on base, and with a hard-hitting team like the Pirates behind him, he will bother pitchers more than ever. There is a question whether Cuyler is as good as he used to be. He failed in the pinches many times last season."

Other baseball men offered dissenting views, not in line with these two individuals from New York. Former Boston Braves manager George Stallings, just selected to oversee the International League's Montreal Royals in 1928, understood McCarthy's reasoning behind making this deal. Stallings supposed that Joe had been looking to increase Chicago's hitting strength, with a lethal trio of Jackson Riggs Stephenson, Kiki Cuyler, and Lewis "Hack" Wilson following one another in the batting order. Pilot William "Derby Day Bill" Clymer of the International League's Buffalo Bisons firmly felt the Cubs snookered Pittsburgh by stealing Cuyler from them in this player exchange.

"They gave him away," said Clymer. "I could have gotten a ball club for him and players beside."[1]

John McGraw's assessment of Sparky Adams seemed legitimate, as he'd exhibited great success as Chicago's leadoff hitter over the past three seasons. However, Pirates manager Donie Bush planned on hitting Adams second in the lineup since Lloyd Waner occupied the batting order's top spot. Through no fault of his own, McGraw's contention that Kiki Cuyler failed in the pinches in 1927 is incorrect. New York's manager didn't have the RISP statistic at his disposal, which is more in vogue now during the current baseball environment. Retroactive research shows that Kiki did quite well hitting with runners in scoring position that year, posting a .361 average. He also possessed solid RISP numbers in 1924 (.336), 1925 (.341), and 1926 (.350). Despite his aversion in 1927 to hitting second in the order, Cuyler batted .341 in the 34 games he held that place in the lineup but struck out 20 times.

In December, Pirates owner Barney Dreyfuss made his final remarks about Kiki's career in Pittsburgh. Dreyfuss offered various opinions about his team's status during a dinner honoring Frank J. Harris, a Pennsylvania state senator. Barney rejected a request to be one of the banquet's speakers, answering it was better to say nothing and be thought a fool rather than talking and then proving that point. After discussing many baseball topics, Dreyfuss commented on the controversy surrounding Cuyler.[2]

> Cuyler is a great ballplayer. I wish him success with the Cubs and feel sure he will have it. But to the Pirates club he was of little or no use.
>
> When Cuyler did not have everything to his liking at the beginning of last season, was not permitted to pick out the place he should play, how he should play it or where he should bat, he became what some folks call temperamental. Right then, instead of confiding his troubles in Manager Donie Bush, or me, Cuyler took the advice of outsiders, listened to them and followed their suggestions. From the way he acted after that it was proof the advice was bad.
>
> No ballplayer has a better friend than the manager or owner he plays for. Cuyler disregarded them and that's the reason the Pirates were glad to trade him. And don't forget—we got a second baseman.[3]

Following a tough first season with Chicago in 1928, Cuyler ascended again to the ranks as one of baseball's top outfielders in 1929, hitting .360 and helping the Cubs win a National League pennant. Another league flag followed in 1932, although Chicago lost both Fall Classics, first to the Philadelphia

Athletics in 1929 and then to the New York Yankees. In 1949, when Kiki returned to the major leagues long after his playing career had ended to coach the Boston Red Sox, sportswriter Regis M. Welsh recalled the former player's troubles in Pittsburgh. Connected for years to various area newspapers covering the Pirates, Welsh offered some evidence and opinion in an article he wrote in the May 1949 issue of *Huddle* sports magazine.

Welsh wrote that club management had railroaded Cuyler out of Pittsburgh during the zenith of his baseball career. Regis also categorized Kiki as an innocent victim of a front-office grudge handed down to two Pirates managers. Welsh claimed that everyone connected to this feud ended up damaged or hurt. The writer also marveled over the support fans extended to Cuyler when Donie Bush benched him in 1927, carrying pennants and homemade banners offering encouragement while constantly chanting, "We Want Cuyler" or "Put Cuyler In." Welsh claimed this to be the most fantastic customer demonstration in team history. Regis also inferred that Pirates management had persecuted Kiki that fateful year.

"That he had courage and ability to overcome the most desperate situation ever endured by a ballplayer was proved by his work in two World Series with the Cubs," Welsh wrote.

Regis also corroborated Bill McKechnie's firing after the 1926 season, having a connection to an immediate problem festering between Kiki and Donie Bush in 1927, surrounding who ran the team; Pittsburgh's new manager or Barney Dreyfuss. Welsh's prose also dispelled the premise that no ballplayer had a better friend than the manager or owner for whom he played. According to Regis, Dreyfuss's early admiration for Cuyler turned to dislike for someone he viewed as a cocky player. Welsh alleged that Dreyfuss's frequent criticisms of Kiki included, "He's a busher hitting over his head," "He's burning himself out grandstanding," and "He's an individualist, not a team player."

The sportswriter also believed Kiki shouldered some of the blame. Welsh classified Cuyler as "Selfish, sensitive and a lone wolf who preferred to be alone to be assured that he was in good company." Regis also stated that Kiki's views on subjects, or "dynamite," as he referred, brought about havoc on and off the diamond. Welsh then cited general stories about clubhouse fistfights, ear-burning arguments, barroom brawls over the favor of a lovely lady, religious feuds, and different cliques in the club to back this claim. In concluding the article, Regis appeared sympathetic regarding Cuyler's bad treatment during his time wearing a Pirates uniform. Welsh felt that in the final analysis, Kiki had been "The victim of the crudest, and most unsportsmanlike maneuvers—a blot on what some still believe to be the 'great American pastime.'"[4]

A little over two months after making the colossal deal with Chicago, another transaction with a possible correlation to the Kiki Cuyler case occurred. This player exchange included a surprising angle, as Barney Dreyfuss decided to work with arch-nemesis John McGraw, something he'd outright refused to do in the past. On February 11, 1928, Dreyfuss shipped hurler Vic Aldridge to the Giants for fellow pitcher Burleigh Grimes, who played for the Pirates at one time.[5] After Pittsburgh's owner announced the trade, skeptical Pirates baseball fans pondered whether the club had moved Aldridge because of his friendship with Kiki Cuyler. Throughout the previous summer, Vic remained outspoken in defending Cuyler, making little clubhouse speeches favoring his friend and teammate at every opportunity.[6] In speaking his mind about Kiki's treatment at management's hands, Aldridge publicly criticized Donie Bush.[7]

Pittsburgh Press sports editor Ralph S. Davis raised the possibility that Vic might've written the letter to that newspaper which Bush read at the last team meeting back in October. In the end, Davis reasoned such a hypothesis to be pure speculation, much like the friendship between Kiki Cuyler and Vic Aldridge playing a role in the pitcher's trade to New York.[8] From a pure baseball perspective, Pittsburgh proved the big winner in this transaction. Grimes signed a contract for 1928 without hesitation shortly after joining the Pirates.[9] Burleigh acted as Pittsburgh's workhorse, pitching brilliantly by appearing in 48 games and posting a 25–14 record, supported by a 2.99 ERA.

On the other hand, Aldridge held out throughout the season's first month. Vic didn't help make a good first impression when he scheduled an appointment to negotiate with John McGraw and never showed up for the meeting.[10] Aldridge finally inked his signature to a contract on May 6.[11] In what ended up being his last major league season, Vic pitched horribly for New York, going 4–7 with a 4.83 ERA.

The moves involving Aldridge and Cuyler proved to be the first significant steps the Pirates' management took in conducting a considerable transformation of the club. As had been the case in recent years, another star performer became caught up in this housecleaning. Once again, the annual event of an accomplished player landing in management's doghouse bloomed brightly like a spring flower. In 1923, Pittsburgh had paid $40,000 to the American Association's Kansas City Blues to secure heralded shortstop Forest Glenn Wright.[12] Besides being referred to as Glenn, Wright also carried the nickname "Buckshot" for his powerful throwing arm, which could also be erratic at times. As a young lad growing up in Archie, Missouri, Glenn claimed he threw at everything to develop his arm. This practice and reputation led to individuals always searching out the Wright kid when someone broke a window in Archie.[13]

Before his first season in the big leagues, Wright conducted a holdout, claiming he deserved to receive part of the purchase price Pittsburgh paid to Blues owner George Muehlebach. After conferring with Glenn in Kansas City on February 6, 1924, an exasperated Bill McKechnie boarded a train for home, vowing to be through trying to deal with the young shortstop.[14] Although McKechnie and Barney Dreyfuss adamantly refused to reveal which players had signed contracts on the eve of spring training starting in Paso Robles, California, sources stated Glenn and fellow rookie Ray Kremer were holding out for the same reason.[15] When the meeting with Wright happened in Kansas City, the Pirates' manager pointed out that if he felt part of the purchase price should go to him, the shortstop needed to take that matter up with Muehlebach. After considering the issue and feeling it unfair to punish Pittsburgh, who'd laid out big money to acquire him, Glenn wired from his winter home in Bartlesville, Oklahoma, that he planned on reporting to training camp.[16]

When Glenn Wright and Ray Kremer initially arrived for spring training, they still hadn't signed contracts but were expected to do so within a week.[17] Upon being interviewed by Dr. Eugene Converse Murdock in 1978, Wright told the historian that Barney Dreyfuss agreed to give him $7,500 in cash when Pittsburgh played a four-game exhibition series against the Kansas City Blues. Before the first contest on April 5, 1924, at Muehlebach Field, Dreyfuss handed Glenn an envelope containing the payment. Wright threw the envelope in the top of his locker and forgot about it when he left for the hotel after the game ended. Luckily, the money was still there the following day.[18] A decent crowd of over 3,000 people attended the first game to watch Glenn and cheer on the Blues.[19] On April 6, the attendance jumped to 12,000 for game two on a sunny, beautiful spring-like Sunday.[20]

Once Wright joined the signed ranks, Barney Dreyfuss reassured those fans worried over the rookie starting at shortstop for the Pirates. Dreyfuss declared that Glenn would do great once he became acclimated to his major league surroundings. Although Wright suffered from an extremely bruised heel as the season beckoned, Barney exuded confidence that the youngster would do just fine since he happened to be a born player who could hit.[21] Nervousness while batting explained Wright's slow start early in the campaign, as he most likely wasn't accustomed to the roar of applause from Forbes Field's patrons when stepping up to the plate. Glenn proved a graceful acrobat out in the field, reminiscent of Fred "Bones" Ely when making strong throws from any position.[22]

Although some baseball scouts had claimed Wright couldn't hit a curveball, he didn't seem to exhibit more of a problem in that area than any of his teammates. It also became apparent early in the 1924 season that Glenn possessed a knack for driving in runs. He continued to sparkle in the field and covered more ground at shortstop than anybody since the days when Honus Wagner played that position. Third baseman Pie Traynor declared that Wright only left him a small swath of territory to ramble over.[23] Glenn experienced a sensational rookie year, batting .287, smacking seven home runs, and knocking in 111 runs. Wright performed even better during the pennant-winning season of 1925, hitting .308 while blasting 18 round-trippers and driving home 121 teammates.

Glenn received justified praise for his performance in the 1925 World Series against the Washington Senators, following Pittsburgh's 6–3 victory in Game Five at Griffith Stadium, on October 12. That evening at the Raleigh Hotel, pundits and other baseball men assessed the Fall Classic up to this point. Many agreed that Wright had been the actual sensation of the World Series. Those who covered American League clubs and hadn't seen Glenn in action considered him a genuine revelation. Individuals from all parts of the country agreed that Wright wasn't just the class of the two competing teams but also one of the best players to break into the big leagues. Among those giving this glowing assessment were sportswriter Damon Runyan and umpire Billy Evans.

This group of baseball scholars agreed that Glenn feared no pitcher, exhibited speed on the bases, and was a superb defensive performer who keenly analyzed plays in front of him. They concluded Wright to be the nearest approach to a perfect baseball player to come upon the diamond horizon in many seasons.[24] Glenn's importance to the Pittsburgh Pirates became readily apparent when he suffered an injury in 1926. While the squad played that fateful series against Boston, Wright hurt his foot in the game at Braves Field on August 6. Favoring a previous affliction surrounding his hip, the foot on his other leg buckled under him, causing a very painful bruise. After remaining on the sidelines for two weeks, where Glenn could do little to no running, he worked out with his teammates on August 20 and found the foot still sore.[25]

Four days later, Wright's limp didn't seem as noticeable. Although nowhere near being in prime baseball shape, Glenn likely could play if asked to do so by manager Bill McKechnie. Wright didn't mind a cautious approach since he felt others had done exemplary work during his absence.

"I am willing to try it at any time now," said Glenn, "but the club is winning well without me and that is the big thing. My foot feels quite a bit better and I'll be glad to start whenever McKechnie says the word."[26]

Glenn Wright finally saw his first action in three weeks as a pinch hitter and defensive replacement on August 28 in a game against New York at Forbes Field. On three occasions, Wright also experienced duty within the pinch-hitting capacity during a critical series against the St. Louis Cardinals at Sportsman's Park. McKechnie feared playing Glenn at shortstop in these clashes because recent rain had led to St. Louis's ballpark being in poor shape.[27] After watching the first few innings between Pittsburgh and the Cardinals in a box seat on September 1, Wright and assistant manager Fred Clarke boarded a train bound for Cleveland, Ohio. From there, the two men expected to make a connection to Youngstown, so Glenn could visit Bonesetter Reese to receive treatment on his foot. If a positive outcome occurred, Wright planned on joining the Pirates in Chicago.[28]

Glenn returned to his shortstop position in the game against the Cubs on September 3 at Cubs Park. When Pittsburgh came back to Forbes Field for a brief home stand from September 6 through September 11, Wright participated in each contest, including four sets of doubleheaders. Although Glenn had returned to the lineup in this time of need, it seemed obvious to most fans that he couldn't play up to his usual standards. Relief to the foot most likely wouldn't be forthcoming during the current campaign, as Wright demonstrated a pronounced limp when walking or running.[29] Glenn appeared in a game for the Pirates for the last time in 1926 on September 17, against the Brooklyn Robins at Ebbets Field. Two days later, the *Pittsburgh Gazette Times* announced Wright had hurriedly left the team to be at the bedside of his sick father, Robert, who sadly died.[30]

Regarding the ABC Affair in 1926, Glenn Wright favored Fred Clarke since he considered him a second father. During his 1978 interview with Dr. Eugene Converse Murdock, Wright declared that some of the fellows on the team resented Clarke's advice because when he told somebody something, the former baseball icon did it in a very straightforward manner, much like Rogers Hornsby. Glenn also referred to Fred as a great ballplayer and a great man. The two forged a strong friendship. After the 1925 campaign ended, Wright joined Clarke for a hunting excursion on Fred's "Little Pirate Ranch" in Winfield, Kansas. Paul Waner, recently purchased by the Pirates from the San Francisco Seals, had asked Glenn for assistance negotiating his first major league contract. Pittsburgh's shortstop invited him to join them at the ranch.

Paul pulled up to Fred's home in his weathered Dodge Coupe as he and Glenn returned from a day of hunting. Waner exited the vehicle wearing a loud purple suit, carrying worn bags containing clothing and another case holding his saxophone. The three men went into the house and drank a highball before dinner. Wright then explained to Dr. Murdock that, as happened to be the case on many occasions after supper when he visited Clarke's ranch, they popped popcorn and sat around the fireplace while Fred's daughter, Muriel, played the piano. In this instance, Glenn asked Paul to join her on the saxophone he'd brought with him.

"You don't have to ask me twice," responded Waner.[31]

In 1927, as Pittsburgh battled to win the National League pennant, a precarious moment in a summer game sent Glenn Wright to the sidelines again. On June 28, the Pirates defeated St. Louis, 9–8, at Sportsman's Park. In the seventh inning of that contest, a pitch from Cardinals hurler Howard Victor "Vic" Keen struck a Pirates batter for the second time. His fast offering in that frame smacked Wright flush in the head. Pittsburgh's shortstop immediately crumpled to the ground, unconscious.[32] Keen quickly rushed to home plate, lifted Glenn's head, and embraced him. Vic hugged and kissed his fallen opponent as several players attempted to pull him away. Keen fought them off and remained kneeling at the side of the Pirates' injured player.

When Vic started becoming hysterical, St. Louis hurler Grover Alexander and coaches Allen Sothoron and Bill McKechnie escorted the pitcher to the clubhouse. After hearing officials summon an ambulance to take Wright to the hospital, Keen broke down and wept like a child.[33] Two spectators sitting in the crowd also fainted after witnessing the incident.[34] Glenn escaped severe injury because the ball smacked him just below the left temple. Upon being examined by doctors after the ambulance rushed Wright to a local hospital, they surmised that if the pitch had struck just a fraction of an inch higher, the blow to the head most likely would've been fatal. The following morning, Glenn appeared to be in good spirits, showing no ill effects from the beaning other than a huge lump where the baseball made contact with his head.

Vic Keen felt relief upon being one of the first people to call on Wright at the hospital and finding out the Pirates' shortstop hadn't suffered a severe injury. Manager Donie Bush announced that Glenn would return to Pittsburgh in the company of another player and that he planned on using Hal Rhyne as a replacement at shortstop.[35] The preliminary prognosis called for Wright to miss at least one week of action. On the afternoon of June 29, Glenn and Pirates pitcher Lee Meadows boarded a train for Pittsburgh, scheduled to reach the city before noon the following day. Doctors recommended resting for a few days so he could be ready to play baseball once again.[36] Although Wright expressed confidence that he would be able to jump right back in and perform at his usual high level, some Pittsburgh baseball fans feared the beaning could cause him to become plate-shy for a brief period.[37]

After missing two weeks, Glenn returned to the lineup on July 14, as the Pirates defeated Brooklyn at Ebbets Field, 6–5. The layoff didn't seem to hamper Wright, as he banged out two singles and drove home a run.[38] Although Glenn posted the lowest batting average of his major league career thus far in 1927, hitting .281, he still knocked in 105 runs. As Pittsburgh suffered a sweep at the New York Yankees' hands in the World Series, Wright couldn't contribute anything better than a .154 batting average.

Bad luck continued to plague Glenn shortly after returning from New York on Sunday morning, October 9. While driving his roadster, the car collided with another vehicle operated by thirty-two-year-old Melvin Morgan.[39] According to police, the impact lifted Morgan's car into the air before hurtling it on top of a traffic beacon. Melvin's vehicle and the traffic beacon ended up being wrecked, while Wright's roadster suffered minimal damage.

An ambulance took several injured individuals from Morgan's car to West Penn Hospital for treatment.[40] Wright walked away from the accident unscathed, while Morgan suffered a minor injury.[41] Police arrested both men and charged them with reckless driving, as Glenn forfeited a $100 bond instead of an immediate court appearance, while Melvin posted $50 on his charge.[42] On October 11, Wright stammered while speaking and seemed very uncomfortable as he appeared before Magistrate John Staley Jr. in traffic court. Glenn explained his side of the story regarding the collision in a very hesitant tone, unable to find a place to rest his hands while moving from one foot to the other. Judge Staley ended Wright's distress by dismissing the case since the two parties happened to be working on a private settlement.[43]

On May 12, 1928, those involved in the accident filed six separate damage suits against Glenn in Common Pleas Court, asking for a total of close to $40,500. All six individuals occupying the automobile driven by Melvin Morgan looked for relief from the court under the original charges levied at Wright for driving recklessly and at a high, excessive, dangerous, and unlawful speed. Besides the driver, the other occupants were his wife, son, W. W. Wright, his spouse, and their boy. Only W. W. Wright didn't suffer some type of injury. Three people asked for $10,000 in damages, while the other two individuals wanted to be compensated $5,000 each for their misfortune. W. W. Wright also requested $400 for damage to the car, which he owned.[44]

This court case added another layer of turmoil for Glenn Wright in what became a somewhat tumultuous season for the shortstop and many teammates.

When the first group of players, including pitchers and catchers, convened for spring training in Paso Robles, Donie Bush didn't pull any punches while delivering an introductory speech to his men in the dance hall above the spring field's clubhouse on the morning of February 21. Bush harshly warned his charges against partaking in intoxicating liquors throughout the upcoming season. While not mentioning the punishment for such an offense, Donie let the players know that things wouldn't go well for anybody who broke this rule. He then discussed bad conduct committed by players in 1927. Bush declared he knew who'd engaged in such wrongdoing last year before remarking that none of those boozers currently held a place on Pittsburgh's roster.

This statement left no ambiguity as to what the punishment would be if Pirates team members didn't walk the straight and narrow path. Donie also intimated plenty of crying would occur after he addressed this topic once again when the remaining players arrived in one week.[45] Kiki Cuyler certainly didn't fall into that category of poor behavior since he never drank alcohol, while Pittsburgh traded him due to insubordination and feuding with management. Besides Vic Aldridge, the club had cut loose Mike Cvengros, Roy Spencer, Emil Yde, and Johnny Morrison since the 1927 season concluded. From this group, Morrison had been guilty of participating in such practices in the past. Bush also affirmed he wouldn't require the services of spies to keep tabs on his players and offer him the facts regarding rule breakers, an indication that he planned on taking care of this matter personally. Donie readily admitted that some players took advantage of him in 1927 because of being a green major league manager.

"But I know the ropes by this time," Bush said, "and any player who doesn't live up to the few rules I make will be severely dealt with."[46]

Throughout spring training, the Pirates' scrappy little manager also doled out positive reinforcement by constantly reciting the slogan, "Repeat! Show the world that our team is as good as the best in the American." During an interview with Philadelphia sportswriter Stoney McLinn of the *Evening Ledger*, Donie stated that the Yankees' sweep over his squad in the 1927 World Series gave him a perpetual headache that lasted all winter.

> I give the Yanks credit for a clean-cut victory in the World Series. But I know that my team was in bad stride on account of the strain of the last few weeks of the race.
>
> What I ask my boys to do is snap into it from the outset this year. If they do, I believe we can win the pennant without burning up our energy near the wire.

Then I would be supremely happy if we could meet the Yanks again. I don't say we would stop them, but I do say we would fight them harder and there would be no four-in-a-row disaster.

Bush also expressed no concern to this writer over the loss of Kiki Cuyler, whom he conceded to be a good player. Not one to live in the past, Donie gushed over what the addition of Sparky Adams meant to the Pirates.[47]

Pittsburgh Press sports editor Ralph S. Davis expressed optimism for a successful season since Glenn Wright appeared to have returned to his old-time form compared to the previous year. Davis stated that Glenn looked healthy and didn't cause Donie Bush any anxiety.[48] When Dr. Eugene Converse Murdock interviewed him in 1978, Wright declared Bill McKechnie was the best skipper he ever played for in terms of real smart managing. Glenn admitted to engaging in arguments with Bush, although the two were great friends. Wright also experienced a pleasant relationship with Barney Dreyfuss. Glenn told Murdock he always kidded Pittsburgh's owner about breaking his finger as a second baseman while playing semi-professional baseball in Kentucky decades ago. Wright also affirmed that occasionally in the evening, Barney and Mrs. Dreyfuss invited him to their house to play bridge.[49]

Hopes of a rematch against the New York Yankees in the 1928 World Series proved to be a delusion for Bush and his players. Once again, the Pirates failed miserably to place a back-to-back pennant in the bank. Pittsburgh experienced a slow start, going 6–8 in April and 12–16 in May. When June started, Donie's squad found themselves in sixth place, 9½ games behind the league-leading Cincinnati Reds. Even Kiki Cuyler's return with his Cubs in a series at Forbes Field that started on April 30 didn't spurn much excitement among fans. Instead of thousands of screaming supporters jamming into Forbes Field, bearing floral arrangements, handbags, an automobile, or other gifts honoring Cuyler, an ordinary Monday gathering entered the ballpark to watch the game.

Many in the crowd loudly cheered when Kiki utilized his blazing speed in the fifth inning to score from first base on Clifton "Cliff" Heathcote's single to left field. Patrons also showered rousing applause in the sixth as Cuyler fired a bullet from right field to the plate, retiring Adam Comorosky, who attempted to score from second on Burleigh Grimes's single. Somebody in the press box jokingly remarked that Kiki hustled from first to the plate on a short single in the fifth frame because "he didn't want to be out on the same field with the Pirates." Chicago manager Joe McCarthy received accolades for being smart enough to ensure Kiki strictly adhered to baseball business while in Pittsburgh.

From the joyous manner he went about playing in this first game of the series, it appeared Hazen loved being a Cubs team member.[50]

Trade rumors started appearing in local newspapers due to the Pirates' poor showing thus far in 1928. One piece of May gossip alleged Pittsburgh hoped to make a deal with Brooklyn to acquire southpaw hurler Jess Petty, who'd pitched for Donie Bush at Indianapolis in 1924. Petty had fallen into disfavor with Robins manager Wilbert Robinson, who subsequently suspended his pitcher for misconduct away from the diamond. It seemed Jess wanted to do his best impersonation of Al Mamaux by not showing up at the team hotel when Brooklyn played in Chicago. Petty admitted he failed to join his teammates at the hostelry, claiming he slept at a friend's house. Petty denied violating the Volstead Act regarding the prohibition of drinking alcohol. When a rumor claimed that Pittsburgh had attempted to trade catcher Earl Smith, first baseman Joe Harris, and pitcher Carmen Hill for Jess, Bush scoffed at the ridiculous nature of this gossip by declaring he wouldn't move the Pirates' hurler even up for Petty.[51]

Like many of baseball's major league clubs, Pittsburgh dealt with the epidemic of colds and the flu knocking individuals out of the lineup. Injuries to pitchers Hill, Ray Kremer, and Lee Meadows compounded this problem.[52] When the Pirates reached Cincinnati to start a series against the Reds on May 20, Donie Bush decided to establish draconian measures to shake his squad from their funk. Bush believed some individuals not suffering from illness didn't seem to be displaying sufficient interest in their work each afternoon. He felt that social pleasures were too high a priority for some of his players. As a result, Donie took things away as a father would do to a child.

Feeling that more regular hours might be helpful, Bush ordered his team not to attend any evening shows or movies or make connections with friends in a particular city. The manager informed his men that he expected them to remain within the immediate vicinity of the team hotel each evening and retire to bed at an early hour. Although some squad members balked over this mandate, serious-minded players felt such rules were reasonable. In a very determined manner, Bush wanted his men to do more thinking about baseball and less ruminating related to outside pleasures. In contrast to not being a taskmaster when assuming control of the team in 1927, Pittsburgh's players now understood that Donie wasn't a man to trifle regarding these orders.[53]

Changes to team personnel continued as the season progressed. On June 8, the Pirates announced they'd traded Joe Harris and Johnny Gooch to Brooklyn for catcher Charles "Charlie" Hargreaves. The team had placed Harris, who batted

.326 one year earlier in his only full season wearing a Pirates uniform, on waivers to gauge interest from other clubs. When Wilbert Robinson submitted a claim for his services, Pittsburgh withdrew the request, and negotiations started between the two clubs about a possible trade. Robinson issued a final bid to add Gooch to any transaction involving Hargreaves. Donie Bush consented to this demand, concluded the deal, and then offered his impressions of the trade that night from Boston, where Pittsburgh had lost to the Braves earlier in the day, 9–5.

"I regret seeing Johnny and Joe go elsewhere," said Bush, "but I wanted Hargreaves and there was no other way to get him. Gooch is a hard worker and a mighty good catcher. Harris still can hit the ball hard and he has a lot of baseball left in his system. I understand Joe's lame leg is mending fast and he will probably join the Robins in a few days. Both are fine fellows, personally, and they are a credit to any club."[54]

Sports editor Regis M. Welsh of the *Pittsburgh Post-Gazette* lamented Johnny Gooch's passing from the Pirates' squad. Welsh commended Gooch's character, saying he confronted financial difficulties head-on this past off-season which weren't his fault. In the same way, he accepted responsibility for making the critical mistake regarding pitcher Johnny Miljus's wild pitch in Game Four of the 1927 World Series. The writer also commented that since Johnny was a solid catcher and great field general, his stellar behavior made him a prime candidate as trading material.[55] As the midnight trade deadline on June 15 approached, an exciting rumor throughout the baseball world claimed that Pittsburgh planned to broker another deal with Chicago involving shortstop Glenn Wright.

In his syndicated column regarding the trade deadline subject, Pittsburgh sportswriter Davis J. Walsh stated that in 1927, Pirates management had engaged in discussion with Wright, warning him to alter his conduct and start being a good boy in the future. According to Walsh, the threat terrified Glenn so much that he quietly submitted to this demand. Since Wright's behavior seemed exemplary thus far in 1928, this quickly forced the Pirates' skipper to admit that such a situation had come about in the first place while offering no comment on silly trade rumors.[56] Glenn missed three games at shortstop near the end of June due to suffering from the flu.[57] Wright returned to the starting lineup on June 28, as St. Louis beat Pittsburgh, 4–3. In the fifth inning, Glenn blasted a home run off Cardinals pitcher William "Bill" Sherdel that landed in the right-field stands.[58]

When June ended, Pittsburgh was sixth in the standings with a 31–35 record, leaving them 12 games behind pace-setting St. Louis. Such a position led to extreme criticism toward manager Donie Bush, coming from Forbes Field's stands and bleachers, often bordering on venomous abuse. Although Donie attempted to ignore these catcalls, it eventually became a challenging exercise since, over time, the negative chorus immediately began when the Pirates took the field to start a game.[59] Patrons and sportswriters also criticized Bush's managerial style. Fans complained that Donie didn't understand how to properly utilize his men to achieve the best results, adding that he never practiced a winning baseball strategy. These rooters pointed to the current rules against viewing movies and partaking in other evening entertainment while Pittsburgh played on the road, causing some players to become antagonistic and resentful.

In conjunction with this belief, fans felt Donie established a stubborn posture of liking or disliking certain team members and refusing to change his opinion when later developments dictated altering that view. In the department of deploying a poor strategy, patrons cited the game against Chicago at Wrigley Field on June 24, which the Cubs won, 8–1. In the eighth inning, with Pete Scott available to pinch-hit, Bush instead sent Glenn Wright up to the plate to bat for George Grantham with two men on base, despite suffering from the flu. Chicago hurler Art Nehf retired Wright on a fly ball to right field. Donie then allowed Glenn to remain in the game at first base, a position he'd never played in his major league career. Finally used by Bush as a pinch hitter in the ninth, Scott doubled with a runner on first base.[60]

Pittsburgh Press sports editor Ralph S. Davis declared that Pittsburgh didn't use a signaling system. When Bush wanted to inform a player about a particular strategical maneuver, he instructed that individual to walk down to the third base coaching box, where the Pirates' manager stood, to receive his instructions. This practice alerted the other team to his intentions, resulting in rival players shifting positions in the field or the opposing manager signaling directives to his men. Donie also didn't receive solid support from some players, who lacked confidence in his decision-making ability. Davis claimed that some older squad members had rebelled when taking orders and outright disobeyed the manager's wishes. A veteran catcher supposedly laughed when receiving directives from Bush and then forcefully expressed strong disapproval. Another player, considered one of the best performers on Pittsburgh's club, also expressed his opposition to Bush's policy on numerous occasions. Although an open insurrection hadn't yet occurred, players lacked confidence in managerial leadership.[61]

The veteran catcher Davis mentioned happened to be Earl Smith. As the 1928 season progressed, Smith and Bush didn't get along, and the catcher routinely started disparaging strategic moves made by his boss.[62] On July 9, 1928, the Pirates' organization handed Earl his unconditional release. Shortly after acquiring Charlie Hargreaves from Brooklyn, Donie intended to cut Smith loose. This stance only intensified the animosity and ill-feeling between these two men. When all the clubs from each major league failed to offer a claim for Earl's services, he became a free agent.[63] Pittsburgh didn't need to grant Smith unconditional freedom due to him not having enough years of major league service to gain this privilege. Nonetheless, management proceeded in this manner. Team treasurer Sam Dreyfuss offered a simple reason for the move, claiming the organization figured they no longer had any further use for the backstop.

Earl Smith quickly landed on his feet as the Cardinals, now managed by Bill McKechnie, signed the veteran catcher to a contract.[64] Later in the season, when St. Louis arrived in Pittsburgh for a series at the end of August at Forbes Field, Smith yelled, "Hello, Santa," to Donie Bush.[65] As numerous team members connected to two pennant winners departed the Pirates' squad, fans pondered whether Glenn Wright could soon be joining this exodus out of the Smoky City. Twenty-year-old shortstop Richard "Dick" Bartell had done fantastic work during Wright's absence due to recovering from the flu. Since Bartell's performance proved so eye-opening, Glenn found a temporary place sitting in the dugout throughout most of July. Bush permanently installed Dick in the lineup because of his timely hitting and brilliant work fielding his position. The Pirates won nine consecutive games from July 7 through July 18 with Wright on the bench.[66]

After Bartell experienced two rough games at the plate against New York at the Polo Grounds, Pittsburgh's manager reinserted Glenn back into the starting lineup on July 26.[67] Ralph S. Davis claimed that the flu and exceptional peppery play from Dick didn't supply the entire reason surrounding Wright occupying a place on the bench. Rumors had abounded for some time that Glenn ran afoul with Pirates management, who wasn't pleased with his work. Davis asserted that in 1927, Wright followed the primrose path of pleasure rather than buckle down to business on the diamond. The sportswriter mentioned his automobile accident after the World Series and a lawsuit still requiring adjudication. Reports from the spring indicated Glenn had picked up where he left off last fall regarding objectionable behavior.

Many fans doubted that the flu had been responsible for Wright's incapacitated condition weeks earlier.[68] They believed Glenn brought this upon himself by failing to follow all of nature's common sense laws and disregarding team rules. Donie Bush and Barney Dreyfuss vehemently denied these charges amidst the belief that Pittsburgh's shortstop occupied management's doghouse.

Wright's solid performance in most cases while in the starting lineup substantiated management's claims.[69] Offering his opinion on Glenn's situation, *Brooklyn Daily Eagle* sportswriter Thomas Holmes declared that earlier in the season, when Pittsburgh's shortstop experienced difficulty rounding into shape, he embarked on a five-day vacation away from baseball. Wright did so without receiving permission. The writer claimed Glenn still hadn't been forgiven by management for taking this unexcused absence.[70]

Another member of both championship squads received his dismissal from the team as the season's end neared. On August 28, the major league career of hurler Lee Meadows appeared to be over, as Pittsburgh released him from the club and placed the veteran on the voluntary retired list. Rather than seek out a new team, Lee planned on leaving immediately for his home in Leesburg, Florida, to access his future. Meadows had only seen action in four games for the Pirates in 1928.[71] Horrible sinus trouble bothered Lee for much of the season and rendered him useless.[72] Meadows, who'd won 19 games twice with the Pirates and posted a mark of 20–9 in 1926, appeared in one game for the team in 1929 and called it quits for good.

Although many Forbes Field fans roasted Donie Bush throughout the season and some team members chaffed over his leadership skills, a group of players offered their admiration through a kind gesture for the man who'd led Pittsburgh to the National League pennant in 1927. When Donie entered the clubhouse before a doubleheader at the home ballpark versus St. Louis on August 31, he noticed three new objects in the dressing room. One was a handsomely upholstered easy chair, the second a stand equipped with humidors and shelves for stocking cigars or pipes, and lastly, an overstuffed footstool. Much to Donie's surprise, super Pirates fan Rosey Rowswell told the manager to sit down in the chair and accept these gifts as a token of appreciation from his players for guiding the team to a pennant one year earlier. Rowswell made the presentation at team captain Pie Traynor's request. Pie's teammates had delegated to him the responsibility of selecting a suitable gift for Mr. Bush.[73]

As the 1928 campaign wound down, speculation heated up regarding a trade involving Glenn Wright. Though newspapers resurrected a possible deal with the Chicago Cubs, Pirates management denied contemplating any such transaction. Despite this stance, rumors prevailed that Wright wasn't in good graces with ownership because his work had precipitously fallen off this year. Ralph S. Davis opined that Glenn possibly had too many friends in Pittsburgh for his own good. Davis also proclaimed Wright hadn't functioned at his best for some time, and people shouldn't any longer regard him as a regular player.[74]

Pittsburgh made it a perfect quadruple, failing to repeat once again as National League pennant winners after appearing in a World Series, finishing the campaign in fourth place with an 85–67 record, placing them nine games behind the champion Cardinals.

Although the season proved disappointing, Barney Dreyfuss praised Bush, claiming him to be the most detailed manager he'd ever worked with in the Smoky City. Dreyfuss also declared that no skipper preceding Donie devoted himself so earnestly to the game. Pittsburgh's owner affirmed baseball as Donie's sole focus, adding that the pilot always tried hard and offered his best efforts. Dreyfuss surmised he could ask nothing more of any man.[75]

Throughout the 1928 season, Pirates officials had discussed the possibility of moving Glenn Wright from shortstop to first base next year.[76] Such a change appeared moot when Pittsburgh selected former Chicago White Sox first baseman Earl Sheely, of the Pacific Coast League's Sacramento Senators, in the major league draft on October 3.[77] This addition and other factors revived tales of Wright moving in a deal with Chicago. Ralph S. Davis once again wrote that Glenn's behavior over the past two seasons would prove a determining factor behind Donie Bush and Barney Dreyfuss's desire to discard him from the team. Davis also reported that during the late-September eastern swing that ended the Pirates' season, Wright's conduct on that trip lowered management's opinion of him even further.[78]

According to Glenn, when interviewed by Dr. Eugene Converse Murdock in 1978, he refused to accompany the squad for an exhibition game against the Toronto Maple Leafs (the contest was against the Montreal Royals), played on September 30, after the regular season ended. Coach Jewel Ens oversaw the team since Donie Bush didn't make the trip. Ens told Wright that if he didn't play in the game, Pittsburgh's shortstop most likely would be punished monetarily. Glenn claimed in his discussion with Murdock that Barney Dreyfuss fined him $500 for refusing to participate in this meaningless contest.[79]

All the speculating and prognosticating received finality on December 11, 1928, as the Pirates shipped Wright to Brooklyn for pitcher Jess Petty and infielder Henry "Harry" Riconda. Robins manager Wilbert Robinson had been dickering for the rangy shortstop since arriving at the league meetings in New York a day earlier on Monday morning. Bush refused to make any deal that didn't include another player besides Petty. Once the two sides hammered out an agreement, Donie notified Barney Dreyfuss, and Pittsburgh's owner immediately approved the transaction.[80] In his column for the *Pittsburgh Press*, Ralph S. Davis declared that two years ago, local fans who at the time idolized

Wright and considered him the best shortstop in baseball would've panned such a trade involving Glenn. Some patrons felt Glenn's downfall resulted from Vic Keen beaning him in 1927. Davis believed Wright's decline stemmed from a failure to realize the importance of remaining in proper condition throughout the season.[81]

Months after the two clubs consummated this deal, a problem arose when it became known that Glenn Wright happened to be damaged goods. In November, at least one month before becoming Brooklyn property, Wright had injured the right shoulder of his throwing arm by running into a wall while playing handball. Robins officials discovered this disability during spring training in Clearwater, Florida.[82] On March 11, 1929, Glenn arrived in Miami Beach, Florida, to start receiving treatment from Dr. Cecil Ferguson, former pitcher for the New York Giants and Boston Doves/Rustlers and an osteopath who studied under Bonesetter Reese.[83]

Dr. Ferguson diagnosed the problem as Wright tearing several tendons in his shoulder when crashing into the wall playing handball back in November. The physician claimed the tendons failed to knit together properly while healing. In a procedure, Dr. Ferguson again tore the tendons and put them back in the correct position so they mended adequately without difficulty. Wright couldn't cut loose throwing a baseball during this recuperation period. Although rumblings over revoking the deal between Brooklyn and Pittsburgh gathered steam, *Brooklyn Daily Eagle* sportswriter Thomas Holmes claimed no precedent existed for forcing Barney Dreyfuss to send Jess Petty back to the Robins.[84] It seemed unlikely that Brooklyn manager Wilbert Robinson even wanted Petty returning to the fold. During spring training, Wilbert discussed voiding the transaction informally with National League president John Heydler and Judge Kenesaw Mountain Landis. They advised against taking this action.

Following numerous pinch-hitting appearances in April, Glenn attempted to play shortstop in three consecutive games at Ebbets Field from May 5 through May 7. Wright appeared to be a former shell of himself in the field when it came to throwing, putting little on the baseball while making tosses around the infield. Glenn seemed particularly dejected after the contest against Chicago on May 7, although he believed his right arm eventually would strengthen while suggesting unseasonable weather had acted as a significant detriment.[85] As hopes faded that Wright could be a major contributor in 1929, Robinson stated Brooklyn made a deal with Pittsburgh because the Ebbets Field fans had clamored for adding a first-rate shortstop to the club. Wilbert declared that when Donie Bush offered Glenn, he seized the opportunity.[86]

On May 9, as the Pirates finished a series against New York, Bush vowed during an interview with Thomas Holmes at the team's Hotel Alamac lodging that they made the December trade with Brooklyn in good faith. Donie affirmed Pittsburgh's organization knew nothing about Glenn Wright's shoulder injury until newspapers had reported it during spring training. Bush also stated he hadn't spoken to Wright since last season. Pittsburgh's pilot considered Glenn a true gentleman and one of the finest young fellows he'd ever met in baseball. While declaring to be sorry over the present condition of Wright's throwing arm, Donie explained why he traded an individual who'd finished the previous season playing standout baseball.

> That deal hung fire for a long while before it was finally completed. That's how much I thought of Wright. I believed that he was to be a great ballplayer for many years to come and I hesitated for a long while before turning him over for even as fine a pitcher as Jess Petty.
>
> Wright's inability to get going in Pittsburgh last season was the reason why he was traded. Glenn hit a slump, the fans "rode" him and a change of scenery seemed to be the best thing in the world for him. That he would be unable to start the season in Brooklyn never entered my mind.[87]

On May 15, Dr. Cecil Ferguson left Brooklyn for his Miami Beach home. The doctor, who received $5,000 from Robins ownership to work on Glenn Wright's shoulder, admitted that initial treatment measures hadn't fixed the problem. The plan now called for Wright to rest and recuperate at his home in Harrisonville, Missouri, hoping the arm improved after extended inactivity.[88] This relaxing time for Glenn included doing some fishing. On July 12, the *Brooklyn Daily Eagle* revealed Wright would undergo a second operation to fix the shoulder issue. After a month of rest, Glenn returned to the club but still couldn't throw a baseball with any velocity during practice. A new specialist employed by the team examined Wright and concluded his trouble to be a chipped bone in the shoulder blade rather than torn tendons.

This specialist, Dr. Armitage Whitman, advised operating by cutting open the shoulder and grafting a piece of material from Glenn's leg to fill the space where the chip occurred. Dr. Whitman guaranteed a complete recovery after six weeks elapsed.[89] On July 24, Brooklyn placed Glenn on the retired list for the season's duration, while the club also announced surgery on the shoulder would be conducted the following week.[90] Almost two months later, the first optimistic sign surrounding the injury occurred when Wright made a trip in his automobile from Harrisonville to St. Louis. Glenn arrived in St. Louis on September 21, as Brooklyn opposed the Cardinals at Sportsman's Park. Glenn appeared cheerful, as the cast on his arm had recently been removed, and desires to play baseball once again filled his heart.

Wright told Wilbert Robinson that doctor reports on his progress following the surgery had been very positive. *Standard Union* sportswriter Henry Richards remarked that Glenn appeared to be in good health while once again possessing a firm and powerful handshake. The incision point from the operation two months earlier had healed beautifully. Continued prescribed exercises to increase the right arm's strength and a one to two-week hunting trip acted as a critical conditioning mechanism toward total recovery. Robinson stated that no attempt to throw a baseball would be permitted until next spring since the team needed Wright to play ball in 1930 and not in the fall.[91] The Brooklyn organization and Robins fans breathed a sigh of relief in 1930. After appearing in only 24 games in 1929, Glenn's comeback one year later reestablished him as one of baseball's top players, as the shortstop batted .321, smacked 22 homers, and drove in 126 runs.

Following Glenn Wright's trade to Brooklyn, only Pie Traynor, George Grantham, Ray Kremer, and Lee Meadows remained from the 1925 championship team. As players arrived for spring training at Paso Robles in 1929, Pirates fans expressed concern over the whereabouts of two members from the 1927 pennant-winning club. The "Poison Boys," Paul "Big Poison" Waner and Lloyd "Little Poison" Waner, had decided to engage in a tandem holdout to receive significant salary increases. The two brothers wanted the club to pay $35,000 between them, and they planned on holding out until owner Barney Dreyfuss met their demand. Neither Paul nor Lloyd intended to sign until Dreyfuss satisfactorily acquiesced to each player's wishes. This situation left Pittsburgh's owner, and rooters, worried.[92]

The strategy of sticking together didn't cross the finish line. Lloyd Waner cracked first, agreeing to join the team in San Francisco, California, on March 21, meet with Barney, and immediately sign a contract.[93] On April 4, Paul Waner held a conference with Pittsburgh's owner in Fort Worth, Texas, and inked his signature to a document for playing in 1929. Although the Pirates wouldn't disclose the terms of the deal, many believed Dreyfuss didn't meet Paul's $18,000-a-year demand. Reports stated Lloyd's contract called for him to earn $10,000 this upcoming campaign. The elder Waner brother intended on having a big season in 1929 and expressed satisfaction over the salary settlement.[94]

Following another slow April start, the plucky Pirates battled gallantly in their quest to win the flag. When July ended, Pittsburgh occupied second place with a 58–36 record, leaving them five games behind league-leading Chicago. As the team prepared to make a push during the pennant drive, a feeling of uneasiness and déjà vu prevailed among fans. On August 6, before a game against the Giants at Forbes Field, Donie Bush decided to bench Paul Waner and played Ira Flagstead as his replacement in right field. Bush changed his lineup to halt a slump where the Pirates had lost five of their last six games.[95] The switch didn't have the desired effect, as New York beat Pittsburgh, 5–3.[96] Donie explained that Paul needed to rest and had been badly shaken up after colliding with George Grantham in a recent game. Sportswriter Thomas Holmes of the *Brooklyn Daily Eagle* alleged a rift had developed between Waner and Bush. Holmes also stated that the latest rumored "Dreyfuss scandal" indicated Paul might be playing elsewhere in 1930.[97]

Brooklyn sportswriter Henry Richards, of the *Standard Union*, likened Paul Waner's current situation to the one involving Kiki Cuyler in 1927. According to Richards, Bush steadfastly clung to his principles and beliefs to the point that some individuals viewed him as stubborn and bullheaded. When Cuyler challenged leadership, Bush took immediate action. Two years later, Donie exhibited the same resolve by benching Waner. Paul must've experienced an epiphany over his supposed indiscretion since he only remained out of the starting lineup for two days. Henry couldn't understand why Pittsburgh's fans didn't think more highly of such a talented and successful manager. The scribe also stated that Bush's fate hinged on how well the Pirates did in the current race. Richards felt Pittsburgh's only chance at making things competitive rested with experiencing great success on an upcoming eastern jaunt.[98]

The opposite happened when the Pirates conducted their eighteen-day eastern tour, starting on August 10. The trip proved disastrous, as the team posted a 5–12 record while away from home. Immediately after the squad returned to Pittsburgh, Donie Bush tendered his resignation to Barney Dreyfuss on August 28. At noon, an announcement came that the Pirates' owner had accepted the resignation immediately. Plagued by misfortune throughout the season, the disgusted skipper had appeared downtrodden during the entire road trip.[99] Dreyfuss named coach Jewel Ens acting manager, with the caveat that he could claim the post permanently through making a strong showing in the season's final month.[100] One report claimed that ownership subjected Bush to severe criticism during the team's recent eastern invasion. Donie offered little insight into any claimed problems when interviewed at his office after resigning.

> There is nothing more to give out than that I have resigned and President Dreyfuss has accepted the resignation. That's all there is to be told. I simply decided to quit. There is no ill feeling between President Dreyfuss and myself, or between any of the players and myself.
>
> I am leaving Pittsburgh with the best of feeling for the fans, the club officials, and the players, and wish the team all the luck in the world.
>
> It was unfortunate we made such a poor showing on the last eastern trip, but it was just the fortunes of war. Everything that we tried went wrong.
>
> But I want to say in justice to the players that every man did his best at all times, and there was never a sign of letting down on the part of anyone.

Barney Dreyfuss exhibited the utmost respect for Donie Bush by praising his former manager.

"There is nothing more to be added," said the team owner. "Manager Bush tendered his resignation and I accepted it. That's all I have to say except that I like and respect Bush and wish him the best of luck. He has been a hard and faithful worker in our service with the best interests of the club always at heart, and I sincerely hope that he will be successful wherever he casts his baseball lot in the future."[101]

Before the 1929 campaign started, Barney Dreyfuss's son, Samuel, had added the title of team vice president to his sports management resume.[102] Sam Dreyfuss still maintained his job as the Pittsburgh baseball club's treasurer. As a team spokesman, Sam hastily made some remarks to reporters about Donie Bush's resignation.

> We didn't ask Bush to resign. He came into the office just after the team got back from its eastern trip, handed his resignation to father and it was accepted. Jewel Ens was immediately placed in charge and he will handle the team the rest of the season, at least.
>
> It may be that the poor showing of the Pirates in the East had something to do with "Donie's" action. That seemed to be the case for there was no doubt but what he contemplated resigning when he arrived in Pittsburgh Wednesday morning. We hated to see "Donie" go for he was a hustler and always had the best interests of the team at heart.[103]

Everything appeared tidy among all involved parties, gift-wrapped with a beautiful big bow on the box. One thing seemed inevitable to those who'd covered or followed events surrounding Pittsburgh Pirates baseball over the past three decades. Something always lurked below the surface, whether it was an inside story or a newfound revelation. Although the walls of secrecy initially hindered discovering the truth, digging relentlessly unearthed additional information, even decades down the road.

Considered one of the best players in major league baseball, injuries hindered the bright career of Pittsburgh Pirates shortstop Glenn Wright. In 1926, Glenn missed time due to suffering from a painful bruise on his foot. On June 28, 1927, St. Louis Cardinals pitcher Vic Keen beaned Wright in a game at Sportsman's Park. According to doctors, Glenn didn't suffer a fatal injury since the baseball struck him just below the left temple. Wright missed two weeks while recovering. Glenn's desire to enjoy the nightlife also became a problem during the 1927 campaign, leading to speculation and rumors one year later that he'd fallen into management's doghouse. In the end, Barney Dreyfuss and Donie Bush traded their topnotch shortstop to the Brooklyn Robins on December 11, 1928. (Courtesy of the Library of Congress).

15

Bitter Holdouts and Tragedy in the Baseball Family

Upon tendering his resignation, Donie Bush stated that he still held owner Barney Dreyfuss in the highest regard. Bush also wished Jewel Ens and the entire team continued diamond success. Donie declared that he had no immediate plans other than returning to his Indianapolis home. Although Ens wouldn't grant interviews to Pittsburgh newspapers, the new pilot offered a statement for the press. Because he'd been a coach under managers who either resigned or ownership dismissed, Jewel selected his words carefully after being named to lead the Pirates.

"The less I say about anything in connection with the club the better," said Ens. "There will be no radical change in the conduct of affairs. We will be on the field every day, trying to win every game possible in an attempt to make up some of the ground lost recently. Results are what count, anyway."[1]

Although winning baseball games mattered most to Pittsburgh's baseball organization and followers, this didn't mean fans couldn't multitask and search out juicy gossip explaining why a player or manager walked out the door. Following Bush's decision to leave the Pirates, *Pittsburgh Press* sports editor Ralph S. Davis alleged that many dissatisfied, grumbling patrons had hoped he'd quit managing the squad. These disgruntled individuals always blamed Donie for everything that went wrong. Davis also stated that people had known for some time that Bush didn't appear happy over how things progressed this season. The writer felt Pittsburgh's skipper panicked as the campaign moved forward by indiscriminately moving his players around in the lineup, hoping to obtain a different result.

Davis also alleged that Donie's poor strategic decisions had been a problem. To prove this point, Ralph cited one of the doubleheader games against the New York Giants on August 24 at the Polo Grounds. According to Davis, Bush ordered several plays that defied current baseball orthodoxy and most likely prevented the Pirates from winning the contest.[2] New York sportswriter Joseph "Joe" Williams believed Donie decided to walk away from his post because Barney Dreyfuss meddled by always offering suggestions to his manager. Williams stated that the Kiki Cuyler case in 1927 started this habit of ownership influence when it came to Bush making decisions. The New York writer believed the Glenn Wright situation from one year earlier also fell under this category. Williams also declared Donie and Dreyfuss disagreed over Paul Waner's contentious holdout in the spring. Joe contended that sources told him Barney ordered Bush to bench Waner, of whose ability Pittsburgh's manager always held a high opinion.[3]

Sportswriter James J. Long of the *Pittsburgh Sun-Telegraph* wrote that Pirates fans never gave Donie Bush a chance to show his ability as a pilot. For the most part, rooters refused to offer him any encouraging words. Long believed Cuyler's falling out and subsequent trade to the Chicago Cubs brought about resentment from the paying public, who held Bush personally responsible for the fan favorite leaving Pittsburgh. The writer pointed out that Donie didn't act alone in that decision, as Pirates ownership fully sanctioned the deal involving Kiki. Long rejected unjustified criticism against Bush in 1929 for failing to win a pennant since most prognosticators in the spring had picked Pittsburgh to finish third in the National League.[4]

In certain instances, time didn't just heal all wounds but also provided some clarity related to past events. Eighteen years after resigning as the Pirates' manager, Donie returned to Pittsburgh on December 12, 1947, to help Pittsburgh's new owners introduce William "Billy" Meyer to newspapermen and radio reporters as the squad's next manager. Bush was a friend and associate of fellow Indianapolis native Frank McKinney, who now acted as the Pirates' team president. During an interview with *Pittsburgh Press* sportswriter Lester "Les" Biederman, Donie declared he almost didn't last more than a year as Pittsburgh's skipper while also providing some insight into what had happened in 1929.

"You know I wanted to resign right after that 1927 season," Bush said. "I wasn't too happy but Barney Dreyfuss talked me into staying. The Cuyler incident was one of those things. I didn't think he was a good ballplayer at the time and I thought he was trying to run things, so I didn't use him.

"The fans thought I was mistreating him and they came to Forbes Field with banners shrieking 'We Want Cuyler,' and they certainly made life miserable."

Bush then told Biederman what had occurred in 1929 while also relating a story about something Barney Dreyfuss did that Fred Clarke considered taboo when he managed the club.

> Barney was a great baseball man, one of the best that ever lived but somehow we didn't hit it off too good. Barney often came into the clubhouse and I didn't think he should. I told him the clubhouse was no place for an owner.
>
> That's the ballplayers' home and he shouldn't come there unless for some special occasion.
>
> He didn't like it when I told him that. Once his son, Sam, told me I had offended his father and I told Sam I was sorry if I hurt his feelings, but that's the way I felt about the clubhouse.
>
> This undercurrent went on for two more years and finally in August of 1929, even though the Pirates were up in the race, I told Barney I was quitting at the end of the year.
>
> "Why not now?" he asked.
>
> I said "now" and that's how it was.[5]

Almost two decades after deciding to leave the Buccaneers' stable in 1929, Donie Bush revealed the secret surrounding his abrupt decision to resign as the Pirates' manager. Less than one month after assuming control of the squad, Jewels Ens's title as pilot shifted from temporary to permanent. Following Pittsburgh's 4–0 victory over Boston at Forbes Field on September 21, 1929, Barney Dreyfuss offered Ens a one-year contract to manage the team in 1930. Jewel promptly attached his signature to the document.[6] Under Ens's leadership, the Pirates went 21–14, giving them an 88–65 record, good for second place in the National League, 10½ games behind pace-setting Chicago. Dick Bartell, in his first entire season as a starter replacing Glenn Wright at shortstop, batted .302

Minor tweaking within the organization continued before the 1930 season started. Proving that all sins truly could be forgiven, team vice president Sam Dreyfuss announced on January 31 that Max Carey had signed to act as a coach for Pittsburgh. This decision came after the Brooklyn Robins gave Carey his unconditional release. Max joined Oscar Stanage, who'd been part of the staff since 1927 when Donie Bush came aboard, to assist manager Jewel Ens. Carey's job would likely include working either the third or first-base coaching lines. The sole role for Max involved coaching since the Pirates' organization didn't register his name on the players' list.[7] Another huge change occurred before the campaign got underway. Barney Dreyfuss turned complete direction and control of Pittsburgh's baseball operations over to his son, Sam.[8]

One year earlier, when offering his opinion on where National League teams would finish in the 1929 standings, sportswriter Norman E. Brown had correctly picked the Pirates to come home second. While engaging in this venture, Brown also stated that Sam Dreyfuss's interference had handicapped Pittsburgh in the team's play and how he orchestrated the views of newspaper journalists so that the organization's narratives on matters made it into print.[9] A challenging situation immediately confronted the younger Dreyfuss in 1930, as pitcher Burleigh Grimes and shortstop Dick Bartell hadn't signed contracts when spring training started in Paso Robles, California. Sam verified on February 28 that both players were holding out. Dreyfuss revealed that Bartell first received a contract back in December, which he returned unsigned. Other efforts toward a resolution had failed, as Dick's rejected document currently resided in the club office's safe.

Burleigh's situation proved different since he currently devoted his time to litigating a nasty divorce settlement with his wife, Florence Ruth van Patten Grimes. While dealing with court proceedings, Grimes couldn't focus on anything baseball related. When pressed by reporters about Bartell, Sam Dreyfuss stated that the peppery shortstop had outright refused to sign a contract. This development surprised other team members, who assumed Dick would join them for the first practice session. All indications pointed to the chasm between player and management being quite broad.

> Dick's salary demands are absurd. He wants a price for playing in 1930 far beyond what the club offered and far beyond what he could possibly get were he playing on any other club.
>
> Negotiations have been going on for several months in the chance that a settlement might be reached. Dick flatly refused our terms and said if we didn't care to meet his figure, he would not don a uniform.
>
> I communicated with him, asking him to come to Paso Robles to talk the matter over. It was then he gave the club the ultimatum of either meeting his terms or ending negotiations. We have given him what we consider a very good offer. If he does not accept, he will not play with the club this year. He refused to come here to discuss the subject.[10]

Besides Grimes's divorce case acting as a roadblock toward a salary settlement, the hurler's demand for a two-year contract aided this impasse since the Pirates' standard organizational policy dictated giving agreements for only one season.[11] When the 1929 campaign ended, Dick Bartell visited Barney Dreyfuss's office. After making the futile trip to team headquarters, Bartell told friends the club's front office hierarchy informed him they weren't ready to talk business. Dick also confided in these individuals that he wasn't satisfied with the treatment afforded him by his employer. Bartell declared to have worked for a minimal salary in 1929 and deserved to make much more money in the upcoming season. Dick asserted that he played good, solid baseball and always gave his best effort on the diamond. He insisted Pittsburgh needed to pay much more than they offered before he would consider joining the squad. *Pittsburgh Press* sports editor Ralph S. Davis believed such a holdout stance by someone so young could prove to be a foolish undertaking that might jeopardize his career.[12]

As a result of Bartell's absence, Jewel Ens allowed William Stuart "Stu" Clarke, Charlie Engle, and Benjamin "Ben" Sankey to battle for the starting shortstop job once camp started.[13] After remaining away from the action for more than a week, Dick broadcast that he planned on making the trip to Paso Robles to discuss his salary situation with Sam Dreyfuss. This announcement followed a telephone call from Bartell in San Francisco requesting a meeting with the younger Dreyfuss. *Pittsburgh Press* sportswriter Fred Wertenbach pondered whether the excellent showing thus far of both Engle and Sankey during spring training had influenced Dick making this decision.[14]

When Dick Bartell arrived at Paso Robles on March 11, he greeted his teammates and Ens. Dick also watched Pittsburgh's players perform an intense workout on the diamond before conferring with the team's vice president. Following this meeting between the parties, Bartell announced his intention to return to his home in Alameda, California, since Dreyfuss once again refused to meet his salary demand. Dick's stance softened after he called his father, Harry Bartell, on the telephone, who advised him to accept Pittsburgh's terms after discussing things with his son. Bartell acquiesced to his father's wishes, agreeing to a deal on March 12. Neither the player nor ownership released a salary figure. Indications pointed to it being below the $10,000 a year Dick had asked for, most likely around $7,000. Bartell participated in the morning practice that day, and the Pirates' manager planned on using him in an afternoon intrasquad game.[15]

Dick's signing left star hurler Burleigh Grimes as Pittsburgh's only remaining holdout. Grimes's battle with the Dreyfusses in this arena reached an acrimonious stalemate when the pitcher made a trip to Pittsburgh at the beginning of March. Whereas Burleigh and management had conducted early negotiations quietly, new vitriol pushed things into the public sphere, causing Grimes to issue a stern warning.

"The club will pay me what I ask, or I will not play ball," said Grimes. "I am not bluffing. I mean it."

Burleigh then disappeared from the Smoky City to partake in training on his own, whether at Hot Springs, in Florida, or at his Wisconsin winter camp. Pirates team secretary Sam Watters commented, "Whoever heard of a ballplayer retiring, as a result of a salary conflict, as long as he could play ball?" Out in California, upon hearing about Burleigh's remarks, an irritated Sam Dreyfuss issued an unyielding and emphatic response.

"Grimes has our final offer," said Sam. "We are not going to dicker with him. He knows what we are willing to give him in the way of a contract, and he can sign at our terms, or not at all."[16]

When Grimes and owner Barney Dreyfuss held a meeting on April 7, most Pirates fans believed this to be a sign that the two sides appeared ready to reach an agreement, and Burleigh would shortly be joining his teammates at the end of the spring exhibition tour. This premise proved erroneous, as animosity only intensified between the hurler and magnate. At that point, management decided a trade needed to be done, with Dreyfuss asking manager Jewel Ens for players he might want in exchange for Grimes. On April 9, the Pirates shipped Burleigh to the Boston Braves for nondescript southpaw hurler Percy Jones and cash. Jones was Ens's second choice regarding two pitchers he desired to acquire in a deal. Since it proved impossible to pull off a trade involving the anonymous hurler Jewel truly coveted, Pittsburgh handed Grimes over to the lowly Braves.[17]

Ens had decided that when Burleigh continued declaring his intentions surrounding a bitter holdout throughout the spring training session, he advised ownership to consider brokering a deal with another team. Jewel figured this approach better than having a disgruntled individual playing for his club.[18] In the salary fight, both sides never resolved the impasse. Grimes wanted $22,000 a season to sign a one-year deal and requested $20,000 each campaign if he'd agreed to a two-year contract. Burleigh claimed the Pirates offered him $17,500, the same salary he earned in 1929. While never divulging their figure, club ownership insisted they'd tendered Grimes a fair document.

Ens confidently declared that Percy Jones would do much better pitching for a pennant contender like Pittsburgh. Besides Boston's interest, reports indicated that Chicago, St. Louis, and Cincinnati had expressed a desire to acquire Burleigh. Many baseball experts felt a second deal with one of those clubs could still occur.¹⁹ This eventually happened when the Braves shipped Grimes to the Cardinals on June 16, 1930. Regarding Jones, Jewel missed the mark on his ability. The Pirates gave Percy his unconditional release on June 23 after the hurler appeared in nine games and posted a 6.63 ERA.²⁰ In fairness to Jewel Ens, Donie Bush and Barney Dreyfuss had blundered when trading Glenn Wright for Jess Petty after the 1928 season ended. Petty went 11–10 with a 3.71 ERA in 1929 and followed that up in 1930 by going 1–6 with an unsightly 8.27 ERA. After Pittsburgh placed Jess on waivers and every major league club passed on his services, the organization sent him to the International League's Newark Bears on June 16.²¹

Such missteps and miscalculations by the management hierarchy didn't help a team aspiring to contend for a National League pennant. The Pirates' performance in 1930 proved disappointing, as they finished in the second division for the first time since their cellar-dweller season in 1917. Jewel Ens brought the squad home in fifth place with an 80–74 record, leaving them 12 games behind pennant-winning St. Louis. As had been the case in past years, related to Max Carey, Carson Bigbee, Babe Adams, Kiki Cuyler, Glenn Wright, and Donie Bush, a purported scandal permeated within the squad that caused management to offer vague responses when questioned on the matter. Shortstop Dick Bartell ended up being the focal point in 1930. In his second entire season as a starter, Dick batted .320 and knocked in 75 runs.

Pittsburgh's baseball fans were surprised when they read in area newspapers on September 25 that management had suspended Bartell for the season. Owner Barney Dreyfuss also announced the team had requested waivers on Dick. Dreyfuss explained this as a mere formality, as September 24 was the final day for this practice until December 1, when the draft season ended. Teams did this to gauge interest regarding potential trades. The owner also affirmed that the list included twenty other Pirates players.²² Asking for waivers didn't seem like a big deal since clubs always retained the option of pulling back this request. Although Bartell had performed brilliantly in the field most of the season, he'd also committed many costly errors. Dick's spunky attitude injected excitement and ginger into sometimes dull contests by supplying constant chatter during a game.²³ Jewel Ens offered little information, as Bartell didn't accompany the squad for their final series in St. Louis because of the suspension.

"Bartell isn't going to St. Louis; Sankey will play short," politely retorted Ens after being questioned on Dick's status.

When approached by reporters, Sam Dreyfuss parroted Jewel, stating Ben Sankey would play shortstop against the Cardinals.²⁴ One day after Pittsburgh's

1930 season ended on September 28, a rumor surfaced alleging that Barney Dreyfuss had suspended and fined Bartell the balance of his salary that year over the charge of "impertinence." This particular tale claimed Dreyfuss and Dick had argued about the player's train fare back to California once the campaign concluded.[25] When Bartell received his punishment, he planned on remaining in Pittsburgh for a few days before starting the drive in his automobile to Alameda with his wife, Olive Loretta Jensen Bartell. If any potential deal with another team gained traction, Chicago looked like an ideal partner since Cubs skipper Rogers Hornsby enormously admired Dick.[26] Some baseball followers believed that Bartell's impertinence could hopefully secure outfielder Hack Wilson and pitcher Perce "Pat" Malone in a Chicago transaction.[27]

Although the Pirates finished fifth in the race, the team decided to allow Jewel Ens to rerun the show in 1931. Sam Dreyfuss didn't announce the terms of the one-year deal to retain Ens. Pittsburgh's vice president explained the rationale behind bringing Jewel back for another season.

"We have confidence that Ens will keep the Pirates in the flag race next year," said Sam Dreyfuss. "We had a fine team this year, but it was unfortunate. The squad for next season ought to be even better. [Lawrence "Larry"] French and [Stephen "Steve"] Swetonic should be better pitchers and we look for much help from Charley Wood, the new left-hander. Moreover, some of the new players may measure up."[28]

Coach Max Carey received a trick rather than a treat on Halloween when the organization announced they'd given him his unconditional release and dropped him from the coaching staff. The Pirates retained Oscar Stanage within that position.[29] Another individual exited the scene on November 6, 1930, as Pittsburgh traded Dick Bartell to the Philadelphia Phillies for shortstop Thomas "Tommy" Thevenow and pitcher Claude Willoughby. During a long-distance telephone call with Phillies officials, Barney Dreyfuss finalized the deal, which had been in the works for some time. When crafting his article for the *Pittsburgh Post-Gazette*, sportswriter Edward F. Balinger confirmed that Bartell and Dreyfuss had argued about transportation money near the season's conclusion. The combination of this incident and Bartell expressing dissatisfaction playing for the Pirates galvanized management to strike a potential deal if they found a suitable partner. Team officials exhibited supreme satisfaction over the players they'd acquired in the trade.[30]

Havey J. Boyle of the *Pittsburgh Post-Gazette* contended in his column that it'd been a foregone conclusion that Dick would find a new home for the 1931 season. Boyle ticked off the points of Bartell holding out in the spring, his employer viewing the shortstop's work throughout the campaign as unsatisfactory, and a late-season argument over some minor financial difficulty as reasons for having that opinion. Havey also opined on Dick becoming a member of a tail-ender like the Phillies, who'd gone 52–102 in 1930.

"He goes now to the salt mines of the league," wrote Boyle, "an exile, until he pulls himself up by his own bootstraps, or until he shows so much stuff that a richer club will offer an amount that will be considered sufficient ransom."[31]

Sportswriter William Braucher believed that Dick Bartell's trade to a last-place team confirmed an argument indeed had happened between the shortstop and Barney Dreyfuss on the subject of paying for his transportation to the Pacific Coast. Braucher concluded that Dreyfuss exhibited a habit of shipping players to basement-dwelling squads when they argued with him about money. The writer mentioned Burleigh Grimes's trade to Boston one year earlier to substantiate this theory. Braucher also referenced the deals involving Kiki Cuyler in 1927 and Glenn Wright in 1928 to lesser clubs, showing Pittsburgh's owner utilized vindictive punishment for those who crossed him.[32] Ironically, Cuyler, Wright, and Grimes made vital contributions to pennant-contending squads in 1930.

Shortly after Pittsburgh traded Bartell, Ralph S. Davis elaborated on the notion that management hadn't been pleased with the shortstop's body of work and attitude in 1930. Davis stated that, like any other player, Dick enjoyed getting his base hits and seemed primarily interested in that game aspect. If Bartell recorded two or three hits in a particular contest and the Pirates lost, he tended to be happy, content, and chatty while teammates felt the defeat's sting. Barney Dreyfuss didn't appreciate this mindset of placing personal achievements above team goals, which most likely sealed Dick's fate in the owner's eyes.[33] Columnist Thomas Holmes of the *Brooklyn Daily Eagle* substantiated Ralph's claim that Bartell cared more about his batting average than the squad's success.

Holmes also discussed a Pittsburgh newspaper cartoonist who'd portrayed Dreyfuss in his work of disposing of an up-and-coming shortstop for two slipping veterans. An additional cartoon caption read, "What was the matter with Whitney, Collins or Benge?" Barney defended himself against this criticism, declaring he needed to receive a shortstop in return when disposing of one. He also tamped down the silly suggestion that Philadelphia would've entertained parting with such stalwart performers as third baseman Arthur "Pinky" Whitney, as well as pitchers Philip "Phil" Collins and Raymond "Ray" Benge.

"Obviously," Dreyfuss added, "Mr. [William] Baker [Philadelphia Phillies owner] could not part with players like Collins, his leading pitcher; Whitney, one of the best third basemen in the league, and Benge, whom he figures as being one of his regular pitchers. To do so would raise a howl from his Philadelphia clientele. Most fans think that a club owner can go out and get the best talent in the league for the asking. They do not realize that every club has certain players whom it cannot let go under any circumstances or at any price."

Holmes also pointed out that Pirates rooters who supported Dick Bartell designated Barney Dreyfuss as cheap for refusing the shortstop's demand that the organization pay the expenses for his wife to travel from California to Pittsburgh.[34] Much like Donie Bush explained the true story behind him resigning as Pirates skipper when talking to Les Biederman in 1947, decades after the incident transpired, Bartell clarified what went wrong between him and management in 1930. In a series of newspaper articles in 1950, where players wrote about their most glaring boner in baseball, Dick selected the topic of what happened when Dreyfuss suspended and fined him in 1930.

> I was yanked out of the lineup more than once in 1930, fined a couple of times. Owner Dreyfuss, you see, wasn't overly fond of ballplayers who asked for more. Finally, Dreyfuss fined me $100 for not covering second base when that happened to be George Grantham's assignment.
>
> Dreyfuss asked me why I hadn't covered. I told him I wasn't supposed to, and I guess he didn't like the way I said it. Anyway, he took my $100, and I wound up being suspended the last five days of the season and fined again for insubordination.
>
> I was on a golf course when Socko McCarey, the clubhouse boy, came and told me the old man wanted to see me.
>
> I always insisted on round-trip transportation and expenses for myself and wife from Alameda, Cal., to wherever I played. A clause in the contract I signed with Sam Dreyfuss, Barney's son, called for that.
>
> "How much have you got coming?" asked Barney Dreyfuss.
>
> I excused myself, went out to a drugstore, called the railroad station and got the price of two railroad tickets and berths to Oakland, Cal., added a fair amount of meal money for two and gave Dreyfuss the figure.
>
> Dreyfuss professed not to know about my deal with his son—despite the clause in my contract, gave me only the price of one ticket and berth and meal money for one.
>
> I protested the fine, suspension and the cutting in half of my traveling expense to John Heydler, then president of the National League. He advised me to take it up with the league's board of directors. The board told me I hadn't filed my claim within the specified number of days, so I was hooked.

On top of that I was swapped to the Phillies in November, had to hustle and sweat it out in Philadelphia for four years before being dealt to the Giants.[35]

From Dick Bartell's account, almost two decades later, Pirates owner Barney Dreyfuss didn't appreciate the shortstop conducting a holdout in 1930 and displaying a fresh attitude when called out for failing to cover second base. The disagreement over travel expenses brought about an unfavorable resolution for Dick through a trade to the Philadelphia Phillies. As Pittsburgh prepared to move on without Bartell as their starting shortstop in 1931, a shocking tragedy rocked the organization and cast it into a deep pall. At 4:30 P.M. on February 22, 1931, thirty-four-year-old Samuel Dreyfuss died at his Morewood Gardens residence on Morewood Avenue in the Oakland neighborhood of Pittsburgh. Sam had been confined to his home for a month with a severe cold.[36] This illness transitioned to influenza two weeks before his death.[37] On February 20, the younger Dreyfuss contracted pneumonia.[38] Barney Dreyfuss was a few feet away from his son's bedside when Samuel passed away.[39]

Besides leaving behind his parents, his wife, Carolyn Wolf Dreyfuss; three-year-old son, Barney Dreyfuss III; and sister, Mrs. Eleanor Dreyfuss Benswanger survived Sam.[40] It had been Barney Dreyfuss's dream for many years that his son would inherit the Pittsburgh Pirates and succeed him as the organization's president. Over the past decade, Barney had rejected numerous offers to sell the club. The proud father always boasted about his son's knowledge related to the game, even in Sam's days as a youngster. When the Pirates conducted spring training, the younger Dreyfuss usually donned a uniform and worked out with the players. Samuel had planned to accompany the squad to Paso Robles but couldn't because he was bedridden with his illness.[41] Those connected to baseball considered Sam one of the best-informed and brightest people.[42] Pittsburgh's owner turned sixty-six years old one day after his son died.[43]

The news surrounding Sam Dreyfuss's death stunned the spring training entourage members as they prepared to conduct their first practice. Manager Jewel Ens canceled the initial session scheduled for Monday, February 23. Ens also postponed Tuesday's diamond drills out of respect for Sam when the plan called for funeral services to happen that day. Jewel offered his thoughts during this sad moment.

> The death of Sam Dreyfuss grieves me beyond words. In the ten years that I have been associated with him I have always found him a great fellow.

He was on his way to becoming a distinct factor in Organized Baseball, fit to follow in his father's footsteps. My heart goes out to his sorrowing parents and his wife in their hour of sadness. I feel that I have lost a friend who was as close to me as a brother.

My relations with Sam Dreyfuss always were on a personal basis and things won't seem the same for some time without him. He had a remarkable knowledge of the game. I can't realize he's gone. It will take me some time to get adjusted without him about.

Pirates captain Pie Traynor, who also happened to be the squad's longest-tenured player, offered his regret over the death of a man he considered a devoted friend.

"Sam was a real leader," said Traynor. "When I came to the club in 1920, Sam made friends with me early. I took a liking to him, too, because of his enthusiasm for the game.

"It is a personal blow to me to learn of his death. I grew to respect his decision on all matters and the fact that not once in my ten years' association with him and Barney Dreyfuss have I ever had a dispute over a contract shows how well we got along."

One of the most heartwarming tributes came from little-known pitcher Andrew "Andy" Bednar, who'd appeared in two games for Pittsburgh in 1930 and would only see action in three contests in 1931. Bednar mourned the passing of a man who'd exhibited compassion and offered him help the previous year.

"At the end of last season," Bednar said, "I was sick in Webster Hall [located in the Oakland section of town]. For almost a week Sam called for me in his auto, took me to the Allegheny General Hospital for observation and brought me back again. Later he saw to it that I got the best of care. I am sorry he died before I got a chance to pay him back for all that."

Throughout his life, Sam Dreyfuss displayed uncanny baseball knowledge. Without hesitation, Sam could offer accurate facts and figures on any person who wore a Pirates uniform, and he possessed a vast knowledge of baseball players throughout the country. Pittsburgh's squad reached Paso Robles on February 22, almost the moment Samuel passed away.[44] As the funeral started in Pittsburgh on Tuesday, February 24, at 2 P.M., Pirates players bowed their heads and held a moment of silence in Jewel Ens's hotel room in Paso Robles at 11 A.M. Pacific time. Local merchants also closed their businesses out of respect. Dr. W. L. Marks, the team physician, gave a eulogy.[45] In the first abbreviated spring practice session, team members wore black armbands paying tribute to Sam.[46] A large gathering attended the funeral back in Pittsburgh, including many baseball men from other cities.

Shortly after Barney Dreyfuss's son passed away, rumors abounded that the grieving father might walk away from his connection to baseball. Dreyfuss dispelled this myth weeks later, declaring no changes to be forthcoming in the policy and ownership of the club. He also told newspaper journalists that reports about him selling the team and retiring lacked any foundation. Although Sam's death dealt Barney a severe blow, the grieving father planned on bravely forging onward, continuing with his life's passion of directing the Pittsburgh Pirates and remaining connected to baseball. Several years before, Dreyfuss had remarked to sportswriter Ralph S. Davis that he expected to die in the baseball harness. Pittsburgh's owner believed that any man who'd been active all his life committed a massive mistake by retiring and giving up his interest in business affairs.

Manager Jewel Ens initially ended up entirely in charge of the spring expedition. Dreyfuss felt Ens's time exclusively should be devoted to preparing his team on the diamond.[47] Barney had hoped to alleviate some of Jewel's burden by joining his squad on the West Coast, but he delayed this decision due to being under the weather.[48] Pressing business at home also prevented this from happening. Instead, Dreyfuss hired John D. Holahan, graduate manager of athletics at Duquesne University, as a temporary traveling secretary until the 1931 season started. The strain had become too great on Ens, who divided his attention between managerial and logistical duties. Holahan's hustling mentality impressed Barney. Pittsburgh's owner became acquainted with John's capabilities when Duquesne's football team played their home games at Forbes Field this past season.[49]

When it came to selecting someone to assume the post of team treasurer that Sam had held, Barney Dreyfuss remained within the family when making a choice. Dreyfuss called on his son-in-law, William "Bill" Benswanger, to accept the position. Bill was a partner in the insurance business started by his father, Edward Benswanger. Although Benswanger enjoyed baseball and had been a Pirates fan since childhood, he passionately loved music, was an accomplished pianist, and held a position on the Pittsburgh Symphony Orchestra's board.[50] In 1925, Bill married Barney's daughter, Eleanor "Fanny" Dreyfuss.[51] When a distressed Dreyfuss requested Benswanger's help, his son-in-law said he would do so if Barney wanted him. After Dreyfuss answered with grief in his heart that he wouldn't have asked Bill if he didn't need him, Benswanger agreed to join the Pirates' organization.[52]

On the field, 1931 was another discouraging season for Pittsburgh, who finished fifth in the National League race for the second consecutive year. The Pirates posted a 75–79 record, leaving them 26 games behind pace-setting St. Louis. Following such a lousy performance, nobody was astonished when Pittsburgh's owner handed manager Jewel Ens his unconditional release on October 8.[53] The Pirates' organization followed standard protocol, not issuing any statement explaining the reason behind Ens's dismissal other than the familiar phrase that both parties had parted on the best of terms. When Jewel arrived in the Smoky City after viewing World Series games in Philadelphia and St. Louis between the Athletics and Cardinals, he refused to discuss the firing other than admitting the club had let him go. Despite back-to-back fifth-place finishes, Ens proved a popular pilot, leaving patrons regretting his release.

When newspapers started elevating former Pittsburgh Pirates catcher and skipper George Gibson as the likely replacement, Barney Dreyfuss cautioned against making such a prediction. Writers based their premise on Gibson and Dreyfuss spending time together for more than one month, viewing games at Forbes Field before George returned to Canada a few weeks later. Barney offered his impressions on the managerial search when questioned by reporters.

"Don't be too sure Gibson is the next manager," Dreyfuss said. "And don't expect a man to be named in the near future. Managing a ball club is an important position, for an investment aggregating several millions of dollars is put in his care. Therefore the appointment will not be done hastily. And if, as you say, you're betting on Gibson, don't bet too heavily."[54]

In the end, those who might've gambled big money on George being named Pittsburgh's manager collected a big payday. On November 30, 1931, Dreyfuss announced that he'd hired Gibson to oversee the Pirates in 1932. After alerting press members to this decision at club headquarters, Barney and his new pilot immediately held a sequestered conference regarding the team's direction. Dreyfuss chose Gibson over other candidates that reporters thought the magnate might hire to run the club. That group included current Cardinals manager and second baseman Frankie Frisch; pilot Arthur "Art" Griggs of the Western League's Wichita Aviators; a Pittsburgh farm team, former Buccaneers scout, and current Mission Reds manager in the Pacific Coast League Joe Devine; Pirates coach James "Doc" Crandall; and former infielder Dave Bancroft.[55]

Before leaving Pittsburgh the following night, with Dreyfuss and William Benswanger, to attend the minor league meetings in West Baden Springs, Indiana, Gibson announced that some potential trades to upgrade the team were already in the works. Fans and newspaper journalists felt some likely candidates in the deals to be George Grantham, Adam Comorosky, and Steve Swetonic. Even Paul Waner's name bobbed to the surface related to trade rumors. George readily admitted that only groundwork on transactions might occur in West Baden Springs, while completing deals likely would happen during National League meetings in Chicago that started on December 8. Gibson advised people against jumping to conclusions when theoretically dabbling in the trade market.

"Don't think, however, that to propose trades is to make them," said Gibson. "We have quite a number of irons in the fire aiming at improving the club for next season.

"The Pirates last season were fundamentally a pretty strong club, but there is much to be done for 1932. There will be new faces on the roster next season, if everything goes right. But it takes two to make an agreement."[56]

Barney Dreyfuss didn't make the trip to West Baden Springs due to contracting a cold on the eve of his departure. Instead, he sent Gibson, Benswanger, and scout Bill Hinchman to represent the organization at the minor league meetings. Rather than risk a more prolonged sick spell by making the journey, Barney decided to remain at home to attend the more critical National League meetings in Chicago.[57] Unfortunately, Dreyfuss couldn't travel to Chicago either, as his horrible cold resulted in the owner's physician advising him to remain in Pittsburgh.[58] To restore his health, Barney traveled to New York City to see a specialist.[59] When Dreyfuss arrived in New York, the baseball magnate told reporters he planned on taking his wife to view some good shows while in town.[60]

In reality, Barney Dreyfuss didn't travel to New York for pleasure. Dreyfuss had been in poor health throughout the past year following the devastating death of his son. Barney just couldn't recover from this stunning setback. Dreyfuss made the trip to New York in the middle of December to consult with a specialist about an ailment not revealed to the public. He returned to that city on December 27 and entered Mt. Sinai Hospital the following morning, with doctors immediately operating to deal with the illness. Reports after the surgery indicated Dreyfuss to be resting comfortably in his room.[61] A group of medical experts had recommended performing the minor operation following a series of examinations. This battery of tests came about following the Pittsburgh family physician's recommendation.[62]

On the afternoon of January 6, 1932, surgeons performed a second operation on Barney at Mt. Sinai Hospital. The Pirates' owner's attending physicians appeared pleased with his condition following this surgery, as Dreyfuss rallied nicely and seemed to be resting as well as expected. Although doctors made no official announcement on the precise nature of Dreyfuss's ailment, the hospital referred to it as a glandular infection.[63] That evening, the organization released news of Barney's surgery to reporters at team headquarters in the Flannery Building in Oakland. After the first surgical procedure in December, which doctors regarded as very encouraging, the surgeons later agreed that a second trip to the operating room was necessary. Dreyfuss most likely would be able to leave the hospital and return to his home after a recuperation period of several weeks. Mrs. Florence Dreyfuss, daughter Eleanor Dreyfuss Benswanger, William Benswanger, and Samuel Dreyfuss's widow, Carolyn, were at Barney's bedside following the surgery.[64]

Sadly, Barney Dreyfuss never returned to his Pittsburgh home. On February 4, the first extreme complication since his second operation occurred when Dreyfuss contracted pneumonia. The baseball magnate, who saw his grit and resolve drained over the past year, didn't have the required strength to win this battle.[65] On February 5, at 11:42 A.M., Barney passed away at Mt. Sinai Hospital, where he'd remained since undergoing two glandular surgical procedures. Upon hearing the news, baseball fans across the country mourned the death of the Pittsburgh Pirates' grand owner for the past thirty-two years, who the National League had just recently re-elected to a second term as vice president.[66] Some newspapers reported that Dreyfuss succumbed to pneumonia following an operation for prostatitis on January 6.[67]

William Benswanger told the press that he planned on taking the body back to Pittsburgh on the night of February 5, with interment probably occurring on either Sunday or Monday after a viewing at the Dreyfuss home.[68] Following the funeral, Barney would be buried next to his son, Samuel, at West View Cemetery.[69] The entire family who'd remained by Dreyfuss's bedside throughout his hospital stay surrounded the magnate when he passed away.[70] Shortly after the announcement of Barney's death, National League president John Heydler paid tribute to the Pirates' leader's human qualities.

"He discovered more great players than any man in the game," Heydler said, "and his abiding faith in the future of baseball continued to the end. He was the senior baseball man of the country. I cannot tell you how deeply I feel his loss."[71]

In Pittsburgh, grieving civic and business leaders, close associates, friends, and baseball officials offered words of sympathy and an outpouring of esteem for the longtime Pirates owner. Team secretary Samuel Watters stated that during his extensive and pleasurable relationship with Barney Dreyfuss, the baseball titan treated him with as much consideration as he would one of his children. Former manager Bill McKechnie, who now held that title for the Boston Braves, ordained Dreyfuss to be a credit to the great American pastime and a sportsman of the highest degree. McKechnie added that it would be impossible to replace Barney in baseball. Newly hired Pittsburgh pilot George Gibson offered a passionate response for the man he'd known most of his baseball life.

> Throughout my acquaintance with President Dreyfuss, which began in 1905. I have found him to be an ideal employer and, after serving practically my entire diamond career with his club, I long ago learned to look upon his as a father. We have had differences of opinion, but the most friendly feeling has always existed between us and his passing is indeed a severe blow to me. I know I am going to miss him, but his absence will cause me to work harder than ever to provide what was his foremost wish in life—a winning ball club. It is my resolve to carry on along the lines he mapped out, just the same as if he still was with us.

Former Pirates skipper Jewel Ens, who now worked as a coach on the Detroit Tigers' staff, said that although news of Barney's death came as a shock, it wasn't entirely unexpected. Ens elaborated, explaining the sudden, unfortunate loss of Sam one year ago proved such a severe blow to Barney that Jewel feared the owner completely breaking down under the burden of sorrow. Ens further stated that Dreyfuss courageously carried on but constantly mourned. Jewel concluded by declaring baseball had lost a great man. In offering his tribute, former star shortstop and friend Honus Wagner reflected on many years.

"I have lost a great friend," said Wagner. "I played for Mr. Dreyfuss three years in Louisville and 18 more seasons in Pittsburgh. I have nothing but praise for the way he treated me. His generosity was remarkable. When we lost the memorable series to Boston in 1903 he gave us a big banquet and then added sufficient to our losing checks to make our amount as much as the winning players received."[72]

Barney Dreyfuss's vision of establishing the first inter-league series by sanctioning a meeting between his squad and the American League champion Boston Americans in 1903 earned him the rightful title of "Father of the World Series."[73] Under Dreyfuss's direction, the Pittsburgh Pirates proved to be a phenomenally successful franchise, and Barney became known as one of the wealthiest magnates connected to baseball. Since 1903, once the National and American leagues settled their differences, Barney had also held the title of chairman of the scheduling committee for the Senior Circuit, a tiring and thankless job that other club officials never envied him over. Dreyfuss became quite adroit at crafting a schedule that avoided conflicting dates in major league cities represented by two teams.

Those players who provided years of faithful service and always played square with him never had to be concerned, as Barney treated them well in times of need, even after retirement. For those who misbehaved by breaking the rules of discipline, Dreyfuss found little use for such men, whether star performers or little-used players. Fellow magnates, especially in later years, considered Barney a bit lucky regarding his ability to turn minor-league players into star major-league performers. Dreyfuss had acquired players such as Paul Waner, Lloyd Waner, Kiki Cuyler, Pie Traynor, Glenn Wright, and others for minimal cost. Within a year after pulling on a Pirates uniform, each of these individuals became top-flight performers at their respective positions.[74]

While offering accolades to Barney in his column on February 6, *Pittsburgh Post-Gazette* sportswriter Havey J. Boyle indicated that Forbes Field would likely be the owner's most significant and enduring legacy. Boyle declared that Dreyfuss had possessed great foresight transitioning from the North Side's unimpressive Exposition Park to a beautiful baseball palace in Oakland that compared favorably with other ballparks nationwide. The writer also stated that Forbes Field became as much of a home for Barney as the residence where he ate and slept. According to Boyle, the ballpark proved a monument to Dreyfuss's faith and confidence in baseball. Since Forbes Field opened in 1909, the Pirates' owner had refused to commercialize Pittsburgh's home grounds. He constantly rejected sizeable offers for placing advertisements on the fences, opting to maintain the ballpark's purity.

Havey also commended Dreyfuss for always surrounding himself with a highly competent and talented staff of baseball scouts. Because baseball happened to be Barney's hobby and job, he followed a course that sometimes puzzled other magnates more interested in the business side of the game. Since the great game tended to be a hobby that transcended daily work, Dreyfuss constantly received a thrill and deep satisfaction when developing homegrown players into stars.[75] Many baseball notables expected to attend the Pittsburgh magnate's funeral, scheduled for 2:30 P.M. on February 7.[76] Unfortunately, Fred Clarke couldn't be there and wired his regrets. Clarke found it impossible to make the necessary railroad connections that would've allowed him to reach the Smoky City in time for the funeral. Fred even attempted to arrange a trip by air but found no airplanes available at any point accessible to his home in Winfield, Kansas.[77]

Hundreds of people filed past Barney Dreyfuss's coffin during the viewing at his home on February 6.[78] Each major league sent beautiful floral arrangements from their headquarters. The National League's consisted of a large blanket of orchids draped over the casket.[79] More than 1,500 people crowded Rodef Shalom Temple on November 7, long before the funeral service started. Judge Kenesaw Mountain Landis, National League president John Heydler, and American League president William "Will" Harridge were the most prominent sports figures in attendance. Besides important people connected to baseball attending, leading dignitaries from the worlds of business and public affairs, along with the owner's friends, paid their final respects. Hundreds of citizens had also passed the casket while it lay in state at Rodef Shalom Temple before the funeral.

Rabbi Dr. Samuel H. Goldenson, who officiated the service, described Barney Dreyfuss's life as epitomizing the highest qualities of fair play, truthfulness, and generosity.[80] Dr. Goldenson declared that Dreyfuss, "so labored in his lifetime in a field that seemed only a pastime for the nation's leisure hours, as to raise it to the position of an outstanding exemplification of fair play and sportsmanship." Goldenson then pointed out how this approach made life better for other people.

"It is fair play we have most need of in the world," said Dr. Goldenson, "and this man made it the object of his life."[81]

Thousands of people crowded Pittsburgh's streets as the large funeral procession involving many automobiles traveled through the city and headed for West View Cemetery.[82] Hundreds of mourners gathered under a great canopy above the grave, bowing their heads in respect as Dr. Samuel Goldenson read the service's final words before laying the body to rest.[83] When Barney Dreyfuss died, the consensus suggested that control of the Pittsburgh Pirates would remain in the family since William Benswanger currently acted as the team's treasurer, while Mrs. Florence Dreyfuss held a position on the board of directors.[84] On February 18, 1932, at a reorganization meeting to select new officers, the board of directors elected William Benswanger president and treasurer. Sam Watters received the title of vice president and assistant treasurer. The club directors also elected Mrs. Dreyfuss as chairman of the board.

Florence Dreyfuss now possessed the controlling interest of the Pittsburgh Pirates as the chief stockholder under her husband's will. Mrs. Dreyfuss planned to leave the responsibility of running the club to Benswanger and Watters. As a young woman in Kentucky, Florence's love for music led her to encounter Barney Dreyfuss. A Sunday excursion train taking them from Louisville,

Kentucky, to Cincinnati, Ohio, for a band concert led them to meet. They wed in October 1894. Logically, the couple's mutual interests included baseball, leading Florence to attend games, although female spectators were rare then. Such a close association with her husband related to baseball had allowed Mrs. Dreyfuss to acquire immense knowledge about the game and an understanding of business matters surrounding the Pirates' franchise.[85]

The Dreyfuss baseball dynasty eventually ended after more than forty-six years of controlling Pittsburgh's diamond destiny. An ownership change occurred on August 8, 1946, when a group including businessmen John Galbreath, Thomas "Tom" Johnson, and Frank McKinney, along with singer and actor Harry "Bing" Crosby, purchased the club.[86] The Pirates didn't claim any National League pennants after Barney Dreyfuss's death and before the sale, as the team came closest to winning a coveted flag in 1938 when the Chicago Cubs nosed them out at the wire. From 1900 through 1931, under Dreyfuss, Pittsburgh secured the National League bunting on six occasions and appeared in four World Series, while his beloved franchise wore the crown as world champions two times. Constantly dedicated to giving Pirates fans a first-division diamond product, Barney's team only finished in the second division six times during his ownership tenure.

Over the thirty-two years he owned and operated Pittsburgh's baseball organization, Dreyfuss employed seven managers and rehired George Gibson months before his death. Of those seven men, Barney fired or released three of them, while the other four either left of their own volition or resigned because of extenuating circumstances. Fred Clarke remained the longest alongside Dreyfuss, working faithfully with him in Pittsburgh as a pilot for sixteen seasons from 1900 through 1915. Fred then returned to the organization as team vice president and assistant manager in June 1925 and remained with the club through the 1926 campaign. Throughout the first decade of the twentieth century, Barney and Clarke worked beautifully in tandem, leading the Pirates to four National League pennants.

Fred acted as the perfect extension for Pittsburgh's owner, especially when doling out discipline when a player didn't follow the rules and precepts established by management. Concerning players who enjoyed drinking and partying, Clarke knew from his experience as a youngster with the Louisville Colonels about the lure of alcohol. When dealing with his players who sometimes misbehaved, Fred remembered Barney Dreyfuss's career-altering talk regarding his lifestyle shortly after joining the Colonels. Clarke had discussed this topic during an interview before the 1911 season started.

I gave up that life, and here I am at 39 years still playing ball in the big league. Whatever success I have had has been due to the sensible talk from my employer. I have tried since I have been a manager myself to inculcate the same ideas into the minds of my players. On account of my own experience I know that the temptations are strong, and I watch the habits of the young men on the team closely. If I find one of them drinking I first warn him, and then if it continues and his playing is affected I hand him his release. It is the only way. One bad actor can do a lot to disrupt a club.[87]

Such bad actors, who didn't live up to the rules of conduct established by Pittsburgh's management, usually found themselves playing baseball in a different city. From Honus Wagner to Paul Waner, many great star performers pulled on a Pirates uniform during the Barney Dreyfuss era. A host of sensational performers also electrified crowds at Exposition Park and Forbes Field with their talent but punched a ticket out of town for assorted reasons. Some, like Jesse Tannehill, Jack Chesbro, Al Mamaux, Max Carey, and Kiki Cuyler, saw their careers in Pittsburgh end because of disagreements or disputes with management. Others, such as Kitty Bransfield and Claude Ritchey, couldn't continue performing at a high level due to the relentless badgering, roasting, and heckling courtesy of gamblers at Exposition Park. These insurgents, embedded at this ballpark and Forbes Field, caused numerous Pirates team members grief and distress for countless years.

Most times, Dreyfuss exhibited extreme generosity and kindness toward his players. In return, Barney expected loyalty, utmost diamond effort, and recognition of the rules, principles, and tenets that made the Pirates one of the most successful franchises in baseball throughout the time he owned the club. Dreyfuss displayed no patience for men who challenged what he believed to be correct and just, whether a player or pilot subverted this credo. Although managers like Fred Clarke received extreme latitude in charting the course of Pittsburgh's baseball fortunes, Barney continuously maintained his status as the final authority on matters.

When George Gibson eulogized Barney Dreyfuss following his passing, the Pirates' newly hired manager vowed to work harder than ever in the great owner's absence. Gibson dedicated himself to achieving this to provide Dreyfuss, even in death, what he foremost wished for in life—a winning ball club.[88] In 1932, George accomplished this goal, as Pittsburgh finished second in the standings with an 86–68 record, four games behind pace-setting Chicago. In the end, achieving victories on the field mattered most to Barney. While the names and faces changed as players retired, found new baseball homes, or happened to be bounced from the club following a falling out with the organization, one thing remained constant: The Pittsburgh Pirates had always existed before an influx of new players continually joined the club over the years. The franchise thrived, flourished, and survived fine without them long after they departed.

In 1930, Pittsburgh Pirates owner Barney Dreyfuss fined shortstop Dick Bartell $100 for failing to cover second base on a play in a game. Bartell responded to his boss that covering the bag happened to be second baseman George Grantham's assignment in this case. Dick supposed Dreyfuss didn't like his straightforward response. Since his acquisition from the Chicago Cubs on October 27, 1924, George topped the .300 mark as a batter each year he wore a Pirates uniform. When trade rumors started coming forward after Barney Dreyfuss hired George Gibson as manager for the second time on November 30, 1931, Grantham's name prominently appeared, along with pitcher Steve Swetonic, and outfielders Paul Waner and Adam Comorosky. (Courtesy of the Library of Congress).

Notes

Chapter 1

1. Circle, "Pittsburg Points: Splendid Weather and the 'Tacks' Battery Causes an Outpour of Fans – Talk about Next Year – Bits of News," *Sporting Life*, October 21, 1899, 10.
2. "Rube Waddell Was Honored: Many Butler County Friends Cheered Him on to Victory," *Pittsburg Press*, October 15, 1899, 14.
3. "The World of Baseball: Vale, 1899 Season – Brooklyn the New Champion of the League," *Sporting Life*, October 21, 1899, 2.
4. Circle, "Pittsburgh Points: Splendid Weather and the 'Tacks' Battery Causes an Outpour of Fans – Talk about Next Year – Bits of News," 10.
5. Pirate, "Donovan Did Well: Got Good Results Out of the Pirates," *The Sporting News*, October 21, 1899, 3.
6. "Baseball Gossip," *Pittsburg Press*, October 19, 1899, 5.
7. Frederick G. Lieb, *The Pittsburgh Pirates* (1948; reprint, Carbondale, Ill.: Southern Illinois University Press, 2003), 23.
8. "That Mysterious Deal: Auten, Kerr and Buckenberger Buy Out Temple," *Pittsburgh Post*, January 24, 1893, 6.
9. "Death Record: William Warden Kerr," *Pittsburg Press*, February 19, 1917, 4.
10. A.R. Cratty, "Angry Owners: Col. Dreyfus' Bed in Pittsburg Evidently Not One of Roses – What the Gossips Say about Pittsburg Club Affairs," *Sporting Life*, December 29, 1900, 7.
11. "Baseball Gossip," *Pittsburg Press*, October 21, 1899, 5.
12. Circle, "Pittsburg Points: Manager Donovan Remains on the Battle Ground and Puts His Time to Profit – A Couple of Youngsters Signed," *Sporting Life*, October 28, 1899, 6.
13. "Magnates Met: Pittsburg Team Affairs Discussed Behind Closed Doors," *Pittsburg Press*, October 22, 1899, 13.
14. "Baseball Gossip," *Pittsburg Press*, October 24, 1899, 5.
15. "Baseball Gossip," *Pittsburg Press*, October 26, 1899, 5.
16. Pirate, "Feigns Surprise: Mr. Watkins Keeps Coming Back to Pittsburg," *The Sporting News*, October 28, 1899, 3.
17. Ibid.
18. "Baseball Gossip," *Pittsburg Press*, October 27, 1899, 5.
19. Circle, "Pittsburg Points: Watkins' Attempt to Buy the Pittsburg Club Frustrated Largely Through Revengeful Local Scribes," *Sporting Life*, November 4, 1899, 5.
20. "Watkins Weary: Thinks He Was Trifled with by Mr. Kerr in the Matter of the Pittsburg Club Sale," *Sporting Life*, November 4, 1899, 5.

21. "Baseball Gossip," *Pittsburg Press*, October 28, 1899, 5.
22. Circle, "Pittsburg Points: Watkins' Attempt to Buy the Pittsburg Club Frustrated Largely Through Revengeful Local Scribes," 5.
23. "Baseball Gossip," *Pittsburg Press*, October 30, 1899, 5.
24. "Baseball Gossip," *Pittsburg Press*, November 1, 1899, 5.
25. "Baseball Gossip," October 27, 1899, 5.
26. Lieb, *The Pittsburgh Pirates*, 44.
27. "Pneumonia after Operation Causes Dreyfuss' Death: Noted Baseball Club Owner Settled in Paducah after Coming from Germany," *Sun-Democrat*, February 5, 1932, 9.
28. Lieb, *The Pittsburgh Pirates*, 44.
29. Edward F. Balinger, "Sport World Mourns Death of Dreyfuss: Pirate Owner Succumbs in N.Y. Hospital," *Pittsburgh Post-Gazette*, February 6, 1932, 14.
30. Lieb, *The Pittsburgh Pirates*, 44.
31. Balinger, "Sport World Mourns Death of Dreyfuss: Pirate Owner Succumbs in N.Y. Hospital," 14.
32. Lieb, *The Pittsburgh Pirates*, 44.
33. Balinger, "Sport World Mourns Death of Dreyfuss: Pirate Owner Succumbs in N.Y. Hospital," 14.
34. "Pneumonia after Operation Causes Dreyfuss' Death: Noted Baseball Club Owner Settled in Paducah after Coming from Germany," 9.
35. Balinger, "Sport World Mourns Death of Dreyfuss: Pirate Owner Succumbs in N.Y. Hospital," 14.
36. "Pneumonia after Operation Causes Dreyfuss' Death: Noted Baseball Club Owner Settled in Paducah after Coming from Germany," 9.
37. Lieb, *The Pittsburgh Pirates*, 45.
38. "Baseball Gossip," October 30, 1899, 5.
39. "Baseball Gossip," November 1, 1899, 5.
40. "Baseball Gossip," *Pittsburg Press*, October 31, 1899, 5.
41. "Late News: Will Be Settled Soon – Pittsburg Deal about Closed," *The Sporting News*, November 4, 1899, 1.
42. "Dreyfuss Has It: Pittsburg's Club Will Be His Property in a Few Days," *Sporting Life*, November 4, 1899, 4.
43. "Baseball Gossip," *Pittsburg Press*, November 3, 1899, 5.
44. "Baseball Gossip," *Pittsburg Press*, November 4, 1899, 5.
45. Ibid.
46. "Another Deal Declared Off: Barney Dreyfuss Will Not Get the Pittsburg Club," *Pittsburg Press*, November 5, 1899, 15.
47. Circle, "Pittsburg Points: A Loophole Spoils the Sale – Kerr Changes His Mind – A Guaranty Cuts a Figure," *Sporting Life*, November 11, 1899, 3.
48. "Another Deal Declared Off: Barney Dreyfuss Will Not Get the Pittsburg Club," 15.
49. "Baseball Gossip," *Pittsburg Press*, November 6, 1899, 5.
50. "Baseball Gossip," *Pittsburg Press*, November 10, 1899, 5.
51. C.L. Moore, "Found a Loophole: Kerr Sidetracked the Big Deal with Dreyfus," *The Sporting News*, November 11, 1899, 5.
52. "Heard in the Corridors: Comments and Gossip Picked Up at the League Meeting," *Pittsburg Press*, December 14, 1899, 5.
53. Pirate, "Buy Dreyfus' Club: This Would Please Mr. Kerr's Pittsburg Patrons," *The Sporting News*, November 11, 1899, 3.
54. C.L. Moore, "Wise and Wealthy: Barney Dreyfus Is a First Class Business Man," *The Sporting News*, November 18, 1899, 4.
55. "Dreyfuss Is at Louisville: Says the Muddle Will Be Cleared at League Meeting," *Pittsburg Press*, November 24, 1899, 5.
56. "Baseball Gossip," *Pittsburg Press*, November 23, 1899, 5.
57. "Another Deal On?: Negotiations for Pittsburg's Club Reported Re-Opened Much to Power's Disgust," *Sporting Life*, November 25, 1899, 4.
58. Circle, "Pittsburg Points: A Brief Lull in the Smoky City Club's Affairs," *Sporting Life*, November 25, 1899, 7.
59. "Baseball Gossip," *Pittsburg Press*, November 29, 1899, 5.

60. "Baseball Gossip," *Pittsburg Press*, December 2, 1899, 5.
61. "Baseball Gossip," *Pittsburg Press*, December 1, 1899, 5.
62. "Baseball Gossip: President Kerr Admits That Another Louisville Deal Is On," *Pittsburg Press*, December 6, 1899, 5.
63. John J. Saunders, "Saunders' Say: Report of a Merger of the Louisville and Pittsburg Clubs – Pulliam Reelected President – After a Berth in Some Other League, Etc.," *Sporting Life*, December 9, 1899, 6.
64. Pirate, "Gigantic Deal: Star Colonels Sold to Pittsburg Club," *The Sporting News*, December 16, 1899, 3.
65. "Baseball Deal Closed To-Day: Pittsburg Paid $25,000 for Pick of the Louisville Club," *Pittsburg Press*, December 8, 1899, 1.
66. "Dreyfuss Leaves Louisville and Will Become President of Pittsburg Club," *The Sun* (New York, New York), December 9, 1899, 5.
67. Pirate, "Gigantic Deal: Star Colonels Sold to Pittsburg Club," 3.
68. Frederick Clifton Clarke, "How I Became a Ball Player," *Anaconda Standard*, August 17, 1913, 2.
69. "Shakeup of the Colonels: Rogers, Manager, Captain and Second Baseman, Deposed," *Boston Daily Globe*, June 17, 1897, 4.
70. "Fred Clarke: The Baseball Capitalist," *San Francisco Sunday Call*, March 12, 1911, 6.
71. "The Trick Turned: Mr. Dreyfus Will After All Remain in the League," *Sporting Life*, December 16, 1899, 4.
72. "Gossip about the Big Deal: Dreyfuss Admits That It Was Practically Closed Monday," *Pittsburg Press*, December 9, 1899, 5.
73. John J. Saunders, "Louisville Laconic: The Big Deal with Pittsburg Expected and Discounted – The Falls City Likely to Remain in the League," *Sporting Life*, December 16, 1899, 4.
74. "Late News: Dreyfus Elected President – Will Control Pittsburg Club," *The Sporting News*, December 16, 1899, 1.
75. "Robison Explains: Reason Why St. Louis Has Bought No Players," *The Sporting News*, December 23, 1899, 4.
76. "Baseball Gossip," *Pittsburg Press*, December 19, 1899, 5.
77. "Trade Talks to Freedman: Dreyfuss and Andy Were Together in New York Yesterday," *Pittsburg Press*, December 11, 1899, 5.
78. "Dreyfuss Has a New Scheme: As Champion of Circuit Reduction He Annoys Syndicates," *Pittsburg Press*, December 13, 1899, 5.
79. Circle, "Pittsburg Points: Likely That Few Moves Will Be Made Until the League Has Decided on the Circuit Matter – Bits of Local News, Etc.," *Sporting Life*, January 13, 1900 8.
80. Circle, "Pittsburg Points: Early Enthusiasm Certain in the Smoky City," *Sporting Life*, January 27, 1900, 6.
81. Circle, "Pittsburg Points: Pittsburg Club Not Alarmed over Any Change," *Sporting Life*, February 3, 1900, 8.
82. Lieb, *The Pittsburgh Pirates*, 81.
83. "Two Good Players Bought by Robison: 'Patsy' Donovan and First Baseman McGann to Join St. Louis Club," *St. Louis Republic*, March 10, 1900, 4.
84. "Changes Will Help Baseball: Reduction of Circuit Makes It Possible to Brace Teams," *Pittsburg Press*, March 11, 1900, 14.
85. "Eight Clubs in the League: Baltimore, Washington, Cleveland and Louisville Dropped," *Pittsburg Press*, March 9, 1900, 5.
86. Circle, "Pittsburg Points: Four of the Surplus Men of the Pirates Have Been Disposed of – Rube Waddell Makes a Hit, Etc.," *Sporting Life*, March 3, 1900, 6.
87. "Baseball News: Mr. Tebeau Is 'In' Good from a Certain Standpoint," *St. Louis Republic*, March 2, 1900, 4.
88. "Gossip About the Big Deal: Dreyfuss Admits That It Was Practically Closed Monday," 5.
89. Circle, "Proud Pittsburg: The Biggest Deal in Recent History Successfully Carried Out – How the Pick of the Louisville Team Was Secured," *Sporting Life*, December 16, 1899, 4.
90. Francis C. Richter, "Dreyfus Dumped: Pittsburg's Club Can't Let Well Enough Alone," *Sporting Life*, December 29, 1900, 7.

91. A.R. Cratty, "Pittsburg Points: Barney Dreyfuss Blocks the Effort to Sidetrack Him – Kerr and Auten May Go into Court – Bits of News," *Sporting Life*, January 19, 1901, 7.
92. Pirate, "Proposed Trade: Kerr Offers Jesse Tannehill for Ed Scott," *The Sporting News*, December 29, 1900, 4.
93. "Baseball: Peace between Western League and American Association in Sight," *St. Louis Globe-Democrat*, November 2, 1902, 14.
94. Richter, "Dreyfus Dumped: Pittsburg's Club Can't Let Well Enough Alone," 7.
95. Cratty, "Angry Owners: Col. Dreyfus' Bed in Pittsburg Evidently Not One of Roses – What the Gossips Say about Pittsburg Club Affairs," 7.
96. "Gossip of the Meeting," *Pittsburg Press*, December 14, 1900, 5.
97. "Jennings May Be the Pirates' Next Manager," *Pittsburg Press*, December 21, 1900, 5.
98. "Base Ball: Caught on the Fly," *The Sporting News*, November 3, 1900, 5.
99. Cratty, "Angry Owners: Col. Dreyfus' Bed in Pittsburg Evidently Not One of Roses – What the Gossips Say about Pittsburg Club Affairs," 7.
100. Richter, "Dreyfus Dumped: Pittsburg's Club Won't Let Well Enough Alone," 7.
101. "Dreyfuss' Deed: He Temporarily Blocks Pittsburg Club Election," *Sporting Life*, January 19, 1901, 7.
102. Cratty, "Pittsburg Points: Barney Dreyfuss Blocks the Effort to Sidetrack Him – Kerr and Auten May Go into Court – Bits of News," 7.
103. Duquesne, "Facts about Deal: How Barney Dreyfus Beat Kerr and Auten," *The Sporting News*, March 2, 1901, 4.
104. A.R. Cratty, "Pittsburg Points: Col. Dreyfuss Gains a Month More on Fellow Owners – The Club Attorney Indulges in a Few Sharp Comments," *Sporting Life*, January 26, 1901, 6.
105. "Baseball Magnates Still Have the Stage," *Pittsburg Press*, January 19, 1901, 5.
106. Cratty, "Pittsburg Points: Col. Dreyfuss Gains a Month More on Fellow Owners – The Club Attorney Indulges in a Few Sharp Comments," 6.
107. "Barney Dreyfuss Made Good Here," *Pittsburg Press*, January 19, 1901, 5.
108. Francis Richter, "Dreyfuss Wins Out: Secures Control of Pittsburg through Purchase," *Sporting Life*, February 23, 1901, 8.

Chapter 2
1. "Gets Pay in Dollar Bills: Pulliam Started the Scheme with Waddell and It Is Impossible to Make a Change Now," *Buffalo Enquirer*, October 7, 1905, 8.
2. "Two More 'Rube' Waddell Stories," *Buffalo Evening Times*, January 16, 1915, 9.
3. "Rube Waddell at His Best: Shuts Out the Cincinnati Red Stockings in an Easy Sort of Way," *Pittsburg Post*, April 24, 1900, 6.
4. "First Game a Record Breaker: Crowd the Largest, Start the Worst, Finish Most Exciting," *Pittsburg Press*, April 27, 1900, 5.
5. "Too Much Jones: Pirates Failed to Find the Southpaw Twirler's Delivery," *Pittsburg Press*, May 4, 1900, 5.
6. "Latest Baseball Gossip," *Pittsburg Press*, May 15, 1900, 5.
7. Frank Menke, "Rube Waddell, the Great: A Pitcher with Greatest Arm and Quaintest Brain," *Evening News* (Wilkes-Barre, Pennsylvania), April 19, 1937, 15.
8. "A Battle of Pitchers: Fourteen Inning Contest at Chicago," *Portland Daily Press*, June 20, 1900, 5.
9. "Pirates Lost a Great Game: Scratch Hit Scored Clingman, the Only Run in Fourteen Innings," *Pittsburg Press*, June 20, 1900, 6.
10. Circle, "Pittsburg Points: A Poor Western Trip by the Pirates – The Entire Schedule at St. Louis Spoiled by Rain – The Row over O'Connor – Clarke in Line," *Sporting Life*, June 30, 1900, 3.
11. "Will Attempt to Stop Giants: Pirates Want to Show Visitors Their Real Game To-Day," *Pittsburg Press*, July 6, 1900, 5.
12. "Baseball Chatter," *Pittsburg Post*, July 8, 1900, 6.
13. "Waddell Suspended: Manager Clarke Forced to Punish the Big Lefthander," *Pittsburg Press*, July 7, 1900, 8.
14. Circle, "Pittsburg Points: High-Class Work by the Buccaneers Results in the Development of Enthusiasm – Excellent Financial Returns – Big Rube Suspended," *Sporting Life*, July 14, 1900, 10.

15. "Waddell's Lay-Off: Clarke Angered by Rube's Statement That He Wasn't Properly Supported," *St. Louis Republic*, July 9, 1900, 3.
16. "Waddell Suspended: Big Rube's Fool Tricks Cost Him a Slice of His Salary," *St. Louis Republic*, July 8, 1900, 6.
17. "Waddell Suspended: Manager Clarke Forced to Punish the Big Lefthander," 8.
18. "Waddell's Lay-Off: Clarke Angered by Rube's Statement That He Wasn't Properly Supported," 3.
19. "Waddell Suspended: Big Rube's Fool Tricks Cost Him a Slice of His Salary," 6.
20. "Latest Baseball Gossip," *Pittsburg Press*, July 10, 1900, 5.
21. "Waddell Jumps Pittsburg: Big Twirler Has Signed to Play with Semiprofessionals," *St. Louis Republic*, July 12, 1900, 4.
22. "Baseball Gossip," *Dayton Daily News*, July 24, 1900, 3.
23. Circle, "Pittsburg Points: The Buccaneers Made a Poor Record at Philadelphia – Cooley Sent to the Bench for Light Stick Work – Waddell Still Running around Loose – Bits of Gossip," *Sporting Life*, July 28, 1900, 5.
24. "Williams Badly Lamed: Pittsburg Third Baseman Hurt His Ankle Very Badly," *St. Louis Republic*, July 14, 1900, 4.
25. Connie Mack, "My Fifty Years in Baseball: Installment No. 19," *Salt Lake Tribune*, September 26, 1930, 21.
26. "To Farm Waddell: Milwaukee Said to Have Secured the Big Fellow," *Topeka State Journal*, July 21, 1900, 2.
27. Circle, "Pittsburg Points: Pirates, Though Playing Good Ball, Have Not Been Winning in the East – Ritchey, One of the Cripples, Goes to Work," *Sporting Life*, August 4, 1900, 9.
28. "Eastern Series of the Pirates: Outlook Is for a Very Successful Trip," *Pittsburg Press*, September 4, 1900, 5.
29. "Milwaukee Won Both: Waddell Pitched Twenty-Two Innings for the Brewers," *St. Paul Globe*, August 20, 1900, 5.
30. J.G. Taylor Spink, "Waddell: Madcap Mound Marvel: Rose to Fame under Mack's Kindly Hand," *The Sporting News*, October 9, 1946, 12.
31. Norman L. Macht, *Connie Mack and the Early Years of Baseball* (Lincoln, Neb.: University of Nebraska Press, 2007), 178.
32. Mack, "My Fifty Years in Baseball – Installment No. 19," 21.
33. "Rube Waddell Joins the Pirates Again," *Pittsburg Press*, September 3, 1900, 5.
34. Mack, "My Fifty Years in Baseball – Installment No. 19," 21.
35. "Rube Waddell Joins the Pirates Again," 5.
36. "Baseball Gossip," *Pittsburg Press*, August 5, 1900, 15.
37. Macht, *Connie Mack and the Early Years of Baseball*, 179.
38. Mack, "My Fifty Years in Baseball – Installment No. 19," 21.
39. Macht, *Connie Mack and the Early Years of Baseball*, 179.
40. Mack "My Fifty Years in Baseball – Installment No. 19," 21.
41. "Rube Waddell Joins the Pirates Again," 5.
42. "Eastern Series of the Pirates: Outlook Is for a Very Successful Trip," 5.
43. "The Games Yesterday," *Pittsburg Press*, September 4, 1900, 5.
44. "Fans Were in a Frenzy: Victorious Pittsburg Baseball Players Return from the East, Are Cheered, Feted and Win Another Game," *Pittsburg Post*, September 21, 1900, 1.
45. Ibid, 6.
46. "Neighborhood Notes," *Butler Citizen*, September 27, 1900, 3.
47. "Good Work by Rube Waddell: Strikes Out 12 Chicago Batsmen with Consummate Skill," *Pittsburg Post*, October 12, 1900, 6.
48. "Sporting Notes," *Pittsburg Post*, October 12, 1900, 6.
49. "Brooklyn Scores One for the Trophy," *Plain Speaker*, October 16, 1900, 4.
50. "Pirates Were Outclassed by the Champions," *Pittsburg Press*, October 16, 1900, 5.
51. "The Punch Bowl Goes to Pitcher Joe M'Ginnity," *Pittsburg Press*, October 19, 1900, 5.
52. "Rube Waddell Kicks over Traces," *Pittsburg Press*, December 22, 1900, 5.
53. "He Is One of the Best: Boston Purchases Release of 'Rube' Waddell from Pittsburg," *Boston Daily Globe*, March 29, 1901, 11.

54. "After Pitcher Waddell: Boston the Latest to Ask for the Pittsburg Man," *Topeka Daily Capital*, April 6, 1901, 2.
55. "Owners and Players Agree: Conference between Zimmer and Magnates Result in Peace," *Pittsburg Press*, February 27, 1901, 6.
56. "Notes from the World of Sport," *Hamilton Daily Republican-News*, March 30, 1901, 8.
57. "Two More 'Rube' Waddell Stories," 9.
58. "Clarke Defends Rube Waddell: Bad Weather Affects Eddie as Much as Other Players," *Pittsburg Press*, April 24, 1901, 8.
59. "Final Practice: Pirates Put in a Busy Day at the Pittsburg College Park," *Pittsburg Press*, April 27, 1901, 7.
60. Alan H. Levy, *Rube Waddell: The Zany, Brilliant Life of a Strikeout Artist* (Jefferson, N.C.: McFarland & Company, Inc., 2000), 76.
61. "Rube Waddell Wild and Erratic: Loses the Game to the Chicago Orphans in the First Inning," *Pittsburg Post*, May 2, 1901, 6.
62. Levy, *Rube Waddell: The Zany, Brilliant Life of a Strikeout Artist*, 77.
63. A.R. Cratty, "Pittsburg Points: Clarke's Men Split Even in First At-Home Series – Rube Waddell Sold to the Chicago Club – 'Truck' Egan's Debut – Bits of News," *Sporting Life*, May 11, 1901, 8.
64. Duquesne, "Not Pennant Ball: The Brand the Pirates Have Been Playing," *The Sporting News*, May 11, 1901, 3.
65. "Dreyfuss Traded Waddell for Stogie," *West Virginian*, January 18, 1915, 6.
66. "Daily Recorded," *Evening Record*, June 30, 1900, 4.
67. Cratty, "Pittsburg Points: Clarke's Men Split Even in First At-Home Series – Rube Waddell Sold to the Chicago Club – 'Truck' Egan's Debut – Bits of News," 8.
68. "Ely Saved the Day: His Homer Tied the Score in the Ninth after Two Were Out," *Pittsburg Press*, June 28, 1899, 5.
69. "In the Days When Bones Ely Batted," *Oregon Daily Journal*, January 30, 1904, 9.
70. Duquesne, "Barney Hustled: Had No Time to Talk about Hard Luck," *The Sporting News*, July 6, 1901, 5.
71. A.R. Cratty, "Pittsburg Points: A Rattling Attendance on the Big Holiday – Showers Spoiled a Record-Breaking Turn-Out in the Afternoon – Bits of News," *Sporting Life*, July 13, 1901, 7.
72. A.R. Cratty, "Pittsburg Points: Seven Straight Victories Counted – Phillies Break the Streak in a Fourteen Round Game – A Leader in Fine Form – Bits of News," *Sporting Life*, July 20, 1901, 7.
73. Duquesne, "Wagner at Short: Leach on Third and Ely a Benchwarmer," *The Sporting News*, July 27, 1901, 6.
74. Dennis DeValeria and Jeanne Burke DeValeria, *Honus Wagner: A Biography* (New York: Henry Holt and Company, Inc., 1995), 94.
75. "Ely Released, Doheny Signed: Pittsburg Club Parted with Its Veteran Short Stop," *Pittsburg Press*, July 26, 1901, 8.
76. "Short Stop Ely Gets His Release: His Services Are No Longer Needed by the Pittsburg Ball Club," *Pittsburg Post*, July 26, 1901, 6.
77. "Ely Makes a Roar," *St. Louis Globe-Democrat*, July 27, 1901, 7.
78. "Pittsburg Comes To-Day: Powell Will Pitch First Game – Sudhoff Not Traded Off," *St. Louis Republic*, July 26, 1901, 4.
79. "Manager Clarke Tells Why Ely Was Released," *Pittsburg Press*, July 28, 1901, 17.
80. "The Pittsburg Players Are Indignant over Fred Ely's Statements: Pirates Angry over Ely's Slurs," *Pittsburg Press*, July 28, 1901, 17.
81. "Baseball Notes," *Brooklyn Citizen*, August 2, 1901, 3.
82. "The Pittsburg Players Are Indignant over Fred Ely's Statements: Pirates Angry over Ely's Slurs," 17.
83. "Ely Signs with Mack: Will Play First Game in American League Tomorrow," *Evening Star*, July 30, 1901, 9.
84. A.R. Cratty, "Pittsburg Points: Stir Caused by Release of Fred Ely," *Sporting Life*, August 3, 1901, 8.
85. "More Trouble for Bob Emslie: Ended Exciting Game by Saying Clarke Didn't Steal Second," *Pittsburg Press*, July 20, 1901, 3.
86. "Clarke Makes Vicious Attack on Bob Emslie," *Philadelphia Inquirer*, July 20, 1901, 6.
87. "More Trouble for Bob Emslie: Ended Exciting Game by Saying Clarke Didn't Steal Second," 3.

88. "Clarke Makes Vicious Attack on Bob Emslie," 6.
89. Cratty, "Pittsburg Points: Stir Caused by the Release of Fred Ely," 8.
90. Duquesne, "American's Agent: Charge of Disloyalty Made against Ely," *The Sporting News*, August 3, 1901, 4.
91. A.R. Cratty, "Pittsburg Points: Air Full of Rumors of a New American League Team," *Sporting Life*, August 10, 1901, 1.
92. Duquesne, "Critical Stage: Pirates May Lose the Lead in Pennant Race," *The Sporting News*, August 10, 1901, 5.
93. "Luck in Baseball: Fred Clarke, Captain-Manager of Pittsburg Pirates, Relates Experiences," *Buffalo Commercial*, August 23, 1905, 6.
94. "How Hans Broke Into the Game: Fred Clarke Tells an Interesting Story," *Evening Free Press*, September 16, 1911, 3.
95. "Captain Kerr Sent for Hough: Baseball Secrets of Last Summer Exposed by Johnson," *Pittsburg Press*, November 30, 1901, 8.

Chapter 3
1. Al Abrams, "Baseball's Stormy Days Are Recalled by Barney Dreyfuss: Local Club Owner Tells of Early Activities of Late Ban Johnson Here; How 'Raids' on Pirate Players Were Staved Off," *Pittsburgh Post-Gazette*, April 18, 1931, 14.
2. A.R. Cratty, "Pittsburg Points: Air Full of Rumors of a New American League Team," *Sporting Life*, August 10, 1901, 1.
3. Duquesne, "Critical Stage: Pirates May Lose the Lead in Pennant Race," *The Sporting News*, August 10, 1901, 5.
4. Francis C. Richter, "Dreyfuss' Doings: The Astute Pittsburg Man Not Caught Napping," *Sporting Life*, August 17, 1901, 6.
5. "Sporting Brevities," *Sunday Tribune*, August 4, 1901, 6.
6. "Jack O'Connor Suspended," *St. Louis Globe-Democrat*, July 2, 1891, 9.
7. "A Columbus Shake-Up: Jack O'Connor Suspended and Several other Players on the List," *Pittsburg Dispatch*, July 2, 1891, 6.
8. "Rough House at Mound City: Catcher Jack O'Connor Knocked Out by Pitcher Murphy," *Pittsburg Press*, July 27, 1901, 3.
9. "Baseball Gossip," *Pittsburg Press*, April 21, 1902, 16.
10. Circle, "Pittsburg Points: Base Ball Men in the Smoky City Enjoy a Rest – Eagerness to Hear of the Special Committee's Doings," *Sporting Life*, December 30, 1899, 11.
11. Ronald T. Waldo, *Fred Clarke: A Biography of the Baseball Hall of Fame Player-Manager* (Jefferson, N.C.: McFarland & Company, Inc., 2011), 52.
12. "Gossip of the Players," *The Sporting News*, December 29, 1900, 2.
13. A.R. Cratty, "Pittsburg Points: Several Champions Playing Better Than Was Their Wont – New Developments in the Desertion Cases – Bits of News," *Sporting Life*, September 13, 1902, 2.
14. Duquesne, "American's Agent: Charge of Disloyalty Made against Ely," *The Sporting News*, August 3, 1901, 4.
15. "Your Old-Timer Dislikes Youngsters," *San Antonio Gazette*, August 4, 1906, 13.
16. Duquesne, "Saved His Stars: Dreyfus Gives List of His 1903 Players," *The Sporting News*, October 11, 1902, 5.
17. Duquesne, "Superb Southpaw: But Tannehill Is in Bad in Pittsburg," *The Sporting News*, September 20, 1902, 6.
18. "Pirates Say Story Is False: O'Connor and Wagner Deny That They Have Jumped to Outlaws," *Pittsburg Press*, June 12, 1902, 12.
19. "Agents of Big Leagues on a Still Hunt for Players: Operations in This Line Are Beginning Unusually Early This Season – Dreyfuss Will Be Hard-Pressed to Keep His Champion Team from Being Wrecked," *St. Louis Republic*, August 24, 1902, 5.
20. "Wagner Rejects Fortune: Star Turns Down Double the Amount That O'Connor Receives for Becoming a Traitor," *Pittsburg Press*, August 21, 1902, 10.
21. "Heavy Rain at Cincinnati: Pirate-Red Half-Holiday Game declared Off at Three O'Clock," *Pittsburg Press*, June 29, 1902, 22.

22. "The Attempted Raid: President Dreyfuss Uncovers a Plot of American Leaguers and Suspends Catcher O'Connor as an Accomplice," *Sporting Life*, August 30, 1902, 4.
23. "Agents of Big Leagues on a Still Hunt for Players: Operations in This Line Are Beginning Unusually Early This Season – Dreyfuss Will Be Hard-Pressed to Keep His Champion Team from Being Wrecked," 5.
24. "Chesbro Receives Big Offer," *North Adams Transcript*, August 20, 1902, 2.
25. "Baseball Notes," *Daily Kennebec Journal*, August 21, 1902, 3.
26. Abrams, "Baseball's Stormy Days Are Recalled by Barney Dreyfuss: Local Club Owner Tells of Early Activities of Late Ban Johnson Here; How 'Raids' on Pirate Players Were Staved Off," 16.
27. "Wagner Rejects Fortune: Star Turns Down Double the Amount that O'Connor Receives for Becoming a Traitor," 10.
28. Abrams, "Baseball's Stormy Days Are Recalled by Barney Dreyfuss: Local Club Owner Tells of Early Activities of Late Ban Johnson Here; How 'Raids' on Pirate Players Were Staved Off," 14.
29. "Pirates Enjoyed Day with Friends at Shore," *Pittsburg Press*, August 16, 1902, 8.
30. "Not a Pirate Was Captured by the Enemy: President Dreyfuss Rescued All Prominent Pirates from Clutches of American League Agents," *Pittsburg Press*, August 16, 1902, 8.
31. "Jesse Tannehill Made Confession: While Under the Influence of Ether He Revealed American League Plot to Barney Dreyfuss," *Pittsburg Press*, November 22, 1902, 10.
32. Abrams, "Baseball's Stormy Days Are Recalled by Barney Dreyfuss: Local Club Owner Tells of Early Activities of Late Ban Johnson Here; How 'Raids' on Pirate Players Were Staved Off," 14 and 16.
33. "Comments of the Day in Realm of the Rooter," *Pittsburg Press*, August 19, 1902, 10.
34. "National League: How They Stand," *The Sporting News*, August 30, 1902, 2.
35. Abrams, "Baseball's Stormy Days Are Recalled by Barney Dreyfuss: Local Club Owner Tells of Early Activities of Late Ban Johnson Here; How 'Raids' on Pirate Players Were Staved Off," 16.
36. A.R. Cratty, "Pittsburg Points: Still Sneak by Johnson and Somers Awakens the Monotony in Pittsburg – O'Connor's Case Reviewed – Bits of News," *Sporting Life*, August 30, 1902, 4.
37. "Wagner Rejects Fortune: Star Turns Down Double the Amount that O'Connor Receives for Becoming a Traitor," 10.
38. "Dreyfuss Exposes Plot: Describes Secret Mission of Somers and Johnson to Pittsburg – Suspends O'Connor for Aiding Them," *Boston Daily Globe*, August 21, 1902, 3.
39. "Wagner Rejects Fortune: Star Turns Down Double the Amount that O'Connor Receives for Becoming a Traitor," 10.
40. "Baseball Gossip," *Pittsburg Press*, August 21, 1902, 10.
41. Abrams, "Baseball's Stormy Days Are Recalled by Barney Dreyfuss: Local Club Owner Tells of Early Activities of Late Ban Johnson Here; How 'Raids' on Pirate Players Were Staved Off," 16.
42. "Wagner Rejects Fortune: Star Turns Down Double the Amount that O'Connor Receives for Becoming a Traitor," 10.
43. Abrams, "Baseball's Stormy Days Are Recalled by Barney Dreyfuss: Local Club Owner Tells of Early Activities of Late Ban Johnson Here; How 'Raids' on Pirate Players Were Staved Off," 16.
44. "Comments of the Day in Realm of the Rooter," *Pittsburg Press*, September 25, 1902, 12.
45. "A Great Grab for Players: Agents Here to Take Up Job at Which Ban Johnson Failed," *Pittsburg Press*, August 28, 1902, 10.
46. A.R. Cratty, "Pittsburg Points: Americans' Raid Seems to be More Than a Pipe Dream," *Sporting Life*, September 6, 1902, 4.
47. Abrams, "Baseball's Stormy Days Are Recalled by Barney Dreyfuss: Local Club Owner Tells of Early Activities of Late Ban Johnson Here; How 'Raids' on Pirate Players Were Staved Off," 16.
48. Cratty, "Pittsburg Points: Americans' Raid Seems to be More Than a Pipe Dream," 4.
49. Duquesne, "Revenge on Mack: Dreyfus' Motive in Signing Burke and Conroy," *The Sporting News*, September 6, 1902, 5.
50. "Planning to Place Team to Oppose the Pirates," *Syracuse Post Standard*, August 24, 1902, 3.
51. "O'Connor Is Released: Dreyfus Turns Him Loose on Learning He Is an American League Agent," *Decatur Herald*, August 23, 1902, 1.
52. "American League Carries War into Pirate's Camp: Jack O'Connor Released; Wagner May Join Browns," *St. Louis Republic*, August 22, 1902, 7.
53. "Baseball Gossip," *Pittsburg Press*, August 22, 1902, 12.

54. "The Accused Retort: Johnson and Somers Admit Their Attempted Raid and Hint at Pittsburg Invasion – O'Connor Enters Denial," *Sporting Life*, August 30, 1902, 4.
55. "No Defense for Jack O'Connor: Player Criticized and Magnate Commended All over the Circuit," *Pittsburg Press*, August 23, 1902, 8.
56. "O'Connor Deserves Sentence: Dreyfuss Commended for Having Courage to Punish the Offender," *Pittsburg Press*, August 24, 1902, 16.
57. "American League Carries War into Pirate's Camp: Jack O'Connor Released; Wagner May Join Browns," 7.
58. "Dreyfuss Has Signed an American Leaguer: Declares that He Has Gone Into the Camp of the Enemy for a Right Fielder," *Buffalo Evening Times*, August 23, 1902, 6.
59. "Brooklyns Took It Easy: Hanlon's Men Enjoyed a Much Needed Rest at Atlantic City," *Brooklyn Daily Times*, August 27, 1902, 6.
60. "Sporting News: National League Heavily Raided by Americans – Some of the Best Pittsburg Players Are Lost," *Topeka State Journal*, September 2, 1902, 2.
61. "Base Ball Notes," *Evening Star*, September 12, 1902, 10.
62. "Strong Team Is Signed for Next Season: President Dreyfuss Announces That Stars of Present Club Will Stay," *Pittsburg Press*, October 5, 1902, 19.
63. "Diamond Gossip," *Washington Times*, August 23, 1902, 4.
64. "Lefty Davis Will Play No More Games This Season = = Has Broken Ankle: Champions Hit the Ball," *Pittsburg Post*, July 12, 1902, 8.
65. "Lefty Davis Let Go by the Club and Jesse Tannehill May Soon Follow: Lefty Davis Is Released," *Pittsburg Post*, September 24, 1902, 8.
66. Cratty, "Pittsburgh Points: Several Champions Playing Better Than Was Their Wont – New Developments in the Desertion Cases – Bits of News," 2.
67. Cratty, "Pittsburg Points: Americans' Raid Seems to Be More than a Pipe Dream," 4.
68. "'Lefty' Davis Released," *Scranton Republican*, September 6, 1902, 10.
69. "Lefty Davis Released: Pittsburg Club Tells Outfielder to Look for Another Job," *Minneapolis Journal*, September 3, 1902, 24.
70. A. R. Cratty, "Champion Chaff: Latest Reports As to Prospective Sliders – Good Youngsters Caught in Recent Baitings – Exhibition Games Next Week – Bits of News," *Sporting Life*, September 20, 1902, 3.
71. "Lefty Davis Let Go by the Club and Jesse Tannehill May Soon Follow: Lefty Davis Is Released," 8.
72. "Davis Released, Tannehill Held," *Pittsburg Press*, September 24, 1902, 12.
73. "Lefty Davis Released: Pittsburg Club Tells Outfielder to Look for Another Job," 24.
74. Ibid.
75. Cratty, "Pittsburg Points: Several Champions Playing Better Than Was Their Wont – New Developments in the Desertion Cases – Bits of News," 2.
76. Duquesne, "Superb Southpaw: But Tannehill is in Bad in Pittsburg," 6.
77. "Tannehill and Chesbro Want the Small Sum of $17,000 for Two Years' Service: Champions Take a Rest," *Pittsburg Post*, September 10, 1902, 8.
78. "Base Ball News: Pitchers Want $17,000 for Two Years Work," *Waterbury Evening Democrat*, September 10, 1902, 7.
79. "Dickering for Grounds: American Syndicate Scheming for a Park in New York," *Pittsburg Press*, September 10, 1902, 12.
80. Duquesne, "Great Advantage: Dreyfus Has Best Pittsburg Parks under Lease," *The Sporting News*, September 13, 1902, 6.
81. "Make Hay While Sun Shines: Big League Ball Players Realize Their Opportunity and Make Enormous Demands in Some Cases – Sporting Gossip," *Butte Inter Mountain*, September 26, 1902, 7.
82. "Final Series of Season: Browns Will Make Last Stand against Chicago Team To-Day," *St. Louis Republic*, September 26, 1902, 7.
83. "Sporting Gossip: Doubts His 'Sportsmanship,'" *Buffalo Enquirer*, October 1, 1902, 4.
84. "Baseball Gossip," *Pittsburg Press*, August 23, 1902, 8.
85. Duquesne, "Hart Protested: Objects to Pirates Playing at Comiskey's Park," *The Sporting News*, October 4, 1902, 4.
86. "Strong Team Is Signed for Next Season: President Dreyfuss Announces That Stars of Present Club Will Stay," 12.

87. "Jesse Tannehill Released: Pittsburg's Star Pitcher Goes to the American League," *Scranton Republican*, October 11, 1902, 10.
88. "Strong Team Is Signed for Next Season: President Dreyfuss Announces That Stars of Present Club Will Stay," 12.
89. Duquesne, "Saved His Stars: Dreyfuss Gives List of His 1903 Players," 5.
90. "Baseball Gossip," *Pittsburg Press*, October 17, 1902, 24.
91. "Pirates' Pitcher Asks $17,000," *Boston Post*, September 10, 1902, 3.
92. Abrams, "Baseball's Stormy Days Are Recalled by Barney Dreyfuss: Local Club Owner Tells of Early Activities of Late Ban Johnson Here; How 'Raids' on Pirate Players Were Staved Off," 16.
93. Cratty, "Pittsburg Points: Americans' Raid Seems to be More Than a Pipe Dream," 4.
94. "Chesbro Bothers Dreyfuss," *St. Paul Globe*, October 9, 1902, 5.
95. A.R. Cratty, "Pittsburg Points: Incidents of the Series between the Champions and the All-Americans – Why Chesbro and Tannehill Were Not Used by the Pirates," *Sporting Life*, October 18, 1902, 7.
96. Hotspur ed., "Baseball War Bitter as Ever: Announcement That More of the National League Champions Will Play in New York This Year Has Raised Ructions in the Older Organization – Time to Call a Halt or Baseball Will Soon Be a Dead Issue – The Situation Reviewed," *Buffalo Enquirer*, October 27, 1902, 8.
97. A.R. Cratty, "Pittsburg Points: Champions Sure to Scoop in Century of Games – Sebring Keeps Up His Neat Work – Bits of News and Gossip," *Sporting Life*, September 27, 1902, 3.
98. Cratty, "Pittsburg Points: Incidents of the Series Between the Champions and the All-Americans – Why Chesbro and Tannehill Were Not Used by the Pirates," 7.
99. "Comments of the Day in Realm of the Rooter," *Pittsburg Press*, October 11, 1902, 12.
100. Cratty, "Pittsburg Points: Incidents of the Series Between the Champions and the All-Americans – Why Chesbro and Tannehill Were Not Used by the Pirates," 7.
101. "Sporting News: King of Pitchers Bounced by His Fellow Players – Jack Chesbro Notified That He Can Be Excused," *Topeka State Journal*, October 11, 1902, 2.
102. "Comments of the Day in the Realm of the Rooter," October 11, 1902, 12.
103. "Sporting News: King of Pitchers Bounced by His Fellow Players – Jack Chesbro Notified That He Can Be Excused," 2.
104. "Baseball Gossip," *Sunday State Journal*, November 2, 1902, 20.
105. Cratty, "Pittsburg Points: Still Sneak by Johnson and Somers Awakens the Monotony in Pittsburg – O'Connor's Case Reviewed – Bits of News," 4.

Chapter 4
1. Duquesne, "Beat the Pirates: Wallace's Great Fielding and Fine Batting," *The Sporting News*, October 18, 1902, 4.
2. "Comments of the Day in Realm of the Rooter," *Pittsburg Press*, November 3, 1902, 10.
3. Hotspur ed., "Baseball War Bitter as Ever: Announcement that More of the National League Champions Will Play in New York This Year Has Raised Ructions in the Older Organization – Time to Call a Halt or Baseball Will Soon Be a Dead Issue – The Situation Reviewed," *Buffalo Enquirer*, October 27, 1902, 8.
4. "Hot Shot from Barney Dreyfuss: Pittsburg Baseball Magnate Pays His Respects to Mr. Johnson-Leach Case," *Butte Inter Mountain*, November 17, 1902, 8.
5. Duquesne, "Traced to Somers: Advance Money Leach Secured from Johnson," *The Sporting News*, November 15, 1902, 2.
6. "O'Connor Says Was No Traitor: Ex-Pirate Tells of His Part in American League Deal," *Pittsburg Gazette*, November 16, 1902, 3.
7. Al Abrams, "Baseball's Stormy Days Are Recalled by Barney Dreyfuss: Local Club Owner Tells of Early Activities of Late Ban Johnson Here; How 'Raids' on Pirate Players Were Staved Off," *Pittsburgh Post-Gazette*, April 18, 1931, 16.
8. Arthur D. Hittner, *Honus Wagner: The Life of Baseball's "Flying Dutchman"* (Jefferson, N.C.: McFarland & Company, Inc., 1996), 93.
9. "Comments of the Day in Realm of the Rooter," *Pittsburg Press*, August 27, 1902, 10.
10. "Even Break at Beantown: Jack Chesbro's Delivery Was Soaked Hard in First Game," *Pittsburg Press*, August 14, 1902, 8.

11. "Johnson, Tempter: American League President Said to Have Gone in Person to Worcester to Take Bransfield from Pittsburg," *Sporting Life*, September 6, 1902, 6.
12. Abrams, "Baseball's Stormy Days Are Recalled by Barney Dreyfuss: Local Club Owner Tells of Early Activities of Late Ban Johnson Here; How 'Raids' on Pirate Players Were Staved Off," 16.
13. Francis C. Richter, "Settlement Secured; Peace Proclaimed!: The Popular Double League System Scores a Splendid Triumph," *Sporting Life*, January 17, 1903, 4.
14. "Harmony Prevails in League: By Unanimous Vote the Magnates Adopt Peace Agreement," *Pittsburg Press*, January 22, 1903, 12.
15. "Jack O'Connor Suspended," *Pittsburg Post*, August 22, 1903, 3.
16. "Jack O'Connor Suspended," *Daily Review*, August 24, 1903, 3.
17. "Under Care of Two Physicians: Fred Clarke Manager of the Pittsburg Champions is a Very Sick Man," *Boston Daily Globe*, July 18, 1904, 5.
18. A.R. Cratty, "Pittsburg Points: Champions Arouse Enthusiasm by Beating the Leaders in Many Combats – Stirring Events Which Bring Money into the Pockets of the Old League Owners," *Sporting Life*, August 27, 1904, 4.
19. A.R. Cratty, "Pittsburg Points: Review of the Series with the Cleveland Club," *Sporting Life*, October 29, 1904, 8.
20. Ralph S. Davis, "Helps the Hitting: Best Suggestion Is to Amend Strike Rule," *The Sporting News*, October 22, 1904, 1.
21. "Late News from All Points: Leach the Leader – In Temporary Command of League Champions," *Sporting Life*, July 23, 1904, 3.
22. "Bucky Veil Taken Suddenly Ill," *Altoona Mirror*, April 15, 1904, 1.
23. "Pittsburg Pirates Release Thompson and Sign Lowe: Phillippe on the Rubber," *Pittsburg Post*, April 15, 1904, 8.
24. Fred W. Veil, *Bucky: A Story of Baseball in the Deadball Era* (Tucson, Ariz.: Wheatmark, 2013), 206-207.
25. "Sebring Denies Deserting: Said He Was Told to Go with Team on Trip or Quit," *Harrisburg Star Independent*, August 4, 1904, 7.
26. Veil, *Bucky: A Story of Baseball in the Deadball Era*, 207-208.
27. "Pittsburg Club Releases Pitchers Veil and Pfeister: Off Day for the Pirates," *Pittsburg Post*, April 26, 1904, 8.
28. A.R. Cratty, "Pittsburg Points: The Premiers' Start This Season Is Not Studded with Brilliancy – Bad Weather and Defeats Seem to Come with Regularity – A Record-Breaking Idle Spell – Bits of News and Gossip," *Sporting Life*, May 7, 1904, 4-5.
29. "Dissensions Hurt Pirates' Chances: Personal Enmities Caused Sebring to Desert," *Washington Times*, August 4, 1904, 8.
30. "Lefty Davis Has Been Forgotten: Jimmy Sebring's Spectacular Performance Makes the Record of His Predecessor Appear Obscure," *Pittsburg Press*, April 24, 1903, 18.
31. "Champs Wallop Boston: Phillippe Had American League Champions under His Thumb, Making Ten of Them Fan the Air Yesterday," *Pittsburg Press*, October 2, 1903, 20.
32. A.R. Cratty, "Pittsburg Points: Notwithstanding Record-Breaking Spell of Misfortune Champs Are Winning Games – Diehl, Cassaday and McCormick Fill Up the Breaches – Phillippi and Phelps Return to Duty – Clarke Is Able to Be Out," *Sporting Life*, August 20, 1904, 3.
33. "Has Sebring Deserted?," *Topeka State Journal*, August 5, 1904, 2.
34. A.R. Cratty, "Pittsburgh Points: Pirate's Spring Tour a Treat to Old-Timers," *Sporting Life*, March 10, 1906, 6.
35. Hittner, *Honus Wagner: The Life of Baseball's "Flying Dutchman,"* 131.
36. Chuck Kimberly, *The Days of Rube, Matty, Honus and Ty: Scenes from the Early Deadball Era, 1904-1907* (Jefferson, N.C.: McFarland & Company, Inc.), 35-36.
37. Hittner, *Honus Wagner: The Life of Baseball's "Flying Dutchman,"* 131-132.
38. A.R. Cratty, "Pittsburg Points: Rumor Starting Easy in Base Ball World Nowadays," *Sporting Life*, December 2, 1905, 6.
39. Hittner, *Honus Wagner: The Life of Baseball's "Flying Dutchman,"* 132.
40. "Dissensions Hurt Pirates' Chances: Personal Enmities Caused Sebring to Desert," 8.
41. Hotspur, "What Our Typewriter Says: Sebring Badly Treated," *Buffalo Enquirer*, August 5, 1904, 8.

42. Cratty, "Pittsburg Points: Notwithstanding Record-Breaking Spell of Misfortune Champs Are Winning Games – Diehl, Cassaday and McCormick Fill Up the Breaches – Phillippi and Phelps Return to Duty – Clarke Is Able to Be Out," 3.
43. Hotspur, "What Our Typewriter Says: Sebring Badly Treated," 8.
44. "Base Hits," *Altoona Times*, June 9, 1904, 2.
45. "Jimmy Sebring Now a Cripple: Will Be Out of the Game for Some Time and Ernie Diehl Slated for Right Field," *Pittsburg Post*, August 1, 1904, 6.
46. Cratty, "Pittsburg Points: Rumor Starting Easy in Base Ball World Nowadays," 6.
47. Hotspur, "What Our Typewriter Says: Sebring Badly Treated," 8.
48. "Sebring's Side of the Story: Pittsburg Player Denies that He Has Jumped Team – Says Dreyfuss Told Him to Quit," *Boston Daily Globe*, August 9, 1904, 3.
49. Hotspur, "What Our Typewriter Says: Sebring Badly Treated," 8.
50. "Sebring's Side of the Story: Pittsburg Player Denies that He Has Jumped Team – Says Dreyfuss Told Him to Quit," 3.
51. "Sebring's Slide: For His Happy Home in Williamsport, PA.," *Sporting Life*, August 13, 1904, 3.
52. "Sebring's Side of the Story: Pittsburg Player Denies That He Has Jumped Team – Says Dreyfuss Told Him to Quit," 3.
53. "Dissensions Hurt Pirates' Chances: Personal Enmities Caused Sebring to Desert," 8.
54. "Jim Sebring at Altoona: Declares He Has Left the Pittsburg Club for Good – Charges Unfair Treatment," *Pittsburg Post*, August 3, 1904, 6.
55. "Sebring's Side of Spat Trouble: Claims That He Has Not Jumped Pittsburg, but Is Laid Up with a Bad Ankle," *Wilkes-Barre Leader*, August 5, 1904, 9.
56. "Triple Deal Made in the National: Donlin, Sebring, and McCormick Change Places," *Washington Times*, August 5, 1904, 8.
57. "Jim Sebring Will Report: Notifies President Dreyfuss He Is Ready to Join the Team at Philadelphia," *Pittsburg Post*, August 5, 1904, 6.
58. "Tommy Leach Expects to Be in the Game at Philadelphia To=Day: New Blood in the Game," *Pittsburg Post*, August 8, 1904, 6.
59. "A Triangular Deal: Sebring, McCormick and Donlin Changes Teams," *Wilkes-Barre Leader*, August 9, 1904, 10.
60. "Tommy Leach Expects to Be in the Game at Philadelphia To=Day: New Blood in the Game," 6.
61. "Sebring May Play with Minors," *Wilkes-Barre Leader*, August 9, 1904, 10.
62. "Phil Comes Home Talks about Team: Says Boys Are Playing Wonderful Baseball and under Great Difficulties – Sebring Has Apologized," *Pittsburg Press*, August 19, 1904, 12.
63. "The Benefit of Change: Ball Players Who Have Been Made Stars by Transfer to New Club," *Houston Post*, December 25, 1910, 17.
64. Ralph S. Davis, "Roasted Wagner: Cheap Gamblers Get after Pirates' Star Player," *The Sporting News*, May 7, 1904, 2.
65. "Splinters of Sport," *Decatur Herald*, May 31, 1904, 8.
66. Ralph S. Davis, "Pirates Chance: Play at Home Almost All of July," *The Sporting News*, June 18, 1904, 3.
67. A.R. Cratty, "Pittsburg Points: Easier Sailing for Champions on Balance of Eastern Trip," *Sporting Life*, June 18, 1904, 4.
68. "Jones' Curves Pie for Pirates: Batted the Ball All over the Lot, Clarke and Bransfield Had a Lively Tilt on Field," *Pittsburgh Gazette*, June 5, 1904, 2.
69. "Pittsburg's Troubles: Looking for a First Baseman and Pitchers Laid Up," *Philadelphia Inquirer*, June 24, 1904, 10.
70. "Dissension in Pittsburg Team: Manager Clarke and 'Kitty' Bransfield Said to Be at Outs," *Minneapolis Journal*, June 1, 1904, 14.
71. Ralph S. Davis, "Bets on His Team: Dreyfuss Thinks Pittsburg Has a Chance," *The Sporting News*, June 11, 1904, 1.
72. A.R. Cratty, "Pittsburgh Points: Champions Run into a Snag in the Series with the Cardinals – Flaherty Downs Them Twice in Hot Contests – Scanlon Given His Release – Mike Lynch's Nice Pitching, Etc.," *Sporting Life*, July 2, 1904, 5.

73. A.R. Cratty, "Pittsburg Points: Champs Fail to Start Well on the First Eastern Trip – Nine Having Poor Breaks – One Game Blamed on Umpire Johnstone – Wyatt Lee Was a Flat Failure – Scanlon Still on Pay Roll," *Sporting Life*, June 11, 1904, 5.
74. Hotspur, "What Our Typewriter Says: Cheap Bettors Worry Ballplayers," *Buffalo Enquirer*, June 25, 1904, 8.
75. "Pittsburg Pirates Thrown ...... Violently Out of the Bus: Bransfield and Miller Get Painful Injury and Are Unable to Play – Players Take the Accident Good Naturedly and Crack a Few Jokes," *Pittsburg Post*, August 9, 1904, 6.
76. Cratty, "Pittsburg Points: Notwithstanding Record-Breaking Spell of Misfortune Champs Are Winning Games – Diehl, Cassaday and McCormick Fill Up the Breaches – Phillippi and Phelps Return to Duty – Clarke is Able to Be Out," 3.
77. "Baseball Is Experiencing a Very Dull Autumn Session: Pirates Will Not Change," *St. Louis Republic*, October 30, 1904, 1.
78. "Pirates' Infield Broken Up," *Evening Star*, October 31, 1904, 15.
79. Ralph S. Davis, "M'Bride at Short: Wagner May Play First for Pirates," *The Sporting News*, November 5, 1904, 1.
80. "Manager Fred Clarke Has All the Say, Says President Barney Dreyfuss: Echoes of the Meeting," *Pittsburg Post*, December 16, 1904, 8.
81. "Ball Magnates Off for Meeting: Clarke Has Plans for Getting a Faster Team for Pittsburg – Bransfield Not to Play with Locals," *Pittsburg Press*, December 12, 1904, 10.
82. "Two New Players for the Pittsburgs: Catcher Peitz and Outfielder Howard Added to the Pirate Ranks," *Pittsburg Post*, December 15, 1904, 10.
83. Ralph S. Davis, "Dreyfuss' Plans: All the Pittsburg Regulars to be Retained," *The Sporting News*, October 29, 1904, 5.
84. "Sam Leever Gets Three Safe Hits in the Game against Boston: Pirates Win a Slow Game," *Pittsburg Post*, July 12, 1904, 8.
85. "Phelps Knocked Senseless: Pittsburgh's Premier Catcher May Be Out of the Game for Some Weeks in Consequence," *Pittsburg Post*, July 12, 1904, 8.
86. "Fans Looking for More Surprises: Think the Prolonged Stay of the Local Baseball Magnates in the East Is Significant," *Pittsburg Press*, December 16, 1904, 24.
87. "Two New Players for the Pittsburgs: Catcher Peitz and Outfielder Howard Added to the Pirate Ranks," 10.
88. "Fans Are Pleased with the Deals: Think Fred Clarke Showed Wisdom in Trading Players – Pirates Made Much Stronger," *Pittsburg Press*, December 15, 1904, 14.
89. "Clarke to Get Another Man: He Declares Trade with the Phillies Was for Two Men," *Pittsburg Press*, December 18, 1904, 18.
90. "Manager Fred Clarke Has All the Say, Says President Barney Dreyfuss: Echoes of the Meeting," 8.
91. "Gamblers at the Ball Game: One Man Fainted When He Realized His Wager Was Lost," *Pittsburg Press*, June 19, 1905, 10.
92. Cratty, "Pittsburg Points: Rumor Starting Easy in Base Ball World Nowadays," 6.
93. A.R. Cratty, "Pittsburg Points: B.B. Johnson's Clever Moves for His Union," *Sporting Life*, December 9, 1905, 8.
94. A.R. Cratty, "Pittsburg Points: Waste of Base Balls Runs Up into Many Dollars," *Sporting Life*, February 24, 1906, 6.
95. "A Double=Header at Beantown on Monday – Yesterday's Game Was Postponed on Account of Rain, Which May Also Prevent Today's Exhibition by the Pirates at Providence," *Pittsburg Press*, September 23, 1906, 18.
96. A.R. Cratty, "Pittsburg Points: Lack of Sportsmanship of Minor Magnates," *Sporting Life*, October 6, 1906, 10.
97. W. Lee M'Ilwain, "New Ball Players for Pirate Team: Abbatticchio Comes to Pittsburg in Exchange for Local Man," *Pittsburgh Post*, December 12, 1906, 10.
98. A.R. Cratty, "Pittsburg Points: Steel City Delegation Pleased with Dovey's Showing," *Sporting Life*, December 29, 1906, 9.
99. "Big Salary for Clarke: Will Be the Highest Salaried Manager in the Business Next Season," *Pittsburg Press*, December 12, 1906, 14.

100. "Fred Clarke May Not Play: Pirate Leader Is Likely to Manage Team from the Bench," *Pittsburg Press*, December 13, 1906, 14.
101. "Big Salary for Clarke: Will Be the Highest Salaried Manager in the Business Next Season," 14.
102. Cratty, "Pittsburg Points: Steel City Delegation Pleased with Dovey's Showing," 9.
103. "Sporting Gossip from Local Viewpoint: The Passing of Claude Ritchey," *Buffalo Enquirer*, December 18, 1906, 8.
104. "Phillippe Signs a Local Contract: Veteran Twirler Is First Pittsburg Player to Get into Line for Next Season," *Pittsburg Press*, January 6, 1907, 18.
105. J.C. Morse, "Ritchey Glad to Leave Here: Claude Says He Asked Barney Dreyfuss Last Year to Trade Him to Boston if Dovey Got Team," *Pittsburg Press*, March 21, 1907, 18.
106. "Ritchey Was Well Treated: Local Fans Object to the Insinuations of Former Pirate That He Was Unjustly Criticised by the Fans Here," *Pittsburg Press*, March 25, 1907, 8.
107. Cratty, "Pittsburg Points: Steel City Delegation Pleased with Dovey's Showing," 9.
108. "Baseball Notes," *Boston Daily Globe*, June 4, 1907, 5.
109. "Base Ball Notes," *Evening Star*, April 23, 1907, 9.

Chapter 5

1. "Big Salary for Clarke: Will Be the Highest Salaried Manager in the Business Next Season," *Pittsburg Press*, December 12, 1906, 14.
2. W. Lee M'Ilwain, "New Players for Pirate Team: Abbattichio Comes to Pittsburgh in Exchange for Local Man," *Pittsburgh Post*, December 12, 1906, 10.
3. "Big Salary for Clarke: Will Be the Highest Salaried Manager in the Business Next Season," 14.
4. "Beaumont Goes to Boston Town: Pittsburgh's Famous Outfielder Gets Release and Agrees to Play," *Pittsburgh Post*, March 1, 1907, 8.
5. L.M. Cadison, "Dreyfuss Planning to Form a Stronger Club: Manager Clark Will Probably Retain Leadership of Pirates, Heavy Betting on Championship Series – Baltimore Wants to Join National League," *Pittsburg Press*, October 8, 1905, 21.
6. "Baseball Nuggets," *Pittsburg Press*, December 11, 1905, 16.
7. "Gossip for the Rooters," *York Dispatch*, December 21, 1905, 11.
8. "Clune Would Like to Be Pirates' Trainer: Declares That When He Saw Some of the Local Baseball Players Last Summer They Appeared to Be Very Stale," *Pittsburg Press*, December 12, 1905, 18.
9. "Beaumont Will Join Team Soon: Dr. Parker Tells 'Ginger's' Old Friends at Beloit That 'Beau' Can Play with Pirates after June 3," *Pittsburg Press*, May 24, 1906, 14.
10. "Gamblers Injuring Game in Pittsburg," *Los Angeles Express*, November 3, 1909, 17.
11. Ralph S. Davis, "Prophets Go Wrong: Dire Calamities Predicted to Deluge Pittsburg Team Have Not Appeared," *Pittsburg Press*, June 23, 1907, 19.
12. A.R. Cratty, "In Pittsburg: Southern Slab Stars Picked by a Posted Patron," *Sporting Life*, August 3, 1907, 4.
13. Ibid.
14. "Comments on the Game," *Evening Star*, June 22, 1907, 9.
15. Cratty, "In Pittsburg: Southern Slab Stars Picked by a Posted Patron," 4.
16. "Clymer Glad to Be in Game: Says He Will Work Hard for Good of Washington Team," *Pittsburg Press*, June 28, 1907, 22.
17. "No Kick from the Fans on M'Closkey's Action: Teams Have Suffered at Hands of the Umpires and a Scrap over a Bad Decision Is Appreciated by Local Enthusiasts," *St. Louis Post-Dispatch*, July 18, 1907, 14.
18. "Chase after Nealon Proves Successful," *Pittsburg Post*, November 14, 1905, 8.
19. "Sporting Gossip: Base Ball Pickups," *Scranton Times*, December 5, 1905, 8.
20. "Pirate Lineup for Opening Contest Is Still Undecided: But the Players Are Willing to Wager That Clarke Will Be in the Fray," *Pittsburg Press*, March 31, 1907, 18.
21. George L. Moreland, "First Day in Vapor City Is One of Work for Clarke's Bunch: Pirates Arrived at Hot Springs Yesterday Morning and Got Busy at Once," *Pittsburg Press*, March 17, 1907, 18.
22. "Baseball Notes," *Pittsburg Press*, April 19, 1907, 26.
23. A.R. Cratty, "In Pittsburg: A Veteran Shows Fine Form As Umpire," *Sporting Life*, September 14, 1907, 7.

24. A.R. Cratty, "In Pittsburg: Pirate Players Must Obey All Rules," *Sporting Life*, February 26, 1910, 2.
25. A.R. Cratty, "In Pittsburg: Better Race in Old League Next Year," *Sporting Life*, October 19, 1907, 15.
26. "New Catcher for Pirates: Schriver, Last Year with Zanesville, Signs with Pittsburg Team," *Pittsburg Press*, February 2, 1908, 16.
27. "Nealon Has Retired: Much Touted First Baseman Fails to Make Good," *Washington Herald*, December 2, 1907, 8.
28. Ralph S. Davis, "Magnates Ready for League Meeting: Clubowners of Both Organizations Will Get Together Next Tuesday," *Pittsburg Press*, December 8, 1907, 21.
29. Ralph S. Davis, "Abuse of Pittsburg Ball Players Is to Be Stopped: 'Knockers' Who Resort to Insulting Language in Addressing Tossers to Be Dealt with by Police," *Pittsburg Press*, July 11, 1908, 5.
30. "Bill Abstein Sure He Will Fill Bill As First Baseman: 'Fred Clarke Need Not Worry about an Initial Sacker' Writes Husky German to President Dreyfuss," *Pittsburg Press*, January 24, 1909, 1.
31. "News from the Training Camp." *Pittsburg Press*, March 28, 1909, 4.
32. "Diamond Dust," *Pittsburg Press*, April 8, 1909, 14.
33. "Fresh Baseball Items Received from Missouri," *Pittsburgh Sunday Post*, April 11, 1909, 1.
34. "Cold Snap Prevents Baseball Game; Hyatt Will Play First Base To-Day: Abstein's Illness May Cripple Pirates at Opening of Eastern Series," *Pittsburgh Post*, May 11, 1909, 12.
35. John H. Gruber, "Game Is Prevented at Cincinnati; Rain: Players Ready to Take Field When it Comes Down – Clarke Disappointed," *Gazette Times*, May 10, 1909, 7.
36. Ralph S. Davis, "Well Fortified: Pittsburg Has Substitute for Each Regular," *The Sporting News*, June 17, 1909, 2.
37. Ralph S. Davis, "Trounced Giants: Three Out of First Four for Pirates," *The Sporting News*, July 15, 1909, 2.
38. Ralph S. Davis, "Giants Out of It: Race Between Chance's Cubs and Pirates," *The Sporting News*, August 5, 1909, 2.
39. Francis C. Richter, "Passing of Pulliam!: The Young Chief of the Venerable National League Shocks the Great Base Ball World," *Sporting Life*, August 7, 1909, 1.
40. "Wagner Weeps: Because He Could Not Attend the Funeral of Harry Pulliam," *Sporting Life*, August 7, 1909, 3.
41. Ralph S. Davis, "Heydler Present: Murphy's Conspiracy Charge Huge Joke," *The Sporting News*, September 16, 1909, 2.
42. "Gamblers Got Abstein: Pirates' First Baseman Was Their Target – Abuse Broke Up His Game," *Norwich Bulletin*, February 26, 1910, 3.
43. A.R. Cratty, "In Pittsburg: Early August Lull Caused Dismay," *Sporting Life*, August 21, 1909, 7.
44. Ralph S. Davis, "But One More Victory Needed by Pirates to Cinch Pennant: Locals Still Lead Cubs by Nine Games – If Pirates Win Today They Can Never be Overtaken," *Pittsburg Press*, September 28, 1909, 16.
45. "St. Louis Boy's Failure Hurt Pirates World's Series Chances," *St. Louis Post-Dispatch*, October 16, 1909, 8.
46. "Who Will Cover Initial Sack," *The Press*, January 4, 1910, 8.
47. "Seventh Game at Detroit," *Evening Star*, October 14, 1909, 18.
48. Joe King, "'The Wonder Man' of Pittsburgh: Life Story of Fred Clarke, Famed Pirate – Part 2," *The Sporting News*, March 21, 1951, 15.
49. "Gambling Almost Fatal to Pirates: Betting Men Got Abstein's Nerve and He Nearly Lost the World's Series," *Sunday Star*, October 24, 1909, 4.
50. "Pirate Rooters Leave for Home of Tigers: Special Train Carrying 3,000 Buccaneer Followers to Third and Fourth Games of World's Series – Remnant of Detroit Delegation Departs," *Pittsburgh Post*, October 11, 1909, 1.
51. "Notes of the Game," *Pittsburgh Post*, October 13, 1909, 10.
52. "Charge Is Made of Baseball Frame-Up: Winning of Games Is Subordinate to Box-Office Receipts, It Is Alleged," *Daily Notes*, October 13, 1909, 2.
53. "Wray's Column," *St. Louis Post-Dispatch*, October 16, 1909, 8.
54. Ralph S. Davis, "Base Ball Crazy: Pittsburg Fans Are Ready for World's Series," *The Sporting News*, October 7, 1909, 2.
55. "Statements of the Managers: Fred Clarke, Pittsburg," *St. Louis Globe-Democrat*, October 15, 1909, 8.

56. "Gamblers Injuring Game in Pittsburg," 17.
57. "Abstein Had Trouble with Pittsburg Fans and Couldn't Play Best Game," *St. Louis Post-Dispatch*, January 8, 1910, 6.
58. "Gamblers Got Abstein: Pirates' First Baseman Was Their Target – Abuse Broke Up His Game," 3.
59. "Gambling Almost Fatal to Pirates: Betting Men Got Abstein's Nerve and He Nearly Lost the World's Series," 4.
60. "St. Louis Boy's Failure Hurt Pirates World's Series Chances," 8.
61. Edward F. Balinger, "Adams Is Expected to Pitch: Youngster Will Likely Be Called upon in Deciding Game of Series," *Pittsburgh Post*, October 16, 1909, 1.
62. Ibid, 9.
63. "Detroit Clubhouse Like Hospital Ward," *St. Louis Globe-Democrat*, October 15, 1909, 8.
64. King, "'The Wonder Man' of Pittsburgh: Life Story of Fred Clarke, Famed Pirate – Part 2," 15.
65. "Adams Scores His Third Victory over the Tigers: Detroit Shut Out in Final Game of Greatest World's Series in the History of National Pastime," *San Francisco Examiner*, October 17, 1909, 45.
66. Ralph S. Davis, "Who Will Supplant Big Bill Abstein in 1910?" *Pittsburg Press*, October 22, 1909, 26.
67. "Adams Scores His Third Victory over the Tigers: Detroit Shut Out in Final Game of Greatest World's Series in the History of National Pastime," 45.
68. H.W. Lanigan, "Clarke Has Adams to Thank for Winning World's Title: Camnitz and Willis Who Won Flag for Pittsburg Not Heard from in the Big Show – Wagner Proved a Better Man in Series Than Cobb," *Butte Inter Mountain*, October 25, 1909, 7.
69. "Pittsburgh Tenders Glorious Greeting to World Leaders: Champion Pirates Are Acclaimed for Hours by Large Portion of People," *Gazette Times*, October 19, 1909, 10.
70. Ralph S. Davis, "Clarke No Quitter: Will Be Back on the Job at Pittsburg," *The Sporting News*, October 28, 1909, 2.
71. "Pittsburgh Tenders Glorious Greeting to World Leaders: Champion Pirates Are Acclaimed for Hours by Large Portion of People," 10.
72. Davis, "Clarke No Quitter: Will Be Back on the Job at Pittsburg," 2.
73. Ralph S. Davis, "First Base Weak: Pittsburg Believes Change Is Necessary," *The Sporting News*, November 4, 1909, 2.
74. "Fred Clarke: The Baseball Capitalist," *Waterloo Evening Courier*, May 4, 1911, 9.
75. A.R. Cratty, "In Pittsburg: Are Seen Harbingers of the Coming Race," *Sporting Life*, February 19, 1910, 12.
76. "Abstein to Go Back to Minor League in 1910," *St. Louis Post-Dispatch*, December 25, 1909, 6.
77. James Cruisinberry, "With Abstein Signed, Browns Are Complete: Hedges and O'Connor Are Now Ready to Start Season, Though They Will Seek Another Pitcher," *St. Louis Post-Dispatch*, January 8, 1910, 6.
78. "St. Louis Fans Happy to Get Bill Abstein: Hedges Thinks That Former Pirate Will Greatly Strengthen Their Team," *New Castle Herald*, January 11, 1910, 2.
79. James Cruisinberry, "Dreyfuss and Clarke Show No Sentiment for Abstein: Barney Now Says Young First Baseman Mixed Play of the Team Badly – Constant Fear of Veterans on Club Undoubtedly Affected Playing of Bill," *St. Louis Post-Dispatch*, February 3, 1910, 18.
80. "Gamblers Got Abstein: Pirates' First Baseman Was Their Target – Abuse Broke Up His Game," 3.
81. "Clarke Tells Why He Let Abstein Go: He Feared That Criticism Would Spoil the Usefulness of the First Baseman," *Buffalo Enquirer*, May 5, 1910, 8.
82. Ralph S. Davis, "Teams Are Not Traveling At Best Gait Yet: Ball Players' Development Retarded by Ugly Weather," *Pittsburg Press*, May 15, 1910, 3.

Chapter 6
1. "Latest Musical Hits," *Pittsburgh Gazette*, September 14, 1904, 3.
2. Ralph S. Davis, "Pirates May Play Minus Star Pitcher: Vic Willis Says He Has Quit," *Pittsburg Press*, January 24, 1909, 1.
3. "Vic Willis Will Pitch for Pirates, Declare Friends in His Home Town: Practices Daily in Delaware College Gymnasium and Arm Is Strong," *Pittsburg Sunday Post*, February 14, 1909, 1.
4. "Willis' Holdout Is Only a Bluff," *Pittsburg Press*, March 28, 1909, 4.
5. "Baseball Notes," *Boston Daily Globe*, March 23, 1909, 5.

6. "Regulars Win Listless Ball Game; Pirates Will Break Camp To-Day: Clarke Affixes Name to Pittsburgh Contract and Hikes for Kansas," *Pittsburgh Post*, April 9, 1909, 12.
7. Sam Crane, "Ha! Ha! Ha!," *Pittsburg Press*, April 5, 1909, 8.
8. Addie Joss, "Tigers Show Their Regular American League Speed in Victory over Pirates," *Dayton Herald*, October 11, 1909, 10.
9. "Muddy Grounds May Prove a Handicap to Tiger Speed Boys: American Leaguers Depend Good Deal upon Bunting and Fast Base Running – Heavy Field May Prevent This Line of Work," *Dayton Herald*, October 11, 1909, 10.
10. "Why Willis Went: Clarke's Method of Punishing Irresponsibility," *Chattanooga Daily Times*, March 2, 1910, 10.
11. A.R. Cratty, "In Pittsburg: Are Seen Harbingers of the Coming Race," *Sporting Life*, February 19, 1910, 12.
12. "'Vic' Willis Is Sold by the Pittsburgh Club," *Chattanooga News*, February 18, 1910, 12.
13. "Reason for Willis' Going: Why Pittsburg Is Willing to Part with Pitcher," *Wilkes-Barre Record*, February 17, 1910, 5.
14. "Cardinals Buy Willis; Jack Miller Signs Up: Bresnahan Seeks Big Pirate Pitcher and Dreyfuss Accepts Offer," *Pittsburgh Post*, February 16, 1910, 10.
15. A.R. Cratty, "In Pittsburg: The National League Schedule Is Acceptable," *Sporting Life*, March 5, 1910, 16.
16. "Must Not Sell Willis to Cubs or Giants: Stipulation Made by Dreyfuss When Big Heaver Was Given to Cardinals," *Pittsburg Press*, April 21, 1910, 16.
17. Brice Hoskins, "President M. Stanley Robison Is All the Word Optimistic Implies: Sage of Vandeventer Park Says Team Has a Chance of Finishing in First Division during Ensuing Pennant Race – Spends Day in St. Louis and Departs at Nightfall for Baden," *St. Louis Star*, February 24, 1910, 7.
18. "Why Willis Went: Clarke's Method of Punishing Irresponsibility," 10.
19. "Canned Willis Because of Row: Change In National League Pitcher's Allegiance Harks Back to a World's Series Incident," *Detroit Times*, February 18, 1910, 6.
20. "The World of Sport: Willis Will Help," *Fergus County Democrat*, March 1, 1910, 6.
21. Cratty, "In Pittsburg: The National League Schedule Is Acceptable," 16.
22. "Wagner Signs with Pirates: King of Backstops Will Play Another Year with Pittsburg World's Champions," *Vancouver World*, March 17, 1910, 8.
23. "Pittsburg Paying Now for Mistakes: Depended Too Much on Young Pitchers When Vic Willis Was Let Go," *Buffalo Courier*, June 13, 1910, 9.
24. "Pirate Pitchers May Lose Jobs: President Dreyfuss Very Angry at Poor Showing of Twirlers," *St. Louis Globe-Democrat*, September 19, 1910, 10.
25. "Giants Here To-Day for Final Clash with Superbas," *Standard Union*, October 8, 1910, 8.
26. "Chicago Cubs Trying to Secure Pitcher Camnitz from Pittsburg: Clarke, after Demanding Brown, Cole and Reulbach in Turn, Is Now Willing to Accept Orvie Overall for His Recalcitrant Hurling Star – Frank Chance Considering Trade," *St. Louis Star*, December 14, 1910, 9.
27. Ralph S. Davis, "Fred a Boy Again: Base Ball Fever Attacks the Pirate Manager," *The Sporting News*, February 2, 1911, 1.
28. Ralph S. Davis, "Hans Is Patriotic: Wagner Will Serve as Juror during March," *The Sporting News*, February 16, 1911, 3.
29. Ed F. Balinger, "Camnitz and Byrne Are Traded to Quakers for Dolan: Clarke and Dooin Finally Put Through Long Pending Deal before Corsairs Depart from Philadelphia," *Pittsburgh Sunday Post*, August 24, 1913, 1.
30. Ed. F. Balinger, "Sporting Chat: Dolan Was in Demand," *Pittsburgh Post*, September 10, 1913, 1.
31. Ralph S. Davis, "'Cozy' Dolan Shows Gameness in First Game at Forbes Field as Pirate: Played Though Injured," *Pittsburg Press*, August 30, 1913, 10.
32. Ralph S. Davis, "Pittsburg Refuses to be Comforted: Defeats by Naps Last Straw for Pirate Fans," *The Sporting News*, October 23, 1913, 3.
33. "Clarke Going to Meeting in Effort to Make Trade: Pirate Manager Is Due in Town Saturday – Should Have Little Trouble in Putting Through Deals," *Pittsburgh Post*, December 2, 1913, 13.
34. "For Fireside Fanning," *The News*, December 8, 1913, 16.
35. "The Hot Stove League," *Standard Union*, December 24, 1912, 8.

36. Ed F. Balinger, "National League Magnates Adjourn – Not a Deal Made: Clarke Tries to Put Through Trade but Fails – Several Amendments Made to Constitution," *Pittsburgh Post*, December 12, 1913, 13.
37. Ed. F. Balinger, "National League Elects Gov. Tener for Four Years: Will Be Inaugurated Today at Big Meeting in New York – Vote Is Unanimous," *Pittsburgh Post*, December 10, 1913, 13.
38. "Koney Grabbed by Pirates in Big Baseball Exchange: Wholesale Deal Sends Miller, Wilson, Robinson, Butler and Dolan to St. Louis for Three Players," *Pittsburgh Post*, December 13, 13.
39. "Which Fared Best, Pirates or Cards?: Clarke Has Completed His Infield, but Outer Garden Is Flimsy," *Pittsburgh Post*, December 13, 1913, 13.
40. "No Chance for Pirates to Secure Ed Konetchy," *Pittsburgh Post*, October 29, 1909, 9.
41. "Huggins' Plans: Cardinals' Manager Will Remain Active," *Sporting Life*, December 28, 1912, 7.
42. Sportsman, "Live Tips and Topics," *Boston Daily Globe*, December 20, 1913, 7.
43. "Sporting Chat: Miller's Amazing Game," *Pittsburgh Post*, December 15, 1913, 9.
44. Frank G. Menke, "Huggins' Predictions Have Now Come True," *Dayton Evening Herald*, September 1, 1914, 8.
45. Ralph S. Davis, "Sixteen Buccaneers Lined Up for Coming Season: Jimmie Kelley Signed," *Pittsburg Press*, January 14, 1914, 28.
46. "President Dreyfuss Secures Mike Mowrey's Signature to Contract: Mowrey Signs Contract after Conferring with Dreyfuss," *Pittsburgh Sunday Post*, January 18, 1914, 1.
47. "Wilbur Cooper a Holdout; Mowrey in for Three Years: Young Pirate Southpaw Considering Going Over to Federal League – Mike Safe Until 1917," *Pittsburgh Post*, January 24, 1914, 13.
48. "'I'll Do My Best' - - - Koney," *Pittsburg Press*, January 14, 1914, 28.
49. "Hendrix and Simon Must Come Back of Own Accord: Should They Fail to Report before Season Opens Will Be Forever Barred from Organized Baseball," *Pittsburgh Post*, January 28, 1914, 13.
50. Ralph S. Davis, "Mowrey Signs Up with the Pirates: Thus Exploding Another Fed Report," *The Sporting News*, January 22, 1914, 2.
51. "Wilbur Cooper a Holdout; Mowrey in for Three Years: Young Pirate Southpaw Considering Going Over to Federal League – Mike Safe Until 1917," 13.
52. Hugh S. Fullerton, "Marvelous Playing of Konetchy and Mowrey Justifies Clarke's Trade," *Omaha Daily News*, May 8, 1914, 17.
53. Ralph S. Davis, "First in League, First in Fandom: Pittsburgh Is One Town That Is Clear Off Feds," *The Sporting News*, April 30, 1914, 2.
54. "St. Louis Players in Golf Links Scrap," *Pittsburg Press*, June 26, 1914, 32.
55. "Baseball Players Escape Arrest in Sensational Raid," *Pittsburg Press*, June 25, 1914, 1.
56. "St. Louis Players in Golf Links Scrap," 32.
57. "Cardinals Said Not to Be Taking Sport Seriously: 'Joy Rides' Galore by Huggins' Stars," *Pittsburg Press*, June 27, 1914, 11.
58. Ralph S. Davis, "Jotted Down While the Corsairs Won," *Pittsburg Press*, June 28, 1914, 1.
59. "'Jack' Miller Is Named in Divorce Suit: Accuses His Pretty Wife and Ball Player," *Pittsburg Press*, July 9, 1914, 1.
60. "Made Home Run Clad in Pajamas: Well Known Big Leaguers Are Involved in Scandalous Divorce Suit Just Filed," *New Castle Herald*, July 9, 1914, 2.
61. "Mrs. Casper Says She Wasn't with 'Jack' Miller," *Pittsburg Press*, July 31, 1914, 20.
62. "Made Home Run Clad in Pajamas: Well Known Big Leaguers Are Involved In Scandalous Divorce Suit Just Filed," 2.
63. Marion F. Parker, "Cards Gain in Race by the Simple Process of Doing Nothing: Huggins Has 4 Pitchers Ready for Use To-Day," *St. Louis Globe-Democrat*, September 10, 1914, 7.
64. Marion F. Parker, "Cards Handicapped by Greed of N.L. Owners: Twice Within Week Have Games Been Called Off for no Other Reason Except That Crowds Promised to Be Thin," *St. Louis Globe-Democrat*, September 12, 1914, 7.
65. "Dolan Exonerated; Miller to Be Tried," *Pittsburgh Post*, October 1, 1914, 7.
66. "Charges Against Miller and Dolan Ignored by Jurors," *Pittsburg Press*, October 14, 1914, 16.
67. "'Jack' Miller Freed from Indictment," *Pittsburgh Post*, January 13, 1915, 12.
68. "Casper Divorce Case Is Taken from List," *Pittsburg Press*, March 10, 1915, 23.
69. "'Jack' Miller Freed from Indictment," 12.
70. "Mowrey Claims He Has Iron Nerves," *Twin City Daily Sentinel*, July 5, 1913, 4.

71. "Buccaneers Set New Season's Record, Making It Eight Straight: Pirates Again Beat Cubs but Contest Is One-Sided," *Pittsburgh Post*, May 8, 1914, 13.
72. Ralph S. Davis, "Tendons Torn In Mowrey's Leg, May Keep Him Out of Lineup Several Weeks: Injured Limb Is Placed in Cast," *Pittsburg Press*, May 21, 1914, 24.
73. "Line Drives from Forbes Lot," *Pittsburgh Post*, July 18, 1914, 11.
74. "Say Mike Mowrey Loafed on Field," *Brooklyn Daily Eagle*, August 19, 1914, 2.
75. "Mike Mowrey Has Himself to Blame: Pirate Third-Sacker Made His Own Bed and Must Lie in It," *Nashville Banner*, November 18, 1914, 2.
76. "'Mike' Mowrey Released," *Boston Sunday Globe*, August 16, 1914, 14.
77. "Say Mowrey Loafed On Field," 2.
78. "Mowrey's Whereabouts Puzzling to Fandom: Pirate Player Disappears after Season Is Over," *Chattanooga Daily Times*, October 19, 1914, 7.
79. Ralph S. Davis, "They All Can Point Faults in Pirates: Players Too Particular As to What They Hit," *The Sporting News*, June 11, 1914, 3.
80. "Clarke Should Get Busy and Replace a Few Regulars: Team, However, Is Weak in Substitutes and Pirate Commander Is Up Against It – New System Needed," *Pittsburgh Post*, June 13, 1914, 13.
81. "Hash from Sportdom," *Reading News-Times*, July 25, 1914, 8.
82. Frederick G. Lieb, *The Pittsburgh Pirates* (1948; reprint, Carbondale, Ill.: Southern Illinois University Press, 2003), 170.
83. Ed F. Balinger, "Koney Had Bad Baseball Year, but Big Train Didn't Lay Down," *Pittsburgh Sunday Post*, October 18, 1914, 3.
84. Ralph S. Davis, "O'Toole Soon Will Be on Move Again: Returned to Pirates by Giants but Not to Stay," *The Sporting News*, October 22, 1914, 2.
85. "Fred Clark Admits He Was Buncoed in Card Trade: 'No Wonder St. Louis Team Finished Last with Players Huggins Gave Me' – Says the Pittsburg Manager," *Owensboro Daily Messenger*, December 6, 1914, 8.
86. "Giants May Land Konetchy: First Baseman Is Said to Be Eager to Play under McGraw," *Fall River Daily Globe*, January 8, 1915, 7.
87. "Owner Dreyfuss Loses Fortune on Konetchy," *Rock Island Argus*, October 17, 1914, 12.
88. Ralph S. Davis, "Koney Played Fed Spy for Months: Fred Clarke Soon Got on to His First Sacker," *The Sporting News*, November 26, 1914, 2.
89. "Marquard Worked Feds for 'Roll,'" *Grand Forks Daily Herald*, December 10, 1914, 11.
90. "Pirates to Fight to Retain Ed. Konetchy: Barney Dreyfuss Says First Sacker's Contract Will Hold in Any Court," *Scranton Times*, December 19, 1914, 10.
91. Robert Peyton Wiggins, *The Federal League of Base Ball Clubs: The History of an Outlaw Major League, 1914-1915* (Jefferson, N.C.: McFarland & Company, Inc., 2009), 166.
92. "Wagner Will Finish Baseball Career Playing Initial Bag," *Honolulu Star-Bulletin*, November 19, 1914, 9.
93. "National League News in Short Metre," *Sporting Life*, December 27, 1913, 14.

Chapter 7
1. W.J. O'Connor, "Fred Clarke Too Nice, That's Why Pirates Look Bad: Manager, Once Known as Hard Taskmaster, Now Acts Don't Care Role," *St. Louis Post-Dispatch*, July 2, 1914, 17.
2. Ralph S. Davis, "He Would Release Jumpers: Barney Dreyfuss Wants Title to Konetchy Established, and Then Would Turn Him Loose," *Pittsburg Press*, December 6, 1914, 1.
3. "Barney Dreyfuss on Fed League: Owner of Pittsburg Club Has Something to Say about New League," *Bismarck Daily Tribune*, December 9, 1914, 8.
4. "Dreyfuss and Clarke Roast Feds," *Bridgeport Evening Farmer*, December 7, 1914, 8.
5. "Pirates to Fight to Retain Ed. Konetchy: Barney Dreyfuss Says First Sacker's Contract Will Hold in Any Court," *Scranton Times*, December 19, 1914, 10.
6. "Another Bluff by Federal: Independents Have No Foreknowledge of O.B. Plans in Regard to Contract Jumping Players," *Pittsburg Press*, April 11, 1915, 3.
7. "Criticise Mike Mowrey," *York Dispatch*, April 24, 1915, 7.
8. "Mamaux, Major Sensation, Was Taught to Pitch by His Father, Former Star," *Salt Lake Telegram*, July 26, 1915, 3.

9. "Death Record: Albert L. Mamaux," *Pittsburg Press*, May 10, 1915, 9.
10. "Mamaux, Major Sensation, Was Taught to Pitch by His Father, Former Star," 3.
11. "Mamaux Signs with Pirates: Crack County League Pitcher to Get Tryout in Major League Company," *Pittsburgh Post*, January 22, 1913, 1.
12. "Al Mamaux Was Given First Lesson in Pittsburgh: Pirates' Sensational Pitcher a Product of the Smoky City and Was Given His First Tryout When Eighteen Years Old with the Wilkinsburg Club," *Philadelphia Inquirer*, August 6, 1916, 3.
13. "Mamaux Signs with Pirates: Crack County League Pitcher to Get Tryout in Major League Company," 1.
14. "Daddy Built Park for Pitcher Mamaux: Father of Pirates' Famous Hurler Knew He Would Eventually Make Good," *Altoona Tribune*, November 12, 1915, 10.
15. "Al Mamaux Was Given First Lesson in Pittsburgh: Pirates' Sensational Pitcher a Product of the Smoky City and Was Given His First Tryout When Eighteen Years Old with the Wilkinsburg Club," 3.
16. "Mamaux Signs with Pirates: Crack County League Pitcher to Get Tryout in Major League Company," 1.
17. "Mamaux, Sensation of 1915 and Star of Pirate Pitchers, Cost Club Nothing," *Lima Republican-Gazette*, August 17, 1915, 7.
18. "Al Mamaux Was Given First Lesson in Pittsburgh: Pirates' Sensational Pitcher a Product of the Smoky City and Was Given His First Tryout When Eighteen Years Old with the Wilkinsburg Club," 3.
19. "Mamaux Signs with Pirates: Crack County League Pitcher to Get Tryout in Major League Company," 1.
20. "Mamaux, Sensation of 1915 and Star of Pirate Pitchers, Cost Club Nothing," 7.
21. "Al Mamaux Was Given First Lesson in Pittsburgh: Pirates' Sensational Pitcher a Product of the Smoky City and Was Given His First Tryout When Eighteen Years Old with the Wilkinsburg Club," 3.
22. "Local Woman Whips Hubby in New York Hotel Lobby," *Pittsburg Press*, October 18, 1914, 1.
23. Ibid, 6.
24. "Must Do Double Penance: Humiliating Position in Which Young Couple Find Themselves," *Daily Inter Ocean*, September 7, 1892, 3.
25. "Dads against Sons Phase in Mamaux Domestic Row: Pirate Pitcher Charged by Father with Threatening His Life – Grandfather Furnishes Bail – Wife Tells Tale of Woe," *Morning Herald* (Uniontown, Fayette County, Pennsylvania), November 18, 1914, 9.
26. "Baseball Pitcher Is Sued by Father," *Pittsburgh Post*, November 18, 1914, 2.
27. "Dads against Sons Phase in Mamaux Domestic Row: Pirates Pitcher Charged by Father with Threatening His Life – Grandfather Furnishes Bail – Wife Tells Tale of Woe," 9.
28. "Local Woman Whips Hubby in New York Hotel Lobby," 6.
29. "Mamaux Is to Have Hearing Late Today," *Pittsburg Press*, November 18, 1914, 22.
30. "Al Mamaux Released; Promises to Be Good," *Pittsburgh Post*, November 19, 1914, 2.
31. "Mamaux Asserts Wife Attacked Him," *Pittsburg Press*, February 2, 1915, 20.
32. "Dads against Sons Phase in Mamaux Domestic Row: Pirates Pitcher Charged by Father with Threatening His Life – Grandfather Furnishes Bail – Wife Tells Tale of Woe," 9.
33. "Divorce Proceedings," *Pittsburgh Post*, December 23, 1915, 12.
34. "Many Opinions Given Out by Higher Court: Lower Court Is Reversed in Mamaux Case and Libellant Granted Divorce," *Pittsburgh Post*, July 21, 1916, 14.
35. "Mamaux Doesn't Want Divorce Case Heard in Public," *Pittsburg Press*, May 17, 1913, 1.
36. "News of the Courts: Actions in Divorce," *Pittsburgh Sunday Post*, May 11, 1913, 5.
37. "Mamaux Doesn't Want Divorce Case Heard in Public," 1.
38. "Master Is Against Mamaux Divorce," *Pittsburg Press*, December 17, 1914, 14.
39. "Mrs. Mamaux Makes Warm Reply to Suit: Asserts Wealthy Husband Deserted Her and That Stepson Was Disrespectful to Her While Father Was Ill," *Pittsburg Press*, May 11, 1913, 1.
40. Ibid, 4.
41. "Mamaux Doesn't Want Divorce Case Heard in Public," 1.
42. "Master Is Against Mamaux Divorce," 14.
43. "Albert L. Mamaux Denied a Divorce," *Pittsburg Press*, March 13, 1915, 2.
44. "Death Record: Albert L. Mamaux," 9.
45. James Jerpe, "Here and There in Sports," *Gazette Times*, March 7, 1915, 4.

46. "This Is Strictly Confidential: New Suit Helps," *Oakland Tribune*, July 19, 1915, 10.
47. "Mamaux, Sensation of 1915 and Star of Pirate Pitchers, Cost Club Nothing," 7.
48. "Mamaux, Major Sensation, Was Taught to Pitch by His Father, Former Star," 3.
49. Ralph Davis, "Ralph Davis' Column: How Mamaux Was Signed," *Pittsburg Press*, August 31, 1915, 20.
50. Ralph Davis, "Ralph Davis' Column: Mamaux Asked for Document," *Pittsburg Press*, August 31, 1915, 20.
51. Chandler D. Richter, "New Side Lights on Base Ball: Mamaux Forces Change of Policy," *Sporting Life*, September 4, 1915, 7.
52. Davis, "Ralph Davis' Column: Mamaux Asked for Document," 20.
53. Richter, "New Side Lights on Base Ball: Mamaux Forces Change of Policy," 7.
54. "Oakes Says Mamaux Made Overtures," *Franklin Evening News*, August 30, 1915, 3.
55. "Mamaux Out for Season," *Boston Sunday Globe*, September 18, 1915, 2.
56. "Appendicitis Accounts for Mamaux's Fall," *Winnipeg Evening Tribune*, October 16, 1915, 2.
57. "Al Mamaux Was Given First Lesson in Pittsburgh: Pirates' Sensational Pitcher a Product of the Smoky City and Was Given His First Tryout When Eighteen Years Old with the Wilkinsburg Club," 3.
58. Ed F. Balinger, "Fred Clarke to Quit Baseball: Veteran Pilot of Pirates Announces His Retirement from Diamond Activities," *Pittsburgh Post*, September 9, 1915, 13.
59. "Fred Clarke: The Baseball Capitalist," *Waterloo Evening Courier*, May 4, 1911, 9.
60. Balinger, "Fred Clarke to Quit Baseball: Veteran Pilot of Pirates Announces His Retirement from Diamond Activities," 13.
61. Ed F. Balinger, "What Fred Clarke Says: Regrets Leaving Pittsburgh – Wishes Successor Well," *Pittsburgh Post*, September 9, 1915, 13.
62. "Callahan Named to Lead Pirates," *Bridgeport Evening Farmer*, December 17, 1915, 14.
63. "Mamaux Ordered Not to Play Gridiron Game," *Pittston Gazette*, December 4, 1915, 6.
64. "Death Notices," *Pittsburg Press*, December 19, 1915, 12.
65. "Pirate Star in Vaudeville: Al Mamaux Follows Manager Callahan's Example and Goes on Stage," *Pittsburgh Sunday Post*, February 6, 1916, 2.
66. "Jimmy Callahan 'Calls' His Pirates for Their 'Parties,'" *Carbondale Leader*, July 28, 1916, 7.
67. Florent Gibson, "They Were Fooling; Al Tells on Himself: Mamaux Spreads News of 'Suspension,' Forcing Dreyfuss and Callahan to Go Through with Their Discipline Bluff," *Pittsburgh Post*, August 21, 1916, 8.
68. Harry Keck, "The Sports Sage's Chat: Kumagae Dangerous in National Tourney; Other Timely Topics," *Pittsburgh Post*, August 21, 1916, 9.
69. "Mamaux Suspended, Threatens to Quit the Pirate Crew," *Lincoln Sunday Star*, August 20, 1916, 1.
70. "Sport Snap Shots," *Hutchinson News*, September 5, 1916, 2.
71. Charles J. Doyle, "Al Mamaux Is Suspended; Breaks Rules: Star Pitcher Given 10-Day Punishment by Manager Callahan," *Gazette Times*, August 20, 1916, 2.
72. Ralph S. Davis, "Pitcher Al Mamaux Suspended by the Pittsburg Club: Is Charged with Violating Rules of the Ball Club," *Pittsburg Press*, August 20, 1916, 2.
73. Ralph Davis, "Ralph Davis' Column: Mamaux's Excuse," *Pittsburg Press*, August 22, 1916, 24.
74. Ralph S. Davis, "Hoke Warner, Dayton Recruit, Reports and Gets into Lineup at Once: Replaces Baird as Leadoff Man," *Pittsburg Press*, August 21, 1916, 24.
75. Davis, "Pitcher Al Mamaux Suspended by the Pittsburg Club: Is Charged with Violating Rules of the Ball Club," 2.
76. Ralph S. Davis, "Pirates and Phillies in Another Double=Header: Quakers Seek Retaliation," *Pittsburg Press*, August 22, 1916, 24.
77. "Pirates Release Costello: Dashing Dan Sent to Toronto, but Doesn't Like Transfer and Talks about Retiring," *Pittsburg Press*, August 27, 1916, 2.
78. "Costello May Quit Base Ball," *Scranton Republican*, August 28, 1916, 13.
79. "Dan Costello Goes to Join Pittsburgh," *Scranton Republican*, September 5, 1916, 10.
80. "Costello Will Enter Harvard," *Scranton Republican*, September 23, 1916, 21.
81. "Pittsburgh Fans and Management Dissatisfied with Work of Jimmy Callahan: Jimmy Callahan on Verge of Losing Out As Leader of the Pittsburgh Pirates," *Evening Ledger*, August 23, 1916, 10.
82. Charles J. Doyle, "Mamaux Will Be Back Soon, Friends Say," *Gazette Times*, August 23, 1916, 8.

83. Ralph S. Davis, "New Pitcher to Report at Once to Aid Pirates against Eastern Foes: Jack Scott Will Arrive Thursday," *Pittsburg Press*, August 23, 1916, 24.
84. Ralph S. Davis, "Carson Bigbee Here after Trip across Continent: Takes Schulte's Place in Lineup," *Pittsburg Press*, August 24, 1916, 24.
85. "Mamaux Affair Helps Pirates: Pitcher Al Mamaux Suspended for Keeping Late Hours and Whole Team Seems Helped," *Winston-Salem Journal*, September 2, 1916, 12.
86. "Pittsburgh Fans and Management Dissatisfied with Work of Jimmy Callahan: Jimmy Callahan on Verge of Losing Out As Leader of the Pittsburgh Pirates," 10.
87. A.R. Cratty, "Pointed Pittsburgh Pennings: Corsairs Kick over Traces but Are Brought to Time by Club Owner – An Unusual Incident of Autumn Hours – Bits of Base Ball News," *Sporting Life*, October 14, 1916, 8.
88. H. C. Hamilton "Callahan to Boss Cubs in Place of Tinker, Is Report," *Seattle Star*, October 25, 1916, 9.
89. Ralph S. Davis, "Dreyfuss Spoils a Fresh Line of Dope: He Won't Sell Out nor Will He Fire Callahan," *The Sporting News*, October 26, 1916, 3.
90. Frederick G. Lieb, *The Pittsburgh Pirates* (1948; reprint, Carbondale, Ill.: Southern Illinois University Press, 2003), 176.
91. "Billy Murray Business Manager of the Pirates," *Evening Ledger*, February 20, 1917, 12.
92. "Player Signed for His Skill, Not for His Bravery," *Edmonton Journal*, March 17, 1917, 19.
93. Ralph Davis, "Ralph Davis' Column: 'Cap' Neal – Business Manager," *Pittsburg Press*, April 13, 1917, 40.
94. Ralph S. Davis, "Strike Worries No One but Players: That's the Way Situation Looks to Ralph Davis," *The Sporting News*, January 25, 1917, 2.
95. "Mamaux to Wed Brooklyn Girl: Pittsburg Pitcher Engaged to Alice Johnson," *Brooklyn Daily Times*, March 8, 1917, 1.
96. Harry Keck, "Al Mamaux to Marry Brooklyn Girl, Report," *Pittsburgh Post*, March 9, 1917, 8.
97. The Old Scout, "Sports and Sportsmen," *Fall River Daily Globe*, June 7, 1917, 6.
98. Paul Purman, "Al Mamaux, Pirate, Has Uncontrollable Appetite; Will Star Heaver Eat Himself Out of Baseball," *Wisconsin State Journal*, July 2, 1917, 5.
99. "Jimmy Callahan Is Released by Pirates," *Titusville Herald*, July 2, 1917, 3.
100. Paul Purman, "Three Managers in Four Days Is Record of Barney Dreyfuss," *Tampa Daily Times*, July 17, 1917, 5.
101. "Mystery-Man of the Baseball, Now Managing Pittsburg Team," *Sunday St. Louis Post-Dispatch*, July 15, 1917, 28.
102. "Cutting the Corners," *Bridgeport Evening Farmer*, July 18, 1917, 8.
103. "Punish Kaiser by Having Him Manage Pittsburgh Pirates – Jimmy Callahan," *Buffalo Evening News*, July 11, 1917, 12.
104. "J. Callahan Grinds an Axe: Has Arranged Financial Troubles with Dreyfuss and is Out," *El Paso Herald*, July 31, 1917, 9.
105. "Punish Kaiser by Having Him Manage Pittsburgh Pirates – Jimmy Callahan," 12.
106. "Twice Failed As Manager: Jimmy Callahan Popular, but Not a Success," *Fort Wayne News*, July 12, 1917, 11.
107. H.C. Hamilton, "Mamaux Suspension Some Vindication of Callahan," *Walnut Valley Times*, August 11, 1917, 2.
108. "Manager Bezdek Rearranges Pirates' Lineup: Pitler and Ward Benched," *Pittsburg Press*, July 23, 1917, 24.
109. "'Bezdek Probably Got Goods on Al Mamaux' - - Dreyfuss," *Pittsburgh Post*, July 23, 1917, 8.
110. "Manager Bezdek Rearranges Pirates' Lineup: Pitler and Ward Benched," 24.
111. Charles J. Doyle, "Al Mamaux Suspended Indefinitely: Erstwhile Star Slab Artist Sent Home for Disobeying Club Rules," *Gazette Times*, July 23, 1917, 8.
112. "Manager Bezdek Rearranges Pirates' Lineup: Pitler and Ward Benched," 24.
113. Ralph S. Davis, "Work of Buccaneers Displeases Few Remaining Patrons: Al Mamaux Not with Outlaws," *Pittsburg Press*, August 4, 1917, 14.
114. Harry Keck, "Al's Mother, Bezdek and Barney Unaware of Mamaux's Jump," *Pittsburgh Post*, August 4, 1917, 6.

115. Davis, "Work of Buccaneers Displeases Few Remaining Patrons: Al Mamaux Not with Outlaws," 14.
116. "Al Mamaux's Name Now on Blacklist," *Pittsburg Press*, August 20, 1917, 24.
117. Harry Keck, "Sporting Chit-Chat: Al Mamaux's Side of the Story," *Pittsburgh Post*, August 21, 1917, 9.

Chapter 8
1. Harry Keck, "Sporting Chit-Chat: Al Mamaux's Side of the Story," *Pittsburgh Post*, August 21, 1917, 9.
2. Frederick G. Lieb, "Ebbets and Dreyfuss Get the David Harum Fever and Engineer Seventh Big Deal of Winter - - - Five Players Involved: Dreyfuss Trades Mamaux to Robins," *The Sun* (New York, New York), January 10, 1918, 17.
3. "Al Mamaux Says He's Glad to Be with the Superbas," *Brooklyn Daily Eagle*, January 11, 1918, 2.
4. "Al Mamaux Admits That He Was Playing Possum When with the Pittsburg Club: Writes to Tell Colonel Ebbets, His New Boss, That His Arm Is as Good as Ever, and That He's Glad of the Change," *Edmonton Journal*, January 26, 1918, 21.
5. Rice, "Mamaux's Small Cut in Salary Can Be Repaid by Good Work," *Brooklyn Daily Eagle*, February 1, 1918, 2.
6. "Mamaux Hurting Himself: Will Forfeit Most of His Salary by Failure to Observe Club's Rules of Discipline," *Pittsburg Press*, July 23, 1917, 24.
7. Rice, "Mamaux Signs Contract and Will Soon Start Training: Gets His Pay for Time He Was Suspended by Pittsburg and Is Pleased to Be with Brooklyn – Uncle Robbie Expects Great Things from New Pitcher – Baseball Gossip," *Brooklyn Daily Eagle*, February 13, 1918, 2.
8. "Pitcher Al. Mamaux Is Reinstated Without Fine by National Commission," *Sunday St. Louis Post-Dispatch*, March 17, 1918, 10.
9. Daniel, "High Lights and Shadows in All Spheres of Sport," *The Sun* (New York, New York), May 3, 1918, 15.
10. "Mamaux Denies Quitting Robins to Avoid Draft," *New York Tribune*, May 4, 1918, 16.
11. "Did Mamaux Desert Dodgers to Escape U.S. Army Draft?," *Wilkes-Barre Times Leader*, May 7, 1918, 18.
12. "Death Notices: Mamaux," *Pittsburg Press*, June 9, 1919, 27.
13. Daniel, "High Lights and Shadows in All Spheres of Sport," 15.
14. "Did Mamaux Desert Dodgers to Escape U.S. Army Draft?," 18.
15. "Al Mamaux Says He's Glad to Be with the Superbas," 2.
16. "Ebbets Hits Back at Casey Stengel: Says Player Talked Enlistment to Force Increase in Salary – Club Treated Him Well," *Brooklyn Daily Eagle*, January 11, 1918, 2.
17. "Casey Stengel to Join Navy; Chuck Ward Now a Sergeant," *Brooklyn Daily Eagle*, June 14, 1918, 2.
18. Ralph S. Davis, "Stengel Will Report to Bezdek at Louisville: Pirate Outfielder Accepts Club Terms," *Pittsburg Press*, April 10, 1919, 36.
19. "Salary Kicker Ousted: Barney Dreyfuss Gets Rid of George Whitted, Pirates Taking Him in Trade," *St. Joseph News-Press*, August 23, 1919, 10.
20. Ralph S. Davis, "Casey Stengel Is Exchanged for George Whitted: Dissatisfied 'Casey' Is Traded to Phillies for Sterling Outfielder, Who Reports to Bezdek at Once," *Pittsburg Press*, August 10, 1919, 1.
21. Ralph Davis, "Ralph Davis' Column: Stengel Will Not Be Missed," *Pittsburg Press*, August 11, 1919, 28.
22. Ralph Davis, "Ralph Davis' Column: Pirates Got Best of Deal," *Pittsburg Press*, August 20, 1919, 36.
23. "The Old Sport's Musings: If You Can't Boost Don't Knock," *Philadelphia Inquirer*, August 11, 1919, 12.
24. Davis, "Ralph Davis' Column: Pirates Got Best of Deal," 36.
25. "Trade of Stengel for Whitted May Mean New Manager for Pirates," *East Liverpool Review*, August 14, 1919, 9.
26. "Hugo Bezdek Ill, Leaves Pirates for His Home," *Evening News* (Wilkes-Barre, Pennsylvania), July 23, 1919, 8.
27. "Bezdek Likely to Retire from Baseball," *Salt Lake Telegram*, August 9, 1919, 12.
28. "Pirate Chief May Resign," *Lima Sunday News*, August 10, 1919, 9.
29. "Bezdek Likely to Retire from Baseball," 12.
30. The Gunner, "Sport Salutes: Bezdek Will Quit As Pirate Coach," *Los Angeles Evening Express*, August 18, 1919, 18.

31. "Few Changes Expected among Major League Managers for Next Year's Pennant Races: Much Talk Has Been in Circulation Concerning Probable Shifts, but Pittsburg Is Only Club Which Is Likely to Have New Leader When Baseball Races Resume – Johnny Evers May Be Found at Head of Pittsburg Pirates," *The Citizen*, November 29, 1919, 8.
32. "Evers Will Manage Pirates Next Year," *Deseret Evening News*, October 25, 1919, 5.
33. "Few Changes Expected among Major League Managers for Next Year's Pennant Races: Much Talk Has Been in Circulation Concerning Probable Shifts, but Pittsburg Is Only Club Which Is Likely to Have New Leader When Baseball Races Resume – Johnny Evers May Be Found at Head of Pittsburg Pirates," 8.
34. Joe Vila, "Army-Navy Tickets Nearly Exhausted: Slight Chance for Civilians to See Football Clash Between Rival Academies," *Philadelphia Inquirer*, November 14, 1919, 14.
35. "Evers Will Manage Pirates Next Year," 5.
36. "George Gibson Signs to Manage Pirates Next Season: Former Backstop Accepts Terms," *Pittsburg Press*, December 8, 1919, 32.
37. "Dreyfuss Appoints George Gibson Pirate Manager for Next Year: Veteran Catcher Succeeds Bezdek as Local Leader," *Pittsburgh Post*, December 9, 1919, 13.
38. Charles J. Doyle, "George Gibson Named Chief of Buccaneer Crew: Former Pirate Catcher Comes Back Manager," *Gazette Times*, December 9, 1919, 13.
39. "Dreyfuss Appoints George Gibson Pirate Manager for Next Year: Veteran Catcher Succeeds Bezdek as Local Leader," 13.
40. Richard C. Armstrong and Martin Healy Jr., *George "Mooney" Gibson: Canadian Catcher for the Deadball Era Pirates* (Jefferson, N.C., McFarland & Company, Inc., 2020), 142.
41. Ralph S. Davis, "Gibson's Going Is Part of Cal's Plan: Pirate Manager's Idea Is to Build Entire New Team," *The Sporting News*, August 24, 1916, 3.
42. Edward F. Balinger, "Maranville Comes to Pirates in Biggest Deal of Season: Southworth and Nicholson with Barbare and Big Sum Exchanged for Boston Star," *Pittsburgh Post*, January 24, 1921, 8.
43. Edward F. Balinger, "Barney and Gibby Depart from City on Quiet Mission: President and Manager of Pittsburgh Baseball Club Leave without Disclosing Destination, but Pilot Declares No Important Deals Are in Prospect," *Pittsburgh Post*, January 31, 1921, 8.
44. Balinger, "Maranville Comes to Pirates in Biggest Deal of Season: Southworth and Nicholson with Barbare and Big Sum Exchanged for Boston Star," 8.
45. "Maranville Is Against Playing with Pirates," *Pittsburgh Post*, January 24, 1921, 8.
46. Edward F. Balinger, "'Rabbit' Maranville Signs Pirate Contract for Next Season: Terms Kept Secret, Except Agreement Is for One Year," *Pittsburgh Post*, February 1, 1921, 12.
47. "Sam Dreyfuss Dies in Home: Son of Pirate Owner Fails to Survive Pneumonia," *Pittsburgh Post-Gazette*, February 23, 1931, 1.
48. "Sam Dreyfuss Dies Here of Pneumonia: Bucs' Vice President Loses Fight for Life," *Pittsburgh Press*, February 23, 1931, 6.
49. Ed F. Balinger, "Sam Dreyfuss Seeks Berth as Army Flyer; to Enlist at Princeton," *Pittsburgh Post*, November 29, 1917, 18.
50. "Pittsburgh to Fight Gamblers: Energetic Campaign Will Be Waged against Bettors at Forbes Field This Summer," *New Castle Herald*, April 21, 1921, 10.
51. "To Fight Gamblers," *Washington Times*, June 9, 1921, 17.
52. "Pittsburg Police Allow Gambling: Charges Made by Barney Dreyfuss, Owner of Pittsburg Pirates," *Akron Beacon Journal*, June 13, 1921, 11.
53. "Landis Will Stop Gambling He Declares: Political Pull Is Releasing Gamblers Caught at Pirates' Park," *Capital Times*, June 21, 1921, 6.
54. "Commissioner of Baseball Is Sore: Landis Raps Magistrate Who Discharged Gamblers Caught at Pirates' Park," *Saskatoon Phoenix*, June 25, 1921, 9.
55. "Babcock Resents Jurist's Remarks about Baseball Gambling in Forbes Field: Not Pittsburgh That Produced Scandal, He Wires," *Pittsburgh Post*, June 22, 1921, 1.
56. Ibid, 3.
57. Ibid, 1.
58. Ibid, 3.
59. "Police Must Pay to See Games at Forbes Field," *Salt Lake Tribune*, July 31, 1921, 7.

60. "Gibson Takes Pirates to Task for Poor Showing Yesterday: Morrison to Twirl Today," *Pittsburgh Press*, August 25, 1921, 24.
61. Frederick G. Lieb, *The Pittsburgh Pirates* (1948; reprint, Carbondale, Ill.: Southern Illinois University Press, 2003), 191.
62. Charles J. Doyle, "Pirates Win Slugfest from Dodgers, 8–2: Glazner Holds Superbas to Seven Safeties," *Gazette Times*, August 31, 1921, 9.
63. Edward F. Balinger, "Pirates Win Final from Dodgers, 8–2 - - - Giants Win Eighth Straight: Robertson's Bat Helps Glazner Win in Eastern Final," *Pittsburgh Post*, August 31, 1921, 9.
64. "Pirate Notes," *Pittsburgh Post*, August 31, 1921, 9.
65. Ralph Davis, "Ralph Davis' Column: Pirates Get the Razz," *Pittsburgh Press*, September 2, 1921, 28.
66. Ralph S. Davis, "Pittsburg in Rage as Pirates Falter: Fans Give Gibson's Crew Razz and Start 'Rumors,'" *The Sporting News*, September 8, 1921, 1.
67. Ralph S. Davis, "Tribune News Idea Not for Pittsburg: Pirate Fans Would Riot If Dope Were Denied Them," *The Sporting News*, September 15, 1921, 3.
68. Chilly Doyle, "Chilly Sauce," *Gazette Times*, September 7, 1921, 9.
69. William A. White, "Should Pirates Be Razzed?: Fandom, Tired of Mediocre Goods, Demands Big Change as Final Battle Starts," *Pittsburgh Post*, September 12, 1921, 6.
70. Ralph Davis, "Ralph Davis' Column: Is This True?" *Pittsburgh Press*, September 16, 1921, 30.
71. Ralph Davis, "Ralph Davis' Column: Charges against Pirates," *Pittsburgh Press*, September 19, 1921, 22.
72. Davis, "Ralph Davis' Column: Is This True?" 30.
73. Ralph Davis, "Ralph Davis' Column: A Suspicious Lot," *Pittsburgh Press*, September 17, 1921, 10.
74. Ralph S. Davis, "Dark Hints against Some of the Pirates: Conduct Not of Sort to Insure Good Ball Playing," *The Sporting News*, September 22, 1921, 1.
75. Davis, "Ralph Davis' Column: A Suspicious Lot," 10.
76. Davis, "Dark Hints against Some of the Pirates: Conduct Not of Sort to Insure Good Ball Playing," 1.
77. Davis, "Ralph Davis' Column: A Suspicious Lot," 10.
78. Davis, "Dark Hints against Some of the Pirates: Conduct Not of Sort to Insure Good Ball Playing," 1.
79. Regis M. Welsh, "Pennant Hopes Dashed, Pirates Must Give Answer to Fans Who Believed in Club; What Has Caused Club to Throw Away Greatest Chance to Bring Series Here," *Pittsburgh Sunday Post*, September 18, 1921, 2.
80. Edward F. Balinger, "'I Do Not Claim to Have a Sabbath School Team,' Says Manager Gibson, Defending Players; Slump, Nothing Else, Caused Club to Lose Lead," *Pittsburgh Post*, September 20, 1921, 8.
81. Ralph S. Davis, "Buccaneers' Failure to Retain Lead Is Severely Criticized: Corsairs Lampooned," *Pittsburgh Press*, September 25, 1921, 3.
82. Ralph Davis, "Ralph Davis' Column: Glad Season Is Over," *Pittsburgh Press*, September 28, 1921, 22.
83. "Pirate Notes," *Pittsburgh Post*, October 1, 1921, 10.
84. "Pirate Notes," *Pittsburgh Post*, October 3, 1921, 8.
85. Regis M. Welsh, "Pirate Machine Bidding Farewell to Forbes Field Today, Leaves Fans Still Wondering Why Pennant Was Lost," *Pittsburgh Post*, September 27, 1921, 10.
86. Ralph Davis, "Ralph Davis' Column: No More Singing, Please," *Pittsburgh Press*, September 28, 1921, 22.
87. Ralph S. Davis, "Perfect Harmony Was Lacking Among Buccaneers: Cliques Helped to Ruin Chances," *Pittsburgh Press*, October 2, 1921, 6.
88. Ralph S. Davis, "Buccaneers Left to Their Dismal Fate: Fans Desert Them and No More Cheers Are Heard," *The Sporting News*, September 29, 1921, 2.
89. Ralph S. Davis, "Dreyfuss Has Plans Ready for Classic: Park Will Take Care of 40,000 If Pirates Are in Series," *The Sporting News*, September 1, 1921, 3.
90. Ralph Davis, "Ralph Davis' Column: Ought to Stop Them," *Pittsburgh Press*, September 26, 1921, 18.
91. Davis, "Perfect Harmony Was Lacking Among Buccaneers: Cliques Helped to Ruin Chances," 6.
92. Ralph Davis, "Ralph Davis' Column: The Secret Is Out," *Pittsburgh Press*, October 3, 1921, 18.

Chapter 9
1. Paul Mickelson, "Sports Trail," *Wilkes-Barre Record*, May 24, 1937, 17.
2. Ralph Davis, "Ralph Davis' Column: Defied Superstition," *Pittsburgh Press*, August 30, 1921, 24.

3. "Was Camera Jinx That Put Buccos in Second Place?" *Pittsburgh Post*, September 20, 1921, 8.
4. Ralph S. Davis, "Pittsburg in Rage as Pirates Falter: Fans Give Gibson's Crew Razz and Start 'Rumors,'" *The Sporting News*, September 8, 1921, 1.
5. Ralph S. Davis, "Shakeup in Pirates Demanded by Fans: Pittsburghers Have Soured on A Number of Players," *The Sporting News*, October 6, 1921, 2.
6. Ralph S. Davis, "Oh Yes, Barney Will Sell His Ball Club: Provided Anybody Comes Across to Meet His Price," *The Sporting News*, October 13, 1921, 2.
7. Ralph S. Davis, "Stock a Pirate If It Can Be Arranged: Cooper One Who May Be Offered for Cards' Third Sacker," *The Sporting News*, November 17, 1921, 3.
8. Regis M. Welsh, "'Saddest of All Is It Might Have Been Here;' Wild Rumors Afloat," *Pittsburgh Post*, October 4, 1921, 12.
9. Davis, "Oh Yes, Barney Will Sell His Ball Club: Provided Anybody Comes Across to Meet His Price," 2.
10. "Pirate Shake-Up Is Planned for Coming Season: Schmidt, Whitted, Tierney, Barnhardt, and Zinn to Be Traded or Released," *Washington Times*, November 8, 1921, 15.
11. Ralph S. Davis, "Branch Rickey Gave Dreyfuss 'Chance': Offered to Trade Stock for Half of Pittsburg Team," *The Sporting News*, December 15, 1921, 5.
12. Segar, Charles, "Robbie and Gibson Unable to Agree on Schmidt Trade," *Brooklyn Citizen*, December 15, 1921, 4.
13. "Holdouts Threaten in Major Leagues for Coming Season: Reported That Several Pirates Will Demand Salary Increases; Barney Dreyfuss Sore," *Great Falls Tribune*, November 25, 1921, 9.
14. Ralph S. Davis, "Ranks of Holdout Brigade Are Said to Be Well Filled: Pirates Have Some Members," *Pittsburgh Press*, January 22, 1922, 2.
15. Ralph S. Davis, "Players of Schmidt Type Are Drawbacks: Pirate Catcher Shows Disposition in Letter He Writes," *The Sporting News*, January 26, 1922, 3.
16. Ralph S. Davis, "Ralph Davis' Column: Gibson's Estimate of Catchers," *Pittsburgh Press*, March 10, 1922, 32.
17. "Schmidt Will Quit Pirates If Not Given Contract of $10,000," *Pittsburgh Post*, March 8, 1922, 10.
18. Davis, "Ralph Davis' Column: Gibson's Estimate of Catchers," 32.
19. "White Sox Beat Pirates 11 to 5: Dreyfuss Declares He Has Reached Limit with Schmidt," *West Virginian*, March 20, 1922, 9.
20. "Late News: Whitted Sold to Brooklyn Club," *Brooklyn Daily Eagle*, March 14, 1922, 1.
21. "Sale of Whitted Has Caused Lots of Talk: N.Y. Tribune Sporting Editor Says Whole Thing Was Done to Humiliate Star," *Twin City Sentinel*, March 22, 1922, 12.
22. "Whitted Blamed by Mates for Crack of 1921 Pirates," *Chattanooga Daily Times*, March 20, 1922, 10.
23. "Owners Lost 1921 Flag, Says Whitted," *News-Herald*, April 20, 1922, 3.
24. Ralph Davis, "Ralph Davis' Column: Whitted Getting in Wrong," *Pittsburgh Press*, April 22, 1922, 12.
25. "Dreyfuss Takes Slam at Whitted: 'Was Released Because He Broke Rules,' Declares Irate Barney," *New York Herald*, April 23, 1922, 1.
26. Ralph S. Davis, "Bars Up against Schmidt: Pirate Catcher Automatically Suspended – Must Appeal to Landis Before He Is Reinstated," *Pittsburgh Press*, April 23, 1922, 3.
27. "Sport Siftings," *Evening State Journal*, May 17, 1922, 8.
28. William A. White, "Walter Schmidt, Corsair Holdout, Reported Ready to Accept Club's Terms: May Be en Route East, Is Rumor Borne by Letter," *Pittsburgh Post*, April 22, 1922, 1.
29. Davis, "Bars Up against Schmidt: Pirate Catcher Automatically Suspended – Must Appeal to Landis Before He Is Reinstated," 3.
30. Ralph S. Davis, "Gibby Hasn't Lost Faith in His Team: Start Was Bad, He Admits, But Watch Pirates Now," *The Sporting News*, April 27, 1922, 3.
31. Ralph S. Davis, "It's Not Peeve That Makes Pirates Lose: Denial of Story That They Are Sore at Dreyfuss," *The Sporting News*, June 22, 1922, 3.
32. "Pirates Have Indian Comedian on Staff: Yellowhorse of Pittsburgh Team Reverse of the Indian of Legend," *Rutland Daily Herald*, June 22, 1922, 13.
33. "Novelty of First Place Nine Rather Trying to Pirate Fans; Barnhardt Playing Good Ball," *Evening News* (Harrisburg, Pennsylvania), June 22, 1921, 15.

34. Jeffrey Powers-Beck, *The American Indian Integration of Baseball* (Lincoln, Neb.: University of Nebraska Press, 2004), 157.
35. James C. Fraser, "Nobody Had More Fun in Big Leagues than Colorful Rabbit Maranville, Who Whipped John Barleycorn," *Sunday Courier and Press*, January 10, 1954, 5C.
36. Frederick G. Lieb, *The Pittsburgh Pirates* (1948; reprint, Carbondale, Ill.: Southern Illinois University Press, 2003), 192.
37. Powers-Beck, *The American Indian Integration of Baseball*, 163.
38. Lieb, *The Pittsburgh Pirates*, 192-193.
39. Ralph S. Davis, "Here's Where Gibby Did Quick Thinking: Decision to Resign Seems to Have Been Quite Sudden," *The Sporting News*, July 6, 1922, 2.
40. Lieb, *The Pittsburgh Pirates*, 193.
41. Davis, "Here's Where Gibby Did Quick Thinking: Decision to Resign Seems to Have Been Quite Sudden," 2.
42. Edward F. Balinger, "Gibson Quits, M'Kechnie Is Made Manager of Pirates: New Head of Bucs Will Assume Reins of Outfit Today," *Pittsburgh Post*, July 1, 1922, 1.
43. Ibid, 10.
44. "Bill M'Kechnie, Ex-Giant, Is Now Pirates' Manager: George Gibson Resigns as the Leader after Team Is Whitewashed," *Evening World*, July 1, 1922, 7.
45. Balinger, "Gibson Quits, M'Kechnie Is Made Manager of Pirates: New Head of Bucs Will Assume Reins of Outfit Today," 1.
46. Ibid, 10.
47. Ralph S. Davis, "It's Plain M'Kechnie Has Big Job on Hand: Easy Going Gibson Left Pirates Badly Demoralized," *The Sporting News*, July 13, 1922, 3.
48. Thomas S. Rice, "Barney Dreyfuss Not to Blame for Downfall of the Pirates; Gibson Seems to Be the 'Goat,'" *Brooklyn Daily Eagle*, July 21, 1922, 8.
49. Squirrel, "Baseballitis," *Miami Daily Metropolis*, July 25, 1922, 9.
50. Ray Coll Jr., "Sports Comment," *Honolulu Advertiser*, July 29, 1922, 4.
51. Mitchell Conrad Stinson, *Deacon Bill McKechnie: A Baseball Biography* (Jefferson, N.C.: McFarland & Company, Inc., 2012), 96-97.
52. Harry Jones, "Baseball's Immortal Madcaps: 'Characters' Fooled McKechnie – Effort to Make Yellowhorse, Maranville Behave Backfired," *Pittsburgh Press*, May 13, 1962, 5.
53. Buss Walker, "Mawnin'!: Yellowhorse, Maranville Were Playboys – Pigeon Hunting, 15 Stories Up," *Chattanooga Daily Times*, August 3, 1951, 21.
54. Ralph S. Davis, "Pittsburg Fandom Like a Burnt Child: Experience of Last Year Teaches It to Play Safe," *The Sporting News*, August 17, 1922, 3.
55. "Bill McKechnie to Lead the Pirates Again Next Year," *New York Tribune*, September 27, 1922, 14.
56. "Walter Schmidt to Manage Pittsburgh Pirates in 1923," *Greensboro Daily News*, September 25, 1922, 10.
57. "Dreyfuss Denies That Gibson Will Be Pilot," *Daily Times*, September 26, 1922, 13.
58. Ralph S. Davis, "Schmidt Denies He Wrote That Letter: Says He Never Had Any Thought of Managing Pirates," *The Sporting News*, October 5, 1922, 3.
59. "Bill McKechnie to Lead the Pirates Again Next Year," 14.
60. Davis, "Schmidt Denies He Wrote That Letter: Says He Never Had Any Thought of Managing Pirates," 3.
61. Ralph S. Davis, "Pirates Turn Deaf Ear to Union Talk: Dreyfuss Knows How to Make Players Satisfied," *The Sporting News*, November 16, 1922, 3.
62. "No Pirate Contract for Catcher Schmidt As Yet," *New York Tribune*, October 12, 1922, 12.
63. Ralph S. Davis, "Pirates Do Well in the Slave Market: Get Two Pitchers Who Should Be of Help to Club," *The Sporting News*, December 21, 1922, 5.
64. Davis J. Walsh, "Bleeding Managers Winter Sport of Ball Players," *Kane Republican*, January 23, 1923, 3.
65. "Phillies and Pirates May Put Over Big Swap: Rumor Has It That Meadows and Rawlings Are Slated to Go to the Oaklanders," *New Castle Herald*, May 22, 1923, 11.
66. Charle J. Doyle, "Glazner and Tierney Traded to Phillies: Pirates Get Meadows and Johnny Rawlings; No Cash Is Involved," *Gazette Times*, May 24, 1923, 13.

67. "Phillies and Pirates May Put Over Big Swap: Rumor Has It That Meadows and Rawlings Are Slated to Go to the Oaklanders," 11.
68. Doyle, "Glazner and Tierney Traded to Phillies: Pirates Get Meadows and Johnny Rawlings; No Cash Is Involved," 13.
69. Ralph Davis, "Ralph Davis' Column: A Good Baseball Deal," *Pittsburgh Press*, May 24, 1923, 28.
70. "Maranville Freed after Accusation by Brookline Cop," *Pittsburgh Press*, May 20, 1923, 11.
71. Ralph S. Davis, "Win Them at Home and Fans Come Out: That's Experience of Pittsburg Club So Far This Season," *The Sporting News*, June 7, 1923, 3.
72. "Rabbit Maranville Is Fined at Boston," *North Adams Transcript*, July 19, 1923, 3.
73. Ralph S. Davis, "Even Split in East Puts Pirates Back: They Hope to Regain Some Lost Ground While Home," *The Sporting News*, July 26, 1923, 3.
74. "Don't Be Too Innocent," *Los Angeles Record*, August 17, 1923, 16.
75. "Fine 'Rabbit' Maranville: Pittsburgh Shortstop Pays $100 for Operating Automobile While Drunk," *Brattleboro Daily Reformer*, July 19, 1923, 1.
76. James J. Murphy, "Rumor That Dreyfuss Wants to Get Rid of Maranville; May Come to Superbas," *Brooklyn Daily Eagle*, August 2, 1923, A3.
77. Ralph S. Davis, "Pittsburg Thinks It Is Now or Never: Time to Beat Giants Is While They Are on the Run," *The Sporting News*, August 2, 1923, 3.
78. Ralph S. Davis, "Pirates Have More Grudges than One: While Settling Those Abroad They Might Work Within," *The Sporting News*, August 16, 1923, 3.
79. Murphy, "Rumor That Dreyfuss Wants to Get Rid of Maranville; May Come to Superbas," A3.
80. Davis, "Pirates Have More Grudges than One: While Settling Those Abroad They Might Work Within," 3.
81. "Fire Maranville: Pirate Star 'Canned' Because of His Attitude," *Capital Times*, October 6, 1923, 7.
82. Westbrook Pegler, "Ball Leaders Hold Annual Debate: M'Graw Hurries Home for Huge Trading Meet," *Illustrated Daily News*, December 5, 1923, 19.
83. "Dreyfuss Refuses Boston's Offer for Maranville: Figures Hub Mere Stopover on Way to Giants," *Buffalo Courier*, January 18, 1924, 14.
84. "Notes from the Training Camps," *Evening Herald* (Shenandoah, Pennsylvania), February 27, 1924, 3.
85. Norman E. Brown, "Connie Mack and Ebbetts Gnash Their Teeth While Barney Dreyfuss Congratulates Self on Getting Wright," *San Bernardino Daily Sun*, July 6, 1924, 17.
86. Thomas S. Rice, "Killefer and McKechnie Utterly Disagree About Future of Maranville," *Brooklyn Daily Eagle*, March 18, 1925, 2A.
87. Brown, "Connie Mack and Ebbetts Gnash Their Teeth While Barney Dreyfuss Congratulates Self on Getting Wright," 17.
88. Ralph Davis, "Sport Chat: And Another Tip," *Pittsburgh Press*, October 9, 1924, 31.
89. "Bucs Wallop Warren, 14-3, In Exhibition: Cuyler and Traynor, With Homers, Lead Onslaught, Adams on Mound," *Gazette Times*, August 18, 1924, 9.
90. Ralph S. Davis, "M'Kechnie Hears Shouting of Mob: Dreyfuss Says He's Satisfied with Bill's Work, However," *The Sporting News*, October 9, 1924, 1.

Chapter 10
1. L.H. Wollen, "Pirate-Cub Deal Leaves Fans Divided: Niehaus Feature Is Question Mark," *Pittsburgh Press*, October 28, 1924, 26.
2. Ralph S. Davis, "Anyway, Big Swap Satisfies Barney: Some Fans Are Inclined to Think Owner of Bucs Got Stung," *The Sporting News*, November 6, 1924, 1.
3. Wollen, "Pirate-Cub Deal Leaves Fans Divided: Niehaus Feature Is Question Mark," 26.
4. "Believes His Team Stronger: Bill McKechnie Confident Improvement Has Been Made by Changes Decided On in Lineup," *Pittsburgh Press*, December 15, 1924, 28.
5. Ralph S. Davis, "Buccaneers' View Is, Let 'Em Rant: Trading Niehaus for Bottomley Just Idle Talk," *The Sporting News*, November 13, 1924, 5.
6. "Caught on the Fly," *The Sporting News*, November 27, 1924, 8.
7. "'Rob' Maranville's Auto Strikes Pittsburg Child," *Altoona Tribune*, November 21, 1924, 8.
8. "Maranville Arrested for Injury to a Boy," *Evening Star*, November 20, 1924, 30.
9. "Caught on the Fly," 8.

10. "Maranville Auto Victim Given $700," *Pittsburgh Press*, January 14, 1925, 22.
11. James C. Fraser, "Nobody Had More Fun in Big Leagues Than Colorful Rabbit Maranville, Who Whipped John Barleycorn," *Sunday Courier and Press*, January 10, 1954, 5C.
12. Ralph Davis, "Maranville Is a Philosopher: Says He Has Learned That No Player Who Drinks and Stays Out All Night Can Compete with Careful Livers," *Pittsburgh Press*, April 30, 1929, 52.
13. L.H. Wollen, "Walter Schmidt Given Release: Pirates Turn Out Veteran Catcher," *Pittsburgh Press*, December 16, 1924, 32.
14. "Schmidt's Release Is Fans' Surprise," *Evening News* (Wilkes-Barre, Pennsylvania), December 19, 1924, 34.
15. "Walter Schmidt Lost Out over Grab for Money: 'Get All You Can While the Getting Is Good,' His Doctrine, Bill Peete Declares," *News-Herald*, December 18, 1924, 8.
16. "Wright Makes Unassisted Triple Play: Pirate Shortstop Thrills Fans with Great Play as Club Loses to Cardinals, 10 to 9," *Gazette Times*, May 8, 1925, 13.
17. Ralph S. Davis, "Pirates of 1901 Beaten by 1925 Bucs: Veterans Are Given Ovation," *Pittsburgh Press*, June 7, 1925, 1.
18. "Clarke Returns to Buccaneers," *Pittsburgh Press*, June 13, 1925, 9.
19. Ralph S. Davis, "Dreyfuss Has Been Fair with His Men: And Yet Two or Three Hold Out on Pittsburg Owner," *The Sporting News*, March 8, 1923, 3.
20. "Clarke Returns to Buccaneers," 9.
21. Ralph S. Davis, "Clarke Goes Back with His Old Team: Former Manager to Serve as an Assistant to Dreyfuss," *The Sporting News*, June 18, 1925, 3.
22. "Fred Clarke Is Helping Pirates," *Kingston Daily Freeman*, July 22, 1925, 8.
23. "Sporting Comment: Rawlings Lost to Pirates," *Standard Union*, September 26, 1925, 10.
24. Lou Wollen, "Absence of Carey Is Felt: Pirate Outfield Lacks Steadiness without Captain; Eddie Moore Is Being Given Time to Think," *Pittsburgh Press*, August 19, 1925, 22.
25. "Sporting Comment: Rawlings Lost to Pirates," 10.
26. "Broken Leg to Cost Pirates Services of Rawlings for Balance of Season: Gritty Infielder, Hero of Recent Spurt of National League Leaders, Fractures Bone in Ankle Sliding into Second Base – Eddie Moore Also Injured in Finale with Cards," *Pittsburgh Gazette Times*, September 6, 1925, 1.
27. "Sporting Comment: Rawlings Lost to Pirates," 10.
28. Charles J. Doyle, "Pirate Hurler Wins Berth as Slab Hero of Diamond Classic: Buc Shortstop and Right Fielder Aid Vic with Home Runs – Schoolmaster's Power and Skill in Clinches Enables Him to Grab Decision over Former Scranton Coal Miner," *Pittsburgh Gazette Times*, October 9, 1925, 13.
29. Hans Wagner, "Eddie Moore Cried, but Not From Pain: Pirate Second Sacker Shed Tears of Regret When Hand Was Hurt, and Assumed Hero Role," *Pittsburgh Press*, October 14, 1925, 25.
30. Ralph Davis, "Sport Chat: Game Little Eddie Moore," *Pittsburgh Press*, October 14, 1925, 24.
31. Charles J. Doyle, "Buccaneers Confident of Winning Deciding Game for Title Today: Corsairs Scintillate in Sixth Contest with 3-to-2 Victory over Senators – Kremer and Moore Outstanding Stars – Oaklanders Now Hold Upper Hand – Traynor Impressive," *Pittsburgh Gazette Times*, October 14, 1925, 13.
32. Davis, "Sport Chat: Game Little Eddie Moore," 24.
33. "Pirates Get Waner and Rhyne, Coast League Stars, In $100,000 Deal with San Francisco: Pittsburgh Club to Give $85,000 in Cash and Three Players for Phenoms of Western Circuit – Lands Sensational Outfielder with Batting Average of .397 and Great Shortstop Who Hits at .313 Clip," *Pittsbugh Gazette Times*, October 14, 1925, 13.
34. Ralph Davis, "Sport Chat: Why Did Landis Delay?" *Pittsburgh Press*, October 15, 1925, 30.
35. Ralph S. Davis, "Burn Gasoline to Dry Forbes Field: Fans Slow Arriving for Deciding Game of World's Series," *Pittsburgh Press*, October 15, 1925, 1.
36. Frederick G. Lieb, *The Pittsburgh Pirates* (1948; reprint, Carbondale, Ill.: Southern Illinois University Press, 2003), 216.
37. Ralph Davis, "Sport Chat: Never a Game Like It," *Pittsburgh Press*, October 16, 1925, 38.
38. Jeff Carroll, *Sam Rice: A Biography of the Washington Senators Hall of Famer* (Jefferson, N.C.: McFarland & Company, Inc., 2008), 140.
39. Davis, "Sport Chat: Never a Game Like It," 38.
40. Carroll, *Sam Rice: A Biography of the Washington Senators Hall of Famer*, 140.

41. Davis, "Sport Chat: Never a Game Like It," 38.
42. Ralph S. Davis, "Pirates Look Good for Years to Come: Team Has Been Built Up Around Ideal Young Athletes," *The Sporting News*, October 29, 1925, 1.
43. Ralph S. Davis, "Winter Fiction, Says Dreyfuss of Report on Moore and Bigbee: Club Has Year to Pay for Rhyne, Waner," *The Sporting News*, November 5, 1925, 1.
44. "Carey Is Confined to Home by Injured Rib," *Paducah Evening Sun*, October 24, 1925, 1.
45. "Max Carey, Captain of Pirates, Is in Hospital," *Daily Notes*, October 26, 1925, 1.
46. "Carey Gets a Thrill," *Indiana Evening Gazette*, October 28, 1925, 7.
47. "John M'Graw Pleased with Showing of Albert Tyson: Eddie Moore's Rumored to Be Involved in Deal That May Send Him West – Tyson Oldest Rookie to Come to Majors," *Richmond-Times Dispatch*, November 8, 1925, 24.
48. Ralph S. Davis, "Carey Still Hears from Injured Ribs: New Pneumonia Threat Laid to Collision in Series," *The Sporting News*, March 11, 1926, 1.
49. "Hal Rhyne May Replace Eddie Moore at Second: Play of New Man at Keystone Sack Pretty to Watch – Smoother Than Moore in Play," *News-Herald*, April 6, 1926, 10.
50. Ralph S. Davis, "Dreyfuss Goes On His Way Rejoicing: Pirates' Bon Voyage to Their Boss Carries Fine Sentiment," *The Sporting News*, June 17, 1926, 1.
51. "'We Can Win Pennant, and We Will,' Is Pirates' Farewell Message to Barney Dreyfuss," *Pittsburgh Gazette Times*, June 10, 1926, 13.
52. Davis, "Dreyfuss Goes On His Way Rejoicing: Pirates' Bon Voyage to Their Boss Carries Fine Sentiment," 1.
53. Ralph S. Davis, "All Isn't So Well In Pirate Menage: Truth Is, Some of 'Em Have Been Cutting Up a Little," *The Sporting News*, July 8, 1926, 1.
54. "Yankees Climb on Tigers with One Run Margin: Late Inning Rally Ties Game for Hugmen," *Selma-Times Journal*, July 15, 1926, 6.
55. Lou Wollen, "Playing the Game with the Pirates," *Pittsburgh Press*, July 15, 1926, 30.
56. Ralph Davis, "Ralph Davis Says: Use of Mailed Fist by McKechnie," *Pittsburgh Press*, July 15, 1926, 30.
57. Ralph Davis, "Ralph Davis Says: Drastic Measures Are Justified – Fans Will Not Stand for Slackers," *Pittsburgh Press*, July 15, 1926, 30.
58. James J. Murphy, "Did McKechnie Err in Farming Out Thompson: Answer Seems 'Yes,' as He Is Outdoing Pirates' Present Keystoners," *Brooklyn Daily Eagle*, July 21, 1926, 2A.
59. Ralph S. Davis, "They'll Be Careful Now, If Not Serious: But Why Must Big Leaguers Be Driven and Disciplined?" *The Sporting News*, July 22, 1926, 1.
60. Ralph S. Davis, "M'Kechnie Wields an Iron Fist to Restore Champions to Order: Rigid Disciplinary Rule Being Followed," *The Sporting News*, July 29, 1926, 1.
61. Lou Wollen, "Playing the Game with the Pirates," *Pittsburgh Press*, July 21, 1926, 26.
62. Norman E. Brown, "Mooring Moore: Reliable Old Banny May Make Eddie Star Infielder," *Wilkes-Barre Record*, August 3, 1926, 19.
63. Glenn Wright, interview by Dr. Eugene Converse Murdock, Cleveland Public Library Digital Gallery, June 23, 1978.
64. "Braves Go on Warpath as Bucs Capture Nat Top," *Reading Times*, July 26, 1926, 14.
65. "Vic Aldridge Fined for Rule Violation," *Bridgeport Telegram*, July 23, 1926, 8.
66. "Aldridge Fined $50 for Absence without Leave: Johnny Morrison Must Face Consequences for Going to Owensboro, Ky., without Consent," *News-Herald*, July 23, 1926, 10.
67. Charles J. Doyle, "Pirates Blanked Twice in Doubleheader: Champs' Attack Wilts as Braves Snare both Games by 2-0 Scores," *Pittsbugh Gazette Times*, August 8, 1926, 2.
68. Lou Wollen, "World's Champions End Eastern Invasion Today: Long Trip Is Profitable," *Pittsburgh Press*, August 11, 1926, 26.
69. Lou Wollen, "Playing the Game with the Pirates," *Pittsburgh Press*, August 11, 1926, 26.
70. Lou Wollen, "World's Champions Windup Successful Eastern Invasion: To Play Cubs Here Friday," *Pittsburgh Press*, August 12, 1926, 26.
71. "Pirates Charter Train but Fail to Arrive for Game," *St. Louis Globe-Democrat*, August 14, 1926, 14.
72. "Pirate-Cub Game Postponed When Teams Fail to Reach City: Players Marooned by Floods in East," *Pittsburgh Press*, August 13, 1926, 28.
73. Ralph S. Davis, "Showdown Near in Pirate Controversy: No Team Can Serve Two Managers, Says Captain Max Carey," *Pittsburgh Press*, August 13, 1926, 1.

74. Wollen, "World's Champions Windup Successful Eastern Invasion: To Play Cubs Here Friday," 26.
75. Davis, "Showdown Near in Pirate Controversy: No Team Can Serve Two Managers, Says Captain Max Carey," 1.

Chapter 11
1. Ralph S. Davis, "Showdown Near in Pirate Controversy: No Team Can Serve Two Managers, Says Captain Max Carey," *Pittsburgh Press*, August 13, 1926, 1.
2. R.M. Wagoner, "Carey, Adams and Bigbee Fired from Team: Three Veterans Let Go, Result of Recent Plot," *News-Herald*, August 14, 1926, 8.
3. "Carey Suspended and Two Released by Pirates Following Row: Move to Oust Clarke from Players' Bench Causes Drastic Action," *St. Louis Globe-Democrat*, August 14, 1926, 14.
4. Ralph S. Davis, "Fans Want 'Inside' Story on Revolt: Carey, Bigbee and Adams Expected to Tell Real Story," *Pittsburgh Press*, August 14, 1926, 1-2.
5. Wagoner, "Carey, Adams and Bigbee Fired from Team: Three Veterans Let Go, Result of Recent Plot," 8.
6. Davis, "Fans Want 'Inside' Story on Revolt: Carey, Bigbee and Adams Expected to Tell Real Story," 2.
7. Wagoner, "Carey, Adams and Bigbee Fired from Team: Three Veterans Let Go, Result of Recent Plot," 8.
8. R.M. Wagoner, "Carey May Get a Place with Giants: McGraw Hasn't Yet Made up His Mind – Pittsburgh Fandom and Writers Divided on Release of Three Players," *News-Herald*, August 14, 1926, 1.
9. "Pirate Fans Express Views on Flareup," *Pittsburgh Press*, August 14, 1926, 2.
10. Ralph S. Davis, "Usual Slow Start for Pirate Champs: Pitching Reaches High Standard, but Punch Isn't There," *The Sporting News*, April 22, 1926, 3.
11. "Pirate Fans Express Views on Flareup," 2.
12. Wagoner, "Carey May Get a Place with Giants: McGraw Hasn't Yet Made Up His Mind – Pittsburgh Fandom and Writers Divided on Release of Three Players," 1.
13. Ralph Davis, "Ralph Davis Says: Pittsburgh's Action Too Drastic – Fandom Stunned at Penalties," *Pittsburgh Press*, August 14, 1926, 9.
14. Ralph S. Davis, "Baseball Fandom Shocked by Upheaval on Pittsburgh Club: Effect on Team May Be Serious," *Pittsburgh Press*, August 15, 1926, 2.
15. "Carey, Adams and Bigbee to Set Forth Their Story of Dismissal by Club," *Standard Union*, August 15, 1926, 12.
16. "McGraw May Take Carey as Fielder for Giants," *Fresno Morning Republican*, August 16, 1926, 6.
17. "Carey, Adams and Bigbee to Set Forth Their Story of Dismissal by Club," 12.
18. "Carey Suspended and Two Released by Pirates Following Row: Move to Oust Clarke from Players' Bench Causes Drastic Action," 14.
19. "Carey, Adams and Bigbee to Set Forth Their Story of Dismissal by Club," 12.
20. "Adams, Bigbee and Carey Not Ready to Talk: Fans Clamor for Full Showdown in Buc Controversy," *Pittsburgh Press*, August 15, 1926, 1.
21. "Carey, Adams and Bigbee to Set Forth Their Story of Dismissal by Club," 12.
22. "Pirate Outcasts Won't Tell 'Other Side': Trio to Await Developments before Citing 'Justification,'" *Pittsburgh Gazette Times*, August 15, 1926, 4.
23. "Pirate Dissension Bared; Clarke Peeved at Small Share in Series: Trouble Between Him and Players Dates Back to Fall of 1925, Adams, Carey and Bigbee Declare – Was Given $1,000, but Wanted to Hand it Back, Alleging 'Ill Feeling' – Moore's Demand Clarke Get Off Bench Resulted in Firing Eddie," *News-Herald*, September 30, 1926, 1.
24. "Carey Suspended and Two Released by Pirates Following Row: Move to Oust Clarke from Players' Bench Causes Drastic Action," 14.
25. Davis, "Showdown Near in Pirate Controversy: No Team Can Serve Two Managers, Says Captain Max Carey," 1.
26. John B. Foster, "'Inside Story' of What Caused the Pittsburgh Suspensions: Remark by Vice-President Clarke at Boston That Carey Was Having Tough Time of It Started Row – Landis Not Likely to Interfere," *Yonkers Herald*, August 16, 1926, 18.
27. "Dreyfuss Denies Revolt Lost Flag: Injuries, Not Scrap, Doomed Team's Chances, Barney Dreyfuss Says, Denying Rumors," *Pittsbugh Gazette Times*, September 27, 1926, 4.

28. Foster, "'Inside Story' of What Caused the Pittsburgh Suspensions: Remark by Vice-President Clarke at Boston That Carey Was Having a Tough Time of It Started Row – Landis Not Likely to Intervene," 18.
29. "Carey Maintains Clarke Is Cause of Buc Scandal," *Altoona Tribune*, August 19, 1926, 8.
30. Charles J. Doyle, "Carey to Meet Judge Landis in New York Today to Protest Banishment from Team: Baseball Czar Willing to Listen, He Tells Players," *Pittsburgh Gazette Times*, August 16, 1926, 1.
31. "Carey Maintains Clarke Is Cause of Buc Scandal," 8.
32. Foster, "'Inside Story' of What Caused the Pittsburgh Suspensions: Remark by Vice-President Clarke at Boston That Carey Was Having Tough Time of It Started Row – Landis Not Likely to Interfere," 18.
33. Doyle, "Carey to Meet Judge Landis in New York Today to Protest Banishment from Team: Baseball Czar Willing to Listen, He Tells Players," 1.
34. "Adams, Bigbee and Carey Not Ready to Talk: Fans Clamor for Full Showdown in Buc Controversy," 1.
35. "Pirates Wrecked, Is Gotham's Dope: Case of Over-Anxiety to 'Get Some of World Series Dough,'" *Pittsburgh Gazette Times*, August 16, 1926 1.
36. Mitchell Conrad Stinson, *Deacon Bill McKechnie: A Baseball Biography* (Jefferson, N.C.: McFarland & Company, Inc., 2012), 125.
37. Lou Wollen, "Playing the Game with the Pirates," *Pittsburgh Press*, August 16, 1926, 20.
38. Ralph Davis, "Ralph Davis Says: Outsiders Comment on Pirate Troubles – A Slap at the Players, Says Kessler," *Pittsburgh Press*, August 17, 1926, 22.
39. Wollen, "Playing the Game with the Pirates," 20.
40. Davis, "Baseball Fandom Shocked by Upheaval on Pittsburgh Club: Effect on Team May Be Serious," 2.
41. "Carey Carries Kick to Landis," *El Paso Herald*, August 16, 1926, 3.
42. Foster, "'Inside Story' of What Caused the Pittsburgh Suspensions: Remark by Vice-President Clarke at Boston That Carey Was Having Tough Time of It Started Row – Landis Not Likely to Interfere," 18.
43. "Will Carey Go Court?" *Pittsburgh Gazette Times*, August 16, 1926, 1.
44. "Pirate Castoffs Gain Nothing by Carey's N.Y. Trip," *Altoona Tribune*, August 17, 1926, 8.
45. "'Won't Resign, No Matter How Case Ends, They'll Have to Fire Me,' McKechnie Says," *Pittsburgh Gazette Times*, August 17, 1926, 1.
46. Ibid, 5.
47. "Another Release Coming?: Rumor That One More Pirate Is to Be Dropped within Week – Reprisal Move?" *Pittsburgh Press*, August 17, 1926, 22.
48. Charles J. Doyle, "Carey May Stay; Heydler Here Today: Pirate Trio's Fate Hinges on Conference This Morning," *Pittsburgh Gazette Times*, August 17, 1926, 1.
49. Charles J. Doyle, "Heydler Clears Players, Upholds Club: Inside Story of Pirate Fuss Untold; Banishment Stands," *Pittsburgh Gazette Times*, August 18, 1926, 4.
50. "Carey and M'Kechnie Clash at Hearing: Manager and Dismissed Player in Heated Verbal Battle at Probe Session," *Pittsburgh Press*, August 17, 1926, 1.
51. Doyle, "Heydler Clears Players, Upholds Club: Inside Story of Pirate Fuss Untold; Banishment Stands," 4.
52. "Carey and M'Kechnie Clash at Hearing: Manager and Dismissed Player in Heated Verbal Battle at Probe Session," 1.
53. Doyle, "Heydler Clears Players, Upholds Club: Inside Story of Pirate Fuss Untold; Banishment Stands," 4.
54. Ibid, 1.
55. "Heydler Clears Pirates' Names: National League Head Refuses to Interfere with Pittsburgh Owner's Ultimatum," *Wilkes-Barre Record*, August 18, 1926, 20.
56. Ralph Davis, "Ralph Davis Says: Sammy Dreyfuss Has His Troubles," *Pittsburgh Press*, August 18, 1926, 24.
57. Doyle, "Heydler Clears Players, Upholds Club: Inside Story of Pirates Fuss Untold; Banishment Stands," 4.
58. "Carey Maintains Clarke Is Cause of Buc Scandal," 8.
59. Lou Wollen, "Playing the Game with the Pirates," *Pittsburgh Press*, August 19, 1926, 28.
60. Ralph Davis, "Ralph Davis Says: The 'Pictures They Turned to the Wall,'" *Pittsburgh Press*, August 20, 1926, 28.

61. Ralph Davis, "Ralph Davis Says: Barney Probably Won't 'Vacate' Again," *Pittsburgh Press*, August 19, 1926, 28.
62. "No Sentiment in Baseball - - - President Dreyfuss: Approves Dismissal of Trio of Veterans," *Pittsburgh Press*, August 22, 1926, 1.
63. Ralph S. Davis, "Not Much Sentiment in Baseball, but Plenty on Part of Fans: Little Mercy for Players," *Pittsburgh Press*, August 22, 1926, 2.
64. "Dreyfuss Will Not Reopen Case of Dismissed Players: Action Stands Says President; Will See Men if They Wish," *Pittsburgh Press*, August 31, 1926, 1.
65. "Dreyfuss Has No Statement," *Pittsburgh Press*, September 1, 1926, 26.
66. Ralph Davis, "Ralph Davis Says: Mr. Barney Dreyfuss Grants an Interview," *Pittsburgh Press*, September 14, 1926, 28.
67. Ralph Davis, "Ralph Davis Says: Denies a Flock of Pirate Rumors," *Pittsburgh Press*, September 14, 1926, 28.
68. Ralph Davis, "Ralph Davis Says: Says Carey's Sickness Was 'Own Fault,'" *Pittsburgh Press*, September 14, 1926, 28.
69. Chilly Doyle, "Chillysauce: Fans Pay Tribute to Carey – Max Appears in Rare Form," *Pittsbugh Gazette Times*, August 24, 1926, 13.
70. "Bucs Victims in No-Hit, No-Run Game: Pirates Fail to Get Safe Blow against Akron Hurler," *Pittsburgh Gazette Times*, August 23, 1926, 9.
71. Richard L. McBane, *A Fine-Looking Lot of Ball-Tossers: The Remarkable Akrons of 1881* (Jefferson, N.C.: McFarland & Company, Inc., 2005), 134.
72. Lou Wollen, "Playing the Game with the Pirates," *Pittsburgh Press*, September 25, 1926, 9.
73. "Stuffy McInnis Gets Unconditional Release," *Douglas Daily Dispatch*, September 26, 1926, 3.
74. "McInnis Blamed for 'Leak' in Pirate Revolt, Fired: Release Seen as Result of Disclosure of Clarke Ballot," *Pittsbugh Gazette Times*, September 26, 1926, 1.
75. Ralph S. Davis, "Murder Will Out, Even with Pirates: 'Misplaced Zeal' Trio Does Some Talking for the Press," *The Sporting News*, October 7, 1926, 1.
76. "McInnis Blamed for 'Leak' in Pirate Revolt, Fired: Release Seen as Result of Disclosure of Clarke Ballot," 1.
77. Ralph S. Davis, "Donie Bush Named to Pacify Pirates: M'Kechnie's Successor Has Fine Record in Indianapolis," *The Sporting News*, October 28, 1926, 1.
78. Ralph Davis, "Ralph Davis Says: The Passing of 'Stuffy' McInnis – Move Does Not Clarify Pirate Situation," *Pittsburgh Press*, September 27, 1926, 22.
79. Chester L. Smith, "Sport Shafts: Where Clarke Failed," *Pittsbugh Gazette Times*, October 1, 1926, 15.
80. Glenn Wright, interview by Dr. Eugene Converse Murdock, Cleveland Public Library Digital Gallery, June 23, 1978.
81. Smith, "Sport Shafts: Where Clarke Failed," 15.

Chapter 12

1. "Little Interviews and Letters to the Herald," *El Paso Herald*, September 24, 1926, 7.
2. "Bill Donohue Lands New St. Francis Job: Big Five Forward and Former Tech Star Named Grid Coach," *Altoona Tribune*, August 27, 1928, 8.
3. "Little Interviews and Letters to the Herald," 7.
4. Ralph S. Davis, "A Ball Player Who Says Prayer Helps Win Games: That's Max Carey – Idealist, Gentleman and Crack Base Stealer – Waived Off Pirates for 'Insubordination,'" *News-Democrat*, August 19, 1926, 8.
5. "Dreyfuss Denies Revolt Lost Flag: Injuries, Not Scrap, Doomed Team's Chances, Barney Dreyfuss Says, Denying Rumors," *Pittsbugh Gazette Times*, September 27, 1926, 4.
6. Ibid, 1.
7. Ibid, 4.
8. Ralph Davis, "Ralph Davis Says: Denies a Flock of Pirate Rumors," *Pittsburgh Press*, September 14, 1926, 28,
9. "Dreyfuss Denies Revolt Lost Flag: Injuries, Not Scrap, Doomed Team's Chances, Barney Dreyfuss Says, Denying Rumors," 4.

10. "Pirate Dissension Barred; Clarke Peeved at Small Share in Series: Trouble Between Him and Players Dates Back to Fall of 1925, Adams, Carey and Bigbee Declare – Was Given $1,000, but Wanted to Hand it Back, Alleging 'Ill Feeling' – Moore's Demand Clarke Get Off Bench Resulted in Firing Eddie," *News-Herald*, September 30, 1926, 1.
11. "Clarke May Quit Pirates, He Asserts: Won't Sit Upon Bench in 1927 or Be Manager Fred Declares," *Pittsburgh Gazette Times*, October 1, 1926, 10.
12. "Pirate Dissension Barred; Clarke Peeved at Small Share in Series: Trouble Between Him and Players Dates Back to Fall of 1925, Adams, Carey and Bigbee Declare – Was Given $1,000, but Wanted to Hand it Back, Alleging 'Ill Feeling' – Moore's Demand Clarke Get Off Bench Resulted in Firing Eddie," 1.
13. "Clarke May Quit Pirates, He Asserts: Won't Sit Upon Bench in 1927 or Be Manager Fred Declares," 10.
14. Ibid, 1.
15. Ibid, 10.
16. "'It's Been Hard Year,' Carey Reflects – Told Pet Canary Is Dead," *Pittsburgh Gazette Times*, October 1, 1926, 10.
17. John B. Sheridan, "Back of Home Plate: Observations of a Veteran Scribe," *The Sporting News*, August 26, 1926, 4.
18. James M. Driscoll, "The Sporting World: Bill McKechnie Is Fired as Pilot of Pirate Club; Fans Demanded It, Reason," *Daily Courier*, October 19, 1926, 7.
19. "Bill McKechnie, Pirates' Manager, Fired: Ax Swung on Corsair Pilot; No Successor Selected Yet," *Pittsburgh Gazette Times*, October 19, 1926, 5.
20. "Fred Clarke, Old Pirate Pilot, May Lead Pittsburgh Again: 1925 World Baseball Champions Will Probably Have the Former Great Outfielder and the Club's Vice-President at Helm Next Year," *Yonkers Herald*, October 22, 1926, 24.
21. Ralph S. Davis, "Donie Bush Named to Pacify Pirates: M'Kechnie's Successor Has Fine Record in Indianapolis," *The Sporting News*, October 28, 1926, 1.
22. Driscoll, "The Sporting World: Bill McKechnie Is Fired as Pilot of Pirate Club; Fans Demanded It, Reason," 7.
23. "Bill McKechnie, Pirates' Manager, Fired: Ax Swung on Corsair Pilot; No Successor Selected Yet," 5.
24. Ralph Davis, "Ralph Davis Says: McKechnie's Release No Surprise," *Pittsburgh Press*, October 19, 1926, 24.
25. "Bill McKechnie, Pirates' Manager, Fired: Ax Swung on Corsair Pilot; No Successor Selected Yet," 5.
26. Charles J. Doyle, "Many Loom as New Manager of Pirates: Neale, Casey Stengel and Fletcher Top Waiting List," *Pittsburgh Gazette Times*, October 19, 1926, 13.
27. Ralph Davis, "Ralph Davis Says: Bill's Successor Not Yet Selected – Bill McKechnie's Successor," *Pittsburgh Press*, October 19, 1926, 24.
28. Lou Wollen, "Naming M'Kechnie's Successor Pastime of Fans: Many Applicants Likely for Place," *Pittsburgh Press*, October 19, 1926, 34.
29. Doyle, "Many Loom as New Manager of Pirates: Neale, Casey Stengel and Fletcher Top Waiting List," 13.
30. Les Biederman, "Donie Bush, Back in Town, Talks About '27 Pennant 'Incidents': Calls Cuyler Case 'One of Those Things," *Pittsburgh Press*, December 12, 1947, 47.
31. "Bush Is Named New Pirate Manager: M'Kechnie's Place Given Indianapolis Team's Pilot," *Pittsburgh Gazette Times*, October 26, 1926, 1.
32. "Donie Bush Will Rule Pirate Club," *Decatur Daily Review*, October 28, 1926, 18.
33. "Bush Is Named New Pirate Manager: M'Kechnie's Place Given Indianapolis Team's Pilot," 11.
34. Ralph S. Davis, "'I Will Hustle All the Time,' Says New Buccaneer Manager: Bush Promises to Give Best Efforts," *Pittsburgh Press*, November 4, 1926, 38.
35. Ralph Davis, "Ralph Davis Says: Fans Declare Clarke Must Also Go," *Pittsburgh Press*, October 19, 1926, 24.
36. Wollen, "Naming M'Kechnie's Successor Pastime of Fans: Many Applicants Likely for Place," 34.
37. "Fred Clarke Resigns from Pirates: Last of Six in Corsair Feud Joins Others; Will Sell Out," *Pittsburgh Gazette Times*, October 27, 1926, 1.

38. "Fred Clarke Resigns Post with Pirates: Former Manager Hands in Resignation as Vice-President of Club," *Los Angeles Evening Express*, October 27, 1926, 29.
39. "Fred Clarke Resigns from Pirates: Last of Six in Corsair Feud Joins Others; Will Sell Out," 1.
40. "Dreyfuss Says He Will Succeed Fred Clarke: Buc Owner to Perform Vice President Duties; M'Kechnie Delays Move," *Pittsbugh Gazette Times*, October 28, 1926, 13.
41. "Bill McKechnie, Pirates' Manager, Fired: Ax Swung on Corsair Pilot; No Successor Selected Yet," 5.
42. "Pirates Good Bet for Next Season: Question of Salaries Will Have to Be Settled by Dreyfuss," *Richmond Times-Dispatch*, January 9, 1926, 9.
43. "Kiki Cuyler Is Holdout," *Mount Carmel News*, January 30, 1926, 3.
44. "Aldridge and Wright May Join Kiki Cuyler in List of Holdouts: Pirate Pitcher and Shortstop Want More Money – They Are Business Men and May Get It," *News-Herald*, January 28, 1926, 10.
45. Charles J. Doyle, "Holdout Threat Not Serious - - Dreyfuss: Pirate Owner Confident His Aces Will Be Back in Fold," *Pittsbugh Gazette Times*, January 29, 1926, 11.
46. Charles J. Doyle, "Pirates Ready for Tuesday's Jubilee: Dreyfuss-M'Kechnie May Satisfy Cuyler at New York Banquet," *Pittsburgh Gazette Times*, January 31, 1926, 4.
47. Charles J. Doyle, "Cuyler May Sign Buc Contract Today: I'll See Kiki If He Wishes Parley, Pirate Owner Says," *Pittsbugh Gazette Times*, February 2, 1926, 13.
48. "Dreyfuss and Kiki Cuyler Due to Talk Things Over," *Altoona Tribune*, February 2, 1926, 8.
49. Doyle, "Cuyler May Sign Buc Contract Today: I'll See Kiki If He Wishes Parley, Pirate Owner Says," 13.
50. Doyle, "Pirates Ready for Tuesday's Jubilee: Dreyfuss-M'Kechnie May Satisfy Cuyler at New York Banquet," 4.
51. "Cuyler Signs a Pirate Contract," *Yonkers Herald*, February 3, 1926, 18.
52. "Cuyler Signs Contract; to Receive about $12,000: Kiki Accepts Terms at Conference with Dreyfuss – Figures Withheld," *Pittsburgh Gazette Times*, February 3, 1926, 13.
53. "Kiki Cuyler Signs, Dreyfuss Announces," *Capital Times*, February 3, 1926, 9.
54. "Kiki Cuyler Got a Boost," *Mount Carmel News*, February 13, 1926, 3.
55. "Bush, Cuyler Sign," *Reading Times*, January 12, 1927, 11.
56. "Many Stars Autographed Biggest Fielder's Mitt," *Logan County Pioneer*, December 16, 1927, 8.
57. "Clarke May Quit Pirates, He Asserts: Won't Sit Upon Bench in 1927 or Be Manager Fred Declares," 10.
58. Irving Vaughan, "Yanks Escaped Cuyler Menace Once, Not Twice," *Chicago Daily Tribune*, September 21, 1932, 19.
59. Clark B. Kelsey, "Temperamental Cuyler Now with Chicago Cubs: Star Fielder and Slugger Who Nursed Grievances on Bench Last Season, Exchanged by Pittsburgh," *Daily Republican* (Rushville, Indiana), November 29, 1927, 8.
60. "'Kiki Cuyler Tells Home-Town Fans about His Troubles: Explains He Has No Ill Feelings," *Toledo News-Bee*, October 13, 1927, 17.
61. Fred Russell, "Sidelines: The Bush-Cuyler Mystery," *Nashville Banner*, October 4, 1960, 14.
62. "Ten Straight as Pirates Defeat St. Louis, 6-4," *Brooklyn Daily Eagle*, May 29, 1927, 2C.
63. "Kiki Cuyler Out," *El Paso Herald*, May 30, 1927, 5.
64. Ralph S. Davis, "Pirates' Gameness Shows in Results: Donie Bush's Crew Fights Hardest When Odds Pile Up," *The Sporting News*, June 9, 1927, 1.
65. Lou Wollen, "Barnhart's Comeback as Slugger without Parallel: Hitting Features Pirate Offensive," *Pittsburgh Press*, July 6, 1927, 26.
66. Lou Wollen, "Giants Score 9 to 2 Victory over Pirates: Fourth Inning Attack Sends Hill to Cover," *Pittsburgh Press*, August 7, 1927, 1-2.
67. Lou Wollen, "Hazen Cuyler Fined $50 by Manager Bush: Failure to Slide in Saturday's Game Brings Action," *Pittsburgh Press*, August 8, 1927, 29.
68. Lou Wollen, "Pirate Owner Backs Manager in Disciplining Cuyler: Bush Is Given Free Rein, Says Barney Dreyfuss," *Pittsburgh Press*, August 10, 1927, 24.
69. Ralph Davis, "Ralph Davis Says: Dreyfuss Laughs at Giants' Opinions," *Pittsburgh Press*, August 10, 1927, 24.
70. Ralph S. Davis, "Pittsburg Divided on Cuyler Incident: In Meantime, Bush Has Backing of Boss Barney Dreyfuss," *The Sporting News*, August 18, 1927, 1.

71. Davis, "Ralph Davis Says: Dreyfuss Laughs at Giants' Opinions," 24.
72. "Dreyfuss Brands Dissension 'Bunk': Owner Laughs at St. Louis Story About Carey," *Pittsburgh Post-Gazette*, August 12, 1927, 14.
73. Regis M. Welsh, "Fining Cuyler Likely Means Passing of Pirate Star: Sterling Outfielder May Be Pivot of Gigantic Trade during Offseason," *Pittsburgh Post-Gazette*, August 9, 1927, 14.
74. Ibid, 15.
75. L.H. Wollen, "Buccaneers Close Giants Series Today: Pirates' Pennant Chances Are Gone," *Pittsburgh Press*, September 25, 1924, 26.
76. Welsh, "Fining Cuyler Likely Means Passing of Pirate Star: Sterling Outfielder May Be Pivot of Gigantic Trade during Offseason," 15.
77. "Dreyfuss Brands Dissension 'Bunk': Owner Laughs at St. Louis Story about Carey," 14.
78. Ibid, 16.
79. Ibid, 14.
80. Ralph Davis, "Ralph Davis Says: Cuyler Proponent Unburdens Himself," *Pittsburgh Press*, August 15, 1927, 23.
81. "Dreyfuss Brands Dissension 'Bunk': Owner Laughs at St. Louis Story about Carey," 14.
82. Edward F. Balinger, "Buccaneers Jolted Twice by Redlegs: Meadows and Miljus Victims; Lose First, 8-6, Second 4-3," *Pittsburgh Post-Gazette*, September 6, 1927, 14.
83. Lou Wollen, "Pirates Did Not Resemble Champs in Labor Day Tilts: Defense Play Is Slovenly," *Pittsburgh Press*, September 6, 1927, 28.
84. Balinger, "Buccaneers Jolted Twice by Redlegs: Meadows and Miljus Victims; Lose First, 8-6, Second 4-3," 14.
85. "Marking Time with Pirates: Up-to-Minute Comment on Baseball – First Game Notes," *Pittsburgh Post-Gazette*, September 6, 1927, 16.
86. "Marking Time with Pirates: Up-to-Minute Comment on Baseball – Second Game Notes," *Pittsburgh Post-Gazette*, September 6, 1927, 16.
87. "Sad but True Story of Buc Defeats: Second Game – Third Inning," *Pittsburgh Post-Gazette*, September 6, 1927, 16.
88. "Pirates and Reds to Make Player Trade: Cuyler and Possibly Morrison to Be Turned over to Cincinnati for Pipp, Hargrave and Luque – According to Reliable Source, after Present Season Closes," *Pittsburgh Press*, September 6, 1927, 28.
89. "Comorosky Will Oppose Cincinnati: Takes Lloyd Waner's Place in Outfield Today; Walter Tauscher Recalled," *Pittsburgh Press*, September 6, 1927, 28.
90. "Cuyler's Position in Field Given to Comorosky," *Wilkes-Barre Times Leader*, September 6, 1927, 1.
91. "Donie Bush Signs Papers to Manage Bucs in 1928: Pittsburgh Manager Says He Benched Kiki Cuyler Because Play Wasn't Up to Standard of Gardener's," *Reading Times*, September 7, 1927, 14.
92. Ralph Davis, "Ralph Davis Says: Jealousy May Have Figured in Cuyler Case," *Pittsburgh Press*, September 10, 1927, 13.
93. Carl L. Turner, "No Orders for Series Tickets Are Accepted: Dreyfuss, of the Pirates, Is Waiting until His Team Is 'In,' before Shouting," *Daily Republican* (Monongahela, Pennsylvania), September 15, 1927, 1.
94. Ralph Davis, "Ralph Davis Says: Donie Bush Will Be Glad When Flag Is Cinched," *Pittsburgh Press*, September 27, 1927, 23.
95. Lou Wollen, "Pirates Clinch National League Flag: Defeat Reds in Weird Tilt," *Pittsburgh Press*, October 2, 1927, 1.
96. "Bill McKechnie, Pirates' Manager, Fired: Ax Swung on Corsair Pilot, No Successor Selected Yet," 5.

Chapter 13

1. Fred Russell, "Sidelines: The Bush-Cuyler Mystery," *Nashville Banner*, October 4, 1960, 14.
2. Ralph Davis, "Ralph Davis Says: Tip-Off on Cuyler's Fate Is Given," *Pittsburgh Press*, October 6, 1927, 27.
3. Les Conklin, "Pittsburgh Fans Await Big Series: City Is Overrun with Baseball Enthusiasts Who Are Paying Heavy," *Evening News* (Wilkes-Barre, Pennsylvania), October 4, 1927, 12.
4. "Cuyler's Son Ill as He Makes Ready for Series," *Evening News* (Wilkes-Barre, Pennsylvania), October 4, 1927, 12.

5. Frank Getty, "Pirates Grim, Yanks Blased, As Series Opener Begins: Corsair Craft, with Donie Bush at Helm, Are All Confidence," *Bristol Herald Courier*, October 5, 1927, 9.
6. "Here and There in Sports' Land," *New Castle News*, April 16, 1949, 14.
7. Russell, "Sidelines: The Bush-Cuyler Mystery," 14.
8. Davis, "Ralph Davis Says: Tip-Off on Cuyler's Fate Is Given," 27.
9. Billy Evans, "Billy Evans Says: A Man of Courage," *Park City Daily News*, October 11, 1927, 6.
10. "Diamond Crucible: Bush a Stubborn Fellow," *Nashville Banner*, October 6, 1927, 13.
11. "Marking Time with the Pirates: Breezy Comment and News on Baseball – Reason, Not Sentiment, Demand Cuyler in Game," *Pittsburgh Post-Gazette*, October 6, 1927, 17.
12. "Diamond Crucible: Bush a Stubborn Fellow," 13.
13. "Marking Time with the Pirates: Breezy Comment and News on Baseball – Reason, Not Sentiment, Demand Cuyler in Game," 17.
14. Davis, "Ralph Davis Says: Tip-Off on Cuyler's Fate Is Given," 27.
15. "Cuyler Isn't Good Enough: Sam Dreyfuss Explains Why Kiki Is Kept Out of World Series," *Nashville Banner*, October 6, 1927, 13.
16. "Here's Real Series Thrill," *Pittsburgh Post-Gazette*, October 6, 1927, 17.
17. Regis M. Welsh, "Pipgras' Great Hurling Gives Yankees Second Straight Victory over Pirates, 6-2: Recruit's Work Earns Big Edge in Series," *Pittsburgh Post-Gazette*, October 7, 1927, 1.
18. Thomas W. Meany, "Mystery of Hazen Cuyler May Go Unsolved: New York Likely to Resent Case as Much as Pittsburgh," *Brooklyn Daily Times*, October 7, 1927, 1A.
19. Lou Wollen, "Pirates Must Improve General Play to Defeat Yankees: Buccos Feeble in All Departments," *Pittsburgh Press*, October 7, 1927, 38.
20. "Something to Remember Him By," *Pittsburgh Press*, October 7, 1927, 40.
21. "Many Stars Autographed Biggest Fielder's Mitt," *Logan County Pioneer*, December 16, 1927, 8.
22. "Bush Shows Courage in Cuyler Case: Ousts Player Despite Protests of Fans – Wins League Pennant without Him," *Bismarck Tribune*, October 7, 1927, 6.
23. Brian Bell, "Yanks Return to Home Town with Half of Title Won: Need Two Games to Win Honors," *Bismarck Tribune*, October 7, 1927, 6.
24. Meany, "Mystery of Hazen Cuyler May Go Unsolved: New York Likely to Resent Case as Much as Pittsburgh," 1A.
25. Regis M. Welsh, "Pennock's Hurling Enables Yanks to Win Third Straight Game from Pirates, 8 to 1: Holds Bucs Hitless Until Eighth Inning," *Pittsburgh Post-Gazette*, October 8, 1927, 1.
26. Ibid, 16.
27. "Morale Broken, Pirate Backers Cheer Yank Win," *Decatur Herald*, October 9, 1927, 10.
28. "Yanks Win 4-3; Sweep Series: Wild Pitch in Ninth with Bases Loaded Ends Pirate's Hopes," *Decatur Herald*, October 9, 1927, 1.
29. Ibid, 10.
30. "Balls and Strikes," *Decatur Herald*, October 9, 1927, 10.
31. Ralph S. Davis, "Yanks Win Series Score 4 to 3: Babe Ruth Hits Homer with One on Base in Fifth," *Pittsburgh Press*, October 8, 1927, 1.
32. "Yanks Win 4-3; Sweep Series: Wild Pitch in Ninth with Bases Loaded Ends Pirate's Hopes," 10.
33. Ibid, 1.
34. Ibid, 10.
35. "Takes Blame for Last Defeat," *Indianapolis Times*, October 11, 1927, 10.
36. "Morale Broken, Pirate Backers Cheer Yank Win," 10.
37. "Bucs May Trade Off Kiki Cuyler: Controversy between Manager Bush and Star Lone Holdover of Big Series," *Toledo News-Bee*, October 11, 1927, 17.
38. Frank G. Menke, "Who Can Tell Why Corsairs Funked Series?: Pitiful Showing a Mystery of Diamond," *Chattanooga Sunday Times*, October 16, 1927, 18.
39. "Kiki Cuyler Expects Pittsburg Club to Use Him in Trade: Manager Bush Will Be Pleased When the Famous Outfielder Is Sent to Some Other Club," *Brooklyn Citizen*, October 11, 1927, 8.
40. "'Kiki' Knows Least about Cuyler Case: 'Whole Thing Mystery to Me,' Says Man in Case," *Chattanooga Sunday Times*, October 9, 1927, 17.
41. Ralph Davis, "Ralph Davis Says: Many Alleged Angles to Cuyler Case," *Pittsburgh Press*, October 11, 1927, 29.

42. Ed Hughes, "Fandom Delves into Depths of Kiki Cuyler Intrigue: Nothing in Baseball Was Ever So Veiled in Shroud of Mystery," *Brooklyn Daily Eagle*, October 12, 1927, 2A.
43. "Pirates Home; Few Fans Greet 'Em at Station: Cuyler Case Expected to Be Taken Up Today," *Morning Herald* (Uniontown, Fayette County, Pennsylvania), October 10, 1927, 10.
44. "Cuyler Convicts Self, Says Bush: Manager Tells Why He Did Not Use 'Ki' in Series," *Pittsburgh Press*, October 10, 1927, 1.
45. Ralph Davis, "Ralph Davis Says: Aldridge Was Friend of Hazen Cuyler," *Pittsburgh Press*, February 15, 1928, 28.
46. "Cuyler Convicts Self, Says Bush: Manager Tells Why He Did Not Use 'Ki' in Series," 1.
47. "Stove League in Full Blast as Bush's Team Breaks Up for Season: Report of Sale of Pirates Denied by Officials; Cuyler's Departure Believed Permanent," *Indianapolis Times*, October 11, 1927, 10.
48. Hazen Cuyler, "Cuyler Tells Why He Was Benched: Hazen's Troubles Start When Bush Forced Him to Bat in Second Place," *Morning Herald* (Uniontown, Fayette County, Pennsylvania), October 10, 1927, 10.
49. Hazen Cuyler, "Cuyler Explains Slump in Giant Series of 1924: Pirate Player Denies He Had Hot Arguments," *Morning Herald* (Uniontown, Fayette County, Pennsylvania), October 11, 1927, 10.
50. Hazen Cuyler, "Cuyler Believes He Has Played Last Game with Pirates; Ends Recital of Troubles: Hazen Doubts He Had Enemies among Pirates," *Morning Herald* (Uniontown, Fayette County, Pennsylvania), October 12, 1927, 10.
51. "'Kiki' Cuyler Tells Home-Town Fans about His Troubles: Explains He Has No Ill Feelings," *Toledo News-Bee*, October 13, 1927, 17.
52. "Stove League in Full Blast as Bush's Team Breaks Up for Season: Report of Sale of Pirates Denied by Officials; Cuyler's Departure Believed Permanent," 10.
53. "Cuyler Case Overshadows Series Comment: 'Ki' Makes Statement; Bush Remains Silent – Bush's Disclosure," *Pittsburgh Post-Gazette*, October 10, 1927, 16.
54. Ibid, 14.
55. Ibid, 16.
56. "Bush Gives His Side of Cuyler Benching Story," *Decatur Evening Herald*, October 12, 1927, 11.
57. "Bush Tells Why Cuyler Was Lifted: Pirate Skipper Recites to Washington Player Story of Famous Case," *Pittsburgh Press*, October 11, 1927, 29.
58. Russell, "Sidelines: The Bush-Cuyler Mystery," 14.
59. Cuyler, "Cuyler Tells Why He Was Benched: Hazen's Troubles Start When Bush Forced Him to Bat in Second Place," 10.
60. "Stove League in Full Blast as Bush's Team Break Up for Season: Report of Sale of Pirates Denied by Officials; Cuyler's Departure Believed Permanent," 10.
61. James Forr and David Proctor, *Pie Traynor: A Baseball Biography* (Jefferson, N.C.: McFarland & Company, Inc., 2010), 100.
62. Glenn Wright, interview by Dr. Eugene Converse Murdock, Cleveland Public Library Digital Gallery, June 23, 1978.
63. Clyde Barnhart, interview by Dr. Eugene Converse Murdock, Cleveland Public Library Digital Gallery, August 4, 1979.
64. "Stove League in Full Blast as Bush's Team Breaks Up for Season: Report of Sale of Pirates Denied by Officials; Cuyler's Departure Believed Permanent," 10.
65. Frank Getty, "'Kiki' Cuyler to Remain with Pirates If Dreyfuss Sells Club," *Decatur Evening Herald*, October 12, 1927, 11.
66. "Wentz Denies Buying Pirates," *News-Herald*, October 12, 1927, 12.
67. "Pirates May Trade Cuyler to Reds for Critz and Wally Pipp," *News-Herald*, October 11, 1927, 12.
68. "Will Trade 'Ki' Rumor States: 'Cuyler to Be Sent to Cincinnati' Remains Unconfirmed," *Morning Herald* (Uniontown, Fayette County, Pennsylvania), October 10, 1927, 10.
69. "Bush Praised in 'Kiki' Case: Other Managers Assert Buc Leader Did Correct Thing," *Bismarck Tribune*, October 28, 1927, 8.
70. Edward F. Balinger, "Baseball Gossip," *Pittsburgh Post-Gazette*, October 28, 1927, 15.
71. Thomas Holmes, "No Other Club Has Approached Dreyfuss on Subject of Cuyler," *Brooklyn Daily Eagle*, November 22, 1927, 2A.

72. "Jimmy Isaminger Raps Donie Bush in Cuyler Case: Carried Punishment to Extreme and Showed Schoolboy Judgment, Phila. Writer Says," *News-Herald*, October 12, 1927, 12.
73. "Scribbled by Scribes," *The Sporting News*, November 17, 1927, 4.
74. "Retort to Dreyfuss Put Kiki in Bad," *Los Angeles Record*, October 19, 1927, 11.
75. "Cuyler Explains Slump in Giant Series of 1924: Pirate Player Denies He Had Hot Arguments," 10.
76. "Man without a Baseball Country," *Paducah Evening Sun*, October 21, 1927, 1.
77. Edward F. Balinger, "Cuyler Is Traded to Chicago Cubs for Adams, Scott: Dreyfuss, Veeck and McCarthy Close Big Deal," *Pittsburgh Post-Gazette*, November 29, 1927, 1.
78. "Acquisition of Adams Gives Bush Experienced Keystone Sack Guardian: Only Future Can Tell Whether Bruins or Pirates Got Better of Big Player Exchange," *Pittsburgh Post-Gazette*, November 29, 1927, 14.
79. "'Even Though Expected, News of Trade Is Shock' - - - Cuyler: Star Outfielder Surprised When Told of Trade," *Pittsburgh Post-Gazette*, November 29, 1927, 14.

Chapter 14

1. "McCarthy May Find Cuyler Poor Buy: Other Managers Appear to Think Cubs Got Stung," *Oakland Tribune*, November 30, 1927, 29.
2. Ralph S. Davis, "Trade Week Meant Little to Pittsburg: Only Real Deal Offered Was One Bush Couldn't See," *The Sporting News*, December 22, 1927, 5.
3. "Sports of All Sorts: Sale of Cuyler Held Result of Temperament – Dreyfuss Says Kiki Is Great Player, However," *Selma Times-Journal*, December 12, 1927, 5.
4. "Here and There in Sports' Land," *New Castle News*, April 16, 1949, 14.
5. Lou Wollen, "Deal with Giants Brings Grimes to Buccaneers: Aldridge Traded to Gotham Club," *Pittsburgh Press*, February 12, 1928, 1.
6. Ralph Davis, "Ralph Davis Says: Aldridge Was Friend of Hazen Cuyler," *Pittsburgh Press*, February 15, 1928, 28.
7. Ralph S. Davis, "All Pirates in Line as Work Is Started: Dreyfuss Finds It Easy Task to Please Burleigh Grimes," *The Sporting News*, February 23, 1928, 5.
8. Davis, "Ralph Davis Says: Aldridge Was Friend of Hazen Cuyler," 28.
9. Davis, "All Pirates In Line as Work Is Started: Dreyfuss Finds It Easy Task to Please Burleigh Grimes," 5.
10. Regis M. Welsh, "Sports of All Sorts," *Pittsburgh Post-Gazette*, April 24, 1928, 15.
11. "Finally Signs," *Pittsburgh Post-Gazette*, May 7, 1928, 18.
12. "Glenn Wright, New Pirate Shortstop, Is a Holdout," *Brooklyn Daily Eagle*, February 7, 1924, 22.
13. "Sports Mirror," John Mooney, *Salt Lake Tribune*, June 29, 1961, 25.
14. "Glenn Wright, $40,000 Star, Is a Holdout," *Park City Daily News*, February 7, 1924, 6.
15. Ralph S. Davis, "Two Minor Buys Are Pittsburg Balkers: Wright and Kremer Asking Part of Purchase Price," *The Sporting News*, February 14, 1924, 3.
16. Ralph S. Davis, "Pirates Leave Cold of the East Behind: First Party on Its Way toward California Camp," *The Sporting News*, February 28, 1924, 2.
17. Ralph S. Davis, "Pirates Get Good Weather at Camp: Pittsburg Team Finds California Ideal for Training," *The Sporting News*, March 13, 1924, 2.
18. Glenn Wright, Interview by Dr. Eugene Converse Murdock, Cleveland Public Library Digital Library, June 23, 1978.
19. Charles J. Doyle, "Pirates Drop Initial Game to Kansas City, 2 to 0: Ray Caldwell Pitches American Association Champions to Victory," *Gazette Times*, April 6, 1924, 4.
20. Charles J. Doyle, "Pirates Turn Tables on Kansas City: Jughandle Johnny Allows but Five Hits; Score Is 7-1," *Gazette Times*, April 7, 1924, 9.
21. Ralph S. Davis, "Bucs Get Acid Test First Three Weeks: Pirates Face Red Pitching Eight Times in That Period," *The Sporting News*, April 17, 1924, 3.
22. Ralph S. Davis, "Pirates Due to Get Morning Practice: M'Kechnie Not Pleased with Way Team Has Been Going," *The Sporting News*, May 1, 1924, 5.
23. Ralph Davis, "Pirates Could Use Several Kremers: One Recruit Who Has Cheering Effect upon M'Kechnie," *The Sporting News*, May 15, 1924, 3.

24. Ralph S. Davis, "Glenn Wright, Pirate Shortstop, Wins High Praise for Stellar Work in World's Series," *Pittsburgh Press*, October 13, 1925, 1.
25. Chilly Doyle, "Chillysauce: One of Many Misfortunes," *Pittsbugh Gazette Times*, August 21, 1926, 12.
26. Chilly Doyle, "Chillysauce: Wright Lame but Ready," *Pittsbugh Gazette Times*, August 25, 1926, 14.
27. Chilly Doyle, "Chillysauce: Glenn Wright Needed," *Pittsbugh Gazette Times*, September 1, 1926, 13.
28. Chilly Doyle, "Chillysauce: Wright to See Bonesetter," *Pittsbugh Gazette Times*, September 2, 1926, 15.
29. Chilly Doyle, "Chillysauce: Best in National League," *Pittsbugh Gazette Times*, September 12, 1926, 3.
30. Charles J. Doyle, "Buccaneers Trounced Again by Dodgers, 3 to 1: Yde Is Victim in Close Slab Battle with M'Weeney," *Pittsbugh Gazette Times*, September 19, 1926, 2.
31. Glenn Wright, interview by Dr. Eugene Converse Murdock.
32. Martin J. Haley, "Cards Get 5-Run Lead, Then Blow Up and Let Pirates Win, 9-8: McGraw Goes to Pieces in 5th; Grantham's Homer off Bell in 7th Wins Game," *St. Louis Globe-Democrat*, June 29, 1927, 10.
33. "Wright's Injury Another Hazard for Buccaneers: Troubles Continue to Heckle Corsairs," *Pittsburgh Press*, June 29, 1927, 24.
34. "Pirates Hit Three Card Pitchers and Strengthen Lead: Wright Beaned but Not Seriously Hurt, Mitchell Trims New York Giants," *La Crosse Tribune and Leader-Press*, June 29, 1927, 8.
35. "Wright's Injury Another Hazard for Buccaneers: Troubles Continue to Heckle Corsairs," 24.
36. "Pitching Weakness Makes Pirates Position Precarious: Lead Only Half Game," *Pittsburgh Press*, June 30, 1927, 29.
37. Ralph S. Davis, "Bucs Take Things Just as They Come: Tough Breaks Only Find Bushmen Fighting the Harder," *The Sporting News*, July 7, 1927, 1.
38. "Cuyler's Single with 2 Out in Ninth Scores Waner with Buc Victory: Wright and Marks Back in Lineup – P. Waner at First Because of Joe Harris's Illness," *News-Herald*, July 15, 1927, 8.
39. "Glenn Wright Is Arrested," *Mount Carmel News*, October 11, 1927, 6.
40. "Glenn Wright Is Arrested after Crash Injures Four: Pittsburgh Ball Club's Shortstop Charged with Reckless Driving, Held in $100 Bail – Other Car Lifted Off Road, Suspended on Traffic Beacon," *Pittsburgh Post-Gazette*, October 10, 1927, 1.
41. "Glenn Wright in Collison," *Brooklyn Citizen*, October 10, 1927, 8.
42. "Glenn Wright Is Arrested," 6.
43. "Glenn Wright to Settle for Auto Crash," *Morning Herald* (Uniontown, Fayette County, Pennsylvania), October 12, 1927, 10.
44. "Six Damage Suits Filed against Glenn Wright, of Pirates," *News-Herald*, May 12, 1928, 9.
45. Lou Wollen, "Pirate Squad Holds Initial Workout of Season: Pilot to Hold Longer Drills," *Pittsburgh Press*, February 22, 1928, 26.
46. Ralph S. Davis, "Bush to Rule Pirates with Iron Hand This Season: No Philandering to Be Tolerated," *Pittsburgh Press*, February 26, 1928, 2.
47. Stoney McLinn, "Pirates, Bolstered by Adams, Hope to Repeat Flag Win and Show Up Yankees," *Brooklyn Daily Times*, March 29, 1928, 1A.
48. Ralph S. Davis, "Pirates Raiding as They Sail for Home: Stop at Many Ports to Collect for Exhibition Games," *The Sporting News*, April 5, 1928, 3.
49. Wright, interview by Dr. Eugene Converse Murdock.
50. Regis M. Welsh, "Sports of All Sorts: Cuyler Gets Back – But Few Realize It," *Pittsburgh Post-Gazette*, May 1, 1928, 15.
51. Ralph S. Davis, "Pirates Whistling to Keep Up Courage: Teams from East Caught Them Short, 'Tis Said," *The Sporting News*, May 24, 1928, 3.
52. Ralph S. Davis, "Fans Still Retain Belief in Pirates: Start Was Slow, but Bush Has Them Coming Now," *The Sporting News*, May 17, 1928, 3.
53. Ralph S. Davis, "Time to Get Going Thinks Donie Bush: So He Begins to Bear Down on His Pirate Team." *The Sporting News*, May 31, 1928, 3.
54. Edward F. Balinger, "Bucs Trade Gooch, Harris to Robins for Hargreaves: New Backstop Likely to Start against Braves Today; Bush Elated in Getting Seasoned Receiver," *Pittsburgh Post-Gazette*, June 9, 1928, 16.
55. Regis M. Welsh, "Sports of All Sorts: Gooch – and His Recent 'Bad Breaks'," *Pittsburgh Post-Gazette*, June 9, 1928, 17.

56. Davis J. Walsh, "Big Trades in Majors Due Today: Pirates Refused to Trade Glenn Wright to Cubs as Other Deals Loom," *Evening News* (Wilkes-Barre, Pennsylvania), June 15, 1928, 21.
57. Edward F. Balinger, "Following the Bucs," *Pittsburgh Post-Gazette*, June 28, 1928, 19.
58. Edward F. Balinger, "Sherdel Beats Bucs in Opener, 4 to 3: Homers by Hafey, Frisch Overcome Lead in Seventh," *Pittsburgh Post-Gazette*, June 29, 1928, 18.
59. Ralph Davis, "Ralph Davis Says: Internal Differences Hampering Pirates," *Pittsburgh Press*, June 29, 1928, 42.
60. Ralph Davis, "Ralph Davis Says: Patrons Attack Manager Bush's Strategy," *Pittsburgh Press*, June 29, 1928, 42.
61. Ralph Davis, "Ralph Davis Says: Manager Has Lost Confidence of Players," *Pittsburgh Press*, June 29, 1928, 42.
62. Ralph S. Davis, "Lady Luck in Love with Earl Smith: Seems He Just Can't Keep Out of World's Series Money," *The Sporting News*, July 19, 1928, 3.
63. "Bucs Release Earl Smith: Run-In with Bush Results in Veteran Being Fired," *Pittsburgh Post-Gazette*, July 10, 1928, 14.
64. Davis, "Lady Luck in Love with Earl Smith: Seems He Just Can't Keep Out of World's Series Money," 3.
65. Regis M. Welsh, "Sports of All Sorts: Not Forcing, but Ready if It Comes," *Pittsburgh Post-Gazette*, August 31, 1928, 15.
66. "Dick Bartell Is Going Great," *Mount Carmel News*, July 24, 1928, 6.
67. Edward F. Balinger, "Following the Bucs," *Pittsburgh Post-Gazette*, July 26, 1928, 17.
68. Ralph S. Davis, "Pirates Win and So Bush Regains Favor: Fortune Turns When Smith and Miljus Are Discarded," *The Sporting News*, July 26, 1928, 3.
69. Ralph S. Davis, "Jinx Hands Pirates Another Hard Blow: Injury of Floyd Scott in Line with Team's Bad Luck," *The Sporting News*, August 2, 1928, 3.
70. Thomas Holmes, "Pirates May Put Glenn Wright on Ivory Market This Winter: Pittsburg May Seek Jess Petty in Trade for Star Shortstop," *Brooklyn Daily Eagle*, August 7, 1928, 4A.
71. "Meadows Put on Pirates' Retired List: Veteran Hurler, Victim of Poor Year, Returns Home," *Pittsburgh Post-Gazette*, August 28, 1928, 14.
72. "Meadows Goes Out," *Salt Lake Tribune*, August 30, 1928, 12.
73. Edward F. Balinger, "Following the Bucs," *Pittsburgh Post-Gazette*, September 1, 1928, 17.
74. Ralph S. Davis, "Much Guessing as Bucs Say Goodbye: Some Hardly Will Be Seen In Pittsburg Colors Again," *The Sporting News*, September 20, 1928, 3.
75. Ralph S. Davis, "Dreyfuss Will Not Delay His Trading: Fans Can Look for a Big Deal Almost Any Day," *The Sporting News*, October 11, 1928, 2.
76. Ralph S. Davis, "Sheely to Replace Grantham at First: Pittsburg Counting on Ex-White Sox Player as Regular," *The Sporting News*, October 18, 1928, 5.
77. Eddie Murphy, "Detroit Gets Good Player in Sigafoos: Kerr, Sheely and Rhyne Also Go in the Draft," *Oakland Tribune*, October 4, 1928, 38.
78. Davis, "Sheely to Replace Grantham at First: Pittsburg Counting on Ex-White Sox Player as Regular," 5.
79. Wright, interview by Dr. Eugene Converse Murdock.
80. Edward F. Balinger, "Pirates Trade Wright for Jess Petty: Veteran Hurler, Riconda Come to Bucs in Big Deal," *Pittsburgh Post-Gazette*, December 12, 1928, 18.
81. Ralph Davis, "Carlson Shouts from Housetops: Famous Coach of Pitt Passers Wants World to Know His Basketball Prospects Are Brighter Than Ever," *Pittsburgh Press*, December 13, 1928, 44.
82. Thomas Holmes, "John Heydler Discourages Brooklyn Bleat on Glenn Wright: Worry over Shortstop's Condition Seems to Be Unfounded from Reports," *Brooklyn Daily Eagle*, March 12, 1929, 4A.
83. Walter Trumbell, "Athletics Stronger Through 1928 Experience, Mack States: 'Younger Players Will Be Better Prepared for Any Hard Series This Year,' Wise Philadelphia Leader Tells Walter Trumbell," *Richmond Times-Dispatch*, March 12, 1929, 14.
84. Holmes, "John Heydler Discourages Brooklyn Bleat on Glenn Wright: Worry over Shortstop's Condition Seems to Be Unfounded from Reports," 4A.
85. Henry Richards, "Glenn Wright Reveals He Can't Play Winning Ball for Robins: Star's Miscues Are Blamed for Robins' Defeat," *Standard Union*, May 8, 1929, 14.

86. Murray Robinson, "As You Like It: Breaking the Fall," *Standard Union*, May 8, 1929, 14.
87. Thomas Holmes, "Bush Denies Pirates Tried to Cheat Robins on Wright," *Brooklyn Daily Eagle*, May 10, 1929, A6.
88. Thomas Holmes, "Robins More Depressed Than Ever in Philadelphia," *Brooklyn Daily Eagle*, May 16, 1929, A8.
89. Thomas Holmes, "Wright's Troubles Diagnosed as Chipped Shoulder Blade – Operation Advised: Vance Ready to Take His Arm Out of Glass Case – Will Work Today," *Brooklyn Daily Eagle*, July 12, 1929, 10.
90. "Glenn Wright Placed on Retired List by Robins," *St. Louis Globe-Democrat*, July 25, 1929, 12.
91. Henry Richards, "Operation Seems to Have Cured Glenn Wright's Ailing Arm: Star Appears Fit for Duty at Shortstop," *Standard Union*, September 21, 1929, 10.
92. "Waners in Unique Brotherly Act," *News-Herald*, February 28, 1929, 13.
93. "Lloyd Waner Due at Bucco Training Camp," *Salt Lake Tribune*, March 21, 1929, 17.
94. "Paul Waner Signs, Plays with Pirate Club Today," *Alton Evening Telegraph*, April 5, 1929, 8.
95. "Paul Waner Benched as Pirates Falter," *Oakland Tribune*, August 6, 1929, 1.
96. "Giants Defeat Pirates Again by Score of 5-3: Walker Effective as Buc Misplays Lose for Petty – Paul Waner Is Benched, Hemsley Spiked," *News-Herald*, August 7, 1929, 11.
97. Thomas Holmes, "Paul Waner Is Center of Latest Pittsburg Internal Dissension Tale: 'Kid Brother' Lloyd Is Now Rated Star of Oklahoma Outfielders," *Brooklyn Daily Eagle*, August 10, 1929, 6.
98. Henry Richards, "Donie Bush Unpopular in Pittsburgh Despite Pirates' Success: Buc Fans Fail to Appreciate Mite Manager," *Standard Union*, August 10, 1929, 10.
99. "Bush Resigns as Bucs' Leader: Manager Gives No Reason for Quitting Post," *Pittsburgh Press*, August 28, 1929, 1.
100. "Jewel Ens Takes over Reins at Pittsburgh: Donie Bush Resigns When Club Returns to Pittsburgh; No Reason Given for Action of 'Donie,'" *Knoxville Journal*, August 29, 1929, 12.
101. "Donie Bush Resigns as Manager of the Pittsburgh Club," *Kane Republican*, August 28, 1929, 5.
102. "Sam Dreyfuss Dies," *Chattanooga Daily Times*, February 23, 1931, 8.
103. Lou Wollen, "Sports from All Angles: Secrecy Surrounds Bush's Resignation," *Pittsburgh Press*, August 29, 1929, 32.

Chapter 15
1. Lou Wollen, "Sports from All Angles: Secrecy Surrounds Bush's Resignation," *Pittsburgh Press*, August 29, 1929, 32.
2. Ralph Davis, "Bush at Sea as Bucs Slumped: Resignation Comes after Failure of Team Had Driven Pilot Almost to Distraction – Donie Not Wholly Responsible for Flop," *Pittsburgh Press*, August 29, 1929, 32.
3. Joe Williams, "Interference Causes Bush to Quit, Claimed: Frequent Suggestions by Magnate Arouses Ire of Buc Pilot," *Pittsburgh Press*, August 29, 1929, 32.
4. "Scribbled by Scribes," *The Sporting News*, September 5, 1929, 4.
5. Les Biederman, "Donie Bush, Back in Town, Talks about '27 Pennant Incidents: Calls Cuyler Case 'One of Those Things,'" *Pittsburgh Press*, December 12, 1947, 47.
6. "Ens Signs to Manage Buccaneers Next Season: Tendered and Accepts One Year Contract; Has Been with Pittsburgh Club as Player, Coach Since 1922," *Pittsburgh Post-Gazette*, September 23, 1929, 14.
7. Edward F. Balinger, "Carey Returns to Pirates in Capacity of Coach: Veteran, Who Served Local Club for 16 Years, Signed to Assist Ens, Giving Bucs Good Strategy Board," *Pittsburgh Post-Gazette*, February 1, 1930, 18.
8. "Barney Dreyfuss, Owner of Pirates and 'Father of World Series' Dies: Veteran of Old Guard Fails after Operation," *Reading Times*, February 6, 1932, 12.
9. Norman E. Brown, "Norman Brown Picks Giants to Take Flag in National League," *Morning Herald* (Hagerstown, Maryland), April 11, 1929, 8.
10. Fred Wertenbach, "Bartell Joins Grimes as Buccaneer Holdout: Dick's Demands Absurd - - Dreyfuss," *Pittsburgh Press*, February 28, 1930, 21.
11. "Rookie Shortstops Please Buc Bosses: Sam Dreyfuss Not Worried over Bartell's Holdout after Watching Charlie Engel and Ben Sankey Workout," *Pittsburgh Press*, March 2, 1930, 2.

12. Ralph Davis, "Bartell's Demands Kept Well Guarded: Pirate Shortstop Has Been Holdout for Months – Youngster Puts Big Value on Services for Coming Season," *Pittsburgh Press*, March 1, 1930, 13.
13. "Fight for Shortstop," *Harrisburg Telegraph*, March 3, 1930, 12.
14. Fred Wertenbach, "Dick Bartell Relents, Asks Salary Parley at Camp: Will Discuss Figure with Dreyfuss Soon," *Pittsburgh Press*, March 11, 1930, 33.
15. Fred Wertenbach, "Infielder Dick Bartell Signs Pirate Contract: Shortstop Quits Ranks of Holdouts," *Pittsburgh Press*, March 12, 1930, 32.
16. Ralph Davis, "Statement Stage in Grimes Battle: Quiet Conflict over Spitballer's Pirate Contract Reaches Open Stage as Official Replies to Burleigh's Emphatic Avowal," *Pittsburgh Press*, March 12, 1930, 32.
17. "Grimes' Trip 'Down River' Penalty for Salary Tiff: Pirate Fans Await Results before Condemning Trade," *Pittsburgh Press*, April 10, 1930, 34.
18. Fred Wertenbach, "Grimes' Deal Startles Mates Who Refuse to Talk: Ens States He Desired Big Trade," *Pittsburgh Press*, April 10, 1930, 34.
19. "Grimes' Trip 'Down River' Penalty for Salary Tiff: Pirate Fans Await Results before Condemning Trade," 34.
20. "Percy Lee Jones Released by Bucs Today," *Daily News Standard*, June 23, 1930, 1.
21. "Jess Petty Veteran Southpaw Waived Out of League by Bucs," *San Bernardino Daily Sun*, June 17, 1930, 15.
22. "Reports Have Bartell Due to Be Traded: Shortstop Not with Club for Vital Series with Leaders," *Pittsburgh Press*, September 25, 1930, 34.
23. "Pittsburgh Asks for Waivers on Bartell," *Daily News Standard*, September 25, 1930, 11.
24. "Reports Have Bartell Due to Be Traded: Shortstop Not with Club for Vital Series with Leaders," 34.
25. "The Nut Cracker," *Altoona Mirror*, September 29, 1930, 16.
26. "Pittsburgh Asks for Waivers on Bartell," 11.
27. "The Nut Cracker," 16.
28. "Jewel Ens Signs One-Year Contract to Pilot Pirates Again Next Season," *Chattanooga Daily Times*, October 29, 1930, 11.
29. Edward F. Balinger, "Carey Dropped as Buc Coach: No Reason Given for Release of Former Outfielder," *Pittsburgh Post-Gazette*, November 1, 1930, 19.
30. Edward F. Balinger, "Pirates Trade Bartell to the Phillies: Bucs Get Thevenow, Willoughby in Deal for Young Shortstop," *Pittsburgh Post-Gazette*, November 7, 1930, 18.
31. Havey J. Boyle, "Mirrors of Sport: The Trade," *Pittsburgh-Post Gazette*, November 7, 1930, 19.
32. William Braucher, "Hooks and Slides: Bartell on His Way," *Cumberland Evening Times*, December 5, 1930, 15.
33. Ralph S. Davis, "Pirates Make Room to Add New Catcher: Bool's Release Regarded as Move toward Another Trade," *The Sporting News*, November 20, 1930, 3.
34. Thomas Holmes, "Critical Pittsburgh Rooters Still Caustic over Bartell Case," *Brooklyn Daily Eagle*, November 21, 1930, 26.
35. Dick Bartell, "Bartell Holds Out on Dreyfuss, Is Suspended, Fined, Traded to Phillies," *Terre Haute Star*, April 6, 1950, 15.
36. "Sam Dreyfuss Dies in Home: Son of Pirate Owner Fails to Survive Pneumonia," *Pittsburgh Post-Gazette*, February 23, 1931, 1.
37. "Sam Dreyfuss Dies Here of Pneumonia: Bucs' Vice President Loses Fight for Life," *Pittsburgh Press*, February 23, 1931, 6.
38. "Sam Dreyfuss Dies in Home: Son of Pirate Owner Fails to Survive Pneumonia," 1.
39. "Sam Dreyfuss Dies Here of Pneumonia: Bucs' Vice President Loses Fight for Life," 1.
40. "Sam Dreyfuss Dies in Home: Son of Pirate Owner Fails to Survive Pneumonia," 1.
41. "Sam Dreyfuss Dies Here of Pneumonia: Bucs' Vice President Loses Fight for Life," 6.
42. "Sam Dreyfuss Dies in Home: Son of Pirate Owner Fails to Survive Pneumonia," 1.
43. "Sam Dreyfuss Dies Here of Pneumonia: Bucs' Vice President Loses Fight for Life," 1.
44. Fred Wertenbach, "Bucs Honor Memory of Sam Dreyfuss: Jewel Ens Calls Off Workouts," *Pittsburgh Press*, February 23, 1931, 13.
45. Fred Wertenbach, "Paso Robles Pays Dreyfuss Homage: Team, Town Will Honor Late Pirate," *Pittsburgh Press*, February 24, 1931, 25.

46. "Buccos Wear Mourning Bands," *Pittsburgh Press*, February 24, 1931, 25.
47. Ralph S. Davis, "Barney Dreyfuss Back in Saddle Assumes Active Charge of Bucs: Owner of Pirates Denies He Will Quit Game," *The Sporting News*, March 5, 1931, 1.
48. Ralph S. Davis, "Pirates Break Camp for Exhibition Tour: Return of French and Paul Waner Gives Ens' Squad New Hope," *The Sporting News*, March 19, 1931, 3.
49. Ralph S. Davis, "Return of P. Waner Sets Bucs for Year: Absence Gave Jim Mosolf Chance to Cinch Utility Berth," *The Sporting News*, March 26, 1931, 3.
50. Frederick G. Lieb, *The Pittsburgh Pirates* (1948; reprint, Carbondale, Ill.: Southern Illinois University Press, 2003), 243.
51. "Funeral Held for Benswanger," *The Sun* (San Bernardino, California), January 18, 1972, 26.
52. Lieb, *The Pittsburgh Pirates*, 243.
53. "Jewel Ens Fired," *Santa Rosa Republican*, October 9, 1931, 6.
54. Fred Wertenbach, "Dreyfuss May Name Another Pilot than George Gibson: Pirate Owner Says No Selection Made," *Pittsburgh Press*, October 9, 1931, 43.
55. "Gibson Made 'Buc' Pilot for 1932," *Pittsburgh Press*, November 30, 1931, 1.
56. Fred Wertenbach, "Trades Loom as Gibson Is Named Pilot: Pirate Head Says Changes Will Be Made," *Pittsburgh Press*, November 30, 1931, 28.
57. Ardee, "Gibson Not Certain about Buc Changes: New Pilot Plans No Radical Moves in Strengthening Team," *The Sporting News*, December 10, 1931, 6.
58. Ardee, "Anticipated Trades by Pirates Lacking: Officials Return Empty-Handed from League Meetings," *The Sporting News*, December 17, 1931, 7.
59. Ardee, "Proposed Buc Deal Likely to Prove Dud: Rivals Coy about Giving Pirates Talent They Covet," *The Sporting News*, December 31, 1931, 7.
60. "Barney Dreyfuss, Owner of Pirates and 'Father of World Series' Dies: Veteran of Old Guard Fails after Operation," 12.
61. Ardee, "Five Buc Twirlers Slated for Release: George Gibson Expects to Carry Staff of Nine Pitchers," *The Sporting News*, January 7, 1932, 3.
62. Edward F. Balinger, "Dreyfuss Goes Under Knife Again: Report Buc Owner Rests Well after Second Operation," *Pittsburgh Post-Gazette*, January 7, 1932, 14.
63. "Dreyfuss Undergoes Second Operation," *Pittsburgh Press*, January 7, 1932, 24.
64. Balinger, "Dreyfuss Goes Under Knife Again: Report Buc Owner Rests Well after Second Operation," 14.
65. "Dreyfuss, Ex-Paducahan, Owner of Pirates, Dies: Pneumonia after Operation Causes Dreyfuss' Death," *Sun-Democrat*, February 5, 1932, 1.
66. Edward F. Balinger, "Sport World Mourns Death of Dreyfuss: Pirate Owner Succumbs in N.Y. Hospital," *Pittsburgh Post-Gazette*, February 6, 1932, 14.
67. "Barney Dreyfuss, Owner of Pirates and 'Father of World Series' Dies: Veteran of Old Guard Fails after Operation," 12.
68. "Dreyfuss, Ex-Paducahan, Owner of Pirates, Dies: Pneumonia after Operation Causes Dreyfuss' Death," 1.
69. "Barney Dreyfuss, Owner of Pirates and 'Father of World Series' Dies: Veteran of Old Guard Fails after Operation," 12.
70. "Dreyfuss, Ex-Paducahan, Owner of Pirates, Dies: Pneumonia after Operation Causes Dreyfuss' Death," 1.
71. "Barney Dreyfuss, Pirates' Owner Dies – Is Second within Two Weeks: Followed National Pastime since 1884 – Was Promoter of World Series in 1903 – Underwent Operation in New York on January 6th," *Standard Sentinel*, February 6, 1932, 15.
72. "Baseball Leaders, Friends Pay Tribute to Dreyfuss," *Pittsburgh Post-Gazette*, February 6, 1932, 14.
73. "Barney Dreyfuss, Owner of Pirates and 'Father of World Series' Dies: Veteran of Old Guard Fails after Operation," 12.
74. "Dreyfuss, Ex-Paducahan, Owner of Pirates, Dies: Pneumonia after Operation Causes Dreyfuss' Death," 9.
75. Havey J. Boyle, "Mirrors of Sport: Barney Dreyfuss – Pride in His Park," *Pittsburgh Post-Gazette*, February 6, 1932, 15.
76. "Notables to Attend Dreyfuss Funeral," *Anniston Star*, February 6, 1932, 6.

77. Edward F. Balinger, "Baseball Fans Pay Respects to Dreyfuss: Thousands View Body at Rodef Shalom Temple," *Pittsburgh Post-Gazette*, February 8, 1932, 14.
78. "Notables to Attend Dreyfuss Funeral," 6.
79. Balinger, "Baseball Fans Pay Respects to Dreyfuss: Thousands View Body at Rodef Shalom Temple," 14.
80. "Bury Dreyfuss in West View: Thousands Pay Last Tribute to Dead Baseball Leader," *Pittsburgh Post-Gazette*, February 8, 1932, 1.
81. Ibid, 4.
82. Ibid, 1.
83. Ibid, 4.
84. "Pirates Likely to Remain in Dreyfuss Family," *Reading Times*, February 6, 1932, 12.
85. Bud Nelson, "Terry Probably Will Sign after M'Graw's Visit: Five Yankees Leave Tomorrow – Mrs. Dreyfuss Made Head of Pirates," *Brooklyn Daily Times*, February 19, 1932, 1A.
86. Chester L. Smith, "McKinney Takes Over as Bucs' Boss: Ray Kennedy Stays as 'Major Domo' in Pittsburgh Office," *Pittsburgh Press*, August 9, 1946, 28.
87. "Fred Clarke: The Baseball Capitalist," *San Francisco Sunday Call*, March 12, 1911, 6.
88. "Baseball Leaders, Friends Pay Tribute to Dreyfuss," 14.

Bibliography

Audio

Barnhart, Clyde. Interview. By Dr. Eugene Converse Murdock. Cleveland Public Library Digital Gallery. August 4, 1979.

Wright, Glenn. Interview. By Dr. Eugene Converse Murdock. Cleveland Public Library Digital Gallery. June 23, 1978.

Books

Appel, Marty. *Casey Stengel: Baseball's Greatest Character*. New York: Anchor Sports – Penguin Random House LLC, 2017.

Armstrong, Richard C. and Martin Healy Jr. *George "Mooney" Gibson: Canadian Catcher for the Deadball Era Pirates*. Jefferson, N.C.: McFarland & Company, Inc., 2020.

Boxerman, Burton A. and Benita W. Boxerman. *Ebbets to Veeck to Busch: Eight Owners Who Shaped Baseball*, Jefferson, N.C.: McFarland & Company, Inc., 2003.

———. *Jews and Baseball: Volume 1 – Entering the American Mainstream, 1871-1948*. Jefferson, N.C.: McFarland & Company, Inc., 2007.

Carroll, Jeff. *Sam Rice: A Biography of the Washington Senators Hall of Famer*. Jefferson, N.C.: McFarland & Company, Inc., 2008.

Cava, Pete. *Tales from the Cubs Dugout: A Collection of the Greatest Cubs Stories Ever Told*. Champaign, Ill.: Sports Publishing LLC, 2002.

DeValeria, Dennis and Jeanne Burke DeValeria. *Honus Wagner: A Biography*. New York: Henry Holt and Company, Inc., 1995.

Doutrich, Paul E. *The Cardinals and the Yankees, 1926: A Classic Season and St. Louis in Seven*. Jefferson, N.C.: McFarland & Company, Inc., 2011.

Finoli, David and Bill Ranier. *When Cobb Met Wagner: The Seven-Game World Series of 1909*. Jefferson, N.C.: McFarland & Company, Inc., 2011.

Fleitz, David L. *Ghosts in the Gallery at Cooperstown: Sixteen Little-Known Members of the Hall of Fame*. Jefferson, N.C.: McFarland & Company, Inc., 2004.

———. *More Ghosts in the Gallery: Another Sixteen Little-Known Greats at Cooperstown.* Jefferson, N.C.: McFarland & Company, Inc., 2007.

Forr, James and David Proctor. *Pie Traynor: A Baseball Biography.* Jefferson, N.C.: McFarland & Company, Inc., 2010.

Freedman, Lew. *Baseball's Funnymen: Twenty-Four Jokers, Screwballs, Pranksters and Storytellers.* Jefferson, N.C.: McFarland & Company, Inc., 2017.

Gaines, W. Craig. *Encyclopedia of Civil War Shipwrecks.* Baton Rouge, La.: Louisiana State University Press, 2008.

Hageman, William. *Honus: The Life and Times of a Baseball Hero.* Champaign, Ill.: Sagamore Publishing, 1996.

Heffron, Joe and Jack Heffron. *The Local Boys: Hometown Players for the Cincinnati Reds.* Birmingham, Ala., Clerisy Press, 2014.

Hittner, Arthur D. *Honus Wagner: The Life of Baseball's "Flying Dutchman."* Jefferson, N.C.: McFarland & Company, Inc., 1996

Hunter, George. *Detroit Tigers Gone Wild: Mischief, Crimes & Hard Time.* Charleston, S.C.: The History Press, 2020.

Kimberly, Chuck. *The Days of Rube, Matty, Honus and Ty: Scenes from the Early Deadball Era, 1904-1907.* Jefferson, N.C.: McFarland & Company, Inc., 2019.

———. *The Days of Wee Willie, Old Cy and Baseball War: Scenes from the Dawn of the Deadball Era, 1900-1903.* Jefferson, N.C.: McFarland & Company, Inc., 2014.

Levy, Alan H. *Joe McCarthy: Architect of the Yankee Dynasty.* Jefferson, N.C.: McFarland & Company, Inc., 2005.

———. *Rube Waddell: The Zany, Brilliant Life of a Strikeout Artist.* Jefferson, N.C.: McFarland & Company, Inc., 2000.

Lieb, Frederick G. *The Pittsburgh Pirates.* 1948; reprint, Carbondale, Ill.: Southern Illinois University Press, 2003.

Louisa, Angelo J. *The Pirates Unraveled: Pittsburgh's 1926 Season.* Jefferson, N.C.: McFarland & Company, Inc., 2015.

Macht, Norman L. *Connie Mack and the Early Years of Baseball.* Lincoln, Neb.: University of Nebraska Press, 2007.

Martin, Brian. *Barney Dreyfuss: Pittsburgh's Baseball Titan.* Jefferson, N.C.: McFarland & Company, Inc. 2021.

McBane, Richard L. *A Fine-Looking Lot of Ball-Tossers: The Remarkable Akrons of 1881.* Jefferson, N.C.: McFarland & Company, Inc., 2005.

Niese, Joe. *Burleigh Grimes: Baseball's Last Legal Spitballer.* Jefferson, N.C.: McFarland & Company, Inc., 2013.

Parker, Clifton Blue. *Big and Little Poison: Paul and Lloyd Waner, Baseball Brothers.* Jefferson, N.C.: McFarland & Company, Inc., 2003.

Powers-Beck, Jeffrey. *The American Indian Integration of Baseball.* Lincoln, Neb.: University of Nebraska Press, 2004.

Selter, Ronald M. *Ballparks of the Deadball Era: A Comprehensive Study of Their Dimensions, Configurations and Effects on Batting, 1901-1919.* Jefferson, N.C.: McFarland & Company, Inc., 2008.

Spatz, Lyle and Steve Steinberg. *1921: The Yankees, the Giants, & the Battle for Baseball Supremacy in New York.* Lincoln, Neb.: University of Nebraska Press, 2010.

Steinberg, Steve. *Baseball in St. Louis: 1900-1925*. Charleston, S.C.: Arcadia Publishing, 2004.
Stinson, Mitchell Conrad. *Deacon Bill McKechnie: A Baseball Biography*. Jefferson, N.C.: McFarland & Company, Inc., 2012.
Veil, Fred W. *Bucky: A Story of Baseball in the Deadball Era*. Tuscon, Ariz.: Wheatmark, 2013.
Waldo, Ronald T. *Fred Clarke: A Biography of the Baseball Hall of Fame Player-Manager*. Jefferson, N.C.: McFarland & Company, Inc., 2011.
———. *Hazen "Kiki" Cuyler: A Baseball Biography*. Jefferson, N.C.: McFarland & Company, Inc., 2012.
———. *The Battling Bucs of 1925: How the Pittsburgh Pirates Pulled Off the Greatest Comeback in World Series History*. Jefferson, N.C., McFarland & Company, Inc., 2012.
———. *The 1902 Pittsburgh Pirates: Treachery and Triumph*. Jefferson, N.C.: McFarland & Company, Inc., 2015.
———. *Pennant Hopes Dashed by the Homer in the Gloamin': The Story of How the 1938 Pittsburgh Pirates Blew the National League Pennant*. Jefferson, N.C.: McFarland & Company, Inc., 2013.
Wiggins, Robert Peyton. *The Deacon and the Schoolmaster: Phillippe and Leever, Pittsburgh's Great Turn-of-the-Century Pitchers*. Jefferson, N.C.: McFarland & Company, Inc., 2011.
———. *The Federal League of Base Ball Clubs: The History of an Outlaw Major League, 1914-1915*. Jefferson, N.C.: McFarland & Company, Inc., 2009.

Miscellaneous
"The Lineage of the Magnificent Nine" – Information about Albert Leon "Al" Mamaux's family courtesy of Bill Lamb, author of the pitcher's SABR biography.

Newspapers and Magazines
Akron Beacon Journal and *Beacon Journal* (Akron, Ohio), August 23, 1902–June 13, 1921.
Alcona County Review (Harrisville, Michigan), October 6, 1927.
Alton Evening Telegraph (Alton, Illinois), April 5, 1929.
Altoona Mirror (Altoona, Pennsylvania), April 15, 1904–September 29, 1930.
Altoona Times (Altoona, Pennsylvania), June 9, 1904.
Altoona Tribune (Altoona, Pennsylvania), November 12, 1915–August 27, 1928.
Anaconda Standard (Anaconda, Montana), August 17, 1913.
Anniston Star (Anniston, Alabama), February 6, 1932.
Arkansas Democrat (Little Rock, Arkansas), January 28, 1923.
Bartlesville Daily Enterprise (Bartlesville, Oklahoma), July 8, 1927.
Bartlesville Morning Examiner (Bartlesville, Oklahoma), March 21, 1929.
Bismarck Daily Tribune or *Bismarck Tribune* (Bismarck, North Dakota), December 9, 1914–October 28, 1927.

Boston Daily Globe, Boston Evening Globe, and *Boston Sunday Globe,* May 29, 1897–September 18, 1915.
Boston Post, September 10, 1902.
Brainerd Daily Dispatch (Brainerd, Minnesota), August 29, 1929.
Brattleboro Daily Reformer (Brattleboro, Vermont), July 19, 1923–October 26, 1926.
Bridgeport Evening Farmer (Bridgeport, Connecticut), December 7, 1914–July 18, 1917.
Bridgeport Telegram, (Bridgeport, Connecticut), July 23, 1926.
Bristol Herald Courier (Bristol, Virginia-Tennessee), October 5, 1927.
Brooklyn Citizen, August 2, 1901–October 11, 1927.
Brooklyn Daily Eagle, September 7, 1902–November 21, 1930.
Brooklyn Daily Times, August 27, 1902–February 19, 1932.
Buffalo Commercial, August 23, 1905–November 11, 1909.
Buffalo Courier, June 13, 1910–January 18, 1924.
Buffalo Enquirer, December 21, 1900–August 21, 1914.
Buffalo Evening News, July 11, 1917.
Buffalo Evening Times, August 23, 1902–January 16, 1915.
Butler Citizen (Butler, Pennsylvania), September 27, 1900.
Butte Inter Mountain (Butte, Montana), June 5, 1906–October 25, 1909.
Capital Times (Madison, Wisconsin), June 21, 1921–February 3, 1926.
Carbondale Leader (Carbondale, Pennsylvania), July 28, 1916.
Chattanooga Daily Times or *Chattanooga Sunday Times,* March 2, 1910–August 3, 1951.
Chattanooga News, February 18, 1910.
Chicago Daily Tribune, September 21, 1932.
The Citizen (Ottawa, Ontario, Canada), November 29, 1919.
Corsicana Daily Sun (Corsicana, Texas), July 4, 1927.
Cumberland Evening Times (Cumberland, Maryland), December 5, 1930–April 6, 1950.
Cumberland News (Cumberland, Maryland), May 22, 1963.
Daily Courier (Connellsville Pennsylvania), October 19, 1926.
Daily Inter Ocean and *Inter Ocean* (Chicago, Illinois), September 7, 1892–October 4, 1912.
Daily Kennebec Journal (Kennebec, Maine), August 21, 1902.
Daily News Standard (Uniontown, Pennsylvania), June 23, 1930–September 25, 1930.
Daily Notes (Canonsburg, Pennsylvania), October 13, 1909–October 26, 1925.
Daily Republican (Monongahela, Pennsylvania), September 15, 1927.
Daily Republican (Rushville, Indiana), November 29, 1927.
Daily Times (Davenport, Iowa), September 26, 1922.
Dayton Daily News, July 24, 1900.
Dayton Herald and *Dayton Evening Herald,* October 11, 1909–September 1, 1914.
Decatur Daily Review or *Daily Review* (Decatur, Illinois), August 24, 1903–October 28, 1926.
Decatur Herald or *Decatur Evening Herald* (Decatur, Illinois), August 23, 1902–October 12, 1927.

Deseret Evening News (Salt Lake City, Utah), October 25, 1919.
Detroit Times, February 18, 1910.
Douglas Daily Dispatch (Douglas, Arizona), September 26, 1926.
Durham Morning Herald (Durham, North Carolina), March 19, 1922.
East Liverpool Review (East Liverpool, Ohio), August 14, 1919.
Edmonton Journal (Edmonton, Alberta, Canada), October 20, 1911–January 26, 1918.
El Paso Herald, July 31, 1917–May 30, 1927.
Evansville Press (Evansville, Indiana), July 16, 1906.
Evening Free Press (Winfield, Kansas), September 16, 1911.
Evening Herald (Fall River, Massachusetts), January 8, 1915.
Evening Herald (Shenandoah, Pennsylvania), February 27, 1924.
Evening Journal (Wilmington, Delaware), November 1, 1904.
Evening Ledger (Philadelphia, Pennsylvania), August 23, 1916–February 20, 1917.
Evening News (Harrisburg, Pennsylvania), July 10, 1917–June 22, 1921.
Evening Record (Greenville, Pennsylvania), June 30, 1900.
Evening Star and *Sunday Star* (Washington, DC) July 26, 1901–November 20, 1924.
Evening Telegram (Salt Lake City, Utah), July 19, 1906.
Evening Times (Raleigh, North Carolina), April 8, 1909.
Evening World (New York, New York), July 1, 1922.
Fall River Daily Globe (Fall River, Massachusetts), March 15, 1907–June 7, 1917.
Fargo Forum and Daily Republican (Fargo, North Dakota), December 9, 1914.
Fergus County Democrat (Fergus County, Montana), March 1, 1910.
Fort Wayne News (Fort Wayne, Indiana), July 12, 1917.
Franklin Evening News (Franklin, Pennsylvania), August 30, 1915.
Fresno Morning Republican (Fresno, California), August 16, 1926.
Gazette Times and *Pittsburgh Gazette Times* (Pittsburgh, Pennsylvania), May 10, 1909–October 28, 1926.
Gothenburg Times and Gothenburg Independent (Gothenburg, Dawson County, Nebraska), December 7, 1927.
Grand Forks Daily Herald (Grand Forks, North Dakota), December 10, 1914.
Great Falls Tribune (Great Falls, Montana), November 25, 1921.
Greensboro Daily News (Greensboro, North Carolina), September 25, 1922.
Greenville Daily Advocate (Greenville, Ohio), July 22, 1929.
Hamilton Daily Republican-News (Hamilton, Ohio), March 30, 1901.
Harrisburg Star Independent (Harrisburg, Pennsylvania), August 4, 1904.
Harrisburg Sunday Courier (Harrisburg, Pennsylvania), September 23, 1928.
Harrisburg Telegraph (Harrisburg, Pennsylvania), March 3, 1930.
Hollywood Daily Citizen (Hollywood, California), March 12, 1930.
Honolulu Advertiser, July 29, 1922.
Honolulu Star-Bulletin, November 19, 1914.
Houston Post, December 25, 1910.
Hutchinson News (Hutchinson, Kansas), September 5, 1916.
Illustrated Daily News (Los Angeles, California), December 5, 1923.
Indiana Evening Gazette (Indiana, Pennsylvania), October 28, 1925.

Indianapolis Times, October 11, 1927.
Joliet Evening World (Joliet, Illinois), August 26, 1913.
Joplin Globe (Joplin, Missouri), January 28, 1926.
Kane Republican (Kane, Pennsylvania), January 23, 1923–August 28, 1929.
Kingston Daily Freeman (City of Kingston, New York), July 22, 1925.
Knoxville Journal (Knoxville, Tennessee), July 26, 1926–August 29, 1929.
La Crosse Tribune and Leader-Press (La Crosse, Wisconsin), June 29, 1927.
Lima Republican-Gazette (Lima, Ohio), August 17, 1915.
Lima Sunday News (Lima, Ohio), August 10, 1919.
Lincoln Sunday Star (Lincoln, Nebraska), August 20, 1916.
Logan County Pioneer (Gandy, Logan County, Nebraska), December 16, 1927.
Long Beach Press-Telegram (Long Beach, California), March 20, 1950.
Long Branch Daily Record (Long Branch, New Jersey), August 25, 1915.
Los Angeles Express and *Los Angeles Evening Express,* November 3, 1909–October 27, 1926.
Los Angeles Record, August 17, 1923–October 19, 1927.
Miami Daily Metropolis, July 25, 1922.
Minneapolis Journal, September 3, 1902–June 1, 1904.
Moline Daily Dispatch (Moline, Illinois), June 19, 1913.
Morning Herald (Hagerstown, Maryland), April 11, 1929.
Morning Herald (Uniontown, Fayette County, Pennsylvania), November 18, 1914–October 12, 1927.
Mount Carmel News (Mount Carmel, Pennsylvania), January 30, 1926–July 24, 1928.
Muskogee Times-Dispatch (Muskogee, Oklahoma), July 28, 1915.
Nashville Banner, November 18, 1914–October 4, 1960.
Nebraska State Journal (Lincoln, Nebraska), July 26, 1926–May 24, 1937.
New Castle Herald (New Castle, Pennsylvania), January 11, 1910–May 22, 1923.
New Castle News (New Castle, Pennsylvania), May 29, 1901–April 16, 1949.
The News (Dayton, Ohio), December 8, 1913.
News-Democrat (Paducah, Kentucky), August 19, 1926.
News-Herald (Franklin and Oil City, Pennsylvania), April 20, 1922–August 7, 1929.
News-Palladium (Benton Harbor, Michigan), July 16, 1926.
New York Herald, April 23, 1922.
New York Times, November 21, 1887–November 28, 1975.
New York Tribune, May 4, 1918–October 12, 1922.
North Adams Transcript (North Adams, Massachusetts), August 20, 1902–July 19, 1923.
Norwich Bulletin (Norwich, Connecticut), February 26, 1910.
Oakland Tribune, July 19, 1915–August 6, 1929.
Ogden Standard (Ogden, Utah), January 28, 1926.
Okmulgee Daily-Times (Okmulgee, Oklahoma), March 12, 1950.
Omaha Daily News, May 8, 1914.
Oregon Daily Journal (Portland, Oregon), January 30, 1904.
Owensboro Daily Messenger (Owensboro, Kentucky), December 6, 1914.

Paducah Evening Sun (Paducah, Kentucky), October 24, 1925–October 21, 1927.
Park City Daily News (Bowling Green, Kentucky), February 7, 1924–October 11, 1927.
Philadelphia Inquirer, July 20, 1901–November 14, 1919.
Pittsburg Dispatch, July 2, 1891.
Pittsburg Gazette, November 16, 1902–April 25, 1914.
Pittsburg Post, *Pittsburgh Post*, and *Pittsburgh Sunday Post*, January 24, 1893–October 5, 1925.
Pittsburg Press or *Pittsburgh Press*, June 28, 1899–May 13, 1962.
Pittsburgh Post-Gazette, August 9, 1927–August 26, 1966.
Pittston Gazette (Pittston, Pennsylvania), December 4, 1915–September 30, 1926.
Plain Speaker (Hazleton, Pennsylvania), October 16, 1900.
Portland Daily Press (Portland, Maine), June 20, 1900.
Portsmouth Daily Times (Portsmouth, Ohio), October 19, 1927.
Portsmouth Herald (Portsmouth, New Hampshire), July 19, 1923.
The Press (Spokane, Washington), January 4, 1910.
Reading News-Times or *Reading Times* (Reading, Pennsylvania), July 25, 1914–February 6, 1932.
Rhinelander Daily News (Rhinelander, Wisconsin), November 30, 1931.
Richmond Times-Dispatch, November 8, 1925–March 12, 1929.
Rock Island Argus (Rock Island, Illinois), October 17, 1914.
Rutland Daily Herald (Rutland, Vermont), June 22, 1922.
Sacramento Bee, July 25, 1923.
St. Joseph Daily News (St. Joseph, Missouri), September 8, 1892.
St. Joseph Gazette (St. Joseph, Missouri), March 5, 1911.
St. Joseph News-Press (St. Joseph, Missouri), August 23, 1919.
St. Louis Globe-Democrat, July 2, 1891–July 25, 1929.
St. Louis Post-Dispatch and *Sunday St. Louis Post-Dispatch*, May 6, 1900–March 17, 1918.
St. Louis Republic, March 2, 1900–October 30, 1904.
St. Louis Star, February 24, 1910–March 5, 1917.
St. Paul Globe, August 20, 1900–October 9, 1902.
Salt Lake Telegram, July 26, 1915–August 9, 1919.
Salt Lake Tribune, July 31, 1921–June 29, 1961.
San Antonio Evening News, January 23, 1923.
San Antonio Gazette, August 4, 1906.
San Bernardino Daily Sun and *The Sun* (San Bernardino, California), July 6, 1924–January 18, 1972.
San Francisco Examiner, October 17, 1909.
San Francisco Sunday Call, March 12, 1911.
Sandusky Star-Journal (Sandusky, Ohio), February 5, 1908.
Santa Rosa Republican (Santa Rosa, California), October 9, 1931.
Saskatoon Phoenix (Saskatoon, Saskatchewan, Canada), June 25, 1921.
Scranton Republican (Scranton, Pennsylvania), September 6, 1902–September 23, 1916.
Scranton Times, December 5, 1905–December 19, 1914.

Seattle Star, October 25, 1916.
Selma Times-Journal (Selma, Alabama), July 15, 1926–December 12, 1927.
Shamokin Dispatch (Shamokin, Pennsylvania), October 26, 1925.
Sporting Life, October 21, 1899–October 14, 1916.
The Sporting News, October 21, 1899–March 21, 1951.
Springfield Daily News (Springfield, Ohio), October 23, 1924.
Standard Sentinel (Hazleton, Pennsylvania), July 26, 1926–February 6, 1932.
Standard Union (Brooklyn, New York), October 8, 1910–September 21, 1929.
The Sun (New York, New York), December 9, 1899–May 3, 1918.
Sun-Democrat (Paducah, Kentucky), February 5, 1932.
Sunday Courier and Press (Evansville, Indiana), January 10, 1954.
Sunday State Journal or *Evening State Journal* (Lincoln, Nebraska), October 12, 1902–May 17, 1922.
Sunday Tribune (Minneapolis, Minnesota), August 4, 1901.
Syracuse Post Standard, August 24, 1902.
Tampa Daily Times, July 17, 1917.
Terre Haute Star (Terre Haute, Indiana), April 6, 1950.
Terre Haute Tribune (Terre Haute, Indiana), November 27, 1975.
The Times (Philadelphia, Pennsylvania), July 14, 1901.
Titusville Herald (Titusville, Pennsylvania), July 2, 1917.
Toledo News-Bee, October 11, 1927–October 13, 1927.
Topeka Daily Capital, April 6, 1901.
Topeka State Journal, July 21, 1900–August 6, 1904.
Tulsa Democrat, July 15, 1917.
Twin City Daily Sentinel or *Twin City Sentinel* (Winston-Salem, North Carolina), July 5, 1913–March 22, 1922.
Vancouver World (Vancouver, British Columbia, Canada), March 17, 1910–March 4, 1911.
Victoria Daily Times (Victoria, British Columbia, Canada), March 4, 1911.
Walnut Valley Times (El Dorado, Butler County, Kansas), August 11, 1917.
Washington Herald, April 24, 1907–February 24, 1913.
Washington Times, August 23, 1902–July 14, 1922.
Waterbury Evening Democrat (Waterbury, Connecticut), September 10, 1902–September 16, 1902.
Waterloo Evening Courier (Waterloo, Iowa), May 4, 1911.
West Virginian (Fairmont, West Virginia), January 18, 1915–March 20, 1922.
Wichita Sunday Beacon, April 9, 1922.
Wilkes-Barre Leader and *Wilkes-Barre Times Leader* (Wilkes-Barre, Pennsylvania), August 5, 1904–March 25, 1938.
Wilkes-Barre News and *Evening News* (Wilkes-Barre, Pennsylvania), April 2, 1909–April 19, 1937.
Wilkes-Barre Record (Wilkes-Barre, Pennsylvania), February 17, 1910–May 24, 1937.
Winnipeg Evening Tribune (Winnipeg, Manitoba, Canada), October 16, 1915.
Winston-Salem Journal (Winston-Salem, North Carolina), September 2, 1916.

Wisconsin State Journal (Madison, Wisconsin), July 2, 1917.
Yonkers Herald (Yonkers, New York), August 16, 1926–October 22, 1926.
York Dispatch (York, Pennsylvania), December 21, 1905–April 24, 1915.

Websites
Allegheny City Society, https://alleghenycity.org
Baseball Almanac, https://www.baseball-almanac.com
Baseball-Reference, https://www.baseball-reference.com
Brookline Connection, https://www.brooklineconnection.com
Chicagology, https://chicagology.com
The City of Pittsburgh, https://pittsburghpa.gov
Cleveland Historical, https://clevelandhistorical.org
Cleveland Public Library Digital Gallery, https://cplorg.contentdm.oclc.org
Detroit Public Library Digital Collections, https://digitalcollections.detroitpubliclibrary.org
Digital Commonwealth – Massachusetts Collections Online, https://www.digitalcommonwealth.org
Find a Grave, https://www.findagrave.com
Free Library of Philadelphia, https://www.freelibrary.org
Google Books, https://books.google.com
Google Newspaper Archives, https://news.google.com
Greater Washington, https://ggwash.org
Historic Indianapolis, https://historicindianapolis.com
Historic Pittsburgh, https://historicpittsburgh.org
Historical Newspapers – World Collection, https://newscomwc.newspapers.com
KeyMan Collectibles, http://keymancollectibles.com
LA84 Foundation Digital Library, https://digital.la84.org
Library of Congress, https://www.loc.gov
National Baseball Hall of Fame, https://www.baseballhall.org
National Football Foundation, https://footballfoundation.org
National Governors Association, https://www.nga.org
New York Architecture, https://www.nyc-architecture.com
The New York Public Library Digital Collections, https://digitalcollections.nypl.org
Oklahoma Hall of Fame, https://oklahomahof.com
Oklahoma Historical Society, https://www.okhistory.org
Paper of Record, https://paperofrecord.hypernet.ca
Penn Libraries – University of Pennsylvania, https://www.library.upenn.edu
Pennsylvania State Senate, https://www.legis.state.pa.us
Retrosheet, https://www.retrosheet.org
Seamheads, https://seamheads.com
Society for American Baseball Research, https://sabr.org
Stats Crew, https://www.statscrew.com
University of Notre Dame – Rare Books and Special Collections, https://rarebooks.library.nd.edu

Index

Numbers in **bold** indicate pages with photographs.

A. Mamaux & Son, 136, 142
Abbaticchio, Edward "Ed or Abby," 86, 105
ABC Affair, viii, 235, 238, 242, 244, 246, 250, 256, 258, 270, 282, 288, 302
Abrams, Albert "Al," 45, 52–53, 58, 70–71
Abstein, William "Bill or Big Bill," 2, 98–101, 103–109, 111, 114–15, 120
Ackerland, Harry, 134–35
Adams, Charles "Babe," viii, 2, 101, 105, **110**, 113, 127, 222, 227–37, 240–44, 248, 250–52, 256–57, 260, 282–83, 326
Adams, Earl "Sparky," 293, 296–97, 306
Akron, Ohio, 245
Akron General Tire (Akron Generals), 245
Alameda, California, 324, 327, 329
Alderdice, Public Safety Director Robert J., 168, 170
Aldine Hotel, 82
Aldridge, Victor "Vic," 204–205, 209–210, 213–14, 216, 218, 220–21, 249, 252, 259, 264, 299, 305
Alexander, Grover Cleveland "Pete," 143, 278, 303
All-Americans, 65
All-Nationals, 63, 66
Allegheny, 30, 55–57, 60, 69, 78, 84, 96
Allegheny County, 141, 216
Allegheny County League, 137
Allegheny General Hospital, 331
Allegheny High School, ix
Allegheny River, 29, 85
Altoona, Pennsylvania, 75, 79
Alvin Theater, 34
Amen Corner, 275
America, 10, 31
American, 242, 298, 336
American Association (major league), 5, 7, 10, 46–47
American Association (minor league), 108, 163, 188, 193, 201, 256–57, 299
American League, viii, 2, 8, 18, 31, 38–41, 43, 45–47, 51–53, 55–66, 68–72, 74, 84, 106, 121, 134–35, 167, 268, 273, 301, 305, 336, 338
American League All-Star, 68
American Leaguers, 54
Anson, Adrian "Cap," 8
Ansonia Hotel, 154, 196
Arbuckle Building, 14
Arbuckle's & Company, 7
Archie, Missouri, 299–300
Arkansas, 292
Army, 161–63
Army Aviation Corps, 168
Ashtabula, Ohio, 33, 72
Associated Press, 197, 274, 276, 279, 281, 283, 285
Asten, George, 267
Atlantic City, New Jersey, 53–54, 62, 150
Auditorium Hotel, 43
Auten, Philip, 7–8, 14, 17, 19–23, 41, 49
Avenue B, 293
Awning and Tentmakers' Association of the United States, 139

Babcock, Mayor and County Commissioner Edward V., 170, 216
Bailey, Milton, 170
Baird, Douglas "Doug," 154, 162
Baker, William, 164, 328
Baker Bowl, 186
Balinger, Edward F. "Ed," 118, 129, 327
Balliet, Frank, 20–21
Baltimore, Maryland, 18, 121
Baltimore Feds, 128
Baltimore Orioles, 11, 18, 45, 63, 65, 121
Bancroft, David "Dave," 201, 236, 256, 333
Barbare, Walter, 167
Barnhart, Clyde "Pooch," viii, 171–72, 182, 210, 215, 217, 249, 261–62, 264, 268–69, 273–74, 276–77, 281–82, 286, 288–89, 291
Barrow, Edward "Ed," 135, 296
Bartell, Harry, 324

Bartell, Olive Loretta (Jensen), 327
Bartell, Richard "Dick," 1, 3, 310, 322–24, 326–30
Bartlesville, Oklahoma, 300
Bates Street, 206
Beaumont, Clarence "Ginger," 14, 50, 75, 85, 88, 91–92
Bedford Springs, Pennsylvania, 58
Bednar, Andrew "Andy," 331
Bell, Brian, 276
Bell, George, 100
Bellevue, Pennsylvania, ix, 202
Belrose Avenue, 140
Beltzhoover neighborhood (Pittsburgh), 137
Benge, Raymond "Ray," 328
Benham, J.A., 55–57
Bennett Park, 101–103
Benswanger, Edward, 332
Benswanger, Eleanor "Fanny" (Dreyfuss), 330, 335
Benswanger, William "Bill," 332–35, 338
Berg, Dr. Gustav, 78–79, 83, 99, 212, 261
Bernheim Brothers, 10
Bezdek, Hugo, 153–55, 157–58, 164–66
Bezdek, Victoria (Benson), 164
Bible, 36
Biederman, Lester "Les," 321–22, 329
Big Apple, 222, 282
Bigbee, Carson, viii, 2, 183, 214, 222, 227–37, 240–41, 243–44, 246, 248, 250–52, 257, 260, 282–83, 326
Bigbee, Lyle, 171
Birmingham, Alabama, 163
Birmingham Barons, 228
Black Sox, 174, 197
Bloomfield neighborhood (Pittsburgh), 33, 142
Boston, Massachusetts, 32–33, 52, 71, 73, 86, 90–91, 99, 144, 161–63, 167–68, 199–200, 223, 246, 249, 253–54, 264, 308, 336
Boston Americans, 39, 72–73, 76, 94, 336
Boston Beaneaters, 5, 18, 33–37, 40, 59, 71, 82–84, 86–88, 90–92, 94, 111
Boston Braves, 150, 167, 175, 189, 199–201, 207–208, 220–21, 232, 236, 240–41, 245, 256, 296, 301, 308, 322, 325–26, 328, 336
Boston Daily Globe, 34

Boston Doves, 91, 313
Boston Post, 64
Boston Red Sox, 116, 292, 298
Boston Rustlers, 313
Bottomley, James "Jim," 210, 212
Boyer Hotel (Hotel Boyer), 58
Boyle, Havey J., 229, 327–28, 337
Braddock, Pennsylvania, 202
Bradley Eagles, 155
Brain, David "Dave," 84, 94
Bransfield, William "Kitty," 2, 37, 48, 71–72, 80–84, 90, 92, 94, 98, 107, 129, 132, 210, 340
Braucher, William, 328
Braves Field, 189, 232, 245, 301
Breitmeyer, Mayor Philip, 104
Bresnahan, Roger, 114
Brickell, George Frederick "Fred," 273–74, 277
Bridgeport, Connecticut, 245
Briggs, Herbert "Buttons," 73
Britton. Helene Hathaway (Robison), 119
Britton, Schuyler P., 119
Brookline, Massachusetts, 199–200
Brookline neighborhood (Pittsburgh), 137
Brooklyn, New York, 20, 51–53, 91, 152, 154, 159, 162, 186–87, 194, 243, 314, 316
Brooklyn Daily Eagle, 148, 162, 186, 193, 219, 282, 292, 311, 313–14, 316, 328
Brooklyn Daily Times, 152, 275
Brooklyn Robins, ix, 128, 147–50, 152, 159–62, 171–72, 183, 185–87, 196, 200, 207, 211, 216, 221–23, 241, 244, 251, 265–66, 275, 292, 302, 304, 307–308, 310, 312–15, 322
Brooklyn Superbas, 20, 31, 33–34, 37, 39–40, 48–49, 58–59, 62, 78, 81, 100, 126, 136
Brooklyn Tip-Tops, 144
Brown, Harry, 198
Brown, Norman E., 220, 323
Brown, Warren, 190
Brunswick Hotel, 199
Brush, John T., 7–9, 13, 19, 65, 72
Buccaneers, 138, 171, 177, 197, 208, 212, 222, 257, 274, 283, 291, 322, 333
Buccos, 209
Buckenberger, Albert "Al," 7
Buffalo, New York, 183

Buffalo Bisons, 219, 296
Burke, Congressman James Francis, 105
Burke, James "Jimmy," 53–54, 138
Burkett, Jesse, 174
Bush, Leslie Ambrose "Bullet Joe," 221, 260
Bush, Owen Donie, viii, 1, 3, 256–58, 260–69, 271–94, 297–99, 303, 305–314, 316–17, 320–22, 326, 329
Butler, Arthur, "Art," 119, 123
Butler County, Pennsylvania, 6, 28
Byrne, Robert "Bobby," 104–105, 107, 116–18

Cain, 26
Cain, Cullen, 239
Calhoun, Police Commissioner John C., 168, 170
California, 94, 96, 141, 178, 189, 194, 260, 325, 327, 329
Callahan, James "Jimmy, Jim, Nixey or Cal," 146–48, 150–51, 153–54, 158–59, 166
Callahan, Josephine (Hardin), 146
Camnitz, Samuel Howard "Howie," 99, 101–103, 113, 115–16, 118
Campbell, Joe, 13
Canada, 92, 333
Canonsburg, Pennsylvania, 228
Cantillon, Joseph "Joe," 63, 93–94
Carey, Aurelia (Behrens), 254
Carey, Max "Scoops," viii, 2, 127, 151, 164–65, 167, 182–84, 209, 211–12, 214–17, 222–23, 225, 227–37, 239–44, 248–54, 257, 260, 265–66, **270**, 282–83, 322, 326–27, 340
Carisch, Frederick "Fred," 81–82
Carlson, Harold "Hal," 182
Carnahan, Judge Thomas D., 125
Carnegie, Pennsylvania, 9, 18, 116
Carr, Lewis "Lew," 37–38
Carroll, Superintendent of Police Thomas, 169
Casper, Clara, 124–26
Casper, William D., 124–25
Cass Lake, 139
Castle Garden, New York, 10
Catholic, 140
Central League, 138
Cerceo, Al, 155
Chance, Frank, 100, 115, 118
Charleroi, Pennsylvania, 86
Charleston Pals, 275

Chesbro, John "Jack, Happy Jack, Algernon or Algy," 2, 14, 18, 27, 35, 46, 57–58, 62–66, 73, 210, 340
Chesbro, Mabel (Shuttleworth), 64
Chester, Pennsylvania, 155
Chicago, Illinois, 7–8, 17, 20, 29, 36, 43, 51–53, 61, 66, 92, 94, 139, 154, 167, 170, 190–91, 205–207, 235, 243, 293, 302, 307, 334
Chicago Cubs, 62, 73, 78, 85, 92, 94–96, 98–101, 104, 106, 114–18, 127, 129, 134, 147, 162, 165, 172–73, 189, 198, 204–206, 208–209, 216–17, 222, 265, 293–94, 296–99, 302, 306–309, 311–13, 316, 321–22, 325, 327, 339–40
Chicago Orphans, 13, 17, 19–20, 27–28, 33, 35–36, 47, 146
Chicago White Sox, 51, 57, 85, 94, 146, 165, 169, 176, 185, 312
Chicago White Stockings, 31–32
Chief Sitting Bullpen, 190
Christmas, 106, 205, 230, 258
Cincinnati, Ohio, 27, 43, 47, 50–51, 54, 72, 78, 80, 99, 106, 121, 143, 165, 167, 220, 307, 339
Cincinnati Enquirer, 9, 63
Cincinnati Reds (American Association), 47
Cincinnati Reds (National League), 7–9, 13, 19, 27, 37, 40–41, 43, 50, 54, 62, 78–81, 83, 92, 94, 99, 107, 113, 126, 130, 143, 162, 165, 168, 172, 182, 209, 218, 221–22, 231–32, 236, 256, 262, 267, 269, 292, 306–307, 325
Cincinnati Times-Star, 11, 14
Circle, 28, 30–31
Civil War, 136
Clancy, William "Bill," 94
Clarke, Fred "Cap or Freddie," 1–3, 11, 14–20, 25–43, 45, 49, 51–53, 55, 57, 59–60, 62, 66, 72–75, 80–84, 86, 88, 90–91, 93–99, 101–108, 111–22, 126–31, 134–38, 142–46, 165, 180, 210–12, 220, 222–23, 225–42, 246, **247**, 248–55, 257–58, 260, 275–76, 291, 302–303, 322, 337, 339–40
Clarke, Muriel, 303
Clarke, William Stuart "Stu," 324
The Clash, 64
Class B, 108

Class C, 108
Class 1A, 162
Clearwater, Florida, 313
Cleveland, Ohio, 54–56, 58, 65, 68, 139, 302
Cleveland Blues, 46
Cleveland Broncos, 54, 69
Cleveland Indians, 46
Cleveland Lake Shores, 46
Cleveland Naps, 74
Cleveland Plain Dealer, 22
Cleveland Spiders, 8, 11, 18, 59, 70
Clingman, William "Billy," 28
Clune, Christmas, 92
Clymer, Otis, 90–94
Clymer, William "Derby Day Bill," 296–97
Cobb, Tyrus "Ty," 113, 194
Cole, Leonard "King," 116
Coll, Ray Jr., 195
Collegians, 35
Collins, Justice Gilbert, 22
Collins, Philip "Phil," 328
Columbia Park, 39
Columbus, Georgia, 152
Columbus, Ohio, 30
Columbus Solons, 47–48
Combs, Earle, 278
Comerford, Danny, 161
Comiskey, Charles, 52
Common Pleas Court, 125, 142, 304
Comorosky, Adam, 267, 281, 284, 288, 306, 334
Concordia Seminary, 248
Conroy, William "Wid," 57, 68–69, 72
Consolidated Traction Company, 23
Constans, Leslie, 166
Coombs, John "Jack," 164
Cooney, James "Jimmy," 210
Cooper, Arley Wilbur, 131, 182–83, 190, 204–206
Corcoran, Thomas "Tommy," 40
Corsairs, 70, 175
Costello, Daniel "Dan or Dashing Dan," 150
Coveleski, Stanley "Stan," 212–13
Craft Avenue, 46
Crafton, Pennsylvania, 137
Crandall, James "Doc," 333
Crane, Samuel "Sam," 112
Cratty, Albert R. "A.R.," 19, 30, 66, 74, 78, 85, 87–88, 114, 151

Cravath, Clifford "Gavvy," 164
Crawford, Samuel "Sam," 101
Critz, Hugh "Hughie," 292
Crolius, Frederick "Fred," 59
Cronin, Joseph "Joe," 245, 250
Crosby, Harry "Bing," 339
Crowder, Alvin "General," 228
Cuba, 178
Cubs Park, 191, 198, 217, 302
Cumberland, Maryland, 140
Cunningham, Ellsworth "Bert," 14, 17
Cup Series, 49
Cutshaw, George, 159, 164–66, 182, 194
Cuyler, Bertha (Kelly), 294
Cuyler, Harold, 272, 294
Cuyler, Hazen "Kiki, King Ki-Ki, Ki, Flint Flash, Michigan Flash or Double O," viii, 2–3, 201, 204, 209–210, 212–13, 215–16, 222, 233, 235, 244, 246, 250–51, 258–69, 271–94, **295**, 296–99, 305–307, 316, 321–22, 326, 328, 337, 340
Cvengros, Michael "Mike," 275, 277, 305

Daily Inter Ocean, 8
Daniel, Dan, 164
Davis, Alfonzo "Lefty," 37, 51–52, 57, 60–62, 64, 69, 72, 76, 95
Davis, Harry, 147
Davis, Ralph S., 82–83, 105–106, 108, 117, 124, 149, 173–74, 176–78, 180, 183, 193, 205, 215, 219, 223, 227, 230, 241–44, 256, 269, 274, 282, 284, 299, 306, 309–313, 320–21, 324, 328, 332
Davis Theatre, 147
Dawson Springs, Kentucky, 142
Deaconess Hospital, 217
Deadball Era, vii, 90, 225
Decoration Day, 129
Delahanty, Edward "Ed," 71
Delahanty, James "Jim," 113
Delaware, 111–12
Delaware County League, 155
Des Moines, Iowa, 75
Des Moines Demons, 215
Detroit, Michigan, 8, 102, 104, 139
Detroit Tigers, 3, 58, 101–105, 107, 113–14, 194, 256, 273, 336
Devine, Joseph "Joe," 258, 333
Devlin, Arthur "Art," 100–101

DeVormer, Albert "Al," 262
Dickson, Fred C., 13
Dickson and Talbott theatrical firm, 9
Diehl, Mayor William, 34
Dillon, Ted, 102
Dinneen, William "Bill," 37
Dodge Coupe, 302
Doheny, Edward "Ed," 73
Dolan, Albert "Cozy," 116–19, 123, 125, 174, 263
Donlin, Michael "Mike," 80
Donovan, Patrick "Patsy," 6–7, 17–18, **24**, 25, 48–49
Dooin, Charles "Red," 116–18
Dormont, Pennsylvania, 2, 136–37, 140–41, 146–47, 152, 163
Doty, Judge Lucien, 86
Dovey, George, 87, 91
"Down the Line," 234
Doyle, Charles "Chilly," 180, 184, 217, 229, 259–60
Doyle, Lawrence "Larry," 165
Dreyfuss, Barney III, 330
Dreyfuss, Bernhard "Barney or Colonel Barney," vii, ix, 1–3, 9–23, 25, 27, 29, 31–32, 35–38, 40, 42–43, 45–49, 51–53, 55, 57–66, 68–72, 74–88, 91–94, 96–99, 102, 104, 106–107, 111–12, 114–22, 126–31, 134–38, 143–49, 151–55, 158–72, 177–78, 182–89, 191–98, 200–202, 205, 208–211, 214, 218–19, 226–28, 230, 234–35, 238–44, 246, 249–59, 263–67, 269, 271, 273–74, 280, 282–87, 289, 291–93, 297–300, 306, 310, 312–13, 315–17, 320–40
Dreyfuss, Carolyn (Wolf), 292, 306, 330, 335
Dreyfuss, Florence, 218, 259, 335, 338–39
Dreyfuss, Samuel Sr., 10
Dreyfuss, Samuel "Sam or Sammy" Jr., 3, 168, 199, 220–22, 225–27, 231, 235–36, 238–41, 243–46, 251, 259, 265, 267, 274, 277, 280–81, 292–93, 310, 317, 322–27, 329–32, 335–36
Duquesne, 49
Duquesne Greys Band, 33
Duquesne University (Pittsburgh College), 35, 137, 332
Durham, North Carolina, 185

Eagan, Charles "Truck," 36
East, 54, 78, 92, 95, 98, 236, 259, 289, 317
East End neighborhood (Pittsburgh), 183
East Liberty Academy, 137
Eastern Canada League, 189
Eastern League, 59, 63, 71, 98, 108, 135
Easy Avenue, 185
Ebbets, Charles, 160–63
Ebbets Field, 128, 152, 161, 171, 211, 302, 304, 313
Edlis, Constable Murray, 140
Edwards, William D., 22
1896 Pittsburgh Pirates, **44**
Elk County, 251
Ely, William Frederick "Fred, Bones or Father Time," 36–43, 46–50, 93
"Ely's Great Home Run," 37
Emlenton, Pennsylvania, 71, 85
Emslie, Robert "Bob," 39–40
Engle, Charlie, 324
English, Councilman W.Y., 170
Ens, Jewel, 199, 222, 312, 316–17, 320, 322, 324–27, 330–33, 336
Erie County, Pennsylvania, 38
Esplen neighborhood (Pittsburgh), 155
Etna, Pennsylvania, 202
Europe, 218, 226, 228, 230, 238, 242, 249
European, 235
Evans, William "Billy," 113, 273, 301
Evening Ledger, 151, 305
Evers, John "Johnny," 165–66
Exposition Park, 2, 5, 26–31, 33–34, 36–37, 39, 41, 43, 54, 58–60, 62, 64, 73–74, 76–78, 80–85, 87–88, 90–92, 95–97, 100, 103, 107, 129, 136, 337, 340

Fall Classic, 102, 114, 212, 271, 274, 276, 297, 301
Farrell, Frank, 87
"Father of the World Series," 336
Federal League, 120–22, 127, 129, 131, 134–36, 143–44
Federal Street, 124–25
Ferguson, Dr. Cecil, 313–14
Ferguson, James Alexander "Alex," 213
Fernando Street, 149
Fifth Avenue, 33, 125, 149, 155
Flagstead, Ira, 316
Flaherty, Patrick "Patsy," 9, 14, 18, 86

Flannery Building, 335
Fletcher, Arthur "Art," 236, 256
Flick, Elmer, 153
Flint, Michigan, 258, 260, 285, 288, 293
Flynn, John, 108
Forbes Field, viii, 2, 99–102, 105–107, 113, 117–19, 123, 126–27, 129, 131, 136, 145–48, 150–51, 164, 168–75, 178, 181, 183, 192, 200–201, 210, 212–16, 219–22, 225–26, 230, 232, 241, 243–44, 258, 261–62, 267–69, 271–77, 280, 283, 287, 293, 300, 302, 306, 309–311, 316, 322, 332–33, 337, 340
Forbes Street (Avenue), 123
Ford, Horace "Hod," 267
Ford River Lumber Company, 7
Fore River Plant of the Bethlehem Shipbuilding Company, 161
Fort Wayne Champs, 138
Ft. Wayne Depot, 56
Fort Worth, Texas, 315
Foster, John B., 59, 232
Fourth of July, 73, 147, 185
Fox, George, 14, 18
Fraser, Charles "Chick," 258
Freedman, Andrew, 13, 18, 65
Freiburg, Baden, 10
French, Lawrence "Larry," 327
French Lick Springs, Indiana, 13
Frisch, Frank "Frankie," 250, 264, 333
Fullerton, Hugh, 122

Galbreath, John, 339
Galesburg, Illinois, 45–46
Ganley, Robert "Bob," 91–92, 94
Gay Lothario, 124
Gazette Times (Pittsburgh Gazette Times), 180, 217, 229, 236–38, 246, 248–51, 259–60, 302
Gehrig, Henry Louis "Lou," 272, 276–78
Geraldine, 254
German, 98
Germany, 10, 218
Getty, Frank, 291
Gibson, Florent, 148
Gibson, George "Gibby," 100–101, 113, 142, 166–68, 171–72, 175, **179**, 181–95, **203**, 208, 211, 257, 333–34, 336, 339–40

Gill, Warren, 98
Gilsey House, 54
Girard, Pennsylvania, 38
Glazner, Charles "Whitey," 171, 198–99
Gloucester, Massachusetts, 246
God Almighty, 249
Golden Jubilee Celebration, 210–11, 259
Goldenson, Rabbi Dr. Samuel H., 338
Gooch, John "Johnny," 183, 188, 251, 271, 277–78, 307–308
Goslin, Leon "Goose," 215
Grant, George, 167
Grantham, George "Boots," 204–205, 209, 213, 217, 246, 249–52, 266–67, 309, 315–16, 329, 334, **342**
Grayber, Al, 155
Great War, 152, 162–63
Greater Pittsburgh, viii
Greek, 269
Griffith, Clark, 19–20, 28, 57–58, 68, 73
Griffith Stadium, 301
Griggs, Arthur "Art," 333
Grimes, Burleigh, 159, 299, 306, 323–26, 328
Grimes, Florence Ruth (van Patten), 323
Grimm, Charles "Charlie," 171, 180, 190, 204–206
Groh, Henry "Heinie," 182, 277
Guy, Richard, "Dick," 248

Hahn, Frank "Noodles," 40
Hamilton, Earl, 182
Hamilton, H.C., 151
Hamilton Avenue, 141
Hanlon, Edward "Ned," 31, 33
Hargrave, Eugene "Bubbles," 267
Hargreaves, Charles "Charlie," 307–308, 310
Harmon, Robert "Bob," 119, 126
Harper, George, 262
Harridge, William "Will," 338
Harris, Frank J., 297
Harris, Joseph "Joe," 213, 215, 307–308
Harris, Stanley "Bucky," 212, 215–16
Harrisburg, Pennsylvania, 120–21
Harrison, James R., 235
Harrisonville, Missouri, 314–15
Harrisville, Michigan, 271
Harvard University, 150
Hawley, Emerson Pink, 8, 31
Hayes, 82

Index

Haymaker, Judge John C., 142
Heathcote, Clifton "Cliff," 306
Hedges, Robert L., 106–107
Hendricks, John "Jack," 231, 236, 292
Hendrix, Claude, 121–22
Herrmann, August "Garry," 78–79, 162
Hershman, Oliver, 23
Heydler, John, 100–101, 178, 223, 236–40, 253, 313, 329, 335, 338
Heyman, D.I., 11, 21
Hill, Carmen, 277, 307
Hilltop Park, 94
Hinchman, William "Bill," 175, 256, 258, 334
Hofman, Arthur "Solly," 116
Hohenzollern, 154
Holahan, John D., 332
Hollenden Hotel, 55
Holmes, Thomas, 292, 311, 313–14, 316, 328–29
Homestead, Pennsylvania, 34, 77
Honey Creek, Wisconsin, 91
Hooper, Harry, 292
Hornsby, Rogers, 176, 210, 231, 256, 302, 327
Hot Springs, Arkansas, 36, 45, 49, 76, 95, 98–99, 111, 122, 138, 153, 193, 211, 325
Hotel Alamac, 314
Hotel Anderson, 140
Hotel Astor, 259
Hotel McAlpin, 138–39, 141
Hough, Frank, 43, 71
Houston, Texas, 108
Howard, George "Del," 84, 94
Hub, 189, 201
Huddle, 298
Huggins, Miller, 119–21, 124, 275
Hughes, Edward "Ed," 282
Hughes, Thomas "Tom," 73
Hughes, William "Bill," 175, 198
Humphries, Albert "Bert," 129
Huntington Avenue Baseball Grounds, 76
Huntington Blue Sox, 138
Hurst, Tim, 54
Hyatt, Robert Hamilton "Ham," 100, 105

Independence Day, 129
Indian show, 31
Indianapolis, Indiana, 9, 32, 256, 293, 307, 320–21

Indianapolis Hoosiers, 18
Indianapolis Indians, 256–57
International Hockey League, 92
International League, 150, 166, 207, 219, 296, 326
Inter-State League, 13
Iroquois Apartments, 252
Isaminger, James "Jimmie," 164, 186, 193, 292–93

J.A. Dubow Manufacturing Company, 260, 276
Jackson, Travis, 262, 280, 285
Jennings, Hugh "Hughie," 20, 104, 174
Jersey City, New Jersey, 17, 21–22
Jersey City Skeeters, 108
Jewish, 293
Johnson, Alice, 152
Johnson, Byron Bancroft "Ban," 43, 45–46, 51, 54–61, 63–64, 68–72
Johnson, Thomas "Tom," 339
Johnson, Walter, 143, 212–13, 214–15
Jones, David "Davy," 105
Jones, Fielder, 34
Jones, Percy, 325–26
Jones, Thomas "Tom," 101, 105

the Kaiser, 154
Kane, James "Jim," 98
Kane, Thomas L., 161
Kansas City, Missouri, 32, 63, 121, 162, 167, 300
Kansas City Blues, 163, 201, 299–300
Kansas City Packers, 136
Karlsruhe, Baden, 10
Kearny, New Jersey, 119
Keck, Harry, 157–58
Keeler, William "Willie," 34
Keen, Howard Victor "Vic," 303, 313
Kelley, Joseph "Joe," 34
Kelley, Michael "Mike," 14
Kelly, 123
Kelly, George "High Pockets," 250, 292
Kelly, Peter, 148, 151
Kentucky, 10, 115, 306, 338
Kentucky Colonel, 10
Kerr, William "Captain or Colonel," 5–14, 17, 19–23, 25, 31, 38, 41, 43, 49
Kessler, Gene, 235, 290

Ketchum, Charles, 245
Kilfoyle, John, 69
Killefer, William "Bill," 205–206, 256
Killilea, Henry, 72
King, Joe, 102
Kingston, New York, 233, 237
Kirby, Alderman J.J., 125, 140
Kittridge, Malachi, 34
Klein, 149
Klem, William "Bill," 100
Koenig, Mark, 278
Konetchy, Aubrey (Seawel), 129, 131
Konetchy, Edward "Ed, Koney or Big Train," 119–22, 126, 128–32, **133**, 134–36, 264
Kremer, Remy "Ray," 201, 209, 214, 216, 241, 245, 249, 300, 307, 315
Krueger, Arthur "Otto," 84
Kunz, Earl, 198

Labor Day, 33, 100, 172, 195, 267
LaForce, Edward "Ed," 74, 107
Lake Erie, 38
Lake Shore Railroad, 139
Landis, Judge Kenesaw Mountain, 169–70, 183, 188, 195, 214, 232, 235–36, 293, 313, 338
Lanigan, Harold, 51
LaSalle Hotel, 139
Latimer, Clifford "Tacks," 14, 27–28, 66
Latrobe, Pennsylvania, 86–87
Lawn Street, 123–24
Lawrenceville neighborhood (Pittsburgh), 46
Lazzeri, Anthony "Tony," 277–78
Leach, Thomas "Tommy," 11, 14, 37–38, 57, 68–70, 72, 74–76, 79, 84, 88, 105, 107, 116, 210
League Park (Cincinnati), 27
League Park (St. Louis), 35, 48
Lebanon, Pennsylvania, 90
Leesburg, Florida, 311
Leever, Samuel "Sam," 8, 14, 34, 72–73, 88, 92
Leifield, Albert "Lefty," 95–97, 101, 103, 115–16
Lelivelt, John "Jack," 256
Leonard, Joseph "Joe," 127
Lewis, George "Duffy," 292
Liberty Avenue, 46
Liberty Bonds, 159
Liberty School, 168
Library Apartments, 57, 64

Library Place, 58,
Lincoln Hotel (Hotel Lincoln), 55, 57, 69
Lindaman, Vivan "Vive," 94
Lindstrom, Frederick "Freddie," 285
Little Pirate Ranch, 254
Lobert, John "Hans," 174
Loftus, Thomas "Tom," 35–36
Long, Herman, 40
Long, James J., 229
Los Angeles, California, 217
Los Angeles Angels, 146
Louisa Street, 231
Louisville, Kentucky, 10–11, 13–14, 16–17, 19, 21–22, 26, 34, 99, 112, 168, 336, 338
Louisville Colonels (American Association major league club), 10
Louisville Colonels (National League club), 5–6, 9–18, 23, 25–26, 70, 146, 168, 229, 339
Luderus, Frederick "Fred," 164
Luque, Adolfo "Dolf," 267, 292

Mack, Connie, 31–32, 36, 39, 43, 46
Maddox, Nicholas "Nick," 101, 115
Madison, Arthur "Art," 14, 18
Magee, Leo "Lee," 123
Magee, Mayor William, 105
Malone, Perce "Pat," 327
Mamaux, Albert Leon Jr. "Al, Abbie, Smokes or the Millionaire Kid," 2, 136–38, 140–55, **156**, 157–63, 166, 169, 307, 340
Mamaux, Albert Leon Sr., 136–37, 140–42
Mamaux, Catherine, 141
Mamaux, Eugene, 136
Mamaux, John J. Sr., 136–42
Mamaux, John "Jack" Jr., 141, 152, 161
Mamaux, Julia V. (Wiseman), 138–41, 155
Mamaux, Nora H., 141–42
Mamaux, William, 161
Maranville, Betty, 206
Maranville, Walter "Rabbit," 2, 167–68, 171–72, 180, 182, 189–92, 196, 199–202, **203**, 204–207, 219
Marietta College, 220
Maripoe Avenue (Street), 142
Marks, Dr. W.L., 331
Marquard, Richard "Rube," 127
Massachusetts, 73
McAleer, James "Jim or Jimmy," 46, 70

Index

McBeth, W.J., 185
McCann, David L., 142
McCarey, Socko, 329
McCarthy, Joseph "Joe," 293, 296, 306
McCormick, Harry, 80, 84
McCormick, William Joseph "Barry," 215
McCreery, Thomas "Tom," 50, 137
McGeehan, W.O., 234
McGinnity, Joseph "Joe," 34
McGraw, John, 45, 63, 65, 112–13, 131, 148, 154, 159, 166, 174, 178, 181, 184, 231, 263, 292, **295**, 296–97, 299
McGuire, James "Deacon," 58
McInnis, John "Stuffy," 209, 213–14, 217, 246, 249, 257
McKechnie, William "Bill or Wilkinsburg Bill," 193–202, 204–205, 208–217, 219–23, 225–29, 231–39, 241–43, 245–46, **247**, 248–49, 251–58, 268–69, 282, 287, 298, 300–303, 306, 310, 336
McKee, J.A., 228
McKee Place, 231
McKeever, Marie "Dearie," 152
McKeever, Stephen, 152
McKinney, Frank, 321, 339
McLinn, Stoney, 305
McPhee, John "Bid," 40
McQuaide, Police Superintendent Thomas, 97–98
McQuiston, Frank B., 65
Meadows, Henry Lee "Specs," 198, 209, 251, 303, 307, 311, 313
Meany, Thomas W., 275–76
"Meet Me in St. Louis, Louis," 111
Memorial Day, 129, 139
Memphis, Tennessee, 112, 292
Menke, Frank G., 279
Mercy Hospital, 206, 216
Merkle, Carl Frederick "Fred," 131
Meusel, Robert "Bob," 278
Meyer, William "Billy," 321
Meyran Avenue, 29–30
Miami Beach, Florida, 313–14
Michigan, 102, 139, 258
Michigan Avenue, 30
Miljus, John "Johnny," 273–74, 277–78, 308
Miller, John "Jack or Dots," 41, 101, 115–16, 119–20, 123–26, 132
Miller, Roscoe, 82

Millvale, Pennsylvania, 30
Milwaukee, Wisconsin, 31
Milwaukee Brewers, 31–32, 256
Minneapolis Millers, 193
Mission Reds, 333
Missouri Lutheran, 248
Mr. McCullough, 173–74
Modesto, California, 184, 197
Monongahela Bridge, 35
Monongahela House, 6, 34, 82
Montreal, Quebec, Canada, 189
Montreal Royals, 189, 296, 312
Moore, C.L., 13
Moore, Graham Edward "Eddie," 201, 204–205, 209, 211–17, 219–20, **224**, 235, 246, 251–52
Moore, Mrs. Susan, 142
Moore, William "Wilcy," 273–74, 277
Moran, Patrick "Pat," 150
Morewood Avenue, 330
Morewood Gardens, 330
Morgan, Melvin, 304
Moriarty, George, 105, 113
Morrison, John "Johnny," 200–201, 209, 214, 220–21, 249, 267, 305
Morrowfield Apartments, 231, 256
Mount Brydges, Ontario, Canada, 166
Mt. Sinai Hospital, 334–35
Mowrey, Harry Harlan "Mike or Iron," 119–22, 126–28, 131, 134, 136
Mowrey, Nannie K. (Hammel), 121
Muehlebach, George, 300
Muehlebach Field, 300
Mullin, George, 103
Murdock, Dr. Eugene Converse, viii, 220, 246, 291, 300, 302–303, 306, 312
Murphy, Charles, 115
Murphy, Edward "Ed," 48
Murphy, James J., 219
Murphy, Michael "Mike," 92
Murray, John "Red," 131
Murray, William "Billy," 151
Musial, Stanley "Stan," ix
Myers, Henry "Hi," 183

Nashville, Tennessee, 290
National Agreement, 14
National Association, 183
National Commission, 155, 160–62

National Game, 14, 63
National League, vii, 2–3, 5, 8, 10–12, 14, 16–19, 22, 25, 32, 34, 37–38, 40–41, 43, 46–48, 53, 58, 65, 70, 72–73, 84–85, 87, 91, 94–95, 98–102, 104, 106–108, 111, 114–16, 121–22, 126, 128, 132, 134, 143, 146–47, 151, 155, 167, 171, 173, 180–83, 186, 188, 193, 195, 197, 201–202, 204, 209–212, 216, 218, 220, 223, 225, 231, 234, 236, 239, 242, 244–45, 249, 255, 259–61, 269, 279–80, 288, 292, 297, 303, 311–13, 321–323, 326, 329, 333–36, 338–39
National League Park, 37, 82, 91, 117
National Pastime, 234
Navy, 161–63
Neal, William "Cap," 151
Neale, Earl "Greasy," 256–57
Nealon, James Joseph "Joe" Jr., 94–97
Nealon, James Sr., 95–96
Nehf, Arthur "Art," 178, 309
New Haven, Connecticut, 222–23
New Jersey, 21
New Jersey Supreme Court, 22
New York, 17
New York, New York, 12–15, 18–19, 21–22, 54, 57, 59, 61–62, 65, 69, 78–79, 83, 86–87, 99, 112, 118–19, 134, 138–39, 144, 154, 161, 165–68, 178, 180–81, 187, 194, 196, 208, 218, 222, 232–33, 235–37, 244, 249, 276, 282–85, 287, 290–91, 296, 304, 312, 321, 334
New York Americans, 65
New York Athletic Club, 99
New York Evening Post, 243, 250, 265
New York Giants, 13, 18, 20, 28, 54, 60, 62–63, 65, 72–73, 80, 84, 98, 100, 112–14, 116, 119, 127, 131, 148, 151, 154, 159, 162, 164–67, 171–78, 180–81, 189, 195–98, 201–202, 204, 211–12, 219, 221–22, 231, 241, 250, 256, 259, 261–65, 268–69, 280, 283, 286–87, 289, 292, 296–97, 299, 302, 310, 313–14, 316, 321, 330
New York Herald Tribune, 234
New York Highlanders, 72–73, 87, 94–95
New York State League, 37
New York Times, 234
New York Tribune, 185

New York World-Telegram and Sun, 102
New York Yankees, ix, 268–69, 271–73, 275–79, 283, 296, 298, 304–306
New York's Battery, 10
Newark, Delaware, 111–12
Newark Bears, 326
Newell's Hotel, 33
Newton, Massachusetts, 200
Niagara Falls, 10
Nicholson, Fred, 167
Niehaus, Albert "Al," 204, 209
1900 Pittsburgh Pirates, **67**
North Side (Northside), 30, 173, 212
Northside Twilight League, viii, ix
North Vernon, Indiana, 121
Northwestern University, 92

Oakes, Ennis Telfair "Rebel," 144–45
Oakland, California, 245, 329
Oakland neighborhood (Pittsburgh), 29–30, 46, 99–100, 123–25, 168, 191, 206–207, 216, 231, 252, 256, 330–31, 335, 337
O'Brien, John, 14, 18
O'Connor, John "Jack or Peach Pie," 36, 46–48, 51–59, 62–64, 66, 69–71, 73, 106–108
O'Connor, W.J., 134
O'Day, Henry "Hank," 48
Officer Tibbit, 124
Ohio, 38, 220
Ohio State League, 138
Ohio Works, 77
Oklahoma, 275, 291
Oklahoma City Indians, 195
Oldham, John "Red," 215
Omaha Rangers, 84
Onslow, John "Jack," 222, 251, 253
Oregon University, 165
Organized Baseball, 131, 135, 155, 158, 188, 197, 331
Ormsby, Emmet "Red," 278
O'Toole, Martin "Marty," 131, 138
Owens, Clarence "Brick," 213
Owensboro, Kentucky, 221

Pacific Coast, 328
Pacific Coast League, 146, 194, 198, 214, 312, 333

Pacific Coast Winter League, 194
Paducah, Kentucky, 10
Palace of the Fans, 78, 99, 126
Paris, France, 241–42
Parker, Dr. Harley, 92
Paso Robles, California, 201, 217, 244, 259–60, 300, 305, 315, 323–24, 330–31
Pawnee, Oklahoma, 189
Pawnee tribe, 189
Peckinpaugh, Roger, 212, 214–15
Peet, William "Bill," 208
Peitz, Henry "Heine," 83
Penn Avenue, 140–41
Penn State University, 165
Pennock, Herbert "Herb," 276
Pennsylvania, 86, 140, 142, 170, 297
Pennsylvania Dutch, 71
Pennsylvania Station (Union Station), 55
Pennsylvania Superior Court, 141
Petty, Jesse Lee "Jess," 292, 307, 312–14, 326
Pewaukee Lake, 32
Phelps, Eddie Jr., 83
Phelps, Edward "Ed," 59, 83
Phelps, Mary (Bills), 83
Philadelphia, Pennsylvania, 7, 30, 38, 46, 54, 79, 82, 93, 99, 116–17, 127, 140–41, 144, 151, 164, 198, 250, 259, 305, 329–30, 333
Philadelphia Athletics, 39, 46, 71, 116, 167, 298, 333
Philadelphia Inquirer, 71, 292
Philadelphia North American, 164, 186
Philadelphia Phillies, 28, 37, 42, 47, 54, 71, 73, 82, 84, 90–91, 94, 99, 116, 150, 163–64, 184, 186, 198, 210, 221, 236, 245, 256, 292, 327–28, 330
Philadelphia Telegram, 88
Phillippe, Charles "Deacon," 14, 65, 72–73, 88, 228
Pipgras, George, 275
Pipp, Walter "Wally," 267, 292
Pittinger, Charles "Togie," 83
Pittsburgh, Pennsylvania, viii, ix, 1–3, 5–9, 11–12, 14–15, 17–20, 22, 26–27, 29–31, 33–41, 43, 45–46, 50–52, 54–61, 63–66, 68–69, 71–72, 77–78, 81–83, 85, 87–88, 91, 94–98, 100, 102–106, 108, 111, 114–18, 120–21, 123–27, 129–31, 134, 136–37, 139, 144–48, 151–55, 159, 161–64, 168–72, 174–76, 178, 182–83, 189, 191–94, 197–202, 204–206, 209–211, 213–14, 218, 222, 226, 228–29, 231, 234–36, 238–39, 242, 246, 250, 252, 254, 256–59, 263–65, 269, 271, 273, 275–80, 285, 287–88, 291, 294, 297–98, 303–306, 308, 310–11, 314, 316–17, 320–21, 324, 326–36, 338–40
Pittsburgh Alleghenys, 5
Pittsburgh Athletic Company, 258
Pittsburgh Baseball Club (Pittsburgh Ball Club), 17, 39, 42, 56, 251
Pittsburgh Chronicle Telegraph, 30, 34, 185, 229
Pittsburgh Collegians, 248
Pittsburgh Dispatch, 65, 82, 87
Pittsburgh Leader, 136
Pittsburgh Ledger, 248
Pittsburgh Nationals, 128
Pittsburgh Pirates, vii, viii, ix, 1–3, 5–8, 11–23, 25–43, 45–55, 57–66, 68–88, 90–109, 111–24, 126–32, 134–38, 140, 143–55, 157–78, 180–202, 204–223, 225–46, 248–51, 253–69, 271–83, 285–89, 291–94, 296–318, 320–41
Pittsburgh Post, 29, 129, 148, 157, 166, 173, 175, 177, 182, 208
Pittsburgh Post-Gazette, 45, 264, 273, 275, 289, 293, 308, 327, 337
Pittsburgh Press, viii, 8, 14, 23, 32, 53, 56, 87, 105, 108, 123–24, 138–39, 149, 173–74, 177, 180, 183, 202, 220, 222–23, 228–30, 234–35, 241, 243, 256, 262, 265, 267, 269, 274, 276, 282, 284, 292, 299, 306, 309, 312, 320–21, 324
Pittsburgh Rebels, 136, 144
Pittsburgh Steelers, viii
Pittsburgh Sun, 229
Pittsburgh Sun-Telegraph, 321
Pittsburgh Symphony Orchestra, 332
Pittsburgh's Chamber of Commerce, 272
Pittsburgher, 46
Players' League, 7, 43
Pocono Mountains, 142
Poison Boys, 315
Polo Grounds, 151, 166, 171, 181, 189, 195, 222, 261, 264, 285, 310, 321
Ponder, Charles Elmer, 189

the Pope, 154
Power, Charles B., 13, 87
Powers, John "Johnny," 146
Princeton University, 168
Probst, Frank, 55
Prohibition Era, 177
Prospect, Pennsylvania, 6, 35
Protective Association of Professional Baseball Players, 34–35
Protestant, 140
Providence, 154
Providence Grays, 98
Pulliam, Harry C., 10, 12–14, 17, 19–21, 23, 25–26, 29–30, 36, 42, 53, 55, 57, 59–60, 65, 68–69, 71–72, 99, 181
Punxsutawney, Pennsylvania, 30–31
Purman, Paul, 153
"Put Cuyler In," 272, 298

Quincy, Massachusetts, 161

Rader, Drew, 191
Ragan, Don Carlos Patrick "Pat," 128
Raleigh Hotel, 301
Rawlings, John "Johnny," 198–99, 211–12, 219, 251
Recreation Park, 46
Redland Field, 130, 143, 269
Reed, Burke F., 228
Reese, Andrew "Andy," 262
Reese, John "Bonesetter," 99, 127, 302, 313
Regulars, 99
Reid, Judge Ambrose B., 125
Rhyne, Harold "Hal," 214, 216–17, 219, 251, 303
Rice, Edgar "Sam," 213, 215
Rice, Thomas "Tom," 148, 186, 193–94
Richards, G.L., 45–47
Richards, Henry, 315–16
Rickey, Welsey Branch, 183
Riconda, Henry "Harry," 312
Ritchey, Claude "Little All Right or Dope," 2, 11, 14, 28–29, 37, 39, 46, 70–72, 84–88, 90–92, 210, 340
Robertson, Davis "Dave," 189
Robinson, John Henry "Hank," 119
Robinson, Wilbert, 160–62, 183, 185–86, 307–308, 312–13, 315
Robison, Frank, 8, 17–18

Robison, Stanley, 8, 114
Robison Field, 120
Rochester Bronchos, 59
Rochester Tribe, 207
Rodef Shalom Temple, 338
Rogers, James "Jim," 15
Rooney, Arthur "Art" Sr., viii, ix
Rowand, District Attorney Harry, 169
Rowe, Norman L., 21–22
Rowher, Claude, 198
Rowswell, Rosey, 311
Royal Rooters, 33
Ruel, Herold "Muddy," 215
Rule 21, 254
Runyan, Damon, 301
Russell, Fred, 290
Ruth, George Herman "Babe," 272, 276–78

Sacramento Senators, 198, 312
Saginaw, Michigan, 55
St. John's Hospital, 212
St. Louis, Missouri, 17, 37, 51–52, 73, 80, 91, 98, 104, 109, 120, 131, 134, 217, 243, 254, 264–65, 284, 286, 291, 315, 326
St. Louis Browns, 12, 36, 46, 51, 70, 73, 106–109, 111
St. Louis Cardinals, 17–18, 27, 33, 35–36, 39–40, 42, 47–48, 75–77, 81, 84–85, 90, 104, 111, 113–15, 119–26, 129–30, 132, 136, 162, 172, 176–77, 183, 192, 197, 207, 209–210, 212, 217, 221–22, 231, 245, 256, 261–62, 265, 268–69, 278, 302–303, 308, 310–12, 315, 325–26, 333
St. Louis Perfectos, 8, 17
St. Louis Republic, 29, 51, 63, 82
St. Louis Star, 39, 48
St. Louis Terriers, 121
St. Marks Avenue, 152
St. Marys, Pennsylvania, 251
San Francisco, California, 94–95, 158, 315, 324
San Francisco Seals, 214, 216–17, 302
Sankey, Benjamin "Ben," 324, 326
Santa, 310
Saratoga Springs, New York, 53
Saunders, John J., 17
Schenley Hotel, 148, 169
Schenley Park, 123, 125, 173

Schmelz, Gustavus "Gus," 48
Schmidt, Charles "Boss," 104
Schmidt, Walter, 166, 171–72, 182–85, 188, 193–98, 201, 208–209
Schoepf, William Kesley, 23
Scott, Floyd "Pete," 293, 296, 309
Sebring, Elizabeth (Milnor), 76
Sebring, James "Jimmy or Jeems," 75–81
Sebring, Mary, 76
Section 5, 55
Selee, Frank, 40
Senior Circuit, 337
Seventh Avenue Hotel, 7–8
Shady Side Academy, 168
Sharpe, Bayard "Bud," 108
Sheehan, Thomas "Tom," 209
Sheely, Earl, 312
Sherdel, William "Bill," 308
Sheridan, John B., 254
Shibe, Benjamin "Ben," 46
Shibe, Tom, 46
Shreveport Pirates, 98
Simon, Jessie Belle (Swarthout), 121
Simon, Michael "Mike," 121
Singing Quartet, 177, 180, 182, 198, 205
Sixth Street Bridge, 58
Sloop, Harry, 245
Smayda, Frank (Smozda), 206
Smith, Chester L., 246
Smith, Earl "Oil," 208–209, 214, 275–77, 307, 309–310
Smith, Harry, 57, 68–69, 72, 75, 78
Smith, Walter, 55
Smith, William "Billy," 290
Smith Building, 64
Smoky City, ix, 5, 7, 9, 14, 41, 51, 58, 111, 117, 123–24, 130, 148, 206, 222, 245, 254, 277, 291, 310, 312, 325, 333, 337
Snodgrass, Frederick "Fred," 131
Snyder, Joe, 216
Somers, Charles W., 54–60, 68–69, 71
Sothoron, Allen, 303
South, 152, 187
South Atlantic League, 275
South End Grounds, 33, 71
South Side Black Sheep, viii
South Side Park, 94
Southern Association, 98, 228
Southern Hotel, 75

Southworth, William "Billy," 167
Soviet, 234
"The Soviet in Baseball," 234
Speaker, Tristram "Tris," 292
Spencer, Roy, 277, 305
Sporting Life, vii, 28, 30, 85, 87
The Sporting News, vii, 13, 49, 102
Sportsman's Park, 176, 217, 302–303, 315
Springfield, Massachusetts, 167
SS *Christopher Columbus*, 218, 242
Staley, Magistrate John Jr., 304
Stallings, George, 296
Stanage, Oscar, 322, 327
Standard Oil Company, 7
Standard Union, 315–16
State Registrar of Motor Vehicles (Massachusetts), 200
Steinfeldt, Harry, 95, 100
Stengel, Charles Dillon "Casey," 159, 162–64, 178, 256
Stephenson, Jackson Riggs, 296
Stock, Milton "Milt," 127, 183
Storke, Alan, 98
Suicide Corner, 175
The Sun, 164, 293
Swacina, Harry, 98
Sweeney, William "Bill," 129
Swetonic, Stephen "Steve," ix, 327, 334
Swetonic brothers, ix
Syracuse Stars, 27

Talbott, Henry, 13
Tannehill, Jesse "Tanny," 2, 14, 19–20, 38, 46–51, 53–55, 57–58, 60–64, 69–70, 73, 122, 210, 233, 340
Tannehill, Lee, 64
Temple, William C., 7
Tener, Governor John, 121
Tennessee River, 10
Tenney, Frederick "Fred," 82, 86, 91
Terre Haute, Indiana, 254
Terry, William "Bill," 262
Thanksgiving, 43, 168
Thanksgiving Day, 146
Thevenow, Thomas "Tommy," 327
Thomasville, Georgia, 18, 87
Thompson, Lafayette Fresco, 212, 219
Tierney, James "Cotton," 171–72, 180, 182, 184, 190, 198–99

Tim Hurst's Irish Fair, 64
Tinker, Joseph "Joe," 100
Toledo Mud Hens, 188, 256
Toronto Maple Leafs, 150, 166, 312
Traynor, Harold "Pie," 201, 204, 210, 216, 220, 227, 235, 251, 262, 264, 266, 277, 291, 301, 311, 315, 331, 337
Trenton, New Jersey, 23
Tri-State League, 80
Troy Washerwomen/Trojans, 37
Turner, Carl L., 268

Ulrich, Frank "Dutch," 292
Union Station (Union Depot or Pennsylvania Station), 33, 55–56, 78, 155
United States, 10, 139, 152, 168, 242
Universal Service, 285
University of Arkansas, 153
University of Pennsylvania, 92
University of Pittsburgh, ix
Upland, Pennsylvania, 155
USS *Lehigh*, 136

Veeck, William L. "Bill," 205, 293
Veil, Frederick "Bucky," 75–76, 79
Vila, Joseph "Joe," 165, 293
Viox, James "Jim," 131
Volstead Act, 307
Von der Ahe, Chris, 12

Waddell, Florence (Dunning), 30, 36
Waddell, George Edward "Rube or Eddie," 1, 3, 6, 11, 14, 25–36, 39, 47, 66
Waddell, John, 6, 31, 33, 35
Waddell, Mary, 6
Wadhams, Michigan, 8
Wagner, John "Honus or Hans," 11, 14, 18–19, 33, 37–39, 42–43, 46, 51–52, 70–71, 74, 76–78, 80–81, 83–84, 88, **89**, 99–100, 105, 116, 118, 120, 127, 131, 142, 151, 153, 167, 210, 213, 228, 265, 301, 336, 340
Wagner, Wilhelm Richard, 33
Waldo, Arnold, viii
Waldo, Charlie "Moxie," viii
Waldo, William "Billy," viii, ix
Waldorf Astoria Hotel, 119, 161, 259
Walker, Dr. E.W., 78
Wallace, Francis "Frank," 243–44, 250
Wallace, Leona, viii
Wallace, Roderick "Bobby," 40
Walsh, Davis J., 308
Walton Hotel (Hotel Walton), 46–47
Waner, Lloyd "Little Poison," 261, 264, 266–69, 273, 276–77, 285, 287–92, 297, 315, 337
Waner, Paul "Big Poison," 214, 216, 245, 251–52, 261–62, 264, 266, 268–69, 276–77, 287–88, 290–92, 302–303, 315–16, 321, 334, 337, 340
Ward, Charles "Chuck," 159
Warner, Hoke "Hooks," 172
Warren, Ohio, 202
Warren Moose, 202
Washington Daily News, 235, 290
Washington Nationals, 18
Washington Park, 81
Washington Post, 13
Washington Senators, 91, 93–94, 212–15, 228, 244, 248–49, 256–58, 290, 301
Watkins, William "Watty," 6–9, 11, 13, 18
Watters, Samuel "Sam," 170–71, 236, 239, 251, 285, 291, 325, 335, 338
"We Want Cuyler," 272–73, 298, 322
Webster Hall, 331
Weldon, Harry, 9
Welsh, Regis M., 175, 177, 182, 264–65, 298, 308
Wentz, Louis "Lew," 275, 291–92
Wertenbach, Fred, 324
West, 291
West Baden Springs, Indiana, 95, 112, 333–34
West Coast, 66, 146, 332
West End neighborhood (Pittsburgh), 155
West Liberty neighborhood (Pittsburgh), 137
West Penn Hospital, 142, 145, 304
West Side Grounds, 28, 98
West View, Pennsylvania, 140
West View Cemetery, 335, 338
West Virginia, 14
Western League, 84, 195, 215, 267, 333
Western Pennsylvania, viii, 30, 58, 102, 140, 174, 189, 202, 285
Western Union Station, 155
Westmoreland Country Club, 149, 172, 195, 238
Westmoreland County, Pennsylvania, 86

Wheat, Zachariah "Zack," 128, 183
White, William A., 173
Whitman, Dr. Armitage, 314
Whitney, Arthur "Pinky," 328
Whitted, George "Possum," 163–64, 166–67, 171–72, 180, 182–83, 185–87, 189, 193, 195
"Why I Was Kept on the Bench," 285
Wichita Aviators, 333
Wichita Larks, 267
Wightman Street, 141
Wilkinsburg, Pennsylvania, 137, 193, 236, 248
William Penn Highway, 236
William Penn Hotel, 236, 239, 275
Williams, James "Jimmy," 45, 63, 121
Williams, Joe, 321
Williamsport, Pennsylvania, 76, 78–79
Williamsport Millionaires, 80
Willis, Victor "Vic," 2, 84, 94, 99, 101, 111–15
Willoughby, Claude, 327
Wilmot Street, 206
Wilson, Helen (alias Mrs. M.E. Sherman), 138–39
Wilson, James "Jimmie," 292
Wilson, John Owen "Chief," 100–101, 106, 117–19
Wilson, Lewis "Hack," 296, 327
Winfield, Kansas, 94, 119, 254, 258, 275, 302, 337
Winter Garden Fashion Show, 152
Wisconsin, 32, 325
Wiseman, Catherine L., 147
Wiseman, Dick, 143
Wollen, Lou, 220, 235, 292
Wood, Charley, 327
Wood Street, 155
Woods, Walter "Walt," 14
Worcester, Massachusetts, 71–72
Worcester Farmers, 71
World Series, vii, ix, 3, 72, 76, 85, 101–107, 113–14, 116, 120, 145–46, 165, 167, 169, 174, 177–78, 194, 212–19, 241–42, 244, 248, 250, 252, 255, 258, 271–73, 275–76, 278–81, 283, 285, 290, 292, 296, 298, 301, 304–306, 308–309, 312, 333, 339
World's Championship, 257
Wright, Forest Glenn "Buckshot," viii, ix, 2, 201–202, 204, 210, 214, 216, 218–20, 235, 238, 244, 246, 249, 251, 258–59, 266, 287, 291, 299–304, 306, 308–315, **319**, 321–22, 326, 328, 337
Wright, Robert, 302
Wright, W.W., 304
Wrigley Field, 309

Yanigans, 99
Yankee Stadium, 276–78
Yde, Emil, 201, 209, 212, 214, 219–20, 235, 251, 277, 305
Yellow Horse, Moses "Chief," 173, 182, 189–92, 196, 198
Yonkers Herald, 255
Young, Denton "Cy," 76
Youngs, Royce "Ross," 264
Youngstown, Ohio, 76, 99, 127, 302

Zanesville, Ohio, 254
Zimmer, Charles "Chief," 14, 32, 34, 59
Zimmerman, Henry "Heinie," 127
Zinn, James "Jimmy," 182
Zuber, Charles "Charlie," 47

About the Author

Ronald T. Waldo is a historian and author who has written nine books about baseball history, with many devoted to examining the Deadball Era and the 1920s. A resident of Pittsburgh, Pennsylvania, his entire life, he graduated from Point Park University in the spring of 1983 with a bachelor's degree in journalism and communications. Following his love and passion for baseball history, Mr. Waldo's first book, titled *Fred Clarke: A Biography of the Baseball Hall of Fame Player-Manager*, was released in December 2010.

Some of his other books include a biography about Hazen "Kiki" Cuyler, a compilation of stories connected to the life and career of Honus Wagner, and team-related works on the 1902 Pittsburgh Pirates, 1925 Pittsburgh Pirates, and 1938 Pittsburgh Pirates. Mr. Waldo's most recent book, published in July 2022, is titled: *Deadball Trailblazers: Single-Season Records of the Modern Era*.

He also participated as a contributing author on the 2018 release *Unlucky 21: The Saddest Stories and Games in Pittsburgh Sports History*, writing the chapter about the 1974-75 Pittsburgh Penguins hockey team, titled "History Gone Bad: Chico and His Men Ruin the Pittsburgh Penguins' 1975 Playoff Party."

A longtime member of the Society for American Baseball Research, each of his five books covering baseball's Deadball Era received nominations for the Larry Ritter Book Award by that organization's Deadball Era Committee. The committee selected *Deadball Trailblazers: Single-Season Records of the Modern Era* as a finalist for the award in 2023. Besides being an avid baseball historian, Mr. Waldo also loves following current baseball, football, hockey, and soccer.

www.ingramcontent.com/pod-product-compliance
Lightning Source LLC
Chambersburg PA
CBHW011751220426
43670CB00021B/2936